T0381558

THE HIEROPHANCY
FILES

Also by Richard Leviton

THE HIEROPHANCY FILES

FILES

A THEFT FROM THE ARITHMETICAL EARTH

RICHARD LEVITON

A Primer on Earth's Geomantic Reality, No. 16

iUniverse®

THE HIEROPHANCY FILES
A THEFT FROM THE ARITHMETICAL EARTH

iUniverse books may be ordered through booksellers or by contacting:

iUniverse
1663 Liberty Drive
Bloomington, IN 47403
www.iuniverse.com
1-800-Authors (1-800-288-4677)

Because of the dynamic nature of the Internet, any web addresses or links contained in this book may have changed since publication and may no longer be valid. The views expressed in this work are solely those of the author and do not necessarily reflect the views of the publisher, and the publisher hereby disclaims any responsibility for them.

Any people depicted in stock imagery provided by Thinkstock are models, and such images are being used for illustrative purposes only. Certain stock imagery © Thinkstock.

ISBN: 978-1-5320-5859-2 (sc)
ISBN: 978-1-5320-5860-8 (e)

Print information available on the last page.

iUniverse rev. date: 09/26/2018

For Judith A. Lewis and Silver Boy

Foreword

The story I relate took place over the course of several months last year, between April and June 2065. I write the story like a mystery in which I am the detective because it certainly seemed like that to me. For a time at least. Something was taken, and we had to get it back, we being a few members of the Hierophancy, a group that works with geomantic matters of Earth's landscape.

I've barely started this book and already I have introduced unfamiliar terms. Hierophancy means a company of Hierophants. This is an old but serviceable term from the Greek and means "Revealers of the Holy Light." What Light is that? The organizational pattern of reality. Light means consciousness. Though the term Hierophant is rather high-level in its suggestions, we are nothing special, more like technicians well-trained to service a vast web of Light.

That is what geomantic refers to, namely, the implicit, designed energy configuration of the planet, with a mythic, geometrical, and even mathematical aspect to it. Geomantic refers to the subtle energy patterns and grids that structure the physical world and all consciousness states within it, all of our ordinary reality. You have to keep up these patterns, keep them vigorous and vital; they are

subject to entropy like all other living systems, including people.

The geomantic pattern typically is studded on the external, visible front with all sorts of structures, cathedrals, stone circles, pyramids, stone avenues, artificial hills, and these sites in turn are floriated with innumerable subtle, otherworldly, not easily visible residences, pavilions, palaces, even cities, made of Light. These are the kind of nonmaterial structures you encounter often in myths, where the gods live and heroes have unusual experiences if they manage to enter that domain. Reality, time, and space are usually different over there.

If you want to be etymological then geomantic derives from *Ge*, or Gaia, meaning Earth, and *mantos*, meaning divination. I take this to have two nuances: to figure out, as in, to divine the pattern, and to render it holy, as in with inspired speech. The geomancer discerns the engineering blueprint of the planet's energy field, he divines the Earth's secret reality, and in interacting with this amplifies its innate holiness: he renders the Earth divine, as it was originally created. Geomancer is a term to denote the people who maintain these Light patterns, who perform this act of *Gaia mantos*. In both ways, then, the geomancer divines the innate hierophantic pattern of Earth. The sacerdotal Earth engineer: that's us.

The phrase "Arithmetical Earth" refers to a certain pattern of Light, an intricate geometry, that envelops the planet like a benefic web, and this involves mathematics. This is the layer behind the mythic one. It can be expressed in terms of numbers and equations. Don't worry: you won't have to learn any mathematics, only to appreciate the Earth's pattern of reality, as organized by Light into geometrical forms and what we collectively call the Light grid, has an arithmetical aspect to it. It's an equation, a big one, admittedly, complicated and thorough enough to run an entire planet and its processes of consciousness. Just to be clear, the planet's geomantic pattern of Light has a numbers aspect. It is the realm referenced by myth, but it is also one determined by mathematics.

Think of the Arithmetical Earth as a separate and distinct version of our planet, as if you could extract all its numbers and equations and see it as a planet. A planet made of numbers and mathematical formulas, like a subtle Light body. To emphasize this distinction, this exact layer of perception I wish to draw your attention to, I capitalize the word Arithmetical. Our Earth is rich in numbers.

Some of my colleagues find this especially intriguing. I struggle with its complexities most of the time, but I appreciate its mental beauty. The energy pattern of the Earth, its geomantic blueprint, or what we routinely call its Light grid, is arithmetical in essence. It is a coded script, a kind of genome of Light, written in numbers. Algorithms and equations figure heavily in this code. Its product, what it generates, is the human being and a planet designed to match, and the levels of perception

and awareness available to us that link us with our home planet and put people into harmonious resonance with the cosmos itself.

Our job at the Hierophancy is to help maintain this system of Light and numbers because it is the basis for the biosphere, all life-forms, humanity, and human consciousness. It is a reciprocating web of Light and awareness coded in numbers and personified by temples made of Light; think of these as interactive architectural spaces constructed from Light, spaces humans are invited to enter.

Yes, you might already be thinking, so consciousness has a mathematical side to it, and I would have to confirm your intuition. Indeed it does. The Light grid I have just referred to is instrumental in maintaining and modulating this field, and our job is to be instrumental in keeping this underlying complex system in optimal working order to keep the Earth in blooming health. I use the word "reciprocating" because the system is interactive and fluidic, full of exchanges and modulations at every level, including the cosmic, planetary, and human. The Hierophant is constantly out in the field making sure this happens. Revealing the Holy Light also entails "fixing" it when it slips out of alignment with human awareness; the arithmetical layer is a key aspect of this Holy Light.

The drama of this book, the mystery, you might say, requiring detective work, was that somebody seemed to have stolen a key arithmetical component of the mathematical system that supervises the planet's grid of Light. Without that component, the entire mathematical matrix that manages the planet's Light grid would start to wobble and, if not remedied with the retrieval of that stolen piece, would falter and lead to catastrophic consequences to the biosphere. Excuse the hyperbole. Except it isn't. The outcome this slight exaggeration points to is real and worrisome. We knew at once we had a major problem on our hands.

We had been tasked with maintaining all aspects of the planet's Light grid, its global geomantic terrain, and the viability of the Arithmetical Earth which I must remind you is keenly tied in to the consciousness structures of the human and in fact to the biosphere in full and is central to all functions and species of Nature. Tasked by who? A consortium of governments and agencies that keeps an eye on planetary viability along these lines, that sees beyond national politics and ethnicities to this common global concern of survival.

This Light pattern I'm referring to is a linked system of consciousness and planet, human body and physical Earth, thoroughly reciprocal, identical in essence, only different in form. It is the common design imprint for both. The system is "plugged" into the galaxy, which adds to the richness of the pattern. The missing arithmetical component manages this system; it is a complicated algorithm that superintends a multitude of processes, and it had taken us years of research to discover then perfect this equation and put it into operation. All aspects of human life as we experience it, expect it, assume it will continue as, were now in jeopardy; the arithmetical aspect of consciousness was in peril too.

None of this is the kind of information that is widely circulated in public. That is partly because of its technical nature and partly because it is inherently esoteric, requiring a broadening of one's concepts of reality and how it works. I always liken it to acupuncture: you don't need to know the intricacies of *Qi*, the meridians, and the many access points to receive the benefits of a treatment. Leave the technical knowledge of this intricate system to the trained practitioner, trusting he will place the needles precisely where they need to go on your body.

So it is with our geomantic maintenance work. We position the "needles" where they best belong, based on our technical knowledge of the planetary system. One of the primary jobs of the Hierophancy is to maintain this body of knowledge and to keep adding to it with new discoveries and innovation in techniques. And to respond immediately and effectively to any disturbances in the Light pattern and take whatever measures are needed to correct them. That well described our current situation: every Light temple on Earth was in peril; all their interlinked systems, the flow of consciousness itself, were jeopardized.

I realize I need to step back and explain what I mean by Light temples. Think of what people used to routinely call sacred sites, pilgrimage destinations, holy places, and power vortexes. These sites of evident higher spiritual potency had many names. The planet's landscape seemed inexplicably freckled with them. Why? The physical aspects of these sites, which often entailed hills, mountains, stone circles, stone rows, pyramids, medicine wheels, churches of various types of religious denominations, were not what the sites were about.

The physical aspects mainly marked the location of subtle aspects, and it was these that gave a location its spiritual charge, or *numen*, as the Romans said. The subtle aspects entailed the numinous presence in architectural form but made of Light of various temples, palaces, cities, even larger assemblages of "buildings" or Light patterns, such as copies of the galactic wheel of stars, and an impressive guest list of advanced spiritual beings and extraterrestrials on hand.

Mostly these structures look like buildings, but they are made of Light. You can go inside them and have what you would likely label "mystical" experiences. This is the otherworldly landscape constantly referenced by the world's myths. This is the place where those wild, crazy, improbable, dreamlike stories took place. All the myths were true accounts, but took place in a *psychic* landscape. If you tried to understand them in only physical terms, you'd never figure them out. You could say they are like waking, lucid dreams in which through your awareness you enter various highly charged psychic atmospheres, walk around, see things, talk to spiritual presences, have edifying experiences.

These architectural forms rendered in Light are called Light temples. The Jewish mystics called them *Hekhalot*, or "palaces," and have a rich literature about the psychic visits of their rabbis to these wondrous locales in the Higher Worlds. The human Blaise's research (I'll come back to who he is in a moment) describes 613 different types of Light temples, and part of the Hierophancy's early work was to identify the locations of each type and correlate these Light edifices with the myths that accurately describe them, or at least hint of their numinous presence. The rabbis and seers who visited those *Hekhalot* became beholders of the divine secrets, the arcane activities of "gods" and angels, of *Yahweh* Himself.

The Light temples were intended to be revelatory—hierophantic— of the higher design principles and to provide glimpses, or at least hints and clues, as to the intent behind it all. Hierophants are the guides to this rich system of temples.

Here's the crucial link: all of these Light temples, and their copies number in the millions, are embedded in the complex, multi-tiered layers of a vast web of Light.

We call that the Earth's Light grid, and it runs all the processes of human consciousness. It runs like a complex living system, and all the Light temples are its components or organs and these have a mathematical tag that defines their operations. The grid has a geometrical and arithmetical aspect, and that's what all the fuss is about, what we're dealing with here. Somebody interfered with the smooth arithmetical management of this Light grid and in effect ran off with the key algorithm that runs the entire Earth consciousness and Light grid show. It's as if an invisible hand reached in and took this key algorithm from the system. My story is an account of what we did to get that management equation back.

Readers of this book will soon observe that our work routinely entails working with representatives from other planetary systems, with what we humans parochially used to call "aliens" or "extraterrestrials." We have finally outgrown that conservatism. It's no big deal. There are aliens everywhere.

A lot of them are our friends and colleagues. The Hierophancy has professional associates all over the galaxy, and even others, and we accept this as normal. Earth's Light grid is "wired" into larger patterns of Light, and these involve other planets across the Milky Way Galaxy. It may surprise you to learn that the Earth was designed this way and was organized with multiple, pre-existing "alien" connections all across the galaxy. The Earth began its life as a cosmopolitan planet; early humans knew this. You'd be astonished to see how many connections and affiliations our planet has with other systems. I was.

The Light grid of Earth was by design cosmopolitan in the true sense of the word, involving the cosmos. In this bit of detective work the theft from the Arithmetical Earth set us upon we worked mainly with five other planetary "families." No, they didn't look like humans, not even vaguely, but they are intelligent, competent, and responsible colleagues, members of the larger Hierophancy that operates at higher levels of geomantic design. They courteously adjusted their forms to a reasonable approximation of a human form. I'm still not sure what they actually look like when they are at home.

They helped us because the theft of our planetary management algorithm had serious reciprocal effects on their worlds and their planets' Light grids. That is because our planets are interlinked in many ways, so we found we had to work collegially to resolve the problem of the theft. It affected six planets in total.

Another aspect of the hierophantic work you will no doubt observe at once is that it requires clairvoyance as a job requirement. Most of what we work on is not ordinarily visible to physical eyesight; it is too subtle, too much made of Light and not dense matter so that heightened cognitive sensitivity is required. I always thought about that in terms of plumbing: a plumber makes a service call to a house that is shuttered and completely dark inside. He has to bring his own illumination or else find the light switches so he can find the plumbing to fix it.

There is no advantage to working in the dark. We work best in full illumination. If you're called out to fix the plumbing, it helps if you can see the pipes. Similarly, to fix the Light grid you must be able to see the Light temples that are plugged into its global "electrical" system. Electrical or plumbing—excuse my wandering analogy, but either familiar domestic system makes the point. You need to be able to clearly *see* the intricacies of the system to fix it. I hope it is equally obvious that you need technical knowledge of the system too. You shouldn't even think about tinkering with this vastly complicated system of Light without a thorough knowledge of its design, purposes, and operations.

Since the big changes brought forward in human consciousness in 2020, this natural skill is not so rare and no longer regarded with either awe or skepticism. Why argue with it? I always say, by way of justification, the Supreme Being invented clairvoyance so why not use it? Stop wasting time doubting its validity or even existence. Start using it. You will encounter a tone of casualness in my reference to things subtly seen. We take those for granted. That is a familiar domain for us. We are plumbers who brought big torches to light the scene. We are electricians who can turn on the lights in the Earth house. We work in houses where you can see all the pipes, drains, fixtures, sinks, outlets, plugs.

I better offer a few notes of clarification on this date. The year 2020 was pivotal. According to the Ofanim, an angelic order in close working relationship with the Hierophancy and which we count among our "friends," on January 1 of that year, now 46 years ago, they began entering the human incarnational stream for the first time in this Life of Brahma, and maybe for many of them. Angels only rarely enter human form. Only four other orders have ever done it, and only for short, proscribed time periods. But starting in 2020 we began seeing Ofanim angels in the form of living humans. What should we call them? Angel-Humans?

They were a completely new formulation of the human archetype because they had no souls, karma, or necessity to rectify or advance their incarnational timeline, and all the other baggage the rest of us old-school humans bring to the incarnational table. Their hands were utterly untied, free to move.

That profound fact shook the Earth mightily. To have that quality of Light walking around in human-appearing bodies was unprecedented in human history, and the Earth has never been the same since. A Life of Brahma, according to Hindu time models, is 311 trillion years, a full cycle of Creation. Ofanim is the Hebrew name for one of the 40 angelic orders; it means "wheels." Incidentally, they had no souls because they didn't need them; they did not need to evolve. They were created perfect as Spirits of Light and remained that way.

Their unprecedented step into incarnation was coincident with the long-awaited beginning of the new *Satya Yuga*, better known in the West as the Golden Age. Finally, and I mean, *finally*, as in at goddam last, the obnoxious, fetid *Kali Yuga* or Black Age lasting 432,000 miserable Dark-Ages-style years was over, finished. The Ofanim picked their perfect moment, the dawn of sunshine in consciousness. Things have been good since then; the tenor of planetary reality has perked up, and a lot of subjects once veiled or forgotten are now in the forefront of world awareness, including, at least to a degree, the Hierophancy. Let's say at least the need for geomantic maintenance of the planet's subtle bits has become public knowledge, though most of what we do is still kept discreet.

Readers will also note a certain fluidity in our movements across time and space. I suppose we are quite used to this, but it may bewilder readers at first. It is not always clear where we are physically or what time it is or which "body" we are operating in and how all that vexing ambiguity happened. I wasn't always clear on that myself. Often I found myself doing things or being present at locations or inexplicably manifesting a multiplicity of body presences and felt unable to account for it in conventional notions of physics or spacetime. Many times I found myself present with equal attention at a number of places at the same moment. I was never sure which was my primary anchoring point. No matter. It didn't seem to do any permanent or even short-term damage to myself, only to my apparently outmoded notion of linear causality and spatial location.

Probably the best explanation is to say, perhaps lamely, that consciousness is far more flexible, creative, and powerful than we routinely assume. Anyway, it's virtually a job requirement in the Hierophancy to be able to get about easily because the nature of a Light grid itself involves multidimensional connections, and if you are going to service it, like a plumber, you need to get to all its parts. Some of these exist in the past or future, and some require multiple plumbers; it's funny because often I need a dozen copies of myself to hold the wrenches steady.

You have to expect your "house" to exist in 4D and even 5D extensions, and you'll need to be able to crawl, climb, or generally reach into these arcane realms. You may find yourself tweaking the valves in the past and the future, never sufficiently clear which time frame you're in or how you got there. Again, you get used to it. My pals and I in the Hierophancy take this fluidity for granted, though, to be honest, it stretches the mind considerably to navigate your way through a 5D Light grid pattern. You're coming, going, and standing still all at the same time, and if you look around, you'll see there's more than one of you.

As for these Hierophancy pals, in case you have seen my previous two books (*My Pal, Blaise* and *The Green Knight Expedition*), you will at least recognize one character who has appeared, however enigmatically, in both books and he recurs in this present account. I refer to Blaise. He is a human, as far as I can tell, a man of average height and modest weight and little hair who looks like he's from the Earth though he has visited other planets and has spent a fair amount of time, at least 20 years, living off-planet, mostly in the Pleiades, and in other bodies, that is, not on the Earth where you accrue gravity-weighted miles on your physical organism and thus aging. In his view, that principally accounts for his unusual longevity. He is currently 116. I am comparatively young at 90.

I don't know what his birth name was. He's never told me, or anyone, probably. His biography is to all practical extents a state secret. I don't know anything about him except what I have directly experienced in his company. I know he is a primary conduit for an order of angels called Ofanim whom he familiarly refers to as Blaise, or sometimes as the Blaises, or, when he feels jocular, as the Blaise Boys. He

has had a long working relationship with them, spanning about 60 billion years, he says, and he isn't joking when he makes this daunting if not, to most sensible people, entirely insupportable claim.

He stands by it. The figure 60 billion is the approximate age of the Ofanim, Blaise says, when God first emanated them out of His infinite vastness, and he claims to remember many of his early days working with these ancient angels. He keeps renewing his job contract with them in sequential Earth human lives, he explains. He says he's worked with them for 60 billion years because this angelic family, along with several others, has an implicit presence in the human design, so if you trace your own origins far enough back, you'll find them there, and you'll find human consciousness occupying the same space as the Ofanim. I know, it is a wild or bizarre notion, but the human Blaise affirms it like bedrock.

I've gotten used to the strangeness of all this over the years. Easier to remember were his early working days from the childhood of this life on Earth. Visits by the angelic Blaises sprouted throughout his childhood. He said they would show up on the roof of his parents' house at night and take him off on interesting expeditions. They would zip up the Rotunda, by expanding the six pillars of Light that supported its golden domed roof, and they would zoom off in a blaze of Light. He got Chariot rides early on. He thought the whole thing normal, going off with a clutch of six wise-cracking angels in their Rotunda of Light; he could have been a *Merkabah* mystic had he been so inclined. The Rotunda, as he calls it, is a mobile upscale gazebo made of Light that the Ofanim suggested to him early on was a suitable midpoint for interactions with them.

I had better put you in the picture regarding these Ofanim. They figure prominently in this story, in the Hierophancy, and, frankly, in all our reports. They are the wheels of the Supreme Being's Chariot or *Merkabah*, which means they move, they *roll*, the Supreme Being's energy about through the universe. They are the embodiment and the constant expression of *Sat Cit Ananda*, Being, Consciousness, and Bliss, said by yogis to be the chief characteristic of the vibrational quality of the Supreme Being. If you were in all charming innocence to ask a yogi what does the Supreme Being feel like, he would likely use these words to describe the unique Ancient of Days's vibrational signature to suggest how you might feel should you be so fortunate as to be in His Presence.

Think of that as an aspect of the wheels. The Ofanim are the second on the list of 40 angelic orders, meaning they were created second but before 38 other families. Order of creation seems to entail a hierarchy of knowledge; the Ofanim seem to be very well-briefed on most matters. They like to take different forms to demonstrate their qualities through vivid metaphors that stick in human consciousness, clever, imaginative god-forms like Ganesh, Hanuman, and Garuda, elephants, white horses, eagles, flying monkeys, august birds. They are principally involved in maintaining the fluidity and viability of consciousness, and they work with all Light imprints and grid patterns that conduct this. They are your go-to angels for all technical questions about energy and Light grids.

Their manifestation package is roughly 40 million copies of themselves. They claim to service 18 billion galaxies with this relatively small staff; and they like to meet with humans in a mobile architectural form we call the Rotunda of Light which is an architecturally smart and elegant gazebo with six diamond-white pillars, a gold domed roof, and a concave diamond geode the size of a sports stadium occupying the central portion of the space and designated as our meeting place. Its size is wildly variable, but let's say your initial impression, stepping into it, is that it measures about 35 feet across and perhaps 15 feet tall. Don't be alarmed, but the Blaises can expand this to the size of the planet itself.

The Ofanim work with all sentient intelligences who interact with this Light grid reality, as geomancers and Hierophants, and that brings in us, and especially the human Blaise who has deep roots and a long professional relationship with these angels. So the Ofanim, the Blaises, are part of this story. I think you'll enjoy the parts when they show up. Oh yes: they have a great sense of humor. They never miss a chance to lob in a levity ball or crack a joke. As the human Blaise has been known to quip, "They're a fun bunch of guys to have around the Hierophancy. They leaven up the dull moments, like anti-gravity."

It is fair to say the human Blaise is the primary mover of the Hierophancy. He has gathered some colleagues around him over the years and infused them with the requisite knowledge and enthusiasm to conduct geomantic business. I suppose it is Blaise's fault that I am no longer an academic, holding a respectable professorial tenure at Dartmouth College. I left that institution decades ago, and readers of my first book, *My Pal, Blaise*, published almost 40 years ago, will no doubt re-experience the amusement my manner of leaving academia provokes. That book was more a product of co-authorship; I edited and annotated a series of notebooks left by the human Blaise just before he left the planet in late 2019.

I ran out the door of my house one morning, recklessly abandoning wife, home, profession, and Ph.D. academic standing. In retrospect, it wasn't reckless. I dashed out the door of my established, comfortable New Hampshire life to pursue the enigmas and mysteries and allurements of this most baffling and intriguing Blaise and the mysterious, intriguing Other World he was pointing to.

I have never since regretted my rash actions. I found that world, and I like it, and that is the basis of my current mode of employment and I even spend weekends there too. I wish you could see my eyes twinkling at the moment. My former Dartmouth peers would hardly see my vocation as constituting employment. It is probably just as well I have no idea how they viewed my sudden departure or what uncomplimentary labels they might have affixed to my presumed mental state. I doubt I could explain myself to their satisfaction.

When I say I "ran" out my front door I mean no hyperbole. I in fact did run. I was answering the irresistible Siren call the human Blaise had let loose from those Ofanim rocks at the threshold of my conventional world and his outré one. I was editing a lengthy manuscript he had left me on purpose even though at the time I had not met him, at least in this life, I think. There's always dreams and the astral world, so I can't be certain about when our acquaintance began. He wasn't trying to lure me out, probably, but as I worked with his words and concepts in what became *My Pal, Blaise*, I found his was the world I wanted. That is precisely what I got. I never regretted it. It has been rich with surprises.

One day I dropped everything (I had finished the editing, so I was not irresponsible as his editor), dashed out the front door, down the lane, and found him there. Blaise was waiting patiently for me, maybe the tiniest of smirks flourishing on his face, and with the insouciance of someone who absolutely knew I'd be along. Regrettably, I created a mystery for my wife, Philomena, and the local authorities, but she repaid it in kind a few years later when she ascended. Yes, the full deal: she turned her mortal female body into one of Light. My colleagues, not that I ever saw them again, no doubt said theirs is a strange marriage, those Atkinsons: running off, becoming Light, up to God knows what.

I must credit Blaise with mentoring me in the geomantic mysteries and protocols over the last four decades. For his part, he credits the Ofanim for similarly mentoring him over the years in the same arcana of consciousness and design, and I suppose it is fair to say I have subsequently done my share of mentoring some younger men and women in these same bright enigmas of the Creation, enabling them to join the Hierophancy as reliable, competent workers.

The human Blaise may have been a Siren to my true vocation, but the angelic Blaises were his master Sirens. Imagine 40 million of them singing alluringly to him from the rocks of the higher spiritual worlds to come join them. Those rocks, of course, were the glittering diamond hexagons of their vast geode. I'll talk about that more in the book, but they plausibly look like rocks of Light.

They made the call to him earlier in his life than he did to me. He said he was in his mid-thirties when they turned his life upside down and made a Hanged Man out of him in which he saw everything from the opposite side of the reality mirror. Or was it a *Heyoka*, a Backward-Walking Man, he became? "I didn't mind that a single bit," he told me once, grinning. "Absolutely loved it."

To be frank, the Hierophancy has made good use of my academic background (my field was comparative mythology), sharpening and refining it in the light of empirical experience and validation. Most of what I once thought was of only intellectual relevance (the vast treasury of myths and folktales from the world) has proven to be keenly relevant and descriptive of the terrain we now work in. I appreciate them now as vivid psychic pictures left by initiates to describe protocols for interacting with the geomantic terrain. I see now that what I once thought were curious mental images is living initiation knowledge. The Hierophancy work requires us to have both clairvoyance and a lot of knowledge.

So none of my formal training and Ph.D. attainment has been wasted or put aside, but I doubt when I started at Dartmouth I could have foreseen my eventual recruitment by the Hierophancy and the metaphysical wildness of our activities and exposures. Did we ever rewrite the book of mythology. Reality has greatly widened out for me since then and I see now how mentally provincial was my Dartmouth life and everything that defined my idea of an educated man.

It could not be otherwise. What the Hierophancy deals with is inherently esoteric. It's not like we're trying to hide things from the public; what we deal with simply does not exist in the physical, seeable world. The Light grid of the planet and the mathematics that run it and the processes in Light and enriched consciousness it produces are subtle by nature, ordinarily invisible, like the wind. They are visible to clairvoyance and pliable to human interaction; you just have to know how to "plug" yourself into the geomantic socket of this realm.

All of this is the backdrop, the backstory, as they used to say, for outer reality. Without the Light grid and its geomantic mechanisms, external reality would end. With it, and when it runs properly, external reality flourishes and shines. The Hierophancy's job is to look after the geomantic mechanics of Earth, maintaining the healthy link between inner invisible and outer visible aspects.

The story I tell in this account is an episode in that maintenance work. It provides a glimpse through a window at what is involved in keeping Earth reality optimized. I know if I had read this file when I was back at Dartmouth, I would have read it with astonishment, disbelief, and, despite this, with delight.

Why delight? Because I would see, convincingly, that reality is well-ordered, complex yet discernible, that it offers numerous ways for people to participate. I would have realized that all these myths I was studying and teaching were field notes of earlier participants in this spectacle of design, Light, and consciousness. Since the changes that began in 2020 and the unique advent of incarnated human-style Ofanim, that is increasingly a common experience, and it is with that understanding that I present this Hierophancy file anticipating it will not strike you, my readers, as too remote from your experience or at least your sense of what might be possible and what might exist behind our daytime world and why it might be of benefit to find out more about that bright realm.

—Frederick Graham Atkinson
Sun Valley, Idaho, August 15, 2066

1

At first we didn't realize what had been stolen. When we finally did, we were appalled. We didn't think it was possible for anyone to do this. But they had and the implications were dire. They had taken the Hierophancy heuristic algorithm for Earth, the mathematical codebook for how to run the planet and its Light grid. Though few knew of its existence, it was the most valuable data set on the planet, the most indispensable body of information the Earth ever yielded.

I was sitting in my office at Hierophancy headquarters outside Sun Valley, Idaho. For those of you who may have heard of this initiative, it was in its second generation. Blaise, my colleague and the senior detective in this small detective firm, had founded the first one in Santa Fe, New Mexico, about 60 years ago. It flourished for a time, up until the time of his disappearance in 2019. Later, his mentors, the angelic Blaises, suggested we relocate the project to southern Idaho.

We did that, and we've been operating out of our new offices here for the last 16 years now. I suppose we are not your typical detectives. We are not actually detectives anyway, not by training, but now we are out of necessity. Professionally, we are geomantic technicians but somebody stole our toolbox.

A mystery confronted us and we had to detect its nature and solve it. We are not typical detectives. Other people our age would be retired, or even dead. Our age doesn't seem to stop us or hold us back in any way. Blaise is very fit for his age. We're also not your typical detectives because we operate under a secret charter with certain esoteric branches of the government which, bless them, finally came to recognize after the momentous world change of 2020 the need for geomantic intervention and maintenance in the affairs of the planet. Not one government, the U.S., incidentally, but several dozen national governments depend on our careful maintenance of planetary geomantic conditions and our regular reports that fill brief them on system status, upgrades, or problems.

We were tasked with investigating and resolving crimes against the Light grid, which you could call geomantic felonies, an altogether new category of offense. When we weren't pursuing infractions, we were in the field adjusting the works. I call us detectives, but we were more like field technicians and engineers and typically the mysteries we investigated, the "crimes" we detected, were geomantic. Something had gotten out of balance with the planet's Light grid and it was our job as repairmen to figure out what it was and set it right. We had to investigate and correct disturbances in the disclosure of the Holy Light. Sometimes they were simply wobbles in the system; other times deliberate acts.

Blaise was out in the field when I discovered the file was gone. At first it didn't look like anything was missing. The file was in place. Then I realized it was a fake one. The numbers didn't look right. They were not heuristically empowered, which is a key feature of the Hierophancy algorithm. I'll get to that. When I say "file" I employ the term out of fondness (Blaise says it's whimsy) for the old-school way of storing information on paper in file folders in a file cabinet.

The file actually was stored in a four-dimensional tesseract holographic matrix, but you can see, I'm sure, it's easier to broach the subject by calling it a file.

I'm not that technical myself, though I'm getting there. I went through a job refit. I used to be a tenured professor of comparative mythology at Dartmouth College, but that was a long time ago, though I do still remember the mythic motifs. As for Blaise, he used to be—after all my years of working with him, honestly, I still have only the sketchiest notion of his early years before this. Probably the safest statement I can make is to say Blaise used to be Blaise, just as we know him today, enigmatic, engaged, funny, and extraterrestrially inclined.

He first came to my attention in 2025 when I edited an unruly manuscript of his, since published as *My Pal, Blaise*, which came to me as nine handwritten notebooks that he left on the lintel of an archeological ruin in Mexico. At the time, he had disappeared under mysterious circumstances, and I mean *utterly* disappeared. In fact, he had left the planet on

December 31, 2019 by stargate, dropping off his bulky notebooks in Mexico on his way out and he stayed gone for almost 20 years. Then he came back, stayed for a while before leaving again and mentored me and set me on the wild course that finds me here today in this office staring at our disaster. He also took me with him back to the Pleiades. I'll get back to that subject later, but I'll tell you, it still astonishes me I did that.

I will note that Blaise attributes his longevity to the fact that he spent about 20 years off-planet, not only free of Earth's gravity but free of occupying a human body. During that time, his Earth body was inactive, in stasis-storage, and no incarnational time-miles were accrued on its treads so it didn't age. I suspect my time off-planet, though far shorter, added years and vitality to my life too. That is a novel way to achieve longevity, though it was never our intent.

There are a few things I should clarify at the outset. We are detectives, but that is to a degree a convenient cover story. Yes, we investigate infractions of geomantic law and order, but that is to veil our true work which is protecting the Hierophancy algorithm. We also maintain and operate it. The main reason we do this is because Blaise created it. It was the product of about 50 years of mental labor, imagination, and deep information recall. I'll come back to this later. I make it sound like this was a file, a unique, singular, discrete information cache, something tangible that could be materially stolen. That's not quite the fact. The danger is in copying it. Worse than that, disconnecting it from its plug-in node. Given the unusual nature of our work, the theft itself is equally hard to explain.

For security reasons, naturally, we have it stored off-site in a warehouse. It is a special site, not easy to access; in fact, it's not even easy to find. As I said, the Hierophancy algorithm is basically mathematical information, coding, a formula. I also said it was stored as a four-dimensional holographic matrix, but you should know this matrix is a 4D cube of Light that measures 50 feet on each side.

The matrix is something you stand inside, like an environment, a psychic atmosphere. Maybe I could better liken it to an illustrated living nervous system. You are in architecture made of mathematical coding. A 4D cube is a cube rendered in four dimensions; that yields eight identical cubes that seem to be moving constantly and in all directions at once. It can be very disorienting at first; your eyes and your mind struggle to make sense of this complicated shape.

The whole shape appears to be revolving too. It's like standing on a 4D merry-go-round. It's moving in a circle, and all its rides are changing their locations. Add to this the fact that the algorithm is displayed upon the edges and surfaces and through the interior volume of this vexatiously complicated moving shape, the "air" threaded with equations written in Light. That's where we make our adjustments and monitor the ones the system makes intelligently on its own. That's why we call it heuristic: it learns, it adjusts, and acts creatively as a result.

You can't steal any of this in the sense of removing it physically from its warehouse, but you can copy and disconnect it or replace it with an alternate script or corrupt it with a virus or stealth-enslave it to run other operations. At least theoretically. We thought we had sufficient safeguards against all these possibilities. To take it out of its necessary operational context that would consist of downloading it into your mind, your consciousness, which is apparently what our thief did. The trouble is that download corrupted the file, which is why, to simplify it, I said the robber left a fake number file in its place.

You will note, I'm sure, it is difficult even to describe the nature of the "crime." The algorithm was stolen from a protected 4D space which in itself starts the mind somersaulting in dizzying conundrums. The algorithm was not exactly stolen, but rendered inoperative, to an extent unplugged from its key arithmetical traction points, and certain spurious, corrupting equations were substituted at crucial procedural nodes. You will likely find this hard to follow.

All this corrupted the file in the sense of contamination. It added a discordant quality to its complex coding, and this started to skew the equations and throw the heuristic aspect of the algorithm out of balance. Its calculation products were wrong and misdirected the system. It is a self-learning and self-adjusting algorithm, constantly receiving input and fresh status data from the planet's Light grid and incorporating this information into its conclusions and then translating its conclusions into effective action to modulate the system.

The best way to explain this contamination is to say that if you enter the holographic matrix the wrong way, without making the correct and precise adjustments and alignments in your consciousness, and you insinuate yourself into its living mental field more by way of jury-rigging this entry, it goes awry. If it were a person, you would say this person is hypersensitive and twitchy or perhaps like a dog nervously attuned to every body nuance you present. If you were a computer coder, you would say this mathematical "entity" was one step short of being an artificial intelligence, that step being self-aware sentience. I think Blaise realized that was a definitive step it would be better if not taken, so he installed safeguards and boundaries in its processing matrix to prevent that.

We had to report the intrusion and theft immediately to our host sponsors. This consisted of a consortium of 45 national governments, though you will appreciate in most cases their contracts with us were so secret hardly anyone in their respective governmental bureaucracies even knew about it. Often their president or prime minister was kept in the dark also, and definitely their public. Public awareness that the Earth's affairs and viability are managed by a complex mathematical formula overseen by a secret cabal of Hierophants in Idaho would be alarming and unsettling, not to mention its mechanics difficult to understand. It's sufficiently challenging to ordinary awareness to entertain the notion the planet is freckled with innumerable subtle Light temples that affect awareness.

The information contained in the Hierophancy heuristic algorithm, its full name, and frankly the full nature of our technical work here, is too recondite, too valuable, too dangerous, too planet-threatening, to afford widespread public knowledge of its existence. It does entail the operational specifics of the Earth and human consciousness. I don't mean to sound histrionic here, but when you understand what this information is and where it came from you'll probably see the sound thinking behind this. Plus it is awfully hard to explain to lay people. At the conclusion of this

case, though, it was decided to publish a public report of the general outline of events. It was time for people to learn about this work. Still, I suspect now it is finished it will necessarily seem only a general overview.

You might reasonably wonder how did we, a small esoteric group of geomancers, gain such a privileged status among 45 major nations of the world? The answer will likely strike you at first as perhaps either boastful or shockingly imperious. We got the commission because we received an imprimatur from the designers of the planet and its complex patterning of Light and Light temples. They insisted that we be given primary responsibility for its maintenance because they had trained us in the mechanics and adjustments of the system.

You could say this cabal of planet designers is the real secret government, but their position is maintained not by power or by being puppet-masters but by their knowledge and wisdom. If you design a piece of complex machinery, you will be at the top of the list of consultants the end-users go to when they need guidance. Despite their repeated public protestations of ignorance, disbelief, or rampant atheist-materialism, there is always within governments a few clued in to reality, who know who the real power brokers are and what the correct story is, what the reality of reality is behind the glamours and deliberate illusions, and where you go to fix these subtle operations and how to make the adjustments. These are the actual and important features present at physical sites labeled sacred, holy, or spiritually powerful. It is their explanation and core reality. In a sense they are all false fronts hiding parts of a vital geomantic global mechanism.

Given the secrecy entailed in this project why ever am I releasing this report? It's true, this report is intended for a controlled, limited circulation. Our simplified declassified report for the public will come out shortly afterwards. Normally, or I should say, up until now, we would have remained mum. But a certain event of pivotal importance and likely impact on both planet and human culture is coming up soon, likely within the next decade, that it was thought prudent to start preparing the public with some sense of its planetary context.

Otherwise, this forthcoming event would appear inexplicable and frightening. Some degree of advanced conceptual preparation is necessary to get people ready and another foggy layer of chronic misperception about the Earth, its history, origin, and why humanity was first placed here, must be stripped off.

Regarding this "we" I just alluded to, we call ourselves the Hierophancy. The term comes from Joseph of Arimathea, rather a grand magus of geomancers. Most people think of Joseph of Arimathea as a wealthy Jew who helped Jesus, provided a tomb for his crucified body, and brought Christianity to England. Our friend and colleague, Edward Burbage, wrote about this important figure in a book he published 11 years ago called *The White Staff Nudge*, in which he reported that this Joseph is probably the planet's premier geomancer, chief of the Grail Knight Brotherhood, and generally the master of all matters geomantic. This Joseph, Burbage wrote, is the epitome of the Hierophant, the discloser of the veiled patterns of Light, the structures of consciousness that comprise our reality.

The Hierophancy is a group of geomancers under his direction trained to act as Hierophants. A Hierophant is someone who reveals the Holy Light and in the process of disclosure, explains it and adjusts it. The Holy Light in this case is the indigenous Light grid of the planet, an etheric web of complex design that envelops the physical world and energizes, directs, and even generates its life. But the Light is also the design itself, the original pattern of reciprocal consciousness and its structures that characterizes the human and our planet. And the Light is also the clarified consciousness that understands and inhabits this pattern, that takes responsibility for its well-being, and keeps it sanctified.

This grid is the master context for what people routinely call sacred sites. It is the design into which all holy and pilgrimage locations are purposefully embedded. It is a copy of the same pattern that characterizes the human design. Hierophancy members are thoroughly trained in planetary maintenance, a discipline that combines formulations of consciousness and Light grid temples. We maintain the reciprocity between planetary and human copies of the design. Perhaps you have heard of the Hermetic Axiom that says *As above, so below*? The full expression is actually *As above, so below, and in the middle too*. It's an essential design congruence, really an isomorphism, between Heaven, Earth, and Human. The Earth is the "middle too" part, bearing a copy of the same energy pattern humans have and which corresponds to the celestial original, the *above* part.

The inescapable fact of the Earth's Light grid is that it is a consciousness web, one that requires—it necessitates, and I'm tempted to say, it *demands*—interaction through applied human consciousness extended from living people. It is a complex nest of Light that directs awareness on all levels of the planet, encompassing human, animal, plant, and mineral realms, and though it has innumerable Light temple and physical landscape correlates, all of which would suggest or dispose one to think the pattern is a material one that could be materially adjusted, the pattern is a complicated weave of consciousness. It can only be adjusted through directed modulations of focused human awareness. The geomancer or Hierophant is somebody trained in how to modulate this.

How did this Light grid get here as a fact of planetary life? It was designed and implemented by a consortium of higher-world experts, but most significantly two: the first was the angelic order called the Elohim; and the second was a contingent of Light grid and planet designers from the Pleiades. The Hierophancy maintains close working relations with both of these groups, and that is principally why we have the exclusive contract with the major governments to manage the Hierophancy heuristic algorithm and to deploy it on behalf of the well-being, evolution, and required cosmic alignment of the planet. You could say, and I don't mean to sound flip, they put in a good word for us.

That, and the fact that Blaise would not have it otherwise. Since he developed this multidimensional living mathematical formula, he controls it. And for good reason: I refer you to his account of various attempts by shadow government agencies to suborn his information for their own dark purposes as published in *My Pal, Blaise*, which I edited and through which I first met Blaise. His last year on Earth, 2019, was marked by all sorts of shadow organization

infiltrations of his projects, attempts to purloin his data, and even to arrest him.

Readers may well wonder why we established the Hierophancy here. I don't imagine Idaho or locales in this under-populated state would routinely show up high on a national list of sacred sites or energized geomantic nodes. Indeed, prior to 2020 the demographics of this state and of the town of Sun Valley specifically would have seemed incongruent with a geomantic Mystery initiative. The state was religious, conservative, and here, hell-bent on skiing. Yet despite this outer disinclination towards higher consciousness and the Mysteries, the landscape was richly endowed with geomantic features which made the site favorable for this kind of esoteric initiative once the landscape got activated.

This started to happen after 2020, and by 2066 things are quite perky here. Bald Mountain, (elevation: 9,150 feet) dominates Sun Valley with its 75 ski runs, in operation since 1935. People flock here to ski; it's as straightforward as that. This domesticated ski-slope peak frames the commercial center of this small tourist town but the geomantic center of this landscape lies behind it to the northwest a dozen miles at Boyle Mountain (elevation: 8,962 feet, part of the Smoky Mountains chain). That's where you'll find the local geomantic "action."

Boyle sports a star dome making it the geomantic center, and this dome spawns several dozens of smaller Light canopies called dome caps that brighten the landscape all around it to a radius of at least 10 miles. In the vicinity is a stargate, a Hollow Earth portal, a Gnome Egg, and a second-tier coiled and wakeful dragon guarding the northern entrance to this landscape of Light. The bulk of the geomantic features lie behind the bright, busy, touristic city center.

In addition there is a feature Blaise calls a landscape Round Table. This is a template (this one is about two miles wide) that is a geomantic generic horoscope with a dozen wedges, each one carrying the energy of the one of the signs of the zodiac. You use this to "joust" with aspects of your own horoscope to balance out the energies affecting your life. You sit in a given wedge, say Scorpio, and experience the energies of that "sign" and engage them interactively by jousting. Though it sounds like a quaint medieval image, it is a way of saying you immerse yourself in the qualities of, again, Scorpio here as an example, to gain mastery. Scorpio challenges you, and you respond, integrating the results. This is an excellent Hierophant training device; we use it with our students.

The area under the dome features a Lucifer Binding Site. Its copy of Lucifer and Sophia were liberated after 2020 and their powerful Light frequency gradually introduced into the area's geomantic and demographic aspects. It is hard to emphasize how vital a liberated feature like this can be to a geomantic terrain. All the original, indigenous powers of consciousness intended to be present and activated in a human are here exemplified, made available in the form, metaphorically, of a pool of sweetwater, as the Polynesians once put it. I'm glad that generally people are less jumpy when news of this feature comes up.

Lucifer and Sophia are the original Hierophants. They are God-appointed Light Bringers, humanity's benefactors from our inception. They are the good guys. They are

the active and passive aspects of the relationship of these cosmic archangels to the field of stars, and they wear the galaxy like a Robe of Stars.

Think of this "pool" as the repository of the primordial Light from the Cube of Space when the Ancient of Days first corralled the formless infinity of His Own existence into a designated bound area in which the Creation would take place and later be known to us as the universe. Lucifer and Sophia, this primary syzygy, dispense that quality of primordial Light to humans. They are the penultimate Hierophants, bringing and revealing the Holy Light. The Supreme Being of course is the ultimate Light Revealer, but the Lucifer-Sophia "couple" bring this Light closer to human understanding. Proximity to this perpetual hierophantic presence is chiefly why we located the Hierophancy here. It provides an excellent consciousness gradient to support all our projects.

With that energy bound up here prior to 2020, and Lucifer-Sophia in a grievous lockdown, the consciousness gradient for this area was steep and in effect blocked. The landscape's geomantic endowment was mostly then "offline," dormant, and ineffectual. Unbinding the Lord of Light in both "its" masculine and feminine valences changed all that dramatically and hierophantic matters have flourished here ever since. It's a place that well reveals the Holy Light.

We saw that long ago this site had been used for Mystery initiations and many people came from afar to participate in its wisdom schools and enjoy its geomantic richness. That landscape use is gradually returning to this area as its geomancy activates further (like slowly turning a dimmer switch), and the sweetwater pool of this liberated Binding Site and its primordial Light and the twin personifications and bearers of that Light as accessible models are keys.

I poured myself another cup of coffee and mentally fretted. The acute question here was how on Earth did anybody break into the matrix and copy it? There's something else I should tell you about it. Your DNA signature is the key card. If the system does not recognize your "signature," you cannot enter. Yet somebody did. It is as if they teleported directly into the holographic matrix and thereby bypassed all the usual entry requirements and checks. They teleported in seemingly from an outside dimension, like it was a secret adjoining room, but they entered wobbling, or incompletely formed, or lacking the right coordinates.

That's why when they made the copy of the algorithm, it deformed the matrix. You operate the algorithm with your consciousness, using it like hands. This deformation made it seem like your "hands" had gone to sleep and you were not able to move them accurately or deftly. Or that you wore thick gloves.

Here is the problem with what has happened, or, should I say, the disaster confronting us this morning. With the Hierophancy heuristic algorithm you can control the planet and humanity. That was not the original intent of this mathematics: it was to provide interactive maintenance and continuous updating of a complex life pattern. The intent was benevolent global system regulation.

The original Light grid or what the Elohim called the "template" resonantly matches human and Earth in a perpetually self-adjusting mode of activity. It is the number code that generates and runs the Light grid. If you were to summarize, in terms of numbers, every functional aspect of this complex design, this would be the algorithm. Blaise worked his way from the Light grid particulars inductively up to this primary coding equation. The Elohim and Pleiadian Light nest designers started with it. The Hierophancy's job is to guard this algorithm now that we have rediscovered it.

In case you're not familiar with algorithms, mathematicians define them as a set of number operations meant to calculate, process data, and reason automatically. The procedure and the name are Persian in origin from around 800 A.D. The algorithm specifies an operation and calculates a function and proceeds towards this goal or output through a series of defined sequential states. A heuristic algorithm is one that is self-learning, one that can update and upgrade itself automatically based on incoming fresh data. It would be incorrect to call this an artificial intelligence, but I suppose it is close. I suspect a heuristic algorithm is maybe one or two steps short of self-awareness.

Blaise tells me every planet with a Light grid has an heuristic algorithm. These number calculations are like headings on file folders kept in the planet design office maintained by the Pleiadians who executed these many diverse designs. The Hierophancy heuristic algorithm is the file heading on Earth's folder. The "file heading" is also the activation, management, and adjustment code, and it is the password that enables you to access then modulate the system in real time. It is the prime method of live and efficient interaction with a Light grid. The algorithm runs the grid's intended processes of consciousness. I hope this background information is giving you an idea of the severity of the problem that confronted us, a sense of what was at stake, the peril to the Earth.

Many years ago, Blaise told me, he realized that the total picture of the planet's Light grid could be expressed and understood in two ways. One was through the psychic pictures known as myths that act as initiation cue cards and describe the site particulars and the optimal modes of successful interaction. Clairvoyance accesses this psychic picture dimension of the planetary design.

The other was through numbers. Everything about the Earth's Light grid entailed numbers, especially the quantities of copies of each type of Light temple. Everything had been precisely counted out; nothing fell off the back of the truck. The bulk of the numbers were extrapolations of the number 9, key to the design. What you might call our higher mind aspect accesses this number dimension.

The quantities of copies of each Light temple were carefully specified. Grail Castle copies, for example, total 144; domes number 1,746; Lucifer Binding Sites, 3,496. You have this degree of specificity for the roster of 613 architectural features that comprise the planet's geomantic profile and Light grid constitution. Each of these different types of Light temples have numbers attached to them, and they can be described and invoked mathematically; so can the entire system.

Since numbers specified all the quantities in the design of the planet grid, it seemed reasonable that this nest of Light might originally have been specified by numbers, spelled out mathematically, which meant it could still be done so. You could invoke and describe and—here is where Blaise got very

enthused—interact with this system through numbers, calculations, equations, algorithms.

All of the Light grid must exist as a complicated math formula, he told me. All the processes of consciousness that its array of Light temples affords must be mathematical in origin; surely, the Light grid must have started out as numbers. Blaise was climbing an inductive ladder back to the original starting point. He was reasoning from details back to the defining principle of the design. You would have one master algorithm that ordered the operation of the 613 Light temple components of the Light grid and their arithmetical processes.

That would be the Earth's Hierophancy algorithm, the perpetually self-revealing number calculation. The heuristic part comes from its ability to self-modulate. It learns from its own calculations and their implications, and it learns from continuously incoming data derived from meteorology, geology (meaning tectonics and volcanism), sociology, astrology, and large collective movements in consciousness—from all possible data sources that reflect current life activities. The system is intensely, minutely interactive and reciprocally self-modulating, and the algorithm is the intelligence that presides over this living concatenation.

Whether it's a destructive hurricane in the Caribbean or somebody's successful accessing of the recondite Grail Castle and a healthy immersion in the unitive consciousness and soul recall of one's own timeline afforded by the Holy Grail or a surfeit of sunspot activities and solar flare eruptions from our Sun, these developments are entered into the algorithm essentially like news reports. The algorithm "learns" from these inputs and adjusts the "output" accordingly. The output refers to the manner of its gently tweaking or nudging the Light grid. The algorithm has pre-established output thresholds, targeted development plateaus that were conceived when the Light grid template was first fashioned.

Think of this as an eschatology built into the system. Not a deterministic, rigidly imposed final outcome, but a general notion, a direction, a suggested tendency to reach and for which much malleability in approach is allowed. What I mean here is yes, there is a desired goal, but the way to it remains fluid. The designers are prepared to be surprised at the novel manner by which we attain it.

The algorithm continuously balances out all the wobbling, staggering, indecisive movements towards that goal. It is exquisitely responsive to geomantic nuances. It constantly adjusts the consciousness "nutrient" feed to the planetary system in response to changing daily conditions. The planet's Light grid or consciousness template is our context for making these evolutionary advances. It needs to be kept in perfecting working order. In many respects this algorithm is the system's superintendent and *genius loci*, its *numen*, intelligence, caretaker, director of activities, mother, and (almost sentient) ensouling presence.

I'm not sure I have yet conveyed to you sufficiently how important this algorithm is. Let's say before Blaise developed it (or rediscovered it), the planet extruded innumerable strings from its geomantic sites and geomancers from the many cultures of the world would pull on their local strings to maintain the local pattern. Shamans, initiates, Mystery candidates, and even secret societies, would do their best to interact with their portion of the world pattern through tailored rituals. Some rituals had an initiation thrust to them for a double benefit. There was nothing coherent or systematic to this interaction, and often it was spotty and inadequate, leaving large areas, whole geomantic provinces, unattended.

With the development of the heuristic algorithm, the complete Earth energy pattern could be maintained at once in a manner that was globally coherent and comprehensive down to local levels. The algorithm accessed the total pattern and all its particulars and all at once, thoroughly and effectively.

Now somebody had taken this invaluable number and left us with a defective fake one. A unique aspect of the Hierophancy heuristic algorithm is that you cannot use a duplicate. If you have a copy of it and somebody else has the original, only the original is viable; the copy will not work. It has no nerve conduction. It is like trying to use a telephone line that is already in use. It's worse, or even more futile, when your "copy" is a defective one and disfigured. Or it's like somebody stole the motor out of your car and left a photograph of an engine in its place. It's laughable. You can't run an automobile on a photograph.

I am up against an inherent difficulty in explaining the predicament. Certainly we had copies of the algorithm written down and filed. It isn't that we cannot remember the algorithm's details. It is the operational context that has been stolen. The algorithm was unplugged, disconnected from its matrix. They stole its operational viability in a kind of mathematical exsanguination. The body remains standing but it has no blood in it, no circulating arithmetical life. The geomantic connections remained in place, but no numbers streamed through the system to invigorate it and geomantic life came to a standstill.

So I sat there in my office, frowning and clenching my teeth. The Earth is fucked, I muttered in one of my rawer, unpolished moments. This was the worst possible breach of security. This number was our point of maximum input and in the 15 years since we had it, we had entered into a smooth, routine manner of geomantic interaction and maintenance with all aspects of the Earth. We had arduously, and at last, successfully, climbed back up the mountain of knowledge that the original planetary designers deployed to create the Light grid and to keep it in top-notch condition in the planet's early days of use. The designers had begun with this algorithm and generated the myriad aspects; we had inductively climbed that pyramid of applications back to the algorithm.

Blaise had spent many decades preparing the foundation for discovering this formula. For a long time the work involved creating an inventory of sites. Let's take the example of Grail Castles. The planet was endowed with 144 copies of this Light temple; these copies were distributed across the Earth's landmasses. To some extent, their existence and location were memorialized in the myths of their host country, and these myths usually served as valuable and reliable clues. French folklore says a Grail Castle was located at the craggy peak in the Pyrenees called Montsegur. It was, but the Grail Castle was an etheric temple above the mountain, in the subtle world accessed at that site. Still, the legend was correct. It correctly told us where one of the 144 copies of this feature would be found.

You find the locations of all these copies, then you draw lines connecting them, thereby revealing the grid that defines their distribution array. Most often this is a complex pattern of connection, here providing us a meta-grid of all the Grail Castles. The pattern is the composite Grail Castle grid. They were all placed purposefully and in accordance with this original geometric design template. It was like a lace doily draped over the global surface, the sites for the 144 copies clearly indicated on it. The grid pattern of their deployment is itself valuable information. It provides a meta-view of the purpose of the Light temple: this many copies working together in this way will generate a likely global effect.

That is a functional unit in itself, and the Grail Castle grid is a Grail Castle conveying the essence of that consciousness process through its geometric shape. Holographically, it is the master expression of that Light temple, the grid itself acting as the master version of the templated Grail Castle at 144 sites. Think of the meta-grid as the master shape, the 144 copies its fractal elaboration. If all the copies were in activated status, you'd be delivering 144 points of identical impact to human consciousness across the planetary body of sites. It would be like 144 members of the Ofanim forming a bright angelic circle around you and talking to you at the same time for 144 points of simultaneous impact in your awareness.

That is a geometrical pattern of influence, and the distribution mechanism implies a mathematical equation that originally specified it. That pattern has a geometry, and that introduces the arithmetical aspect, its coding. Do you follow?

We work inductively upwards from myth, to Light temple, to location, to all the locations, to a map of these locations, then a grid of their array, then the arithmetical aspect that created that grid pattern in the first place. The geometry of the distribution grid yields an arithmetical code, its key design signature. Then we do this for all the types of Light temples (our current count is 613 types), compiling many grids and these revealing their innate mathematics. This way we generate 613 sub-algorithms, from which we derive the master one. This is the heuristic algorithm; it supervises the totality of these Light temple grid patterns.

You may appreciate that a great deal of research was involved in this, a combination of scholarly and clairvoyant investigation, a painstaking inventory. Each of these Light temple distribution grids can be specified by a calculation, and the complete planetary distribution pattern of everything, the full geomantic array, can be specified by a calculation, though it is an intensely complex one. You could regenerate the Earth and its Light grid from this master algorithm. If you were an entirely mathematical species, for whom arithmetic was your prime language, you could look at our algorithm and derive the entire planet from it. I mean you would see the mental or abstract form of the planet and its Light grid. You would see the mental architecture that precedes all the metaphors and grids.

Take away the visual impressions of Light temples and all the mythic narratives and psychic interpretations (the metaphors) and you reveal the naked substrate of numbers that code it. Behind every Light temple and Light temple distribution grid are the numbers.

These numbers reflect the coding mechanisms by which the forms were created. Whatever codes something can also be used to maintain or upgrade that system; that's the algorithmic function. That's what the Hierophancy heuristic algorithm performs. You see why it's a disaster it's gone?

The Hierophancy had been looking after this system for 15 years at this point, except now our hands were suddenly, shockingly, dangerously empty.

I said at the outset that initially we didn't know anything had been stolen. We only found out routinely on a Wednesday morning when we instituted our daily updates and the system didn't respond. In fact, it didn't work at all. It went through the gestures of working; it initially looked like it was outputting correctly, but then nothing changed in real time or in real terms. It was all fake. Or it was like entering data on a computer file then when you go to save it, no trace of what you just entered remains on the document. It did not register. It was like writing a document on water. It only looks like you are writing, but the surface fails to retain any vestige of an imprint. That's what the algorithm did (or, more properly, failed to do) the morning we discovered it had been stolen.

Blaise was away from the office at the time. He was in Budapest making personal inspections of a few Light temples near the city center. He said they had appeared wobbly and unanchored the last time he "looked" at them from a distance. He is a very accomplished clairvoyant and often works this way. When I notified him of the development, he was silent on the phone line for a while. His reaction was similar to mine: it was a greater mystery how someone had acquired the algorithm than who the perpetrator was, though that was key too.

He suggested we insert a tracker data set in the algorithm by way of queuing it up in the inputting schedule. The authentic algorithm, because it was by nature holographic and thereby functionally encompassed the entire planet and its data, would collect this new data and incorporate it, even if this input did not register in our flawed and basically fake extant version. The real one would get it, and through that we could start tracking where it was and who took it. It was far worse than we initially thought, Blaise said. It was stolen six months ago. I don't know how he arrived at that startling discovery, but he was proven right.

Now I was silent for a few moments. Shit. That meant we had been dealing with a spurious version of the algorithm for that time and didn't know it. The inputs entered during that time failed to hit their mark. Other contrary or slyly deviating inputs had taken their place, and their mark on lived reality was the one that the "soft wax" of the Earth's Light grid registered. The Earth's Light grid had been drifting in an incremental entropic manner all that time. Six months of accrued subluxation—that was a momentous, worrisome deviation.

Please note my use of the word "lived." It is crucial to understanding the Light grid. It is a pattern of Light that directs and regulates all aspects of awareness, from bodily to spiritual; it structures and infiltrates all expressions of matter, including the five elements and through them the Periodic Table of Elements, as we live them, as they inform the daily feeling quality of this life. It is, by analogy, the planet's and humanity's collective etheric body, the woven imprint that precedes and thus generates and sustains all physical expressions.

If you take away the etheric body from the physical human form, it will die at once. It is similar with the planet: if you compromise or vitiate its etheric field, all its natural processes will wobble, weaken, and quickly expire. The Light grid's mathematics are the blood that circulates through this etheric body. The world's inventory of mythic pictures are the vivid points of heightened self-awareness and meaning rising up within this etheric web.

I mentioned that on that Wednesday morning our inputs had failed. But up until that time, we had assumed, based on reasonable observations and performance standards, that our inputting was proceeding correctly and effectively. Only now can I appreciate how for six months a slight divergence between input and output had been steadily growing; now it was a major gap.

The algorithm was undergoing a slow-motion hijacking over those six months, a kind of incremental information poisoning of its mathematical matrix which was basically undetectable until it reached an inflection point, and then we saw it. I would have to notify our worldwide network of Hierophancy field members, as well as our local staff of 25, except what if one of these people was the perpetrator? Our security was breached so we would have to be circumspect about who we told and how much we disclosed in case we were aiding the thief. I don't wish to sound alarmist, but if you can manage the planetary and human consciousness through this algorithm you can also control and suborn it as well.

Blaise said, just before we ended our conversation, that he was going back to the

Pleiades to consult with the senior designers of Earth's Light grid, but I was to tell no one of his departure. He said he might first come back to Sun Valley and leave through the nexus there. "Keep it secret. I want the perpetrator to assume we are stymied and paralyzed as to effective corrective action. Which is probably not too far from the truth at present. My colleagues back home will help us figure this out. They might even have anticipated it. Keep an eye on what the hidden tracker we put in the system reveals about its location or operation."

Our Pleiadian senior colleagues maintain a file of planetary algorithms. It is not physically like a file cabinet with file folders, but a data inventory of the key operational number sets for thousands of planets with Light grids, all of which they designed. Our Earth has a file that contains its heuristic algorithm. With this number, you can summon a virtual representation of a planet's grid, study its complete body and layerings of systems and consciousness streams. It also gives you access to its operations and enables you to adjust its systems. That points to what is both the maintenance advantage and the serious risk of misuse.

Of course, we hadn't "lost" our number. We had many copies of its mathematics. The problem was it had been unplugged and was no longer connecting to the Light grid system, at least through our Idaho operations headquarters. The subornation of our system had been exceedingly clever. It still looked like our inputs got entered and started adjusting the actual planet. We remained entranced in this intended manner until one day I saw a wrong digit.

Say you have a number sequence that has perhaps 30 digits on each side of a decimal mark and you notice that one digit is changed. It is not the one specified for that location. It was like coming to work and finding a new employee that nobody remembered hiring. I stared at that wrong digit for five minutes as if mesmerized by this impossible development. Imagine looking in the mirror one morning and finding your face was radically different. You don't think it is possible that your algorithm can be manipulated but there it is before you: it has, one deviation, just one changed number, one that spelled disaster.

I hope I have not conveyed the impression that this algorithm is like a number sequence you can jot down in a notebook. You can, but that undersells its complexity. It is a living 4D reality, and to stand within its holographic matrix you'd feel certain it was a sentient calculation, even, if you felt metaphysically daring, a self-aware one. I mean self-aware to the extent it looks after its own welfare and is aware of itself doing so. To stand inside this matrix is like residing in a hyperdimensional expression of a planet and phylogeny itself, like you're standing inside the complete *idea* for the expression of both human and Earth, inside an arithmetical architecture that codes the manifestation of both forms.

It keeps you on your mental toes monitoring the complexity of this 4D array. You can pull out of this vast mathematical construct the coding specifics for any Light temple subset, such as the array of Grail Castles, Cities of the Gods, or Ray Master Sanctuaries, among the huge repertoire of designs. We have catalogued 613 different types of Light temples with many copies of each. Each type has its own coding specifics and calibrated effect on consciousness.

The end product of the heuristic algorithm is to constantly update and calibrate the reciprocals of consciousness, natural conditions (floods, fires, volcanic eruptions, earthquakes, severe weather, and their effects on human awareness and the collective emotional body), with the planet's Light grid. There are so many inputs to collate. It makes continuous adjustments, down to the most minute level, to reflect progress in the evolution of human consciousness, new galactic and solar inputs, information downloads from the angelic and Hierarchical realms, and changing grids of influence from the other planets in our solar system and the Sun as well. Somebody remembers the history of their soul in a Grail Castle, and that trembling in the collective consciousness becomes a fresh input. The system is exquisitely reciprocal and requires exacting oversight.

I went into Sal's office to check on the status of things from his view. Salman Johnstone is our resident data inputter, adjuster, tweaker, and monitor. I suppose those are all nontechnical terms. With his advanced degrees in mathematics, I'm sure he has more appropriate if arcane designations for what he does for the Hierophancy. He once jokingly said, "Call me your resident algorithmic topologist." We do, but we also call him Sal for all numbers issues.

He showed me all the data sets ready to be inputted and ran through an input session. He could run a simulation here of the official inputting in our 4D hologram. We watched in subdued horror as they failed to reconfigure the number matrix. You could practically see the glaring gap between fresh data formulation and the intended destination of that new information in the matrix. Mostly, the holographic array failed to respond to the input; it wobbled, and, if it were a living person, I imagine we'd be hearing moans and perhaps a few sighs.

Sal has been with us for nearly ten years. Blaise brought him in, after, I think, trawling the top universities for math geniuses, but ones willing to see things differently or perhaps whose minds were bent correctly since their birth. The mental framework required for the Hierophancy challenges conventional norms of quotidian reality; even with the momentous changes to the world psyche since 2020, what the Hierophancy is and deals with still stretches the mind. Sal is, at least compared to Blaise and myself, blushingly young, a mere 45. I wondered for a while if he were one of the Blaise babies, 35 years old when we roped him in, but Blaise says he isn't though he may have lived in proximity to some of those unique, newly fashioned angel-humans now walking among us.

Before Sal came to the Hierophancy he had been working on advanced mathematical topics. These included spatial and geometric algorithms, visual analytics, computational algorithms, and topological algorithms, all of which, in my layman's approximation, involved the application of complex algorithms to the generation, maintenance, and manipulation of geometric objects from 3D and up, especially into arcane domains of higher dimensional space like Light grids. As I just indicated consciousness is a shapeable space with its own topology, so Sal's expertise in managing topological mathematics was pertinent to our work.

You can see, I trust, how his skills would be relevant to our Hierophancy work which increasingly has involved topological modeling and algorithmic computations. Sal is the one who showed us how to "attach" the algorithms to the grid models. That way we could get the master Hierophancy algorithm to monitor and adjust the planetary Light grid. He said it had to do with "topological consanguinity." His work gave our master heuristic algorithm a point of workable traction within the total grid; it affected Light temples and their grids through their mathematical forebears within arithmetical space. We knew modulation was theoretically possible; Sal made it work in real terms.

Blaise has had Sal working on a special project, in addition to all his other copious math-related Hierophancy tasks. This project pertained to figuring out the theoretical infrastructure of a presumed second-tier Light grid based on prime numbers. Blaise had noted that nearly all the numbers for the quantities of features in the Earth's Light grid were composite numbers; only a few numbers out of hundreds of quantity designations were primes. What did that mean? The mysteries of the primes would have to wait. The missing algorithm was topmost, though for readers intrigued with this, I'll return to a prime numbers grid later.

"Do you see the input has only an inconsistent, you might even say only a trembling effect on the data set," Sal said. "But it lacks all real-time traction. It's like saying you extend your hand to shake somebody's hand and yours has somehow fallen asleep and you can't move the fingers. It's now just a limp hand. That's what happens with our fresh data inputs. They don't shake hands with the algorithm.

What we have here is a ghost version of the Hierophancy number. Even the paralyzed-hand effect seems to take place in slow-motion, as if, to make matters worse, our algorithm and its 4D display run in a time-dilation field."

Sal paused and his face took on a grim expression. "It's worse than that. Devilishly clever, actually. I realized this morning the degradation effect is running backward. It is not just that we cannot input any data and get new tractionable effects; the system is now working backwards. Soon the system will resume inputting, but it will be for negative outcomes, ones that start to degrade the planet's Light grid. What I see scheduled is a systemic number poisoning.

"The wrong numbers will be entered into the system and they will start taking apart the algorithm and damaging the physical planet and all its life systems. Our algorithm will start feeding in negative numbers to the holographic matrix, and that will start taking apart the complex architecture of the Light grid itself. To use a different analogy, this is rewriting the Light grid's DNA script."

I used to listen to the daily inputs into the Light grid. It would be at 3 a.m. I found myself getting up early to be awake and attentive when it started. It was like a gardener fascinated with datura which blooms in gorgeous white blossoms during the night. You figure somebody should show it the honor of observing the nocturnal beauty of these moonflowers. They line up their blossoms for the night like a series of long white torches ready to erupt at dusk. You get curious what their nocturnal blossoming ritual might be all about as if they are botanical priests running an all-night meditative vigil on our behalf.

I would sit here, at my desk in the hyper-quiet of the Idaho early morning, and listen to the inputting. That's not accurate: the inputting was silent, but the uptake was noticeable. It was like hearing water circulating through a plant's leaves and stems right after you watered it. You sensed a vast global body of consciousness being reassured and corrected, taking on clarifying information that adjusted its complex systems to changing conditions. Did you ever listen to a houseplant thank you for watering it or moving it into or out of the bright sunlight? They do, you know. The Light grid responds like that. According to Blaise, once the Earth's Light grid was comprised entirely of plants. Planet Plant, they called our planet back then: for a long time the plants were the geomancers.

The algorithm supervised all the homeostatic regulatory functions of this global body. It adjusted the proportions and flow rate of elemental and angelic consciousness through the human system, which, you must remember, is at the highest level the complete Earth-Human phylogeny. Blaise calls that Albion.

The inputting took into account the modulations of fluctuating astrological influences, the continuous dance of squares, oppositions, conjunctions of the other restive solar system residents, where they were in relation to one another and to the Earth and the effects these alignments had. Then it adjusted the reaction of the planetary system to these altering impacts, tempering that reaction to balance humanity and biosphere.

The algorithm factored in the subtle influence of what acupuncture calls the stems and branches, the delicate flows, ebbing and cresting, of cosmic *prana*. On a single human body level, this is the flow of *Qi* through the major meridians, and the algorithm delivered to it what amounted to a daily acupuncture treatment. The algorithm adjusted the daily proportions of the different necessary flavors of consciousness, including angelic, Hierarchical, elemental, alien, and human.

None of this precluded regular field-delivered Light grid adjustments. The Hierophancy was constantly sending out teams to recalibrate the individual geomantic nodes as required and to participate in the year's real-time geomantic downloads from the celestial world, such as Epiphany, Michaelmass, and others. These are part of the annual geomantic liturgical calendar of scheduled events. Everybody loved these assignments: it was like a trip to a gorgeous waterfall, they often said, when the celestial energies flowed down like the purest water. Nobody wanted to stay at home or in the office when Epiphany came around each year; everyone on our staff flew out the door to the designated grid node.

Dark inputs still showed up at sites and had to be purged by our experts. This might be 46 years into the Golden Age but it hasn't erased the option to commit evil from the polymorphously perverse human unconscious. Evil got committed, and we had to periodically clean out its effects from particular geomantic nodes. It wasn't always evil-intentioned pollution deposited at the sites; often it was the product of misdirected attempts to tune in or interact with the sites and their attendant deities or ill-advised participation in the affairs of low-level astral spirits using those sites to trawl for recruits for their glamours. Still, these were routine taints and nothing of any serious import. We purged the sites, polished the Light temples, adjusted their illumination, and then moved on.

Global consciousness is a single hypersensitive living awareness body. It isn't just being aware of the Earth's heartbeat, what they used to call the Schumann Resonance, a frequency emanation of the physical planet and its systems. It isn't only being cognizant of the co-presence of Gaia and Pan, the planet's two primary regents of all natural systems and their many elementals. It is awareness of human sentience as a living presence as vivid as breathing. The planet, geomantically, is the Human, only expressed in a different form. The awakened, self-aware, totally sentient, telepathic Human is its end product. The Light grid in all its complexity is the womb in which this Human gestates. The Hierophancy heuristic algorithm is the mathematical midwife who will birth it.

One name for this collectivity of awakened, vital human sentience is Albion. It has taken the entire life of the Earth to date to awaken this colossus of Light, and birthing it has always been one of the prime objectives of having a Light grid. Think of the Hierophancy heuristic algorithm as the mathematically constructed physiology of this collective planetary spirit. It is the interactive, self-adjusting system that runs all the processes of this Light grid personification. Albion is the face on the planet's Light grid, and arithmetic is its physiology. With the heuristic algorithm that runs this cosmogonic face now taken out of the picture, can you see the peril that act has imposed upon planet and humanity?

This sentient global awareness was supposed to be taking in the vast life of the solar system, galaxy, and cosmos, and all levels of existence were alive in this. The system is fluid and open-ended, yet you felt, expanding yourself into this planet-sized version of the human, wide-awake to the greater cosmic life, watching all of it, feeling its myriad influences bathe over you and prickle your skin like carbonated bubbles, you *knew* at the same time you were this immense epiphany. You were this, everything you were watching and enjoying defined your true identity. Even better, you felt safe, assured, confident, knowing your well-being was looked after by benevolent celestial intelligences. Albion is the global version of each of us, and we are miniature walking-around Albions.

Prior to 2020, we were so grimly accustomed to the seeming absence of that assurance. The benign celestial agencies were still there, but the dark conditions prevailing on the Earth usually blocked much of their influence getting through to daytime consciousness, or it distorted it or cut its potency by 75%. But now within this global sentience beamed the eyes of billions of humans wide-awake to the spectacle of Light that is their life, the algorithm monitoring it.

Except now it wasn't. Now the algorithm, perversely, was destroying this.

"It's like a case of daily, incremental erosion, and soon the cliff will be gone," said Sal who could say insightful remarks and furiously type in numbers at the same time and not lose track of either coherence or his unfolding formula. "Well, obviously our Light grid is the well-built mansion on the edge of the cliff, meaning the cosmic abyss of no Light grids or coherent organization, little null pockets where the Supreme Being didn't get around to building something nice. Whoever did this to our algorithm left some clever booby-traps in place.

Every time I try to tweak the eroding system or make even a tiny adjustment, it degrades faster. My intervention acts as a decohering arithmetical accelerant.

"Even worse, it spins off a fake branch of the algorithm, as if it is distracted. It looks like the main line, but if you study the configuration carefully, you see one or two key numbers have been changed, yielding a different, more wrong result. These 'more wrong' results seem to be exponential: each new wrong one delivers a far worse outcome than the previous wrong result. The wrongs are getting stronger. If this were a classic detective-mystery story, it's like tampering with the brakes. The chief witness is getting too close to the truth, so we'd better derail him, take him out of the picture before he can incriminate us."

Sal smiled, as if he had discovered something that cheered him. We certainly could use some good news. "They didn't find my back door. Excellent. I installed a bolt-hole in the system, not so much for escape or hiding but for secret entry. Normally, as you know, we stand in the holographic matrix display, try not to feel dizzy from the constantly invaginating cubes and the general complexity of the system displayed as a living organism around us, and mentally make adjustments, interacting directly with the heuristic mind of the system.

"I put in a number of secret doors embedded like grace-notes which you access by inputting an equation like inserting parentheses in a sentence. That has the effect of making the interior display seem to bulge and gape, yielding a wide-open door. It resembles a big open mouth, like it's yawning or about to swallow you. The tricky part is this grace-note sits in the fifth dimension of the algorithm. It's like walking in the higher-dimensional walls behind the main gallery of a cathedral then suddenly emerging into the 3D expression of this physical space.

"The 4D matrix is challenging enough, since past, present, and future are present, like fans spread out in a sports stadium or a vast art gallery with everything hung in the one big room. But in the 5D backdoor level of the system you have many secret access points to this all-present timeline. Providing you can keep track of where you are, not lose your bearings in this hyper-complex expression of the algorithm, you should be able to adjust the lower 4D. It's like performing a high-wire balancing act in a form with 40 3D cubes and 10 4D cubes, all tumbling, turning inside out, shuffling about like a frenzied crowd."

Everything I ever knew about myths, the entire world curriculum and yearbook of players and roles, the roster of mythic pictures the many cultures had recorded, was swallowed up and digested in this number funhouse, or to a layman, this madhouse of numbers turning inside out in a hyperdimensional space. Each of the functions in consciousness the myths alluded to and which the matching Light temples delivered could be reduced to number codes, Blaise had determined. Here was our planet's Light grid in full expressed as mathematics.

All the mythic pictures, image codes for the identity and operation of the Light temples, had been transformed into numbers and those fed into the algorithm, and here it was, the master key to planetary reality and human consciousness, and that key, I reminded myself, was now twisted and broken.

Years ago during our many outings together Blaise talked about the two primary ways of describing the planet's Light grid. "First you can see it as an array of psychic pictures, coded images that detail interaction patterns and modes. These comprise the key elements from the world's myths; these are the face cards in the Supreme Being's deck. You still have to interpret the pictures, though, see through the metaphors the images pose, figure out their meaning.

"The second way is that all this reduces to numbers and equations. The Light grid is a numbered reality; you can describe it then access it through the numbers. If it's a number matrix, then there must be a number that encapsulates the system. This would be a password, the summary of all specifications, and the means of optimal interaction. That's how I developed the Hierophancy heuristic algorithm. I wanted to see what that number looked like. I wanted to try it out."

Blaise made good on his intention. First we inventoried all the mythic pictures, trimmed away superfluities accreted over time, streamlined the picture to its core. Then we abstracted all the numbers from these pictures, though this was in terms of the quantities of their copies and any operational codes we deduced, especially from their master distribution pattern. Their global array pattern was geometrical and that yielded numbers in an equation producing it.

Here is the logic behind this approach. Picture 144 copies of the same Light temple placed all across the planet. Draw lines connecting these points. That yields a geometric pattern, a distribution grid. That was the basis for their original placement, and

it comprises numbers and these imply equations that organize and run them. The distribution pattern of the 144 copies is itself a Light temple and its geometry yields numbers and formulas that generate the shape.

Do this with the 613 other Light temple designs the planet's geomantic pattern exhibits. Other numbers may be derived from exposure duration, how long typically it takes to be inside such a temple to get its intended effects. The combined distribution pattern of the 613 components is itself a Light grid with numbers. With 613 different Light temples and their copy arrays, we derived 613 operational equations. Then on this information basis, Blaise put the heuristic algorithm together. This algorithm was the command equation for the system.

I suspect his Pleiadian colleagues helped him in this work. They were the master designers of nests for Light and consciousness. That's probably why he bee-lined for the Pleiades as soon as this theft was disclosed. Before this, there were times when he was deep in thought about the Light grid numbers and he started to look like a Pleiadian: his face, his eyes, his expression, transfigured. You began to see his true backstory, his place of origin, his original phylogeny. He would clearly look like someone else, like he came from somewhere else, another planet certainly where the mind was stronger, broader, and deftly comprehended more of the complex design of reality, planets, and humans.

For a long time, he gave seminars in Hierophancy matters, educating all our members in the protocols of geomancy and Light management. He would be absent for long periods too, never explaining where he went or why, just suddenly back again ready for more classes or field trips. Certainly Blaise was exceptionally long-lived, but he was not, I don't think, immortal, at least not yet, so it made logistical sense to pass on his knowledge while he was here among us.

I wondered how he was making out back there. He was in the 4D matrix assessing the damage. Then soon after we discovered the breach, he returned to our offices, entered the holographic coding matrix, then when he stepped out of the cube, he asked me at once to drive him to the nearest stargate. He knew their locations and destinations, the way a seasoned traveller knows airports. It took us longer to drive to the stargate than it took for him to reach the Pleiades. He would have arrived within seconds of stepping into the shimmering portal. He had, in fact, been making many trips back there in the last two years, as if he was part of a planning committee for something coming up in Earth's near future. He didn't talk about his work there, but then he was circumspect about many things.

He often joked about how frequent travel to the Pleiades added years to his life. That's because his human body was dissolved, freed of Earth gravity, while he was there, and his borrowed Pleiadian form did not accrue any biological aging. That's the odd thing about stargates: you cannot arrive in your departure body. The human form would not survive in these alien atmospheres, so our transiting consciousness assumes the generic sentient life-form of that world. Blaise leaves as a human, arrives as a Pleiadian, thus saving tread-wear on his mortal physical human body and thereby contributing to its longevity. The stargate downloads arriving consciousness into an available generic form and the biological aging clock on his human body stops for the visit's duration.

I realize I should not assume prior knowledge of stargates on the reader's part. A stargate is a device enabling almost instantaneous physical relocation from a site on Earth to a site on one of 300 planets in our galaxy. Our planet was originally equipped with about two million stargates in its geomantic patterning.

There is much redundancy in destination, just like with terrestrial airports where you can fly to key places like Los Angeles and London and Paris from multiple airports. The stargates are not physical devices as we know physicality, though they produce physical translocation; on average, they are the size of a small house and they exist in a complex but describable pattern all across the Earth. They were dormant for many millennia during the advent of second-generation humanity, and that dormancy was a direct correlation of the degree of binding for Lucifer and Sophia, as their Light and consciousness energize the system since their cosmic forms include all the stars the gates open up to.

As we drove to the stargate, I thought about how Blaise wanted to find that master number and try it out. He did, though it took years. It worked. It was like taming a wild horse, not that either of us were cowboys or even riders, but the analogy seems pertinent. I refer to the collective consciousness of the Light grid. It was feral, a stranger to itself, having lived for so long outside the corral.

By this I mean the intended operating parameters for the planetary system. It was used to being skittish, undisciplined, rogue, even if it was self-destructive. It behaved that way because of the unruly influence of humanity's collective unconscious, the nonintegrated, still inchoate nature of the sleeping Albion. But as the Hierophancy algorithm started to take control of the planet's Light grid, you felt the world start to settle down on its springs, no more rearing and neighing. Reality calmed down; its innate rationality became apparent. As Albion completed his wake-up process after 2020, the Light grid grew tranquil.

That's the biggest problem geomancers face, namely, we know Earth reality was carefully planned, but with its innate geomantic body hidden from public view and understanding, for a long time it was difficult to convince people of its good purpose, or even, in many cases, of its existence. Gradually, planetary consciousness started to come awake to itself, take its bearings, and begin to appreciate the intelligence behind its own design and even glimpse its future. Finally, now we can point to the evidence that makes us say Earth makes sense, and we can reasonably expect a fair number of people to understand us.

Discordant emanations from the undisciplined subconscious of the collectivity of humanity started to diminish, particularly their aberrational effect on the Light grid and its components, such as weather and geology. Did you know human emotional turbulence can precipitate earthquakes and volcanic eruptions, that ungrounded collective human feeling can wreak storms? The Earth has to channel those strong disorganized waves of group emotion into a planetary system, like lightning rods on a house safely grounding an electrical discharge. Albion's sleep was perpetually disturbed by all this commotion for millennia, but now, awake, and with humanity somewhat pacified, he is calm.

Sustained but unbalanced emotional releases seeped out of the collective human psychic field the way the noxious chemicals once used to preserve new carpets would come out as gases when you walked on the carpets, and these human releases would disrupt the delicate ecosystem, perturbing the weather, inciting drought and rain cycles, and usually darkening the emotional tone of people everywhere. Often they would produce "natural disasters," social eruptions, and interpersonal turmoil, from fights to wars. It gave the physical world and the feel of human life a chaotic, hostile, unpredictable, crazy aspect. People would walk about sickened, either bodily or mentally, and not know it.

Now with the algorithm we could regulate these two components, human exudates and planetary receptor-regulatory systems, to minimize the chance of disorder and sickness. It was like finally putting your hands on the controls for machinery that had been dangerously running amok and without sensible management for millennia. Now we could compensate for heightened human collective emotionality by adjusting the geomantic systems, and these in turn would reciprocally tone down those human psychic eruptions; gradually, both would come into balance, and instead of storms you'd have graceful minuets. The managing algorithm rendered the system tremendously reciprocal in which every human input produced a corresponding geomantic adjustment for balance.

Fortunately, with the planetary changes precipitated by events of 2020, governmental "scientists" had stopped trying to jury-rig and weaponize the planetary ecosystems to fit their futile total world-control agendas. Their inept attempts had been crude and incrementally destructive. They gave them up. They stopped spraying the upper atmosphere with toxic chemtrails; they halted bombarding the lower atmosphere with radionic and electromagnetic pulses; they ended using earthquakes and violent storms as coercive forces; they stopped lighting massive summer forest fires to stimulate jobs for firefighters. Scientists' ill-advised attempts to control physical phenomena only generated global chaos and further separated consciousness from its rational context.

The installation of the heuristic algorithm finally took this aberrational, chronic distortionary input out of the Earth's system. Regulation, not crude control, became the order of the day. Earth reality de-stressed and eased up. Gradually, people started to develop a fresh appreciation of their planet as the algorithm began to harmonize human, ecosystem, and Light grid relations. This same string of numbers, our 4D algorithm expressed in a holographic matrix and that provides us access to the planet as a sentient body of Light, now was revealing that complex, beautifully designed world to all its living members.

The algorithm was making the planet hierophantic. The Earth itself was revealing the Holy Light everywhere, the high spiritual intelligence comprising its design. The Earth, disclosed in its Light grid complexity, is this body of Holy Light. The Earth is hierophantic, and it is itself the embodiment of that Holy Light it is perpetually revealing. It always has been as far back as when this blue-white planet was only a concept in the brilliant design minds of the Pleiadians who created its Light architecture.

But people forgot, didn't see this anymore. So it would take a positive Apocalypse to reveal this original pattern to people. The algorithmic management system was enabling people across the planet to appreciate they too were manifestations of this same Holy Light. With the advent of human-form angelic incarnations in 2020, humans started seeing themselves as hierophantic, the human form, human presence, the gestures of consciousness, were hierophantic. Religions had always taught this, but it had been only a mental concept; now it was real, and you could easily see this hierophantic disclosure every day.

I don't mean to sound spiritually precious here. I mean this in a Hermetic sense. The human design replicates the planetary design; they are isomorphic grids. They both reveal the *same* Holy Light, and that Light is the perfection of design. The human form and the planetary pattern are reciprocally hierophantic designs. As the planet's Light grid is perfected, meaning as its original form is revealed and validated by interactive consciousness, this beneficially feeds back into the human version of the same design, and the human starts to awaken to its true nature, and consciousness finally breaches the horizon as a glorious sunrise. This reciprocally feeds back into the well-lighted planet, and the cosmos takes notice as Earth and its reciprocating sentient life-form at last knows itself.

Albion is the name for this reciprocally awakened and self-aware appreciation of the Holy Light. Albion is its body and consciousness, the fulfillment of the human and planetary design. Albion is the hierophantic ideal. Human design and corresponding planetary design are fulfilled in our Albion.

Prior to this, our collective karma had been distorting the pure pattern. Unresolved compulsions from the past and current mental oblivion had blocked general human awareness of this reciprocating pattern of Light. The delicately beautiful woven pattern of Light was blackened and distorted by dark lightning flashes, storms, and eruptions in the collective psyche, obscuring the design. You caught glimpses of this Light occasionally, like you would during a fretful summer's day in England, when if you were lucky you'd see the Sun for a moment amidst the veiling, troubling clouds that blanketed the land and psyche.

It was the polarized world of sacred and profane, as mythographer Mircea Eliade had characterized it. Some of the geomantic nodes preserved the atmosphere of sacrality as a sanctuary you could escape into from the roiling profane world. Now that dichotomy was resolved and, geomantically speaking, the whole world was now sacred, all of it a sanctuary, all of it the Holy of Holies prolifically rich in the Holy Light in which the original hierophantic gestures and rituals of the gods were revealed in their timeless freshness, as Eliade said.

We had waited 432,000 years for the advent of this most recent Golden Age, for the infernal *Kali Yuga* to be finished and gone, not wanted and not missed. That's how long the Dark Age, the Black Time, what Hindu time-philosophers called the *Kali Yuga*, lasted, the long epoch of the dark grid, Antichrist, and awful conditions for consciousness, when the world could only tolerate 25% of the Truth, the rest occluded and nonincarnate. The years leading up to 2020 saw Kali squeezing the last dregs of darkness out of her *Yuga*.

The Hierophancy heuristic algorithm was now brightening this fresh Golden Age's prospects. Finally, we had a free hand. In this new time, fully 100% of the Truth was present.

The Hindus personified Truth as *Dharma*, a celestial being with four legs of truth. We finally had all four of his legs confidently striding across the planetary landscape. Four-legged *Dharma* walked among us.

The newly hierophantic Earth was the world all the myths I used to study alluded to but which had, until 2020, out of deep, melancholic memory, seemed irrecoverably only in the past and increasingly foreign to our so-called modern, deadened sensibilities. Now this was illuminated all around us, and the planet had become a living archive of psychic images and mythic tableaus, and these now comprised our world, even as they always had though long veiled to us.

The Earth was mythopoeic now. It had transfigured into a geomythic planet. The planet was floriated with mythic picture scripts demonstrating how to use the sites. Every script, as Blaise discovered, had on its flip side the specific number coding that generated it originally; Blaise collected these codes as raw data to input into his emerging algorithm. You could rightly declare, as Blaise often did, that the Earth is arithmetical. It is a world spun out of numbers. That's why the Hierophancy heuristic algorithm works. It maintains the Arithmetical Earth. It was the culmination of Blaise's life work, and that has been a long life.

He told me once he was so glad when 2020 finally arrived. He was 70 then. He had coped for many frustrating years with the obdurate thickness of human comprehension under the heavy literalness of the Black Age. "It was just about impossible to get most people to understand what I was showing them regarding the Earth's energy design. Brick walls stood between them and this reality. It wasn't their fault. I even found it hard at times to conceive of Golden Age frequencies during the last decades of the *Kali Yuga*.

"You have to remember the original Light settings for the Earth's grid were *Satya Yuga* conditions. That is difficult to even imagine during the Black Age; it is too contrary to consensus reality and our ingrained habits of perception. Forget about introducing people to the hyperdimensional nuances of 4D, 5D, and 6D aspects to the Light grid, of which there are many, good examples being domes, stargates, and wormholes. Before 2020, accepting the existence of a Light grid run on numbers with grids and temples was too much."

I returned to Sun Valley. Jocelyn came into the office. She is our resident librarian and scholar. She knows all the myths, frontwards and backwards, and can recite their details flawlessly on demand. She has an eidetic memory for mythic images. We often consulted her when we needed the accurate picture story that opened up a geomantic site to our understanding. If we were back at Dartmouth, she would be the brilliant head of our department in a flash. If Eliade were alive, he'd be courting her to join his faculty, to co-write breakthrough books. Jocelyn Blake is 65 and has studied the world's myths since she was eight.

She had done this in copious, even stupendous, detail. She had compiled permutation charts depicting all the different story variations, character nuances, and cultural guises of the archetypal figures in myth, and she had correlated it to varying geomantic locales across many cultures. Take the permutations of character and locale for the Arthurian heroes, all the sites across the British

Isles traditionally associated with King Arthur, Gawain, Lancelot, the Holy Grail. It is a long and bewildering list, all the different names affixed to the archetypal faces.

For Jocelyn it was like charting the progress of a troupe of consummate shapeshifters through a myriad of different cultural personae, and through this she had extracted the archetypal essence of each mythic gesture. She knew how to recognize each shapeshifter despite the changing guises he took. When we needed any information on a character, motif, or location, we hustled over to her station and she gave us the full, truly awesome, mythic briefing.

"So, it appears we have a modern-day Autolycus on our hands," she said.

See what I mean? Sal looked puzzled, but I got the reference and laughed. "The wolf itself. That's the meaning of his name. He was the son of Hermes and a master thief. Almost the archetype of thievery. He stole the helmet of Odysseus, his grandson, and he stole Sisyphus's cattle herd while he stood by, apparently distracted. Autolycus had been awarded the precious gift of never being caught for his thievery. He even managed to transfer the blame for one theft to Heracles. He owned a helmet that made him invisible and he was credited with enjoying turning black into white and hornless animals into ones with prominent horns."

"The difference here," Jocelyn said, "is that what our thief has stolen is far more momentous, even calamitous, than anything clever Autolycus got away with. It's not a war helmet or some cattle. It's the well-being of our planet itself."

"I'm getting the impression our Autolycus is a slow-motion thief," said Sal. "I am finding indications of an incremental stealth incursion into our system over the past few years, evidence of small perturbations and adjustments made to it. It's like stealing a bank by taking pennies every day. Eventually, you'll get it all. If I can stretch this analogy, these pennies cast a magnetic field over the larger denominations, and when Autolycus nicked the pennies, he pulled out the big bills too as if they stuck to the pennies and he pulled them by sticky strings. Our thief has been positioning himself for the big theft for years. We never saw it while it was happening, because it was like the proverbial perceptual futility of watching paint dry, and now we only see it from behind, as it speeds away."

I asked Sal what he meant by a slow-motion theft. He replied: "A slow replacement of individual integers. At first, it's not noticeable, nor does it affect anything crucial or seemingly anything in terms of algorithmic output. Then it does. Our Autolycus made these tiny withdrawals and substitutions over the last five years, then all he had to do was pull on the skein once and he took it all and left us with a defective version that if we even could get it to work it would only produce the wrong results and start incrementally damaging the entire system.

"Here's an example. Take the measurements for landscape zodiacs. They have predictable patterns to the right of the decimal point where usually at the third integer the numbers start repeating in twos, seemingly forever. Here are some representative sample measurements: 2.28*7272*; 3.84*3030*; and 17.95*8181*. These are measurements given in miles; the pattern is consistent across the list.

"Let's say you change any of the two numbers preceding that, or perhaps just the third. That will throw off the repeating pattern or at least throw the measurement number off balance. Do this effectively, then the algorithmic inputting that would favorably adjust the zodiacs starts to skew; screw with a dozen numbers this way, and the frequency system of all 432 zodiacs starts to wobble and you are facing an entropic negative cascade and arithmetical degradation. Eventually, human consciousness feels it. Nature probably sooner. The formerly coherent frequency input meant to address the 72 different sizes and 432 total copies will now be subtly incoherent, growing more so every day."

So somebody had hijacked our algorithm in stages, as if nibbling a dinner in tiny increments until the entire meal was consumed. Maybe this serial stealth removal was to keep us from noticing. It worked. We didn't notice. But I kept coming back to the core problem, the one that baffled me. You have to physically be in the 4D matrix and have your DNA signature scanned for entry before you can input anything, before the system even turns on its display for you.

Then you still need the Hierophancy access password, itself a 5D matrix formulation which acts as a key to open up the 4D matrix. You also need the precise inputting language format which was created by Blaise's Pleiadian colleagues which presumably is difficult if not impossible to penetrate without a lexicon. With all that in place, then the algorithm generates the 4D interactive inputting space which your DNA signature affirms through certain lock-in features.

Given these five entry restrictions, *how* on Earth did somebody hijack our algorithm, "hack" into its arithmetical matrix, as they used to call it? Don't misunderstand me: I was equally interested in *who* did this, and here again I drew a blank. The mental sophistication required to pull this off was rare. But the how question had priority because it highlighted a major security weakness. It meant somewhere in the system there was an unlocked door.

"It's as if somebody stole the Earth itself," said Sal, looking downcast. I knew why he said that. Already I sensed the dismay and discontent of our host constituents in the planet's Light grid, the Nature Spirits, elementals, Light temples and their attendant *devas*, even, to a degree, Gaia and Pain themselves. They felt restive in this Light grid perturbation underway and building every day. It was like the way dogs grow restless and anxious during a fireworks display or summer electrical storms. It is a vague, pervasive threat they cannot understand. The collective consciousness of humanity, only recently awakened and quickened, acted like a person who waits uneasily for the other shoe to drop.

I went back to my office, pondering this. I found myself frowning, almost grimacing, when I realized we couldn't call anybody for assistance. We couldn't report the theft to the authorities because *we* were the authorities and our project, our work, our algorithm, the existence of the Hierophancy, were classified at the highest level. Hardly anybody knew we were doing this work. We could only call ourselves and we'd drawn a blank. Blaise appreciated this quandary at the outset which was why he left instantly for the Pleiadians and their consortium.

One of the reasons our work was super-classified was the difficulty in explaining its conceptual basis to most people, not to mention the mathematical aspects. I understood these in principle, in the broad strokes, but only Sal and a few others in our group could find their way amidst the many abstruse data sets and equations. Another reason it was classified was that it held the safety and well-being of the planet in its hands; this algorithm ran the Earth and its affairs.

It's not the kind of reality you want wantonly advertised. It is likely to invite inquiry, and that inquiry may eventually entail questions for those who might wish to commandeer the system for their own advantage or notion of world rulership. Knowledge of the planet's Light grid and how it runs has political implications and potential dark applications; it could be misused to the detriment of humanity and planet, so it is prudent to restrict this knowledge.

Sure, the Golden Age advent and widespread Ofanim incarnation of 2020 upgraded the quality of awareness on the Earth, but people could still be tempted. Take enough intelligence, a helping of avarice or lust for power, and you're off and running as the next potential world-control manqué using geomancy's power over consciousness to run world affairs to your agenda.

Discretion was imperative, though we offered public programs on external topics like comparative mythology, the spiritual topography of sacred landscapes, and other introductory themes, which sometimes steered a few likely candidates our way for a possible introduction to the outer edge of the real geomantic mysteries. Please don't think us elitist in this hermetic seclusion of knowledge; it has always been this way in the Mystery tradition as genuine knowledge is dangerous. Consciousness must be carefully prepared to accept the responsibility this living initiation knowledge entails, and that excludes many.

I will try to clarify this issue. It occupies a perilously subtle position. What we do here is not control but regulation. Through the algorithm we act as a sentient homeostatic reciprocal interactive presence within the Earth's Light grid. Try to keep in mind this is the externalized infrastructure of all the processes of consciousness that constitute a human being; the Earth's Light grid is a colossal Human displayed in the form of myriads of Light temples and conduction lines.

This system enables people living on the planet to get the maximum advantage of its consciousness design features, or to whatever degree less than that they wish. Our job is to keep the grid operating in top condition, minutely sensitive and responsive to daily fluctuations in all the physical reality vectors, such as weather, tectonics, volcanism, and solar events like flares and sunspots.

There is a fine line between maintenance and manipulation, though, and whoever stole the algorithm had crossed it and was presumably intent on imminent world domination. What other motive could they have? The algorithm was the perfect way to do that domination. You only had to use it darkly. It's like magic: you have white and black, but it's the same generic energy involved. This theft was not a matter of national security, but global viability, affecting everyone and all countries without discrimination. It was a matter of Earth security.

I shivered. As Sal intimated, you could make inroads on world control merely by working with the list of the Earth's 432 zodiacs. That's only one of the 613 types of Light temples on our list. That list of the 432 is

a frequency table itself, lending itself to all sorts of uses, depending on your moral framework. You have six copies of 72 size models, each of them originally calculated in megalithic yards, which is an old geomantic nomenclature for the mathematical constant *e*. That is an exponential table, the base of logarithmic expansion, a harmonic cascade. It can exalt embodied consciousness into the empyrean or enslave it.

On the one hand, the attainment of the algorithm was the fulfillment of the mandated responsibility for humanity to geomantically maintain its own planet. That was a cornerstone in our collective agreement with the Supreme Being for us to be awarded this special planet, though most people have forgotten. On the other hand, since this is a free-will planet, it offers those morally dubious people an opportunity to take control of world affairs and global consciousness to their own advantage. Humans are free to choose good or evil actions, however dire the results. The proposition balances on this exquisite razor's edge, and I think some people were about to get cut on its keen blade. The *Kali Yuga* saw enough slices and gouges to fill a hospital emergency ward.

Frankly, it felt like I would be among the first to get sliced. I could not think of any likely suspects. I went through lists in my mind, and all the names fell off. The degree of sophistication required to pull off this heist was awfully exclusive and self-limiting. I immediately ruled out any of our government contacts; they were only officious if well-meaning bureaucrats. They had no mathematical expertise and no access. Members of the Hierophancy staff?

It was unlikely. They had been intensively vetted then monitored for years, even slipped subtle inducements or opportunities, analogically like unlocked office doors, and nobody had showed any indication of wayward or seditious tendencies. Blaise periodically scanned their psychic fields with his own clairvoyance to look for any deviant signs or newly intruded dark energy fields or untoward spirits. He did this every two months, and to date he had discovered no indications of drift. The angelic Blaises kept an eye on people too.

Motive aside, who *could* do this? Blaise could do it, but he already had full access to the system and I could not conceive of any benefit to him to altering his orientation towards this maintenance work. He had spent his life developing this algorithm to serve the planet and its geomantic pattern and his responsibility for both. World control did not interest him, other than as a risk he had to guard his algorithm against. Some of his Pleiadian contacts?

Certainly they would have the ability, but their job was to design Light grid nests for evolving consciousness on physical planets. Control of the Earth and its evolving consciousness would be a trivial pursuit for their level of intellect and orientation. They could generate convincingly real holographic copies of the Earth any time they wished and they could simulate any Magister Ludi inclinations they might have using this copy. But they were beyond that.

It would be a time-waster, a distraction. They didn't have those control inclinations. The chief "bad guys" we'd dealt with in the past few decades, the Pleiadian dark spirit called Andron, the Druj, the Andromedan disaffected Klingsor, had been defeated and packed away ineffectual into a holding space. For information on these malfeasors and our work against them, I refer you to my previous books and those of Edward Burbage, which recount the episodes.

A good detective never rules anybody out automatically. I should not rule out myself as a suspect. Yet it couldn't have been me. I didn't have the complete access or password. My access was linked with Blaise's as a general safeguard. I did some of the preliminary inputting, data preparation for the each day's adjustments, so I was allowed in the 4D algorithmic workspace. Maybe I knew more in my sleep and I sleepwalked my devious self into the matrix and took the algorithm. I laughed at the absurdity of that possibility. In all the years of my marriage to Philomena, she never once said I got up and walked in my sleep. Though, now that I think about it, I have had dreams in which I ran the shop.

In the dreams I took it for granted that I directed algorithm activities, ran the Hierophancy, trained recruits, administered programs, basically ran the planet. In these dreams I never questioned my right to do this, my appointed status. In emergencies I made the adjustments; in cases of planetary wobble, I corrected our axis orientation. I dispatched field agents to targeted grid nodes.

It's funny, but I don't remember Blaise being part of my dream version of this place. Maybe he was out of town, gone off to the Pleiades, I don't know, or retired, but he wasn't here and he didn't factor into the scope or execution of my responsibilities. Maybe I was dreaming of my far future when Blaise was out of the picture purely from his age and I officially had been given the mantle of the Hierophancy. Ever since I met him in 2026 (a year after I started work on his notebooks), Blaise had been my mentor, my initiator, my facilitator. Even before I met him in person, he had influenced me deeply—disturbed me—through his writings as I edited his nine notebooks that later became the book *My Pal, Blaise.*

Those notebooks and what he said in them were the cause of my profound life change when I ran out the front door of my house and academic life in search of at least the outer fringe of the Mysteries he had alluded to. What he took for granted, what was normal reality for him, wound me up until I irresistibly sprung out of my ordinary professor's life and leaped into the woolly unknown with him. No, in my daytime personality structure, I had no wayward suppressed desires to replace Blaise and put myself on the top and in charge.

Yet my body winced and I noted my face now wore a frown. I felt petulant. It's that damn unconscious we lug around with us. It was restive. Would Blaise always be my mentor and would I always occupy the second seat? Was I the plodding Hastings to his brilliant Poirot? I didn't really think so.

I moved with such ease and fluidity in those dreams, with unquestioned confidence. I took action when it was required, fixed problems, resolved difficulties, managed the staff, and supervised data acquisition and deployment, as if I was born to it. The Earth survived nicely under my leadership. I am confident to say it clearly flourished when I ran the Hierophancy. Maybe Blaise had retired. He is 116 now, a year after the events in this book concluded. Even for somebody as lithe and vital as he, those years must weigh on him now. If he hadn't yet retired, maybe he ought to, I remember thinking in my dreams.

You know how it is with vivid dreams, you are certain the time is now, that all the action takes place in the actual and vivid present moment. Dreams do not present themselves as theoretical or speculative, but as accomplished facts. They seem very lax on daytime morality boundaries and definitions. Anything goes. In one of these dreams, and it was only a few months ago, I had modified the 4D matrix entry password. I had found a way to increase its security aspects by adding another mathematical tangent to the way you enter the number code. I didn't think I could do that in my daytime self. I lacked the mathematics. Yet there I was in my dreamtime space, an arithmetical wizard changing the codings.

I had not yet told anyone else at the Hierophancy about this new number formulation. I'm not sure why I neglected that; maybe I was still testing out how well this new version worked. Maybe I liked being sole possessor of the keys to the kingdom. I had a list of improvements I had conceived for this kingdom, our client planet. Some of the Light temple systems (the total distribution pattern of all copies of a Light temple) needed upgrades; they were running sluggish, slow to respond. I had some ideas to implement that would accelerate the Light flow.

I wasn't sure Blaise would approve of these, consider them appropriate or useful. That irked me. I had been around the planet's Light grid long enough to understand how it worked and how to tweak its settings to tease out improved and brisker performance, to make its response to our inputs more snappy, more instantaneous. I found myself having to wait ten or even 15 seconds many times now until it responded. It felt like I was using a computer that was outmoded.

It's an old analogy, but I do remember the feeling before the 2020s when before you knew it your "brand new" computer was suddenly a derelict, supplanted by a cleverer, superfast new one with sleeker, faster software. Earth's Light grid was starting to feel like that: old, outmoded, plodding, dense. The 2020 upgrades were merely a beginning, an overture perhaps; surely it was time now to launch the first act, get those adjustment arias glowing in the Light grid.

I was startled and confused to hear a voice warbling on about something. I was in the middle of making the day's input in the holographic matrix and was installing faster response time programming keyed to my entry signature alone and somebody had turned on an irritating sound system emitting a bleating voice. Somebody's finger gently tapped me on my right shoulder and my vision cleared. It was Sal. He had entered my office and apparently had been trying to get my attention for some moments. His voice didn't sound bleating anymore.

I was about to say, give me a minute, I must finish this data inputting, but I wasn't in the matrix but slouched in my office chair seemingly staring at the near wall. As Sal began to speak, or maybe it was as my brain started to make sense of his syllables that had been accosting me already for some time, I lost track of the data input scene I had been immersed in. It was gone. Then a few moments later I didn't even remember being in the matrix. That was gone too. Then I forgot all about being confused by Sal's discordant harsh clamoring voice. Frankly, I was surprised I was no longer in his office. When had I left? I thought I was still in there discussing the theft situation with him. Jocelyn was with us too.

"We've heard from Blaise," Sal said. "He wants us to run dual diagnostics. I will continue analyzing the arithmetical matrix from outside and from scratch, looking for possible entry or tamper points. I will review its theoretical basis and number infrastructure. You will analyze the holographic matrix from the inside. Inside the box. Since you are not a mathematician, Blaise thinks you might notice certain broad alterations that I, in my minute focusing, might overlook. He sent the access codes for you. He suggests you test the system while you're inside it.

"He says look at some of the individual Light temple systems and their configurations. He's in conference with his Pleiadian colleagues going over lists of possible intruders, 'people,' I suppose I should say, who have the ability to steal this. He says since 2020 and the Light grid upgrades since then the Earth has become even more a planet of interest to various galactic groups with empire designs. So he would like you to investigate these Light temple array grids for possible intrusion points already exploited or now positioned for exploitation. I think in conjunction with his Pleiadian cohorts he's thinking off-planet in terms of identifying likely perpetrators. There are a number of extra-planetary groups that have been keenly watching our progress here; maybe they've made a move."

We keep the holographic matrix in a separate building, though it is close by. The algorithm's operation requires special shielding as it generates strong electromagnetic and radionics fields that would disturb our other operations. As I mentioned earlier in my first attempt to describe this place, you enter the 4D holographic matrix through a 5-cube door. This can be initially a bewildering perceptual experience. You feel you have cubes (40 of them in the 5D door) opening and closing all around you, coming at you from every angle, and your eyes cannot resolve them into a fixed image. Imagine being on 40 intersecting merry-go-rounds all pitched at different angles yet connected to the one axis. Or 40 revolving doorways, also dovetailed at 40 different angles to one another, and you are trying to pass through all of them at once, or maybe just go through one, but it's like a hall of mirrors in which the one door is multiplied into 40 copies.

From a 3D perspective, nothing past 3D is a fixed shape. The 4D tesseract and the 5D penteract seem to be in constant motion which is an artifact of your overworked 3D eyes and brain telling you they cannot register and thus see all of these complex shapes *at once*, and the struggle to resolve the image generates the impression of constant motion and unfolding shapes all wildly shapeshifting. Your 3D-trained eyes convert spatial simultaneity into a crude linear sequence; the trouble is that conversion perpetually leaves you a dozen steps behind the reality unfolding before you. You don't catch up; you end up a cognitive laggard.

The complexity of this system itself is an excellent security factor. The degree of cognitive dexterity you need to negotiate this 5D space eliminates most people. I'm not suggesting I am any kind of operational prodigy here, by the way; Blaise had trained me considerably in managing the protean higher complexity of this system. I was not new to this; I just had not before had unsupervised access. You could say I had been up until now a trained co-pilot.

I entered the password and stepped down into the operational 4D space. Though a 4-cube is simpler than the 5-cube, with only eight cubes turning inside out all the time, our display space included 613 different Light grid systems and their arithmetical correlates. As mentioned, that is the number of different Light grid temples in the grid, and each has its own mathematical specifications displayed before me. The total of copies of Light temples in these 613 systems runs into the millions. Knowing this, you appreciate the comparative streamlined simplicity of using numbers to denote and then access their reality. The details were colossal and likely to overwhelm most people if they saw the full spread.

All you had to do was put your attention on any of these 613 systems and your perception enlarged the display until, for the time, it filled your perceptual field. It is a neuronally correlated interactive holographic system keyed to our mental constructs and thought commands. If you wish to see the distribution grid for the 144 Grail Castles, you think that and the system displays it for you.

Your attention controls the zoom-in and zoom-out function, and you can mentally hypertext to an arithmetical display only, and simplify that to only managing algorithms and all the way out, or up, to the master heuristic algorithm. The operational principle of this system was the original design reciprocity between human and Earth in terms of a shared geomantic template.

The higher octave of our genetic code contains an imprint of this primordial geomantic template and that facilitates our human geomantic interactions with the Earth. We simply made an interactive Light temple or arithmetic laboratory out of this pre-existing design fact, just like the Light grid is a projection of our own form. In many respects, I was now standing in Earth's pre-eminent Light temple, the one master facility that subsumed them all, could regenerate them. This is an entirely mental space; it is the Earth-Human template in numbers.

Here was the Earth's Light grid in miniature, and here too was the structure of human consciousness, and here too the plan for their conjoint reality. This was Blaise's true Grail, this plan for the complete and original design of Earth and human reality that he had sought his entire adult life. Knowing him, he probably dreamed about it as a child, or, more likely, plotted wakefully to find it while other kids his age played baseball or got distracted by girls. Well, he had found it, reassembled this complex but beautiful pattern for consciousness, and we and the planet had enjoyed 15 years of living under its operational brilliance until some malcontent was clever enough to figure out how to steal it.

Ironically, it was just like the Grail Quest, as he himself discovered and reported. You *start* with the Holy Grail then quest around the Light grid learning how to use it. You don't have to find the Grail; the angels give it to you at the beginning. The quest is to learn how it works and to understand its nature.

Similarly, he started (at his first human incarnation, that is, when he left the Pleiadian phylogeny) with the complete Light grid schematics (when you factor in his Pleiadian origin and heritage and the fact the Pleiadians created the design), but he had to remember it, retrieve its many details across the Lethean boundary he submitted to in becoming a human. That is the vexing, sometimes irritating, memory veil put between our current incarnational self within this phylogeny and our vast preceding history, the soul's discoveries and knowledge over time. In Blaise's case, this was the full engineering package for the Earth, which he helped draft. He often complained about these blocks in his memory, finding them a nuisance in his work; he needed to remember everything now.

As I stood inside the holographic matrix, I wondered, how big is this space? Experientially, or perhaps I should say in functional terms, it is far larger than the physical housing the matrix occupies. That's a relatively small building. This space is as big as the Mind. Here you are inside the mental construct of a resonant human-planet design, keyed to crucial solar and galactic design factors. You are in a Mind-space, the architecture of your own consciousness, in fact, of everyone's, displayed in real time, as if it were breathing, progressing along its time-line of evolutionary unfolding. Every second it adjusts to changing conditions, like a 4D version of all the world's stock markets in one display with all their fluctuating prices. But that is a simple, primitive version of what is here.

You're looking at a generic version of your awareness itself, human bedrock, the essence of what constitutes a living human and what it can achieve. This is far more than our ordinary notion of consciousness and its possible range. That is embarrassingly, or perhaps charmingly, parochial. The full range extends into areas most people have neither experienced nor yet conceived of, yet which comprise the Complete Human, the full design package of our capabilities.

Don't forget you are standing within the extrapolated template of the Elohim. It's like being at Avebury stone circle in England: those old wonky eroded stones were precipitated out of the ethers by the Elohim; the stones still carry their vibration. So does this arithmetical laboratory of the human-Earth geomantic template. You feel like you are standing inside their celestial Mind, a field of angelic creativity. In here is Elohim creative mental space. It almost feels like if I touch anything with my attention I will get an electric shock from them.

This is the anatomy of the Holy Light the Hierophancy reveals and works with but which is also rendered in basic form as a number matrix, like I have before me. Part of our Hierophancy induction training is our gradual exposure to this range of expression, the Light and its reciprocal arithmetical coding. It is a slow dilation process to see it; proceed too fast and you risk unhinging the mind.

The key fact here is that this is not just a map of Light temple arrays. That will sound abstract and removed from daily experience to most people. But it isn't. This is the etheric blueprint of all aspects and operations of the biosphere. It is the vital *pranic* underpinning of the physical world and its life processes. I could take any human inside this 4D matrix and show them the display and say, Behold yourself. They might feel overwhelmed, but this is their truth. So if this Light grid falters or gets corrupted, biological life and material conditions suffer.

The situation is like living in a 100-room mansion and you only occupy three small rooms in the front and think you live in a modest cottage of three tiny rooms. The 100-room truth of the full scope of intended human awareness has to be introduced to people incrementally. The shock of the discovery can be overwhelming. We deal with this full scope every day in our Hierophancy grid modifications. I keep reminding myself how big a revelation this would be to a person unfamiliar with the Hierophancy and its work: here you see the reciprocating pattern of human and planetary design, identical except for shape.

It is the same consciousness architecture deployed in two complementary forms. Inside the holographic matrix, the algorithm executing its calculations all around you, you stand in the arithmetical heart of this design for free-willed awareness. How did it get here, you ask, incredulous. It was all designed. No, not an accident of the cosmos or blind mechanical forces, but the Designer-in-Chief commissioned it, paid for it, loves it, gave it the Official Seal of Approval. Did they transport it here in a massive fleet of trucks? No. They magically precipitated it from the arithmetical template I was now standing within.

All this likely would come as a shock to those culturally conditioned to a mechanical world poorly run by chaotic, soulless forces for an unfathomable end in death. You could look through this wonderful design and see the Face of God Himself. Not that He looks like anything you could see, but you get my meaning: you would encounter irrefutable proof of the existence of this Higher Authority, this alleged Authority about Whom you had heard so many unsubstantiated rumors, and now here it was, the proof, and He was right in your face, smiling.

I knew I would be in here for a while. I planned to review the number specifications for the 613 main components of the system, the Light temple arrays. You have to be careful with your mind in here because your directed thoughts organize what is displayed; you don't want your attention wandering. The system was sufficiently detailed so that as an operator you may pull up a 3D map of all the locations of a given Light temple within a composite array and view physical 3D aspects, 4D nuances, and any 5D harmonic octave versions. Nothing exists singly as a fixed 3D substantiality; all temples have their echoes.

Say you're looking up Grail Castle locations. You could summon the display of the 144 sites and glimpse their physical locales as if through a surveillance camera. I checked their number specifications and calculations. They were good. You could also see the geometric configurations of the Light grids around these temples and how they slightly adjusted themselves nearly every moment in coordination with subtly changing exterior conditions and the fluctuations of human collective consciousness such as current human access.

It is an intricately, meticulously calibrated system, and I marveled at its livingness as I stood there checking data. Every time somebody accesses a Grail Castle and conducts Grail Knight business there in the correct manner (occupying the original Grail, simulating a healing of the Wounded Fisher King, chatting up the Grail Maidens), it reciprocally affects all the copies of this feature. They brighten and move their Mysteries a little closer to human understanding. These changes move through the arteries of the Grail Castle Light grid system.

Yet I started to feel chills as I discerned slight subluxations in the system. The geometric pattern for the Grail Castle array, for example,

was marginally deformed. You could easily miss it if you weren't trained to recognize its distinctive pattern. It was as if somebody had dropped it and bent its girders. Now that I saw where to look, the alterations appeared glaring and large-scale.

The quality of the Light emission from its geometric infrastructure looked slightly dirtied or off-color, as if it had been minutely diluted with brown or gray. The number displays were skewed by a few digits. If I may use an analogy, it was as if you're expecting these number displays to be irrational numbers, with an infinite repetition starting at a predictable digit, and instead you have a quite ordinary natural number sequence that has no pattern of digit repetition. The Mystery numbers have been removed and quotidian, inert ones substituted.

Let's stay with Grail Castles for another moment. You have a number calculation that specifies the Light grid shape and details for its array pattern. You have another number sequence that arithmetically describes an individual Grail Castle, specifies its architectural details even though they are expressed in Light. Then you have another one that details the operations of the Grail Castle, its function and process as an "organ" within the global body of consciousness.

I have already said these number sequences were slightly off. In terms of architecture, it was as if in framing the Castle, the way carpenters put up the two-by-fours first, nothing was a perfect right angle. All the corners were slightly skewed and not at 90°. They were 88°. That is too big a deviation. This meant that our adjustment inputs would never be perfectly resonant; they would hint at the frustration or incongruity of putting a round peg in a square hole, and the current-condition input would fail to achieve system coherence and the system would be slightly disconnected and out of alignment, operationally subluxated.

You'd sense the system wobble or send off tiny sparks as its configuration appeared fuzzy, as if drifting out of focus, its fine edges blurred. Blaise told me he once encountered a Ray Master Sanctuary of Ray Master Magdalene-Brigit that was sitting at an angle to the landscape and she was floating above it. He knew the problem wasn't at her end, but due to a distorting veil between her geomantic reality and what he was able to see through the bizarre distortions. Discordant energies had been inserted between her pure reality and human perception, and humans had to struggle to see through this interference layer.

This meant the consciousness process it modulates would similarly feel indistinct. Do this enough times to a sufficient number of geomantic systems and soon the collective consciousness of humanity and that of its individuals would feel disoriented, like it had an inexplicable hangover or woke up feeling prickly, sensing stormy weather in its subconscious, wayward seductions arising, or like every planet in the solar system had gone retrograde at once, like a delegation storming out of a conference room, their papers testily flung everywhere.

It might feel like someone who had sworn off heavy drinking and had refrained for months, maybe years, suddenly gave in to the old compulsion and had a scotch. Then two, then the whole bottle. Or, after 45 years of delicious alignment with the Golden Age grid conditions, you suddenly tasted the stinky acrimonious greyness of life as usual in the earlier Dark Age, making your foray into Light conditions seem like a child's hallucination, as if reality had reverted. Or, and this was worse, what I feared was inevitable and which may already have started, you felt you were being led somewhere unknown against your will, that something unlawful had happened and you were its next recipient in line.

The numbers were suggesting this. I knew enough about how the formulas ought to appear to realize deformations were appearing in them. This was a serious problem, yet even as I took note of the potentially dire consequences of that intrusion into our system, I felt a ripple of delight in my body. I couldn't quite account for this, or even explain it, but it felt validating.

I *should* be here, in the algorithm's heart, assessing it and making adjustments. Oddly, it reminded me of the delight I felt (I'm tempted to call it a thrill, but I will refrain from formally using that designation) when I did something that pleased or even surprised my parents, maybe riding my bike without training wheels earlier than expected or getting impressive ratings at school or on a test. You know how it feels when you're doing exactly the right thing, in the right place at the right time, anchored in your genuine life purpose? It's a solid feeling, packed wall-to-wall with existential certainty. It feels great.

Here was a number that was incongruous with the rest of the display. It was in fact a number set, containing many numbers as if in invisible brackets. It was subtly flashing behind the main displays, like a faint piggy-backed signal. This number set was different, as if color-coded out of resonance with the rest. As in espionage, it was like getting a coded message from a deep background, but here this antecedent context used different equations, different number orders. I studied these equations for a while in bewilderment. Then it flashed in me what they were. They denoted a Light grid component that was off-planet.

It was off the physical planet anyway, on one of its seven subtle landmass extensions. These extensions are not widely known, if known at all. They were recognized by some of the older cultures such as the Vedic which called them *dvipa* and the Persian which named them *kešvar*, or, more formally, *Sapta-dvipa* and *Haft-kešvar*, both meaning "Seven Region." They were an Earth secret. Still, it looked like I was finally handed a clue to get started on. That was something.

The words mean island, peninsula, or continent, though *kešvar* is often translated as "clime." These seven land-climes extend at right angles from the physical Earth, and unless you're clairvoyant, an initiate, or a *Siddha*, you are unlikely to see them or be able to enter their domain and walk about. They are regarded by the seers in these traditions as ancient divisions of the Earth's surface comprising "the Earth of Seven Climes." These climes were generated at the beginning of Creation by the star Sirius in Canis Major, Persian lore says, which rained on the Earth, producing the *kešvar* oceans and the seven climes. I think it unlikely this bright star created these extra continents; it seems more likely the myth alludes to its organizing and anchoring role in the life of these lands. Logically, they would have been part of Earth's original geomantic design.

When you're there, they seem real and solid enough, but from a 3D physical body perspective, they are purely etheric and dreamlike, lacking substantiality. Yet they

formed a coherent aspect of classical Vedic cosmography, land maps of the esoteric Earth, obviously known to the seers who recorded their details, each clime more remote and harder to access as you moved out from the first one, closest to our world, called *Jambudvipa*, Rose-Apple Tree Land.

Imagine seven veiled, etheric lands, as a big as continents, existing in the hyper-reality of the Upper World, yet legitimate extensions of our own planet Earth. Topographically, our planet is about double the size we normally think it is. These continents lie at right angles to the Earth, like a sheet of plywood leaned up at a 45-degree angle against a beachball. Pardon the crude image, but you could potentially see this higher octave expression of our familiar Earth suggesting you could walk off the surface of Earth and onto its slanting surface.

The Vedic model of the *dvipas* was something I was familiar with from my studies in comparative mythology, although those were, now I was 89, some 65 years ago in my post-graduate days before I started in at Dartmouth. These seven concentric island-continents were said to be circular, each separated by an encircling ocean. The cosmic mountain called Mount Meru rose toweringly at the center of these seven concentric rings of immense though veiled landmasses and acted as a universal umbilicus, defining and anchoring the seven continents.

The key fact of this hidden topography is that the Earth has much more landmass than we ever suspected, though this newly revealed landscape is not physical in the way we are accustomed. It has a higher Light component to it. It corresponds to what Buddhists call a Pure Land or Buddha Field, a terrain so infused with the Holy Light as to almost eclipse the substantiality of matter.

Jambudvipa, the "Land of *Jambu* Trees," usually translated as rose-apple trees, lay closest to the center, encircling the vast cosmic peak which rises 80,000 miles. That terrain is the one reputed to be closest to human consciousness and the possibility of access. Blaise said he had been there a number of times. The *Jambu* tree is enormous: its trunk is 15 *yojanas* wide (120 miles), its branches spread out for 50 *yojanas* (400 miles), and it stands 100 *yojanas* tall (800 miles).

The *Jambu* tree supposedly yields fruits the size of elephants. When they ripen then rot then fall from the boughs they generate a river of juice called *Jambunadi* which flows down from the mountains and through the continent. The human inhabitants drink this river-juice and gain enlightenment and longevity. While *Jambudvipa* has nine zones (*varshas*) and eight mountains (*parvatas*), Vedic cosmography says this *dvipa*, closest to the paramount universal mountain, is where humans may attain enlightenment and therefore it is the most desirable.

Apparently, all the famous mountains inventoried in the Puranas exist here. I used to read these clairvoyantly wild documents and wonder where do they keep all these awesomely celestial peaks teeming with *Siddhas* and Masters? I couldn't find them anywhere in our conventional topographical world. I laugh at my naïveté now. That's the 3D mind vainly trying to grasp a 4D spiritual truth. Even Tibet's famously spiritual Mount Kailash exists in its true form only in the *dvipas*. The bright, snow-clad peak in western Tibet is only a physical-world reminder, a place-marker, a

clone of the original exalted Light-infused holy mountain, among many others, found there in the sublime *dvipas*.

The Persians say only this one continent was ever inhabited by humans and was the fabled *Eran-Vej* (or *Airynaem Vaejah*), original home, cradle, or seed of the Aryans who peopled Iran. It lies in *Xwanirah* (also written as *Xvaniratha*), the greatest and most prosperous and central of the Seven Climes. Each clime generated a pair of twins who became humanity's first couples.

Other cultures such as the Aztec similarly claim they derived from this extra-planetary landscape, for them known as *Aztlan*. That tradition calls the extra-continental aspect of the Earth *Chicomoztoc*, "The Place of the Seven Caves." Aztlan is one. Collectively, the Aztecs that emerged from these seven continents or caves are called *Nahuatlaca*, the *Nahua* People, their language was *Nahuatl*, an ancient tongue in Mexico. So these three cultures point to the same higher world of seven climes, islands, or caves, from which certain ancient peoples emerged.

Vedic tradition says *Jambudvipa* measures 10,000 *yojanas* in extent, probably meaning its diameter, and that yields a distance from eastern to western oceans of 80,000 miles, unarguably vast. The physical, visible Earth's diameter is a mere 7,917.5 miles, so *Jambudvipa* is about ten times broader, and there are still the other six islands which swell the extra-continental landmass. Persian lore says Iranian hero-kings claimed sovereignty over all seven regions of higher Earth and that each *kešvar* will yield a world savior when it's time to renovate material Earth reality. He will work under the direction of the *Saoshyant*, the prime renovator, which I take to be the Persian Messiah. It's possible a fair bit of our ancient mythology took place in this Higher World.

During the Golden Ages, called *Satya Yuga*, the Vedas declare, humans could access any of these seven regions in *Bhu-mandala*, their name for the composite septenary invisible, higher octave extension of Earth. I suppose in the other three Ages it would constitute the mysterious dark matter shadow of the planet, a rumored but never verified additional mass of the planet. As you can see, you can justifiably go back and forth between Persian, Vedic, and Aztec descriptions, as they indicate the same extra landmass dimension of our Earth. They all claim it's there, and that they originally came from there. It also suggests that at one point, long ago, awareness of this Earth extension was commonplace and early peoples understood their point of origin was in this Higher Earth.

I knew all this, as intellectual book knowledge. It's the kind of information you collect as a scholar of comparative mythology. I never thought it was real, though. As with most of what you find in the Vedas, Puranas, Avesta, and other old Hindu or Persian texts, it seems rife with exaggeration. I can cite its details, but I have never been sure whether to credit any of it as real. The size of the *Jambu* tree seems outrageous. Where could such fantastic, improbable lands really lie? I didn't know. But Blaise could vouch for the existence of these arcanely recessed, mythic continents. He knew they were real. He had visited *Jambudvipa* some years ago and knew the island well. He'd seen that big tree.

It is possible, I suppose, advanced souls might visit these continents in physical bodily form. Blaise had gone in psychic extension, in his Light body, in the company of Ray Master Lao Tzu, Lord of the Yellow Robe; apparently, he is a guide for humans to these hidden lands. So I had it on reliable authority that *Jambudvipa* was real, despite the haze of its hard-to-verify Hindu attributions. Anyway, it had better be real because that's where we were heading; that is where the first plausible clue regarding the arithmetical theft from Earth led us.

I cannot claim to understand what I was seeing. The arithmetical aspect of the Hierophancy algorithm was not my specialty. But it seemed another Light grid and its number coding was becoming apparent behind the main one. It was a shadow version of the algorithm, though I don't mean it was in the dark. If anything, it was brighter, like a sunrise suddenly appearing on the horizon. Or maybe I could better say it was like a higher octave version of the algorithm. In a strange manner, it looked like a grace-note door you could step through right out of the algorithm that we normally thought occupied the complete display space.

I was about to leave the 4D matrix display space and call for Sal to see if he could interpret this background number display. Then I realized somebody was standing next to me. It was Blaise. He was back from the Pleiades. He grinned as he tapped me on the shoulder with his palm. "Pack your bags, pal. We have to make a trip into *Jambudvipa* and trace this anomaly to its source."

2

It was the Golden Age again now, so I supposed we had a reasonable chance of entering *Jambudvipa*. It was sanctioned by the advent of the *Satya Yuga*. Blaise, as usual, was jaunty and flip in his manner, full of confidence and assurance. He explained a little of the *Jambudvipa* mystery to me as we set out.

"*Bhu-mandala* is like a huge Frisbee the size of the solar system set at right angles to the Earth's axis of rotation at the South Pole. That's where you enter. Esoteric tradition alludes to this stealth-veiled land as the Supreme Country, and I suppose real estate magnates, if they knew about this land extension, would be salivating over the sales and developmental possibilities. *Jambudvipa* is at the center of this and Mount Meru, the cosmic peak, at its center, with the eight Celestial Cities or *varsas* arrayed on its slope, with a ninth, Brahma's, at the top.

"The Meru set-up is a necessary holographic version of the center of the universe. It makes sense. Mount Meru in *Bhu-mandala* is a hologram. The Earth's Light grid is mostly a copy of the important features of the higher spiritual worlds and galactic, even universal, structure; it is a pure-form microcosm. The Earth's Light body conducts consciousness back to its source. It works the other way round too. *Bhu-mandala* is the code that writes the code that specifies the Earth's Light grid algorithm. It's the mother algorithm or algorithm generator.

"Plato would call it Earth's *eidolon* or original Idea form, its prototype in Light. The name *Bhu-mandala* means the structured, labyrinthine pattern of the Earth, but obviously it is the Higher Earth, the cosmic, primordial Earth, *Bhu*, the way the Greeks meant it when they said *Ge*. They meant cosmic space. Earth as the cosmic etheric space in which the Creation took place. Not the planet. It's the mother country and home base of the Arithmetical Earth. If this were the British Empire around 1880, we would be going back to London—no, more than that. Back to Buckingham Palace, to the heart of Queen Victoria's domain. So if we have a problem with our code out in the Colonies, we go back to its source."

I mostly understood him. I took the opportunity of our traveling together to ask Blaise a question. I was never clear on how an algorithm could affect our material reality. How could a string of numbers, albeit a super-intelligent self-learning one, do this? I knew, from hints Blaise had let out, no doubt purposefully, that his Pleiadian colleagues had helped with this a great deal, that they were the shadow members of our Hierophancy group. But they always preferred to stay in the background. What mystified me was that not only were numbers describing our physical reality through the interface of the Light grid and its arithmetical displays, but they were affecting it, managing it, changing it, exerting actual traction on our material condition, modulating it constantly. My question was elementary: How did the mathematics affect our material reality?

"It works through the mental sphere," Blaise said. "This is where numbers, number patterns, Magic Squares, and algorithms rule reality, the arithmetical realm. Think of the mental sphere as constituting a complex Magic Square, one whose numbers and combinatorial possibilities direct reality. Numbers are sentient, and they have a sonic, pronunciatory aspect as well.

"Think of how the Qabalists ascribe numbers to each of the 22 Hebrew alphabet letters. The flip side of each letter is a number, like two sides of your hand. That means every word is also an equation or at least its seed. Every word codes a reality; that's why the Qabalists regard Hebrew as a magical language. In a Magic Square you can invert the numbers and get the letters and pronounce them. They have reality-producing, primary creative effects, as Jewish tradition states. In Judaic lore, the letters combined into words generate actual realities.

"That means the numbers do also, equivalently and simultaneously. They are pre-connected to subtle and material reality, like puppet strings. Our algorithms comprise numbers and thus the sound-matrices behind them. But more profoundly, or perhaps more simply, the mental sphere plans reality, lays it out like an engineering schematic written in arithmetic, and it uses numbers to sketch out, specify, codify, then generate our reality. The letters-numbers command reality to comply. It is like writing computer code that specifies a program or an image, or, more fun, a holographic reality in Light. The language itself is algorithmic, coding a function to produce an end result.

'What activates this is the alignment of your consciousness with the complete grid pattern. It is as if you inhabit the design, infuse it throughout with your awareness; then as you 'think' the numbers, run the algorithm mentally, at once it distributes itself through this pattern of Light and adjusts its number settings. You could say the complete Light grid pattern, the mental or Higher Mind aspect of Earth and human consciousness, is held in the awareness of a higher being. Some call this the Primordial Buddha.

"The Blaises once told me the Buddha holds all the 'strings' of Earth's Light grid in his hands, meaning our Light grid reverts to Buddha-Mind. To a degree, the Pleiadian Light grid engineers also maintain portions of this array. They are very mental from our perspective and work in the higher chakras. They design and implement Light grids directly from their minds. No paper, no sketches, no hands are involved. It is a direct mental transmission.

"In Qabalistic terms, in the Tree of Life model they operate in the *Sefira* of *Hod*, the realm of perfect and absolute intelligence, the source of all mental images and magical forms. It is the pure form expression of the *Manipura*, City of Gems, or solar plexus chakra. They create nests of Light within the tetrahedrons of fire, more commonly recognized as pyramids. Ray Master Hermes is associated with this.

"As I said, the other side of this pattern is its number equivalents, like numbers on the back of a picture postcard. You just flip it over and access the numbers. Do you see the mechanism? If you fully suffuse your awareness through the pattern, then your thoughts, your calling up of changed numbers, change the pattern. This is where the mental sphere is also the creative zone. You have to be extremely careful in how you tweak the planetary system. Even minute adjustments, as you judge them, can alter the planet's direction too much.

"The Buddha's Light grid maintenance over the millennia has been mild and miniscule. Now that we have the Hierophancy, we are enabled, actually expected, to make bigger, bolder adjustments. The times are ripe for this. You could say the Buddha has acted as concerned caretaker while the estate owners were away. Now they're back, *we* are back, and we can assume our mandated duties. It is part of the human contract with the planet designers to take on Light grid maintenance responsibilities. We're expected to. Most people don't know this. The danger now, the extreme risk, is that a hostile agency seemingly has possession of the algorithm and can make unwarranted changes to the grid.

"That 'agency' can nudge the algorithm in undesirable directions, redirect its self-learning mechanisms to acquire data or output computations against the well-being of humans and where our collective consciousness is trying to evolve to. The Hierophancy algorithm is a geomantic tool; over time and much research we developed this algorithm to help us in our work of revealing the Holy Light. The peril is that this invaluable tool has been taken up by unfriendly hands. It can wreak distortions in that Holy Light, apply filters, and install splotches."

Blaise seemed to shift gears and his face now glowed almost with rapture. He got like that now and then when he was inspired, when the sudden force of revelation or the truth or maybe a powerful insight rose up in him like a sunrise.

"To continuously reveal the Holy Light, as the Earth's grid does, means to continuously reassert our true identity as humans and the planet's true nature too. That each is a clear mirror reflecting the primordial truth of the other. The Earth shows us our true nature, and we reveal to the planet its true condition. They are reciprocal, simultaneous revelations of the Holy Light, the Holy Idea. Both are coded, written in letters and numbers, equations and algorithms. The Hierophants' job is to keep polishing the mirror to ensure the clear reflection. In computer language, we keep tweaking the programming to improve the results.

"Both reveal the divinely made Face. This is a perpetual infusion of *prana* or consciousness force into the planetary system. It is a reiteration of what the Buddhists call *Prajna-paramita*, the perfection of transcendent wisdom. This is the wisdom, the nondualism of the primordial Light, reality's true nature, that transforms the Earth into a Christed planet, or, if you prefer, one possessed by Buddha-Mind, its Buddha-Nature of primordial Light shining out across the solar system so that it seems the Earth itself has become a sun blazing in its designated tier in the solar system's gravity well of planets. Imagine. Our Earth.

"No longer merely a material planet, the Earth has become radiantly self-aware, empty of separate selfhood, nondual, *awake.* Rudolf Steiner once said the Earth's destiny is to become a sun. That sun will be flush with Buddha-Mind or Christ Light, its equivalent. The Light grid will birth it and we will help that."

Blaise laughed. "You'll have to excuse my excess. I get carried away with the picture of this possibility, this, I hope, eventuality. It's the whole point of the algorithm, the achievement of this condition. Our algorithm, our Hierophancy, serve this goal. The Archangel Michael or the Buddhist Bodhisattva Manjusri who supervises the disclosure of this Light on the Earth, slices through the armor of our selfhood to reveal the Holy Light. The Holy Light reveals our truth within.

"Michael's sword is the force of celestial consciousness that precipitates this disclosure, that dissolves the veil of selfhood and physicality to reveal the Light inside us and the Earth. His sword discloses the Elohim's template. His sword renders the Earth hierophantic. Then we understand our true condition. The algorithm directs this Michaelic sword of truth to slice through both realms, especially where both humanity and planet are asleep in illusion or fantasy or nightmare, in a perpetual slow-motion gesture that reveals the Holy Light in us and within the material face of the planet. It is a two-way perpetual Epiphany. The Archangel Michael makes the gesture, then our algorithm emulates the gesture. The Hierophancy's job is to keep both of these operating harmoniously.

"The algorithm is an arithmetical version of Michael's *Prajna-paramita* sword held blade-edge facing us and Earth to reveal the primordial truth of what we are. That's the purpose of the Light grid we and the planet share: it reveals this. The algorithm keeps the Light grid in balance and trim so it can reveal this Light. Just as Michael's sword is hierophantic, so is the algorithm. Can you feel that patient urgency the Creator has to eventually reveal this Holy Light?"

Blaise looked a little grim, though his eyes still twinkled. "But it still totally sucks that somebody has nicked our algorithm. It jeopardizes all this."

I agreed. The Light grid was in jeopardy as long as the algorithm was in the wrong hands. It was still the biggest mystery to me how that had happened. I suppose a lesser mystery was how Blaise proposed we get to *Jambudvipa.* Years ago he let me know he disliked physical travel. It was slow and boring, certainly the conventional style when you had to depend on an airplane, train, or car to transport your body. He didn't even bother to hike up hills or mountains anymore; he went by the Ofanim's Rotunda of Light, a convenient mode. He used to say, with a touch of mischievousness, why climb the mountain? The Light temple is just as invisible way up there as at ground level. So see it from here and save your body the perspiration to climb up to where it invisibly is.

He had abandoned those cumbersome means for something faster, more streamlined, with less travail on the physical form, and free. He used wormholes, stargates, the Rotunda, and when necessary, his own astral body. To facilitate his preferred lifestyle, he had discovered and mapped the complete transportation system and locations of the first two venues; the astral body was easier to come by. It came with the set of seven bodies you get as an incarnate human being. The stargates and wormholes came with the Earth, so I suppose that's equivalent.

So when I say we set out for *Jambudvipa*, basically we walked out on the Hierophancy property to a special meditation building Blaise had outfitted for this. It was quiet and guaranteed privacy. You just activate a little sign on the outside that discretely flashes the message "Occupied." It reminded me of television and radio stations that would have a neon sign over a door, "On the Air," meaning don't come in and disturb us. We would travel from here. Ironically, it should say "Unoccupied" because if we were travelling in our astral body, our physical form would be basically unoccupied by our consciousness.

To outward appearance, our travel mode was low key and unremarkable. We sat down in comfortable chairs, but not too lushly comfortable: we had to stay awake or at least not lapse into what the body would recognize as sleeping. Blaise told me we'd be met by Ray Master Lao Tzu once we got to *Jambudvipa*.

Blaise took the lead. He had been there a number of times. Our manner of getting there struck me as odd the first time, but Blaise said it was customary. Once we set our intentions to go to *Jambudvipa*, and I suppose the angelic Blaises helped us build up a focus and pointed us in the right psychic direction, we saw before us a table of feasters seated at a banquet table that encircled the planet. It was not a rowdy bunch; it was more like a meal at the High Table at an Oxford college, subdued and mannerly, though they weren't wearing academic robes.

These people, I gathered, were guardians of the gateways into *Jambudvipa*. For all I knew, the feast they were enjoying was the fabled Messianic Banquet. Behind them were the portals, like large open doorways that at first looked like they existed in many copies, but then I realized it was just the one open gateway that appeared wherever I looked past the feasters. No matter. We went through it. Probably in some subtle manner these banqueters had checked our bona fides.

Maybe they were not feasters. Perhaps they were more like judges, a panel of adjudicators making sure whoever passed into *Jambudvipa* was worthy of that. They all looked at us, concentrated as a group on us, then we passed through the gateway, seemingly moving right through their conjoined faces which in turn resembled or maybe constituted the portal itself, and they ushered us along, almost whisked us through by their approving attention.

I'm tempted to call them portal *devas*, a higher-level version of landscape angels that guard sites. In fact, I was beginning to think these "judges" were also tour guides and had just offered us (downloaded subliminally?) an accurate orientation to the landscape. Probably they were *Siddhas*, highly advanced spiritual beings, and the impression they gave of banqueting was meant to indicate their consciousness was already fully comprised of the exalted qualities of the Messianic Banquet, pure Light. They were the Christed "Perfected Ones."

Lao Tzu was waiting for us, as promised. He was smartly dressed in his Ray Master's Yellow robe. He stood next to a giant tree. I assumed this was the original *Jambu* tree for which the continent was named. It was bigger than the biggest redwood tree I had ever seen, but as I looked at it, the tree impression started to dissolve and be replaced by that of a towering *deva* of Light, and where the branches and leaves should be was instead a fountaining of

Light, splashes of Light in all directions like water falling on rocks from above. Maybe that tree-*deva* was actually the reputed spiritual leader who occupies each clime, as the Persian *Bundahišn* reported, he who will be one of the seven world-saviors.

The land surrounding us in all directions was flat, like an empty plain. I then surmised that maybe we hadn't quite arrived, that this was a transition zone. It was, for Lao Tzu gestured we follow him as he stepped into the great tree. We copied the gesture, and I realized even the impression of the *Jambu* tree as a *deva* was incomplete. This was a portal, a dimensional passageway, into *Jambudvipa*. We passed through this figure as we had through the feasters.

I realized both represented threshold exemplifiers of the frequency domain. I mean they demonstrated the quality of consciousness in operation there. They were not feasting on it, but the gesture indicted they were comprised of this quality already. The feasting became metaphorical. They had eaten *Jambudvipa*, and their bodies and consciousness were gorged on that Light. We matched that quality, then passed through it as easily as moving through a door.

When we entered the *Jambudvipa* landscape the Light it emitted dazzled. This is what the Buddhists must mean when they talk of a Pure Land or a Buddha-Field. The seemingly material aspects of perceivable reality were so suffused with Light that everything solid and tangible seemed ethereal and made only of Light, as if all of reality were a vast Light temple. The Persian mystics had a name for this realm: they called it *Hurqalya*, Earth of Visions, Celestial Earth. Instead of Mount Meru, they described Mount Qaf, the Emerald Peak, at its core.

The Persian mystics called *Hurqalya* the "Earth of Resurrection" and "Earth of the Seven *Kešvar*," implying this purer version of Earth would redeem the physical one by presenting a vision of the original Landscape of Light intended for us. Earth is an Angel, the seers said, saturated with the Light of Glory. Persian lore says originally the Earth was a continuous whole, a kind of Pangaia model that included these extra-continental landmasses, but due to demonic oppression it became divided into the seven *kešvar*, of which only one clime, called *Xvaniratha*, "Luminous Wheel," is now accessible to humans.

It was the same place, just with different names, I was sure. I stomped my foot to see if it passed through the ground. It didn't. The ground felt hard and solid as you would expect it to under normal terrestrial conditions, yet I could see through it, see its constitutive elements, and all of this was radiant, as if lit from within by brilliant spotlights of white Light. No, it wasn't white exactly, more like a blazing diamond-like fire flushed in white. But even this color was not its true appearance. Its true appearance was that of consciousness itself, which meant it was more for me to experience than to see. I was standing on a landscape made of wakeful consciousness, Buddha Mind, primordial Light. I could throw lots of names at this, but the fact was it was shockingly wakeful. You just felt so rivetingly aware, present, focused, and blazingly conscious.

The people were like this too. I started seeing some humanlike forms. They looked like humans, but they too were more Light than matter. I felt like I was walking around inside the

Buddhist and Tibetan iconographic depictions of the celestial realms, with enlightened spirits enhaloed in great globes of Light. They wore elegant robes, opulent jewelry on their ears and around their necks, and their heads seemed to be crowned. I realized these features were not literal. I was seeing an expression of their auric field, their consciousness signature expressed as these seemingly physical appurtenances; it wasn't jewelry and crowns. It was the state of their awakened awareness that took the visually metaphorical form of this opulent array. I felt more awake just looking at them.

I felt something slam into me. It jolted me momentarily, then I felt thicker. I could see more clearly. Everything was suddenly brighter and more vivid.

"Our astral bodies just arrived in a rush, as it were," said Blaise. "You'll start to feel more grounded and substantial now. Soon you won't even notice it."

"I know what this place is called, but what is it really?" I asked Blaise.

"Think of *Jambudvipa* as Earth's Higher Self, the land that remembers Earth's true condition, which our dear old planet has not yet attained, but will. This is an Earth of Light, of awakened consciousness, a Pure Land, a landscape which is identical with the Buddha, which means it is thoroughly awakened and nondualistic. Landscape, life-forms, and consciousness are all the same thing.

"This condition is the fruit of the completed Light grid of *Jambudvipa*. It sets the example; it holds this example forth in brilliant illumination, for its lower self, our planet Earth. Our planet's Light grid is primed to produce this same state. It can seem staggering, even shocking, at first, this perfection of existence,

but it is the point of things, why Earth has a Light grid and why the Hierophancy exists. Our physical Earth will one day become a Celestial Earth, like this place."

"Why did we come here?" I asked. Before I had thought I knew. We were chasing down a clue, that number discrepancy I found. Now I didn't know why.

"*Jambudvipa* has higher-level geomantic settings for the Earth's Light grid, a kind of pure, antecedent condition, the original parameters, you might call it. Even though fundamentally this is a state of consciousness and not a material expression, we established a safe house here, a fall-back geomantic archives that inventoried our Earth settings and its arithmetical constructs in case something went wrong or the system got skewed, or as now, the Earth got screwed.

"We set up this safe house to act as a reference point in times of grid aberration. This is why we stashed all the jewels and family heirlooms in this inviolate landscape of Light and *Siddhas* against a time when the Earth might be robbed. You might think of this as a higher-dimensional form of the heuristic algorithm."

I was thinking of how I used to stash all over the place multiple back-up discs containing copies of important computer files. I'd put them in my car, in the barn, around the house. Blaise had stashed a back-up of our algorithm here. We headed towards a building that looked like an observatory. It was rounded, like a half-sphere set on the ground, but as we got nearer, I found it hard to keep a clear focus on its shape. It seemed to keep shifting its form. If you weren't careful, you would conclude your eyes had gone screwy, but it wasn't that.

It was the building that was screwy. Except it wasn't screwy exactly. It was not rooted in the third dimension, or at least not exclusively. That's why it looked odd. Gradually, I realized it was like watching a cube shapeshift to 4D, 5D, then 6D forms, then back again to an approximation of 3D. Maybe the shapeshifting was only an artifact of my hobbled, slow-motion seeing and its true shape was permanently higher dimensional, which made it hard to see.

Though *Jambudvipa* was a Pure Land exhibiting the perfection of Light and awakened consciousness, you still needed security protocols for a safe house. The *Siddhas* (enlightened celestial spirits in humanoid bodies of Light) would have no interest in breaking into our arithmetical sanctuary, but that wouldn't preclude others who managed to get to *Jambudvipa* with the intent of stealing or corrupting our Earth codes. You didn't need a visa to get here, only the psychic means to do so. Whoever had tampered with our algorithm might be among those who would be interested in compromising our fallback archives here.

The security in place initially consisted of a sphere of Light around the "observatory." If this were a science fiction movie, I'd be tempted to call it an inertial wall or force-field, but it was more sophisticated than that. It was more than just a barely discernible shield of plasma; it was a consciousness membrane, an armored, impenetrable skin made of focused awareness molded into a canopy that enclosed the building in 360 degrees. It was under it as well. The archives building was completely englobed by this concentrated force-field.

This defense shield extended about 100 feet beyond the edge of the building, and it emitted a slight hum, like you'd hear from a swarm of bees at a distance. When I touched its glimmering, almost invisible, surface, my hand bounced off it like a kicked soccer ball. It was immediately repulsed, as pliantly bouncy as a backhanded tennis ball. It didn't hurt. My hand didn't feel anything. It just wasn't on the shield any longer, but several feet away, like it was flung. I looked to Blaise for suggestions on how to get past this formidable force-field.

Blaise grinned. "It's easy, though it may seem a little odd at first. You picture that it is you who is projecting this shield and it surrounds your body."

I did this, and I was surprised to find it worked. The inertial wall was around me, pulsing and humming as an impermeable barrier. Then I noticed something else. I was inside it. I don't mean just the spherical inertial shield I had pictured around me. I had passed through the shield around the whole building. I had pictured a reversal of my seeming relationship to it, and this had changed everything, including my apparent location in space and the conditions it had. Reality and consciousness and their interactions were fluid, even magical, here in *Jambudvipa*. I would have to get used to that extreme ease in modulating the apparent "facts" of the external world. It seemed everything was negotiable here.

Blaise knew what I was thinking. "It's simpler than that. You reversed your position in relation to the inertial shield-globe because you created it. So did I. Everyone in the Hierophancy who has come here created it originally. What that means is that at some time, as part of one's induction into the Hierophancy at this higher level, you come to this safe house and learn the entry protocols. They remain implicit in your psychic and mental field, available for reactivation. Don't start wracking your memory banks for when you came here in this life. The balance of good karma gets carried forward. It was in some earlier life you came, but that information, the tangibility of that contact, remains active in you."

I saw what looked like a shadow version of myself standing at the core of this building starting to move outward executing the security protocols in order. In fact, I realized this building was only a layer in a larger building or reality. This shadow version did not look like myself, though it appeared to be human. This must be an example of what Blaise just alluded to, balances carried forward from past lives, though in this case it was valuable security information. It was as if the codes that activated or turned off these security measures had been buried like a computer chip in my karmic body and were made available to me now.

I know my language is inexact when I say "karmic body," but let's postulate that there is some carry-over mechanism by which consciousness transfers forward what it has attained or acquired as specific knowledge to a future incarnation. Think of it as like book royalties that you can keep collecting in future lives. I saw several earlier versions of myself, possibly dozens. This information was passed along forward on my soul's timeline like a lineage. I was observing the line-up of some of my prominent ancestors, my previous versions.

These shadow versions of myself must be my forebears within the Hierophancy, earlier expressions of my soul's abiding commitment to the Light. That must explain why it seemed easy, even effortless, to reverse myself in relation to the force-field sphere and transfer myself to the other side of it. In technical terms, I never passed through it or penetrated its inertial wall. It was more like stepping momentarily into subspace (outside 3D anyway) where it didn't exist, then stepping out of it to be on the inside of what had moments before been outside. It was easier to do it than to put it into clear words now.

When I was finished marveling over my hyper-physical adroitness and patting myself on the back as if I had just scored a dunk in a basketball game, I realized another obstacle now confronted me. It was a dark geometric grid. It looked like a screen door that had been bent and contorted to form a spherical fence. Still, it showed signs of being a coherent geometric form, just complex.

As I studied this "fence" more, I realized I was mistaken in calling it twisted or bent. It was highly regular, ordered, even symmetrical though in an arcane dimension. My eyes were spinning, and I had to remind myself these were my astral body eyes which presumably were designed to make visual sense of complicated forms like this. Take a screen door minus the frame and fit it around a cube. Do this to 30 more screens. Overlap these 31 screens upon one another but at different angles. Spin it so it rotates continuously; then try to see it.

Blaise was chuckling. Evidently, he knew what we were confronted with. "The technical name for this next security shield is a cantellated 5-demicube, one of the uniform 5-polytopes also called a runcicantic 5-cube. Look familiar? Any seasoned geometer would recognize this figure and smile. Not smiling? One reason your eyes feel like they're spinning trying to get a lock on this fantastic shape is that it has 480 vertices, 1,040 faces, and 1,000 edges. That's formidable."

Come to think of it, that sounds like a lot more than just 31 screen doors. The way I got through this second defensive layer still confounds me. I found myself holding a cube of Light, but it was the size of an accordion. I was massaging its shape the way you would squeeze then open an accordion to play. Each time I flexed this protean shape it suddenly expanded in all directions and dimensions, as if it was self-generating more cubic shapes from out of itself. These cubic forms ballooned out of any semblance to 3D reality and veered immediately into the more dizzying, hyperdimensional terrain of crazy shapes. They were not genuinely crazy, but seeing them morph like this made me feel crazy, like my perception and cognitive processes had no handle on reality now.

I caught a reflection of myself in one of the glasslike surfaces of the morphing cubic shape. It was not myself I saw there. It was not even a human.

What does a nonhuman sentient life-form look like? That's a challenge even for a psychic to decipher in visual terms. Let's say they (I saw myself accompanied by others with the same form) looked generally humanoid, that is, upright, with two arms, legs, standing maybe six or seven feet high, and a with head of sorts, and eyes, mouth, some form of nose, but it was as if their craniums were transparent and you could see through them to the brains, except it wasn't brains you saw, but their higher psychic centers, a number of them packed neatly into a shared space. Their heads looked like they were adorned with jewelry and crowns.

It suggested the Cyclopes, or an evolutionary stage on the way to that refinement. Cyclopes were not stupid, hirsute, one-eyed chumps living in damp caves on Sicily, the way the Greeks pictured them. I think these impressions connoted their residency in higher-mind landscapes, that their consciousness was mostly mental. The Greeks rendered the Cyclopes safe by demoting them in terms of their evolutionary status and portraying them as moronic and hideous.

As soon as I figured this out, I saw the way through this complicated "fence." I had to line up a mental copy of the same form so that the centers corresponded. This would reveal the door and unlock the passageway. The center of this form indicated its point of origin, its geometric seed that spawned this confusing complexity of lines, faces, vortices, and edges. I just had to find that seed within my own mental sphere, my higher mind archives, to unlock it.

I didn't have to worry about the rest of this figure which, frankly, was defeating my perception. Paradoxically, the easiest way to do that was to stop thinking about it. The answer was not in my 3D professor's mind, but in some higher-up locale in me. I forgot about it, relaxed, and allowed my awareness to find the center. When I did, it felt like I had stepped onto dry land out of a raging ocean. The complex fence-grid fell away or opened up and I was past it now.

The humanoid figures (I was starting to realize they must have been past lives of mine, conducted in different sentient life-forms on God-knows which planets and for the purpose of broadening my education and level of experience) applauded me, and I was sure they grinned as they did so, though only slightly. Then they pointed to something in front of me which I hadn't yet noticed.

It was another shield layer I would have to get past. But this one was even weirder than the fence. It looked like a shimmering, vibrating pale purple loop folded in on itself in numerous ways yet also flowing like a river through a contorted channel. It looked like a loop expressed in 4D, or maybe worse, 5D. It seemed alive. It was flowing, twisting, as if it were some sentient creature with a loop for a body. Charting its topology would be like riding a rollercoaster in 4D.

Blaise was laughing. "That confounded me too when I first saw it. That was when the Blaises first showed me a Pleiadian ship occupying what they called an interdimensional portal. I could not see the damn thing at all at first. I knew it was there, but it was a blur. My mind and eyes were baffled, like yours. It was not so much an object with a fixed shape, but a type of living process in 6D. I later found that physicists modeled such moving forms as interdimensional membranes and even named their perplexing forms after themselves, such as the Calabi-Yau manifold space, but the clever names didn't make it any easier to see this. They thought they were demonstrating ramifications of their string theory. They didn't realize they were modeling what a Pleiadian spaceship looked like."

I saw a group of Pleiadians standing behind this twisting alive form. I knew they were Pleiadians because for one, Blaise had described them to me often, and for another, I had seen them during the few times Blaise took me back to his original home base. They were tall, robed, hairless, with large craniums; you could say they looked like humans, but they seemed ethereal, physically indefinite, as if occupying fixed material forms was not their top preference. They were primarily mental beings, and manifesting or exhibiting a bodily form was more of a courtesy on their part and not a big part of their self-definition.

Somehow I saw them as if I looked through the 6D twisting membrane. The Pleiadians mostly appeared as faces gazing indifferently through this form at me. I wouldn't say they looked friendly, but they didn't look unfriendly either. Theirs was a gaze more of neutrality than any partisan position on our presence. I assumed this was the last security device I had to get through to enter the core. Despite the apparent coolness of their presence, I was cheered by the fact that they were friends of Blaise, colleagues, even old pals from home. If he were British, he'd probably say we went to school together, old chums from Eton.

I turned to Blaise so he could see my bewilderment. He didn't look bewildered. "Remember your algebraic topology. That will get you through."

I didn't know what he meant, at first. I had never studied algebra, other than when forced to in high school and I quickly forgot everything I barely learned. Yet something was rising up in my mind, some vague understanding quickly sharpening into crystalline insight. Manifolds like this 6D Calabi-Yau manifold space, this interdimensional membrane twisting in higher space before me, could be generated by algebraic equations. Mathematicians had been experimenting with these forms for more than 100 years and had created an estimated one-half billion variations of shapes with these extra dimensions. "A manifold is a topological space that in a local sense looks like flat, Euclidean space near each point that generates it." My mind made that arcane declaration.

Before I had time to ponder where that bit of abstruse mathematical knowledge came from, I understood how to get through this vexing 6D shape. I saw a flat space in this twisting, rotating loop; in fact, I saw a myriad of flat spaces. I stepped onto one and the entire shape stopped moving and flowing. It looked as if it had flattened itself out to first a ring shape then a checkerboard. Then it was simply a matter of walking through this flat, now open, space. What had been a complicated twisting 6D form hard to see was now merely a thin wall made of squares, each of which was open and passable like a wide-open door.

I went through that door and entered a space that seemed filled with numbers, as if they were hung by invisible threads in the air around me. Stranger than that was the impression there were multiple Fredericks in here with me. I saw myself in dozens of copies standing amid these number matrices. They formed Magic Squares, quadratic algebraic equations, complex geometric forms. These numbers were like letters; they wrote scripts, spelled out codes for shapes.

One of these Fredericks stepped forward and whispered a phrase in my ear. It was an activation code, I saw, after I mouthed it myself. It caused this seeming jumble of shapes, squares, planes, number matrices, and geometric forms to leap into a coherent assemblage that, as I studied it, began to resemble the Earth's Light grid when you viewed all its complexity at once. I regret that I must keep this activation code a secret, but the Fredericks insisted on this when they told me. I couldn't help grinning. This code rendered the shapes obedient, as if you had a roomful of unruly dogs and you said a few words and they all sat.

It looked like the Earth Light grid model we kept at the Hierophancy in Sun Valley, but it was somehow brighter, more sharply defined, as if it were expressed in a higher octave that refined and clarified all its features in Light. It was like seeing your best friend's father, or maybe grandfather: you saw the continuity of facial architecture, the physiognomic similarities, but in older, purer versions, like you were seeing the original face pattern for your friend.

This representation of the Light grid, which, by the way, showed all the signs of sentience, possibly even to a self-aware degree, displayed its particulars. You could zoom in on any feature, any type of Light temple, either individually or in its distribution array, and bring it forward into close-up focus to consider. The various displays of numbers were also available as a background you could call up. I tested this feature and marveled at the mathematics underlying it.

I had expected to find Blaise's Pleiadian colleagues here since I had seen them in outline form before I made it through the twisting loop security shield. I still saw them, but their presence was faint, as if projected here from elsewhere.

"They aren't here in any material sense," said Blaise. "They are in the Pleiades, and we'll have to go there when we finish up here. They project images of themselves into this space as caretakers, watchers, and, when needed, helpers. Think of them as like reference librarians in a big college library. They can put their hands immediately on any volume you request, meaning any question you put to them regarding Light grid operation, since they are the prime designers.

"You could see them so easily because you have some history with the Pleiades too. You didn't realize that they were stealth-veiled; not everyone would have seen them, but you did so effortlessly. You have a Pleiadian karmic seed inside. You found that seed, touched it, turned it on, and it got you through the barrier. It remembered the mechanics of that barrier and got you through it.

"You couldn't see this, because you were inside it, but this Pleiadian seed in you expanded to occupy your entire manifestation space, and you passed through the twisting loop barrier as a Pleiadian. That older part of you accessed the mathematical protocols to disassemble the 6D twisting membrane. That identity worked like an automatic pass-through security clearance. Otherwise, you would have stood there baffled and remained permanently locked out.

"You are still in that Pleiadian form, incidentally—you just need a mirror to confirm it—and the multiple Fredericks you are witnessing, both to your amusement and bafflement, are Earth-human lives in which this seed was similarly activated and are now able to instruct you in Light grid mechanics. That twisting hyperdimensional membrane was put there to discourage, quite definitively, access to the system by anyone not qualified or professionally entitled, meaning it only lets certified Hierophancy members through its field. It is likely to dismay all other potential intruders; they'll never get past its shape.

"What we have in this chamber is the Earth's Light grid in *eidolon* form. Its perfect, original design, its ideal expression, including its intended final form, and some higher octave expressions of the same mathematics. As you know, the Light grid is both a fixed and an open-ended design. The designers pictured a desired end-goal, but left the system sufficient flexibility to arrive there through any number of surprise possible directions and novel evolutionary moves.

"So the design presents the original explicit pattern and the implicit outcome. That's why I likened this place to a reference library. It's where they stored the blueprints for Earth's design. The Hierophancy heuristic algorithm at our Sun Valley center is the field-application model, the many-times folded and stained and crinkled and weathered copy the engineers and builders take into the site to make their daily system adjustments. Here's the original. No creases."

I hadn't realized until that moment that Blaise was looking suspiciously Pleiadian too. His human form fluctuated with the Pleiadian overlay, with its big cranium, wispy, ethereal, tall body and general impression of strong inner Light. I noted that when he pointed out to me that I was exhibiting Pleiadian body indications, I felt a shiver, as if a black shadow had momentarily stood behind me, fringing the edge of my aura in a cold darkness. Strangely, I had forgotten this immediately, and soon after I remembered it there it slipped away again. I shouldn't have been surprised to find this Pleiadian involvement, in both us and the Earth's Light grid. They are the primary Light grid designers in this galaxy, and since the human design matches the planetary, the Pleiadians are there too.

I was standing inside a hologram of the complete Earth Light pattern. I could walk around inside it, point to an area and cause it immediately to zoom up and fill my perceptual field, then I could enlarge any details within that area. I only had to tap a given area twice to disclose the arithmetical version of the pattern; the numbers and equations that specified the feature were implicit in it.

That's what Blaise and I started doing, zooming and tapping. We were going over the whole of the mathematical specifications for Earth. We were looking for a defect, an area where something was missing, distorted, or written wrongly. I was aware of Pleiadians standing ethereally around the Light grid display. They were chaperones or perhaps cicerones awaiting any inquiries we'd have. They were not "physically" here in *Jambudvipa*, but I suppose that didn't matter. They "were" wherever their attention was focused; it was focused on us.

I didn't expect the Pleiadians to say anything. They weren't big on speaking. But they were showing us images; telepathy was their preferred mode of communication. I saw groups of "aliens" examining the Earth's Light grid pattern somewhat in the casual but engaged manner of museum visitors. They were studying it for its Light and consciousness conduction systems, for how awareness traveled through the system like an electric current through wires to illuminate sites and their corresponding processes in consciousness.

A few poked and prodded some of the Light lines and tried to lift up the Light temples, possibly to see how they were attached to physical matter. With wires? Their curiosity was intriguing, though a few of them were more than curious. I had the impression they wanted to make copies of the pattern or insert data into it or reorient the facing of some of the Light temple arrays like satellite dishes. I suspect most people living on the Earth would

still be surprised to discover the degree of interest by extraterrestrials in our Light grid design. Public knowledge of the existence of a complex landscape of Light temples was still scanty so we were dealing with two layers of esoteric information and reality.

Even within that specialized community, notions that our specific planetary pattern is of particular interest to other intelligences will come as a surprise. But it is the case. Earth's Light grid is special, a subject of great continuing interest. Other intelligences routinely study Earth's pattern; there are few like it, I hear from Blaise, and the Pleiadians certainly excelled in creating this one. That degree of galactic public interest explains why some of these intelligences might go further than aesthetic or mental appreciation of the beautiful design and may take steps to tinker with it, or worse, attempt to add it to their roster of colonial acquisitions, as if stuffing it in a pocket.

The trouble with this line of inquiry, as naturally we'd have to consider this area as a place to look for potential suspects, is that the alien intelligences could look but they couldn't touch the Light pattern. At least we thought so; that was our assumption requiring system security. It was unlikely they could penetrate the multiple defense shields I had already encountered; the only way I got through was, apparently, because of my pre-existent Pleiadian background. I could not realistically take credit for that endowment; it came with my body. Still, was this protective system absolutely inviolable to uncredentialled parties?

We were here, investigating the security system, because apparently it was not secure. Someone had managed to get through, either here or at the Earth end. Our investigation was the psychic version of looking for fingerprints. If someone had tampered with our algorithm at the *eidolon* expression of it and the Light grid it specified, we should be able to find traces of their intrusion.

The equivalent of a fingerprint would be a slight tilt to a system array, a tiny deviation in the expected digits in the coding specification for a Light temple, or even a minute slowness in the zoom function of a grid display when I ordered it. Apparently, by the fact that I, new to accessing the system at this arcane end of it, was not regarded by this system as an unwarranted factor, I surmised that I could investigate possible anomalies without myself creating and depositing one.

I had to keep pushing away, discrediting, the traces of alien surveillance on this system. Just because they were watching did not mean they'd invaded it. They could peer through the window, but it didn't offer them an unlocked access. I felt the presence of their attention; it was watchful, earnest, a bit contemptuous. I could feel the disdain emanating like heat waves from some of the alien minds at the presumption of awarding a second-rate phylogeny like humans such a masterful Light grid. What did humans ever do to warrant such a Light pattern?

I felt surges of hostility, ripples of ire that wanted translation into sharp kicks. If they could, many of these hostile alien minds would pummel our Light grid out of envy, disagreement, or just bad manners, like aristocrats mistreating the help. I noticed that though I had penetrated three layers of security to be able to stand here within the Light grid display, it had more defensive measures. It was being protected, even insulated, by Pleiadians, even if they were off-site. Apparently, they were in the Pleiades somewhere, maybe on Blaise's host planet, and they projected their guardianship from that location to this facility. Still, that projected presence was keeping the hostile alien minds at bay and outside.

Though they must be in physical terms hundreds of light-years from this place (precisely, it's 444.2 light-years from Earth to their star cluster, or 2.6 quadrillion miles), I felt their acknowledgement of my thought, as if, standing only a few feet from me on the other side of this constantly modulating pattern, they nodded their subtle heads. That erased the quadrillions of miles between us. They knew every aspect, every geomantic nuance, every option, of this pattern. I had to admire that level of engineering knowledge and the talent to create this. Their presence here suggested they could easily erase the spatial distance between where they were in the Pleiades and where we were on Higher Earth.

The Pleiadian overseers indicated that I should look behind the Light pattern. This was not as straightforward as it sounds. The grid display was constantly moving, adjusting its shape, and turning inside out. The "behind" part of the display kept flowing towards the front and then back again so it was not like walking around to the other side of the barn to inspect the woodwork.

I had to access the "back" of this system in a different way. I projected the image of a circle of large adjacent mirrors about 30 feet tall to surround the modulating grid display, but I set this circle slightly out of alignment with the Light pattern, deliberately introducing asymmetry. The asymmetry allowed me to see the back side of the system, and when I did, I saw a skin of numbers poised to bite into it.

I know that's an odd way to put it, but these number clusters looked like insects hovering in preparation for biting into someone's rich human skin. These numbers were deployed in anticipation of entering the grid pattern from behind. I may have imagined this part, but I thought I saw the hostile aliens who were launching this intrusion, as if their galactically outlaw fingers still held the numbers, as if the contrary numbers and equations extruded from their fingers were puppets or perhaps arithmetical *avatars* and through them they could walk into our system and make small changes that would gradually corrupt it.

The Pleiadian overseers for the moment were preventing this penetration by way of a thin but evidently powerful transparent force-field the aliens couldn't crack. Their numbers, as if they were sentiently empowered, kept nipping at the shield. The Pleiadian shield was made of laminations of mutating algorithms operating in four dimensions, all layers mathematically correlated.

The intruding aliens would have to unlock each layer and its connection point, and since the algorithms were mutating and I presume self-learning, it would be the arithmetical version of Herakles trying to cut all the heads off the Hydra and failing as the monster kept generating three new ones for every head he severed. Add to this the fact the system was keyed to a Pleiadian genetic signature which cannot be faked or simulated, so these unlawfully probing alien exacerbators would fail and with all my best wishes they could bloody get lost.

My cocky assurance was short-lived. I saw another alien intrusion poised for launching into our system. It was clever, I'll give them that. It appeared as a duplicate of the Light grid display, as if our display was reflected perfectly in a mirror. This duplicate was trying to convince our display that it was its proper context, its housing, or even, in an odd quasi-spiritual sense, its true self. It was trying to tease, cajole, seduce, or maybe yank our display into merging with it, suggesting it was its true home, perfect expression, and favorite lounge chair.

I saw the veiled tactic. As soon as our Light grid model touched the fake duplicate, previously invisible "arms," in the form of arithmetical devices and geometric shapes, would immediately launch to penetrate the system, grabbing it from the inside and taking control of it entirely. It would be as if 10,000 long tendrils made of activated numbers would extend into the genuine system and commandeer all its mathematical processes, erase them, and install its own.

If you don't mind a completely different analogy, the Light grid display was surrounded by a series of fierce-looking bear-traps ready to clamp shut. One false move, one slip in the security protocols, one wrong computation, and they would. These aliens could wait as long as necessary, centuries, even millennia. Maybe they had no other pressing engagements; or maybe they had sent automatic holograms of themselves and duration of presence didn't matter. The goal was too desirable for them to indulge in fits of impatience or hurried tactics. So our back-up copy of the Light grid mathematics was under jeopardy, though it seemed the infiltration scripts had not yet penetrated our numbers system.

Something about this "bear-trap" scenario was tugging at my memory.

"Blaise, this set-up bears resemblances to the Valles Caldera mechanism."

He nodded. He wasn't grinning this time. We both remembered that well.

It was June 2030 and that site had recently been declassified. Normally, declassification is something a government agency did; this one didn't fit that model. Hardly anyone in the U.S. government, or any national government, knew about it. The declassification came from higher up, from the Great White Brotherhood, our galactic government, that decided the site was now safe.

Prior to the major turn-over in planetary reality that started on January 1, 2020, the Valles Caldera site (more specifically, a node within the large sprawling site) was too dangerous, both in physical terms, but more acutely in psychic, geomantic terms, for any public knowledge of it, its history, or what was buried there, to be in circulation. The Hierophancy was tasked to supervise the site declassification. You have to appreciate the irony that almost nobody knew this was a restricted geomantic site. To the eye it was just a broad pasture-like field.

Valles Caldera is a 13.7-mile wide grassy caldera or circular depression surrounded by mountains and lava domes up to 11,000 feet, located in the Jemez Mountains of northern New Mexico, a dozen miles from Los Alamos National Laboratory and about 50 from Santa Fe. The valley-like caldera is what remains of a supervolcano that erupted about 1.47 million years ago. A caldera is the collapsed crater-like core left from an erupting volcano,

and geologists say the Valles Caldera formed over several earlier calderas that now lie buried under it.

The huge grassy area of the caldera, elevation about 8,000 feet, has hot springs, streams, fumaroles, natural gas seeps, and volcanic domes, as you would expect if you were a geologist. Many come to study this special site. Wild elk graze, tourists visit, Western-style movies were once filmed here, and in 2000, the 89,000 acres of Valles Caldera became a protected national preserve. Navaho and other Indian tribes once used the caldera for hunting and probably for ceremonial purposes and sometimes still talk about regaining ownership of it.

It challenges my imagination to walk inside the collapsed core of a formerly huge volcano. It spewed tuff out to 50 miles from here. Geologists say it is dormant, if not extinct; still, you wonder, is it truly quiescent? This bowl-like depression of the caldera was once inverted, the peak of a towering mountain that overlooked much of northern New Mexico long ago. That's the physical aspect of the site, but it had a geomantic feature as well, deep down. The Valles Caldera geomantic node was declassified, but it was still protected; its truth and history were still kept cautiously on reserve, on a need-to-know basis, and for many people, once they were debriefed on it, they wished they didn't know.

That's the outer story. The inner story is startlingly different. Blaise told me the first part of the story, based on his visit here in the summer of 2010, about 16 years before I met him. The second part of the story took place in 2030. He said he drove into the caldera along the rough two-mile long dirt access road, found a place away from the visitors to sit down and tune into the site. He was curious. He suspected the site might have geomantic significance. He was surprised, he said, that when he started to clairvoyantly "read" the site he was blocked. Not by his own capabilities, but by the site itself: it repelled seeing. It was holding a secret it did not want anyone to see. I impute intelligence and agency to the site only to make the point: somebody had put a shield over it.

"I was investigating the site at ground level," Blaise had told me, "which meant about 8,000 feet lower, from the time before the volcano rose and the land itself gained its current high elevation. Remember, originally, the planet's surface was flat and there were no mountains. It was like excavating straight down into the Earth to reach ground level. I had a hunch if the site had a Light temple or some geomantic feature it would appear to reside at ground level. Well, it did.

"The surprising fact was I could not see it. I couldn't penetrate what appeared to be a strong defensive shield that kept deflecting my clairvoyance. It looked like a tightly-sealed crystalline pattern, as if an entire city had been walled up on all sides, including its top, making it impenetrable, keeping outside observers out and whatever was inside this city from escaping into the world. I managed to get through the outermost "skin" of the tough defensive shielding.

"It looked like a carpet of ruby facets, but later I realized it was more like bloody skin. That is mostly a metaphor. Something catastrophic must have happened here before the volcano arose, and whatever that was then was sealed off for perpetuity to protect the future of the planet and the humans living on it. Knowledge

of what this catastrophe had been was too dangerous for the public. Even to hear a rumor or a vague reference to the existence of this was prevented. It seemed to be a kind of Pandora's Box, disastrously opened, then barely closed. The Higher Authorities did not want humanity to ever hear about this Box again.

"Naturally, that intrigued the hell out of me and I wanted to know everything about it, and naturally the Blaises and Ray Masters prevented that. That was the first time they had refused to help me see something and actively opposed my efforts. They should know humans better than that. All their resistance did was intrigue me further. I had to find out what was buried there. Don't ever tell a curious person they are not allowed to see something hidden.

"My analytic and imaginative faculties went into overdrive. Whose wouldn't? What could it have been down there? A weapon capable of destroying the planet? A global plague? A mini-black hole? Whatever it was that led to the sealing, it took place millions of years ago, like an echo of the Supreme Being's destruction of antediluvian Sumerian sites like Sodom and Gomorrah. Those were human settlements, but I suspected Valles Caldera was an alien one.

"This mysterious early 'city' was buried multiple times under volcanic eruptions. I'm not sure it was a city; only that it was large, and the spiritual authorities wanted it gone from human memory. I wonder if the Ray Masters even precipitated the volcano to rise up as an expert method of site burial; what could be better than burial under 8,000 feet of rock? It was a huge explosion: an estimated 95 cubic miles of molten rock were blasted out into the atmosphere then settled across northern New Mexico as volcanic ash which condensed into tuff. Add pyroclastic lava flow to that and you have a good burial mechanism.

"For a while, a lake covered the circular caldera. First they sealed off the site, or city, or whatever it was in actual fact; then they caused the supervolcano to erupt several times to fully bury their burial; then they flooded the caldera. It was like having three locks on a door. Then they refused to ever speak of it or let any information about the event enter public knowledge or perhaps even esoteric databases. Not even the geomancers should know about this old disaster. They prevented people from seeing it, and probably wiped the notion from their minds if it ever arose. That's a fourth lock on the buried secret, isn't it. I first found this site by accident, or so it seemed at the time. Later, I suspected the Blaises wanted me to find it. Well, it seemed possible. Were they ambivalent?

"The Blaises refused to tell me anything about the site when I first discovered it. Clearly, it was classified at the highest level, seemingly from all of humanity. Nobody was to know about it; that knowledge itself could be dangerous. It would be unsettling to the mind to know what this site was about. If it was a weapon that threatened humanity or the planet, knowledge of it as a fact of possible existence, in other words, that such a thing could be done, would be disastrous. It would be like relaunching a pandemic infection, letting a terrible biohazard loose, stirring up no end of fear and catastrophe pictures in the mind.

"Either people would try to duplicate it or they'd lose sleep—that's an understatement: they would live in a permanent panic—because they knew it was possible and it once had been deployed or blocked on this planet and could,

theoretically, be revived and launched again. I imagine it was like having a crazy, mad ancestor in your family lineage and you spend your life afraid you'll get infected with that madness and go crazy too and get locked up in the attic.

"This is an *old* secret too. We know we can rarely trust scientific estimates of dates. Typically, they are wildly off and far too conservative, based on too few factors. If we credit the geologists, then the event here took place more than 1.47 million years ago, but that's not far back enough. The mountain as a volcano was already here. Our event preceded the rising up of the mountain itself. It was pre-orogenic. The city or artifact or installation was buried at ground level back then, which meant ground level had to be accessible. Then they rose up the volcano. Yes, I admit, openly and frankly, I am not *that* old, at least not in this body. But I did eventually access the case file for this event. I can tell you what happened.

"What is the biggest threat to a planet like our Earth? It's not physical colonization or population decimation. Those are trivial, primitive approaches. No, the worst thing, the cleverest approach, is to commandeer the Light grid. Change reality without people knowing it. Covertly modulate their daytime consciousness. Send the planet's evolution and physical, elemental parameters in another direction, deliberately deviating it from its intended, designed course.

"That's worse than going crazy. At least you know for a while you're going nuts. But if you have your reality stolen from you, and you don't notice it, it is akin to having somebody commandeer your soul and force it into an alternate evolution. You've been taken over by an alien consciousness and don't know it. You are no longer yourself and fail to recognize this alteration. Technically, your free will becomes enslaved and your consciousness managed by an outside authority with you oblivious to the infiltration. Horrifying. What was buried at the base of Valles Caldera could make that awful change happen.

"It has the same logic as an expert bank robbery. Get in, get the money, be invisible. Leave fake money or some kind of electronic artifact behind that resembles money. It's all digits in a computer file anyway. The superior robbery is when nobody knows it ever happened. Do the same with a Light grid. It's even consistent with folklore: leprechauns awarding a human fool's gold. It looks like gold, for a while, then it disappears the next day and you don't even have dust. If you steal the Earth's Light grid, change its programming parameters, you have lifted human consciousness out of its rightful context, erasing its intended body.

"To start with, the simulacrum was a mutating, self-learning, self-veiling hyperdimensional algorithm installed like an intelligent machine, virtually an artificial intelligence, but also exhibiting biological tendencies you could liken to a plant's germplasm. It could grow like a plant emerging from a seed and extrapolating its own genomic signature, and it could self-direct its growth through its adaptive intelligence, and it could camouflage or even shapeshift its appearance. And its body was made of numbers, assembled in clever equations. I would liken this formulation to a poisonous plant, like deadly nightshade. It has a pretty flower, even an alluring blossom, but it can kill you if you imbibe it. This algorithm was innately hostile, set against humanity's welfare and well-being.

"In many respects, it beggars our own notions of what an artificial intelligence can do. Millions of years ago, it far exceeded anything our scientists have come up with today or have even conjured in their fervid imaginations, at least per the public record. It was clever and infernal and extremely dangerous.

"The implanted system had a front and a back. The front ran the apparent planetary systems. The back commandeered them covertly for other purposes. The front was a veil of multiple layers, each attesting to its own authenticity. The back end of the system was like a team of bank robbers conveying all the gold bars out of the depository and nobody saw them or even suspected the heist. We thought this system was an adjunct to the Earth's own arithmetical regulation; the Hierophancy brought it in believing it to be a complement, a system upgrade. We did not realize at first it was a devilishly clever Trojan Horse in our midst.

"My concern today is that someone has managed to unearth that buried algorithmic weapon and set it in motion again against the correctness of Earth's Light grid. Also they're drawing on this precedent when our arithmetical system was breached. That's why your attention and mine were suddenly drawn to this.

"It has the ability to deconstruct our present reality, recode the geomantic status quo, and basically commandeer our Earth as we know it, replacing it with a vile simulacrum and so cleverly masked hardly anyone will notice it. That appears to be what the current intrusion has in mind. That's probably what you were picking up on, the similarity in design and intent in the current assault on our system and this earlier one. We can't have it happen again. To pick your pockets of all your currency, replacing it with play money like from board games such as *Monopoly* or with folded newspapers cut to money size.

"It would transfer us into a false reality on an illusory planet without a Light grid. We'd be transferred to an illusory reality and never know it. That is way worse than merely being dead from some physical cataclysm. At least it's still *you* that is dead. *You* can start over, do another life, get back into the game. Here it wouldn't be you anymore at the center of your own action. You'd be a substituted you, and you wouldn't know it. Terrible hall of mirrors that. It would covertly cancel our free will and sever us from our own karma and any hope of resolving it and completing our Earth evolutionary plans. Think of it as an arithmetical reality erasure weapon no bigger than a canister. It contains a programming code lethal to our planetary Light grid parameters. Game over.

"I found it interesting and a bit spooky that this reality erasure algorithm was situated only a handful of miles from where, much later, though now in our past, the secrets of the atom would be breached and the first atomic bomb created. I am referring to Los Alamos National Laboratory. You could say they came up with another kind of reality erasure algorithm. Clearly, there is an arcane geomantic reason for this coincidence of two potentially world-destroying energies in proximity to each other, one that erases, the other that vaporizes. As a geomancer, you might think the landscape energetics inspired this conjunction. Throw in the supervolcano as the third erasure agent: it erased the existing contours of the landscape and even part of itself for many miles around,

converting a volcanic peak into a mellow bowl-like caldera. A lot of erasures.

"We were deceived then, though it was a long con, one that built itself incrementally, like watching a glacier move. Your eyes won't see it, but time-lapse photography will catch the gradual, inexorable advance of the massive sheet of ice, in this case, the progressive infiltration and decisive capture of the Arithmetical Earth, the whole grid. You'll note I'm saying 'we,' implying I remember. I do. It took a while to summon up the recall, but I did. You were there too. You never could have gotten into this place if you hadn't been there.

"The memories are carried forward across the succession of incarnational bodies. The Hierophancy straddles a vast stretch of the timeline, certainly all of Earth's. We had better do a security check in present time on the Valles Caldera vault and make sure it has not been breached or any of its contaminants released. Ray Master Lao Tzu will facilitate our fast travel to that location in the Jemez."

If you are not in your physical body in the first place, it shouldn't surprise you if you quickly transition to another location with no effort, which we did. Blaise and I stood at the center of the grassy Valles Caldera. Nobody was about. Then it seemed as if we instantly took an express elevator straight down 8,000 feet to the vault that had originally captured Blaise's unsanctioned curiosity. It felt like how it might be (putting aside the physical unlikelihood of this) to investigate a site where nuclear waste had been buried underground or perhaps to visit a mass murderer or serial killer at his maximum security prison cell. You felt you were up against something feral, utterly against humanity's welfare, immorally dangerous at a cosmic level, and it was emitting hate waves on you.

It reminded me of a science fiction story I once read. A man spoke a command sentence that shut down another man's consciousness completely. It killed his brain with just a few words, but the right ones. It also reminded me of a chess gambit, an introductory tactical move that announced the game plan. It reminded me of Gandalf warning people not to listen to Saruman; his hypnotic voice would lull them into a trance-state of submission and agreement. I realized I was nervous about visiting this ancient site and examining its buried nastiness.

It was as if I could see the implicit architecture this illicit arithmetic would produce, as if at some mental level it already existed, had already generated the capture forms, and was just waiting its moment to start rewriting Earth reality. My mental-psychic "immune" system would recognize it, wrongly, as friendly, and start incorporating it again or acting under its ill-intentioned programming.

An advantage of moving about in your astral body is you could walk through walls. The vault was a physical protection barrier, compounded of many layers and electronic defense shields and modulating electromagnetic currents, but it was to us as if it wasn't there. Two steps and we were inside the vault, amidst the roiling numbers. It was an arithmetic Hell realm from Hieronymous Bosch. It didn't look it, but I knew it was a terrific ontological contaminant.

It could spell the end of the Earth and humanity as we knew both. Blaise studied the mathematical architecture of the churning numbers, like he was a trial judge following a lawyer laying out the complex defense motion in a crucial court case. He knew how the arithmetical script was supposed to look, so he was studying it carefully for any elisions, amendments, or substitutions. It seemed fully intact, capable, and ready to launch its total rewrite of human and Earth reality. I was in my astral body, which you would think would be exempt from the usual physical body reactions, but I felt myself shivering with the cold. It felt like somebody was pointing a cocked pistol at my head and I didn't know why.

Blaise nodded. He appeared satisfied. "It looks the same as it did the last time you and I were here, inspecting it before the vault was sealed up forever."

When Blaise said that I suddenly flashed into the details of my timeline. I saw us there, back then, vastly long ago yet as vividly present as if it were right now in 2065, investigating this nefarious Light grid intrusion through what is now known as the Valles Caldera node. We were in different bodies of course; they were human forms, but they seemed ethereal. I would guess these were our Light bodies. Strangely, we didn't seem to be on the planet's surface but inside it and deep down. It wasn't that we were in a cave or some subterranean passage; we were in a well-developed dwelling *in* the Earth, as if the topside had been inverted and put inside the Earth as a viable, livable landscape for humans.

It seemed almost like living topside. It had the same sophistication of buildings, lighting, plant and animal life, atmosphere, weather, sunlight as you'd expect on the surface of the Earth, and even the people looked about the same, though perhaps brighter and more Light-filled, except we were far down within the Earth's "innards." I laughed when I realized how obtuse, how brick-headed, my mind was being. I knew there was an alternate human civilization living inside the hollows of the planet; Blaise had briefed me on that important fact. I was surprised, almost perplexed, that I had entirely forgotten that crucial fact. Then I remembered I, Frederick, in this current lifetime, was recalling an event a much earlier version of myself participated in; what we each knew differed a lot.

We were down there meeting with our Inner Earth colleagues because the machinations topside with the planet's regulatory algorithm were negatively affecting conditions inside. If it put topside humans in a fake, dream-world, imitation reality it would likely transfigure the Inner Earth people similarly. We had to warn them and, we hoped, come up with a joint workable plan to stop it.

We still have colleagues in the Hierophancy drawn from the Inner Earth population. We always have. The Light grid that ran consciousness and physical parameters in the Hollow Earth was a type of grace note to the topside grid. The inside-Earth algorithm was like a bracketed number set within the topside's algorithms. It ran mostly independently and autonomously, yet it shared key linkages. Modulations in our topside grid always nudged the inside-Earth grid. The commandeering of the topside, principal Earth Light grid was destabilizing interior Earth conditions—they are still living on the same Earth as we topside humans so collectively we were threatened with a dark reality transfiguration.

Perhaps I shouldn't take so much for granted. Knowledge of the Hollow Earth is still not widespread, still subject to disbelief, or worse, inflation and unsubstantiated attributions and glamours. The residents are people, just like us. Blaise's pals, the Blaise angels, once said they were Gaia's fallback plan for humanity, an alternate human civilization, modest in numbers but set up as a reserve in case topside humanity irrevocably screwed up all their life conditions. They had even provided a population count: about 17,000 humans lived in here.

Native American myths routinely speak of their origin being inside the Earth, that they climbed up ladders to arrive on the surface of the Earth long ago, and their tribal myths maintain knowledge of the location of these emergence points. Many of their rituals, and even the design of their *kivas*, reiterate and honor this primal emergence story. Naturally, almost no "white" people believe any of this, though geomancers know it's all true and I can show you a map detailing where the 360 ladders down to the Inner Earth are located. Our friend, Ray Master Lao Tzu, is humanity's official tour guide for expeditions downward. Blaise tells me that this Ray Master accompanied him on his early forays inward.

The head of the Hierophancy was down here waiting for us. This Ray Master routinely instructs topside and inside humans. History will remember him as the Greek boundary-god Hermes and the Egyptian Thoth or Tehuti. He was the teacher of measurement, the science of numbers, science itself, magic, geometry, land surveying, astrology, astronomy, writing, the alphabet and hieroglyphs, and the deployment of rationality. He was psychopomp to the dead, fleet mediator and messenger between human and divine realms, patron of thieves, a consummate trickster. Myth says he made the calculations for the establishment of the

Heavens the stars, planets, and Earth, and all they contain.

Esoterically, this came down to the Arithmetical Earth and its Light grid mechanisms that structure consciousness and reality which he oversaw with us as a prime activity of the Hierophancy. Hermes was the chief brainiac of our already hypermental outfit; he ran the numbers. He was the chief rationalist. Now I appreciated Jocelyn's clever reference to Autolycus as our numbers thief. He was the son of Hermes, and Jocelyn was hinting at the inevitable appearance of our hierophantic mentor in the arithmetical and Mind Mysteries we had been forced to plunge ourselves into when we discovered the algorithm was stolen.

To the Egyptians, he was *Djehuti,* "the one like an ibis," the ibis-headed god. They regarded the ibis as a sacred bird, so it was an honorific for him. He was the superintendent of the Mysteries of the Emerald Tablet, the Emerald itself (the secret Heart chakra), formulator of the Hermetic Axioms, superintendent of the Mystery rites of *Wesak* held during the Full Moon of May each year.

The Emerald I refer to is the Qabalist's Cube of Space seen tilted 45° to create the impression of a double-terminated upright crystal tower. The mental component comes in with the fact the Cube of Space is the repository of the five Trees of Life and the 50 *Sefirot* or Light containers of the Creation. That is the entire psychic architecture of higher reality with all numbers attached to it, and Hermes was our guide to its mental complexities of design and operation, not to mention the laws or axioms by which this fabulous complexity operates. He is our Mr. Wizard to all the geomantic and higher rationality Mysteries of reality.

Hermes was the guide to the Underworld, even for the gods, and you have to interpret Underworld to mean everything below the Absolute or Pleroma, the material 3D world, and for us that is the *Upper* World of the more refined dimensions. It's confusing, but the Underworld and the Realm of the Dead where Djehuti is the guide and adjudicator of karmic balances lie *above* the human crown chakra. It's *up* from this world, not below, as in below ground. The launching point for death Mysteries is the crown chakra; the Underworld is up.

The role of Hermes as mystagogue entails much technical knowledge, of mathematics, algorithms, and enough rationality to make sense of it and to explain it. He presided over the Weighing of the Heart ritual in the Judgement of the Dead, which meant he was a prime psychopomp to the recently deceased soul trying not to get lost in the *Bardo* and get immediately sucked into another dismal womb-door, as the Tibetans dolefully put it. In other words, he shows up in Egyptian and Tibetan models of after-life procedures, and he knows the topography of the Underworld's afterlife realm; he might lend you his map of the terrain and list of the main players and give you tips on who to best avoid.

Further, he directs the Transfiguration phase of the Christed initiation which takes place in the Emerald. That's when the explosion of primordial Light from inside the Emerald utterly changes your manifestation form and you assume a Body of Light, emulating Jesus on Mount Tabor when his true nature and form were shockingly revealed. He is one heavy-handed mental Ray Master.

We knew him as Ray Master of the Green Robe, one of the 14 Ray Masters operating galactic Light out of the stars of Ursa Major. I don't know what we called him back then. It was long before Egypt. I don't even remember what I was called, or Blaise, or any of the others of the Hierophancy, or what we called our initiative then. The function was the same. I suspect it was not names as we know them today anyway; a lot of our communication was telepathic.

This was millions of years before Egyptian or Greek culture. In recent centuries, this Ray Master was known as Djwhal Khul and he was associated with the metaphysical writers Helena Blavatsky in the 1880s and Alice Bailey in the 1930s, both of whom credited him as the channeled Higher World source of their intellectual metaphysics and their long (Blavatsky) and copious (Bailey) books.

Technically, the Ray Master of the Green Robe we worked with these millions of years ago was a different spiritual intelligence than Djwhal Khul. Blaise says there was a change in personnel in this Ray leadership around 1900. The one who had been Thoth was promoted upwards, and a new Ascended Master was elevated to Lord of the Green Robe. The Ray qualities and assignments remained constant, but the master of them was a new spirit. In the old days I refer to we worked with the Ray predecessor to Djwhal Khul, but whatever his name and personality is, this Ray Master directs the Hierophancy.

The Ray focus and themes remained consistent. Thoth had a feminine counterpart, sometimes called his daughter, wife, or sister. This was Seshat, "She who scrivens." Seshat had many of the same attributes as Thoth in wisdom, knowledge, writing, and mathematics. She was the "Mistress of the House of Books," which is fitting when you consider the size of Blavatsky's books and the quantity of those published by Bailey. Her priests ran the scroll library which preserved the most important knowledge and spells (protocols). Probably the brother-sister arrangement alluded to the archetypal syzygy pattern of deities where each manifested a masculine and feminine, *yin-yang* valence. We have already observed that with the Light Bringer with Lucifer and Sophia faces.

Thoth was "married" to Ma'at, and I suppose Seshat was too, because marriage here means alignment with, acting as a conduit for, and Ma'at was the name for the principle of the cosmic correctness of the original design of the Light grid. Ma'at was the goddess of truth, balance, order, harmony, law, morality, justice, and the basic equilibrium of the Creation. She regulates the stars and the actions of mortals and gods; she set the universe into order to rescue it from primal chaos or a tendency to relapse into chaos. Ma'at personified all this, and *ma'at* was its abstract, non-deific form. The Greeks called her Themis, but the principle is consistent: Ma'at is full knowledge of the Arithmetical Earth, the master regulator of the Earth's Light grid and its host solar and galactic grids.

The marriage designation is apt and illustrative. To say Thoth is married to Ma'at means a prime function of this Ray is to convey Ma'at to the world. It says this Ray and its Ray Master is the psychopomp conducting the soul into the mysteries and revelations of *ma'at*, the precise mathematical order of Creation. You get strong hints of that correlation in the linkage of Thoth-Hermes with the Emerald Tablets and the allegations (or rumors) of cosmic laws they describe. You could say the function of the Hierophancy, in Egyptian terms, is to explain the details and mechanisms of *ma'at* as they work in the phenomenal world. The Hierophant reveals the Holy Light of the goddess Ma'at as she scripts reality. The Light grids of Earth and beyond are the manifestation forms for this *ma'at*.

As I said, I don't remember what we called the Green Ray Master then, but let me revert to at least an older name than the Egyptian. The Babylonians knew him as Nabu, a male god of literacy, the inventor of writing, the rational arts, scribes, and wisdom; he rode a dragon called *Sirrush*, and was associated with the planet Mercury, the domain of the mind, the Roman name for Hermes.

An earlier Sumerian name was Nisaba and personified the Ray Master as a female deity. One image of her shows a woman holding a gold stylus and studying a clay tablet bearing an image of the starry Heavens, the array and ordering of the stars. She was the scribe of the gods, which meant she was fully briefed on their divine program which is virtually saying she upheld the correct and holy cosmic order. That evokes the arithmetical realm of reality because the holy order, the *ma'at*, necessarily entails numbers, and Nisaba knew them. It also suggests she briefed humans or at least Hierophancy members on the cosmic plan, the details of the *ma'at* infrastructure that ran Earth and cosmic reality, as if she showed us the arithmetical, Hermetic game-plan writing on her clay tablet.

All this aside, the easiest approach is to call "him" Ray Master Hermes, as we do routinely. I digressed a bit to present some details of his

(and her) résumé to indicate we had excellent help in our work and deep roots and time continuity in the work. Who better to deal with vexations to the Arithmetical Earth than this *Ma'at* Man? Who better to act as prime mentor to our Hierophancy than the master of the Hermetic Mysteries? If we were going up against these "evil" master math brains of the cosmos, we needed to up our mental game too and enlist the best coach in the league. Surely he had moves we'd never heard of.

We needed a fresh technical briefing on the Mysteries of mind, patterning, mathematics, energy, and probably, at this rate, applied white magic: "spells." Once we had identified this intrusion algorithm at Valles Caldera millions of years ago we consulted with our colleagues inside the Earth, as we were doing again now in 2065, because the programming intrusion implicated their well-being, and we brought our grid expert, Hermes, to help us plot our tactics. I don't usually like caves or enclosed spaces, but down here, inside the Hollow Earth, it felt spacious, uncrowded, and I could almost believe I was still topside.

We were consulting with our Hollow Earth counterparts to see if anything was missing from their sub-routine algorithms and if they had heard anything about ours. As mentioned, the two systems work reciprocally, but if the topside equations get compromised, it spells major trouble for the inside mathematics.

Our Inner Earth Hierophancy colleagues ran the numbers that manage their interior Light grid. They did this in their holographic projection room. We were inside the display, and watched it run its algorithmic processes, intricate computations, and constant adjustments. It seemed intact, though we discerned it appeared to run a little slower than usual, almost as if it stuttered or hesitated when it had to iterate certain computations. We noticed specific delays and even omissions, some data not getting through, in the processing linkages between the topside arithmetical system and how it correlated its products with the inside.

Overall, the system seemed to be running too slowly, shambling along instead of jogging, compared to how I remembered it, as if it was burdened with an excess of bytes or was running too many simultaneous programs or perhaps trying to run programs computationally incompatible with its own parameters. This condition suggested the inside system might have memory lapses or gaps in its cognitive processing syllogisms, like pieces were missing or had been taken out. This told us the Inner Earth Light grid numbers structure was being affected by the problem we were chasing down on the topside: the theft of the algorithm.

Meanwhile, being down here inevitably brought on a vivid recall of that first time at Valles Caldera and our assessment of the degree of the intrusion.

The foreign intrusion into the Light grid system stealth-installed at Valles Caldera then had been a replicating capture algorithm that operated in correlated dimensions. It was like a predator made of numbers, and its teeth were arithmetical incisors, and it was a marauder possessed of all the sly cunning and determination a predator needs. As I understood it then, this capture algorithm had seven tiers. Business (to us that meant trouble) began at the fourth level. It exhibited a Siren-like call of seduction to the existing self-regulating series of equations. This system would misread the new

number sequence and accept it as current-time input based on mutable conditions.

It would input the data which then acted like a number version of a capture virus. That would immediately lock in the first four tiers of the Light grid, the three physical parameters of material reality, and the fourth dimension of fluidic time. The Light grid, if I may personify it for a moment, would not realize this capture had taken place; it would operate like a submarine that had been boarded on the outside by a larger submersible that clamped on to its sides.

This capture algorithm extended its arithmetical "net" over the live algorithm. It would start rewriting its equations, first changing certain key digits. This process of capture, expansion, and number recoding continued until the original Earth Light grid had been captured up to the seventh level or dimension. Each new layer added to the complexity of the arithmetical capture sequence. In retrospect, maybe we were seeing the hypothetical deployment of this capture algorithm like a preview of what it was designed to execute, while the fact of the matter was that most of it had not yet been released and we stopped it in time.

Picture how the geometry of a cube gets more complex as it moves from a hypercube or 4-cube to 5D, 6D, then 7D. Then picture this in terms of number matrices, each one thoroughly locking down its layer, commandeering it like a virus. A 7-cube or hepteract is a seven-dimensional hypercube with 128 vertices, 448 edges, 672 square faces, 560 cubic cells, 280 tesseract (hypercube) 4-faces, 84 penteract 5-faces, and 14 hexeract 6-faces. Try to picture that in terms of number matrices. That appeared to be the shape of the arithmetical capture net set over the grid. This was like a master virus primed for release at the touch of a button; it would exponentially spread across the world and sicken everyone. Except here it was a computer virus, a capture-erase algorithm ready to launch.

I remember at the time I could barely grasp the complexity of that, even when we created the equivalent of what we would now call computer displays presented holographically as rotating Light projections over a large worktable. It had the Light grid in a complete stranglehold; if this were wrestling, it was a pin-down in which the Light grid "body" could not even wriggle its big toe.

The capture system, we quickly learned, would be aware of any of our attempts to reacquire the algorithm and execute predetermined containment measures to stop it, even to the extent of adding more number matrices to increase control. The intrusive device was a series of locks and clamps, each operating in a successively higher dimension, meaning there were more facets to deal with. The clamping mechanisms were operated by the algorithms and worked like roots whose veins infiltrated everywhere, their numbers increasing.

The worst part, or perhaps I should say the mathematically cleverest aspect, was that other than we in the Hierophancy who were versed in the mathematics of the Light grid, it seemed unlikely that any of the beneficiaries of this number-based Light grid system were aware of this definitive capture by intruding alien minds. The beneficiaries are the human population of billions on Earth. Reality would still seem, feel, and operate more or less normally to them. The physical world serviced by the Light grid would persist. This arithmetical weapon was like a bomb primed to go off anytime, even if it wasn't for millions of years; it would stay perfectly primed, waiting for that single finger-tap.

But to us that "less" than the quotidian normality of reality was crucial. It was a huge "less." It was more like a negative number. We had Hermetic eyes that saw the capture. It was our job to. But it was dismaying to see this. The planet had been captured and its modulatory affects on consciousness had been rudely hijacked. Still worse could happen; it was scheduled to. The operating parameters were being incrementally altered, like redirecting the path of an ocean liner so subtly that nobody notices until you hit that gigantic iceberg. You think you're steaming towards Liverpool; instead, Valparaiso lies straight ahead.

The relevance of this to the landscape later known as Valles Caldera was that the intruding alien intelligences had installed their arithmetical capture device there in the center of what millennia later would be this 14-mile wide grassy area. If you looked at it quickly you might visually interpret it as a small radar dish; look at it longer and you'd start to be dazzled by its fractal geometry.

First you might see a circle of adjacent duplicated radar dishes numbering in the hundreds, and you might even wonder if your sight was blurred and your eyes suddenly defective. You'd see one radar dish, then you'd see a thousand like it. The thousand would seem to be inside the one, and you'd see the reverse too. It was difficult to get a visual purchase on the actual details of this radar array, and even then you had to remind yourself this was a visual metaphor: it was not radar dishes you were seeing, but some complex, higher-dimensional broadcasting system, and it was broadcasting the capture of Earth's Light grid.

Then this multiplicity of copied, dovetailing radar dishes took on a crystalline aspect in which each parabolic dish assumed a complicated, faceted geometric pattern. If you tried to put your hand on this system, it would pass right through the array. This level of the array was not in the physical world, not even in the etheric. It cast an auric field out in all directions for many miles; this field resembled an ice cloud saturated with ice crystals, each a geometric shape.

You felt you could cut your mind on these diamond-edged crystals in the cloud. This crystal cloud perpetrated the spread of this arithmetical virus outwards across the topside Earth's multi-tiered Light grid and downwards into the inside Earth's subsidiary Light grid; it was forcefully and completely commandeering both. It was chilling to contemplate numbers and math sets deployed as contamination vectors, as if they were the foul exhalations of a truculent demon-god of numbers who was intent on seizing the planet and changing the manifest order of human and Earth creation into something different. It was setting the planet on a retrograde direction, taking it apart. You have to realize some alien intelligences deeply resented the largesse of humanity. They thought God was mistaken and misguided to award such bounties to us.

The intent may have been the sign of a hostile planetary takeover, yet its symptoms and any evidence of its presence were still hypersubtle. The intrusion had so far gone undetected by the bulk of the Hollow Earth population. Only the Light grid managers, the inside-Earth Hierophancy members, detected the unholy distortions this number capture system was spreading.

I say "unholy" because as an attack against the planet's Light grid it was aggression against Ma'at and the cosmic order and balance she represented and the Light grid provided. It was an affront to the pattern of reality the planet's Light grid maintained. It defied the commissioned intent of this consciousness-bearing planet. Perhaps I should put it in more mechanical, geomantic terms: this ancient Valles Caldera contaminant was a distortionary input made of numbers, and it was an aberration that skewed all the intended algorithmic end products.

We were working in great concentration to map its pattern of intrusion. It was a tricky encroachment and highly responsive to any attempt to penetrate it. If it detected our probing presence, even on a mental level, it immediately propagated more tiers of grid entanglement, like a tree spawning more roots. That was its defensive posture; on the offensive side, it was rewriting the number script of the Light grid, specifying new details of Earth reality and consciousness.

It was strange and unsettling to see numbers set to a disequilibrium purpose. In the Hierophancy we worked with numbers, equations, and mutating algorithms all the time, but it was always in the context of serving the Light and its grid patterning. I don't mean to sound precious, but this number service was always in support of *ma'at*, the inherent, intended, designed holy intent of the Light grid system. Hierophants reveal the Holy Light, and the *ma'at* or cosmic order was the chief characteristic of the divine radiance of Ma'at, the perfect rationality of the Creation and its arithmetical coding undertaken for our benefit.

But now we were examining a shadow, unholy form of this numbers deployment, like a mathematical version of Dorian Gray, hideous and infernally aged in his true body form. It was as if the numbers were stained with iniquity. We were witnessing reality itself being corrupted at a fundamental operational level, and it was our job to undo this corruption, disentangle the numbers and equations from the still faceless devilry that had grabbed it to steal the planet.

I kept sliding back and forth along the timeline from the present incursion of 2065 to the ancient threat at Valles Caldera. It seemed the same hostile intelligences might be involved with both intrusions, and the threat to the planetary Light grid was of equal intensity at both times we were investigating.

This devilry might be faceless, but perhaps not nameless. Ma'at had a perpetual enemy. He was called Isfet, though again the Egyptians were personifying an abstract tendency, in this case one towards disorder, chaos, dissolution of form and order, injustice, violence, and entropy. His name meant "to do evil." Other nuances to his name and character included that which is difficult, troublesome, and disharmonious. He is the embodiment of anti-*ma'at*.

What we had before us at the site later known as Valles Caldera was not chaos or entropy. It was an exceedingly orderly Isfet-capture of an orderly Ma'at-flavored system for the purposes of commandeering human consciousness and redirecting its evolution, or, more practically, derailing or ending it. It was orderly in both directions, but one was holy, the other unholy because it was unsanctioned.

It may not have been Isfet directly, but his spirit was influential.

The Egyptians believed that when Isfet gained the upper hand, the world would start to decay and become separated, even estranged, from the cosmic order. The Pharoah's job was to combat Isfet and keep reality always aligned with Ma'at and thereby prevent the ordered reality of Earth and human life from degenerating into primordial chaos, as it were, falling apart into raw disorder. The Nile would fail to inundate the lands at its appointed time and famine would ensue; then society and the natural order would start to fall apart. The Pharoahs, when they accepted that task, were members of the Hierophancy. We worked with them in their struggle to reestablish the reign of *ma'at* against Isfet.

Now in present time, Blaise, myself, the members of the Inner Earth Hierophancy, and Ray Master Hermes assembled in a circle inside the Earth. We wore the robes of the Hierophancy, a deep emerald green that sleekly draped the body from neck to ankles, and we wore a bishop's mitre type of headpiece of the same color, Hermes's Green Ray. Before us stood a six-sided Emerald as large as a three-story green building. I capitalize this word because it was not an ordinary emerald I was seeing. It was crystalline in appearance, but it was more than that.

Picture a cube seemingly made of the emerald gemstone, its six sides sheer, glassy, and brilliantly green. Then tilt this cube 45 degrees and elongate it so it becomes a double-terminated upright green crystal with six sheer glass sides. Then fill it with blazing Light. That is what we had before us. It was a holographic replica of the Cube of Space, or what we call the Emerald.

Our Inner Earth colleagues kept one permanently projected as a hologram so they could access it any time. It was like keeping the office lights perpetually on. This Emerald can be projected at any size. In the human, it's a mere two inches long; externally, it can be the height of a skyscraper or even the size of the Earth. We adjust the Emerald's projected size to meet the requirements of the job.

In Qabala's model of the Creation, God originally sealed space in six directions, and filled this implicit primordial cube with the Light of Creation. Qabalists called this the Cube of Space; medieval mystics termed it the Green Stone; we know it as the Emerald. I capitalize it to distinguish it from the gemstone. All humans within the second generation of humanity received a holographic copy of this, and yogis knew it as the Heart within the Heart, the *Hridaya*, or the Heart. They didn't mean the organ. It is the third and secret part of the heart chakra, a unique doorway in and out of existence for consciousness.

The Transfiguration happens when you open the Emerald and release this Light. It completely changes the nature of your manifestation as a unit of awareness. It floods your awareness and drowns it in Light. You become a blazing Body of Light, a nondualistic radiance without separate selfhood any longer, like Jesus Christ standing on Mount Tabor, and according to the Ofanim, you enter a nondualistic state as you and reality are one. I was cheered that the same Ray Master, Hermes-Thoth, superintended the *ma'at*-flavored revelations of the Emerald Tablets and the sublime Christed initiation. It's in the same

temple. You get the perfect rationality of the cosmos explained and rendered as a blueprint and you get the absolutely purified, primordial consciousness to step into as you digest these Mysteries of the Creation and the Clever Mind of God.

Geomancers know that the Emerald exists inside humans and across the planet as a Light temple and more acutely that it contains the Emerald Tablets. These were alluded to in the Gnostic and Mystery traditions as a body of ancient knowledge attributed to Hermes and containing the operational secrets of reality. They were the basis of the Hermetic tradition and its geomantic applications.

The exact location of these Tablets apparently was a secret, one highly classified, or over time perhaps people forgot where they were. Well, they were right in front of us. Here was the mystagogue Hermes and his Emerald Tablets. We could touch them, run our fingernails over their glassy sheer surface; we could peer through their translucent walls and glimpse the Mysteries. Soon we'd be in there. That's why I brought up this summary of the Emerald, its links with Hermes, and its works so you could appreciate what I am about to say next.

The Tablets are the walls of the Emerald. They are hidden in plain sight, though there is an irony in that statement. Not many people yet know about the Emerald or how to access it. Within the human energy field it is tiny, barely more than two inches long, situated to the right of the sternum at the second rib down. In that place is a miniature version of what we had before us in large form, though they are the same in essence and design. The projected size is adjustable. The easiest way to access the

Emerald within is to project it large outside of you in psychic space then enter it that way. We would enter the walls for the Tablets.

From the outside all you see is sheer green glass walls, as if you are standing before a skyscraper made of the clear part of quartz crystal. It looks solid and impenetrable, but it isn't. You simply walk into these walls and remain there, not proceeding further into the main chamber of the Emerald. Inside, the wall appears as spacious as a warehouse yet you feel you're inside an electronic brain or an advanced computer with all its computations displayed around you. You are not holding Hermes's Emerald Tablets; you are wakefully *inside* them. The Tablets are a surprising combination of supercomputer and Delphic Oracle.

Those are crude images to evoke what I was seeing. You had the visual sense the "air" around you was filled with script and number equations written in Light. It was an information matrix and you activated it by asking a question. I suspected you could ask virtually any question and it would formulate a living answer. The display screen for the answer was in front of you; better, you were standing in it. It was like you were standing in an unlimited information field.

It was immediately responsive and vastly knowledgeable and could instantly configure its "display" presentation to answer questions. It was in a sense an artificial intelligence if you credit that to mean an abiding intelligence behind all the answers, a super-intelligence regarding the mathematics of Light grid design. To stay with this analogy, this computer was equipped with all the specifics of *ma'at*, the design specifications and mechanisms of reality and Light.

You will appreciate that this was exactly the kind of top-notch information source we needed to consult, a higher authority on the arithmetical realm now in turmoil. We had consulted the Emerald Tablets millions of years ago for advice on the Valles Caldera weaponized algorithm, and we were doing the same now about the Hierophancy heuristic algorithm theft. That's probably why I was remembering our earlier visit. This place is outside spacetime and has a kind of eternal, no-time specificity to it, and your normal sense of time flow goes out the window, so once you're in here, it seems like all the times you've been in here. There were a dozen of us in here (Blaise, myself, Hermes, and nine Inner Earth Hierophancy colleagues), but there was no crowding. We prepared our question.

Our question was obvious and immediate. How can we stop this grid intrusion? We saw it displayed before us, like an X-ray. I felt chilled. It looked like a picture of a cancer metastasis seen in speeded-up motion taking over the body, spreading roots and capturing body mass. The alien intrusion was doing the same to the Light grid pattern, infiltrating it, clamping it down, rewriting its code to start changing planetary reality. It was aggressive and thorough in this.

It was changing the numbers that ran Earth reality, shifting all the equations. We saw next to this degraded system display a copy of the original pristine grid programming, and we saw this superimposed over a specific geomantic node. It was fascinating, when I regained my mental composure, that the earlier Valles Caldera intrusion and the algorithmic theft we were currently pursuing seemed to blur together. Both entailed aberrations to the smooth processing of the arithmetical matrices in place. I suppose they were chapters in the same book, although it seemed to most resemble a well-crafted horror story.

The system gave us an answer in pictorial terms. Relaunch the system.

I know this is an old analogy, but it used to be with computers, when I was young anyway, that sometimes their operating systems would get so stuck and entangled they ended up going in a loop with no apparent resolution. That's when you would unplug the computer, switch off its electricity, then start it up again. That's what the "Tablet" was suggesting: relaunch the Light grid.

In practical terms, that meant going back to its starting point, the untainted energetics of its inception, then entering and dissolving the intrusion from a place of geomantic seniority. Logistically, that meant returning to the original Blue Room and then the planet's primary umbilical point at Avebury in England. That was the specific geomantic site the Tablets showed us, but the Blue Room visit would come first because that preceded the grid inauguration of Avebury.

We would make these contacts in consciousness. We wouldn't have to travel bodily. But let me try to clarify the timeline. When we discovered the Valles Caldera intrusion the first time, we visited our Hollow Earth colleagues, then consulted the Emerald Tablets after which we set off for the original Blue Room headquarters and then Avebury, the planet's Light grid umbilicus and primary geomantic coding "station." We would do the same again in 2065, retracing a few of those steps in the arithmetical syllogism of how the planet was generated out of mathematics and in what order the equations proceeded to accomplish this; knowing this gave us a way to a solution. I was remembering ancient events at the same time we were repeating those early steps now in the present moment. What worked before might help us resolve the present issue.

The Blue Room is a casual term the human Blaise uses to denote a central design and planning office for the planet's Light grid. It was established in what we now know as northwestern Siberia near the Laptev Sea several billions of years ago. I assure you I do not exaggerate. It was established in the early days of the planet. It is a subsidiary, an Earth affiliate, of a master geomantic design office in the galaxy located on Mount Meru in the domain of Brahma, whom the Hindus know as the Creator god and who has a celestial city on that peak. Brahma is equivalent to the Judaic Ancient of Days and the Supreme Being, although I've always conceived of Brahma as like God with His sleeves rolled up, an engineer meeting with you on a Saturday morning to review plans.

Our Blue Room operates under the auspices of this executive Brahma. His universal residence is called *Brahma-pura*, "City of Brahma," or *Brahmavrinda*, "Abode of Strength," located at the top of this celestial first mountain. Eight other Celestial Cities of the gods flank the slopes of that golden mountain. God-names tend to be fluid and interchangeable, so the Hindu seers also know him as Visvakarman. In that role he acts as prime executive designer and artificer of all Light temples, god residences, and schemes for realities that support incarnate consciousness. He's the original of what Henrik Ibsen calls the "master builder." For Blue Room geomancers and Hierophants, he is our Chief Executive Officer.

Visvakarman or Tvastr, as he was known in the earlier Vedic pantheon, is respected as the divine architect, lustrous chief artificer, master engineer of the world, supreme craftsman, the all-accomplishing maker of everything. He was equivalent to the Egyptian Ptah and Freemasonry's Grand Architect of All That Is. He has five heads or prime attributes, and with them he conceived the plans and created the palaces of the gods, their chariots, weapons, and thrones. He has eight arms, by which he can reach into numerous worlds and hold them steady. I suspect this specific number was also a clue to his correlation with the eight-sided inner heart chakra, the *Ananda-kanda*, or Abode of Bliss. Everyone carries this in their chest, filled with the nondualistic Christ Light as a thoughtful gift from the Creator.

From the field-working Hierophancy's point of view, his was the principal design office and archives of all universal designs. I know that sounds grand, but it's accurate. You went to his office, his celestial city, his realm, when you needed clarity on a design. If you were a Hierophant or geomancer, it was the central office, equivalent, though on the ultimate scale, of a municipal office that registers the construction blueprints for all buildings put up in its jurisdiction. If we're talking libraries, his office is the Library of Congress, and our Siberian Blue Room is the local branch library, smaller, more modest in scope, basically similar.

Here you will find the engineering schematics for all the galaxy's Light grids and Light temples and the crucial processes of consciousness they managed. In Earth's Blue Room you find the engineering schematics for just our planet. The best part is that Visvakarman's domain is absolutely inviolate

to intruders. His "city" is untouchable and incorruptible there at the summit of the cosmic mountain. Our Blue Room installation in Siberia was an abridged hologram of the original vastness of his universal design office, but it had the special advantage of facilitating trips back to central headquarters. The easiest way to reach Visvakarman's original office is to go through a planet's local one. All Visvakarman's local planetary branches are hyperlinked with his central one.

Initially, you might, as I certainly did, find Visvakarman's main office cognitively daunting. It is so vast it seems impossible for your mind to take it in. This is the place where, as Brahma, he Mind-generated reality and all its parts. Here is where he deployed the arithmetical domain to code innumerable realities. It seemed to me as if I stood within the innumerable blazing diamond-white fiery crown chakra petals of an immense white head and on each petal burned the design for a planetary Light grid, itself a script for a nuance of consciousness. This prolific head seemed to present what I would estimate to be millions of designs, like an architect's filing cabinet of his career's productivity, except in this case it is the Premier Architect with a prodigious work history.

Alternatively, I saw an upright white pinecone with at least a million petals, with Brahma looking out through each, infiltrating each of his Mind-created worlds. I say alternatively because my "mind" or psychic equipment was struggling to condense this vastness into some kind of steady, comprehensible image, and failing. You felt Brahma looked everywhere; probably that's why he was portrayed with five heads, just as the Qabalists modeled an ultimate reality of Five Worlds, five Trees of Life with all their complexity, each tree more arcane. Brahma has a head through which he can observe each of his Five Worlds, and those are entire, vast universes of multiple component worlds and life domains.

Attentive scholars will point out Brahma has only four heads. Originally, he had five heads, but Shiva chopped one off. I'm going with Brahma's original condition. He's a Five-Head Guy, and while I'm at it, I know, blushingly, I vastly underestimate the number of his completed designs. Millions? Far more, I should think. Here is the archive of all Brahma's creative projects, mock-ups for complete phylogenies, including ours on Earth and Earth itself and its Light grid. Here is where he manifested creative visualizations, as we might lamely call them, energizing them to the degree they were fully animated with life and motion sufficient to carry them forth through eons of incremental development.

Here he foresaw and planned the intended if eventual outcome of a self-aware consciousness, what it could, and, he hoped, would, gradually shapeshift itself into. In the case of Earth, it would be our Albion, awake, self-aware, and cosmically mobile. Visvakarman's notion of a teleology for one of his evolving consciousness designs would outstrip our ability to conceive of it but perhaps not ultimately to achieve it; only then would we become aware of the full plan.

The easiest way to describe Visvakarman's architectural archives is to liken it to a huge library in which everything is immediately at hand. You specify which plans you want to examine and they manifest before you, as if summoned out of the air where they are stored holographically. Yes, you could say that Visvakarman's library of Light grid forms was a single hologram and you could pull down from this vast array the precise details you sought and the "reference room" in which you did this would fill with the desired complete pattern. I used to think our Earth's Blue Room was complex, packed solid with too much data. From a normal human viewpoint, it is, but Visvakarman's design office staggers that in detail, information volume, the overwhelming prolific creativity it shows.

On a more practical level, putting the ineffable aspects of this place aside in favor of some concept of it that I could work with, this design information would appear in two tiers. One was for the architectural shape of the planetary grid or Light temple; the other for the number specifications that coded those forms, though this could easily lead to complications as the designs were linked in a manner similar to what was once called hypertexting in computer language.

These many designs were like stepping stones, one leading to the next, getting you across a great pond. These forms were accessible in their multitude of evolving and adapted patterns, the way back-up modules for computers used to automatically store new content every day so you had a stratigraphy of slightly different versions of the same file. The mockup for a consciousness phylogeny included a myriad of incremental steps by which that form became self-aware. Here you could access that phylogeny at any stage of development, then hypertext yourself to any adjacent, congruent, or related planet systems.

Here you find equations parenthetically inserted within larger equations. Think of written sentences that have long dashes and parentheses, giving you additional contingent data within these interstices of the main thought exposition. These parenthetical equations branched off into many higher dimensions of form, and here it's helpful to think in terms of branching octaves or cascades of harmonics, realities expressed at different levels of complexity.

You could call up all the modulations ever made to a Light design, and you could see a display of the potential or contemplated shape alterations not enacted but which remained as possibilities should they be needed, like understudies for actors in a stage play. You could see this in number form too. Physicists would call this the quantum possibility field.

Let's say you have 500 players available for a baseball team, but you only need nine. You select your nine ball-players and the 491 reserve players remain on stand-by. As the coach, you run through all the possible permutations of player combinations to see which yields the best outcome, a victory in the game. This is my layman's inept analogy for describing this quantum possibility field. You could see the equations and algorithms for all these possibilities, and these number displays themselves had forms of an almost sculptural grace and detail. This Bright Guy had plans within plans inside plans. He kept track of all of it.

I never would have thought I'd be the proper person to send into a place like this. Mathematics was not my strong suit; it wasn't even my weak suit. It didn't come much into play in my studies of comparative mythology, but in the years in which I've travelled and studied with Blaise I have nudged myself cautiously into the field of numbers and equations so at least I don't trip over them anymore even if I can only lamely describe them. I was like a pinch hitter in a baseball game, one who hadn't been called on for some time. I had to get a hit. I had one or two moves that might work, and they'd better; the team was counting on me to come through with something. In this case, it was Team Hierophancy.

One attribute that is consistent across the different names for this engineer god is that he, as Ptah, Brahma, or Great Architect of the Universe, generated reality and all its edifices, Light grids, godly palaces (and cities, such as the legendary Lanka and Dwarka), and what we call Light temples, from his Mind. They are Mind-born, arising out of his pure thought. He conceived them mentally then energized them, establishing their reality, with the "magic" of his "word," which suggests a vibrational signature awarded to each.

This deity in his various cultural formulations is the patron of architects and craftsmen, but that understates the degree of his involvement in primal designs. He is the master of geometry and proportion, but as soon as you say that you're in the realm of numbers, equations, and algorithms that generate all realities. You could say, if you'll pardon my flipness, Brahma is the master numbers man. Hermes is a professor, but Brahma is the department chairman.

I saw this mind in action. I felt I was standing inside his mental processes. First there was a cloud of fire in which a command seemed to resound, like a declaration. I couldn't tell the shape of this cloud but it clearly had a signature. It was an atmosphere with a definite quality, a framework, as if chaos and quantum flux had been suddenly commanded to assume a clarified shape.

Then I saw that this shape comprised numbers, and these numbers expanded into equations and were like the skeletal system of the commanded shape. These numbers in turn generated shapes and geometric forms which were harmoniously inter-nested. I realized I was now inside an architectural structure made of directed Light. Then it was as if this geometric shape with bones made of equations exuded a specific vibration. It was like striking a bell and you stood inside its sound, expanding yourself in its cascading wave trains. This was the process, the condition, of consciousness this mental thought generated. It was the desired reverberating result of Brahma's mental engineering sequence: a temple.

That was just one Light temple's generative sequence. A planet's Light grid was similar, only vaster, and I realized the Light temple individually was a fractal of the whole pattern. I realized that this creation process was continuous and still happening. I was not observing an historical event, but one performed live, right now, before me. Visvakarman was perpetually creating the myriads of Light temples in their Light grids. He kept thinking about them, or I should say, maintaining his steady focus of thought that sustained their reality each moment.

Maybe it was more like chanting and the words and syllables he intoned perpetually reinfused shapes with reality. These shapes were not just the Light temples for Earth's grid; they were for universal reality and all its planets, though there was some overlap as Light grids sustained self-aware intelligences and these,

despite having different biological forms, still had much in common.

I need to clarify a technical point. Here at Visvakarman's design office you see the original, archetypal, or, should I say, generic designs for Light temples. The extruded primal concepts taking form as constructs of mental atmosphere, arithmetic, structured Light form, and consciousness process. For many planets, especially our Earth, you then have the Pleiadian fine-tuning of this pattern. The Pleiadian planetary Light grid designers used these raw materials to construct Light grids that delivered the precise consciousness calibrations called for to insure the likely evolution of consciousness and intelligent, self-aware life-forms on the host planet. Visvakarman created the raw materials; the Pleiadians then "cooked" with them, preparing tasty, nutritious "dishes" made of Light temples.

What I had to do was find the exact mental extrusion stream that coded the Light temple feature that was being hijacked through the Valles Caldera node—wait: I was checking the original records for the correct formulation of our master algorithm, in present time, wasn't I?—and then redirect it (in a sense, copy it) to that site as a corrective measure. To use the old computer language, this would be restarting the system with the original program, and the insertion of the original programming should remove the node corruption. Blaise and Ray Master Hermes were with me, and the nine Inner Earth colleagues, but everyone was standing around calmly waiting for me to act. Things had fallen into my lap.

It was like standing in a room with thousands of electrical wires hanging down from the ceiling. I was picking through them like a traveler in a rainforest slashing and pushing his way through a tangle of vines. I felt I was covered in numbers, that arithmetical factorings enveloped—cocooned?—me thoroughly. I hope I am conveying how unsurpassingly odd this experience was, but I kept my focus on the goal, looking for the precise strand that coded Valles Caldera.

I was operating on two parallel lines. On one, which I was remembering, I was trying to fix the Valles Caldera problem from millions of years ago. On the other, I was looking for the pure form expression of our master algorithm which somebody had just stolen in the year 2065. The two problems and the two visits seemed to blur in my perception, like two episodes in the same chronic problem. This venture, the one I believed I was aware of, was as far as I could tell taking place in present time, right now. The two timeframes, the two episodes of adulteration, and my goals ran parallel yet they seemed to blend together.

I was going back over tracks I traveled the first time we had a problem like this current one. Maybe there had been other forays here I hadn't yet remembered. It was like Mircea Eliade said of sacred sites and holy time: you are in the timeless, archetypal eternally present moment of the creative gods and their generative gestures when reality was manifested in its pure idea form. This is truly sacred space because it is outside of the phenomenal world's timeline. Except I was in Isfet time, when the holy order of sacrality was totally fucked up.

It was like standing in a shower of pure, invigorating water. I was energized by its abundance of *prana* as it made such a striking contrast with what I now perceived as the polluted, dirtied shower water of the corrupted

node. You have to remember that ultimately Light temples are processes of consciousness; that is their purpose, to deliver structured, which is to say, scripted, pristine nuances of awareness. You appreciate this vividly when you can immediately compare a pure form with its tainted version. I shuddered as I realized this taint was being distributed across the planet through the Valles Caldera node, like a dirtied house air filter. And the absence of Earth's dominant algorithm was similarly delivering a distorted reality to its "customers," humans on the Earth.

I was looking at the inventory of pure designs for Light grids that would structure and run realities and sustain consciousness. But they were as yet unfitted to actual life conditions. To use an analogy, they lacked their wirings. The grids have to be scaled down and adjusted to local planetary conditions. The Earth's Light grids, especially the ones that template Celestial Cities, are clearly reduced in size; the cosmic originals, according to the Puranas, were vast in scale and would not even fit on the Earth in the number of copies prescribed. The temples have to be scaled down to fit the planetary context, individually adjusted (think of this in terms of a dimmer switch: how bright do you want it?), then collectively integrated into the whole pattern which is more adjustments.

How would I get this correct copy of the node transferred back to the site? I would be its carrier. I laughed as I realized I would have to emulate Brahma. I would carry this Mind extrusion of the Light grid shape and specifications and relaunch it at Valles Caldera as if I were Visvakarman himself thinking it up fresh. To use an analogy, I would carry it back on me like a patterned cloak; then I would take off the cloak and drape it over the site, and the pure form would erase the corrupted form, as it was the senior expression of the original idea. Similarly, I was referencing the original form of the planet's algorithmic structure to give me insight on how to restore the missing components. How we handled the first major perturbation was a model for how we should proceed now.

The pure form would excise all the branching networks, eradicate the hyperdimensional tiers already being extrapolated from the alien seed intrusion into this site. It was growing rapidly and its take-over shape was gaining in complexity, yet exposure to the original pattern had inexorable seniority over all secondary corruptions. If not, the Earth would have been in serious jeopardy, and eventually its entire Light grid would collapse and probably the planet would implode and vanish. I am grateful smart people designed this system and made astute accommodations for future inevitable dire problems such as this.

I had the correct uncorrupted file, but before I could install the pure form of the geomantic node back at Valles Caldera, I had to immerse it in the equally pristine first Light at Avebury. I'd have to take it there as my mission's second step. This is the site of Earth's umbilicus, the planet's version of the Blazing Star that sits at the core of all physically manifest humans and represents the condensed presence of the Ofanim, better known as the human Blaise's pals, the Blaise angels. It is the pure Light that like holy water washes any taint clean.

Avebury, in case you've never visited it, is a 28-acre stone circle in Wiltshire, England, about 100 miles west of London. The stones are very old, tall, heavy, ponderous, wild looking, like they were quarried by a scruffy sculptor who perhaps needed glasses. Many of the original 96 stones are physically missing, though their etheric bodies remain upright in place; they encircle what looks like a vast concave diamond geode comprising 40.3 million facets. It looks as large as the biggest outdoor sports stadium, facets taking the place of seats.

This umbilical node, facilitated by the presence of this diamond geode, links the Earth with the galaxy and links humanity with its source, truth, and life purpose. The angelic Blaises were always telling the human Blaise that among their forms they are the Blazing Star, a tiny point of Light inside each human just above the navel. When you peer into this Blazing Star you see the diamond geode. Either way, it is a spiritual umbilicus. Avebury is that for the whole Earth.

Avebury, site of the planet's copy of the Ofanim's Blazing Star, is the Earth's geomantic umbilicus. It is the planetary fetal sac bearing the complete programming for Albion. It is umbilically hooked up with our two cosmic parents, Sirius and Canopus. Lines of Light come down from both these stars to this site, gold father energy from Sirius, silver mother energy from Canopus. Its umbilical function enables Avebury to be the central engineering field office for the Earth's Light grid, the repository of its geomantic genetic code for humanity. It has all the buttons and switches and levers that run the planetary Human, though probably a more apt analogy would be to say it runs all the geomantic synapses. Avebury is the geomancers' downtown, the Hierophant's pilgrimage destination, the place of maximum instruction all geomancers need to visit.

I will offer a few clarifications here. Visvakarman's design office holds the original designs for Light grids, the specifications prior to field installation. Think of these as the pure forms, the *eidolons*, of the Light grids, factory fresh. They haven't been field-tested; there is no wear on the tires, no paint scrapes on the car's enameled surface. Avebury is where the ideal form was plugged into the living actual planet and turned on, like a car's motor. To press this analogy further, Avebury is where we first started to drive the Light grid car. You can see all the components of this planetary "car" in living operation. The only thing Avebury is lacking is the Hierophancy heuristic algorithm. That was added to the system, even though it was implicit in the system's manifestation.

At the time of the first Valles Caldera episode, we went to Avebury to reground ourselves in the correct original geomantic pattern, to refamiliarize ourselves with every last minute particular of the planetary design. This time in 2065, it is for reassurance and inspiration, to stand again in that *eidolon* of the template, that perfect design for human and planet, to have it refresh my mind. And I had to immerse the retrieved blueprint from Visvakarman's files in the holy baptismal "waters" of Avebury's incorruptible Earth geomantic template.

Avebury, as the Earth's umbilicus with the cosmos, contains a perfect hologram of the entire geomantic system. You find a miniature Earth with all its geomantic systems running in real time at Avebury. The blue-white planet in just 28 acres is infiltrated like a capillary network with the force of pristine Ofanim consciousness. Here is the root seed of human awareness in all its eventual flowerings, and here is the geomantic mechanism to shepherd that great floriation of synoptic awareness. It's an image of the potency of consciousness in the geomantic infrastructure that maintains it and all the engineering blueprints.

The alien gods can't steal this, that's for sure. They can only look. But we had to make sure the geomantic blueprint was intact and uncorrupted and see if there was any miniscule loophole or system backdoor we had overlooked that the alien intelligences or whoever it was who stole the algorithm used to enter.

What is it like to stand in a stream of numbers, in a purely arithmetical atmosphere? It's like being inside the command center for organizing reality; it feels like the abstract outline for a pattern of instant connections, a system, a body perhaps, in constant motion that gives the impression of shapeshifting, a protean fluidity, or like you're inside a seemingly endless syllogism, a logical chain of linkages. On a mental level, it seems correct, appropriate, and inevitable, a pure-form rationality. It's like you are a "smart" hotel, its presiding self-aware intelligence, and you experience all the personnel systems running flawlessly, perfectly orchestrated, dovetailing, neatly complementing one another, all necessary communication being effected, all linked tasks completed smoothly.

I stood within the Avebury diamond geode of the Ofanim and felt the purity of their original, never tainted Light wash clean, like a baptism, the geomantic cloak of the original programming I'd brought from Visvakarman's place. It was like standing in the shower with my raincoat on, another crazy image. I felt, as if on the outskirts of this main perception, the way the taint had started to shift the global psyche sideways, rendering it incrementally deranged. It moved into this pattern of disregulation in slow-motion, tiny steps, but I felt it.

You felt your brain was being taken apart cell by cell, your certainty wobbling. The correct alignment established your anchorage in the core of reality, the way the Supreme Being had intended it; in fact, you felt anchored in that highest deity. In contrast, the taint felt demonic, cold, artificial, like a leering simulacrum, like you had just been kidnapped by a hostile antihuman agency. Both taints felt about the same, the disregulation of the system and the theft of its managing algorithm. I felt like I had become the angry battlefield for a definitive encounter between Ma'at and Isfet. I stood inside Ma'at, but I felt Isfet pressing upon me from all sides. I felt Avebury was the salvific antidote to this animosity.

I got the pure form immersed in the Avebury Light, though the Isfet taint hovered menacingly on all sides. I brought this geomantic correctness back to Valles Caldera and installed it. In some subtle manner I downloaded the correct sequence into the node. The node immediately adjusted itself back to operational normalcy. The algorithms were running correctly now. You could feel the rightness of reality restored. The global psyche was settling again onto its proper seat. The only problem was the event had left a scar on the Light grid pattern there, like a geomantic miasm, a taint in the genome the site coded reality for. I groaned. My success was in the past. I still had the corrupted form in the present.

The site would have to be buried, made inaccessible to any future human or alien intrusion. We would have to effectively erase all memory of its existence from the public record, even to the extent that we ourselves would cease to remember it unless we applied great efforts of recall, as Blaise had done when he encountered this place in 2010. He had requested the Lethean memory erasure.

A miasm, medically speaking, at least in terms of homeopathy, is an etheric disease taint, a tendency to develop disease within a designated category, like illnesses in the respiratory system or those pertaining to the skin or mind. It is carried forward through generations of a family, lying in wait as a seed, what we might call an etheric genetic aberration, one that could influence our genetics. The disease residue of this geomantic aberration would similarly be borne forward through this site and its intricate connections with the rest of the grid which was why we were here again at Valles Caldera investigating its possible role in our current Light grid corruption case, the theft of the master algorithm.

So we could not fully eradicate it and a trace of it remained that, given the right circumstances, could repropagate itself like a cancer rendered dormant but not extinct. That's why we sealed the place up so snugly that even we, showing up millennia later, had difficulty prying open the lid we had put there ourselves. The Earth would bear this infection possibility, this taint, into its future. Still, though the planet and the phylogeny, and we as well, would bear the miasmic taint of this early perturbation, our success in handling it would also carry through time and, I hoped, fortify, even instruct us, in dealing with the new one.

We were in that future now, many millennia later on the planet's timeline, confronted with what seemed another episode in this geomantic disturbance, the master algorithm missing and the geomantic system in operational peril, so we would have to be careful and exercise considerable circumspection in our work. Avebury's system integrity was intact, its geomantic data undefiled, which meant we still hadn't gotten to the core site of our system's infiltration and corruption, the crack in the wall they slipped through, though we were carefully retracing all the steps in the mathematical syllogism by which Earth's arithmetical Light grid was originally constructed. Now where should we look?

3

We had to go back to the Pleiades, to Blaise's home planet and the headquarters of his Pleiadian Hierophancy colleagues. It was where he had vanished to back in late 2019 and to which he had taken me a few times since. We'd have to bring our physical bodies for this trip, so we headed back to the physical Earth and took his same route of wormhole and stargate to get there. I know, I refer to this marvelous mode of transportation with an air of flippancy, but as you know, by this time, in the 2060s, use of it has become more routine, at least for members of the Hierophancy and our geomancy field-work colleagues.

All I can say is, thank God for the stargates. One day I calculated how long it would take me to walk to this star cluster 2.6 quadrillion miles away. I figured I could do 10 miles a day, or 3,650 miles a year. It would take me 712,328,767,123 years to get there on foot. I know, it's a useless calculation, but I was trying to get a bodily feel for how far away Blaise's favorite stars were. We had just traversed that awesome distance in seconds by stargate folding of space.

I'll have to set the context for this visit by explaining what the Pleiadians do. Well, not all Pleiadians; the special branch within this phylogeny that attends to planetary Light grid designs, the ones who spend their creative time making Light nests for evolving consciousness, such as they did for our Earth eons ago. They design consciousness structures for planets; they oversee their installation and then remain available for maintenance calls and routine system updates.

Blaise's Pleiadians are not a talkative bunch. Mainly, they communicate by telepathy, sharing mental pictures and projecting holograms of their thoughts out in front of them so the others in the group can study the models of Light. I could readily see the advantage of this; understanding was better and faster. Anyway, judging by the size of their craniums, you would expect something like this, some high-level mental existence in which, as if emulating Visvakarman and his mind-directed reality creation projects, they lived in their creative ideas.

We got started immediately upon our arrival. Why wait? I understood the Pleiadian grid designers had engineered safety and monitoring protocols into the Earth Light grid system; these were capable of detecting intrusions and alterations made from outside the system and which would distort the pattern. You could liken this to an immune response with geomantic white blood cells. They would detect foreign intrusions (the arithmetical equivalent of antigens) and take immediate corrective measures, dispatching the "phagocytes" to terminate the disruptive code and undo the effects of extrapolating algorithms.

It seems such encroachments had happened many times before, as if alien intelligences were constantly testing the defensive measures of our Light grid. You have to appreciate the fact aliens at this level play the long game: to them, the flow of time is leisurely and they think (and plot) in no rush, in terms of eons. They have the patience to wait until the prime moment arrives, then they take it. It seemed like the Pleiadians had foreseen every likely contingency, every nuance of infringement on the integrity of the Light grid system, yet we had before us the evidence of an apparently successful invasion and stealth removal of our Hierophancy algorithm that ran all Earth affairs. What had they overlooked?

As I mentioned, the Pleiadian grid engineers use the generic Light temple designs generated by Visvakarman as raw materials for creating planetary recipes for consciousness. I hope you will indulge me with my lame analogy, but they assemble the diverse types of Light temples in combinations calibrated to deliver specific nuances of awareness and possibilities for conscious experience. The Pleiadian engineers had this wealth of design plans laid out before them, as it were, displayed in the airspace around us as dozens of illuminated holograms.

I may have understated the complexity of what they were doing. They had displayed before them thousands (not dozens, which was my first conservative impression) of Light grid designs, as if someone had torn all the pages out of a vast encyclopedia and placed them

into the air around us. The Earth has, without exaggeration, millions of Light temples, and most of these exist in clusters of other geomantic features, hence my use of the word recipes to evoke the sense of a diversity of combinations and awareness results. Most geomantic nodes consist of a layering of temple features, like multiple skins.

If you were a Qabalist, you'd be tempted to explain this in terms of permutations. Qabalists are always exploring the nuances of the extrapolated meanings of words and numbers and what they convey when put into different combinations. The Earth grid's design is like that, a concatenation of expanding permutations, even if they were exponential which are far more complex, and the Pleiadian designers dealt with thousands of such concatenations, not just ours.

The Pleiadian designers had embedded certain trigger hypertexting codes into this system. The clusters of the Earth's Light temples were inherently linked by design; the entire geomantic system is one vast interconnected web of Light and consciousness. But the designers had installed hidden backdoor triggers, stealth entry points, and command centers enabling them to discretely access the system. They were examining these esoteric "grid doors" now for signs of intrusion or tampering or, worse, subtle rewriting and algorithmic corruption. If we were ordinary flat-foot detectives, we would say they were meticulously examining the crime scene for footprints, residual traces, and miniscule clues.

Blaise looked like he was following most of their mental examinations. I couldn't say the same for myself. I watched their adroitness with awe. They were running the equations in their mental space and the airspace around their heads was the display screen. The atmosphere tingled in arithmetic. I imagined it was like being inside a computer, in the actual binary computational space where the device ran its programs and worked the myriad equations, though I think in this case, it was a quantum holographic computer. Binary simplicity was left far behind. The Pleiadians were paging through thousands of algorithms, the complete mathematical script for Earth, the planet's engineering blueprints.

The Hierophancy heuristic algorithm is the master or meta-algorithm, running all the others, but these others constitute a large group of complex equations. I felt I was witnessing the display of the complete mental schematics for the planet, our Arithmetical Earth, displayed here in its foundational mathematical sense. Here was the reality of the Earth, the idea of the planet, its coding, expressed as a mind projection before anything physical had been created, including humanity, though both aspects of this linked system were accounted for in the equations. People think of DNA as the bedrock design expression of the human phylogeny, but this was antecedent. This was the mathematical coding that, further along the numbers syllogism, would generate the human genetic and planetary geomantic scripts. This far preceded DNA.

As I marveled at this revelation, I noted the Pleiadians ran through their code checking dispassionately. They had done this countless times. They had roamed the galaxy as itinerant geomantic "tinkers," master engineers who fixed the pots and pans of reality—their name itself from the Greek means the "wandering ones"—creating and maintaining nests of

Light for evolving consciousness in a variety of life-forms. It wasn't that they didn't care; they cared, but it was a professional caring, the way a plumber installs your hot-water heater with attention to details, but he doesn't get emotional about it. He doesn't jump up and down with delight over your new heater or pull his hair out in despair over the old one's awful brokenness; he installs it in an attitude of professional neutrality and clinical detachment.

When it comes to numbers and the algorithmic aspects of the Arithmetical Earth, I am decidedly an outsider, mostly foreign to this abstract world. Or so I thought at the time; later events would show me a different picture. Still, from my years with Blaise and his occasional mentoring in the arcane area of the mathematics of the planet's Light grid, I gleaned a few facts, and I think I understood them. One of these was the enigma and extent of prime numbers. I briefly alluded to this earlier as a special project Sal was working on for us.

Pertaining to the quantities of copied Light temples or any of the quantity specifications for features in the grid pattern, very few are prime numbers. These primes appear in the quantity list: 3, 5, 7, 13, 23, 47, and 613; all the other quantity numbers for the 613 Light temple features are natural or composite numbers.

I always wondered what that meant, this scarcity of prime numbers in the geomantic quantity list. Mathematicians regard primes as special, curious, even mysterious. They try to figure out their distribution patterns. It turns out there is another number grid behind the primary Light grid and arithmetical display: it is a prime numbers grid and, by analogy, it's like an auric field for the main one which is dominated by ordinary, everyday, rank-and-file composite numbers.

Nobody knows how many primes exist. Some mathematicians say it's at least 50 million and through computers they have worked out the integers for these, the largest a few decades ago, the last time I checked, consisting of 23,249,425 digits. It's like getting an eye-opening glimpse of the vast extent of the higher worlds. In case you're unclear about primes, it is a number that can only be divided by itself and 1 without producing a fraction; or, put differently, it is a natural number greater than 1 that cannot be formed by multiplying two smaller natural numbers. You can see how these criteria eliminate many numbers.

Blaise said you could liken these few prime numbers in the main grid to genetic markers. In biology, a genetic marker is a gene or DNA sequence at a known location on a chromosome; it stands out like a neon billboard on a highway. DNA researchers call these markers descriptive variations, possibly due to mutations or creative variations in the normal gene sequencing; they serve as observation nodes. In the geomantic coding, these markers are more like doorways or perhaps grace notes or even bolt-holes that allow passage upwards.

You're not trying to escape so much as effect an exit upwards through an arcane passageway coded into the system. The Pleiadians were now studying these prime number bolt-holes for any signs of deliberate arithmetical mutation. These could serve as potential stealth access sites for intruding alien minds. That prospect is dizzying, and standing there as the Pleiadians explored the prime number bolt-holes in the Earth grid pattern, I had a mental glimpse (or maybe it was a vivid imagination) of an infinitely expanding roster of prime numbers, of how the Earth was threaded into this unending series which soared like a kite.

I tried to imagine what the consciousness conditions would be in that higher octave prime numbers grid. To be surrounded by a teeming crowd of only primes. Surely that would put one closer to the Mind of God. Each prime like a mysterious stranger portending revelations. Mathematicians call the complete number set of primes P; that would be the ultimate Light grid expressed arithmetically. I wondered how close to that end point to an infinite progression the Pleiadian grid designers had reached in their modeling and exploration. If the Supreme Being and His Mind were infinite, the extent of P must be infinite.

Prime numbers are the building blocks of all natural numbers, which in geomantic terms must mean the primes are the grid's parents, possibly akin to stem cells. I felt a shiver of excitement as I began to wonder what it might be like to have a body and live on a planet of primes, maybe known as Planet P. Yes, I know, not a planet or even a body exactly, at least not as I think of them, but a landscape, a domain whose infrastructure was comprised of prime numbers.

Then a notion flashed in me from somewhere in my karmic background where I must have once enjoyed a deeper immersion in mathematics. The optimal place of alien insertion would be in the calculation process where a prime number generated or "birthed" a natural number or where a natural number was analyzed to reveal hidden primes. Mathematicians call this the factorization into primes and they employ prime factorization algorithms to produce these results. The number grid integrity seems to be vulnerable in this transition phase because one arithmetical expression is morphing into another and neither is yet fixed and steady. In this tentative in-between moment lies danger. I felt the Pleiadian engineers telepathed me their agreement. This would be a perfect manipulation point for the intruders to gain traction.

I suddenly felt lucid, like I knew my way around prime number grids. The Pleiadians must have given me a mental boost, or maybe I was now walking around in their shared mental atmosphere as a guest visitor sampling the number arrays. Algorithms might be employed to work with or identify primes, but prime numbers in themselves were beyond that operational level.

I compared them earlier to genetic markers. Maybe they are more like mileposts, large-scale phylogenetic precursors or summary forms or perhaps germplasm, like the rarified realm of archangels compared to the copious realm of angels. Within each algorithmic display I saw the prime numbers highlighted in gold. I watched the algorithm run its operations, the primes in it highlighted. It was like seeing Pleiadians highlighted in gold as they mingled within crowds of ordinary humans. You'd see these gold figures at odd intervals amidst them.

I had the notion to position myself in that vulnerable in-between zone where prime numbers generated natural numbers and those disassembled themselves to reveal prime numbers. It felt like standing under a waterfall. It was full of dynamic energy, a sense of churning, turning inside out, shapeshifting. It felt like I was mid-stride, executing a broad, bold step, my leg still raised. I felt I was mid-way between one step and the next in an arithmetical syllogism. I

felt I was involuntarily holding my breath at the top of the inhale: everything paused.

I have to keep resorting to analogies here to convey my impressions of this nonmaterial, abstract realm of higher numbers. If this were a platform, it seemed slightly, perhaps only minutely, tilted, or its flooring was perhaps a little warped. It felt like for only a fraction of a second the whole edifice shook slightly, the way a platform might shudder and wobble momentarily when a weight settles on it. I assumed this was my perceptual way of registering the number transformations.

I couldn't tell you why or in what manner but I suspected my presence was crucial to that shift from natural to prime numbers within the ongoing algorithm. For some reason, Blaise stood to the side, seemingly aloof, and let me do the work of standing in the numerical "waterfall" of this live algorithm, anchoring it. It seemed I was standing at the nexus of a world of connections, that this algorithm connected us, consciousness itself, to a vast web of linkages that exceeded the scope or necessities of our Earth and included much more. I appreciated the fact (it startled me, actually) that if an aberration were introduced here, it could ramify throughout the extended web of connections.

I saw Sal and Jocelyn as if they were standing within this Light web. I don't know why I suddenly saw them. They both dealt with topologies, Sal with algorithmic topologies and Jocelyn with thematic ones, charting number and picture landscapes. These two realms were inter-related, even reciprocal, and both are keyed into the Earth's Light grid. Blaise always says you can describe the grid either with numbers or mythic images. These colleagues had mapped both domains in great detail and knew where all the doors were to enter it. The landscape maps of both realms, the numbers and myths, were operational keys; both showed you how to interact with the system, through running algorithms or by entering the mythic images and enacting the protocols they represented.

Blaise's Pleiadian pals put these building blocks together into nests of Light. The result is an Earth Light body that exhibits both numbers and myths. But what concerned me was why did I suddenly see my two Hierophancy colleagues at the moment I plugged myself into this system here to restart it? Were they in some way connected with the theft of the Hierophancy algorithm? It seemed impossible, utterly unlikely, yet why was I seeing them just now? If they had not done anything overtly, had they somehow been covertly accessed? But then I could pose the same question to myself: How come I was in this zone?

As if I were back in the Sun Valley office, I saw both of them running their programs. Sal was scouring all the algorithms that comprised the Hierophancy meta-algorithm, looking for number deviations, however slight, that would indicate an intrusion node. Jocelyn was reviewing all the consciousness protocols she'd extracted from the mythic tableaus from world cultures to see if any dealt with a theft on the scale we were witnessing or suggested ways of dealing with unlawful entries and appropriations. Once you took the myths seriously but realized they were descriptive on a psychic and geomantic level, they suddenly became exceedingly practical, and you saw they are guides to using the nodes.

It may seem like a stretch, but you could see the algorithms as abstract versions of the mythic characters interacting with one another at their godly palaces, as a kind of austere, stripped-down action script that coded the grid's mythic actions. The algorithms are abstract, arithmetical choreographies of the processes of consciousness the myths portray and their characters enact, and the Earth's Light grid, its geomantic terrain, is the stage for this live performance.

I didn't like what I saw next. I felt I was getting paranoid, too suspicious. I saw Sal alter a couple digits about 20 places to the right of the decimal point in a key second-tier algorithm. Even so slight an adjustment could skew everything. I saw Jocelyn delete two locations from the geomantic roster of key Light temple arrays, so that instead of tabulating the complete list of 144 locations of the same "photocopied" Light temple, her list now only tallied 142; this threw off the geometric distribution pattern the location of the copies implicitly revealed.

It would be equivalent to badly stacking heavy crates in a moving van. The uneven weight distribution could cause the truck to lean to one side or even topple over. But had my friends done what I just saw? I couldn't believe they'd betray us. But what if they had done this under duress, the equivalent of a gun to their heads?

Blaise tapped me on the shoulder. He had seen I had grown distracted. But another thought grabbed me. Something niggled me. How well did I know Sal and Jocelyn? We had vetted them thoroughly of course before hiring them and nothing suspect had shown up. Still, you can find ways to hide anything. There is a transition clamp that joins their reciprocal topologies. Transition clamp is my nontechnical term for something I'm sure mathematicians have a name. But it's the place where the terrains of numbers and myths join up. That could be an insertion point for our thief. It is a vulnerable in-between zone where somebody clever and exceedingly devious could acquire our heuristic algorithm.

That was my next point of investigation. I stood in that transition clamp. This is a place where Sal and Jocelyn often stood; in fact, they worked here in this zone of connection and transition, securing the smooth linkage of equations and psychic pictures to the functioning Light grid model of the Earth. It was an elegant complementarity and a necessary reciprocity that kept the planet healthy.

For me, it was a cognitively odd experience, at least at first as I entered this zone. I saw algorithms and quadratic equations running about with numbers forming skeletal systems for faintly outlined figures, and I saw richly delineated deities and human heroes flushing transparent, revealing they were comprised of numbers. Their actions were choreographed by arithmetical necessities, and the cool, abstract conclusions of long calculations were fleshed out by opulent gods.

People tend to underestimate the potency of mythic images. They are not irrelevant, outmoded artifacts from a fanciful childhood of humanity. They are vivid protocol choreographies showing us precisely how to interact with Light temples. They are psychic photographs of earlier, archetypal interactions; they are like highlighted dance steps and body postures, *avatars* or virtual reality bodies for our consciousness to move into and effect maintenance or upgrades.

The numbers aspect specifically spells out the design details and frequencies. You could say they delineate the time and spatial aspects of these movements. In both cases they are modelled gestures of great potency and dependable guides. They are metronome and digital timer combined. Through them we can emulate the mind-generated aspects of Brahma. We step into his creative mind and walk around in the living reality mock-ups he made.

So we are well advised to treat these numbers and myths with respect. They are capable of modulating reality and thereby our consciousness, and this means, alarmingly, in the wrong hands, or in good hands gone wrong, gone dark, they can be used against our best interests and subtle changes can be introduced without our knowing it until reality, like a great ocean liner, has shifted course by a few degrees, but by just enough to send us off elsewhere.

My concern, my rising, uncomfortable paranoia, was that Sal and Jocelyn might have done this. Certainly where they worked would enable them to, but would they? If you alter anything in the transition clamp you could then hijack the algorithm, and we knew somebody had taken the algorithm—well, not exactly: taken our algorithm's traction on the Light grid and the potency of its interaction, extracted its real-time and real-body presence within the Light grid, disembodied it, taken away our ability to use it—which was why we were here.

I felt like I was in the middle of a shapeshifting zone, intensely busy with transiting back and forth between the two forms of expression, sorting the forms. The numbers were like a ticking metronome, or thousands of them, or like conductors tapping their music stands with their thin batons, and the mythic figures were the dancers and balletists, pirouetting, leaping across the stage. I started to extend my arm and flex my fingers in anticipation of touching—what?

Then I laughed and realized hands have no utility here. This is a mind space. I was in the mind-generated reality of Brahma; it was my mind that was reaching. Here was the actual fabric of mental creation, the first fleshing out of thoughts because Brahma had extruded these two realms as intertwining strands of Light and the Pleiadian arithmeticians were the choreographers of this ballet. Brahma was the universal bard intoning the universe, generating it in syllables, the Pleiadians directing the dance troupe in their leaps and twirls, and I was poised to insert a syllable of my own—or had Sal or Jocelyn already done that?

One form looked shredded, like somebody had slowly ripped it apart. Threads were dangling, though you could easily miss this as they were very thin. I reached out to touch it. I touched it. It felt subtly electric, gave my fingers a tingle, or I suppose to be more accurate, it gave my mind a little zing of attention. It was odd but it seemed the numbers comprising its form drooped as if wilted.

Even though this dance fugue of numbers and personages is meant for human edification, to touch them, or touch them ineptly, is to alter their progression, a bit like when a surgeon disturbs your intestines and it takes days for them to reset. The difference is excruciatingly precise: you are to stand within these adumbrations of number and picture as if in a shower, participate in their revelation, receive their nutrient download as guides for consciousness, but you are not supposed to actually touch them, slightly adjust their angle or location.

That throws them off balance, disturbs their numbers, ruffles their myth images. I know this must sound exceedingly strange and unbearably precious, *diva*-like—how can numbers be so excessively twitchy and hypersensitive? They require human contact, but through consciousness and not the body, to anchor them into human and planetary reality, but there they can still be thrown off.

Blaise gestured for me to withdraw from this interaction zone, though he studied me with a concentration that was slightly unnerving. He was always like that so I suppose it was nothing special. Then he grinned and said, "Like the shower? Your skin is coated in numbers and pictures: the arithmetical man."

Blaise's Pleiadian colleagues stood behind him, attentive but silent and very tall, like sleek barkless trees, and with big craniums bulging with brains and chakras supporting higher awareness. I wondered why they didn't just resolve the case for us, identify the thief, and retrieve our algorithm. Surely that was in their range of competency, yet they held back, facilitating our investigation but not particularly moving it along. If they knew the identity of the culprit, they weren't saying. There was meaning in this cool aloofness, there had to be; these guys did nothing without clear purpose, but at the time I couldn't fathom it.

I finished the check but felt I had to shrug my shoulders. I didn't notice anything suggestive of an actual intrusion. The prime numbers factorization nodes seemed intact, untampered with. The transition clamps between numbers and images were intact and unviolated. That shredded form I saw must have been a mental hiccup and thus unreal. I saw where it might have been done, but I found no evidence it had been. The prime numbers coding zone was a clue, but I didn't know where to take it now. It just remained suggestive, but inconclusive. As far as I could tell, the algorithm thieves had not penetrated this system level.

Blaise was noncommittal, the Pleiadians steadfastly treelike and cryptic. Our checkpoints were coming up empty; we were clueless. On the other hand, though our algorithm was based on sophisticated mathematics knowledge, theoretically it was possible and easily conceivable that intelligences more advanced than us could find subtle intrusion points beyond our ken. I was up against the limitations of my knowledge of mathematics. They could enter the system and I would not see it, not even know to look there. They could have snuck in and pinched our algorithm through number doors I never suspected, but then wouldn't Blaise or the Pleiadians have detected these egresses?

I have to say it is mentally stimulating to the point of being almost overwhelming to spend time with these Pleiadian designers. Their heads are filled with Light grid designs and they access these as easily as a fast computer opening up requested files. You could easily find yourself believing their mental space, the true site of their minds, is around them, that they use the airspace around their forms, perhaps extending out for dozens of feet, for plan storage. No, not just for storage: it's as if their auric space is a wrap-around display screen onto which they project their designs, geometries, or engineering details.

This is different than being around merely very smart people, humans with high I.Q.s who spend their time working tough mental problems. The minds of these Pleiadians are suffused—leavened, levitating—with spiritual Light creating a condition better called Higher Mind as it takes in actual conditions of reality. There is nothing theoretical or speculative about their Light grid modeling. The components they work with and use to build their Light nests are arrestingly real, and "real" in this sense means comprised of Light and the ideal image behind it. To the layman's mind (me, in other words), these guys are master magicians. They spell out new realities from their mental space.

I tried to imagine what it would be like to perpetually live in this world of perfect forms, to have your awareness saturated in this recondite design field, to have a mind so sharp, so creative, so immediately responsive to intent as to instantly generate changed reality conditions and new designs for the Light. This was not a case of being mentally abstracted from life, of just living in one's head, aloof from the concerns of real living, as people would put it. No, not at all: this is where life itself comes from; here is the mental infrastructure of reality itself.

This is the vital framework in which embodied awareness, including our habitual human-style awareness, has its home. It is the well-built home itself, and these Pleiadians dwelled in its core design level, and they had, it seemed as I looked around them, hundreds of such home designs stored in their mental field archives, as if the space around them was populated with architectural renderings with their math specifications ribboning the plans.

Here's the part that caught my attention, like a slap in the face. Usually, we walk around the world, oblivious to its subtle or maybe it's better put to say its secret infrastructure. We take our reality, the appearance of the world, the condition of our consciousness, the fact we are and have it, for granted. These Pleiadian reality engineers live and work in that secret, veiled infrastructure. They don't take it for granted; they create it in the first place. They are many steps closer to the source of reality itself than we customarily are. They perpetually reside within the etheric, formative framework for multiple realities.

I briefly experienced that closeness. I found it bracing, revelatory, alluring. If I lived in that mental space, surely I would see at once who stole our algorithm. I felt like a detective who finally stumbles upon a witness, who senses they might have the answer to the vexing mystery, but then realizing this witness is unavailable or will not testify for us or is speechless or constrained. They know but cannot say. Something troubled me, though. I had the strong impression the Pleiadians could tell us who stole the algorithm, that they knew, saw it clearly, had from the start. But they chose not to let me in on this. And that they could fix the problem its removal caused, but they chose not to at present. Why? I didn't understand. I thought that would come under the heading of helpful colleagues.

Despite the epiphany of the Pleiadian higher mental life, I knew we were nowhere in our investigation. Somebody had stolen the algorithm and we didn't know who or how and we had so far been chasing down clues that dead-ended. I suppose I could say we were eliminating suspects, ruling out possibilities. Still, it seemed a logical proposition that whoever it was must have been involved originally in the design or implementation of the planet's Light grid; it

would have to be someone, some agency, that was well-briefed on its details. It would have to be one or a group extremely competent in the grid's higher mathematics.

Otherwise, they wouldn't know where to look. They wouldn't even know what to look for, and possibly, on a technical level, they would not understand it. They would have to be able to operate at this Pleiadian level, which is why we thought our Pleiadian colleagues might know their identity. We archived a short and recondite list of people with this competency in the Hierophancy files and we have excluded most of them already so who is left? On the other hand, Blaise maintains a private mental list, or perhaps the complete one, longer and more detailed than our office's official one and possibly containing names of players too hermitic, too much in the deep background, for the rest of us to be aware of.

I had a thought and turned to Blaise to offer it to him. "We need to remember everyone who was there, you know, back in the Earth's Blue Room, when we were first setting things up, assigning tasks and implementing plans. Review every participant, see if we have overlooked someone, somebody silent. Possibly someone has gone rogue and is operating against us from the shadows."

Blaise nodded. He probably already had the thought and was tactfully waiting for me to catch up. Still, it was a valid approach. Everyone there, briefed on the complete picture, would have had comparable competency levels. It was a crew of great technical ability and knowledge. Fortunately, we didn't have to travel to the Blue Room, go all the way to northern Siberia up near the Laptev Sea. The answer wasn't there in the present. The answer was back there, millions of years ago, when we first assembled in that planetary outpost of the galactic Blue Room, Visvakarman's central design office, to set up the Earth's Light grid.

Someone may have shown early signs of defection back then. We could examine everything with that in mind. We didn't have to relocate our consciousness, or astral body, or whatever the body mechanism was, to the Blue Room in space; we would access it within us on our own timeline. We would remember it together and walk around in it wide-awake in our joint memories.

The Pleiadians helped us with that. They raised up a platform under us, and this platform had the ability to project pillars of Light around us. The remarkable part was what these thin translucent blazing pillars did for us. Somehow they facilitated, even sharpened, our ability to access the far past. They converted our memories into a living projected interactive holographic display. It enabled us to participate in what you might call a shared lucid dream space. We could watch our projected memories like a movie, and we could walk around in them as well, study events and people from different angles and perspectives.

The Blue Room's period of heightened field relevance lasted 2.7 million years and began approximately 4.5 billion years ago when the planet's surface was viable (which is to say, its surface sufficiently dried and hardened) to begin the second round of geomantic installation. It took about 2.7 million years to implement all the Light grid features. The first deposition of features, such as the dome network and 15 Oroboros Lines that circled the planet, had been implicit with the creation of the Earth itself, forming the etheric shell out of which the physical globe had been extruded, like pouring wet clay into a pre-shaped mold.

Blue Room staff came and went regularly from the Siberian office, commuting, I assume, from all sorts of other locales and projects. You simply can't rush an installation like this one. The etheric blueprint and the physical manifestation of the Earth had to slowly be put into harmonious resonance and reciprocity with each other, a slow process. All the parts had to work together, and we had to continually monitor their interaction as we activated the grid.

Siberia then was not cold, frozen, and barren as it is now. The whole planet in fact was temperate; the seasons hadn't started because the mountains hadn't risen up yet to perturb the equanimity of the moderate global climate. The planet had not been tilted off its intended axis. The Light grid was perfectly aligned with the material world. The Light grid turned on the number 360 and its derivatives. The landscape was flat, the whole planet was like Kansas in terrain.

It was a flat surface topography, except for the domes, the planet's original mountains of Light rising blisterlike up 16.5 miles high. They were not physical landmasses, but half-spheres of translucent Light conveying star presences to the Earth and eventually to human consciousness, when humans started arriving. They were Earth's primordial mountains, and they rose up at once, coming to it from afar. Earth's mountains of Light arrived on the planet from what in the vernacular we would call outer space, suddenly blinking brightly upon the planetary surface—imagine: all 1,746 domes here all at once.

As I remember it, one reason the Blue Room was installed here was its proximity to the planet's magnetic North Pole, but I can't yet remember the other reasons. I do remember what it felt like back then on the pristine Earth. It was so pure in fact, karmically chaste, brand new and unused, the geomantic "glue" hadn't dried yet. Some Native American myths allude to the Earth's primordial "green earth" condition when the surface was mudlike. That didn't affect the Blue Room installation because, as I said, it wasn't physical. The Light grid wasn't a physical "device." You didn't need to set it into the muddy ground.

The best way to put it is to say it fluctuated in-between Light and matter. It was primarily an etheric manifestation. But that isn't the main point I'm remembering. What I remember is how quiet the planet was, how still it felt, devoid of noisy life, devoid of all life. That hadn't started yet. On a psychic level the planet was marvelously, deliciously serene, unperturbed by any incarnation-based human thoughts now amplified by billions of alive minds.

The Earth has never been as quiet since those primordial days when we were the only ones on the planet and as we were not in physical bodies but in advanced Light bodies, for the most part we didn't make any sounds either, vocal or even mental. As anyone incarnate knows well, it's the physical body and corresponding self that is incessantly opinionated, providing a continuous commentary on life events.

I could compare the sensation to being a member of a crew in the pre-dawn setting up facilities for an outdoor wedding or concert or huge picnic. It is wonderfully quiet; the audience, the wedding party, the picnickers, are not here. That's what we were doing, though it took 2.7 million years: setting up the gear for a huge outdoor party known as human incarnation on a replacement planet.

Maldek was fucked and we were scrambling to outfit this substitute world for our Maldekian clients. They had lost their planet; their grid engineers had blown it up by mistake, and these displaced, disembodied souls needed a new planetary context, and quickly. Earth was designated as their new planet. Despite the seeming extreme length of our set-up time, we were rushing to meet the deadline set by Visvakarman.

Think of the 2.7 million years as the time required for the cement to harden, all the paint to dry, the Light temples to adhere to the etheric realm of the Earth and make viable connections with the physical world (it was like sound-testing amplifiers at an outdoor concert to make sure they worked properly). We needed that time to field-test all the equipment, namely, the global inventory of Light temples and their processes.

The mechanics of Light temple projection are interesting, I think you'll find. First we projected the mathematical topology of the intended architecture. I am referring to the arithmetical coding, the algorithms that specified the type of consciousness process the architectural shape of the Light temple would produce. That topology was a shape in itself, as the integers directed the ethers. So first the planet was beribboned in these hosts of algorithmic projections. It was an Arithmetical Earth, with the mathematical aspect its first manifestation. This was Sal's specialty: algorithmic topologies, contoured in mathematics.

The algorithms spelled out the details of the Light temples they would oversee, and the Light temples organized the processes in consciousness they would deliver to the planet and the incarnating humans when they started to arrive. I imagine we felt somewhat like geomantic magicians computing Earth realities in accordance with our master blueprint from our design warren up here in the far North. The Light temples would eventually establish a system of congruent correlations with observable physical and landscape aspects, creating a geomantic topography. But there was yet another layer to this complex system.

Take a landscape template with numerous different types of Light temples. Blaise calls this a Landscape of Light; you could compare it to a star cluster in the galaxy. It is a bright zone in the planetary landscape. It may consist of a dozen or several dozen Light temples arrayed in a specific pattern, with some temples dovetailing their neighbors, others laid in like delicate skins giving the geomantic array a palimpsest quality. This pattern has a design.

You could call it a landscape mandala or, more abstractly, an ideogram, from the Greek "idea-writing." In practical terms, it is a graphic symbol that conveys information. The information in this landscape temple array pertains to an aspect of the structure of human and universal consciousness. The ideogram of a Landscape of Light conveys information about all the structures of consciousness and their inter-relationships, what they reveal about the universal design of Light, and how they convey this illumination to Light temple users. The level below this is the geometry of the Light temple array pattern; the one above it is the pure process in consciousness this ideogram

delivers to its users, and above that one is the arithmetical coding and the algorithmic management.

The domes (about 85,554 when you count the major and minor ones) would mark the spots of higher consciousness gradients and convey a rich star presence to the Earth and its biosphere as it started to develop. These were our first mountains and on a technical performance level, nothing else was required. The arising of actual physical mountains, the momentous orogeny, was from our design point of view irrelevant, unnecessary, and a grid interference factor. When the mountains finally arrived, it was as a symptom of a grievous geomantic subluxation, the planetary disaster resulting in the tilting of its axis.

That sounds strange today of course, so accustomed are we to mountains. But originally they were not part of Earth's landscape; only the Light temples were. The domes served as mountains, uniform in size, and in fact massive at 16.5 miles tall and 33 miles across, with 1,746 of these huge canopies of Light in total. Picture it: these mountains of Light each stood 87,000 feet tall. The Earth's tallest mountain today is Mount Everest which stands a mere 29,035 feet high.

Add to this the second-tier smaller canopies we call dome caps, these numbering 83,808. Some of them stood 4.5 miles high, or almost 24,000 feet tall. The effect was to create what looked like from above a blistered landscape, these many blisters of Light each filled with the hologram of a star. The planet would have been utterly silent if it wasn't for the pervasive humming of these domes; everywhere you went you'd hear this sound of swarming bees. I think it was the contact of these extra-physical, higher dimensional domes with the elemental material reality that created the impression of a constant hum, perhaps vaguely like the cruder sound once heard near high-tension electrical towers. Maybe I'm shortchanging the sonic beauty of this: 85,554 star-*divas* singing to the Earth.

Blaise and I ran through all the Light temple projection scenarios. That was 613 different features, so it took us some time, though I couldn't say how long that was. We studied each projection for any flaws or deviations, any blemishes or minute insertion points we might have overlooked the first time we did this and that could have provided our "thieves" a devious entry point. I laughed. It was like a magician going through a spell book to check whether the summoning methods were still viable, had not been tampered with or edited. We didn't find any design deficits; the Light forms manifested correctly per design.

The Blue Room was holographically projected all around us like a film. I should mention it was far larger than a room. Our name for it is idiosyncratic. It would be better called Visvakarman's geomantic field office or whatever formal name is attached to his headquarters. In scale, the Blue Room was more like an alien university modeled in 4D, but Blaise had originally called it a room with a predominant sky blue color to its crystalline walls, so the name stuck. He told me when the angelic Blaises first took him there all he saw was one large room and its walls were crystalline sky blue, so in simplicity it became the Blue Room.

It was, as far as I can tell, never physically manifest in the way we think of that. You couldn't walk up to a wall, tap it, and expect to hear a sound like you would if you tapped something

physical. Still, the overall "university" complex looked physical, structured, and architecturally well conceived. The Blue Room was made of something subtle, ethereal, in between manifest matter and Light, just like the domes, like a midpoint between a hologram and physical substance.

I always thought the place looked like an alien spaceship that had landed and sunk itself about a third into the landscape. Its 4D shape is hard to see or describe. Let me suggest a four-leaf clover presented in 4D or with a dozen overlays, each slightly phase-shifted from the next. Well, I said it was hard to see.

As an Earth field office of Visvakarman's master design office, it has divisions that deal with all aspects of the Earth's Light and its operation. I would be shamelessly 3D materialistic to describe it this way, but I must: there were mapping rooms where holographic displays modeled the Light grid design in progress; libraries; meeting rooms; geometric modeling chambers where we could experiment with combining the Platonic and Archimedean Solids; walk-through holographic projections of selected aspects of the Light grid, that is, selected by us, the designers, such as individual Light temple grids, for the domes, for example. We could pull up and zoom in on any level of its detail.

Again, I am sure things were not this solidified and objectified, but let's say there was some form of individual computerized workstations, file cabinets containing an archives of all the planetary designs we and our antecedent colleagues had done, and, the most valuable part, the specifications for the Earth's Light grid. Everything, how many domes, dome lines, Grail Castles, and where they went. As for "staff," my impression is that the original Blue Room had hundreds of staff members, drawn from a number of planets and occupying Light bodies for the purposes of illustrating their presence in spacetime, in other words, so we could see one another, though most communication was telepathic. This, principally, was what we had come back here in memory to survey. Were any of our former Blue Room colleagues suspects in the theft of the algorithm?

There were a lot of Pleiadians about too, for they were the principal grid designers. They appeared in their characteristic form with large craniums, hairless, tall, broad bodies, and a searing sharpness to their gaze, suggesting an intense mental life. They moved about the place in auric fields of arithmetic.

As "people" we were never physically manifest either. Human bodies had not been perfected yet; they might still be in the developmental stage. We were there in our Light bodies, and some of the Blue Room staff never had bodies in the first place. I refer to the archangels Michael, Gabriel, and Uriel. They were among the august members of our wide-ranging talent consortium. As for what kind of Light bodies we had, I presume they were crafted from our home planets and copied the dominant life-form we occupied while living there. Should I see myself as I appeared back then, I would probably be startled at the strangeness of form I was occupying; the same with all my colleagues from then. It is quite likely I would not at first even recognize myself or any of my friends.

How many members were present in our Blue Room consortium? At least hundreds based on what I was seeing. Here's the strange part. None looked precisely the way humans do today; that's because Earth humans hadn't been manifested yet and all of us were there in our antecedent or current Light forms. It is probably more accurate to say we looked like thoughtforms of bodies. Etheric space vibrated as we moved through it, but our forms were indistinct.

Some of our colleagues, as I said, looked like Pleiadians, tall, thin, willowy, with huge heads and sleek forms. Others, the Sirians, for example, were also tall and slim, but they had cone-shaped heads, like you suspect must have been under those tall headpieces the Egyptian gods like Nefertiti and Akhenaten wore. They were Sirians. They had cone heads. All the Sirian heads are elongated cones. Also present were representatives from the angelic orders Ofanim, Elohim, and Serafim, a potent celestial trinity still usefully influencing humans.

There were representatives from other star systems, including Ursa Major, Cepheus, Arcturus, Orion, Cygnus, and Canopus. There were eight star systems with central involvement in this project. I couldn't tell you what any of these intelligences originally looked like. It might be fascinating, but ultimately, both for this report and for our group technical work there, it is not important. I suspect our psychic apparatus contrived a general, plausible form for them and left it at that. We mostly interacted telepathically and with shared psychic images so specificity in body image was not necessary for that type of communication.

So as I remember it, these various spirits took on plausible quasi-human Light forms for the purposes of visibility, or maybe I just construe them that way now out of convenience or for reassurance against the feral otherness of it all from my now entrenched human perspective. Most of our work was psychic and holographic and bodies and talking were not a big part of that. We traded thoughts, just as we shared blueprints. It was an instantaneously shared reality, like we stood before the Pleiadian wrap-around display screens seeing the same information. The Blue Room team walked about with design patterns and their corresponding numbers displayed around them like auras fluttering in banners.

You didn't have to ask your colleagues what was their special area of responsibility. You could see it whenever you wished, flashing around them like a neon billboard. Nor did you have to look over their shoulders to examine their architectural renderings spread out on some worktable; these renderings vividly enveloped them. I don't remember any worktables, chairs, drawings, slide rules, pencils, computers, calculators, draftsmen's tools, though as I said above, I am tempted to impose this materialistic image over it. The work was done in mental space. Probably there were no office tools, papers, or furniture at all, just minds.

With the full roster of Blue Room colleagues now displayed before us as a seemingly living presence, Blaise and I studied each for possible deviance. Had we overlooked something back then, some little clue that might now be glaring? Some little seed of deviance that over time sprouted and grew into betrayal?

I know we both felt uncomfortable with even the suggestion of indicting our fellow workers from that pristine time, but we had to rule them out as suspects and to do that we had to first consider they might each be a culpable party. First indict, then acquit, as

uncomfortable as it might feel. We reviewed each colleague, observed their area of work, even assessed the unique direction of their thoughts and mental images which wreathed their heads. We came up empty-handed with them all. I looked at Blaise and shook my head. He agreed.

I have the impression many of us did not have the complete blueprint for the Earth, only segments relevant to our supervisory assignments. Maybe that was good, because the Earth Light grid design is appallingly, beautifully complicated, so it might have been mentally overwhelming to possess the complete schematics. Don't think in terms of us holding printed-out patterns.

These blueprints, the geomantic schematics we were tasked with, were mentally implanted by thought transference. I think that's how the angelic Blaises put it. You arrived here at the Earth's Blue Room and discovered your mind was already briefed with the plans, at least those relevant to your assignment; then we had to adjust the general plans to the specific field (i.e., planetary) conditions. I like to think the Blaise angels, certainly the archangels, had the complete plans, knew what the complete "building" would look like.

Who else was present? Visvakarman, of course, and a retinue of his key assistants. He was an architect with a lot on his plate, so he would flicker in and out of manifestation with us as we needed his overview and suggestions. He was running many simultaneous planetary design projects throughout the universe. I shiver even as I put this so jocularly: his scope of responsibility is awesome and the number of construction plans he must hold in his head is staggering, and he could dispatch a thoughtform semblance of himself to multiple locations at once.

Several Ray Masters were present, including the one I earlier called Hermes-Thoth, Lord of the Green Robe. A number of Ascended Masters accompanied him. Sanat Kumara, the six-bodied Cosmic Logos, periodically was with us; he seemed to flash in and out of our awareness as he was keeping an eye on developments because several billion years down the planet's timeline when the Light grid began its momentous transformation to a more complex shape (starting in 1986 and already underway now for about 80 years) his supervision would be crucial to shepherd the Earth into its next geomantic life-phase.

I have to keep reminding myself that I am now, as an embodied human with a long résumé of past lives receding behind me or perhaps I should say crowding up upon me insisting on the perquisites and continuously reinforced habits of human-style incarnation, approaching the Blue Room reality from a human 3D perspective. But when we were there we had come to it from higher dimensions of experience and intelligence with a radically different set of assumptions and life experiences, all of which was, at least, in 4D as a start point. We hadn't come from the Earth; it barely existed; it was virginal ground. So if I expected to have any success in retrieving long-ago memories of the Blue Room, I would have to reverse my perspective and start out fresh and be there in 4D.

It's hard to convey how weird this experience was. Here I was, the 89-year-old human-bred and habituated Frederick occupying a pre-Frederick Light body from billions of years ago that was also and even more legitimately myself, or, more properly, my soul-self, and standing in an environment I had never beheld as this human-acculturated Frederick, except a few times in aloof vision. That means, with Blaise, I saw some aspects of it like looking through a window.

Now I was there as "I" had been originally long ago, with a radically different headspace, background, expertise, and framework of expectations and plans. That pre-Frederick had no Earth timeline yet or karmic record, but "he" had a huge history and backstory that led up to this pivotal moment. The actual Frederick could look back over his (my) accrued karmic timeline to that virginal moment. What comes next? Share an espresso? I got past that wonderment (or whimsy) because it wasn't helping me remember anything. I'd file it under thrilling moments of existential disconnection and maybe review it later.

I knew we had just come from several other projects much further along. The Hierophancy undertook multiple overlapping projects. You could only do a finite amount of installation and adjustment at one time; you had to let the system settle and ripen, to use a couple inexact analogies. During that 2.7-million-year stretch in setting up the bulk of the Earth's Light grid, we came and departed frequently; it was like being a commuter, except we didn't have to board a train or a spaceship. We relocated our consciousness and congealed a plausible, walking-around body then dissolved it when we left. We snapped back to our origin.

It was as if we welled up into a subtle form of manifestation then shimmered off, the way P.G. Wodehouse described Jeeves. He said of this consummate British valet and gentleman's gentleman that he would shimmer soundlessly into a room precisely when his jackanapes employer, the feckless Bertram Wooster, required his awesome brain, and make a slight cough like a sheep heard on a distant mountain, Wodehouse said, to indicate his availability.

One aspect of this 4D framework is you see the past, present, and future as a single wrap-around environment, in this case the intention and evolutionary expectation of the newly outfitted planet. This triple perspective timeline view is part of the geomantic mock-up Visvakarman equipped his "helpers" to make real. Those helpers are the present crew in the Blue Room, angels, Pleiadians, and possibly one bad seed waiting for the right moment to steal the key equations.

The Hierophancy heuristic algorithm was implicit in the Blue Room. We brought it with us as a future possibility. That's why Blaise and I were remembering those days. We were looking for clues. Places of vulnerability, access, seduction, the earliest signs of trouble. The Earth, humanity, and the Light grid would have to reach a certain threshold level of development before we could deploy this Light grid management algorithm, but it was part of the plan. By 2050, it had and we did, but some four billion years ago it had not.

Had someone waited that long, been that almost inconceivably patient? Apparently, yes. It was like waiting for the Earth to produce a diamond then plucking it. It isn't the algorithm itself that is the key element worth stealing. Naturally, we have copies of that, like a code or password you have a few people memorize. It was the clamping infrastructure, the layered installation it needed.

It was the ripeness of the Earth, the maturity of its geomantic systems, and complexity of its awakening Albion that made the heuristic algorithm desirable. It's the self-learning knowledge "products" the algorithm achieved as it deepened its interaction with the planetary Light grid since 2050. That history of engagement made it much more than a mere mathematical abstraction, a clever formula. It was everything it had learned from this interaction. It was enriched. It was only 15 years, but it was expanding its capacities almost exponentially. It's like waiting until a prodigy has attained her Ph.D. before offering her a top job.

But it raises the question of why we had to forget the algorithm. We came here knowing it; its mathematics informed all our Light grid installation work. After the introductory period of 2.7 million years, we all drank from the Lethean stream and forgot we knew this master management equation. I think it makes sense if you see it this way: we, on behalf of slowly evolving humanity, had to gradually reacquire this algorithm, building the incremental syllogism of steps leading to it, so that when we, again on behalf of all our human fellows, got it again we would have attained the requisite spiritual and incarnational maturity to handle this vital information wisely.

Our awareness would have grown consonant with humanity's adjustment to the Light grid parameters and a growing consensus reality awareness of its existence and operation. We had to pace ourselves, in terms of full recall, walk much slower than our usual gait, progress with the rate at which humanity was moving so when we reacquired this management algorithm, humanity was in Hermetic congruence with the Light grid and the geomantic reality of Earth. The collective consciousness of humanity had to be growing in conscious alignment with the Light settings in which their creation and evolution had proceeded for millennia; there would be no advantage to doing this prematurely, with a big differential between humanity's evolutionary status and the Light grid settings.

We had been checking in on these layers of the Light grid patern, seeing if the intrusion point lay in any of the clamping strata. You can't (you don't need to) steal the clamps. Each of these clamp layers has its own executive algorithm; the Hierophancy heuristic algorithm is the meta-equation that manages all the secondary ones. You don't take them, as if hiding them in your pockets. You acquire exclusive access to them; you "enslave" them to your altered purposes, then when you run the algorithm it manipulates these suborned clamps to your agenda. When we try to run the algorithm, nothing happens; the car motor fails to start; we open the hood, there's no engine there. Our nimble thief had been acquiring the necessary traction points to enslave the algorithm; at least it seemed he must be though we hadn't yet found any evidence of the intrusion.

I tried to frame the thief's tactics. He would have put them into place the minute the Earth-humanity project got the green light to proceed and when the Hierophancy was dispatched by Visvakarman to begin the planning phase. I shivered as I contemplated the foresight that entailed, to see the desirability of the likely end product of a Light-grid-outfitted new planet. The thief would have studied the plans to find optimal intrusion and traction points. If he were part of the design or implementation team, or had access to their schematics, that would have greatly aided if not guaranteed his success at stealth acquisition of the plan. I could have known the guy and accepted his smiles as he pinched the key parts.

I walked in my memory through the offices and among the people of the Blue Room. It was like strolling through a hologram in which all the actors were freeze-framed, halted in their motions, and it was like being there among the quick as everyone moved and thought (remember: it was mostly a mental space, so thinking was the dominant form of motion) about their work assignments. I saw Blaise scrutinizing everyone, like a chief of detectives suspecting everyone.

I was pleased to see I understood a great deal more about mathematics then than I demonstrably do now. Part of the design complexity the team was working through was to dovetail the algorithms and number specifications for individual components, such as individual Light grid systems and their arrays, with one another and with the entire system. All these different arithmetical levels had to be made congruent and compatible with one another, and that meant a constant monitoring of output and making minute adjustments to it.

In practical terms, that meant the numbers, especially digits to the right of the decimal point in the equations, had to be constantly modulated to higher or lower denominations, at least during the crucial design phase. That role would later be taken over by the Hierophancy algorithm, but here—then—we were still creating the Light grid "body," assembling it like a puzzle made of organs, bones, and veins, and this arithmetical body, this planet made of equations, required constant minute modifications, and every one of these tiny alterations was a point of vulnerability when an access door was temporarily wide open.

At that time, naturally I was not fine-tuned to looking for a thief's nimble fingers ready to pluck the key interstices in our meta-algorithm for Earth, and no doubt since the fingers were mental and not physical he would have used misdirection, sleight-of-hand, and all the cognitive tricks of the expertly devious. He could have pulled it off right under our noses while we were doing something else or while he cleverly distracted our attention. Even better, he could have phase-shifted himself, stepped out of our normal 3D spacetime world, aligned himself precisely, stepped in, nabbed it, stepped out. The idea sounded plausible, except as we were in 4D, he'd have to be in 5D.

Each of the designers had his own signature in the system. I suppose we would call this a password today, but it was a mathematical code we entered every time we interacted with the system or made adjustments appropriate to our brief. The intent behind this was not to classify individual work against the intrusion of others, but to guarantee our full attention to all its details and to serve as a kind of inspector's approval signature on the work as it progressed.

I saw something that disturbed me. Within my signature and the scope of my responsibility as a Light grid designer then I saw a stealth tunnel, like a slow-motion wormhole that threaded its way through a series of interlinking systems. That tunnel was supposed to be there; it was a type of hypertext link across dimensional expressions of the Light pattern, but if left unattended, it could be compromised, and possibly it had been. It was a "door" you're supposed to always close after passing through it. Possibly mine

had not been or maybe it was someone else's, I couldn't tell, as all the designers had similar access hyper-portals through the grid arrays they superintended. That was suddenly many risky access points, open arithmetical doors, that seemed alarmingly exposed.

As if my vision had been suddenly augmented, I saw these tunnels as if they were framed in fluorescent green. The design room was floriated with green portals. They were like broad straws leading up through everyone's grid infrastructure. They were vulnerable, places of potential inimical access, if you weren't carefully monitoring them. Our designer passwords wouldn't protect against that because these were like grace note bolt-holes, phase-shifted off the main vibrational spectrum the designers worked with. Our thief could use them.

These were not actually tunnels or bolt-holes I was seeing. They were at most the products of arithmetical processing going on, equations running their number necessities. The mathematics created the tunnels through the array. What I call a tunnel was the master algorithm, but within that there must have been a couple dozen more constituting number steps, each equation, executed, generated a step, but this turned inside out (like doing a backwards somersault but looking transfigured when it returned to its starting point meaning, I suppose, this strange action took place in 4D), then linked with the next one.

That linkage looked, at least superficially, like rings on a bracelet, but I think it was more subtle than that, more like an equation yielding a number result. I saw the end result as a tunnel because these sequential equations within the master algorithm moved something upward through it. What? A person?

I moved myself into this tunnel column to see what happened and how it felt. The fact I was not in a physical body certainly eased my passage; maybe it was required. This may sound odd, but it felt like being in a birthing process: you go through a series of changes that feel like a sharpening of clarity, a riveting of focus with each step, the completion of each secondary calculation, creating it. It also felt (I ask the reader to not laugh, or at least not too much) like being a car moved slowly along a wash ramp getting soaped, brushed, waxed, and buffed. Here's another way to put it: It was as if reality itself moved in wrenching steps, each one a new configuration dictated by the changing relationship of integers.

As I moved up this pseudo-tunnel I felt I was touching the live numbers. Not in a tactile sense, but a mental one, as if I moved within the domain of each. That experience, if you will indulge yet another stumbling analogy on my part, was like being a piece of clothing tumbling around in a dryer. I felt myself inside, gripped by the abstract reality of the components of an equation running its steps. I could also liken it to being a chess piece in a game of speed chess in 4D. I felt like I was being moved about by expert, terrifically competent, fast hands, that each finger touch on my mind redefined me. I was a shapeshifting marvel.

But I felt somebody watching me, attention deriving from a source other than the necessary handling by the unfolding numbers in the equations. Somebody was studying my movement through this arithmetically generated tunnel, scrutinizing it for the optimal handhold for a time when they would repeat my steps but with a different project in mind. I was studying the sequencing to see how somebody might use it to steal a clamp component for the algorithm. The invisible watcher was studying it to see how "he" could steal it.

The trouble was none of the Blue Room crowd had eyes in a normal human sense. It's not like you can survey a roomful of people and look for shifty eyes. This group was consummately mental, here only in vaguely defined Light forms. The only thing likely to appear shifty would be their minds; they could hide that. I couldn't identify anybody suspect merely by seeing shifty eyes. Nor could I observe somebody mentally acquiring access to this arithmetical ladder because the mind is invisible, quiet, capable of parallel and multiple-track functioning, and I assume our thief, if "he" were even here in the Blue Room, would also be adept at misdirection, sending my attention, should it succeed in grabbing onto anything, off in the wrong direction, chasing empty shadows.

Then it dawned on me. I wasn't looking back in time far enough. Yes, the Blue Room represented a node on Earth's timeline that was billions of years behind us now, but I was registering an attention antecedent even to that. It was like surveying a crowd for one person who had unusual, focused attention, then realizing the place I should be focusing on lay far behind the crowd itself. A basic question arose that I realized immediately was a door opening into that vaster past. Why were we outfitting the planet Earth with a Light grid in the first place?

You could say it was because Visvakarman asked us to and it was our job. Well, why was an Earth Light grid needed and why was Earth needed? I knew the answer but until now I had not given it sufficient weight to factor into the problem. Earth was a replacement planet. It was the fallback option, the bench and understudy. That sounds harsh; it isn't meant to demean the value of the Earth. It's just a fact. Earth was outfitted with a Light grid for humanity to replace the destroyed predecessor planet known generally as Maldek. People who used to fear catastrophic events on the Earth were in fact remembering the destruction of Maldek; it's a dark memory embedded in human consciousness.

You'll know it now as the asteroid belt between Mars and Jupiter. Those asteroids are the grim remains of a blown-up planet, destroyed billions of years ago through a dark confluence of seduction between proto-human inhabitants and grid engineers tasked with maintaining that planet's Light grid and physical power production which coincided topographically at the key geomantic nodes. Maldek ran hydrogen power plants at the geomantic nodes, overlapping its physical power production with the Light grid maintenance sites; it was a powerful yet logical confluence of the two layers of planetary reality. It was efficient and maximized output, but it was a point of vulnerability for Maldek. It put access points to both levels of its planetary system in the same place.

Outside influences took advantage of that vulnerability. The planet imploded and the millions of evolving human souls needed a new place to continue their incarnational safaris through the Underworld of matter. Earth was selected; it was closer to the Sun and thus warmer and potentially more favorable to human-style biology. We would try out new Light grid configurations, partly to support the newly refashioned humans and partly as

security measures against another total end-game fuck-up on a Maldekian scale.

So when we were working in the Blue Room to design and implement a fresh Light grid for the Earth and its arriving Maldekian souls, plus the diversity of souls coming from many other locations throughout the galaxy, we had this Maldekian presence looming over us. It was like an ocean liner of refugees and displaced persons waiting for resettlement; we were the rescue vessel sent to collect the survivors of the Titanic disaster. We felt their anxiety and impatience to resume their odysseys through the human phylogeny now set in a new key. We appreciated the urgency to prepare the replacement context and to secure a safe and incorruptible new planet for these souls to continue their evolution on.

The politics of the Maldekian disaster were that an outside agency, advanced "aliens" as we might charmingly (and parochially) call them, had manipulated events and human consciousness and seduced the responsible grid engineers to make incremental grid adjustments that culminated in the definitive implosion of the planet. Apparently, the grid engineers managing the system got bored, found the movement of evolution on Maldek, its spin rate, too slow.

They regarded the Maldekians as too pokey in their spiritual progress and wanted to hasten the pace. They wanted to speed things up, maybe relocate Maldek to an upscale zone of the solar system or maybe to another one, upscale meaning with a higher consciousness potential likely to be reached sooner and where the spin rate of consciousness was a lot faster than this retrograde pace.

It was a dangerous impatience, one that was vulnerable to just the right kind of seduction. That's precisely what happened. The grid engineers made some ill-advised alignments with advanced aliens, and the planet imploded. Its Light grid, dovetailed, rendered thoroughly congruent, with its physical power grid, based on hydrogen, meant when the Light grid system got overloaded, it fed directly into the physical grid and both exploded inward, ending Maldek.

It is unlikely that any Maldekians were culpable, either in the destruction of their planet or the theft of our algorithm much later.

They were still too young as souls, still too immersed in the wonders and bewilderments of life. It is more likely that the outside "alien" agencies I alluded to were central to this, like an invisible hand reaching from the past straight through into today's Sun Valley.

I felt that hand within my mind. It was cold and dark, and seeing it I felt chills. Was I with the Maldek backstory now at last on the track of the infringers in Earth's algorithm? It made sense: if you manipulate one planet, why not do it again with its successor? Somebody was definitely trying to do that with Earth.

4

All those dead rocks—I could still hear the shouts of dismay from them. The asteroid belt, the exploded remains of Maldek, comprises an estimated 1.1 to 1.9 million floating rocks larger than 3,200 feet in diameter and 200 larger than 60 miles across. For a long time scientists talked themselves into believing none of this derived from a blown-up planet but they finally outgrew that inept notion.

Maldek had been there, as earlier scientists had demonstrated since Kepler. Maldek *had* to be there. Johann Elert Bode, a German astronomer, in 1772 had come up with a plausible math theory proving its necessary placement between Mars and Jupiter. Bode's Law predicted the mathematically necessary placement of planets within the solar system. The dwarf planet-asteroid Ceres now occupies a small residual or vacated planetary position of the destroyed Maldek. But it's only a fragment of what was once there. Can anyone believe that the founder of the universe left this space empty? Certainly not, Bode reasoned.

Bode provided a convincing mathematical formula for demonstrating Maldek's necessary location there between Mars and Jupiter, but we at the Blue Room already knew it was a fact because we had to factor in accommodation figures in our Earth design to handle the solar system displacement occasioned by the removal of Maldek. Probably, though I haven't yet remembered this in any detail, we had helped plot and install Maldek's Light grid before it was inhabited. Its destruction had upset the extraplanetary geomantic ecological equilibrium of the solar system and certain emanations expected to reach Earth from Maldek were gone. It has been ever since a ghost astrological presence.

The Earth's Light grid design now had compensatory formulas in place for that. So the moribund Earth scientists could wax on with their fantasies of no planet ever existing there while on the factual level we had already made adjustments for it. We had a complete math program that accommodated its ghost presence in the solar system web. But the real problem, the reason I was hearing these moaning voices, was that Maldek still exerted a dark Siren call on Earth-anchored human awareness. It was the spectral voice of our antecedents. More to the point, it was there, I now suspected, we would find clues to the thief.

The so-called scientific modeling that discounted the likelihood of the asteroid belt originating from an exploded planet nicely served to hide the reality of Maldek and its revelations of the history of Earth humanity.

I suspect such a clever scheme as this type of obscuration was orchestrated by the same alien intelligences that corrupted Maldekian grid engineers and quite possibly extended a long feral hand right into our Sun Valley offices. Why ever should they stop their machinations just because they ruined one planet? Far better to have Maldek exerting a shadow presence on the Earth human psyche than anything overt or publicly recognized; subliminal results are always better.

This meant it was unlikely I would see the actual malfeasors in the Blue Room. At best I might catch sight of their long intruding hand, their devious mind. Had he worked through any of us? What if he was only surveilling, not manipulating, through our planning activity in the design office, waiting for the opportune moment to lift key equations or linking algorithms as we used them? Even more basically, I didn't know whether to attribute a singular or group agency to the theft of our algorithm. How many "malfeasors" were at play? I have been saying "he" but it's just as likely it is a collective veiled "they."

Then it occurred to me maybe "he" could piggyback on some of the carry-over algorithms from the Maldek Light grid. What we were creating for Earth was significantly different than its predecessor, but it did borrow some of the arithmetical infrastructure commands we used in designing Maldek's grid. The phylogenic characteristics had to shift since Earth is much closer to the Sun than Maldek and thus has different starting material conditions. But the human essence that we designed the Light grid for would be isomorphic with the original idea the Supreme Being and Elohim had in mind when they started. In practical terms, "he"

didn't have to do anything; "he" could do a Trojan Horse on us and already, soundlessly and undetected, be here in the new design.

Yes, we had designed Maldek's Light grid. We had a Blue Room on that planet, an outpost for geomantic affairs and a staff consisting of many of the same people as we had with us now. Remembering that stretched my mind, and details of that project now started coming back to me. There were strategic reasons for selecting Maldek over Earth as the starting point for the human experiment in this solar system. I tried to imagine living out beyond Mars.

We must have chosen Maldek over the Earth for practical reasons. Its greater distance from the Sun assured a weaker affective base for the incarnating human, cooler blood, more possibility of cerebration. It's funny: for decades people used to obsess about possible earlier life on Mars, and invading or visiting "aliens" for a long time were construed as Martians in the popular imagination. But why didn't anyone ever talk about life on Maldek? That actually had been a fact, and a provable one, at least by the Hierophancy. Maldek always got left out of the conversation, as if there was a classified moratorium to never bring the subject up or make references to this former human habitation. Better to propagate intriguing fantasies about a noninhabited planet than admit the truth of the earlier human habitation and self-destruction of the actual one.

As with Earth, when we finished the Light grid installation, many of us stayed on hand as resident geomantic technicians to fine-tune the system once the newly manifested people started using it, interacting with the design's Light temples. I am compressing many thousands of years of cultural development here, but I remember we trained selected Maldekians in running the hydrogen power plants which coincided with key Light grid nodes, so that these trained managers oversaw the conjoint operation of Light grid and physical power grid.

I did that for a few hundred years (Or was it thousands? I am not sure.), though I can't yet remember whether that was continuous employment in one life or spread over many. Maybe I commuted there between running other lives elsewhere. The Maldekians lived long lives there. I trained many technicians in the subtle and tricky interplay of power plant and geomantic mechanics; that involved dimensional shifting from 3D to 4D thinking and interaction modes, but the Maldekians took to it with easy fluidity and with their longevity they remained in their professional superintendency posts for a long time assuring good continuity of operation and management and very few technical mistakes.

In retrospect, we could look upon the Maldekian design as the prototype for what we unveiled for the Earth, but at the time it seemed like our prime Light grid design for a human-type phylogeny and not just a first attempt. You don't go into a complex design project like this expecting it will fail or be corrupted within a few million years of its installation and brilliant launch time.

The system allowed a great deal of freedom to incarnate consciousness, far more than current Earth humans, even in this new *Satya Yuga* of the 2060s, now enjoy. It was comparable to the cognitive largesse afforded to first-generation humans on Earth, but, as we know, they screwed up this gift royally and it was rescinded and second-generation humans

have lived under tight supervision and initial limitation, the "Original Sin" consequences of their predecessors' abuses.

The Maldekians did not show signs of abusing their abundant privileges and powers of consciousness, but on the other hand, their purity (or was it naïveté?) was an open door for shadow-side manipulation and, sadly, as we all know now, their eventual seduction, corruption, and complete ruination. Maybe they didn't have enough time to fuck-up their condition and ruin the planet on their own.

The "bad guys" targeted the brightest among the geomantic engineers maintaining the power plant-geomantic node interstices and played on their fresh eagerness, gradually converting it into incipient impatience, showing them how much better conditions would be if consciousness moved faster, if the planet spun faster, if the pace of conscious evolution was speeded up, maybe if the planet itself relocated to a higher-frequency solar zone. Why not? To be fair, however, the majority of the seduced Maldekians were actually the original Pleiadian oversight engineers charged with managing planetary development.

There were certain key algorithms we used in the Maldekian Blue Room that were carried over into the Earth's Blue Room that bore a taint of this intended corruption. It was as if the malfeasors had inserted certain management integers in brackets into the algorithms and these hidden digits were instructed with other algorithms to alter or even seize control of the equations when told to. Earth's algorithms bore certain Maldekian mathematical ghost traces the way geneticists say our human DNA bears remnants of ghost species or lineages. I suspect people might be surprised to learn that some of the mathematics that run planet Earth and its Light grid processes derive from its predecessor.

I know mathematicians will likely wince at the ineptness of my layman's way of putting this, but whatever the number mechanics, certain control mechanisms were inserted into key equations and left there until activated at the right time. This gives Original Sin another taint. The arithmetical original taint from Maldek got brought forward like a credit into the Earth's operating mathematical system. The means to capture Earth's heuristic algorithm was introduced long ago into the planet's operating mathematical system, like a defective gene or, better (if you are the tactician plotting this, worse if you are us), a genetically altered gene that would lay dormant until a time of activation.

I looked at Blaise. He nodded. He apparently had been following my long cogitations on Maldek and now agreed with my assessment that we must reinsert ourselves into the integer cascade of the Maldekian formulas to watch for the crucial but presumably stealth moment of alien integer insertion. It would be like the security team for a building watching closed-circuit surveillance tapes to catch the intruder, thief, bomber, or whatever, precisely as he enters the site.

"We took the calculations that coordinated gravity and the chakra hierarchy within the human form on Maldek and transferred them to our Earth calculations," Blaise said. He must have "said" this telepathically because I didn't have the impression I heard his voice. His thoughts simply registered in my mind. "We had to modify them for the transfer as the gravity quotient for Earth was different and thus the coordination of chakras, gravity, the physical form, and the flow of consciousness were also different, though essentially still congruent with Maldek conditions. But in that transfer, as one system is shifting to the next, as the arithmetic runs the changes and transfers digits, you have a point of exposure, of vulnerability. We have to watch this for any alien egress.

"Maldek also had fewer Light temples than Earth, but the ones it had were mostly more sophisticated. Some were only slightly modified forms of Light temples you have on the Pleiades, which are high-end consciousness inducers. We never used them on the Earth; its starting point was lower, the gradient less steep. We had to deliberately dial back the freedom and fluidity quotient for this relaunching of humanity. Still, starting conditions for the first round of new Earth humans far exceeded what second-generation humans got.

"In a sense, we had to dilute the potency of the Pleiadian Light temples and multiply and spread them out for the Earth design, and that let a lot of doors remain open, and through these doors our clever 'malfeasors,' as you charmingly call them, could deftly slip themselves or their integer modifiers into the mix.

"Their intent was not to damage or even corrupt our algorithms, but to position itself for an immediate stealth take-over when conditions were optimal. They set in motion a means to trigger certain command algorithmic structures that would seize the unfolding arithmetic of the Light grid and enslave it to their purposes, but to do this slowly, incrementally, and quietly, so we wouldn't notice at first, or maybe not even for a long time. Then it would be too late. The Light grid mathematics would have been sufficiently rewritten or overwritten to make it unlikely we could undo it; this is basically what happened. This gave them an edge to get into the minds and calculations of the resident geomancers.

"By the way, Frederick, the reason you haven't been able to see these guys is they don't have bodies, at least not routinely. They can project a form, if necessary, or hint at one or suggest in your mind they have one, but they prefer working in the shadows, and I mean this literally. Their visible presence is fainter than humidity in the air—can you see? They are primarily a mental presence. I suspect they disdain taking forms of any kind and prefer a formless mode.

"They are primarily a mental species. They have many manifestations in the mental realm, but don't expect bodies like you're accustomed to. They are Mind-based, and you might find yourself being stared at by an invisible mental force-field but not any discrete perceivable life-form. They're more likely to show up as some slightly offbeat algorithm; at first it looks normal, but you know something is peculiar about it; the integers are placed strangely. That's only if you're a trained mathematician and know what to look for; otherwise, they veil their unorthodox arithmetical presence with familiar ones."

Blaise was right. I couldn't see these guys, at least not in a bodily sense. But I did note the idea of a face as a carrier of attention and focus glaring at me. That attention was the beam projected from a mind operating in multiple levels. You don't expect a mind to have feelings, but this mind emanated hostility, or I should say the direction of its plotting and calculations was inimical to humans. It was running its own algorithmic programs that were unfavorable

to humans and I suspect to more sentient, intelligent life-forms, almost like it bore a huge grudge against any bearers of this endowment from the Creator of all life-forms, as if it were protesting all intelligent life and opposing it with their arithmetic.

Then I took stock of the obvious but which up until now I had overlooked. Blaise seemed to have identified our perpetrators, at least in general terms. We were starting to form some sense of the agency involved in our grid problem, though our personification of it fluctuated between an arithmetical and an "alien" mental presence, as if "they" could be both numbers and attention. You couldn't say these "minds" were present in either of the Blue Rooms, but they were surveilling it and somehow projected their sharp intelligence into it. I was sure I could hear their minds churning, like a machine quietly humming, though they could well be operating off-planet, elsewhere in this or even another galaxy.

For every algorithm we set in motion, they countered with one that changed it. That is, they immediately conceived its alternate or opposite form, but didn't launch it; they held it as an open option, like a chess master considering moves or a poker player building up a hand of excellent cards. We were suddenly engaged in a struggle for the freedom of consciousness and were waging this in the arcane arithmetical realm which actually maintained reality. Physical battles, political or economic conflict, were irrelevant and ineffectual compared to the results that could be achieved by working the dichotomy here.

I had the impression they concocted hundreds of alternate moves for every one we the designers introduced into the system, and these potential, considered moves hovered about their minds and the implicit heads that would house them like a coronal fog filled with calculations and their integer products to change reality. They hung in the mental air like predators ready for a dive towards prey. I emphasize that just because it was mental doesn't mean it was without effect. These minds could undo our geomantic designs and hijack a planetary reality and all they had to do was deploy the correct mathematics. They could capture and command a planetary system with one clever algorithm and before anyone realized it conscious life there would move differently.

I saw clearly that they could do this, commandeer a planet with numbers. But I didn't understand why they would want to, why they would exhibit such sustained hostility towards phylogenies being awarded smart new Light grids.

"They resent all life-forms with free-wheeling, self-aware consciousness pre-loaded with all the potencies of awareness, the chakra powers called *siddhis*," said Blaise. "They have done so from the beginning. It's in the *Mahabharata*. There's a memorable fight scene in which Garuda, my pals, the Blaise Angels, tarted up in their favorite majestic bird form, is storming the halls of the gods to steal the Soma. Garuda knocks a lot of things over, breaks stuff, and trashes the gods' clubhouse. He acquires the Soma, meaning awake consciousness, and gives it to humanity, supervising its installation and its later development in them.

"The *Mahabharata* says he stole the Soma to free his mother who had been captured, but Blaise tells me the Supreme Being commissioned them to award the possibility of wide-awake, fully dilated divine consciousness, known then as Soma, to a new life-form, now known as us, human beings. This was long ago. The business about saving his captured mother was just after-action fluffery.

"The gods are more than peeved by this rash action. Their presumptions of the privileges of power and the limited distribution of the potencies of consciousness are wildly affronted by this act of cosmic largesse. Whose act? The Supreme Being's of course, but they don't care. They disapprove; they dislike it; they positively hate this brash development. They focus their waspish opposition upon Garuda, traitorous malefactor. Later, humanity will get some of that bile, and all the pals of Blaise across time will get spewed with this opprobrium too. I have always noticed a penumbra of opposition and enmity from the periphery in my work and travels with Blaise over the years. Their enemies become mine.

"The true politics are this: The Supreme Being commissioned Garuda to install the Soma in the newly created humans and to superintend its activities. Garuda didn't steal the Soma and technically he didn't trash the gods' clubhouse. But the gods' presumptions of exclusivity were trashed by this bold, outrageous gift of a potentized consciousness package to the upstart new human phylogeny. They strenuously opposed it; they fractiously protested the endowment; they went about in great huffs and flounces of irritation and vows to get reprisals. It was like extending the right to vote to the great mass of the unwashed or opening up membership to an exclusive Piccadilly club to Cockney dockworkers.

"The gods were in an enflamed state of agitation and outrage. They declared that Garuda was a shit and pronounced him their enemy forthwith forever. He had upset their niceties and proprieties, their imperial, aristocratic presumptions of the powers and privileges of higher consciousness. That would not be tolerated. They would not stand for this usurpation of their elite status.

"As for the Supreme Being, well, He should have His big white Head examined *stat*. Possibly an emergency lobotomy might be in order. Or call the Old Man up on charges, incompetency, gross enfeeblement, something of that sort surely. Get a vote of No Confidence enacted by Parliament. Call for immediate elections to replace the Supreme Being. That organized, sustained, *long-term* enmity has been transferred to all Garuda's agents, like us, the Blue Rooms, the Hierophancy, Maldekians, and all Earth humans naturally, though I think the professional geomancers working with the Ofanim get its brunt."

"So these mental guys basically have been fighting God ever since?"

"Indeed, it's a long match, winning some, losing others. It's still a draw," Blaise replied, "but it is a constant undermining influence, a kind of psychic erosion force. You would think opposing God is futile, ill-advised, the straining of stupid people against an unmovable force, but erosion itself is a powerful influence, inexorable, if you give it enough time. They've had enough time. This certainly establishes a clear motive for the possible algorithm thieves. Retaliation against God and every stupid consciousness phylogeny He rashly created.

"It was like monarchical Edwardian England contemplating a proposed independent India. Lose Queen Victoria's Jewel in the Crown? Preposterous. Gandhi was demanding what? Out of the question. Throw the mendicant in jail. So, to compromise the Earth by stealing its managing algorithm is a cool revenge. They pull off an adroit end-run; what they can't legislate away, they steal.

"They stole the Hierophancy algorithm. That's a win. With it they can neatly undermine all the geomantic integrity of the Earth, subvert its geomantic ecology, corrupt its Light grid, dirty the Light temples in a manner akin to spraying illiterate graffiti on clean walls or releasing pathogenic agents. They can commandeer humanity's psychic apparatus, lead the human soul grievously astray, dismantle the hierarchies and potencies of consciousness genuinely awarded to humanity, or, even better, rewrite them, reorienting consciousness, and offer up a big extended middle finger fuck-you to the Top Man in Charge.

"You would assume, as a human, that this prolonged choleric opposition to the intended plan for higher intelligent life-forms such as humans would be fueled by roiling emotions. It wasn't. These gods were entirely dispassionate. On a mental level, they said this shall not be, it shouldn't be, it will not be. God had introduced a disagreeable thought into the pure mental field of these older gods. Humanity, now possessing this precious Soma, was a pack of inept sorcerer's apprentices. It was offensive and bound to lead to disaster, likely quite soon.

"To them it was noting an objectionable mathematical procedure, a set of algorithms that yielded an inelegant result. The proof was suspect. It offended their sense of arithmetical propriety. It was like an editor observing the repeated wrong use of a semi-colon or a chronically misused past tense of a verb. It was incorrect usage, and that was for them a mental irritation. Multiply this by a million. Or maybe it was like a pack of former illiterate farmers presuming to write like Marcel Proust or Henry James, flaunting their convoluted syntax. So they conjured up ways to undo this outrage. They are skilled in doing this.

"The tricky part, the part where the Hierophancy has always been direly challenged to keep on its toes, is that these alien oppositional gods could make changes without them being apparent. It would be like editing reality overnight, deleting people and conditions and any memory they had ever existed. You wake up the next morning and take the changed conditions as the long-enduring status quo, absolutely familiar, totally quotidian, exactly as you left things yesterday, and you don't suspect that your familiar reality is a sham and the real one has been hijacked, rewritten, *abridged*, and returned to you as a lobotomized ghost form of itself, you now living under seriously changed circumstances.

"It's *QED*, as the smug British aristocracy used to say. *Quod erat demonstrandum*, 'what was to be demonstrated,' as in the end of a mathematical proof, or, in the vernacular, 'which was what we wanted.' I could imagine the 'posh' aliens *QED*-ing one another on this, tipping their glasses of port, tapping their cigar ends, and smiling imperially. 'We *QED*'d those little fuckers, put those upstarts in their place, quite nicely, I can tell you. Put a tidy end to that little rebellion as fast as possible, which was precisely what we wanted and we got.'

"The timeline has been altered, your history recast because they changed the algorithms running both. Dangerous and devilishly clever of them to do this. All the roads now go somewhere else than they did yesterday, but you don't know it. Consciousness starts moving in a different direction with a new tone and you have not been notified. They have countermanded the Supreme Being's orders. Nobody sent you the memorandum, and nobody ever intends to. They fully expect nobody will notice the substitution of reality conditions. Awesome."

"How did these oppositional gods get that way, so adept with numbers?"

"I wondered that myself. Then I asked the Blaises. As you know, they are walking, joking encyclopedias. They know all the *QED*s! Their memory has deep roots. These errant gods, they told me, were trained in numbers; they were entrusted with the arcane knowledge of mathematics by an angelic order originally commissioned by the Supreme Being to superintend the domain of arithmetic. These are the Arithmetical Angels, though they are a hidden order.

"Think of this order as comparable to the angels that look after or perhaps are in essence the creative-fire letters of Hebrew. Those we might, cautiously, term the *Autiot* Angels, primordial creative spirits whose celestial bodies are the fire-letters. Most people do not think of the *Autiot* spirits as angels, but in their functions they are. Then these, our current troublemakers, the ones who look after the vital numbers, we might call the Angels of Arithmetic and their bodies are compounded of arithmetical computations, equations, and holy algorithms.

"Think of it as a body of knowledge, the inventory of all mathematical formulas and calculations within the infinite Mind of the Supreme Being. Well, *nearly* all, for a created intelligence cannot be comparable in knowledge to an infinite one, so the Supreme Being keeps a few things back for Himself alone. He has to, otherwise He'll end up sharing infinity and then infinity won't exist any more and He'll be out of a job because He has no special distinction any more.

"As I said, the Qabalists regard their alphabet, the *Autiot*, as hypersentient spiritualities who superintend every aspect to do with using these potencies to create realities. They exist as an activated crown of fire around the Head of God. This other angelic order does the same work but with numbers, equations, and algorithms. This is construed as a sanctified language, the formative arithmetical realm, and this group is charged with superintending its constituents and uses. It's like two sides of the one hand: one side is fire-letters, the other fire-numbers.

"Mathematicians would delight in this knowledge, if they could believe it. Imagine having the definitive list of all prime numbers that exist. Every one. To the absolute end of the enumeration. This is God-knowledge. Only an infinite being can know the end of an infinitely expanding number. It's exhilarating just to consider the possibility. Such a list must exist. I'd love to see it. God must know this, and the arithmetical gods too, I speculate, or they're intending to. Mathematicians would realize they are not making up all these theoretical formulas; they actually exist in reality and have a divinely appointed purpose.

"They have in fact higher reality coding applications than they ever suspected. They represent the command language of reality, magic, creative force in the guise of equations. They describe, script, and catalyze movements within reality at the core level of basic infrastructure. They are the original codes that program the crucial processes of consciousness.

Infrastructure and process are their products. It's just that those programming codes deal with levels of reality and perception that far exceed where people normally look for arithmetic.

"The angelic order looks after this realm of number knowledge, and at some point a very long time ago they instructed our oppositional gods in this knowledge. They were not oppositional at the time; they deviated later. It was the same widescale tutoring you read about in the apocryphal ancient texts like the *Book of Enoch*. The text refers to various angels (200 are mentioned and their leader) from the Fifth Heaven known as the Watchers, those angels who were awake and watchful and who guard. In Greek the name became *Egregoroi*, then later egregores; in Aramaic, they were the *'iyrin*, Holy Ones, or *qaddiyshn*. They were supposed to watch over humanity and presumably the heavenly secrets too, keeping them separate. Eventually, the Watchers became the collaborators.

"They passed on arcane angelic knowledge to early humans about astrology, metals, and most aspects of the magical arts. This group I'm describing got the arcana on mathematics, the full arithmetical disclosure. The *Book of Enoch* makes it clear this was unauthorized by God, though I always find it hard to understand how angels can be disobedient, can act independently of the Supreme Being's directives, act against the Old Man's directives. They aren't free like humans but are compelled always to act in alignment with His wishes. If that's true, then it sounds like the Old Man leaked the information through them.

"Let me stop for a moment to explain a few assumptions. I don't know if what this book says is true and accurate or distorted and mirror-reversed like everything else we've been encountering. It could just be more editorial animus by some dogma-obsessed Christian clerics. They seem to delight in having the gods fall due to moral transgressions. It's like high-end gossip about celebrities. I decided to use the statements offered in the *Book of Enoch* as a creative thought-experiment, to proceed tentatively, letting it be provisionally true for a while.

"The angels let these newly tutored gods use the numbers. They gave them some test assignments to see how they handled them. They did well. The angels expanded their scope of responsibility, detailing them with bigger tasks. The inevitable happened. Their proximity to this formative and formidable creative power seduced them, swelled their heads. These gods fell and started abusing the privilege, running special operations with their arithmetical means.

"I call them 'gods.' Technically, they are not gods, merely long-lived mortals. As humans, we tend to label intelligences 'gods' when their level of development and access seem to so far surpass ours as to be hard for us even to conceive. Armed with this mathematical knowledge, they became certainly god-like, and after a while their black-ops arithmetical deployments shifted into frontal applications and they no longer felt any need to run their formulas in the dark. They were creating a new, justified arithmetical empire to endure forever.

"Like collectors, they became proprietary, acquisitive, about their mathematics knowledge and considered it their privilege, duty, and frankly, their ardent desire. It became a monolithic mental lust, you might call it, to acquire any and all new modifications of the basic reality operating algorithms. All numbers belong to us, no questions asked, no disagreements tolerated. The Hierophancy heuristic algorithm came to their attention and they desired it. It was supposed to be theirs, and it would be. So they stole it, and it was theirs."

"So you've known all along who took it?"

"They were the most likely suspects. The Pleiadians agree with this. It is also possible that, first, it was the tutoring angels themselves who were the tainted arithmetical gods and the advanced humans who took up the alluring mathematics were corrupted by secondary exposure; and, second, these humans who became the arithmetical gods may have infected the angelic tutors with their own messianic obsession with preserving the purity of the numbers realm, and the difference between the two groups has been blurred by subsequent writers. I suppose I should add a third caveat: maybe none of this is the least bit true.

"What we have been doing, Frederick, in our search for the algorithm thief, is testing the various traction and input points in the master algorithm to see if these gods accessed them, or even tried to, tested them for vulnerability. Who might have stolen our algorithm is of secondary importance though naturally it is hard to resist speculation about their identity. The fact that it *could* be stolen highlights previously unsuspected vulnerability points in our system. We need to identify those exposed number loopholes and seal them up. In the process we might reason our way through arithmetical logic and syllogisms to an answer to how this valuable piece of mathematics was extracted from our grid, and from that to an accurate identification of the perpetrators, no more guesses."

"Are they smarter than the Pleiadians?" I earnestly hoped they were not.

"No, more like comparable in intellect but with different orientations. The Pleiadian engineers are interested in the field applications of mathematics and geometry. They regard this number knowledge as a useful tool in implementing their designs for Light grid nests for consciousness. In contrast, the oppositional gods look upon the arithmetical trove as connoisseurs, and they regard the formulas more from an aesthetic, contemplative viewpoint. They are meant to be displayed in pristine, inviolate condition in glass boxes in rooms dedicated to their appreciation by only the most refined of collectors.

"This does not preclude their occasional polishing and fine-tuning these formulas when they discover an inelegant or inefficient aspect to their number sequences. Or let's say, in a mood of petulance and self-absorption, you wish to not be disturbed in your hotel room by anyone yet interruptions keep arriving: you use a convenient algorithm at hand to stop all interruptions and their irritating agents. In practical terms, you start rewriting performance aspects of local reality, changing the programming codes to stop undesired behaviors.

"They are not interested in deploying this arithmetical knowledge to create anything. They merely want to own them all, like butterfly collectors wishing their collection to include every extant species. They are museum curators for a fabulous collection of arithmetical examples. They want them all. Or I should say, they want them all *back*, returned to them for careful curating. They want them all to themselves; they don't want visitors asking to see the collection, to borrow equations, test algorithms, or even to inquire about them.

"If someone or a group like our Hierophancy has an algorithm they don't, they immediately and autocratically desire it and set out to acquire it by whatever means necessary, direct or devious. They are passionate, ruthless collectors, though it is a dry, cold, mental passion; simply, they do not want others to have these formulas because they believe they are likely to corrupt them, sully their mathematical beauty. Alternately, they may regard this algorithm as already theirs but one being used by extraneous parties without permission; or maybe they once allowed or condoned this, but now do not.

"Of course, if the upstarts of the cosmos can't (and shouldn't) have these arithmetical powers, then they will also not have the realities these formulas generate, and that suits these gods nicely. They regard most consciousness-bearing phylogenies as unworthy cosmic parvenus. They should never have received access to the precious arithmetical formulas, and that ancient wrong is now being corrected. Lower consciousness forms should not even be aware of the arithmetical realm; that is restricted knowledge. They are not privileged to have it. They prefer the Supreme Being never granted any of them their Light grids and thereby access to the arithmetical scripts that code and generate these patterns. All those enumeration scripts are immediately recalled to source."

I had to stretch my mind and imagination to conceive of their motives, their frame of mind. It wasn't conquest, the drive toward physical enslavement of species, the acquisition of resources, territory, or wealth, not even of the lure of achieving total intellectual and dogmatic supremacy against all other beliefs. It was not about power and control, total world domination and other fantasies. It was none of that. Those are all petty goals. Irrelevant. Trivial. They wanted all the numbers and set about attaining them in great concentration and, I would like to say but cannot justify it, feverishly. No, their desire was cold, like ice. It was indifferent, without dogma, purely logical: an act of sheer mental efficiency.

"What's driving their zeal to collect all the algorithms they can find? What do they plan to do with this mathematical horde when they finish collecting?"

"I think you'll be surprised to hear the answer. They're building a Magic Square. The biggest one possible, one that includes all the numbers, equations, and embedded algorithms. It is the master arithmetical matrix, everything in it. Okay, first, what is a Magic Square? It's a mathematical construct. A Magic Square is a square grid in an *x-y* axis with a varying number of cells with distinct, nonrepeating numbers and in which the sum of integers in each row, column, and diagonal is equal. This total is called the magic constant or magic sum.

"A Magic Square of the Sun, for example, totals 111 for each line and 666 for the entire shape. This is what it looks like: six cells or boxes in a row, a number in each; six rows of these six cells, both across and top to bottom, giving you 36 cells. The total of the numbers in each row is 111. The total for the whole Magic Square is 666. Users of Magic Squares regard these totals as significant, even magically powerful. The number 666, as well as other Magic Square totals in reference to the planets,

is a command number, they suggest. A potent one.

"Esotericists say it has something secret to do with the actual Sun, that it possibly has a type of invocatory or manifestation function. They like to put out the false notion it is the Number of the Beast and therefore terrible, toxic, and to be avoided. That's nonsense, a smokescreen. It's a power number. There are Magic Squares for all the planets in our solar system, each with its key number. The Mercury Magic Square turns on the number 8 and uses all the numbers from 1 to 64; its magic constant is 260, and the sum of the Square of 2080. The Moon uses the number 9, Venus 7, Saturn 3— these are complex arithmetical matrices.

"Humans have been making Magic Squares since at least 650 B.C. in China, then, not much later, in Persia and India. In all cases, presumably, it was as a form of recreational mathematics, something clever to occupy the mind. Perhaps, but that's the way nonmagical, non-occult scholars would see it. The Magic Squares for the planetary energies of the seven classical planets in our solar system, magicians claim, are grids denoting accessible potencies. Mathematicians have concocted Magic Squares for all sorts of extended, abstract purposes, seemingly just to see what kinds of arithmetical permutations are possible, how big they can become, how many variations on this principle and its parameters they can come up with, and because the challenge is fun.

"These alien gods are not making theirs for recreation or fun. Their Magic Square is for controlling all reality. Everywhere. Actually, for recalling reality by sequestering the numbers that code it. They want to control reality by stopping it; then they won't have to think about it anymore and control is irrelevant.

"Each integer in its cell is a false front for an algorithm, similar to how for Qabalists a Hebrew letter is also a number, and that in turn is linked to a special background or shadow Magic Square consisting of thousands more algorithms in a kind of branching tree array. That's why people consider Magic Squares to be magical invocation devices: each number in a cell is also a Hebrew letter with all its creative fire-letter power. These are power devices. Here's the scary part: Each Magic Square has a magic constant dependent on the order n and has its own mathematics formula for calculation, and these are in effect magic summonings.

"Magic Squares for the numbers 3 through 9 are correlated with our solar system's planets, and mystics believe they can attract planetary influences and their attendant angels or demons when the Square's energies are properly focused. Others say you can draw down favorable astrological influences or cause illusory palaces to appear over your head with these Magic Squares.

"At least three of the Watchers were credited with teaching the humans about astrology and the esoteric aspects of the Sun and Moon. Astrology is not only about interpretation and prediction; used in reverse, it has a control aspect, a planetary influence management system. It is not a trivial pursuit. More potent than any spiritual intelligences present or parlor tricks are the number arrays and their calculation matrices. That's where the power of Magic Squares lies.

"Picture it like this: behind the elegant numerical symmetry of the integer cells lies a fierce hand reaching out to grasp whatever the Magic Square lures to itself. Picture this inexorably strong grasping hand as behind all possible Magic Squares. That is a lot: You can make 880 of 4 X 4 Magic Squares; 275,305,224 of the 5 X 5 ones; for the 6 X 6 style, the number of examples comes to 1.8×10^{19} Squares. What distinguishes these copies is the order of the integers in the cells.

"There is another type of Magic Square construction called multiplicative Magic Squares of complex numbers. There is apparently no top limit to how many of this type can be constructed; they are complicated even to look at. Mathematicians have figured out (or maybe it was discovered) how to make Magic Squares of prime numbers, such as one with 13 rows of 13 integers.

"So when you study any of these tables and reflect that the grasping hands and acquisitive minds of the arithmetical gods lie behind them, you begin to see their power to control reality by their grip on the numbers that run it. Still, it is not the lure of acquiring the cell integers that drives these number collectors. It is what the integers are connected to, their live traction points across realities, the reality processes they hook into and run with their many avaricious hands. Tempting. I think ultimately they don't want the Magic Squares to run anything.

"This is a master Magic Square of hands within hands set to control everything. They want the numbers and they want what the numbers control. It's like telling people to stop singing, to stop using their voices or language. Our Earth is set to be a cell in that vast Magic Square. That's why they stole the algorithm that runs our planet's Light grid. It enables them to fill this cell slot. It's like this:

Imagine you are cranky and impatient with how things are going. You have the means to recall the numbers everywhere that code reality. Your attitude is basically 'The hell with reality everywhere.' And you have the means to make good on your petulance. You can effectively recall all the coding digits."

For a moment I saw this master Magic Square with the Earth inside a cell. It felt like a prison cell with the wrong kind of universal connectivity exhibited. It was one that enforced compliance rather than enabled freedom; it was grim regimentation, not interdependence. I wasn't sure if this was a natural pattern gone bad or an unnatural pattern unnaturally born and dark at its inception. I moved that problem aside for a moment because I saw something much worse.

This master Magic Square was now exhibiting depth. I realized I had been seeing it primarily as a 2D phenomenon, a flat array of numbers in cells. That had expanded to add depth and it was now a 3D Magic Square, like a stationary Rubik's Cube. Then it became a confusing shape. It was moving, turning inside out, what was on the right shifted to the left, what was on the bottom rose up to the top. I felt dizzy. Then I think my eyes figured out how to see this roiling form and I realized it had upshifted to a 4D shape, a hypercube of eight cubes. Its cells contained what seemed like millions of Light grids and enwombed planets.

In a flash I understood how this could be, but I didn't like what I now understood. The algorithms run the planets through manipulable, modulating traction points on their Light grids. The master Magic Square represents those algorithms in a live form; therefore, the Magic Square controls those

planets and they are effectively in it. The algorithms grab them and hold them fast in the Square. That's the meaning of all those fiercely grasping hands I saw earlier.

This vast Magic Square was the meta-algorithm for all the Light grid algorithms. It seemed to be the master coding equation for everything. It's hard for an Earth mind to understand how an algorithm can grasp a hologram and hold it fast in a cell within a Magic Square, but that is precisely what I saw. The only part I wasn't sure about was whether the Earth had been grabbed yet.

I did see, or at least sense, the rapt presence of these alien minds behind their master Magic Square. In a dry, cerebral manner, they delighted in this burgeoning acquisition campaign. They were like coldly ruthless collectors intent on acquiring every last available example of their desired collectible. They would stop at nothing to complete their collection; they felt entitled to possess all of it.

Their entitlement was unshakeable, like bedrock. No one would presume or dare to challenge it. No algorithm coding a planet's Light grid would remain out there. From a human perspective, it seemed outrageously selfish, but I doubt they saw it that way or could even comprehend how we could attribute that quality to their collection work. It was necessary; they were equipped for it. From their viewpoint, everything mathematical necessarily belonged back with them.

Had these strange guys stolen our Hierophancy algorithm? Probably. I took solace from the fact that in their astonishing revolt against all reality and its arithmetical infrastructure they would still never get all the algorithms. They couldn't. The Supreme Being was infinite, His arithmetical generation was endless, and ultimately the master Magic Square that managed all the deployed algorithms was without limit. Whatever master Magic Square these recalcitrant rebellious arithmetical gods were assembling would still fall short of His Square.

These aliens would never acquire all the calculations. They could never reach the end of the warehouse housing them, so full control of the numbered reality would always elude them. They could only inch forward over the eons, assuming they were that long-lived and irascibly single-minded to keep at this one project and do nothing else and acquire ever more equations to fill the burgeoning cells of their Magic Square, but they could not expect to get all of it.

Still, what they had, and it was already vast, could do a lot of systemic damage. Their finite Magic Square that sequestered all the deployed algorithms would still effectively shut down the Creation because all of infinity, every last possible permutation, was not incarnate in that manifestation, as vast as it may seem, which means in practical terms if they retrieved all those algorithms already in service of the Creation, those deployed in the finite world, that would be good enough. They didn't need to extract all the algorithms from the infinity field; they only needed to get back ones on-line, activated, in service of reality.

Meanwhile, the algorithms they had secured continued to run their manipulation programs. I saw hands, or maybe they were threads of numbers, reaching out from each cell to the captured planet those numbers were running. I guess you could say the grids of these many planets were running on autopilot for the

moment; all their essential life systems were properly maintained, but no forward-provoking evolutionary-level inputs were for the moment introduced.

Their Light grids modified planetary conditions as extra-planetary inputs changed. They responded ably to changing planetary factors as well, such as weather and sociological tendencies and tidal movements in consciousness. But I had the impression that despite this competent, responsible degree of regulation, most of the planets were being maintained at stasis, treading-water containment. Since all planetary systems and their Light grids were interdependent and richly connected on many fronts, this containment was producing galactic stagnation.

This master Magic Square was acting like a universal inertial wall halting progression in consciousness across the worlds. It was universal Stop sign, a red light at a busy traffic intersection that would stay on red for the calculable future. The best way to inject a hospital patient with something you want them to have but to which they might not agree is to hold them down, tight and steady. That's what the master Magic Square was doing: pacification through containment and stultification to enable the introduction of catalytic factors the alien minds chose.

But I did notice six planets were squirming, resisting this externally forced becalming. If they were people, they were scrambling away from the grasping hands. Their cells in the Magic Square were suffused with a pale blue light, blue like the sky. One of these resisters was the Earth. The others I didn't recognize. They could lie anywhere in the Milky Way Galaxy or possibly far beyond in another one.

I would have to check with a mathematician on this but I had the impression the planetary algorithms for these six were linked, causally related. These six planets seemed energetically connected by an implied hexagon; each planet occupied a vertex in this six-sided figure that seemed to span galaxies.

As you ran the number processes for Earth it would affect and trigger the other five. This reciprocal process cascaded throughout this implicit hexagon of cells. Not one of the six itself had the primary center of gravity for the hexagon; it kept shifting, as a new one among the six took the primary position, but the definitive anchoring point, the true center of gravity, was the whole system of six planets itself. In some way I couldn't yet discern, these six planets were different than all others. The product of their algorithms was special, and, it seemed, rare.

There seemed to be a constantly reciprocating relationship between algorithm and planetary process and the condition of embodied intelligent consciousness. Their algorithms were creatively and minutely modulating effects. The algorithms of the rest of the planets in the master Magic Square were only holding conditions steady, maintaining the dominant status quo, staying put. I got the impression the fate of Earth's master algorithm was intimately tied in with that of the other five similarly outfitted hexagon planets. Similarly, if the alien gods had targeted their algorithms for ruthless acquisition then Earth's condition would be imperiled as well. The six were in this together. The alien gods would have to acquire all six at the same time to get full control.

The Light grids of these six seemed more fluid, protean, and more quickly modulated than the other planetary Light fields I was observing in the cells. Cells? I realized I was starting to regard these planets and their algorithms as if in prison, and the cells in the Magic Square looked more like prison cells than simply boxes for digits. I had just arrived at this maximum security prison and was assessing my new environment. I was observing six inmates who were less docile than everyone else and more proactive about changing their imprisoned status or, better, staging a successful break-out and leaving this prison behind.

Meanwhile, studying these six, it was like watching ballet dancers whose nimble movements surpassed those of all other dancers in their performance troupe. I reminded myself I was watching the modulations of a collective consciousness across a planetary phylogeny, geomantic twirls on the dance floor of a Light grid, and I realized the regulating algorithms must be commensurately fluid and instantly adaptable. These six were not acquiescing to the alien gods.

I started to feel admiration for its designers, then I laughed. I was standing amidst them. The Pleiadians, of course. What I still didn't understand was what distinguished these six planets to such an extent they formed a rare, possibly unique, hexagonal cabal of activity far exceeding the gifts of the other cells. What was so special about this hexagon of six planets and their grid mathematics?

Blaise provided the answer. "There are only six planets in the Creation awarded this degree of free will and a correspondingly flexible Light grid. If this were a school, you could say these are six promising students with exceptional opportunities. It is not that the students themselves, yet, are prodigies, but they might be. But they have been sent to the topmost school and given the best teachers. Now everybody sits back to see what they make of these opportunities.

"This also means the regulating algorithms for these six planets are special. Highly refined, terribly complex, creative and bold, daringly, brashly experimental. These six are top prizes, irresistibly alluring for the alien gods' collection. They must acquire them. They look upon them with the same acquisitive zeal with which collectors once regarded Fabergé eggs. That's why they are expending all effort and tactical input to acquire them, and that's why it is imperative the Hierophancy stop them and prevent this acquisition. They want these six for their inert collection; we need to preserve these six because universal reality needs them. It would be disastrous for them to go out of circulation. We're getting help from a familiar quarter in our attempt to stop this outcome."

Blaise gestured to what looked like a honeycomb of hexagons of Light surrounding each of these six planets and somehow also the six of them together. Thousands, possibly millions, of identical hexagons like an array of diamond caves surrounded each of these six planets (our Earth too, I feel drawn to remind you), and standing inside these caves were translucent figures like monks in their hermit caves, meditating or chanting to save the world.

But these figures weren't meditating, at least not in any sense we would think of it. They were wide awake and focusing Light and attention on their designated planets. They looked like top-level angelic administrators dispensing conscious regard and pure attention to these planets and their phylogenies, including Earth's humans.

"You're looking at my pals, the angelic Blaises, the Ofanim in their Og-Min Brotherhood guise," said Blaise, with a touch of pride. "That's a guise they used for the Tibetans principally, very arcane, secretive, highly competent, their work so rarefied it was hard even to speak of it, as Tibetan Buddhists hinted.

"The Taoists mentioned them too, saying they live in their Cave Heavens or astral *shiens*, residential holes or cavernous pockets in the galaxies. Og-Min means 'No Down,' meaning they do not descend into the phenomenal realms. They operate at the most pure and rarified levels of reality to maintain the lower phenomenal ones, all of which has been ironical since 2020 when in fact some Og-Min did go down and against all tradition and definition entered the human incarnational realm. I refer of course to the momentous, unprecedented mass incarnation of the Ofanim into human forms that began in January 2020. The No-Down Boys are now the Gone-Down Ones, and some are here to rescue things.

"For those remaining above, for not all the Ofanim or Og-Min descended into our midst, it's like they stand and operate the controls at the top of the universal Light grid and its fractals and look after affairs of consciousness from the top down. They are within reach of definitive Buddhahood and world transcendence, but they refrain from taking that ultimate step to help those still embodied. They can't sneak into the offices of the alien gods and reacquire the algorithms; God won't let them. But they can point out where they are and provide tips and lighting. They are our pals, faithful allies of the Hierophancy. They are giving this hexagon of the six special planets a little uplift in Light."

The Cave Heavens of the Og-Min Blaise Brotherhood surrounded each of the six planets like a singular cavern of Light made of thousands of mirrors. Each planet, including our Earth, was encased in this wraparound sphere of facets with the Blaise angels in their more cosmically serious mode as the Og-Min. They reminded me of the Pope standing in his balcony above St. Peter's Square in Vatican City giving an Easter blessing to the penitent and pilgrims assembled, though I suspect the Blaise angels would not see their work as bestowing a blessing nor would they miss any opportunity to slip in a good joke. If the human Blaise joined them, you'd better expect some stand-up routines. And in this version, there was not one Pope, but thousands of presiding Og-Min.

It was strange, an almost comical symmetry I was observing. The Og-Min by the thousands in their diamond Cave Heavens were meditating to preserve the continuity and force of commissioned consciousness in the arithmetical realm, their numbers occupying designated cells in the master Magic Square and its myriad of permutations across the universe. The Og-Min were managing reality processes. It was metaphysically alarming, too, when I thought about it, this mirror imaging of the two realms, one protecting awareness, the other guarding numbers. Was it a stalemate I was witnessing or an intended reciprocal symmetry?

Was it even symmetry at all, or was it more truly an asymmetry? Maybe the Ofanim as Og-Min inherently had the upper hand from the start. The Og-Min, the Blaises in their Cave Heavens in their exalted *Akanishtha*, the Highest Pure Land and Buddha-Field and Unsurpassed Heaven than which nothing is higher, according to the Tibetans—there they were uniform throughout their multiplication of copies. That is a very spiritual realm they occupy, one of pure consciousness, "Below None," the Buddhists say, and "in the *Ains*," says Blaise. It was always a Blaise angel inside a hexagon cave, dependably, whether they chose to appear as an Og-Min "monk," Garuda, Hanuman, Airavata, or Ganesh.

The impression of Cave Heavens teeming with Og-Min is consistent with their name. It also means, or at least denotes, the "thickly-formed" or "densely-packed realm," the impression that a great many of them are crowded together. If you picture the Ofanim's diamond geode with its 40 million identical hexagon diamond facets, or caves, each filled with one Blaise angel, or Og-Min, it is not a visual stretch to construe this as a thickly-packed zone, yet one dwelling in the highest reaches of created space, "that which is not inferior or under any other realm," the Tibetans say. The Og-Min, our pals, the Blaises, are "that which is not below," except for when they come down to visit, help, advise, joke, or incarnate.

The arithmetical gods, for their part, also dwell in a pure realm, but it is a mental one that emphasizes quantities, numerations, and what can be done with them, and not one of consciousness. But with the numbers in their cells in the master Magic Square, they appeared in wild, protean diversity, as if revealing their inner selves, the innumerable variations of Magic Squares into the millions of permutations, as in the example I gave earlier of 275,305,224 alternatives of the 5 X 5 Magic Squares. In each cell, within its resident number, you'll find a different Magic Square.

On the other hand, evidence for symmetry lay in the shared disinclination for incarnation in the lower phenomenal realms. For the Ofanim, it was (until 2020) a professional job description; angels work the higher worlds principally. They don't Go Down; the Supreme Being doesn't allow it, normally. For the arithmetical gods, as I would see, they strenuously disliked the created, contaminated worlds, even though their numbers were deployed to sustain them. They would never go down; the Go-Down Realm was contaminated. They wouldn't go down if you paid them, or even if the Supreme Being shoved them.

They regarded their abstract numbers realm as inviolate. They wouldn't go down; the Og-Min and the angelic families couldn't go down. As I contemplated these two seemingly opposed but commensurate realms, I wondered why couldn't the Ofanim help us, Gone-Down consciousness, penetrate the numbers realm, comprehend it, possibly master it? Can they? As always, it's a matter of permission and divine commission and not competency.

Something else was present in this image. It wasn't beatific. A thin hand with long fingers extended into each of the planetary Cave Heavens. The fingers were stretched out in a gesture prepared for grasping something. This was a suggestive though literal image, I knew; the reality was more subtle.

"The strange thing about these alien gods," said Blaise, "is they are not inherently evil, not in any sense in which we construe the term. They are not evil like the Antichrist, Druj, or even that failed Grail Knight, Klingsor, who spent his days in petulant resentment against the Supreme Being and the Grail Knights.

"No, these guys are neutral or amoral. They're not for or against the Supreme Being or any of the phylogenies. Maybe they once had a partisan position, resentment against the Supreme Being. Not now. If anything, mortal conscious life is simply irrelevant to them, inconsequential. A waste of good numbers. They regard it as a possible field application of their numbers, like a child's doodling on paper, but they see no inherent point to it nor do they ascribe any need to ensure its longevity or even persistence. It's like somebody whistling while they wait for the bus to arrive. It merely passes the time and is quickly forgotten when they get on the bus. Then they recall all the scripting numbers, and drive away with the arithmetical realm safely strapped into the bus seats.

"They consider it a logical necessity to acquire the complete set of algorithms, to finish their master Magic Square. To them, it is unarguable that all the algorithms belong in their proper cells in the Square. They *should* be there; it is incontrovertibly logical. You could liken their mental state to the amoral programming commands of a sophisticated computer, one that borders on artificial intelligence; it operates inexorably on binary logic. Numbers are not meant to do anything, certainly nothing as gross and improper as coding a reality. Who would want to enter such a deformed, transient realm where all the numbers were hidden, as if stuffed into the pockets of fat stupid slow people?

"These gods were probably once mortal or at least phenomenally expressed, I'm pretty sure, and not computers as such, but even then they were excessively mental, more mind than soul, though they had self-reflective awareness. They were role models for computers, you could say, their cosmic prototypes. It's just that their soul level got eclipsed by their dominant mental preoccupations; introspective self-awareness, individuation, and the rigors of spiritual awakening to them seemed irrelevant or outmoded and unlikely to yield anything mentally pleasing or useful. I said they are not evil, but they do seem to lack empathy and any likely flowering of their empathic tendency is superceded by the unarguable necessities of building the master Magic Square.

"Empathy is perhaps to them an optional mental gesture, a logical response when not opposed by the more senior considerations of completing their Magic Square. I suspect they cannot understand opposition or resistance from any parties to their work of acquiring the algorithms. It would not make logical sense to them. The trouble here is that because they are basically amoral and not, technically, evil, because they don't recognize that category or even the polarity of good versus evil and acknowledge and validate only the necessity of completing their master Magic Square, they are harder for us to appeal to.

"Someone committing evil still retains a seed of goodness that could, if activated, become a moral compass again, but for these alien gods, no such seed ever existed. There is no mental argument, no syllogism, no logical chain we could deploy that would have any influence on them. In a sense they do not see the world in these binary terms, black and white, evil and good. To them it is just too obvious. The Magic Square must be completed; it's like tying your shoelaces. Why ever would you want them untied? You'll trip over your own shoelaces.

"Why ever would we not want to complete the Magic Square? That's how they think. Letting it remain incomplete would be like tolerating a wrong answer to an arithmetical puzzle. It would be an affront to the proprieties of Mind, an error, a wrong calculation. The system cannot run with a wrong calculation in it. To these mathematics-obsessed alien gods any attempt by the Hierophancy to reacquire the algorithms would be construed as an irritating intervention in their work and would likely be opposed right away by whatever convenient means.

"Keep in mind they didn't steal the algorithm, assuming these are the ones culpable for the theft, but they acquired the means of controlling its output. That's all that counts, all you need. The arithmetical traction points on the system. That's why you saw the image (I saw it too) of a hand with long fingers reaching into the Cave Heaven of the six planets made by our pals, the Blaises, to take the algorithms. This was a way of seeing their minds grasping the necessary traction points, the secondary, reciprocal algorithms that constitute the main one. They took the palpable vital numbers and left us their empty ineffective shells.

"Their intent, ruthlessly, single-mindedly pursued, is to complete their Magic Square. I suspect that drive to completion lay behind the destruction of Maldek. That planet's Light grid was designed to facilitate a high degree of free will, comparable to that reset for its replacement planet, our Earth. That made their master algorithm desirable and necessary for the alien gods' Magic Square. I don't think it was they who directly, or shall I say, 'personally,' interfered with Maldek and seduced its Light grid engineers with illusory prospects of faster evolution. They worked through intermediaries, cut-outs, field agents, or, perhaps less flippantly, let's call them covert operatives, as in espionage."

As Blaise spoke, I watched the constantly churning Magic Square. It was beautiful and horrifying. An elegant, hypersymmetrical design, but a prison too. Its movement was hard to discern at first because it was at least 4D in nature. This may be inexact, but I would liken it to watching a torus-donut shape in perpetual motion, turning inside out, except this was happening at a 4D level, which meant you saw multiple toroidal churning motions. It made me dizzy.

It was a crazy, multidimensional labyrinth, a maze full of planets and their Light grids fastened to their respective square cells by their operational algorithms. Talk about a puppet-master, this was the pre-eminent shadow manipulator, the secret operator working the strings. Here was a picture of universal connectivity, of reciprocal relationships and linked Light patterns, but it was perverse, a dark, corrupted version of a holy idea. It was without blood.

How was this different than intelligent management? It looked like the alien gods were competently managing the algorithms and their host planets. But something was missing, some alive factor, at least from some of the cells. What I saw seemed synthetic, forced, even stultified. It was a straitjacket on a planet's Light grid and consciousness processes. It wasn't the Light touch they needed.

The intent of Light grid supervision is you were supposed to be more like a dance instructor, a ballet master delicately showing new dancers how to hold their form, angle their elbows, pirouette, leap, keep their balance, and to impart this instruction with the gentlest of touches. The alien gods instead had laid a heavy coercive hand on the consciousness of these many planets; they pressed down hard on the muscles and limbs of the dancers, but the system was designed to run on only the lightest of tweaks and nudges. It was meant to be a delicate, constantly reciprocating interaction of the two, moving to the "music" of free will and the continuous evolutionary expansion of awareness and possibility on each world. The alien gods crudely clamped all that down.

This was especially so with the six planets within the Blaise's Og-Min encasement of hexagonal diamond windows. The alien gods were having difficulty getting a secure lock on those systems; the free-will dispensation that characterized those six made their consciousness fields slippery, like wet soap. The free-will endowment made the reciprocal dance between the evolving consciousness patterns and external management exceedingly refined.

The management structure, the superceding master algorithms, had to be so fluid as to seem as if they were being rethought, reinvented every second. It reminded me of watching the minute fluctuations of share prices on the stock market from many years ago when my father introduced me to that wild world. It was wild, I had thought, because nothing stayed stationary but kept changing.

The consciousness patterns of these six planets seemed constantly one step ahead of the grasping aliens. Was this the Supreme Being's secret edge, where He'd out-thought the deviously clever aliens, seen around an extra corner? I realized the question was embarrassingly inane: nobody can outthink the Creator, but I guess what I was mentally staggering towards was the notion that the Supreme Designer had anticipated this likelihood and added a provision to both pique the avarice of the Magic Square-obsessed aliens and to assure they might not succeed in their mental colonization of all the arithmetical designs for reality. Was this a high-level cat-and-mouse game I was being introduced to?

The operations of these six special planets were intimately interlinked. That meant if you stole one algorithm, gained its traction points on the Light grid, you would simultaneously gain access to the other five, at least a partial control. Conversely, it meant the six could form a defensive shield against intrusions, like a conjoint immune system from five consanguineous sibling bodies in a family. They should be able to repel most antigens.

Then I saw something that had until now been veiled to me. It was another algorithm. This sequence ran the free-will endowment for each of the six planets. It was a secret, embedded arithmetical countermeasure against hostile intrusion, such as we were witnessing today from these acquisitive, Mind-focussed alien gods intent on owning all of reality. Free will is a discrete quality with quantified parameters, so it had to have code written for its presence in a planet's Light grid, even if all that code did was allow heightened system flexibility, letting a system stretch further, respond creatively. It was a layer in the design. For the Earth, this free-will algorithm was a subset of the primary Hierophancy heuristic algorithm, like a data chip buried inside another one.

This meant if we expected to be successful in retrieving Earth's stolen algorithm we would have to protect the other five from being stolen too. Blaise gestured for me to stand inside that Cave Heaven made by the Blaise angels. It was odd being in there. It felt like I was standing on six planets at the same time, that my head

was immersed, saturated in, the Light grids of six different planetary consciousness patterns and that my awareness was doing a fast dance, a weird combination of Sufi twirling, ballet, and *qigong* moves from martial arts. Or how about if I put it this way: I was playing six wild games of tennis in 4D.

Blaise stepped into the playing field. That made it a two-man tennis match in a 4D court. It didn't stop there. Four more figures entered the space. Now it was a six-man game of hyperdimensional tennis with algorithms for tennis balls and us playing in an arithmetical arena made of a Magic Square and an audience comprising morally ambiguous, human-hostile alien intelligences.

What was even stranger was that all this seemed transparent and that we were also, inexplicably, back at our Sun Valley Hierophancy offices and Sal and Jocelyn were cheering us on, following every tennis serve and smart backhand. The entire hologram of the Cave Heaven, the six free-will planets, the six tennis players dashing and leaping all about the court, and the mentally abstracted aliens intent on thorough data acquisition, was there like a bubble in our offices.

No, it was more than that. It was present in six offices. Six offices corresponding to geomantic command posts presumably on five other planets. The Hierophancy extended this far? I looked at Blaise. He anticipated my question. He nodded yes. I mentally asked him, You knew about these other five? He nodded again. I didn't feel left out or not read into the program. I was simply astonished. I hadn't suspected the Hierophancy extended beyond the Earth, other than into the domains of its adept consultants like the Pleiadians.

But here was the Cave Heaven hologram displaying simultaneously in six locations. I couldn't even guess how many light-years these other five planets lay from the Earth, and I didn't bother trying because the distance didn't matter. Apparently, consciousness erases all spatial distinctions and seeming distances. Alignment was everything and evidently that was preordained with the design.

I saw Blaise standing at the core of the Light grid pattern and algorithm traction points of the other five planetary systems. I deduced from this that he had been to these five recondite locations. I wasn't too surprised. I knew he had been to many places after he left the Earth at the beginning of January 2020. It wasn't just to the Pleiades and his antecedent planetary home that he traveled.

It seems he went to these other five locations, though I admit the *how* intrigued me. The angel Blaises or perhaps his Pleiadian colleagues or maybe the Ray Master chief of the Hierophancy had briefed him on these prior multiple Light grid alignments and the necessity to keep the six free-will planets in reciprocating, intimate correspondence. If Earth was in jeopardy, the other five were too. Somehow they facilitated his travels to these five related planets.

Now there were five other figures, each occupying a node in this space. Blaise had stepped back to stand next to me. Apparently, he had been holding the space for that other planet until its designated geomancer had arrived. I watched that figure. There was a delicate dance between his form and the planet's Light pattern, perhaps like a hundred simultaneous tennis matches, with Light, thoughts, or focused consciousness continuously exchanged between them.

I wouldn't say the figure looked exactly like an Earth human, though he was upright, had two arms, two legs, a large head, and thoughtful, focused eyes. He was taller and leaner than the typical Earth human, maybe as a product of gravity. The best way I can put it is to say it was like hearing your favorite piece of music played in a different key and with different, perhaps antiquely tuned instruments, so it sounded different than you would expect. He looked both feral and familiar. I shrugged. He was a Hierophancy colleague. I'd leave it at that.

The other four were also strange in appearance, but I accepted the fact we shared this working relationship and that I as an Earth human living in the gravity well of this blue-white planet probably looked odd. Appearance was of secondary importance, if it had any at all; what was crucial was our shared, reciprocal, interdependent alignment with this Cave Heaven. I suspected, if vaguely, that I was mistaken on two counts. First, I think there were more figures present than I was seeing, that some planets had more than one representative; and second, my impression of a humanoid appearance was probably a familiar conceit of my human mind and that they did not look that way or close to it, that their true forms might be too bizarre or incomprehensible for me to see at all.

It was like singing in an *a cappella* sextet in a cathedral made of diamond facets. Each of the six voices was necessary to complete the tonal architecture. This conjoint expression of self-aware, evolving free will on planets with sophisticated Light grids was somehow necessary for the rest of the created worlds.

These six were not the only ones with free will; as Blaise had explained once, it was the degree to which this free will was allowed to be flexible and self-directing that made its expression on these six planets unique and noteworthy. You could say, if you'll pardon the dog analogy, these six walked off-leash, while the other sentiently inhabited planets had leads of varying lengths. These six were experiments, or maybe they were like exceptional students put in their own class to excel at their own rate and follow their own intellectual preferences.

It was clear that if the "bad guys" wanted to steal Earth's algorithm, they would have to acquire that of these other five planets as well. It was a package. As I've tried to make clear, it is not the arithmetical aspect itself that was to be stolen, but the traction points between the planet's Light grid and that equation. Here I saw clearly how those traction points lived in the consciousness fields of each planet's prime geomantic administrator, namely, these six working figures.

The Og-Min Cave Heaven framework kept these six in top-notch focused acuity. They seemed to be broadcasting a continuous emission of sharpened attention. That was a hallmark of the Ofanim, as the human Blaise had often told me. Sharp, bladelike, unwavering attention on a topic, person, place, or condition. I saw the master algorithms that each planet and their designated geomantic "dancer" operated; they were like umbilical threads made of number strings. The Og-Min presence worked like bright spotlights on these numbers. I couldn't explain how but it seemed the spotlight accelerated the arithmetical unfolding of the algorithms, both clarifying and speeding up the procedures. It was like watching the energy of clarity itself, refining the focus of awareness.

The six figures, including myself, seemed thoroughly busy, absorbed in this geomantic "dance" work under the clarifying spotlight of the Og-Min. Yet somehow another version of each of us was standing attentively in a circle regarding one another. Or maybe we had shifted to another space, some kind of office or meeting chamber. Blaise was with us, and so was Ray Master Hermes.

He was the chief of the Hierophancy after all and certainly needed to be here. He stood in the center of our circle of seven, his emerald robes bright and sparkling. As for the five other "exotics" or "aliens" (or whatever their true number was as I still couldn't tell), they had considerably contrived to assume plausible adult humanlike appearances, comprised of Light; they had heads, faces, and mouths, as you'd expect, but I knew our communication would be telepathic. I didn't mind. I was getting the hang of talking with only my mind.

We had tactics to discuss. The Earth, even at 4.5 billion years old, was the youngest of these six planets and the most vulnerable, the one most in jeopardy. That was because the arithmetical umbilicus holding the planet's Light grid to its superintending algorithm was the sixth and last number "button" to be "snapped." Please excuse the clumsy analogy. The six free-will planets were like buttons sequentially snapped on a jacket of Light; Earth was the top button. When it was snapped or activated the system was complete; derail it, interfere with the button snapping, or better, steal the button altogether, you stopped the system and derailed the geomantic operating modes of the other five planets.

My attention flickered back and forth between this quiet assembly and the comparatively frenetic geomantic dance operation inside the Cave Heaven. That experience was one of being yourself plus five other consciousness points, or like sitting on a merry-go-round ride and jumping onto five other adjacent rides and experiencing them all at the same time. It was being in six places simultaneously. Or it was like playing cello in six string quartets at once, each duplicate cello bowing neatly through a different Mozart composition.

I laughed. I wasn't sure why at first, then I understood. This must be what Sanat Kumara experiences as Cosmic Logos, at least in a tiny part. He has six heads. The myths say he either has six heads on one youthful body or six identical youthful bodies with equal shares of his cosmic consciousness. But he was sixfold, as I was, though he was probably used to it and saw no need to laugh about it. It was normal for him. So, pardon me (the six of me, actually) for my (our) youthful delight in this novelty of manifesting in six identical forms.

I stopped laughing because now my eyebrows suddenly arched and my mouth fell open. I wasn't the only sixfold operator. The other five were also. As my awareness shifted from one to the next in this six-person circle, I realized each of these figures was also experiencing their geomantic operations in a sixfold way. I'd have to check with Sal on the numbers, but didn't that mean my attention was now distributed across 36 frames of reference all at the same time?

Now I was beginning to understand angelic copy multiplication. The 40 angelic orders each have their own permitted number of self copies. The Blaise angels could occupy 40.3 million simultaneous consciousness points, and probably more because the human Blaise was always carping about how they cheat on the numbers and clearly have far more copies than a mere 40.3 million. He used to detail how it seemed impossible for the Ofanim to do everything they claimed to be involved in and have comparatively so few copies to use for this.

As I pondered this, momentarily I was amidst the millions of Cave Heavens, inside one of the facets that formed the single Cave Heaven surrounding the six of us. I was both the 36 simultaneously distributed and active forms of myself and at least one of the Blaise angel points of focus, or maybe co-present with all of them, amazed within a crowd of 40 million angels. I needed a seating plan to keep track of my copies and their locations.

I saw the array of numbers around me like a mental atmosphere. The algorithms were generating their arithmetical products in slow motion. At the same time, the totality of these calculations formed a grid of Light, a discrete pattern, though I won't pretend it was easy to see or figure out. The geometric pattern and the number calculations were two aspects of the same reality, and they kept shifting from one to the other, or maybe they were both present at the same time. I realized there was a subtle interface that linked these expressions.

It was what I might call a gesture or posture of awareness. Mine. I saw it was the same with the other interacting humanlike figures. The traction point that activated this system was when my awareness locked into this array. It was more than merely seeing it; it was when I reached out for it with my mind and moved my awareness into it as if it were a habitable body, when I enlivened it with self-aware consciousness and which I now saw included the Cave Heavens presence of the Ofanim, whose proximity heightened my clarity and focus. It came down to making the correct alignment, and that was in consciousness. The algorithms required a consciousness-bearing life-form to render them active, and the Ofanim's presence helped me, and I presume the other five, reach this focus.

I shivered. I also saw how the alien gods could get in here and steal the algorithms. All they had to do was distract me, seduce my awareness with a thought, or just strong-arm their presence into my psychic field and take it over. Did you ever wake up in the middle of the night, check the clock, find it was 90 minutes before your planned get-up time, and think you'd lay there for a while? Then you wake with a shock and realize several hours have passed and you're late, but, worse, you didn't know you had fallen back to sleep, not until now? I'm trying to say something like that happened to me next and I didn't realize it until some time later I snapped out of it with a shudder and wondered how I lost it.

The "it" means the continuity of my attention based on where I believed my body and awareness were anchored. Because I seemed to have slipped out of "town" on both counts without realizing I had and did a kind of sleepwalking. I was in a cube made of numbers. The cube had innumerable identical cells, too many to count. I thought, weirdly and with a vaudvillean enthusiasm, had the Supreme Being converted the Cube of Space into affordable condominiums?

Each cell was made of equations, like tenants, and each cell had a building superintendent, which took the form of a command algorithm. This pattern was repeated endlessly through the arithmetical condominium I was studying. You know how in some types of dreams you can see the strangest, most bizarre things and not even question the ontological legitimacy of your perceptions? It was like that. It didn't occur to me that this must be out of *Alice in Wonderland*. It got still weirder. My job was to add two zeros to each cell and then three ones to each algorithm solution. It was like a factory job, repetitive and very boring, where you stand in an assembly line and add something or fold a flap or affix a stamp to a product moving past you on a conveyor belt. I added these numbers.

Somewhere in my addled awareness I understood this was saving the world, providing a first-aid fix to the Creation itself. The awards ceremony hosted by a grateful Supreme Being was scheduled to take place when I finished. I knew my friends and colleagues would be proud of me, though oddly I could not remember their names or faces. Their identities were a blur in my mind. If my brain or mind or whatever was pretending to be either was working even a little I would have realized I was conducting my mental processes as if I had just sustained a concussion and everything was spinning, blurry, vague, indefinite. Somebody I was sure I knew but could not place at the moment stood behind these burgeoning number fields reading from a book of stories about the gods. Somehow their stories were relevant to the arithmetical mayhem playing out.

As that person I knew but couldn't identify kept reciting the mythic accounts and these formed moving images around each cell, I continued with meticulously placing my zeroes and ones into their designated slots. I was doing this with what seemed an exaggerated precision and assiduity, the way we used to plug wires into the backs of computers or insert "flash drives" for copying. I was reaching for my teacup before my tea got cold and was about to ask Philomena about her upcoming music recital and I noticed the maple trees visible out the window rustling and fluttering with bright afternoon sunlight.

I was turning the page in a book by Mircea Eliade when as I reached for my teacup I missed it and stuck my finger in the cup rather than my hand around it and spilled it on the table. As I watched the tea stain the tablecloth, I realized (finally, I say to myself now, shaking my head in disbelief at my staggering opacity) that something was wrong, very off, utterly incongruous.

Philomena? Tea at the big breakfast table in our New Hampshire home? She couldn't be here with me now. She had been gone from the human realm for 32 years already, and I hadn't seen her in about that much time too. It wasn't divorce or death; she had left the planet and dropped her human body. The technical term for her transition is ascension; she turned her body into Light.

I heard some laughter and a trickle of applause, as if I had been a stage actor and had just delivered a punchline that predictably generated laughs and applause. Maybe they were applauding my awesome dexterity in fitting those numbers in, like I was a figure skater and I'd done a flawless triple toe loop.

I saw the hands coming together at the palms to make the clapping sounds, then I saw the faces full of mirth and attention, and then I saw the wings. And then I came back to myself. I snapped out of this fantastic

trance I'd been in. I recognized them: it was the Blaise angels, standing in their opera boxes more professionally known as the Cave Heaven cells in the gigantic Cave Heaven La Scala that surrounded where we were. Then I remembered where we were and who "we" were. I started to remember myself, who I was thought I actually was.

There was the human Blaise, studying me with interest and amusement. There was Ray Master Hermes, not exhibiting any kind of emotional reaction. And there were the alien gods just nimbly jumping back from my mind as I regained focus and I suppose like a riled up dog snarled at them to back off. That was nasty, I thought. I had not even noticed I had become entranced, that my attention had been deftly commandeered and rendered dopey and hallucinatory.

I hoped I hadn't screwed things up, that my shocking inattention hadn't allowed an undesirable egress into the system. I had felt the alien gods edging their awareness as close as possible to me where I stood within the number array. I knew their tactics, their intent, was to occupy the precise space I was standing in, which means, in practical terms, to occupy and dominate my consciousness and through that control the number sequences I was managing.

It was impossible to know how much time had passed. Aside from the human Blaise's slightly smirking expression, everything looked the same. Had he been the only one, besides his angelic counterparts, who had witnessed my distraction? The other five planetary representatives were still standing in place. Holograms of Sal and Jocelyn were still in attendance, and now I saw these five humanlike planetary representatives were flanked by two assistants as well. These assistants seemed to be providing numbers or pictures as required just as our Sal and Jocelyn were doing. It was as if they were holding the basic syntax required for the work of the geomancers, that of arithmetic and mythic images, that the two were not only complementary, but front and back of the same hand.

Ray Master Hermes stepped forward and started speaking. "The images and the numbers are both needed. They cross-explicate each other. The pictures show embodied consciousness paths and models for interaction, likely results. The numbers guide the geomancers and engineers in their maintenance work. These conditions are fairly constant across created planets. This is what the ancients meant when they attributed the arts and science of architecture to me. This is the inner, hermetic aspect of buildings, measurement, and geometry."

I have never found Ray Masters to be particularly personable or jokey. But I was sure I detected the slightest twinge of a grin when Hermes said "hermetic." I had a momentary amusing image flash through my mind: Ray Master Hermes walking around in a bulging green cloak made of the Emerald and packed with all the arcane codes of Creation stored in the Emerald Tablets, and him grinning. But I also saw something that took the grin off my face. I saw some of the planets these alien gods had destroyed by recalling their coding numbers, leaving those worlds withered and abandoned, the phylogenies they had derailed from their evolutionary course gone from the planet and set on regressive or recursive disembodied pathways or in many cases their evolution ended summarily.

It wasn't any of our six, though the troublemakers were continuously looking for inroads and weak spots in our respective planetary grid systems. I saw our five planetary colleagues vigilant and prepared for their insidious actions, and I saw them taking defensive, evasive, or misdirecting maneuvers. We could learn something from these elder planets on how to fend off the bad guys. The other planets I saw were not so fortunate. They were already ruined.

These planets had a different Light grid design, but I surmised that these designs began with an initial greater degree of limitation on mobility of consciousness. These structural limitations were instituted as necessary discipline for freshly incarnating consciousness, not in any way as a punitive measure, but more like guidelines, like a short leash for walking a frisky dog.

But the alien gods managed to convince the incarnating "humans" that they were prison bars and that they, the new intelligent life-forms, should rebel against this unwarranted, insulting incarceration. The aliens got the new "humans" to fight against their supportive, nurturing Light grid, to see it as jail bars; unfortunately, that was as ill-advised as a fetus fighting against the uterus and its mother while its body is still forming, when it still has seven months to get through before it can expect to be discharged into the phenomenal world.

Despite the validity of any political perspective, such as whether in fact the Light grid parameters were drawn too severely, this was a slow-motion suicidal act and it led to inevitable and dire consequences. The Light grid fractured, unraveled, slipped into entropic confusion and cognitive disarray. All the numbers got skewed, the algorithms ran amok, producing wrong results.

Maybe these are not the most precisely technical ways to describe the ruination of the planet I was watching, but something like this happened. Its grid fell apart. The "humans" walked about as if they had all sustained concussions that flowered into amnesia; they were forgetting who they were, walking about confused, in sensory disarray, in a burgeoning nightmare perception of reality.

Their planet was wobbling off its axis, its weather and climate now chaotic. It was as if the key that ran their consciousness and Light grid had been removed from the lock and they no longer could access their own Light grid to make the adjustments. They could not enter the system. They were locked out. It was like being barred from your office when you desperately needed access. You had to call the police, fire department, or paramedics and report a disaster, but they couldn't do anything: the programming algorithms had all been removed.

I saw another devastated planet, also designed for humanlike forms. Here the results were less overtly catastrophic, but more spiritually homicidal. The "people" were now living in a hallucination-modulated planetary reality. They were misperceiving almost every aspect of reality; their consciousness filters were skewed and off-center, covertly commandeered by the alien gods. It would be as if your television had captured your awareness and now ran it while you still assumed you were casually watching it for news or weather reports. What you were watching was controlling and altering what you thought you were watching; the "television" or Light grid became your eyes you used to see it.

Their Light grid was feeding them wrong information, misleading directives, and they did not realize it was carefully manipulating their lives. It was supposed to be midwifing their spiritual evolution; instead, it was stillbirthing it. It was worse than that. The people on that planet didn't know what was happening. They thought they were living healthy, productive lives, making steady gains in consciousness and in mastering its powers. That was a lie. The reality was they were living in a contrived dream world, all illusory. It was as if their consciousness had been covertly hijacked, relocated, and set into an artificial environment that simulated their original planet but was fraudulent. That is a terrible thing to do to incarnate consciousness and the souls in bodies.

The alien gods had taken that planet's managing algorithm and left the planet reeling. They didn't care; they never cared; they were unable to care. It was like pulling a pin that kept a planet steady; now it was reeling in the psychic version of gimbal lock. They wanted this planet's master algorithm to fill a cell in their master Magic Square, and they took it, and these were the consequences.

It reminded me of science fiction shows I had seen decades earlier in which automated spaceships start terraforming an entire planet, regardless of the presence of any life-forms. It looked ruthless, but from the computer's point of view, it was merely a logical necessity: this planet must be refashioned. I looked at Blaise. He was shaking his head, sharing my dismay at the travesty we saw.

I saw another planet that seemed to be spinning too fast. Everyone living on it showed signs of hyperactivity. Their body processes ran too fast, and their cognitive ones looked like they were in a perpetual sprint. Life was frenetic. Here the alien gods had turned up the planetary speed several notches by altering the ruling algorithm. I suppose from their point of view it was a valid experiment; from the vantage point of the embodied intelligence forms, it was a disaster they couldn't get out of. They were doing a Maldek number on them.

It was like being swamped by a tsunami every day. They couldn't leave the beach, and they couldn't drown, only be tidal-waved in a perpetual Groundhog Day of the same awful event. The alien gods didn't care. They probably fed the geomancers of that planet the same seductive lie they did on Maldek: let us speed up your planet's processes so you won't be so bored. I think their tactic was to speed up the spinning of the algorithm so it would break loose and spin off the planet and into their waiting collection box for the Magic Square.

My thoughts shifted back to something that had started to engage my attention before I saw the wreck of these three planets. Blaise knew these guys, the other geomancers and their assistants in this special Cave Heaven realm.

"Blaise, how did you ever meet these managers of the five planets? They are from worlds a vast distance from the Earth, right? Even in other galaxies."

"What you're really asking is how big is the Hierophancy's reach," he replied. "It extends through all created worlds and galaxies and has many branches. It's a kind of countermeasure installed with the generation of the planets. You need a maintenance system and a group of trained practitioners to look after these many sentient planets and their intelligent life-forms. Say you manufacture complicated heating systems for houses. You need to train people in how to fix these systems when they don't work correctly, which will happen.

"To answer your specific question, Ray Master Hermes made the introductions for me and over the years escorted me on focused diplomatic visits to many planets. I use the term 'diplomatic' with suitable irony. It's more like meeting colleagues and alumni from the same school. You already have a bond. We were all already members of what Ray Master Hermes no doubt will be pleased to hear us call his Transworld Hermetic Collegium. It was understood from the beginning, and I suppose I'm referring to the master designer here, Visvakarman, that planets would need maintenance and upgrades and that they would occasionally be the focus of targeted assaults and acquisitions like this.

"They would reach a point at which their master algorithms caught the interest of older intelligent life-forms who would have no scruples about acquiring them. These arithmetical thefts, or at least attempts at such, have been perennial. It's only recently that our Earth has fallen into this domain of targeted planets. The trouble is because Earth is one of these six specially endowed worlds with the optimal free-will quotient installed in their Light grids, the consequences of an inappropriate acquisition of our master algorithm are dire.

"That's why we're here, and why these other Hierophancy experts are here. Everything is intricately and intimately connected, as you know, part of the same vast pattern, so the outcome of this investigation into the arithmetical theft from the Earth has consequences throughout the complete planetary pattern."

Blaise looked at me, a slight grin on his face, and asked me an odd question. "Tell me, Frederick old pal, what do you remember of any of this?"

The question was odd because I didn't understand what my memory had to do with this theft or our investigation, and, for that, I wasn't remembering much at all. How could I remember an event that was only happening right now? As usual, Blaise had deftly confused me with a single sentence. Well played, old pal yourself. Still, I felt something stirring in me, like an old motor that hasn't been turned on for a long time but still, surprisingly, works and turns over and hums.

Everyone seemed to be looking at me. Sal and Jocelyn were staring at me. Blaise cocked his head slightly and watched me. What was I supposed to recall?

I started to see images of Light grids. I laughed at first. They looked like screen doors, hundreds of them, probably many thousands, stuck into large bins the way painters would stack finished canvases before preparing them for an exhibit. Such a diversity of patterns, such complex geometric forms. A Light grid, after all, is a geometrical pattern, as is a screen door with its tiny squares comprising the screen; they make a simple *x-y* axis, the basis of the grid.

Numbers swirled around in these grids like swallows looping through barns. Designs for consciousness, scripts for evolution of self-awareness, patterns and processes that would contribute to the awakening of the universal Cosmic Man. The screen-door grids flashed their scripted Light like bright garish signs. Arising out of each numbered grid pattern was a face in Light, representative of the achieved, awakened state of that planet's phylogeny and cosmic seed origin. Here was the face of the fulfillment of that planet's Light grid and phylogeny, the self-aware consciousness "product" generated by the planet's mathematics.

You can see I was impressed with what I saw and that I readily sensed the implications. I found myself rooting through these many Light grids as if I were a wealthy, discriminating art buyer selecting the next treasure for my personal art gallery. I still didn't know what I was looking for specifically, why Blaise expected me to pull something important out of this picture hunt. I did not recognize nearly all of these picture displays; they were the faces of exotic life-forms though I appreciated amidst their diversity the similarity of life purpose. Wake up, become self-aware, unify your planet, join the cosmic conversation. And try to avoid the grasping fingers of these algorithm-stealing alien gods. That was the mandate justifying and directing the existence of these many forms.

As I was rummaging through these Light patterns, I felt less like an art buyer and more like somebody with a faulty memory trying to remember where I put an important item, and, embarrassingly, I can't remember what it is. I felt the attention of my colleagues on me, Blaise, Sal, Jocelyn. The Ray Master too though he was discretely hiding it by appearing to be looking out elsewhere or meditating or looking cosmically regal. Did he just wink at me?

The Blaise angels in the massive Cave Heaven that framed us were watching me intently like I was a favored player in a chess tournament and they'd bet heavily on the outcome and eagerly awaited my next move. Make it a smart one. Checkmate those irritating mathematics fuckers. I doubt they really thought this, but it amused me to think it. I did feel I was losing this chess match. I won't even mention again the steady pressure of the fate of the universe apparently resting on the outcome of my fevered, amnesiac search in the files. And I was looking through files of Light grid paintings by artists I didn't know.

Then I saw something, finally. I didn't know if it was what I was looking for, if you can tolerate the ambiguity of that. It looked like a seed. It was small, dark, and tightly packed with content. It was like a plant seed, but it was not. I thought my mind was just being clever or maybe it was slurring its speech when it announced, "This is a planet seed." I picked one up and examined it. I saw an entire planet and its Light grid inside it, as if it had been radically miniaturized.

I realized it had not been rendered small. It started out tiny and was waiting to be expanded to full size. This was the germplasm for a planet. It was the planetary equivalent of the genome script for a human or any life-form you'd find on Earth, its complete genetic code plus the intended outcome, expressed fully but in a tiny form, yet you could see what it would unfold into, the *eidolon* all this genetic scripting was intended to produce, its mature planetary face.

The surprising vista didn't end there. There were thousands of such seeds in this "bin" that I was rummaging through. Now I saw them displayed like colored beads on a single, vast necklace worn by the Supreme Being and with a smile. I disbelieved my impression at first. It seemed too improbable, too whimsical. The Supreme Being, ultimate Creator of everything, had made all these colored beads, each a planet germplasm, and now in an arts-and-crafts-flourish of cozy domestic design, He had strung

them appealingly to make a folksy necklace to wear. For some reason Blaise was laughing enthusiastically.

"All He needs is a tie-dyed shirt and alfalfa sprouts hanging off His beard and He'd be a perfect rendition of an early 1970's hippie back-to-the-lander."

It sounded a bit irreverent, though I took Blaise's point. Personally, I couldn't remember any of that as I had been born in the late 1970s, but Blaise would have been a man in his mid-twenties and lived through it, beards, sprouts, and all. The Supreme Being did look a bit like He'd just wandered in from a country commune. His necklace of planet seeds was draped over His lengthy beard and He was grinning. Was He parodying a 1970's hippie? I shook my head. Surely I was concocting this picaresque image myself. The Old Boy must have some *gravitas*.

I knew from my professional academic studies years ago the Creator could not have any fixed form or image, that all you could have was God-images, as C. G. Jung once put it, metaphorical renditions of only minute aspects of the Ultimate Presence that at best poorly suggested aspects of an infinite existence. Tie-dyed tee-shirt, hippie-style scruffy beard, and a copiously beaded necklace? No way. Yet the human Blaise had always remarked that the Supreme Being had a great sense of humor, liked jokes, just like the Blaise angels, that it runs in the family. Was the Old Man, the Ofanim's Dad, spoofing Himself?

I tried to put the whimsy aside and get back to the serious matter at hand. I also tried to not look at Blaise who was putting forth a very competent smirk. Even at age 115, he was still an inveterate, dependably snickering smart-ass.

I probably haven't made this part clear yet. These planet seeds were at the center of each Light grid design, the ones I first referred to as being like screen doors stored in bins you'd expect to hold finished art canvases. With the seed at the center of the Light pattern, it changed the shape to more like a vortex with the seed at its bottom, though functionally the Light pattern emerged from the seed, and its arising itself shaped the vortex walls. You could see the fully expressed planet in each seed.

Each one I looked at, even for only an instant, yielded an immediate full-bodied image of the completed planet, its dominant intelligence-bearing life-form, and its intended face, what on Earth we call its Albion, our cosmogonic Human. All the numbers, the algorithms we were obsessing about, were implicit in the seed. No, it's more subtle than that. The numbers were identical with the concentrated design and planetary genomic script; the numbers were its "flesh."

It was reassuring to know that at this level a planet was entirely inviolate, immune to any machinations or acquisitions by these insidious alien gods. But somewhere between this inviolate stage and the extrapolation of the germplasm into Light and physical flowering a planet was susceptible to their interference. That was the crucial interface where a planet's intended direction could be hijacked and redirected, or its algorithm extracted and the planet abandoned. That was where I would have to be especially careful, even circumspect, in handling any of the Light designs, including Earth's, to not expose it to them. I wasn't sure I would be able to touch these planet seeds anyway. They were emitting a strong energy, throbbing with power and Supreme Being essence.

I am up against a fundamental Mystery here. What does the Supreme Being feel like, if you were able to nudge your attention right up against a manifestation of His Presence? That's what I was confronted with in these planet seeds, fistfuls of Supreme Being primordial essence, the potency of pure Light. You can see why these germplasm cores were utterly inviolate. Even the "good guys" can't touch them; we can only witness their power and original purity.

Mimicking Jimmy Durante's famous 1929 quip about his endless supply of corny jokes, the Supreme Being says of His planet seed designs, "I've got a million of 'em." He's not kidding. Here they all are, millions of fully executed designs for planets and their intelligent, flowering, self-aware life-forms, such as humans. Here was Earth's, like an ultrasound impression of a fetus, the plan for the arising of consciousness on our home planet and how we got to the present moment, laid out in advance like a flow-chart. Could we enter this planet seed?

Before I had any time to consider this question, I was already inside the seed. I guess Blaise took me by the elbow and escorted me into it. Instantly, we were bodies of fire, our forms consumed with blazing white flames, yet not burning us up the way fire burns wood, but more like a permanent condition. I was inside the planet's life-story, beginning, middle, and end, its final destiny. All that was implicit in here, extrapolated in holographic miniature. Here are the briefing papers for Albion, the classified file he can read when he fully wakes up.

I saw that our Earth was based on the planet seed design of Maldek. We knew that, although I was seeing the truth of that now revealed in staggering detail. What I didn't know was that the Maldek design had antecedents in the plans for the other five free-will-bearing planets, as if they formed a stepped pyramid of intention and execution and the Earth's planet seed was its latest permutation. I saw the tiers of the arithmetical cascade that started with these earlier planets and culminated in the bold experiment known as planet Earth.

"You see what comes next," said Blaise. "We have to go back to that first planet, the original attempt. Study its design and find the hidden egress points."

5

It wasn't just Blaise and myself who would make the journey to the original planet. Two representatives from each of the other five would come too. I hadn't noticed they were standing inside the planet seed in bodies of white fire. We were in this together. I don't mean just the blazing planet seed. I mean in the predicament of the arithmetical assault on our planets' master algorithms. The outcome of that destabilizing action directly affected their planets and people.

We would be a traveling, fact-finding group of 18, as the Ray Master Hermes would accompany us, in search of a key to preserve the integrity of the Earth. We comprised the four of us, Hermes, and 13 of our extra-planetary colleagues from the five planets, but if you added the Ofanim, the number was suddenly huger. Where did the 13 come from? For the five compatible planets, three had one representative, one had two, and the last had sent eight people. My blurry vision had finally cleared and I could count how many colleagues we had.

There was an alpha and omega aspect to our expedition. We, as the representatives of Earth, the most recent expression of the algorithm of free will, stood at one end of this continuum. The planet we proposed to visit was at the other, and it was the source or first expression of this complicated set of numbers. Mathematicians will wince at the technical incorrectness of this, but in a sense, this first planet's arithmetical design was the square root of Earth's algorithm. Multiply this planet's number set by itself and you get the Earth's.

In this first planet we should expect to see the core arithmetical and design features that led to, were extrapolated into, Earth's lushly complex Light pattern. If I were to liken this to a detective's case investigation, this was perhaps like interviewing the suspect's grandfather to get a character reference and family background. Yes, detective, it's true, our grandson may be a billionaire, but we started out as humble immigrants with one ragged suitcase and a poor command of English, but with a strong belief in the necessity to stand in the truth, to always speak the truth, and to demand the same from people we meet. What I mean here is that possibly in examining this first planet with its simpler, straightforward free-will design, we'll be able to identify traction points for potential hostile acquisition that are harder to see in the more complex Earth.

I asked Blaise why it was necessary for the "people" from the other five planets to join us in this investigation. Did the outcome matter to their planets?

"Very much so," Blaise replied. "The cascade effect works in both directions, from the first planet outward to Earth and from Earth back to it. The six planets, because they share this unique design imperative, are fully linked. Despite the great physical distances between these six planets, they comprise a collective Light grid. Their individual Light grids are part of a larger single one. The theft of our algorithm is bringing this pre-existing linkage of the six planets into visibility. It has always existed, of course, but this event emphasizes it. Anything affecting the Earth, its Light grid and mathematics, immediately transfers these effects to the other five and precipitates a cascade of more effects.

"You can see then how if you extract a key mathematical component from one planet, it destabilizes the complete six-planet Light grid. It's then in the best interests, no argument, for the other five planets to help remedy the theft. Their well-being is jeopardized, and the quality of collective consciousness, what you might call the higher octave of the six planets constituting a single flavor of consciousness, is in turn thrown into peril. So Earth has five stalwart colleagues. We're all part of this linked system and have been since we were first designed."

"Is there a master algorithm that manages this collective of six?" I asked.

"Indeed there is," Blaise said. "That algorithm coordinates the cascade of interactions among the six. Earth's algorithm is a subset of that larger one, which means the master one has a kind of antecedent seniority and mathematical primacy that might prove helpful to us in retrieving and reinstituting Earth's. You can derive Earth's heuristic algorithm by working down or backwards

from the one that runs the Light grid of the six planets. What is missing from our system is implicit in this larger calculation, assuming the alien gods didn't get to it. I'm pretty sure they should be unable to hack into this algorithm. I hope so."

Blaise's little tag of doubt at the end of his sentence disturbed me. It felt like a black cloud suddenly appearing on the horizon. I hoped he was wrong.

"Do you realize that this is not just about capturing a planet," Blaise was saying. Somehow I missed a transition for I found I was now sitting at a large table with Blaise and the other 13 planetary representatives and the Ray Master. "It is about acquiring an arithmetical slot in the mathematical matrix of Creation. If this were a roulette wheel, it would be equivalent to owning a slot, like red 12. The physical planet itself, even its Light grid, would be of secondary importance.

"You would now hold the copyright on all expressions of this specific numeration. If the alien gods succeeded (or had they already?) in acquiring Earth's 'red 12,' it would mean they also had gained strong options on the slots of the other five number categories and control of their respective planets. Then all six free-will planets would be in jeopardy, if not already badly compromised, or worse. That is a potentially disastrous outcome we must strive to prevent."

As we sat at the table I saw that the room was enveloped by a complicated Light grid, as if sketched in the air itself. I surmised it was the geometric pattern formed by the intricate relationships among the six planets, their individual planetary Light grids integrated into the composite pattern for the six. There was something curious and intriguing about this display. From where I sat, the Earth's grid was predominant, as if written in brightly flashing neon ink.

When I moved my attention to where the next person was sitting (this proved remarkably easy: our awareness was terrifically adroit in here), the grid pattern for that planet was now highlighted and the patterns of the other five took on a secondary role, as if they were functional subsets of this major one. The array seemed a variation on the classic geometer's nesting of the five Platonic Solids, a complicated but geometrically rational display of these elemental forms.

I doubted whether many people on the Earth today know our planet is inextricably part of this geometric array of five other planets, however distant. I didn't know until this moment, though Blaise probably did. Earth's destiny, humanity's future as a free-will-endowed species, is tied up with the fate of five other planets that nobody on Earth has heard of and which lie light-years away. Let me emphasize we're probably talking up to billions of light-years away. Not too long ago the furthest known galaxy from us lay 13.4 billion light-years distant, and our five collegial planets are positioned across this universe of galaxies like single bright buttons on a vast cloth spanning all these light-years. I am guessing the light-years, but I'm certain they are a great distance away.

On the other hand, this pre-existing bond means we have five staunch allies to count on in times of peril, such as now, when the alien gods steal our algorithms. The consciousness gradient we share among the six of us, as planets, means we can expect near instantaneous telepathic presence despite the vast physical distances involved. That's why we appeared together in this room. Wherever all of us actually, in a bodily sense, were, was of no consequence. I sat there and marveled at the ramifications of this secret arrangement. I didn't realize how entranced I had gotten in my thinking until Blaise rapped the table.

I have given the initial impression that these 13 extra-planetary colleagues had humanlike forms. I started to realize that was an illusion, though it was a semblance not meant to fool me but rather to reassure me of collegiality. The physical conditions of their planets were radically different than ours, so the structure of their life-forms had to be comparably different too, as what the ordinary human mind would consider excessively exotic or, frankly, alarming. No matter how egalitarian we might feel, bodily otherness can be discomfiting. Even seeing the Pleiadians, who were basically larger human-type beings with huge heads, was startling; I felt my own body cringe a little at their strangeness.

I couldn't see what their true forms were, and probably if I had it would have been disturbing. That meant, logically, they were not seeing my actual human form for the same reason, but a plausible likeness congruent with their planet. The same exchange pertained to language and probably thoughts as well; there must be a cognitive translation program running for us to understand one another both in terms of visual appearance and communication language.

Free will is a generic condition with constants that will transfer across phylogeny borders, but language and thoughts that express that will differ greatly. Still, we were all accredited members of the Hierophancy and here we were working on the ramifications of a vexing and serious problem. It was humbling to realize my human form, so familiar, so taken for granted on the Earth, might be a source of cognitive disturbance to differently constituted souls.

I assessed our situation. The alien gods appeared to have stolen our algorithm by accessing the various traction points that secure it to successive operational levels. We don't know where they "put" it, though that of course is too physical a way of expressing the problem. I suppose they put it in their master Magic Square, but as I said it is not as discrete as hiding a single equation. They hadn't stolen the algorithms of the other five free-will planets, but their well-being and arithmetical integrity were jeopardized by Earth's new condition. The mathematical design and function of our six planets were interdependent. I had a sudden hunch that maybe there was an opening for us in that linkage.

"Blaise, is there a kind of mathematical link between the six algorithms?"

Blaise turned to the Ray Master who nodded, then said, "It is too complex to explain here, but let me say by way of simplification that each planet's master algorithm has some elements, certain integers and their functions, that are equivalent to those in the algorithms of the other planets. Think of these equivalencies as overlap nodes. These equivalency nodes provide the implicit linkages. They are the mathematical equivalent of grace notes in music or hypertexting data-sets, hidden but accessible backdoors that get you from one algorithm to the next. Or more simply, they are like stones laid across a pond.

"If this were cryptography, you'd say each had embedded in it certain key integers, perhaps a digit cluster that had a repeating size or that repeatedly appeared, enough so that an attentive cryptographer would notice these arithmetical plants. These hidden cryptic identifiers, for the moment, are still inviolate. They have not been interfered with. That is largely because in the design of your six species and their corresponding Light grids for the planets these secret backdoors were encoded as a backup in your DNA. Not exactly your physical genomic script, but an etheric, parallel, higher-frequency version of it."

"We need to access that secret node within us," said Blaise, his gaze sweeping across the table to include the planet representatives. "All of us must."

We set to it. It was like meditating, or maybe it was more like highly concentrated thinking. It vaguely reminded me of the focused atmosphere in a classroom when it was examination time, all the students furrowing brows and clenching their minds to recall the correct information or formulate their critical thoughts. I had the impression of the 17 of us rummaging through hundreds of file cabinets in our minds, pulling out folders, surveying our genomic script, scrolling through the 3.2 billion nucleotides that comprise the human genes to find the crucial linkages, the veiled repeated digit patterns encoded in this.

I didn't know how many nucleotides our extra-planetary colleagues would have to sort through, though I was finding the job not overwhelming, as I would have expected. It was like going through a sack of marbles in which only one marble would be lit up like a flashing neon globe. It shouldn't be that hard to find the one marble that was pulsing out bright Light. The marbles were pretty. It was pleasant to look at them, to examine these bright genetic scripts.

We had an additional factor working in our favor. I just noticed it. The Elohim. The master designers of the genomic script for humanity and the other five phylogenies whose representatives sat with us at the Hierophancy table. The Elohim designed the template that matches species with their Light grid, and that meant they knew all the specifics of the geomantic "nucleotides" and where that buried arithmetical backdoor lay within the vast coding array of these different nitrogenous combinations.

I saw that many Elohim surrounded our table and stood in front of their characteristic cobalt blue monolithic pillars that you see at their citadels. That's the architectural name Blaise assigned to their planetary residences, although to call them residences can be misleading. They are Light citadels, and they don't live there, because angels don't have to live anywhere, but they are for humans places to meet with their phylogenic designers and get useful briefings. I presume that for the Elohim these sites are also focal points and entry nodes for their continuing work on Earth's Light grid and template. To be blushingly simplistic about it, that's where they keep their screwdrivers and duct tape.

Here's something you need to understand about the Elohim: their name. According to the Blaise angels, the Elohim are the many forms of *AL*, or *EL*, a name denoting a creative potency capable of generating a multiplicity of forms. Qabalists will tell you *AL* is the God-Name for the *Sefira* called *Chesed*, which corresponds with the human crown chakra, and it is an expansive realm, what astrologers would probably call Jupiterian in the lushness of its abundance.

The Elohim are the form makers, the template designers, planet Light grid installers. They make the forms, they wear the forms, they compose the forms out of *AL*. The many worlds are full of their *AL*-infused forms, even our *AL*bion, dear old boy. He has the Elohim signature in his form too. I counted 30 of them standing a short distance from us in a circle around our table. They looked like a majestic combination of human and angel, expressing both human genders in a generic form in body appearance but strongly humanlike in tone and valence. They were tall, regal, serene, attentive, kings and queens out of the oldest myths.

These were the creative intelligences who designed everything geomantic and megalithic, including all of the Earth's stone circles and rows, including the pre-eminent ones at Avebury, in Wiltshire, England, standard holder for the megalithic yard, the basic principle of measurement for all geomantic features. They were the clever ones who worked the higher mathematics behind the stone circles, not some plucky Neolithic potato farmers who stacked big stones on the weekends. If you want to know why the Avebury circle is the standard for this mathematical value and where the megalithic yard (about 2.72 feet, virtually identical with *e*, which is 2.711828…to infinity) came from in the first place, ask the nearest Elohim. They have all the mathematics at their mental fingertips.

They are the Light grid's pre-eminent mathematicians and geometers. I fantasized them with front shirt pockets stuffed with compasses and slide rules, very 1950's-style brainiacs, maybe thick black glasses pinching their nose bridges. Predictably, they would run their calculations instantaneously in their minds, the roster of mathematical and physical constants at hand, all this data displayed on endless aisles of poster boards parading across their mental space.

My point here is that the geomantic template is arithmetical, as well as genetic and pictorial, and the Elohim are adept at any matters involving mathematical complexity, along with these other two categories. They even stood for photographs now and then in various cultures, those old images appearing as mythic fragments of giants, Cyclopes, and ancient Earth shapers and builders. Now they stood around us, acutely attentive, all their pencils sharpened.

Another thing it is useful to know about the Elohim is their television. That was the human Blaise's whimsical reference to a kind of fourth-dimensional viewing screen the Elohim use to run multiple permutations of likely scenario outcomes. I don't know how they do this on other planets, and I presume in their primary angelic state, they do not require any interface to perform these variations, but on the Earth they created 6,300 cyclopean stone constructions. You see remnants of some of these in the stone ruins at Baalbek, the Wailing Wall in Jerusalem, and the big stones at Peru's Sacsayhuaman, Mycenae, and Tiryns. These function as the screens for what I lamely or whimsically call Elohim TV.

The term "cyclopean" comes from the archeologists because myths attribute the construction of these features to the mythic Cyclopes, giant in stature, except, naturally, the archeologists don't believe that for a second.

They just like the name for these; they'll take the literary allusion but not the fact. Cute metaphors are okay, but God protect us from any metaphysical truth lurking behind them. That would be disastrous to our intellectual edifices. Still, they have no sensible theories for how these huge stones got moved into place. The ancient myths use Occam's Razor: big people, giants, carried the big stones. Scientists, though they affirm this principle as the bedrock of the scientific bedrock, run as fast as possible away from any of its metaphysical conclusions.

These sites consist of massive piled stones that form what seem to look like enclosed spaces roughly the size of large buildings as we know them today. It's *as if*, the archeologists daringly propose, they were built by antediluvian giants, you know, the ones with a single large round eye ("Cyclopes"), just as Homer described them. Surely, they were big and strong enough to heft those huge stones. But if course we do not credit that childish myth with any factuality for a second; no, it's only a quaint old belief. Cyclopes never existed, God knows.

Except they did, and still do. They were standing around us. There are two key facts you need to know about the Elohim: first, the single round eye business. That means they never lose sight of unitive consciousness, all chakras are fused into one, or the original unified perception unfallen and fragmented into the multiplicity of chakras we take for granted. That's their single round eye. It comprises the 49 aspects of all seven chakras and their nuances fused into one.

Another way of accounting for the single round eye, as Blaise told me, is that all seven chakras associated with the physical body merge into the sixth chakra, the one of psychic sight in the forehead. The potential perceptions and powers of the seven chakras and their 50 petals or wheel spokes are rolled into a single round eye that sees all reality from a condition of unitive consciousness, not separate from God, not fragmented into the insect-style distributed sight of the seven chakras and that we take for granted, paradoxically, when we have mostly forgotten the chakras even exist. That fullness of one eye is the cyclopean perception; all the Elohim have it because they are Cyclopes. It's something humans can look forward to reacquiring at some not distant point.

Second, they were for a time actual physical giants standing 18 feet tall. This largesse was commissioned by the Supreme Being and their size was required by the work and for their safety. The angelic Blaises once vaguely hinted it was because of the dinosaurs. Some were quite large and apparently ill-behaved and not socially well-adjusted. So if you stand 18 feet tall and probably weigh 2,000 pounds, even if you're lean, you are unlikely to be intimidated by any pre-existing indigenous cranky large animals on the order of dinosaurs or other antediluvian monstrosities of matter and animality with poor social skills.

It's funny because the mythic allegation is so simple, so childishly stark, and completely true. The giants did build all the megalithic features including all the cyclopean walls and buildings, ruins of which still lie in heaps across the Earth. These were products of the Elohim long ago terraforming the planet and setting up the basic geomantic and megalithic infrastructure, the mysteries of which we now live in. They never had to lift a single stone either; another advantage of this unified round-eye business is you can move stones with your mind alone. They used these structures, the massive, shaped stones, perfectly fitted despite their tonnage (some at 15 tons), places still extant as ruins, as a flat-screen TV to view permutations of likely outcomes of varying reality alignments.

I mention this because the Elohim were watching their 4D television now. We were too. They were flipping the channels, so to speak, letting us witness the many different scenarios they had studied, accounted for, and included in their design package in a manner that suggested parentheses or perhaps footnotes. Here are the probable outcomes when the algorithm is discovered and used properly; here when it remains hidden and the planet drifts unattended; here where the algorithm has been discovered, used, then taken off the playing field. They even had probability simulations for precisely right now, the Hierophancy representatives from the six free-will planets meeting here to fix the problem of the conjoint algorithms that run our planetary Light grids being in jeopardy.

Hebrew letters swirled around their heads like enthusiastic birds. These letters were on fire, or maybe they were fire itself, shaped into alphabet forms. The Elohim around us were using these fire-letters to create shapes and patterns, as if the letters were building blocks like atoms constituting the emerging forms. They were directing this creative deployment of fire-letters with a massive upright sword of Light. It was as tall as a tower and the Light cast was brilliant.

I wouldn't say that I saw any of the Elohim holding this sword. Rather, it appeared that the sword was an expression among them of their own sharp concentration. It was mind-generated and directed the letters. They manifested themselves as this sword and it was flashing out letters and forms. They were building Light temples, architectural spaces made from these letters, with the easy fluidity of accomplished chefs following their own tested recipes, their hands and minds moving in complete assurance and certainty as to results.

"Why are they doing this?" I asked Blaise. I noticed the other planetary representatives were watching this creative spectacle with rapt attention.

"Watch," replied Blaise, frustratingly enigmatic from my point of view.

Numbers, equations, and algorithms started appearing within these forms, not as content but more as the "bony" structure of the Light temples. The buildings looked substantial, despite the paradox of being made of the subtlest casting of Light, yet they were also clearly compounded of number sequences.

Then I remembered the Qabalists say each of the letters is also a number, as if the reverse side of each fire-letter shape has a number written on it. That is too spatially literal; it is more that the number and letter occupy the same space, and these "hands" of letters and numbers were weaving a vast tapestry-like shape before us. It was as if an endless supply of long elegant hands with nimble fingers were putting together a complex form in Light of letters and numbers.

The resulting pattern was a bizarrely beautiful weave of equations and letters. Even stranger, the letters were speaking, sounding their own Hebrew names, and this generated more letters and numbers as they spelled out these spoken names. That was strange and arresting; it meant when I heard the letter *Bayt*

(for the English "b", pronounced BETT), I was hearing the digit 2 intoned. It also meant God is still pronouncing or singing the infinity of letters-numbers in *pi*. It was an aria that would never end, at least not before this Age of Brahma was concluded and the *prima* baritone lay down for His songless *Pralaya* nap.

This combined pattern kept cascading out in further iterations of itself, numbers and letters singing a lovely duet or maybe one voice with an octaval echo. Qabalists who delight in permutation studies would surely revel in this bewildering display. They might squirm a little, as I was, at the sound effects. It was a hall of echoes as names pronounced themselves in a waterfall of digits. It was as if every conceivable permutation of letters-numbers was spelled out in this cascade, and that meant somewhere in this riot of names was Earth's own algorithm presumably in its pristine, original condition, before it was stolen.

As soon as I thought that, I saw a complicated math formula highlighted. It was as if it was suddenly surrounded in flashing neon. That was ours, our precious "rock," now lying visibly and recognizably amidst this river of "rocks." Everything our algorithm specified was shown linked with it in a grid pattern. This was the core design of the Earth in a mathematical sense, brightly revealed as if under a strong spotlight. I saw its implicit connections to the grids of the other five free-will planets, all of this a secret pattern of relationships, secret in the sense that unless highlighted like this, it would be immersed in the richness of possible grid patterns, this vast arithmetical torrent of design ideas. But here's the surprising thing: our Earth algorithm was changing itself.

That is the meaning of the descriptive term heuristic. It is capable of learning and adjusting itself. That's what I saw it doing. In algorithmic terms, it was generating new number specifications for extending its processes, but in visual terms it looked like a tree sprouting branches and new leaf patterns. As I mentioned earlier, as far as I could tell, our algorithm was not an artificial intelligence, but it appeared to be perhaps just one step short of that. It was deliberately, purposefully constructing new applications of its basic program, modulating its arithmetical "product" to meet the changing circumstances.

One of these circumstances was the encroachment of the alien gods trying to steal it. The algorithm was not recursively, contemplatively self-aware, regarding its own awareness as a self-existing unit of consciousness observing itself; it was one level below that lucidity, doing its actions in a pre-coded mechanical manner. It was adjusting its outputs in response to evaluations of constantly though minutely modulating circumstances. Except the alien gods' intrusion was a major circumstance, requiring big adjustments in the numbers.

It seemed like a crazy idea, but I wondered if we could communicate with it. I didn't have the impression, yet, that this algorithm was self-aware, only that it was a very efficient adapter and was rewriting some of its operating code to better fit the reality modulations appearing around it. But it had some awareness. I saw the Elohim, their quick, protean, and endlessly creative minds, within it, and I saw the infinite Mind of the Supreme Being within that agile mentality. The numbers and letters and everything you can do with them, the realities you can generate, all derive from this Mind and thereby carry its watermark within them.

I had a kind of whimsical picture of this Mind being like a large country estate, the Elohim its architects and building maintenance crew, and the algorithm its staff, butlers, valets, maids, cooks, and the rest, keeping the place in top form. The realities of the many planets and their Light grids and the types of intelligent life-forms occupying those created worlds were the weekend guests.

I don't know how I did it, but now I found myself inside the algorithm. My mind, my attention, wore it like a complex glove, one designed for somebody with a thousand fingers. I realized that not only was this algorithm awesomely and instantly responsive to changing conditions, it was proactive, ahead of them. It seemed to anticipate reality modulations in advance and make adjustments before these modulations even arose, thereby short-circuiting their unbalancing effects. The algorithm's proactive nimbleness rendered it predictive. The inevitable next step was that this algorithm was starting to direct outer reality, to shape and influence it and in many cases suppress its incipient modulations using the speed of its predictive capacity to adjust reality before it happened.

It's as if it stifled the wobbling and wriggling in reality that would lead to a change. It was starting to take charge. Not only was it regulating its own affairs, namely, those of the host planet's Light grid, it was managing the planet's embedded context, the source of all perturbances, and quelling them before they even arose. It had taken on a management role and was handling it capably. It seemed to be running reality permutation scenarios and timeline projections like the Elohim, extrapolating logical and likely outcomes given a variable set of factors, then adjusting its algorithmic parameters to accommodate those projected changes. It was doing this exceedingly fast, like a hyperdrive game of ping-pong or seemed like a superfast game of chess played against itself.

I next saw that this constantly "dancing" algorithm was linked with another one, like adjacent 4D snowflakes. I realized I had been seeing only the Earth's controlling algorithm, but I was reminded the six planets have a shared overarching algorithm and I was starting to see its outline. I'm struggling for suitable visual metaphors here. If I said it was like watching six expert figure skaters all doing triple toe loops at once, landing in such a way that they held hands and continued pirouetting, would that help convey the idea?

The six planetary algorithms were generating patterns out of themselves. Each algorithm was a Light grid and this spawned billions of copies of the dominant phylogeny the Light grid served. In the case of the Earth, it was humans, generically portrayed as a seemingly endless unfolding of identical forms. It reminded me of when children cut paper dolls then unfold them and you have a line of 50. Here it numbered in the billions. I saw the same with the other five planets, as their dominant consciousness-holding species was represented in vast numbers of identical forms. The planet's algorithm was keeping all of this in motion, alive and responsive, and the master algorithm kept the six in animated motion. The numbers were running the planetary shows.

I have only described the "show" as it pertains to the six free-will planets. As complex as this display was, it was only a minute portion of the complete array within the Elohim's presentation. There were millions of other similar Light patterns being run by numbers and their algorithmic processes. I think I was glad at the time that I was not able to focus on these others in much detail. Even this briefest of glimpses of this arithmetical universe was overwhelming. But it gave me a glimpse of what you could do with unitive consciousness.

Let me spin you around even further, as I was spinning around upon realizing this, and say these algorithms were self-learning, adapting and refocusing according to new input. Which meant the universe, certainly our tiny six-planet section of it, was in constant dynamic motion and change, upgrading itself following a primal mandate to stay current and on top of changing status.

I had never seen anything like this, it was so complex, yet so full of primal life. The master algorithm for these six planets kept track of the changes the algorithms for the individual planets were making and made adjustments on that basis. The result was you had local planet and system-wide modulations as the need arose. The representatives of the other five planets were inside this complex arithmetical weave of instantaneous adjustments just as myself and Blaise were, and it was as if we were both still and observant, watching this frenetic but perfectly controlled dance of adjustments and being at their heart as well, as if it were our hands, made of equations, our minds made of numbers, that executed these minute and sequential changes within the deepest core of reality—actually, it was in the deepest core of ourselves too, as Blaise had said.

I stood inside the master controlling algorithm, the one that oversaw the operations of the six in this special linkage. Then I was standing on its planet. This meta-algorithm seemed to have its own home base, like a planet or perhaps actually a planet, from which it ran the arithmetical operations of the six others. I wouldn't have expected this, under normal embodied conditions, but as I stood on the surface of this truly foreign planet I could see its controlling algorithm wrapped around it, dancing, weaving, turning inside out, parading its numbers. Vigorous, shape-shifting, expertly under control, an arithmetical atmosphere—it was the life-script of this planet, its consciousness body expressed in numbers.

The numbers were not only above me, like arithmetical clouds of processes. I saw that this number matrix extended throughout the volume of the planet. It was continuously generating and regulating all aspects of this world's reality, managing the spectrum of its life from consciousness to material expression. Seen at this level, the planet was a unified field of algorithmic processes. This was the mathematical heart of the outer physical manifestation of the planet. If you asked what is the true nature of this world, the answer would be its numbers.

I could compare this revelation of bedrock function to walking around in a human body and being able all the time to see your internal organs and bones as you move. That would probably unnerve most people, myself included. Still, it is the truth about our body. Here the perpetual disclosure was of the number scripts running your reality. You lived here within a finely calibrated reality marked by the inexorably intelligent mechanism of arithmetical calculations.

I thought about how some people would regard that disclosure as cold and chilling, reality run by an abstract intelligence, but I was cheered to see the rationality behind all existent phenomena. I much preferred knowing reality was implicitly intelligent, that rationality was a quality that thoroughly permeated all spectra of existence, from the overly physical to the subtlest design layer. That implied (maybe it proved) purpose, design, intention, and good will. The dark side of this same fact was that this arithmetical matrix could be hacked. You could gain unlawful backdoor entry into its number calculations and change them or remove a few or substitute some others. Play rationality against itself.

It was a rational plan from a rational designer for a rational purpose, even if all this expanded our model of rationality into areas we never suspected could be explored. In that world the framework of rationality is bounded by the Hermetic Axioms, which given half a chance, will rewrite everything that passes for science and reframe how we view reality. Not being sure of these underlying rationality factors undermines the mental poise and certainty of many people, and what passes for official orthodox science is a child's caricature of the truth.

Still, this raises a question. What does consciousness want? What is the point of this constant concatenation of starting circumstances? Why bother? Why did the Supreme Being commission the Elohim to generate individual units of awareness and set them within this constantly fluctuating arithmetical world? What did the Old Man expect us, anyone, to do? Why not keep things in stasis?

Reality may be saturated with rationality, but the Chief Designer is still an enigma. His motives for creating consciousness-bearing life-forms like humans are still a Mystery of the first rank. Possibly the only way to get an answer, the answer itself, is to return to the Supreme Being, pass back through the Throne. Then you'll be anchored again in the Mind of God and presumably understand. You may forget you even had the question; you're being immersed in the full briefing package, the Official Explanation for everything, all questions answered.

It reminded me of when I was a teenager, maybe 14, arguably not the most polished of ages for a maturing consciousness. I would lie on my bed and stare at the ceiling, an open book placed on my chest where I had put it moments ago when I took a break from reading. My parents would look in to my room and tell me to go outside and play baseball, run around, meet my friends, do something. Why? I didn't see how that would be any improvement over what I was doing, just another flavor of distraction, keeping me from answering this fundamental question: What was I supposed to do with this consciousness and whose end product apparently is myself earnestly asking this question?

So now I was standing amidst the arithmetical mechanisms of this consciousness. I was inside the machinery that maintained awareness and a world for it to perceive. The same question was relevant. I couldn't say I had ever answered it satisfactorily. Maybe nobody can. Let me be clear that I do not mean this in the usual sophomoric, nihilistic sense of bemoaning the futility of life and action. I mean it in a philosophical, even engineering, sense: To serve what purpose is this intricate arithmetical plotting, planning, and gridding?

I hadn't arrived at an answer yet, but I saw something new to this spectacle. The distances between these six special planets potentially spanned 18 billion galaxies. That's the number of galaxies in the universe, according to the human Blaise who got it from his pals, the angelic Blaises. I am speculating, but I presume these six occupy different galaxies, since their qualities are so rarely bestowed; this means, at least theoretically, they could be at opposite ends of the spatial extent of the entire universe. Yet here they all were, holographically throbbing around me, five from elsewhere accompanying Earth, the sixth one.

It was as if vast distances across universal space had been stitched together to meet here in one drawn patch of skin, as if different zones of the body had been knitted together to coincide at the belly button. Each brought its own operational algorithm, which was still running its affairs within the master one. Six wildly separated planets, occupying locations light-years from one another, were for the moment all drawn tightly together into this small operating space.

Physicists will likely squirm at this next comparison, but it struck me as being like a six-gated wormhole. It wasn't we who had traveled but the wormholes from their respective planets to this uniquely defined topographical node. Space had been folded, distances erased, and the six planets were right here. We could travel back through these holographic presences that were like wormholes to their actual material planets, but we had a problem on our hands.

Several dozen long, thin, black hands were reaching into this holographic display of planets, Light grids, and operational algorithms, poised to snatch them. It was the alien gods. They had found this supposedly sacrosanct zone, this special hidden room that exists only in hyperspace where the "six of us" get together. The integrity of the arithmetical arrays of our six special planets was in peril. Yet the hands were frozen in their gestures; even their grasping fingers were halted, as if in some kind of fundamental stop-action or radical slow-down. They didn't need to remove the algorithms; they only had to seize and hold them in place. It would assure control over their operations. That was the actual theft. We still had time to take effective action against their in-reach. But to do what?

Since the forward movement of these obnoxiously grasping alien hands was for the moment apparently halted, I thought I would investigate this first planet I found myself, as I now discovered, standing on, at least in my Light body. Don't ask me how I determined this but I felt the pull of gravity was much weaker than we have on Earth. I felt like you could easily bounce along the surface of this planet, like you wore the bounciest, jumpiest of new sneakers.

I felt a corresponding lightness in my thoughts, as if my mind were floating. I don't mean spaciness, fuzziness, or disorientation, but a delightful ease of carriage, as if the quality of my thoughts and awareness was feather-light. I felt far less pulled down by the heaviness of Earth-Human concerns. I hadn't realized how weighty, even ponderous, the reality of Earth life had been. It had been some time since I had left the planet, and the Pleiades never felt like this, so I concluded I was registering the psychic absence of all aspects of Earth gravity.

All of us were bouncing along the surface of this very pleasant first planet. Even Ray Master Hermes had a bounce in his step, though I had learned from the human Blaise that Ray Masters tend to preserve their decorum and gravity. They don't want to be observed tripping along like school kids on a pleasant summer's outing. Still, you felt here as if you were inside the Supreme Being's intention for the granting of free will, and you realized it was a serving of His own lightness of being, the sense, almost giddy for me, of being unconstrained.

You could do virtually anything, and you had the means, the creative power, to do so, and, I believed, though again I don't know how, you had the requisite maturity to do this properly, wisely, and not intemperately muck it up big time. When I say "first planet" it was my impression we were visiting the first of these six planets, the one first created and given the free-will allotment.

You felt as if your clothing was dotted with a hundred colorful buttons and these buttons seemed ready to burst and pop off your chest and arms and torso. I am referring to the chakras, all 81 of the complete set, and on this virginal planet these cognitive centers seemed primed to their fullest extent, fully topped off. They were brimming with vitality and power, and you felt you could create anything with them, that each was a magic wand and you knew all the spells.

Reality itself seemed poised to respond to your intentions, like a dog squirming to chase that stick at full-throttle acceleration as soon as you throw it for him. Or should I say reality stood at the ready like the most attentive restaurant waiter, pen poised over the pad, waiting to take your order and rush off to the kitchen. Even more striking than this was the sense that reality, if I may personify such an amorphous abstraction, seemed glad to see you, happy to brightly surround you. Hey, how are you doing? Good to see you again, pal.

I concede this is probably an odd thing to say, but I noted I could not remember ever feeling this on the Earth, certainly not before 2020, and not too strongly after that pivotal date. Can you imagine this? Reality pleased to see you. Welcoming you, as if your presence had been accounted for in advance, and the servants of this cordial reality were rushing about making your visit wonderful.

My companions on this pleasant investigation seemed to have picked up on this quality. They were walking around as if the intangible air itself possessed great fascination and was brimming with information. It was flower-scented and, again, I know this will sound odd, it was exceedingly pleasant to breathe, as if with each inhale you took in more than the requisite oxygen, a glad feeling. Did you ever feel that inhaling on the Earth, even when the air was reasonably fresh? I didn't, not even in New Hampshire where Philomena and I once had a country estate, surrounded by lush trees and mountain views, so long ago now. I always felt that along with the oxygen I was inhaling the dark psychic vapors of disgruntled, confused, angry, suffering humans emitted across the planet.

What I especially liked as far as the design of this planet was concerned was that reality was displayed as an accessible palimpsest. You could see its constitutive layers. Outermost was the physical sensory realm, the air, birds, sunlight,

the feel of your feet lightly touching the ground as you walked along. Then you felt you could discern the button-like chakras bursting with *prana* and the reciprocal welcoming gestures of outer reality waiting for your commands. Then you could make out the arithmetical layer, the algorithms running reality.

It was like standing upright underwater, but here the water was mathematical. You stood within an arithmetical reality, its numbers managing all your affairs. It was as if you had a complex, extremely agile computer right before you in the air. You could check the calculations, make adjustments, tally results right there. Reality itself was computational, the equations right at hand.

This next observation even struck me as weird at first, though delightful. You felt that you could change places with outer reality and observe yourself walking through this arithmetical Light grid of breathable air and expectancy. I felt like I had walked into a mirror. Now I stood, without discrete form, within the Light grid and its number processes that kept scripting this planet's reality. I enveloped this human body that vaguely reminded me of myself with geometry.

I was scribbling math equations all over its *pranic* field, like writing on water, but here the scribbling was retained by the corporeal surface and its energy field. I dispatched secondary-level equations to compensate for various changing light conditions and certain wobbles and shifts in magnetic field frequency of adjacent planets in this solar system and the occasional restiveness of its sponsoring sun. I was continuously modulating this walking upright man's relationship with his arithmetical context, and I was serving him different equations, ever new ones, fresh variations, alternate programming approaches.

My mind felt fluidly engaged in all aspects of apparent reality. It felt like a flock of barn swallows swooping adeptly everywhere at once, wherever needed. I felt like I was a thought, focused attention, touching the leaves, causing them to quiver, and I was all those leaves receiving the energizing touch of intention. I think the strongest impression I took from this immersion in planetary reality was the astonishing feeling that it all made sense. It added up to something intelligent, well thought out, and moving forward with a firm, clear purpose.

You felt you were saturated in the implicit rationality of its creation, and I mean by that term, usually such a dried, fustian concept employed by merely mental professors and guaranteed to irritate the mystical and sensitive who know reality responds to subtler inputs, the indwelling pure intelligence of the Higher Mind. Think of this as a combination of analytical, logical intelligence and the sharpest clairvoyance set in the context of a God-mandated purpose using a perfect design to achieve it and then to display it proudly to the world.

This reality was rational, reasonable at its core, and organized by the most metaphysical Mind conceivable to deliver a multi-tiered alive reality. It's just that it was hyperdimensional in nature, which means your concept of a causal chain, the reality syllogism that helped you understand events, had to be pitched cognitively higher. Particular events were happening because of a multitude of coinciding factors. But still that was rational, though you had to stretch your mind. This reality was suffused with the absolute permission of free will. I could take a step forward or I could remain standing; either way, reality awaited my next move with the rapt fascination and approval of a circus audience watching a tightrope walker performing an awesome balancing act at 100 feet above them.

You will, I trust, permit me my shamelessly wandering metaphors. You can perhaps appreciate the fact that this place was hard to account for mentally. Its construction seemed perfect, flawless, and, contrary to my experience to date, delightful and welcoming. How often can you ever say that of Earth reality, though, granted, things have improved considerably since 2020, but not like this. No, I'm quite sure, Earth reality does not yet feel like this, or even close to it.

The purity of this realm was arresting, and I think it was frustrating the alien gods. Their long black tendril-like fingers (it also looked like they were wearing sheer black gloves) were flailing and grasping futilely on the edge of our world. They were failing to make contact, to grasp what they sought. It seemed we were encased in a transparent though somehow palpable glass sphere or energy wall. I only became aware of it when I saw the black hands trying to gain purchase on us. They couldn't penetrate the crystalline sphere surrounding us.

That was a relief and I paid them no more mind for now. I was too absorbed in the instantaneous co-presence of the Creator within this pristine created world. Within these layers of physicality, Light grid, and arithmetical processing, you felt you were inside the Mind of the Supreme Being, sharing the minute fluctuations of thought and intention that apparently characterized His inner life. I know, that is metaphysically an inane way to put it, but when you're up against an infinite being probably anything you say will sound juvenile. I felt I was enmeshed in the concatenation of thoughts and suggestions arising in this infinite mind and that reality was so perfectly responsive to it you'd swear it was outer reality that had come up with these clever modulations and not God.

As for my companions, the 13 extra-planetary members of our delegation seemed to be conversing but I wasn't sure they were using a word-based language. It seemed more an exchange of pictures. It was certainly telepathic. They stood in groups, appearing as humanlike figures, and these groups were conversing. I know this because I saw some of the pictures they shared.

The groups were arrayed in a circle, but in the center of this circle stood a copy of each of these figures and they were exchanging a different set of pictures. They did this by impressing the reality and full extent of the picture into the awareness of the others, and it looked like they did this by temporarily co-occupying their psychic space, as if standing in the same space as their bodies. They didn't show one another the pictures; they enabled one another to enter these images and experience them as if they had arisen naturally within them. That made failure of communication an unlikely prospect; it was an efficient way to share information and assessments, far more effective than verbal speech.

I hope this image isn't confusing. I'm saying these 13 spirits comprised the circumference and the center of the same circle. In fact, so did Blaise and me. We were engaged in some complex conversation, many-stranded yet unified. Yes, telepathic, naturally, but it was holographic, almost to the point of, to me, incomprehension. How many simultaneous tracks can you follow at once? These people could follow more than me, though Blaise seemed to be keeping up.

Images of their respective planets framed these spirits, the way parents might stand proudly behind their children who had just done something amazing. Then they were standing in their planetary image, a Light body they wore like a cloak. These kept shifting around from one group to the next, like passing around an *hors d'oeuvre* tray at a party. Everyone got to "taste" the flavor of the planets.

I mentioned earlier that these six planets, including our Earth, enjoyed a special linkage. You could liken this connection to a geometric pattern, a Light grid with six nodes. When one planet overshadowed you, you saw the rest of the pattern from its perspective; then you saw it from the next planetary node. You went around the grid in this manner until you had fully experienced the array.

At the same time this felt like an arithmetical riot, like you were in a room of 13 mathematicians feverishly running their algorithms and reveling in their numbers. This was a level of reality most people, certainly myself, never experience and probably never thought of or could even conceive. Why would anyone? It is too recondite, too abstract, too remote from daily concerns, even though the cycling of these equations maintained the quotidian reality we're immersed in.

I had to remember the basics, though. The theft of our algorithm. Would this display, however arresting it was to my mind, however much it held my attention in rapt engagement, help us retrieve Earth's Hierophancy algorithm? As far as I could tell, the Light grids of these planets and their individual energy patterns were inviolate against the alien gods' intrusion; only ours wasn't.

They had gotten through our security measures and stolen our algorithm. That's why we were here. Their skinny black-gloved hands kept flailing and grasping at the outer glasslike edges of this composite Light grid and failing to penetrate it. Yet, according to the holographic logic at play around me, access to Earth's algorithm would immediately put them inside this shapeshifting grid pattern. They would be able to co-occupy the node Blaise and me were holding and conduct further covert operations and incursions into the composite algorithm. If my assumption was right, it meant they were already in the house. That in turn meant my earlier assumption was wrong: the others were not inviolate to their intrusions and were vulnerable and in jeopardy right now.

Normally, under ordinary body-based conditions, we worry about our body. We construe threats directed at us in terms of potential bodily harm, or perhaps to our property, or maybe as peril to our environment or the planet. But this threat was altogether different. It was a threat to our reality itself and our consciousness that perceives and interacts with it. The alien gods didn't wish to destroy anything, not our bodies, environment, or planet. They wanted to commandeer our reality by grasping the algorithms that ran its Light grid that in turn managed the ecosphere and all the physical parameters of our Earth lives. I think they didn't want our reality; they wanted its arithmetical underpinning. They apparently didn't care what happened when they extracted the numbers.

I tried to imagine what that would be like. The very way I was perceiving all this, thinking about it, even registering these thoughts as I stood inside this complex holographic array of six planets and their arithmetical infrastructure, would be changed, possibly in such a way that I would fail to notice the theft. Hindu cognitive philosophers talk about five generic aggregates or "*skandahs*" that manage our perception and interpretation of the outer world; they are fundamental to humans. The alien gods were vacuuming the life-force out of this basic operating platform; we would be rendered cognitively dumb, our mind and consciousness inert because the cognitive mechanism of reality was gone.

Let me contrast our working relationship with the assigned agents of reality with how the alien gods were going about things. The Hierophancy works closely with planetary designers, Elohim, Pleiadians, and Visvakarman, the Master Architect. Now, with these six planets, we have a meticulously designed free-will operating system with careful calibrations, constantly updated, that regulate the interplay of initial parameters and evolutionary freedom. In this context, you feel like you're doing a perpetual slow-motion dance with the Supreme Being's Mind, His idea for these planets and for your consciousness.

It feels legitimate and you know it is properly commissioned. Yes, you can move, adjust, and generally modulate these Light grid parameters, these consciousness boundaries, as you approach them in your experience. You know you are aligned with something perfect and ultimate, with bedrock. You are co-modulating reality conditions with the Ineffable Mind Who made it. You are dancing with the Ultimate Authority, and you trust the wisdom of this. He won't step on your toes or spin you around precipitously. You'll keep your balance.

It's not that way with the alien gods. They are not in this alignment. They don't wish to be. They are in disregard of it. They are not trustfully waltzing with the Great Ballroom Dancer. They are chilly collectors of algorithms. They want to snatch yours and put it in their Magic Square because that is their vocation. They don't care what the Divine Mind has in mind for us, or any other planet, and certainly not for this juvenile array of the special six planets. Free will? To them it's a recess permission slip awarded to precocious children. I suspect they regarded this geometric array I was standing amidst with disdain and contempt. To them it stood in the way; it used arithmetical materials that belonged to them.

Just as I felt this cold indifference to everything the Hierophancy stood for, the black grasping hands suddenly penetrated the glassy sphere around me. It was as if I had been arm wrestling and our two arms were poised in an upright stalemate; then in an instant my hand slammed down onto the table and I lost. My opponent got up, took the prize that had lain between us, and walked away.

I couldn't see the other people in my group, nor Blaise, nor the Ray Master. They seemed to have disappeared, as if they had been surreptitiously swiped. I felt a dark, powerful mind start to grow tendrils into the "dance floor" I had just moments ago been twirling around, my hands demurely clasping the Supreme Being's waist. Please excuse that overly literal metaphor, but I suddenly felt I had been disconnected from the rightness and correctness of Being and was unanchored to reality, tossing upon a roiling chaotic sea lacking structure and rationality because the numbers that code those qualities had been sucked out.

I mentioned tendrils. These were extensions of the alien gods' intention to acquire Earth's algorithm, and the other five thrown in as a surprise bonus. These tendrils were rapidly growing around all the components of the algorithm, staining the numbers and distorting the arithmetical product, uprooting it. They were loosening the algorithm's hold on Earth reality, and the work of the tendrils was unfastening it from its traction points, like it was pulling up a long carrot.

I saw people on Earth, the sensitive ones anyway, look up in surprise, then anguish, as something essential was extracted from their perception of reality and self. The continuity of the constant reciprocal exchange between these two was disrupted. They felt a strange combination of amnesia and concussion aftermath. They felt they had forgotten how to make sense of the world. Light temples started to tilt, their Light diminish, their bulk thinning out as if drained of life-force. The bridges between these temples and the outer physical world started to collapse, the fords across the dimensions collapsed, and people began to be unable to find these temples or even to see them on the river's other bank.

I felt like I had been soaking wet, saturated with the water of alignment. Now the alien gods were using suction pumps to extract every last molecule of wetness from my body, leaving me desert dry. Let's take that water as life-force. I started feeling droopy, wilted, a plant neglected for weeks, badly water-hungry. Reality was making less sense, as if I had received a concussion and my head was spinning. I saw things but I couldn't make any sense of them; they were mere raw phenomena without significance or meaning. My mind was dazed.

Many others were suffering in a similar manner, their cognitive acuity punctured and draining. I couldn't remember what the Hierophancy was or how I had ever heard that strange word. The numbers in the algorithm were growing faint and ethereal. The Earth was wobbling, far more than its "normal" 23.5 degrees. It was like a spinning top falling off its axis, wobbling deliriously, about to tumble over, then roll a bit, then come to a stop, and with it, all Earth reality.

I heard somebody mumbling. It might have been Blaise. He was saying something like "... not the end of the...alignment intact until we...Frederick!"

I snapped awake. Everything was as it had been, aligned, dancing, the algorithms running, and the 18 of us standing about with attention and interest. If I had sustained a concussion and reality had been vampirically drained, all that was suddenly reversed, as if it had never happened. Maybe it had not happened. Had the alien gods been playing a mind game with me, simulating their successful intrusion and theft of the ruling algorithm? It seemed that way.

"They were testing the integrity of the boundaries and defenses," said Blaise. "It was clever. I'll give them that. As best I can tell they thought if they could convince you their simulation was in fact real and get you to experience their steadily encroaching presence and acquisition of the algorithm, you would start to fall into alignment with them. That would put them in an overlap position with your consciousness and its traction points on the algorithm, and through that they could reach right through you, as if claiming the use of your arms and mind, and grab the algorithm, even though, technically, they had not penetrated our glassy sphere of defense. Their simulation would have fooled it."

I looked around at our group. The other 13 planetary representatives looked a bit bedraggled, probably the way I appeared. Apparently, they had been similarly conned into believing the alien gods' devilishly clever mind game. That explains why I couldn't see them. They had been whisked away into separate bubbles of illusion, taken off the conjoint playing field we had been enjoying. It was as if the alien gods had walked through glass walls to snatch our numbers, cocooning us in convincing but glum, despair-filled hallucinations.

They had cast a glamour over us, making us believe they had penetrated our defenses. As soon as we accepted that as the changed, new reality, then they could actually seize the algorithm, having tricked us into opening the doors. I realized their simulation had not failed. They had identified the traction points by which our attention was fastened to the arithmetical grid of computations. It was like the way bank robbers used to pretend to stage a robbery to study the response time, reaction points, and vulnerabilities of the bank's security system.

Then it happened again. I shuddered. The remission with Blaise and the other planetary spirits had been the illusion. I had hallucinated that reprieve. The alien gods in fact had stolen the algorithm, that was the real part, and I was now reeling with the collapse of the Earth's Light grid and its arithmetical infrastructure. We'd been hacked. The proper geometry of the Light grid was starting to unravel, fall apart, deform, whatever way you choose to describe its destabilization and form loss. All the number bones were taken out of reality.

My head was spinning. The Earth was spinning. The Light grid was disassembling. This was disastrous. Wasn't this what the Hierophancy was created for, to prevent this acquisition and safeguard the grid? We had failed, goddam tremendously failed in that responsibility, and the catastrophic results of that ineptitude surrounded me. The Earth's Light grid was in ruins, its equations appropriated by hostile alien gods who regarded our free will with disdain. I assumed the same had befallen the other five planets and their grids.

These alien gods were starting to reassemble the grids but in different, bizarre patterns. It was like a piece of literature translated from English into an exotic language that had no phonetic counterparts with the original tongue; the translation could not possibly convey the same meaning, and the images and moods it evoked, its pace and rhythms, would be entirely different and probably, to we speaking English, mostly unrecognizable and even grating on our minds.

There wasn't much for us to do. We watched as our planetary realities were taken apart and reassembled in a different fashion, the processes and products of consciousness for our respective worlds subluxated from their original design. Imagine, though it might seem frightful, you suddenly shapeshifted from your human form into a bizarre four-legged animal, bizarre because it hasn't been seen on the Earth before and its features are unfamiliar. Your consciousness now feels crude, feral, predatory, boxed in, though somewhere your original, wider awareness sits torpidly like a bound prisoner.

My mind felt numbed, as if anesthetized. I couldn't input any Hierophancy numbers. Worse, I couldn't even remember them. The definition of an algorithm itself was starting to fade in my mind, taken away by the current of growing oblivion. It's some sequence of numbers that does something, right? Yet, oddly, it was as if the water or something around me was shouting my name.

"….up, Frederick….not real, but only…. *Frederick*, snap out of it now!" These words were being flung at me by a voice that was obnoxious yet familiar. It was Blaise, again, yanking me out of a second round of hallucinations that only moments ago I had taken for irrevocable reality. None of that had been the case.

With relief, I realized the alien gods had not seized the Light grid algorithms, but slipped another simulation of that into my mind and, foolishly, I bought it again. I felt like a hand puppet that the alien gods kept trying to move around in order to grasp the algorithm. When they flooded the hallucination through my mind, that was equivalent to slipping their nimble fingers into the puppet glove; then they could move the puppet forward, me, the unsuspecting Frederick, lost in the dream, accepting the dark hallucinatory scenario as truth, to grab the equations. It was clever and awful and I was getting very tired of this.

Blaise looked at me and nodded. I took that to mean he agreed with my analysis and that he had followed my wobbly syllogism telepathically. As to why they were picking on me specifically, Blaise shrugged his shoulders, but for some reason I couldn't figure out then I suspected he knew but wasn't telling me now. But he did tell me something new, and it startled me until I understood its logic.

"The next time these guys seduce you with a horror show of total acquisition, work it backwards," Blaise said. "Use their apparent control over you to work in the opposite direction into their minds and plant something. While they think they're picking your pockets, which are empty, because this is an illusion they've spun over you, pick theirs which are in fact full of riches and not subject to illusory conditions at all. They are far more vulnerable than you."

It was funny, the situation I was now in. Maybe even ironic. I was waiting for the next hallucination to grab me and yank me into the ocean of delusion after which I would slip something into the pockets of these pain-in-the-ass gods. Yes, Blaise's tactic sounded feasible, though I wondered why he was starting to look bent, as if he wasn't standing up straight, and come to think of it, his expression seemed petulant all of a sudden and he was looking like a stranger.

I reflected on how he always thought he knew best, had the superior concepts, that we should always follow his lead, though I can't see that he had earned this or that his ideas, really, were that topping. And, add to that his tendency—I was starting to feel dizzy and fuzzy in my head. I felt like I had fallen over, or gotten banged on the head without noticing it

until now, and as I righted myself, my head was spinning, my balance lurching and seriously off. I couldn't see Blaise or anybody else at the moment and reality felt rickety.

I vaguely remembered I was supposed to do something clever and sneaky, but I couldn't bring it fully to mind. It was like a rumor heard faintly at a distance. I started counting, I don't know why, up from one to ten; then I started reciting the prime numbers from two to 101, again, for no clear reason I could fathom. I started throwing prime numbers at some unseen antagonist, and I don't even know why I felt this animus, but they were limp and feckless like sloshy mud pies created by a six-year-old. I lobbed 29 like a limp Frisbee, then gave 67 a strong underarm thrust, and finally connected with 89 in the face. Somebody's face anyway. The prime numbers hung off the rest of the body belonging to this face like dented ornaments inattentively hung on an old tree.

I heard laughing. It seemed to come from a distance. Somebody found what I was doing funny? It seemed like serious man's work, nothing to laugh at. I felt something like a hook grab my neck and yank me away from where I was lobbing prime numbers. Then I shook my head, quite like how a big dog would. There was Blaise staring directly into my face, a glare and a smile on his face.

"They got you again," he said. "They roped you into another hallucination and you never suspected it, and then you had that charming prime number mud-pie fight. You carried on like a concussed field agent or else a dead drunk who forgot his mission and couldn't even remember his cover story, who he was pretending to be, and regressed to the whimsicality of a six-year old spy. I have half a mind to put your consciousness on a short leash and to keep it taut."

Blaise was right. I had botched this round utterly. He was critical, but it was a good-natured jibe at my easy seduction by the alien gods' hallucination. But something puzzled me. I hadn't thought to bring it up until now. So I did.

"How come I am the one who has to go into their mind-games field?"

Blaise studied me before he answered. I felt like a junior reporter at a press conference given by a busy president. "It is important that it is you who makes this level of contact. I can't say more about the reason for that just now."

It didn't explain much, but at least he agreed with the question's relevance. Meanwhile, I was aware of the alien gods waiting for the next round. It was as if they stood inside a squash court and were ready to start flinging the ball against the cramped walls of the playing space, waiting to outplay me again. The fate of the arithmetical universe came down to a game in a squash court?

It would be a game in which one player had a hard time staying awake and couldn't tell when a hallucinatory veil was slipped over his undiscerning head. I felt I should be embarrassed at the nincompooperies on my part. But I wasn't. I was laughing. The minute I set myself, squared myself up for the engagement, I was already hallucinating and didn't know it. It started before I even began to engage them. That was a serious handicap I was starting with.

I thought about complaining that the alien gods enjoyed an unfair advantage. Basically, they could manipulate my perception of the squash court itself, as if they had nimble fingers on a perception dial, making the playing court outlines grow faint and fuzzy or leap into sharp relief, expertly confounding me. The dial was the algorithm, and they had their usurping hands all over it which meant they controlled reality itself, modulating it at will to suit their advantage.

Change the numbers and everything was suddenly different, running west when you had been romping east, walking backwards on your hands when you had been confidently striding forward. Was there some place I could stand that was senior to all these manipulations of reality and my perceptions of it? It's the kind of question Philomena and I used to ponder over tea. What is behind reality, and who do I see about getting an invitation to visit that fabled land?

It wasn't a question of hiding my body. My body wasn't here. I had to hide my consciousness, veil it somehow so the alien gods could not throw another glamour over it. I had to find a place antecedent to all numbers. This was tantamount, it seemed to me then, to slipping out of this dimension and finding another adjacent one from which I could conduct business, which in this case meant reverse pick-pocketing, to slip something into the alien gods' pockets without them noticing the intrusion. What was that anyway? I looked at my hands as I realized I was holding it. It was a complex miniature grid pattern comprised of numbers set out in equations that built an algorithm. The grid was alive somehow, the numbers as if scurrying about the place like attentive butlers.

But where to hide? I had to put aside the other vexing question of why me, why I had to dart into some kind of nothing place then sneak out and put this contraption in the alien gods' pockets. A place where they couldn't see me? Now I saw it: Blaise often spoke of this, the business of following your attention back to its own roots and then disappearing yourself into the emptiness of it.

You find that quiet place where attention resides. It is behind all the phenomena of yourself you are accustomed to, behind all perceptions and self-definitions. You marshal your attention to pay attention to where you're paying attention from. The Vedantists call it the No-Self zone. It is a singularity of consciousness in which you as the perceiver and the world as the perceived become one thing. I know, it can feel like you're a puppy frantically, futilely chasing your own tail. Still, you find that place, walk into it as if striding through an invisible wall of glass, and when you are fully in that wall that isn't a wall, have passed through it, you find you have disappeared, there is no wall and never was, and "you" are no longer filing reports on the conditions you find. You could send out a search party to look for yourself, but there's nobody there.

It is a slow-motion vanishing trick. Even you can't find where you are. Just before I lost track of myself, I laughed again at the absurdity of this version. I should expect to lose myself again, this time in a self-spun hallucination without imagery. I would slip a veil over myself, although more truly I was removing all veils leaving only an invisible nakedness beholding itself in a grand vanishing act. Behold, the disappearing Frederick. He was never here. He's gone beyond.

It must have worked. It's like falling asleep. You usually only know this has happened when you wake up again and look at the clock. I don't remember telling myself to do this, but I found myself poking my newly reformed head out of this nonexistent glass wall to spy on the alien gods, to see if their attention was focused elsewhere. Miraculously, it was. I slipped the numbers grid into their pockets then yanked my head back into the void and disappeared myself again.

All that took no more than a few seconds, but if my awareness was like a recording camera, it seemed to have registered hours of footage at slow speed. This empty space I had slipped myself into as a kind of self-erasure of form and identity was a zone superior or antecedent to the numbers realm. There were no numbers in here; numbers were not needed to code this zone. It was utterly without code. There was nothing at all: lucid wide-awake empty awareness. It was the zone of nondualism about which I cannot say anything without contradicting its nature which is that everything is one: twoness doesn't exist. Twoness and dualism are out, against the law, inadmissible, and impossible.

All the numbers swirled outside this nonexistent glass wall divider between self and no-self, between Frederick and who's that you're looking for? In a strange way I still cannot quite explain, "I" was able to see this arithmetical realm that lay outside the wall, but it was within me, not outside at all, and this "me" I refer to was not Frederick but more of a naked nonpersonified global awareness. It is difficult to explain this without lapsing into vexing, impersonal abstractions that reek of the old dualism and its conceits of inside and outside.

I did figure out the alien gods had no interest in this personality-free zone I was in. Devoid of numbers it held no interest for them; they ignored it. In those moments when

I returned to myself I marveled that the current work of the Hierophancy, usually all about numbers, grids, and Light temples, had come to this: erasing yourself in a void zone beyond the reach of the algorithmic world, emptying your consciousness of everything arithmetical then disappearing.

I tried to muster some dignity befitting my age, but I was full of hilarity. In this radically expanded zone of total emptiness I was pick-pocketing myself. I was the electrical engineer working the stage lights for a theater production. I had to get the lights working again; they had fallen into a fit of inoperability. I laughed again: the Hierophant is the revealer of the Holy Light, and here I was, the engineer behind the stage props trying to get the infernal lights switched on. I heard the words "Find the algorithmic trigger and trip it." It must have been Blaise somehow finding a way to insert his voice into all this silent emptiness.

Mathematicians talk of algorithms spontaneously triggering unexpected results, such as stock market price-change cascades. But this was different. I knew by algorithmic trigger Blaise meant something that would activate the algorithm itself, trigger it into an action sequence to produce expected results. There was more cause for mirth: when I was in the empty zone, I couldn't remember anything, and the "I" that I took for granted seemed dissolved, and when I was outside it momentarily, as if poking my head out of a hidey-hole, my mind was suddenly switched on and I was beset by a flurry of frenetic thoughts.

When I was facing outward, I was holding the trigger. When I slipped back into this universe-wide emptiness zone, the trigger was gone as were my hands. The place where I was immune from the alien gods was also the place where I lost myself in this universal wide-awake void zone. You see why I laughed? The only truly safe place for me was a region in which I did not exist.

In my occasional moments of mental lucidity, I understood that the algorithmic trigger was a deeper, antecedent function to the various traction points I had been exploring on this outing with Blaise in search of our algorithm. The traction points were how the algorithm hooked into the Light grid system, but the trigger part was the "on" switch for the functioning of the algorithm. I suppose you could compare it to the car key that turns on the algorithmic motor. You're not going anywhere and the algorithm will fail to grip its constituents if you don't have the trigger key. Which I did, and which the alien gods wanted.

It looked like a tangled ball of yarn, but the yarn was made of numbers. I had many odd impressions at the same time: it looked like a holographic maze, intricately folded, paths leading in many directions at once; it looked like a bird's nest in which the individual fibers of plant substance were sub-equations comprising the algorithmic trigger; it looked like a Qabalist's permutation table of all the possible combinations of certain letters in an order. More than any of these impressions, it seemed alive, throbbing with animation. It was shapeshifting through a repertory of forms and yet remaining true to itself. It kept casting out different form impressions, yet its number form stayed steady.

I realized I had no idea how the algorithmic trigger had come to be in my possession, me holding it like a magical toy of great potency. It just appeared in my hands right after Blaise telepathically made the suggestion to find and trip it.

I had a spontaneous memory of working in a laboratory with some colleagues. For some reason it suggested the Baghdad cabals of the time of Harun al-Rashid which was about 800 A.D. I had read about this in the writings of Rudolf Steiner; he was always citing this figure as someone of importance. He was the "Rightly-Guided" or "Aaron the Just," and during his life as the Caliph of Baghdad (the chief Muslim civil and religious leader), the city enjoyed a Renaissance of culture and high intellectual inquiry and discovery comparable to the later Quattrocento of Florence. It was, I learned, a good time for arithmetic.

His library, the *Bayt al-Hikma*, the "House of Wisdom," was renowned, and it was also known as the "Storehouse of Wisdom." It curated many old and valuable works from Arabic and the earlier Greek culture on philosophy, medicine, astrology, and astronomy. It was more than a library, though; the *Bayt al-Hikma* was an innovator in many areas of intellectual study and application and became known for its mathematical advances. It was a study house, a Mysteries center, and akin to what people used to call a "think tank."

No surprise here because the guy who invented the algorithm and moved the discipline of algebra forward, Muhammad ibn Musa Al-Khwārizmi (780-850), was a mathematician working in the House of Wisdom. He wrote a treatise on in algorithms in 825 and then he made a breakthrough which is probably why I am remembering him now. For a time this Arabic think tank was the epicenter of advances in mathematics, medicine, geography and map-making, science, astrology, and

Ptolemy's geometric model of landscape and urban coordinates, contributing much to world knowledge.

Again, it was not really a surprise, because as Rudolf Steiner noted, Harun al-Rashid was another guise of Saint Germain, and Saint Germain, as Blaise told me, is one of the 14 Ray Masters. So our study house was overseen by a master of the Mysteries, esoteric rituals, magical ceremonies, alchemy, and other abstruse but highly important procedures in consciousness conducted under the Lilac Ray and its administrator, the "Holy Brother."

I sat at a large wooden table. It was covered in parchments and scrolls, and all this "paper" was covered in numbers and equations, like arithmetical tattoos. I looked at my colleagues. I counted seven around the table. I made eight. One of them presumably was Al-Khwārizmī; he seemed to have numbers sprouting out of his fingertips. Arithmetic was his passion, algorithms his exploratory edge. He was on to something important, and we were helping him formulate it.

Say you had a set of algorithms, perhaps 10 or even 20, he said, when we got started on this project, and you wanted to start them all working at once. Might there be a trigger that would ignite the complete set at once and set them going? He seemed to think in numbers; his mental processes were not verbal but arithmetical. The rest of us loped, ran mentally, to keep up with his thoughts.

When we completed the project, the algorithmic trigger looked like a lace doily made of numbers. It was thin, elegant, intricately patterned. Al-Khwārizmī held it up before him to study and admire like a beautiful tapestry. With this we change the world, he said. We take hold of essential processes. This was some months after we began the research; many hours had gone into this. In my present form as Frederick, I appreciated the symmetry: back at Dartmouth, I had worked with graduate students, assigning them aspects of a large research project I undertook. College professors do that all the time. Back in that study room, I was one of the eager graduate students ready to help my teacher.

The study room was aswirl in numbers. It was as if I could see them roiling in the mental atmosphere all around us, projected from our teacher's brilliant mind. Presumably, we spoke in Arabic, but our real language was algorithms. These complex sequential equations had their own syntax, and with them we were attempting to move the mountains of physical reality by launching arithmetical commands at their obdurate inert mass, and succeeding. I suppose today we would liken this language to computer code, but our prolix arithmetical discourse was more sophisticated, more elegant, more refined than that, and it worked directly on physical reality, not on an electronic interface.

I'm not sure Al-Khwārizmī or anyone in our study group knew about master algorithms controlling the Earth and its linkage with the other five planets. I suppose it's possible; often teachers do not speak of the full extent of their esoteric knowledge, especially to students. But I was certain that he was pursuing a lead to wherever it directed him. He saw a mathematical thread and he pulled on it slowly and steadily to see what number product it generated.

He knew that mathematics underlay the world around us and was its secret hidden code. He wanted the full revelation, and he intended to capture this in numbers. I had never felt (or

enjoyed) this level of commitment and ardor in any of my Dartmouth seminars. Maybe it was my shortcoming, but I think students in my time of professorship didn't have this degree of passion about a subject. The study topics never imparted this sense of vital connection to reality.

One day Al-Khwārizmī told us a story. He had been thinking about the rules for reality, about the dictates and seeming commands of astrology, how the constantly changing planetary placements affected our life and consciousness, favorably and badly. He asked the Supreme Being if He liked rules or had any? In other words, was the Supreme Being, bound by any rules or did He have an absolutely unbounded free hand? The question was almost tautological because it was He Who made all the rules, so we were asking, perhaps cheekily, can You disregard Your own laid-down rules?

"The Tree of Life is My rule book," was the answer. The Tree was the Qabalist's hierarchical model of reality consisting of four trees and 40 levels of reality, or sometimes five trees and 50 levels, but these are hyper-arcane. The "trees" are an abstract way of representing the energy hierarchy of reality and consciousness as having four major zones, many components in each, and critical transition thresholds. Think of many spheres attached in a symmetrical pattern to three upright pillars, then stack three more of these trees on top of that one.

We weren't Jews, but we were aware of this model and referred to it often. It was useful in our studies, and we were as ecumenical in our studies as we could find research materials from other disciplines and cultures. The Supreme Being said next, "I follow these rules I have laid down so I don't hurt the Creation by getting destructively in its living space. It would be like an elephant squeezing into a child's dollhouse. It would crack and shatter and be ruined."

That Tree, mused Al-Khwārizmī, is like a waterfall with 40 platforms. The water, the absolute consciousness, spills down these 40 levels, simplifying at each one. "The bottom tier is our physical reality from which we look up and try to see the complete cascade. Mathematics are our eyes, arithmetical processes the mechanisms of our perceptions. We are using numbers, equations, and these algorithms, to climb back up that cascading waterfall of 40 levels. These numbers are the footholds, ropes, ledges, and the muscles of our bodies as we climb."

Al-Khwārizmī's eyes blazed with a passionate zeal for this arduous ascent. The Supreme Being had written these rules, generated this waterfall, with numbers. These numbers had relations with one another, and algorithms were a key to it, and under Al-Khwārizmī's tutelage we were determined to find them.

Periodically, Harun al-Rashid would visit us and check on our progress. He was genuinely interested in all aspects of attainable knowledge, and he appreciated the potential cognitive reach of mathematics. He never spoke about it, but I suspect he was aware of the complexities of the planet's Light grid, the master deployment pattern of its innumerable Light temples and holy locations, and that it was possible to model this pattern through arithmetical descriptions.

After all, we were living on the outskirts of a once legendary geomantic landscape, the Land of Shinar, or Sumeria, and its antediluvian cities. Baghdad, too, once participated in that Land of Light and had its own numinous

profile. He was, as we all agreed, Rightly Guided in a true sense, and I thought perhaps he envisioned the possibility of managing world affairs geomantically and arithmetically from the cultural high point his center in Baghdad represented.

We had arrived at this controlling algorithm in a manner different than the route Blaise had taken in the years leading up to 2050. He had extrapolated it out of the palimpsest of the 613 secondary-level algorithmic grids; in the study house, we had arrived at this formulation on a more theoretical basis, not from geomancy. But then again, since our master algorithm was not tied in to the geomantic infrastructure, maybe what we developed was a proto-formula for controlling algorithmic tiers and the geomantic algorithm was an application. We had approached it as a logical mathematical possibility, proving it possible as a way of demonstrating control over a set of algorithms; Blaise in contrast had developed his for the practical purposes of planetary Light grid management.

As I said, we completed the master control algorithm here, and with it the Hierophancy heuristic algorithm, though at first it seemed Al-Khwārizmī did not fully appreciate the magnitude of our completed task. Perhaps he had not seen the likely outcome but was diligently following each clue in a syllogism whose full articulation was not yet revealed to him though it definitely was now. I could almost hear the indrawn breaths as we contemplated the ramifications of this.

So did Harun al-Rashid. He recommended we commit all the algorithmic details to memory and burn all paper traces of our calculations and arithmetical results. He said knowledge of this scale was dangerous to the world if it fell into the wrong hands. The best way to prevent that was to destroy its physical traces. He must have anticipated that one day we would have precisely the problem we had now. Intelligences with inimical intentions would seek to steal and misuse the information and thereby imperil the world and the geomancy of the Earth.

In retrospect, he must have been aware of the full geomantic implications of this algorithm, how it could manage or suborn all the affairs of the Earth's Light grid, that the planet had such an energy and Light infrastructure, that it was vulnerable to interference, both from people on the Earth and those on other planets or realms. If the only record of these results was stored in human memory, this would make any hostile acquisition of the algorithms difficult.

Of course, it would also make it likely that sooner or later none of us would remember anything, that, finding ourselves in different bodies and in cultures with different interests, we would be unable to remember what we had memorized or worse, not even remember we had memorized it, as I, the entirely non-mathematical Professor Frederick, had found in myself before this moment.

The procedure of committing this information to memory was itself algorithmic. It followed the sequential, unfolding process logic of an algorithm. We assigned key activation words for each tier of the algorithm to be memorized. These were in Arabic and held significance beyond, or perhaps before, we assigned them as memory triggers for number sequences. It made sense to us then; to me, American, English-speaking Frederick, it was linguistically foreign.

We arrayed these trigger words like steps in a pyramid. One unlocks the next in order, but the crucial word-lock would be the first. I etched its syllables into my mind like a sculptor carving a name in a granite block. I would never forget it. The "I" that vowed perpetual full recall was of course not the Frederick currently tasked with remembering the algorithmic trigger. That Arabic and mathematical Frederick was shelved somewhere in the archives of my many past lives. Now in 2065 I fluctuated between the two incarnate identities across 1,240 years on my timeline, mathematical Arab and mythopoeic American.

Suddenly Al-Khwārizmī's face loomed hugely before me. His eyes beamed. He was speaking. He said "I speak Arabic." I thought, of course you do. What's the big revelation in that? I pondered that for a while, knowing I was missing something important. The Frederick part of me was puzzled. The Arabic part of me got it. Al-Khwārizmī made his statement in Arabic. It went "*atakallam al-'arabiya.*'" He was hiding and revealing the algorithmic trigger in plain sight.

The phrase had 18 letters and each one unlocked a tier in the algorithmic cascade. The series of linked equations unfolded like the revelation of a stepped pyramid, as if it had been veiled in fog or some kind of stealth covering, pardon the mixed metaphors. Now it sparkled in the mental air around me, all its parts disclosed. I was laughing too. I remembered Al-Khwārizmī used Arabic as a code word for our arcane mathematical explorations. "I speak Arabic" meant "I do algorithms." In Al-Khwārizmī's study house, we all spoke Arabic every day.

6

We were back at the Blue Room headquarters in Sun Valley, all of us. That included the 13 representatives from the other five free-will planets. Sal and Jocelyn were working in the room. Sal looked at us in puzzlement. "I thought you guys were going somewhere. You haven't left yet? Who are your friends?"

I thought my remembering the algorithmic trigger would resolve the problem. Apparently, all it did was bounce us back to our starting point while introducing another conundrum. It had seemed we were gone a long time. To Sal and presumably Jocelyn too we hadn't even left the institute yet. I guess that's the cost of doing business in a body other than your physical one. Time gets screwy, elastic, and hard to pin down; it may not even march forward, or perhaps in our case it progresses so sluggishly as to seem like slow-motion. Sal's comment implied a tiny portion of time had elapsed since he had last seen us.

Ray Master Hermes had journeyed back with us as well. He gestured for us to give him our attention. We followed as he walked out of the cramped research room into the conference room and we sat down at the large table and waited for him to speak. The "people" from the other planets were unperturbed. I felt fidgety. I wanted to look out the window and see if Earth reality was still stable; after all, the managing algorithm for its Light grid had been stolen. From what I could see in the conference room, everything seemed still normal. Sal and Jocelyn were not wringing their hands and running around distraught. Not yet.

"You have just completed the first run through of the Hierophancy protocols," the Ray Master said. "You have seen many of the algorithm's traction points and potential places of vulnerability, but not all. Look around in this."

He was referring to an array of points of Light and strings of numbers. He had inducted us into the Emerald Tablets again, so smoothly I hadn't noticed. I felt like I was inside a mainframe computer, walking among myriads of bytes. Here were the building blocks, the atoms, of all possible realities. The numbers were alive, but it was a different kind of animation than in biological life-forms. As we had seen before, this packed environment was immensely responsive to commands; here were the "obedient electrons," as one writer had once said.

"Frederick, speak Arabic," said the Ray Master. I did, though I couldn't explain how I knew what to say or how to say it. I had never studied Arabic. I watched with fascination, as if I was observing somebody else perform a trick. The individual letters of the Arabic phrase "I speak Arabic" were assembling a complex Light grid. Not only was this phrase a coded mnemonic for recalling the algorithmic trigger, each of its letters was also somehow an activation key for it.

Enunciation of each Arabic letter released its implicit stored grid pattern. I didn't think the Arabic language implicitly was invocatory in this manner, but it seemed we had encoded its letters to restore the Light grid pattern when we commanded it to. We packed the coding equations into the numbers, just as we had for the complete phrase to trigger our recall. I say "we." Maybe I had done it. I felt like a Qabalist running wild with his permutations of letters and numbers. Each Arabic letter generated more letters and Light grids; it kept branching out like proliferating snowflakes spawning new ones. This Arabic was generative!

I saw before me now an orrery of the interconnected Light grids and algorithms of the six planets. Each of these letters released its code to build this Light pattern, and it secured the connections with adjacent grid patterns, just the way the letters in this simple Arabic phrase worked together to deliver a composite meaning. I glanced at my fellow Hierophancy members, including the new acquaintances we had brought with us. Nobody was especially impressed.

But this was a particular kind of indifference. I think they expected me to retrieve this knowledge because they knew it was my speciality, even if I didn't know it. It's the last thing I would have expected of Frederick the Dartmouth professor. But apparently for

whatever my name was within Al-Khwārizmī's House of Algorithms, this was normal for me. It might even have been my assignment to remember this arithmetical sequence over time, to release it again right now, for the Arab buried in my subconscious to rise up and speak Arabic.

I couldn't tell you what the composite geometric shape I was generating was called. It was probably too complex even to have an official tag. But it was the Light body and geometric and mathematical infrastructure of six conjoint planets bound in this special trans-karmic relationship across time and Creation. I saw its forms and equations, like seeing the soul within a human body.

I assumed we were, finally, immune to the intrusions of the alien gods. I was mistaken. I felt their presence as if looming over my shoulders from a distance. They were not in our Hierophancy offices but they were surveilling us from nearby. I saw their long black snaky fingers starting to grasp at our Light grids. I had a thought that chilled me and gave me shivers. What if they were merely waiting for me to activate this Arabic-embedded arithmetical code? They knew I had it and they didn't, so they waited for me to intone the trigger. On the other hand, Ray Master Hermes did not seem alarmed or even perturbed. His calm, even complacency suggested he held a wider view of these actions, saw around more corners than I suspected, and anticipated a different outcome. Well, of course he did. What I mean is I was coming into contact with that assurance.

Then I had a funny thought. I was a singer performing before an audience of raptly attentive heads. The alien gods followed my every syllable with delight. Their black elongated fingers framed their large peering heads as they watched me. Their hands resembled dark ivy leaves veining around dormer windows. Yes, ivy tends not to grow on roofs, but their heads projected out like dormers.

I was the tenor singing an aria from an unfamiliar but arresting Arabic opera, until now unknown to the world. Strings of numbers were tumbling out of my mouth like precision acrobats. My thoughts were growing silly, possibly crazy; they teetered around in my mind. Arabic opera? Maybe I'm not a human being, not a former comparative mythology professor, but a computer, a mental construct capable of spewing out vast sets of numbers. They kept streaming out.

The alien gods didn't care what I was or what self-definition I settled on. They wanted the master algorithm. They waited, catlike, ready to pounce on it. Then it got even more confusing. I seemed to be back in that hyperspace where we first met the 13 planet representatives. I didn't seem to be in Sun Valley. It seemed I was bouncing back and forth between the two locations, then they were superimposed, and I realized I was straddling an occupancy in both domains.

Another inversion happened. I was on the outside, like the dormer windows, looking in to a realm in which the alien gods already had possession of all our protected algorithms. The game was over. I had failed. I watched as they deftly manipulated the equations and played, again catlike, with the fate of the Earth. I had the impression, maybe I made it up, or they made it up, of the alien gods insouciantly juggling the algorithms like colored rubber balls.

I heard voices. I figured it must be those of the 13 representatives, like coaches calling out

shots to a player, me, running and scrimmaging on the field. No, it wasn't that. I saw equations streaming out of their mouths. They were calling out their algorithms as a defense measure to shore up my position. Ray Master Hermes (it was amusing to see this) was conducting their intonations as if they comprised a choir in some majestic Bach oratorio. This put me back on the inside, as if clutching the precious algorithms, and the alien gods, no longer sneering in triumph, were on the outside, scratching at the walls. It was beginning to resemble a chess game, my move and their countermove. There was no longer a discrete inside or outside. I was a globe of tumbling numbers.

This is the arithmetical realm, I said to myself. But how did I know that? It was not a realm of forms or people. I couldn't say exactly how I was in there. I saw no traces of my body, any of them, whether subtle or manifestly solid. I was there, but only in a sketchy, vague sense, as if I were standing aloof at a distance taking notes on an event but not presiding in the swirling heart of its action.

I heard a sound like finger snapping. I knew it must be from something else. There were no hands in here to click. I felt I was immersed in water, a lake maybe, through which dozens of divergent currents vigorously rushed in all directions. Then it seemed I was in the midst of a circus of shapeshifters in which dozens, perhaps hundreds, of performers constantly changed their shape and costumes all at the same time, as if choreographed in advance to do this.

Yes, very strange, I know, and my analogies probably don't impart much clarity. I was in the stream of numbers, flowing along with their calculations. That makes it sound too linear.

It was more like multiple starbursts of number sets. I found myself halved then halved again, in jumps, until whatever volume my presence possessed had been reduced many times from a mountain down to a mere point. This was the running of square roots. Then suddenly I proliferated into hundreds of copies of whatever form I had, like I had emptied a bag of marbles. Each marble generated a hundred. This was the multiplying of integers.

Then I seemed to extend and expand indefinitely, like an echo that kept going and didn't lose any vitality along the way, and I was racing along with this extension into dizzying infinity. This was the exhilarating life experience of the irrational numbers, like *pi* and *e*. I was the continuous effect of exchanges and processes. I was ploddingly climbing a pyramid when it doubled its size and the number of steps, then it doubled that again, and several more times. That was the expansion of number sets. I felt like I was jumping across the squares on an asymmetric checkerboard that receded into the unseeable distance. That was the infinite grid of prime numbers unevenly distributed throughout the array of natural numbers. It was like a game of hopscotch designed to test my balance.

I was a member of a performing theater troupe that every second changed its faces and clothing so that I never saw any authentic faces. Everything they showed the world was symbolic, and this was the bewildering dance of algebra. Then I was a slew of syllables in a mellifluous phrase that kept being intoned and that seemed to have no end and made a widening circle. As for the alien gods, they treated this like a riotous baseball game. They were the catcher landing the pop up in the fat glove; they were the outfielder snagging a high fly ball. They were the shortstop mitting the zooming ball and flinging it to first base. They were the pitcher receiving the hardball flung back lightning fast from the catcher. Me? I was the ubiquitous busy baseball, my number innards unraveling sloppily.

Was there anywhere in this crazy realm of numbers and equations I could stand immune to the prying hands of the alien gods? I laughed when I saw it: 0.

I could hide inside the zero. Nobody had any interest in this empty non-entity. I knew I was invisible inside the zero; the alien gods couldn't see me, or if they did, they discounted my presence and attributed no potency to my new position. I could watch them with impunity, though I was powerless to stop them as well. I thought, maybe the alien gods would regard the zero with the ambivalence of the classical Greeks; they were uncertain as to its ontological status. How can nothing as represented by this empty digit stand for something, be a value? They studied the zero as if it were an unfathomable, potentially dangerous mystery. American professional basketball players used to wear 0 or 00 on their uniforms, apparently believing the oddness of this designation distinguished them. Their zeroes seemed as substantial as other normal digits.

In algebra, mathematicians call zero a root, and a zero of a function is an input value in an equation that generates a product of zero. I'm not sure what that means, though I remember Al-Khwārizmī immersed himself in algebraic complexities and he must have pondered, if not explored, the zero function because though I could not articulate anything sensible about this abstruse function, I felt I understood it enough to use it in the field. The zero means no objects are present; it is neither positive or negative; it sits on the *x*-axis of a graph where the line, representing the amount or function, crosses it with the result that the value and function of *x* at that point is zero. It sounds vacuous to the layman, but I was going to use this empty zone to hide from the alien gods.

I made myself into the zero of a function. First I was holding all these numbers in my hands, like strings of pearls made of integers— the algorithms. I dangled these before the acquisitive arithmetical gods to catch their interest. Then as they reached out for these number pearls, I ran the zero of a function routine, which in practical visual terms was more like a magic trick in which the numbers in the algorithms progressively vanished as if erased right before them. Then I disappeared, as far as the alien gods were concerned. I was in the zero.

There was nothing to acquire and nobody holding it. It was an empty space, yet, since I was still self-aware, it was more like I was wearing an invisibility cloak. You couldn't see me, and you couldn't observe any numbers, but you might, if you were very sensitive, have sensed my lurking but veiled presence in the zero. I was a one inside a zero. It was like wearing a deep-sea diving suit to protect me against the extreme water pressure at ocean depth. If I could pull all of numbered reality into this zero with me, we'd all be safe, but then reality would have no traction within existence and might as well not exist. I would still be chasing my tail within this unresolvable paradox, going nowhere.

Meanwhile, they seemed to be taking number sets and threads of equations and stringing them like beads on a long chain of gold. It was like an avaricious publisher scooping up available copyrights, locking down all publishing rights on books. These were ruthless collectors who would stop at nothing to acquire everything. As such, they were entirely inimical to what the Hierophancy stood for. They wanted more than the Hierophancy heuristic algorithm for Earth; they wanted all the numbers, even before they were combined into the equations that ran reality. They wanted to commandeer the arithmetical raw materials of the Creation itself, picking the deep pockets of the Creator Himself. They wanted no numbers to remain extant in the world.

It was an ambition so vast I felt all I could do in the face of it was laugh loudly. I did, and the egglike zero I was hiding in wobbled and wiggled like a gelatin. I laughed more when I reflected on how far all this was from looking after Light temples and matching old mythic images with the secret function of these sites and developing inventories of locations and equivalent descriptions. It seemed a long way from our usual work of revealing the Holy Light, which meant keeping the temples in operational trim as mirrors of cosmic realities.

Now we were working at the arithmetical realm that made the existence of these Light temples possible, the fundamental math equations that generated them. If the Light temples were compromised or erased altogether when their underlying arithmetical foundations were removed, our processes of consciousness would falter and dry up. We would no longer have the identity mirrors they provided and we would lose all possibility of self-awareness that characterized our lives and epitomized what being a human was all about.

In effect they were stealing the possibility of our standing in the Holy Light itself, removing that from our planetary reality. Take away the numbers and the Light temples collapse, and with that goes our life. Standing hidden inside a zero might be affording me a measure of safety, but it would not be the basis for reconstituting an arithmetically scripted world. The whole world couldn't stand with me inside this zero. That would be like non-existence. So I was safe and blushingly clever inside the fortress of my zero, but the rest of reality was still exposed to the deprivations of these mathematical predators.

That led to a disturbing thought, one I could not settle in my mind. Had we dredged too deeply in looking for and securing the heuristic algorithm that could manage all geomantic and physical affairs on the Earth? Had we disturbed a basic level of reality we were not meant to access and thereby upset all balance?

Obviously, if we hadn't developed the master algorithm, the alien gods could not have stolen it. That is too self-evident a casual chain. What I mean is had we ill-advisedly exposed an operational level behind reality that then grabbed the attention of these conscienceless acquisitive collectors of all arithmetical modes? Had we heedlessly probed into the realm of forbidden knowledge and touching it like a button never meant to be exposed or activated set in motion events that could lead to the end of reality?

In developing the algorithm, we had definitively taken charge of our human consciousness by mastering the mathematics that ran all processes of human and Earth, but at the same time we had rendered this precious level naked and vulnerable. I had the impression the alien gods could not have revealed it on their own; maybe they couldn't be bothered, or only we as the recipients of this arithmetical largesse could dig that deeply and uncover the secret equations and we had just found their much desired buried treasure.

We had to intemperately cross this forbidden boundary, touch the recondite algorithm, then the alien gods could sweep in and neatly scoop it up. Or maybe our digging it up was the requirement, even the fulfillment, of our having free will, to reach this degree of taking responsibility for our human consciousness, to boldly seek out, find, and apply the managing number script, interactively manage its processes in all its fields, both bodily and planetary. As you can see, the question vexed me and I had no viable answer, no certainty.

The odd part here was the alien gods were not in any classic sense of the term evil, though their actions clearly would have evil consequences. They did not dislike intelligent life-forms like humans and our extra-planetary colleagues. They did not like them either. I think they had no attitude about us at all; they just wanted our arithmetic. They were spirit beings of zero affect. It didn't occur to them, or maybe it did and they dismissed it as irrelevant, that in acquiring the arithmetical realm that ran our realities they took out our bones. They extracted the skeletal system that held up our forms, supported our minds, and, in doing this, presumably assured our eventual dissolution and death.

That must have been the insight Ray Master Hermes wanted me to have. I was back at our

Sun Valley offices again where I had been, I guess, moments ago. Before I even thought about it, I was out the door and walking across the land. One of the planetary representatives was with me in a plausible semblance of a human form, adopted, I think, mostly to fit in and not be overtly conspicuous. I have no idea what "his" name was in "his" home language, but we managed to agree that I should refer to him as L2, meaning his planet's second emissary. We agreed to call his planet "L" since its actual name was untranslatable in English. As for the "his" and any gender attribution, my impression is their gendering was beyond my understanding and male and female differences might be moot.

That said, L2 and I walked up the lower slopes of the north side of Bald Mountain. That is the big ski slope mountain in Sun Valley, and it has been since 1934 when people first started skiing down its slopes. The mountain, known familiarly as Baldy, its south surface quite earnestly etched in ski runs, stands at 9,150 feet, dominating this town (and nearby Ketchum and Hailey), which has organized a busy commercial center around the skiing industry. Ketchum is still noteworthy for being the former home of Ernest Hemingway, and Hailey boasts the early presence of a famous American poet, the iconoclastic Ezra Pound.

The important geomantic advent of 2020 did not dim America's capitalist drive, though I have noticed in recent years more people inquire about the possible "spiritual" nature of this mountain so clearly sacrificed to human pleasure. The north side is quiet and remote, flanked by more mountains and steep ridges. The noise, physical and psychic, from the clamor of the skiers and the equipment skiing

requires doesn't reach out here. Here we felt the mountain.

We perched on the lower grassy slopes of Baldy and looked out. It was a pleasant, high elevation mountain view. We were a little above 6,000 feet. The weather was pleasant, a mild 60° F with a slight steady breeze. We hadn't cracked the case of the arithmetical theft, but we were taking a break. At least that's how it seemed. I didn't feel like I was orchestrating much of what I did at the moment. I didn't mind having time off from those vexing alien gods. It was nice to be back in my physical body, to feel the pull of gravity, and to assume the customary rules of physical incarnation pertained again and I could trip and fall if I wasn't watching where I put my feet. I enjoyed breathing again. I spent some moments following my breath and studying my sneakers. They were scuffed.

L2 didn't talk but he did communicate telepathically, mostly in pictures. Despite for him the evident physical strangeness of our planet, it was familiar. Apparently, they had pictures and diagrams of our Earth in their geomantic offices, the equivalent of our Hierophancy. They had Light grid models of the six free-will planets, and members of his group were well-briefed on the designs.

They were several steps ahead of us, or maybe it was of just myself. Maybe Blaise had seen diagrams of their planets and their Light grids and never mentioned it. It didn't even seem strange to me that as I looked out across the mountains I saw superimposed on them the Light grid patternings, and on those, the arithmetical codes that scripted and maintained their physical existence. L2 saw this too. I know this because in an odd but easy way I could share his visual point of view. We were seeing the landscape as the product of an engineering diagram and its arithmetical coding, and we were seeing its physical side too. It was like seeing simultaneously three stages in a linear sequence, plan to reality.

Earth didn't seem to be falling apart yet, even though the algorithm that ran it had been stolen and no doubt was now being installed in an infernal Magic Square. On the other hand, I thought I detected a slight gap, a fissure almost, between the Light grid patterning and the physical composition of outer Earth reality. Was this an early sign of the essential alignment of matter and Light pattern starting to falter? The alien gods' vacuum pump was sucking out all the arithmetic underpinning our reality 24 hours a day now; soon it would be gone.

It wasn't that unusual for me to be meeting with "people" from other planets. The 2020 Light grid upgrade had brought vitality back to the stargate network and the Earth was slowly becoming a galactically cosmopolitan planet *again*, even if only small numbers of people at present appreciated this trend. People were intensely surprised that the Earth had been designed to be a cosmopolitan planet with regular travel back and forth among 300 linked worlds. That's what the stargate network of two million nodes facilitates: great mobility.

I had met with many representatives of other planets pre-linked in this system and always on matters of Light grid design or rehabilitation, but not about its theft. These extra-planetary representatives routinely came and went through the stargate not far from here and called in at the Hierophancy offices. The stargate system was once again working the way it was designed to. It was the next stage in diplomacy and scientific exchange, Earth now enjoying relations with 300 other planets in this system, ones whose chief phylogeny sufficiently overlapped ours or shared enough design consanguinity to justify our relations.

L2 showed me a set of pictures meant to illustrate how their Light grid interacted with their physical forms which, I noted, seemed much more subtle than ours, more couched in Light than dense matter. The "people" on his planet walked about with a greater basic perception of the overlapping of reality layers. That meant they could see the Light grid designs that shaped their physical forms. They saw the minute fluctuations of Light intensity in these enveloping grids as their own thoughts and emotions modulated them; even their breathing could impart a classic "butterfly" effect on the status of the Light grid patterns.

They registered incoming astrological influences and saw these grids bend and twist and even rotate under their attention, though these influences were short-lived. They kept track of the regular tidal flows of time from the future and past into their present reality configuration. Essentially, their reality worked in 4D, and time currents and influences from the past and future were normal.

They would well up and gain significance for a while the way a composer would periodically reiterate or maybe build on certain themes in a symphony. I saw how on L2's world you could routinely see evidence of how things had been, where things were going, and the current progress status. It was like watching a single fluid movement, a gesture like picking up a bucket, even though this motion comprised aspects of the past and future.

On L2's world the people tended to be aware of when higher celestial intelligences "touched" these grids or when angelic presences fanned their wings on them to quicken the life-force and the consciousness gradient of the souls living within them. L2 helped me understand they had their own terms for these presences; while "angelic" is a term with human meaning, from his viewpoint it was more like a circulating toroidal field (it could resemble the fanning of wings) with an acute unformed celestial presence that delivered this beneficent gesture.

Nomenclature was not of primary importance, L2 indicated. The frequency of influence was paramount. They saw themselves as like living in a shallow tide pool such as you see among flat rocks with a small depression filled with salt water close to the ocean's edge. You're constantly immersed in the life of the water as well as the tidal rhythms that roll the water in and sweep it out. The water is the extended consciousness field of the celestial and galactic realms, and the swells and ebbs of its flow were the time currents from past and future. Regarding these mountains before us and ski-slope-etched Bald Mountain behind us, L2 saw these as masses of consciousness, as higher-frequency hills with physical matter as a place-marker for these lucid points in consciousness.

I suppose that is equivalent to how a geomancer sees domes and their mountains. The domes give the physical mountain its numinosity, but for L2 the dome was the mountain, and even the dome wasn't necessary: here was a rise in awareness. He saw that consciousness gradient as the mountain. Paramount was this elevated zone of consciousness where reality was quickened. Dome and mountain or neither—anyway,

it was the arithmetical code scripting both that was the origin of this terrestrial reality. An algorithm directed where both aspects of the phenomena were to stand as it ran their activities.

L2 and his world did not distinguish the layers of reality in the sense of keeping them separate. We still did. Our Earth mind was still slowly moving into the unified field of the Golden Age and its cognitive upgrade to the Light grid, physical matter, and our sense of awareness. I still saw the mountain, its devic host, then the dome, then the contents of the dome, then the host star and its denizens and the Light temple they worked in. I saw these as sequentially perceived layers. L2 saw them all at once as a unit and cut to the essence of the phenomena: here is a zone of quickened consciousness, his attention confirmed.

Perhaps when the domes make their momentous and forecast fourth presence on the Earth, not too long from now, in fact, our cognition will catch up with L2's. For the moment, I was enjoying the rank physicality of sitting on this mountain slope, clearly (as far as I could tell) back in my physical body, and liking that, and I didn't mind peeling through the layers of reality like flipping book pages. L2 absorbed the book at a glance and skipped all the page flipping.

L2 showed me his hand. He held something in it and he wanted me to see it. It looked like a pulsing hypercube. That is a four-dimensional cube. It's a complex shape and hard for the human eye to perceive it as it consists of eight cubes that seem to be somersaulting, turning inside out, and generally acting wild and crazy in geometrical terms. Fortunately, I was familiar with this shape, though this one was made of Light. It was like holding a fairy in your palm, grasping something from another evanescent, ethereal world in the physicality of your hand. I didn't get this initially, but the image first appeared as a tattoo on his palm; then it leapt into a Light form, like a square tennis ball resting in his palm. Then it expanded into a four-dimensional moving shape, like a live being.

Numbers and equations were inscribed upon the geometrical edges and surfaces of this constantly convoluting and shapeshifting form. I suspected the device also worked as a hand calculator, maybe even a computer with significant byte capacity. L2 indicated the numbers on the edges and surfaces as the reason he was showing me this image. Some were familiar; the rest were not. I realized this hypercube was not the algorithm, only a container for it, like a magic treasure box whose constantly altering shape was part of its security measures. It was a hand-generated computer and holographic projector displaying algorithms.

"We generate a false Magic Square for our greedy collector gods," he said, though I'm sure it was a telepathic sharing of thoughts, obviating words on his part. "Note the small changes in some of the calculations. A few of the key digits have been altered, but otherwise the components look correct though the product will be misleading. Still, it is enough like the master algorithm the alien gods seek. We let them acquire this simulacrum and keep the real, correct one safe. They still have not acquired the complete algorithm. We have managed to withhold it from them this far. Now we pretend to let them take it from us.

"We will allow our Light grids to temporarily degrade to a small percentage to support the illusion we have surrendered the correct managing algorithm. These will seem like routine perturbations to the system resulting from transient celestial phenomena. We have the advantage that these collector gods do not know the full shape of the algorithm, all the numbers in their correct order. Since that is what they've been trying to get from us, they might accept the false version and not know it until they put it into operation. Maybe not then."

I appreciated L2's devious mind. His plan might work. If we were spies, you'd call that good tradecraft. We couldn't remove these gods from the playing field, but we might trick them into accepting an illusory algorithm for the real one. L2 would have to sit down with Sal to work out the mathematical specifics. I realized, a little chilled, that the alien gods were after the algorithms of our six collegial planets, meaning all six of us were now in a shared jeopardy state.

I was beginning to see that the alien gods' inimical interest in our Hierophancy heuristic algorithm was a natural and unavoidable consequence of our having achieved it in the first place, having ascended to this developmental threshold. It was an evolutionary milestone that put Earth on the map of planets of interest. We had identified ourselves as new players on the field, like a planetary culture mastering warp drive in the *Star Trek* language of years ago. Mathematical innovations detected anywhere immediately caught their interest and they set out to acquire them and remove them from the operational field.

No, it wasn't quite that. We had acquired the algorithm centuries ago back at the House of Wisdom, but its existence and use had remained secret. Maybe we hadn't appreciated what we had discovered then or how to operate it. Now we were a chartered official agency, working relatively openly though on covert projects, even if few understood what we did or how we did it. Many didn't care or regarded our projects as tame assuring us some protection from scrutiny.

Still, even that small amount of public visibility was probably what alerted the alien gods to our ripeness. Maybe the operation of this management algorithm left a specific etheric signature that they detected. The Light grid was what made the lush physicality of Earth possible, and the algorithm was what managed the life of this Light grid and the consciousness field it supported, humans, and which we took for granted as our personal and external reality which we expect to be waiting for us each fresh morning when we get up.

I was enjoying breathing, smelling the air, and feeling the hardness of the rocks around me. On the other hand, this physicality was the wholesome expected product of this reality engineering and arithmetical modeling. I wondered if we could calculate the arithmetical structure of these rocks, if we could run the algorithm that generates solidity as an Earth feature. What? I didn't know why my thoughts took this sudden turn into the philosophical.

Then I did. Somehow Blaise was now sitting next to me on the hill. I hadn't seen or heard him approach. He seemed to have suddenly appeared. I had subliminally registered his arrival by the shift of emphasis in my thoughts.

That was just like him to do this, and I shouldn't expect any explanation from him. He always went for the deepest backstory he could

access; surface details were never sufficient for his probing, Scorpionic mind, for this ontological Sherlock Holmes. He was dedicated to the Earth, to the fulfillment of its Light grid, since he had helped design it long ago, but he was also aloof, a wanderer, no longer content to remain only here. After all, he'd spent almost 20 years off-planet in the time between 2020 and 2040, much of it in the Pleiades, his home. I could sense his restiveness, his desire to move on soon, return to the Pleiades.

"Show him how it works, L2," Blaise said to my companion on the hill.

He was referring to the hand-held hypercube. Suddenly it expanded to the size of a large house and we were inside its confusing shifting geometry. Storage device, calculator, and now clearly a holographic projector, what had first appeared as a curious tattoo on L2's palm was now a structure of Light. It was as if somebody had built a large summerhouse on the side of this hill. If you ever find yourself inside a live version of a hypercube, don't focus on the complex movement of all the cubes; it will spin your head around too much. Find a steady point and keep your attention there. I did that and soon the shifting geometry was less unsettling to my perception. I studied the numbers.

The structure was like being inside somebody's mind. It was instantly interactive. If I thought of our Earth, it appeared at once, complete with its Light grid and all the arithmetical aspects. The same was true for the other five free-will planets. If I wanted to zoom in on one algorithm or even an aspect of one, that happened immediately, and I could follow its intricate interconnections with the many other calculations inside this composite. I only had to think the request. It was as if L2's brain was outside his body, accessible like a handheld computer; more surprising was the fact other people could access his mind this way as well. And here we were, walking around inside his mind projected as a big house.

I noticed that a number of the many edges within this four-dimensional cube were highlighted in red. They seemed to throb insistently, drawing my attention. As soon as I looked more closely at them, they revealed layers of mathematical calculations, as if I were interviewing them and they were gladly cooperating with my inquiry, showing me documents and all the relevant data.

"These are the areas they are particularly interested in," said L2. "They seek earnestly to swoop in and collect those calculations highlighted in red."

"If we think in terms of manufacturing," said Blaise, "these red-lighted calculations are raw materials, like the 17 rare-earth metals or trace minerals vitally needed to complete a product or to run a chemical sequence to make the product. Their progress is stalled as long as they don't have these components. Our job is to stall them out permanently. We don't want them to finish their product which, as you know, is not a product at all but a master Magic Square. That Magic Square, when activated, will be inimical to all sentient intelligence, especially to those possessing high levels of free will and Light grids to match it."

As Frederick, I examined these red-lighted equations like a foreign language. In other words, I made little sense of them. But as the former Arabic mathematician in the Study House of Al-Khwārizmī I understood them at once. They were clever, original, and

arithmetically adroit; they specified abstruse sub-processes within a Light grid's overall operation. The level of thinking and the mastery of algorithmic calculation behind them were impressive. I noticed that these red-lighted areas were slightly glaring in their Light emissions, like neon signs, as if they were trying to block me from seeing something else. But I did.

Behind them I saw some calculations done in green. They were less immediately impressive and did not draw one's attention the way the red-lighted ones did. But they had a welcoming modesty, the quiet familiarity of your hometown greeting you after a long absence. I recognized these. They pertained to the Earth and were important. I might have helped generate them.

They were familiar and surprising, the way you might feel if you had a powerful dream, swore you'd never forget it, forgot it, then remembered it years later. It returned to you with a shock of familiarity and the sense of an urgent message. Almost like you had vowed to do something, write a book, compile arithmetical maxims, do something anchored in an important level of truth, and you forgot you intended this, forgot you even knew this information, until now. As soon as this registered with me, the green mathematical coding got blocked and the red-lighted ones returned to their place of visual prominence.

"Do you ever have to provide fresh input to your heuristic algorithm?" asked L2. His question subtly pulled me away from what I had been watching. I noted that the question came immediately after the green codes got blocked. Did L2 not want me to study those recessed calculations highlighted in green? I wondered why fleetingly, but then the subject disappeared from my mind like somebody erasing a blackboard that had been covered in writing. I forgot about it and respectfully considered his question. Blaise's expression revealed nothing.

"We used to, in the early days of its inception," I replied, "but then it entered into a reciprocal exchange with outer reality and made its own data collections regularly. As the term heuristic suggests, the algorithm learned how to do this on its own, then proceeded to get ever better at it, gaining competency. Now it routinely gathers data on weather, climate, geological conditions, volcanology, astrological factors, sociological trends, electromagnetic field fluctuations, solar flare emissions and any Sun-related activities. We will monitor its data acquisition, look for omissions, sometimes add a few factual nuances, and generally almost every day check to make sure it is functioning well.

"It can even quantify the degree of human interaction and consciousness investment in any aspects of the Light grid across the Earth and in all countries and cultures and include this in the overall computation. Mass spiritual or pilgrimage events like India's regular *Kumbh-Mela* that attracts millions go into these figures. The annual *Haj,* the Muslim pilgrimage to Mecca, and the regular processions along the Santiago de Compostela route across Spain are factored into the computations. Similarly, mass events, guided by the media, to distract people and herd them into a cognitive null zone of frenzy and gossip, are included because they drain off the sharp focus gained from the pilgrimages. They are a kind of geomantic

bloodletting which weakens the planetary patient.

"The effect of annual Light grid top-ups like Epiphany and Michaelmass, even though poorly attended by human awareness, still represent significant moments of celestial input and are added to the computations. They are like blood transfusions to strengthen the patient, if you will allow the analogy. Over time, our algorithm developed exceedingly fine, broadscale data collection abilities to sentiently sense anything new or altered in the planetary domain.

"It then adjusts the flow rate and relative quantities of angelic, celestial, and terrestrial inputs, balancing them against the electromagnetic field status, like a consciousness-nutrient feed for the planetary Light grid system. There are 238 geomantic nodes across the planet specifically designed to do this. Blaise calls them Control Bubbles and likens them to geomantic thermostats and adjustable flow valves that regulate a balanced infusion of celestial energies. These are primary regional input nodes for the heuristic algorithm; they work in both directions, sending current data to the algorithm and inputting its changes."

L2 pointed to a region within the holographic house-sized algorithmic process we were sitting inside on the mountain slope. Some of the equations seemed active, flushing with Light and urgency. "Those are collecting fresh data right now back on our planet and making immediate Light grid adjustments. The data collection mesh is so sensitive it can register when someone reaches a deep space of clarity and cosmic alignment in a meditative state. When they touch the bedrock of consciousness, this registers as significant, positive Light grid input. It is like adding a sparkling gold coin to a pile of them at a public fountain. Then everyone benefits, however slightly, from this addition, this Light contribution. This proves that the contribution of a single person can affect the whole system."

Then the queerest thing happened. It was as if L2 extracted a carpet of numbers out of himself, like a huge, extended tongue rippling with calculations, and this moved into the holographic house and carpeted it from the inside. I told you it was strange. It looked like a carpet or tongue but it was comprised entirely of numbers in organized fashion, algorithms, arithmetical formulations, all that. The numbers glistened on the extended tongue like saliva. I realized, gradually, as I overcame my shock at this feral impression, I was seeing arithmetical DNA.

In some arcane manner of design, the tongue of numbers enabled L2 to instantly reprogram any aspect of the system. This system was immediately responsive to this manner of input, and in this way L2 extended an arithmetical *avatar* of himself into the holographic display of his home planet's Light grid system. Bear in mind that just as I am basically translating non-English statements from L2 into plausible English syntax and meaning, so did my mind recompute the images. God knows how L2 conceptualized this numbers tongue.

Meanwhile, L2, with his magical numbers tongue, was making real-time adjustments to his planet's system through this holographic version of it, even though, technically, in spatial terms, it lay an unfathomable number of light-years away in another galaxy. Did that mean he was changing the reality conditions of his planet's inhabitants right before me? L2

registered my question and responded without my having to voice it.

"The system runs simulations and receives actual inputs," L2 said. "It can do either, as I choose. I am now running simulations. They will not have any impact on my planet's reality conditions. They merely show me what an impact will probably look like. I have to add another element, this green ribbon, to implement the simulations and have them produce a real-time palpable effect."

This green ribbon, which I had seen only in part before now, glared like neon. It too, like the tongue, was packed with numbers and computations, but it reminded me of an ocean-borne troop carrier (officially known as an LCVP, a landing craft vehicle personnel boat widely used for military amphibious landings), loaded to the maximum with numbers, approaching a shore (I thought of the beaches of Normandy in 1945), everyone poised to instantly disembark.

I couldn't quite picture a boatload of prepared algorithms in this personified way, yet when L2 gave the word or whatever his manner was to signal engagement, they would disembark, rush the shore, and start reorganizing reality on his planet and its Light grid would adjust accordingly. It was like an army invading France and then utterly re-arranging its culture and landscape. L2 was a one-man planetary grid geomancer. That was a lot of power, knowledge, and responsibility in one person's hand, I thought at the time. Was it at all risky?

"They're using a generative algorithm to trigger the real-time inputs." It was Sal, our resident mathematical wizard, suddenly standing next to me. "That green ribbon," he said by way of explanation, pointing to it, "runs a generative algorithm which models how data is produced (the new input parameters and specifics) in order to categorize and dispatch a signal (the new input that is implemented). It's clever and efficient. It displays the whole logic train.

"The operator, or geomancer in this case, prepares all the calculations mentally. The green ribbon stores them, like an arithmetical launch vessel, then releases them when the correct command is entered. L2 does the calculations himself. That's quite a talent, and it's a marvel too, when you think about it: a planet's entire geomantic life and maintenance managed by just one adroit numbers mind."

"On the backside of these number displays are pictures, like images painted on rock surfaces you used to find throughout the American Southwest." Jocelyn had joined us inside L2's holographic house of arithmetic. "They are like an image commentary on the abstract activity of the algorithms, very sophisticated glyphs. Here's one, for example: it shows a humanlike head, like the way L2 appears to us, but the cranium is larger and more cone-shaped.

"A hand extends out of the top, and it has numerous long fingers, dozens of them. On the hand numbers ripple, looking like animated water beads. These numbers send sparks and lightning bolts into the outside world. The image shows people running away from them, trees leaning over, waters rising. Clearly, this arithmetical activity is regarded as powerful, controlling, maybe a little scary. Isn't this marvellous? We're looking at a mythic image from another planet. We could enroll it in a new xenomythology department at a school."

Despite our close proximity inside the numbers-house hologram, Jocelyn said to me privately, "This image rather disturbs me with its implications. That is a great deal of power vested in one individual with control over a planet's grid."

I took her point. The difference in approach was significant. Our heuristic algorithm only required occasional deliberate input from us, its administrators. Then it ran its program and made adjustments in response to changing Earth conditions. But for L2's set-up, his mind, his interactive consciousness, was a prime component of the system, like a football coach who also plays quarterback or a movie director who also plays a character in the film. He doesn't call the shots from the sideline, bellowing out plays; he is out on the field directing the burly players from among them, ordering where the ball goes, even carrying it.

L2's administrative algorithm is dependent on his continuous input for its deployment which means he must maintain rigorous purity of intent and objective focus. Jocelyn was suggesting that perhaps this was not the case on his home planet, or maybe she was just hinting that it was a point of vulnerability. It demanded optimally high standards of integrity and incorruptibility by L2. Of course, she couldn't help but view this set-up from the human perspective, and the knowledge of humanity's basically duplicitous, ambivalent moral nature. It didn't automatically mean L2's phylogeny was equally morally undependable.

That's as far as I got with this thought at the time. My attention was diverted to that tongue of numbers I mentioned earlier when L2 called my name. We had been standing on it; it had seemed enough like a carpet to not warrant too much disturbed thought about its real nature. Now I saw that when it was activated it roiled in numbers and equations like a pot of boiling spaghetti, the long algorithmic calculations resembling thin straws of white pasta. It was a sea of potentialities, innumerable possible arithmetical combinations and outcomes.

It was like a think tank packed with clever people coming up with sharp ideas. The range of applications spanned minute cosmetic adjustments to radical overhauls. L2's job was to select which level of adjustment the system required. The set-up reminded me of a radio disc jockey who could choose any record and particular song among hundreds of albums available to play for his audience. My point in using this antique example from my parents' generation is that what was played, the music broadcast, was at the emcee's discretion and his sense of musical syllogism. The listener was stuck with it; the emcee hoped he'd like it.

But I saw how L2 could direct the flow and moods of his planetary consciousness. The Light grid system was instantly responsive to his tailored inputs. To use still another analogy, he was the nurse adjusting the contents and flow-rate of the IV-drip; he could modulate the analgesic input for more lucidity or sleepiness. L2 had great responsibility and considerable latitude in this work. I did wonder at the time whether L2 could be liable to subtle outside influence. If in effect he was the heuristic element in this system, could he be manipulated by external thoughts or suggestions and perhaps not realize this input was in play? I didn't know, but I appreciated that if the alien gods wanted to grab L2's planet's arithmetical matrix they'd have to breach this complex of tongues and cubes.

Now another representative stepped forward. I hadn't realized he was even with us on the slope. We agreed to call him R1. I apologize again for the inept sounding names we've given these "aliens," but there is no plausible, pronounceable English equivalent for their actual names. This one was the first of two representatives from the planet called (simplistically, by us) R.

R1 extended his right index finger and it seemed to turn into a long wand. This wand then projected a sphere filled with many upright copies of itself, like pillars. These pillars, which were ruby-colored, contained numbers; they were packed solid with numbers like a straw which has just drawn up a full volume from a glass. The numbers filled the straw-wands like effervescent bubbles eager to be released into the world. This apparently was the algorithmic depository for this planet. I waited to see what R1 would do with this arithmetical abundance.

I should note that at first I thought this was a vision, a shared mental image passed around within our small group. I was mistaken. It was a hologram manifested out in front us, as large as a building, like L2's, adjacent to his in fact. We were now standing inside it, surrounded by these curious straw-wands. I wondered what "ordinary" people in Sun Valley would make of this bizarre double apparition of a holographic house shaped like a sphere filled with numbers, but it was more likely they wouldn't see it as it was probably phase-shifted from normal human sight, or (maybe additionally) there was a stealth mirror around the whole backside of Bald Mountain deflecting all attention.

I was only seeing this now, as I thought of its likelihood. We were well shielded from any public gaze. L2 and R1, who only had vaguely plausible human shapes, would no doubt strike alarm in the unprepared eyes of casual hikers or bird watchers or whatever might bring people to this non-skiing side of the mountain. Maybe nobody came here. There was no reason to other than the recondite one that brought us here for privacy and this abstruse arithmetical modeling of our respective planetary Light grids. But was it abstruse?

I remember Blaise telling me not long ago that he was beginning to favor the mathematical description of Light temples. The psychic impressions of palaces, cities, godly residences, and the deities themselves were too indefinite, too fluctuating, too inherently unformed, too mercurially protean, too much approximations contrived by a mind struggling to describe ineffable realities.

No matter how strong or precise your clairvoyance was, you were up against the fundamental epistemological problem that these processes of consciousness, whether they were personified as gods or palaces, did not inherently have any fixed form, only approximate ones, yielding plausible visual metaphors for us. They were alive, dynamic, shapeshifting and modulating constantly; to cognitively force them into a single fixed shape shaves off too much of their reality. Arithmetical displays were not subject to this variability. Thankfully they are fixed, nailed down, permanent. They are a reality baseline you can always count on.

"I used to think they were equivalent and interchangeable, cross revelatory, reciprocally revealing, psychic-mythic images or mathematical formulas," Blaise said at the time. "You could pursue either for insight. But now I regard the arithmetical version as

deeper and antecedent, more revealing. The mythic pictures are filtered through a person's clairvoyant but still subjective experience, a picture formulation of how the energies or processes affected them. They are at best plausible visual metaphors, even if generated by the gods. But look at how different cultures have formed these metaphors in reference to the same geomantic features. You don't have that fluctuation with the numbers. The mythic-psychic side is too subject to variation. I mean, consider the Blaises.

"Metaphor masters, I call them, with no end of different plausible forms to take, such as white horse, elephant, angel, giant bird, flying monkey. They are all suggestive images, but what is their true form, their actual, correct appearance? None of these, and none at all. That's my point. There is no absolute, solid ground with them, or the realm of psychic images. These are relatively correct, but none are unequivocally, definitively descriptive. They are not unchanging like numbers. It's as if they say, with a shrug, well, let's say we look *like* this. Let's say our energy and consciousness can be represented this way. Like it?

"We still have to see through their metaphors, the likenesses, to the pure, steady arithmetical realm. Only the numbers and the equations they are coded from stay the same. I'm not saying the Blaises are the product of a math code from God, but I was using their example of protean metaphorical expressivity to make the point. The arithmetical dimension of a geomantic node is neutral and fixed. The algorithm remains the same tomorrow, and the day after that, no matter who is looking at it. Mathematics do not need plausible visual metaphors. As a matter of epistemology, that strikes me as closer to basic bedrock than myths."

So we stood inside this second holographic space, surrounded by these tall red pillars packed with bubbles that were number clusters. Sal and Jocelyn were inside with us, along with R1, L2, Blaise, and our other 11 colleagues. R1 was the ringmaster for this circus. He stood still, meditatively alert. I didn't see him move, but he must have made some kind of head gesture or generated a thought command, because the pillars started releasing their number hordes. Numerous thin strands extruded from the pillars; numbers encircled these strands like beads on a string; and these numbers started to form into equations. It was like watching the letters of an alphabet spontaneously start to write words.

These words were now generating life-forms to populate the planet. It was a display of all a planet's phylogenies sketched in the air like vivid paintings. The numbers and their equations scripted these images, then disappeared into the background, managing these newly created realities quietly from the shadows. The forms were strange from an Earth perspective, but in essence they included what we would call animals to live on the ground, forms that flew in the air, and the dominant consciousness-bearing shapes that vaguely resembled humans. They were taller, leaner, hairless, their heads elongated and oddly transparent.

The planet's Light temples were modeled in the air too. Architecturally, these were bizarre because their designs were so original from my Earth view. Their geometry was hard to make sense of, as if designed by M.C. Escher to deliberately occupy overlapping dimensions, both transparent and nonlinear. After studying

them for a while, I began to see their congruence with the consciousness structure of R1's planet's dominant phylogeny, the quasi-humans.

Clearly, they were crafted from the same hand as their design style was consistent. I saw how these various Light temples were projections from aspects of the body, how they modeled these crucial body and mind processes for the souls. That's where you get the Light temples from after all: it's like you disassemble the consciousness-bearing phylogeny and project its constituents across the planetary landscape as Light temples. The Light body of this taken-apart phylogeny then constitutes the architectural inventory of a planet's geomantic landscape, and the purpose of working the Light grid is to reassemble this form through serial conscious interactions with the individual Light nodes.

On our Earth that form is Albion and the 613 different types of Light temples we have inventoried are components of his terrestrial Light body. Blaise uses the term "Walking in Albion" to denote the experience of consciousness finding itself in this distributed dismembered cosmogonic body of Albion that is our Light grid. The Hierophant's work is to illuminate this distributed form and to supervise its reassembling in human consciousness by connecting the nodes.

Walking in Albion is the experience of wakeful consciousness touring this reassembled, completed body, like an owner proudly strolling through his newly-built home, except we walk in Albion knowing we are the same as Albion. Any progress or illumination in consciousness we make is transferred to him, and any new inputs from the solar system, galaxy or cosmos from Albion are automatically downloaded into human awareness. It is a very fluid relationship. Humans are the many little Albions, and Albion is the one big Human, and the Earth maintains a reciprocal, interactive reflection of both aspects of this reality.

That seems to be a consistent design principle in correlating Light temple design and dominant consciousness-bearing life-form, that they must mirror each other. Outside, they create a world and spell out its diversity; inside, they comprise the necessary components for consciousness and biology, knitted together with Light. Outside and inside versions generate bridges to link up.

R1 was managing bridge-building at the moment. Maybe he cast out the bridges. He wrote the choreography for this elegant ballet of reciprocity of outside and inside versions, and he stands in the stage wings directing the complex dance steps. The principle of geomancy is the same on any planet, it seems: the inherent reciprocal correlation of planet and consciousness, human and Earth, R1's people and their planet and the process of waking up the planetary expression by humans or the intelligent life-forms interacting with and illuminating the distributed nodes of that planetary consciousness body. That way the consciousness-bearers keep congruent and integrated with their world.

That brought me back to another comment Blaise made that day. He was asking what precisely does a geomancer do, once you penetrate to the core arithmetical and algorithmic level of planetary Light grid maintenance? Provide cues and choreography hints to the players when they falter or forget their lines?

"I was having a consultation with the Architect-in-Chief one day, at least in my mind I thought I was," Blaise said, "and I was wondering what the goal of the Earth's design and successful evolution was. Where is it all going? A reasonable question, surely, that any thoughtful geomancer will raise. Then I saw something. Maybe the Chief gave me a little vision, or maybe it was the Blaises who did this because they figured in the impression I had, as they always do.

"I was standing in my naked awareness with no form amidst the millions of hexagonal diamond facets that comprise their composite Light form. This is the stage I call the Phoenix Cloak, where you wear the *Nimitta* diamonds like a robe around your consciousness or when you occupy the body of the Simorgh, their majestic, divine Bird of Light form, saturating yourself in the total vibrational manifestation of this angelic order, namely, their *Sat Cit Ananda*.

"You need to be inside your white staff to do this, having enlarged it to Light pillar size. The diamond array is the tray upon which the White Crown rests. That's the top of the white staff, the white diamond-fire flaring crown points, the flowering part. This is holy ground, where the 22 creative fire-forms of the *Autiot*, the Hebrew generative alphabet, reside respectfully wreathing His Head, awaiting His use to create reality or perhaps extend it or modify it, and according to Qabalistic lore, each is petitioning The Chief to be used first.

"I don't want to lose you in the complexity of this impression, but what happened next tended to answer my question. Or at least it addressed its concerns. The totality of the Earth's Light grid design, its idea and completion, was raised up and placed in the midst of these White Crown points of His Head. It was the Emerald, filled with all the particulars of the Light grid, and its personification, Albion, awake, Christed, lucid, ready to journey and converse. It sat like a diamond geometrical egg in a bed of feathers made of divine Light. You will, I trust, permit me my wandering metaphors. It's hard to evoke the quality.

"The Holy Letters were like tongues of fire that licked the Emerald. The 231 Gates, a secondary level expression of the *Autiot*, comprising all the two-letter combinations possible and looking like a dragon's treasure cave of criss-crossing Light lines joining the two letters to make new third-level expressions, also enveloped the Earth's Light grid with rivers of fire. It was a benediction and a validation, and I think it was also a topping-up of vital consciousness life-force.

"The Earth's Light grid had returned to its place of conception to be honored by its parents, in this case what I like to call Mr. and Mrs. God, in Person, joined by their creative staff, the fire-letters, as well as the 24 Elders and the Holy Beasts. Think of this as the Supreme Being's inner circle of advisers and holy courtiers. I stress the word 'holy,' not a word you want to overuse, to suggest the purity of this presence and the uniqueness of the gesture and place.

"The Earth, through its Light grid and summarized in the Emerald as its form, was presented at court upon the myriad diamond facets of the White Crown. It was an oroboric moment but with an alpha head and omega tail, the completion not identical with the inception because then it was idea, now a finished reality. The slight asymmetry here was crucial; it is

where the learning happens. Albion was awake and lucid, ready for his cosmic peripatetry. The Christ Light was circulating like the finest blood through the grid system.

"Our work as geomancers, as workers in the Hierophancy, seemed done. The Earth had achieved its maturity, and it was now a self-regulating system. The Hierophancy heuristic algorithm could handle matters from here on. I was outside when I had this impression, and it was dark out, after midnight, and the innumerable stars above me seemed to be making a point. I had been thinking only of one planet until now. What about the 18 billion galaxies and their stars?

"How many stars is that? The Milky Way has maybe 250 billion and the Andromeda Galaxy a trillion, though nobody has ever gotten into either to take a full census. Reasonable guesses, perhaps, or maybe wild ones. Let's take 500 billion stars as the average count for a galaxy. Multiply that by 18 billion galaxies. Astronomers estimate the universe has 100 billion galaxies, the Ofanim say 18 billion, but they may have actually counted them, the astronomers not.

"At 18 billion galaxies, that's a total head count of about nine sextillion stars, and God only knows how many planets associated with them, presumably each with its own Light grid and landscape of geomantic nodes. How long would it take me to count them all? The real question, I gradually realized, is the Supreme Being must be aware of all nine sextillion *at once*, as a simultaneous, panoptic appreciation of His progeny, with no need to count them. I sat enrapt in the marvel of that consideration, to be aware of that many stars at the same time.

"Whatever is true for the Earth as one planet has to be true for all of them, at least in general terms. The Supreme Being, to be a fair father, must honor all His creations equally, even though they are all at different levels of soul evolution, and some are brighter, quicker, faster than others. I saw the way the Qabalists portray the Supreme Being, as a White Head, a blazing cranium. It was like a clubhouse, even, I thought whimsically, a child's tree house. Inside were these nine sextillion stars and their Light-gridded planets. They were strung up like lights, pasted on the walls like postcards, floating in the air like pointillist pixels, alive with awareness; all were present, accounted for, on display, *known*.

"This White Head was the size of the complete universe, the master container. The stars were inside this Head, which is to say, within the Architect's awareness. It was a unified, coherent structure. The stars and planets are neurons in His 'Brain.' The human brain has 100 billion neurons. The Supreme Being has nine sextillion. They run the processes of His universal consciousness, His Brain the size of the universe, including all of it, and ours, though smaller, runs on the same principle. It is a holographic fractal of the Complete Brain, as the Qabalists might term it, and so are the other innumerable planets and their parental stars, all displayed up there in the White Crown.

"Our hierophantic work is to enable a single neuron to wake up and function, to put one completed jewel there, the Earth awake in its activated Light grid, fully *on*. We are like Ganymedes, cup-bearer and wine-pourer for Zeus, serving the Great Chief these delicious portions of achieved Light and awakened consciousness. We reveal the Holy Light that is the design of the planet and its Albion, facilitate its awakening, sentience, and self-awareness, supervise the completion of the reassembly of its constitutive parts, and present it upwards.

"Ganymedes is our model as a Hierophant. He serves up the revealed Holy Light to its Creator. We disclose the Holy Light so its Generator may take pleasure in this, to see that His Idea was sound. It's as if every time we or any Hierophant does this it's like saying, Yeah, we got the idea, Old Boy. Did it. Here it is. Do you like it? See all the bright stars all over it. Damn impressive sight."

I wondered if R1 saw things this way. He seemed adept at managing his numbers and grids. The display of circumferential pillars and the open interior space had inverted. Now the pillars were bunched together like a clutch of tied-together upright straws, and the Light grid particulars were outside this. The pillars were still releasing bubbles of concentrated numbers, and these were unpacking themselves, extrapolating themselves into complicated algorithms.

R1 stood motionless amidst this spectacle of organization and deployment, but I knew his mind must be active. I thought at times I could see his thoughts extend out from his mind like long arms directing numbers and grids to make changes. I had the odd impression that a copy of his head was attached like a bulb to the end of each extended arm which now seemed more like a stalk and through this bulb he looked at every detail, every niche and nuance of this managed world. R1 looked through his executive numbers to see the world these numbers were managing, but not controlling, for this was a free-will planet, and the management was flexible and open-ended enough for this.

His planet's master algorithm enveloped this array of pillars and stalks as an arithmetical environment. It throbbed with life as it coordinated the processes. But what exactly gave it this animation? It coordinated the activities of weather, tectonics, electromagnetic and astrological influences with sentient consciousness and all the life-forms it assumed on that planet, but those were the effects of this animation, its recipients. More primally, there was an original stirring of Mind that sought to set a system in motion, directing it with numbers in a sequence.

It was as if the Chief Architect kept coming up with ideas for created worlds and wrote out these ideas in mathematical script which then birthed the worlds. The Architect was the prime permutationist, entertaining Himself with these seemingly endless variations, exciting (to Him) number combinations. He merrily spun out scripts for planets like a chef having a great creative afternoon in his kitchen making up recipes for his staff to prepare that night. Then He assigned talented spirits, like R1 and L2, to supervise these creations and to oversee their deployment as their planet's Light grids. Say R1, He might say, would you mind looking after this nifty algebraic coding formulation for a self-evolving planet I came up with yesterday during teatime? It sure looks like fun.

The planetary realms of R1 and L2, holographically displayed in miniature before us, were adjacent on this mountain slope. They were also inter-related. This was managed by an intermediary webbing between the two spheres. It reminded me of a diplomatic neutral zone where countries might parley away from the polarities and vicissitudes of their own home environment and politics. Or maybe a better example was a gentleman's club, like in Victorian London days, when writers, business leaders, or members of Parliament might exchange views and policies in a private, comfortable environment. So here we had a quaint example of a geomantic version of Henry James's Reform Club.

This intermediate zone was where the two planets could exchange data, sample changing conditions, keep in reciprocal contact for their mutual benefit, report upgrades, and reset their own conditions in response to alterations underway in their neighbor. A separate algorithm ran this in-between zone, like a well-trained, discrete valet, trotting capably back and forth between the two.

I reminded myself that a main reason we were looking at our respective Light grids and arithmetical configurations was to find any points of egress that the alien gods might use, or already have exploited, to compromise our systems. So far I hadn't seen any, but I worried that I was not discerning enough, that maybe some subtlety of mathematical computation, some tiny adjustment, had slipped past my attention and was already running a covert hostile take-over.

I looked at Blaise. He was gazing keenly at one area within R1's configuration. I looked there and saw that a particular number sequence seemed to be winking in and out of clarity, somewhat like a pulsar, but with the effect you found yourself alternately squinting and opening your eyes wide as its emitted light changed. The number sequence seemed, in an odd way, unbalanced, like a poorly loaded moving truck where too much weight was shifted over just one wheel and axle. This number sequence seemed to be hiding something, as if perhaps another arithmetical process was running within it.

It had the quality of a covert probe, an algorithm running behind the scenes, like somebody had slipped a tracking and emitting device in your coat pocket and you didn't notice it and meanwhile it was sending out locational signals and running number sequences to capture all your computerized systems. It was hacking your phone, your global web access, all your IDs.

Blaise drew R1's attention to this hidden probe and R1 studied it with dismay. I'm guessing it was dismay because R1's consciousness style was mostly mental, so maybe I should say I detected R1 making a slight mental frown as he discovered his numbers system had been deftly breached and compromised. When you burrow into one system, you potentially contaminate all linked systems which meant R1's contiguity with L2's might now be tainted by this, and if it tainted that one, it could spread through the other four in our linked array.

It looked like the algorithm was running one set of numbers, which generated a reality, but another algorithm operated behind it, in the shadows, projecting a different set of conditions. The two versions vied with each other for supremacy. Two versions of one planetary reality ran simultaneously, like parallel worlds. R1 seemed to be tracking this, like following two concurrent tennis matches. As I've suggested, R1 wasn't the kind of "guy" who showed his emotions, if he even had any as we understand them in Earth-human terms. But he did seem concerned, vaguely frenetic, as he tracked both manifestations. I

had the sense the difference between the two competing reality versions was blurring, and he was losing his grip on the original, correct planetary version.

Blaise was taking proactive steps, putting himself into the tricky game. While I had been studying R1's handling of the crisis of intrusion and deception, Blaise had generated a holographic version of the Earth and its Light grid and was activating its various tiers of management algorithms. You could say he was running security checks for breaches in its defensive and operating systems.

There was our entire Light grid, displayed in miniature form before me. Looking at it, I could zoom in on any feature, Celestial Cities, Grail Castles, the domes, landscape zodiacs, and bring them in full detail to the forefront. I saw the Hierophancy heuristic algorithm running its numbers and handling affairs. I saw Albion and all his fractal copies watching us watching him in a reciprocal loop of attention and cordiality. He was by this time in Earth's life dependably awake.

I turned to Blaise and was about to say, "That means you're—"

He nodded. Grinned. "Call me E1. The first of two representatives from planet Earth, as part of this cozy colloquy of concerned planetary managers. Care to guess the identity of E2?" He waited while I puzzled over his question. I was used to Blaise always being several steps ahead of me, and enjoying it— him, that is. Blaise pointed to me. "Hello, E2. Care to step up to the algorithmic plate?"

I suppose I shouldn't have been surprised to learn this. I had already discovered I could speak Arabic and all that it meant, including the arithmetical interpretation. That's the thing you have to always keep in mind about your own past lives, the likelihood that occasionally you did stuff that would quite surprise you in your present life, exceeding your modest expectations of likely past accomplishments. I would have to get used to being E2 later; Blaise expected me on the job now. I would have to act like I was E2 and knew what I was doing.

He showed me something when he saw I gave him my full attention. I mentioned Ganymedes earlier and how the planetary Hierophant was like the Olympian cup-bearer bringing the ambrosia to the exalted Top Dog of the gods. I said that for the Earth, the completed Light grid was like an Emerald jewel set on a bed of the petals of the White Crown to which the Ofanim raised the Light grid. As Hierophants for Earth we participated in this elevation of the achieved grid to the inspection and, we hoped, delight and validation of the Boss-in-Chief.

What I saw now was that as the dual Ganymedes Blaise and I did not only present the completed Light grid to the Supreme Being but we enveloped it with our Christ alignment. The result was that the Emerald and its complicated patterns in Light and scripts in numbers was inside us, which is to say, inside our joint consciousness like a node of pure Light as we stood there in the Holy Presence. We were up there in the White Crown presenting the Earth as the completed, awakened Light grid, like a precious jewel that we bore inside us.

I'm trying to make clear that we and the Light grid were Ganymedes. It's funny in a way: it gives the term Hierophant, as Revealer of the Holy Light, a new twist. The Earth too is hierophantic; it reveals the Holy Light that comprises it. The Earth is a Hierophant,

we are Hierophants, the Holy Light itself is hierophantic, revealing, ultimately, its consummate creator, the Supreme Being. As the planetary Hierophants we disclosed the Holy Light to the Boss. We're all Ganymedes, presenting and revealing the Holy Light to its sponsor. He's the kind of celestial spirit whom we hear appreciates a fine piece of irony. "Oh yes, looks vaguely familiar. It's coming back to Me. *Yes.* I remember this Light!"

My flippancy aside, I reflected that we beheld—in fact, we were holding it with our minds and focused attention—the Light grid and its arithmetical underpinning that generated and sustained what people on Earth took for reality, including myself in earlier days before I got re-introduced to all this. Here was the context, the theater, I was tempted to call it, for many billions of incarnational dramas played out every day by our planet's residents.

The Supreme Being sat back and watched avidly how all these souls made sense of their inexplicable bodily incarnation and bewildering presence on the Earth with the mandate to make something of the gift of their individualized existence. The Old Boy, I suspect, has great patience for clichés, always hoping for the bright spark of something truly original, unexpected, a surprising twist to the pattern.

Most people might not see the Light grid and its many temples or even know of it, but it was the energetic and mathematical bedrock of their home planet's existence, and it was the theater with stage lights, props, and costumes (and audience) in which they performed their ardent personality-incarnation dramas and odysseys for meaning and self-validation every day. Here was the seed of that grand spectacle, a complex crystalline Light form right in my hand. I too was playing a bit piece in an off-Broadway production, reviews not yet in.

In those long-ago but halcyon days of relative ignorance when Philomena and I enjoyed our afternoon high tea at the New Hampshire farm, everything that constituted that extended delightful moment as we construed it came from this Light grid I saw before me, that Blaise and I, as E1 and E2, were responsible for. When I was a teenager I used to walk out on a winter's night and look at the neighborhood including my family home and see the lights on and people inside. I saw my own room, and I imagined looking through my bedroom window observing myself going about my activities which then were mostly reading.

At that moment of heightened attention, looking in on myself from the outside, I took stock of my essence, my qualities—yes, it was proper adolescent narcissism. But it was also an epiphany, if on a minor, domestic scale, a revelation of my essential quality, a minor hierophantic moment, if you will. I'm sure many of my readers have had this experience of heightened self-awareness.

I bring this up because as I observed the entire Earth and the life field of its billions of inhabitants I realized I was participating in a much larger epiphany involving the lives of all humans. There they were, there it was, our full incarnational pageant. It was as if I was holding a snow globe of the Earth complete with its grid. All the affairs of humans, Nature, the Light grid, and our collective consciousness personified as the colossus of Albion, were in there.

The Light grid and its tiers of arithmetical management formulas running it, and E1 and E2 and the rest of the Hierophancy supervising that management work were within this snow globe, this crystalline seed for an entire world. The Light grid of the Earth comprised the windows, its arithmetical aspects the mechanism of my looking through the windows, the human lives the drama of evolving consciousness which was the intended end product of the whole set-up.

Meanwhile, the scene on the mountain slope was beginning to resemble the way people used to say a world's fair looked, circa early 20th century perhaps, with pavilions from numerous countries representing in miniature that nation's essence, quirks, strengths, and specialties, enticing people to have a look. Our Earth hologram now occupied a space adjacent to R1's and L2's spheres. I couldn't see any details, but I imagined R1 and L2 were similarly observing the spectrum of intelligent life underway on their respective planets within the Light grids their math formulas this minute were upholding. I'm sure they realized that. I laughed. Bald Mountain and skiing-obsessed Sun Valley were missing out on this high-powered alien life disclosure broadcast happening in their midst.

Even though our management algorithm had been stolen, the Earth's planetary affairs and Light grid operations seemed to be running normally. I studied the grid geometry and its number cascades for any shimmies or aberrations. I thought maybe if reality seemed at all blurry or fluctuating in intensity these might be indicators of dysfunction, but I saw evidence of neither.

The geometrical pattern had numerous "buttons" installed along its edges and these enabled contact with the other planetary grids in this six-planet system. The buttons extended threads of Light to similar buttons on the other planetary grids and periodically sent updates in the form of compressed data bursts to keep them linked and briefed on changing circumstances or system upgrades. These threads resembled transparent arteries, numbers being the red blood cells, but one of these arterial threads was kinked, its numbers jumbled.

This particular artery was threaded into a new holographic display, that is, one I hadn't seen until this moment. It wasn't easy to see either. Let's start with its color. It was a bright sky blue, as if suffused with the white fire of diamonds. The planet looked spherical but the Light grid display was like a hypercube. This 4D shape of a cube, as I've mentioned, contains eight cubes that seem to be moving in and out of themselves, entering from the left then coming in from the right, hard for the 3D-accustomed eye to comprehend visually.

The arithmetical display for this planet was done in hypercube fashion. Picture a standard *x, y, z* axis; string numbers and calculations on it, like party lights. Now expand that into 4D so you have axes, like cubes, extending into eight directions but working with 32 edges on which you can string numbers. Run algorithms through that complex, dynamically active hyperdimensional form and you get an idea of what I was trying to see for this next planet.

I wasn't surprised to discover that the dominant intelligence-bearing life-form for a planet with this kind of complicated Light grid and math formulary was equivalently complex. They were airborne spirits; they lived in the air.

I wouldn't say they looked like humans, or birds either, for that matter. Let's say their shape was rather indeterminate in terms of human form expectations.

They still had souls that required individuation and they still generated karma in the process of achieving that goal, so in that respect they were like we Earth humans. Just forget about trying to get a clear, steady image of their form. Maybe I should say they looked like beautiful, elegant birds that when you went to see them you only saw a faint trace of diamond-fire fluttering in the pale blue sky, the air retaining a quickly fading form memory of where they had been moments ago, like the legendary Russian Firebird disappearing in a fire flash.

Naturally, the holographic display for this planet was in the air before us. It was not on the ground, the way the other two were, like bubbles lightly bouncing on the hard physical surface, but basically stable and anchored in place. You could spend a lot of time, and probably get lost six times, following the number cascades that ran this planet's Light grid. I should think its complexity would give the avaricious alien gods a proper headache trying to grab it. You had to follow the integers and their combinatorial permutations across a hyper-Escher landscape of interdigitating cubes that wouldn't sit still.

I mentioned buttons a moment ago. One of the buttons securing an attachment of this airborne Light grid with the Earth's and presumably the others had been monkeyed with. It looked the way a lock would after somebody had tried to wrench it open with a strong screwdriver then banged it with a hammer. It showed signs of a failed attempt to open it, and even that attempt had thrown its mechanism slightly off kilter so that the number cascades associated with this button and the area of the hologram it served seemed to shake off static sparks. I had the impression that whatever the number stream Earth was sending out to this airborne planet was getting adulterated along the way, arriving skewed. This might have been a point of covert access and manipulation by the aliens.

"Acquisition of the algorithm for one planet is not their prime objective," said Blaise. "They want the controlling algorithm for the six-planet system. We haven't seen all the details of that array yet. Still, they nibble at the local ones."

What Blaise called a nibble to me looked like a gouge. I didn't know if the representatives from this air planet had noticed the intrusion. It's not that I could see them; they weren't simulating humanlike forms or making it easy to see them. I had an impression of eight linked heads, like a sheet of cut-out identical dolls. They were not, strictly, heads but an abstract rendition of an awake mind.

There was not one or two of these, but eight, possibly one for each axis in the hypercube-style array of their Light grid. I suppose I should call this planet A, for air, and the representatives (I now saw two minds clearly delineated) as A1-4 and A5-8. I take responsibility (or blame) for the ineptness of this personnel designation, but they weren't helping. Within each single representative I saw three more. The four heads in the composite "system" seemed to be facing the cardinal directions, almost as if they were keeping a lookout for any hostile intrusions. You can see it was exceedingly hard to have certainty about them.

I said I can speak Arabic and that means generate and read mathematical formulas, but what this group of extra-planetary consciousness forms was up to was beyond me. A calculation going out in eight directions was beyond anything we dealt with in the Study House. But Blaise and Sal were making sense of it. They were conferring about the algorithms, examining certain threads of its exposition, as if holding the number strings up for close analysis, making sense of them apparently. Sal looked delighted; this was like a lunch buffet for him.

For myself, I was making a little progress in seeing this group. Now they looked like one form with eight identical heads, as if arrayed in a circle around a single implied cranium. You see depictions of certain gods this way who each have multiple linked heads, Brahma with five, Sanat Kumara with six, and Visvakarman with five. The one with the most heads, so far, was the "demon" of the *Ramayana*, Ravana; he sported ten heads, gazing into the 10 dimensions.

I was wondering what it would be like to live in the air without a body. At least a body in terms of how we know them, arms, legs, eyes, and your daily knowledge of the heaviness of matter and the gravity pull of the planet. These air spirits lacked human-style gravity-observing bodies, but they still had to perform their individuation requirements and honor that great gift of free will. They still had to honor their Ganymedes hierophantic obligation to the Chief.

I had the impression that regarding the arithmetical aspect of their existence they were not mathematicians as such but processed the number sequences as routinely as breathing, recognizing the complicated computations as natural elements in their environment. For us in contrast it was a mental skill, one we had to master and not an environment we naturally found ourselves in. These air spirits were born already knowing Arabic and, apparently, thinking it was nothing special. My impression was we had to learn Arabic the hard way.

We had two more planetary systems to put up their holographic displays. The first to go was what I call the Yellow Ones. I have to tell you it was strange. Picture several dozen yellow doors imposed over a sphere. The doors are closed. They are rimmed in mathematical calculations, algorithms streaming over their surface like ivy leaves on a building's brick wall. You put your attention on the algorithms, enter their sequences with your mental attention, and follow them through as if you were running along a pathway. This opens the door which is to say it reveals the interior of the Light grid for this planet. Everything is in yellow. The upright rectangular shape is maintained at this next level, minus the door.

These door shapes seem to frame geomantic provinces, and I counted 36 of these. Inside this framed space were all the specifications for Light temples in that area. They were packed in there, concentrated like a complete genome. Obviously, the geomantic design was fractal, a design pattern I've seen many times, including for our Earth, the repetition of a design at hierarchical levels.

As for the planetary geomancers, I saw two figures, though somehow they framed all 36 doors. Imagine a humanlike countenance taking up the rectangular space of a doorway. You see the eyes, ears perhaps, and the impression of a smile or at least some kind of cordial expression on a face. Then make 17 copies of this for the doors. It wasn't a question of having multiple heads; just that somehow these two representatives had copied themselves in full so that each stood at 18 of the doorways. You won't be surprised to hear I labeled the group Y1 and Y2.

The mathematics parts of their planetary reality seemed initially to be part of their minds, as if the number sequences were extrapolated directly out of their "brains." It was a series of layers once you got past the doors: the arithmetical specifications, then a mythic-pictorial version of those numbers, next the actual Light temples or architectural spaces in which the resident consciousness life-form could conduct its individuation business, then the physical details of the material planet. This same pattern was repeated 36 times across the planet, and each repetition was supervised by either Y1 or Y2, as if standing in the doorway.

Incidentally, the transitions between these four layers, or five if you count the doors themselves, was lightning-quick. I should think that would make the prospect of nicking the arithmetical treasures by the alien gods much harder. In all, it looked like you could enter the consciousness reality of this planet by any of 36 doors; you could also expect to be greeted and accompanied by Y1 or Y2. Somehow the fractal nature of this planetary grid design seemed to preclude the possibility of stealing the number sequences. They were too well embedded in the geomantic system to easily extract. Perhaps this yellow planet was exempt from the hostile incursions of the alien gods; their algorithms looked like they were wrapped in an impenetrable cellophane coating, perhaps an inviolate wax.

The sixth planet was a pale orange and its Light grid had a complicated geometry. This included squares, pentagons, and equilateral triangles somehow congruently fitted together over an implicit sphere. I walked around the holographic projection of this exotic Light grid and tried to count these shapes. I tallied 20 triangles, 30 squares, and 12 pentagons, plus 60 vertices and 120 edges. I kept in mind that this complicated geometric pattern shaped the quality and processes of consciousness on that planet; with an overarching system this complex, the conditions of incarnate consciousness must be similarly advanced.

Let me emphasize that though this pattern was visually bewildering, it still struck me as coherent and symmetrical, and thereby well-organized and rational. It had that kind of regularity and repetition of form you find in the Platonic Solids, but this shape was beyond any of those five comparatively simple forms. I tentatively called the sentient representative from here G1, for first-rate geometry, or surpassingly complex geometry, or geometry beyond me.

"Rhombicosidodecahedron," called out Sal, as if I knew what that meant. "It's one of the 13 Archimedean Solids. They are the next level geometric expansion after the Platonic Solids, their upgrades. The Earth now has one of them, the icosidodecahedron with 20 triangles and 12 pentagons, 60 edges and 30 vertices; it's far simpler by comparison with less repetitions to keep track of than this one. The advanced planets apparently get these upgrades once they reach a certain plateau of development. Blaise told me Earth got hers back in 1986. The mathematics formula that generates this shape is very interesting, elegant, really. Lots of square roots of two and five involved. I'll tell you about it sometime. Did I ever tell you I *love* square roots, even dream about working them on occasion?"

Sal strolled around the hologram of this Solid appreciating its shape and poking his head into the vertices and running his hand along the edges, like the way somebody might examine a brand new car, feeling the sleekness of the metal. It looked as if he was finger-reading the arithmetic like it was in Braille.

Now I saw this same complicated figure raised to the fourth dimension. If you think a hypercube is hard to see, try this one on for size. The number of moving facets you get when this is in 4D can quite overwhelm your cognition. The mathematical component matched this complexity, and I had glimpses of formulas and equations running across a dizzying distribution of axes, like a hundred butlers and waiters scuttling through a restaurant designed by Escher.

It made me appreciate how much more advanced these "people" were in their mental capacities and general level of consciousness than we Earth humans. Our planet's Light grid was not yet anywhere close to being this complicated. But it told me that the intelligent life-forms on this orange-gridded planet must be able to perform all sorts of simultaneous and multidimensional functions in their awareness, like juggling 40 balls or playing 30 games of tennis at once.

Our sixth planet had projected its Light grid hologram and its arithmetical processes, so the array of the six worlds could start revealing the implicit pattern of their relationship and the composite algorithms linking them. All six had many points of intersection and congruence in their Light grids, and the inhabitants of these six planets, despite the great distances laying between them (in other galaxies, millions of light-years apart, no doubt), shared in the consciousness life of one another, dwelling in background proximity to them.

No doubt the psychic and hypersensitive people of any of these planets would be more acutely aware of this background presence. The outer details and forms of these inhabitants might be radically different, but the congruence of the mathematics running their Light grids would assure certain constants and generic conditions among the six worlds. An algorithm is not language-dependent and will run the generic exchanges of a life-form with its environment. The result, whatever the design complexity and phylogenic forms, exhibits rationality. You live there and you know you're saturated in a world of high rationality.

I probably need to qualify this statement. The Light grid imparts rationality to a planetary reality; it is rationality embodied, but that is at a bedrock and infrastructure level. You have to learn to read this causal chain at its correct level, which is 4D minimum, where many causal factors coincide. The causal chain leading by syllogistic logic to the present events and conditions is the result of multiple inputs on your 4D timeline coinciding—arriving simultaneously—at the present moment. That is not a linear, straightforward coincidence, from the normal 3D notion of causality, and it may straddle three time frame inputs (past, present, and future), but you know it still makes sense.

The inherent rationality is set at a higher level of complexity than we are used to. When you learn how to read this multifactorial causal chain, you see the rationality. Events have their causes, but these causal chains span multiple points of input. Some elements of the causal syllogism may occupy different nodes in the timeline, and the outcome may exceed what you would interpret as the immediate needs of the moment. Remember, the Chief Planner plays the long game, and current "products" of any algorithmic calculation may serve an obscure teleological goal far larger than the small outcome you were hoping for.

Another factor confounding rationality is the human free will component. Here we have a perpetual dance (I'm tempted to call it an antic hay, after Aldous Huxley's clever use of that old term) between free will and Light grid necessities. The human factor, incompletely understanding the syllogism of events, may confuse the field, draw wrong conclusions, refuse to comply with their own life plans (drawn up under rational conditions), and you end up with a social and psychological reality that seems devoid of rationality or perhaps like a typical British summer day when it's mostly overcast and blowing with a little Sun. So we'd better say a planetary reality like Earth's is implicitly rational but we may have to work at it to comprehend the details of its logical, intended syllogism.

I did see some perturbation in one of the Earth connections with the master algorithm that was managing the relations of these six planets. Sal noticed it too and was already standing next to it, as if examining the number wiring. One of the formulas seemed to keep flipping over and running in reverse, as if the "electricity" running a circuit going to a lamp kept sparking or shorting out. This equation kept inverting and running backward, and it did this very quickly. I could see Sal loved problems like this, solving a mathematical conundrum at this level of expression was not something an Earth mathematician got every day. It was a stimulating challenge. Sal looked concentrated but he was smiling.

As if to underline the importance of this six-planet grid consanguinity, the Ofanim projected a huge version of their diamond-faceted array underneath us. It was like a flower made of thousands of diamond hexagons rising slowly up under us to include the array of the six planets; Blaise angels stood in each facet.

Let me explain this image a little. Picture a tray covered in diamonds; then give this depth, like it is a half-sphere geode of diamonds. Then expand this to the size of a sports stadium, deepening and widening the scope of this vast crystal cave. Put an angel form in each diamond hexagon, like an angelic monk meditating in each, and the whole thing looks like a chalice of diamond caves and also like a royal cloak that wraps around your consciousness and radically brightens you. Please excuse the meandering analogies and metaphors, but I am trying to evoke the sense of majesty and focus of this diamond vortex array.

The effect of this was as if somebody turned on a thousand spotlights illuminating our six planet Light grid array on the mountain slopes, though I was fairly certain the Ofanim's diamond-faceted manifestation was not physical and thus seeable by human eyes in nonpsychic people. I say "fairly," but I wasn't certain because since 2020 when the Blaises started incarnating as humans in bodies, everything had changed, and what used to be reserved for only subtle manifestations now had a tendency to be overt and materially right in

your face. Plus there were Blaises in human form now walking around the place and if you were inattentive you might come up against a Blaise Human and fail to notice it until, I suspect, you start to wonder how come you suddenly feel so marvellous.

I was just starting to wonder what angels looked like to our colleagues on these other planets, whether they would see them at all the way we do, when the human Blaise started pointing to an arithmetical node in the display. It was sparking and fluttering, and I saw ghostly images of the alien gods in it. One of the algorithms seemed to have had a few of its digits removed and it was failing to compete its calculations, like an electronic device signaling "computer error" and freezing itself on a single page or blanking out the screen.

This malfunction due to a deficit in required digits was creating an arithmetical cascade along the algorithmic chain affecting the other five planets. The master algorithm linking the six was faltering, and the other five individual planetary algorithms were also flickering and teetering, if you can say that of equations. If a calculation can be arithmetically hobbled, then this one was.

"I think it comes down to a problem with the design," said Blaise.

As he said this I became aware that we seemed to be in a rising elevator. It was not that we were ascending off the ground, but rather we were moving upwards through the frequencies of reality. Maybe I could better put this in terms of rising up through Qabala's Tree of Life. It was like viewing levels of a building where each was a completely different reality than its lower or higher neighbors, or each one seemed to be more starkly disclosed, with more details available, but its processes were more complex with each succeeding level.

Anyway, our elevator service was provided gratis by the Ofanim who, as the human Blaise has often told me, are the archetypal umbilicus within the Creation. An umbilicus connects levels, and that's what the Ofanim do, and are doing, and likening their uprising function to an elevator is a justified if simple analogy. Qabalists talk of the *Kav*, the Line of Light that threads through the Vacated Space and contains the 40 or 50 *Sefirot*. The Blaise elevator runs in that.

Where we they taking us? It appeared we were back in Visvakarman's offices. All of us, Blaise, me, Sal, Jocelyn, and the 13 "guys" from the other five planets, were now standing in a large circular room whose walls comprised a complex engineering diagram. Imagine taking the blueprint for an electronic circuit and laying it out laterally, as if taping it to a curving wall, except this circuitry specifies the design and operations of six planets and their Light grids.

It seemed to be a continuous design, which meant the circuitry of our six planets was somehow part of one complicated system displayed before us on the walls. To call this design pattern a circuitry drawing is misleading. It was all numbers. The arithmetical specifications of the six planets were laid out seemingly in 2D mode. It reminded me of what the 3D Platonic Solids look like when they are unpacked and displayed in flat 2D. A cube, for example, is a crucifix shape.

I say seemingly because of the remarkable statement Blaise made next. "It's all about sphere packing. The matter of our six planets and their relations pertains to the close-packing of equal spheres, six planets around a seventh.

The seventh is a composite planet made of these six; it is implicit, at the center of the sphere packing across the 18 billion galaxies that our six planets span. Invert this and you have a single planet made of six packed spheres. That's what we have here. That's why the alien gods regard the acquisition of its number sequences as paramount in their program of control and management. This is a rare layout.

"The dense arrangement of congruent spheres in a regular arrangement or lattice has intrigued mathematicians for centuries. They even have formulas to calculate the greatest fraction of space that these close-packed spheres can occupy. They study the density of these different forms of lattice packing. What is special about this close-packing of six spheres that are planets is the distance between them across universal space. That is not a factor the mathematicians worked into their formulas to calculate the density of packing. They assume their spheres are physically next to one another, not spread out across the universe.

"This sphere packing is what we would have to call hyper-spatial. You'd almost have to turn the universe inside out to get the six planetary spheres in one relative area to surround the seventh. In physical spatial terms, they lie vast distances from one another, and the pattern these distances make is asymmetric and can appear distorted to 3D eyes. Plus the six planets are all different sizes.

"But I emphasize the generation of the seventh is what this is all about. It's the key. Here's the vital number: the greatest density for sphere packing is 0.740480489. This derives from a formula for calculating the density of cubic close-packing and was figured out by Carl Friedrich Gauss, a German mathematician working in the early 19th century. But don't worry about the mathematics here. Just keep in mind there is a number that defines this packing.

"The issue is the alien gods want to skew that density equation so that the close-packing of the six planetary spheres is thrown off and the universe itself will quiver because when you think about it this sphere-packing of our six free-will planets around the implicit seventh is at the core of the universe of 18 billion galaxies. It's like a special, even secret, project Visvakarman devised to cohere the universe; he put a special veiled infrastructure within the cosmos of galaxies.

"The Designer wanted to pack these six congruent spherical planets as densely as possible around an implied seventh which is really the composite of these six. This seventh postulated planet is comprised of the meta-algorithm that runs the relations and algorithmic processes of the linked six planets. Sphere-packing is the mechanics of this six-planet relationship. The alien gods want that algorithm; acquire that and you unravel this unique seven-planet nexus."

"This is why we were projecting and modeling the Light grids of the six planets down there on Bald Mountain," said Sal. "I think the significance of our display and commentary escaped us at the time, but I see the relevance of it now. We're dealing with a mathematical constant, a fundamental design formula. On a technical level, the equation for sphere packing is *pi* divided by three times the square root of two. That is what yields this special number of 0.740480489.

"In the 17th century, Johannes Kepler laid the groundwork for Gauss's original formula in what's known as the Kepler Conjecture. Later, Carl Friedrich Gauss helped provide the proof for this conjecture. If you randomly drop spheres in a container you will get a density of about 65%. That's a pretty loose configuration. That means the random distribution of the spheres will manifest a 65% efficiency in close-packing, that is, in terms of how tightly they compress their shapes into the available space. You will agree 65% is a loose packing job.

"Pack them in closely and properly and you get the maximum ideal density expressed as 0.740480489, or 74%. That's a red light flashing throughout the arithmetical universe; it vexes the alien math gods like a red flag to a bull. It's the perfection of a mathematical and geometrical principle, this 74%. It reminds them they do not have this in their collection; it is out there, in the wild, performing a perfect mathematical move but not under their jurisdiction where it ought to be, and they will collect it and remove it forever from the playing field.

"That number actually continues for a lot more digits. Maximum density means you have the maximum number of spheres that can occupy a given space; here the seventh planetary sphere is the composite of the six. Kepler didn't discuss that possibility. The density of the arrangement of the six spheres equals the collective volume of the six planetary spheres divided by the volume of the container, or the seventh. The Designer was exquisitely precise about this set-up.

The exciting point here is that the digits in 0.740480489 secure and hold fast the 3D spatial connection among the six closely-packed spheres, our six planets.

"This is where the innate congruence of numbers and Light grids is clearly demonstrated. This equation specifies the packing, commands it, you might say, makes it happen. Any number sequence less than 0.740480489 and the close packing starts to falter and loosen. It's like a screw not tightened sufficiently to hold in place. When it corresponds with this number, it is at its ideal, densest possible state. That's when you manifest this perfect composite seventh sphere. You're standing inside this number that expresses the perfect optimal packing. For a mathematician, for me, anyway, that's like experiencing God firsthand.

"Now for the problem. By compromising the master algorithms running our six planets the alien gods have destabilized this mathematical constant and thrown off the ideal density. They're causing the numbers to slip, the packing to go slack. The six planetary spheres would no longer be perfectly and optimally closely-packed in a regular lattice. That loosening of the optimum close-packing lattice would then quickly cascade backwards through the six affiliate planets and their Light grids and algorithms. The congruence of Light grids and material planets would similarly start to erode, their systems falling into subluxation. Similarly, mess with only one of the six algorithms, that of Earth's, and you skew the whole system, introduce instability and algorithmic product degradation."

I had to concentrate to get all this straight in my mind. In spatial terms, these six free-will endowed planets were not anywhere near one another. They were spread out across unfathomable reaches of universal space. But in terms of intention and function, in the shared allotment of free will to this high

degree, they were energetically close to one another and you could, without twisting your mind into anomalies of spacetime and logic, say that holographically they were closely packed around a seventh larger sphere, which was their totality. It seemed likely that though the physical planets varied in size, their Light grids could be scaled larger or smaller like an aperture to fit the material conditions and did not require an exact and constant size application to the recipient planet.

Though the physical planets no doubt vary greatly in size and volume, and their Light grids clearly diverge considerably in shape, dimensionality, and color, within this energetic unit they are identical in size, in their design essence equal spheres suitable for close-packing in a way that demonstrates the greatest density possible for equal-sized spheres and as indicated by the mathematics. I suppose that meant it was their ideal form expression that was being closely-packed, the essence of their Light grid design imposed upon a sphere. At this level their designs could be rendered as equal spheres, even though as physical planets their pattern was scaled upwards appropriate to their plan. Maybe it will make more sense if I say it was their Light bodies, their etheric forms, all rendered to the same spherical volume, equal spheres, that were densely packed.

These six planets constitute a composite seventh, a conglomerate planet, and within this arcane layer of universal reality they were closely-packed spheres. Physically, they were not closely-packed but greatly separated, but energetically they were and entirely congruent, forming this esoteric hyper-planet. It was, perhaps, like being a conventional, successful businessman and belonging to a secret lodge that met regularly with members from other supposedly normal sectors of society and neighboring towns. You manifested your true identity when you rejoined your fellow lodge members once a month, or, better, you conducted these meetings with everyone in their astral bodies.

This lodge had its set of rules and these correspond to the algorithms running this seventh planet, and this is what the alien gods were zealously targeting. Its algorithm contained elements of the six planets' algorithms, and its own unique combinations of processing approaches. For an arithmetical collector, it was a very desirable item to add to one's treasury. As far as I could tell, this composite planet was unexplored territory for me, or was it? Something about it started to feel familiar, tugging at me, though I had no exact memories.

Apparently, the engineering diagrams that covered the curving walls of this study room were details of the arithmetical relations of these six planets and the specifications for generating the implicit, composite seventh hyper-planet. There were certainly enough numbers and equations on display here to interest our intrepid arithmetical hijackers; it would be like a cornucopia of available purses and wallets for a team of nimble pickpockets working a busy crowd. The mathematics of sphere-packing can seem abstruse and complicated to the layman, involving cosines, square roots, the mathematical constant of *pi*, lots of numbers packed inside parentheses, and the letters *x*, *y*, and *z* performing secret functions and not revealing their identities to outsiders, such as myself.

I wasn't the only person perplexed by the mathematical scripts I saw all over the walls. "Does anyone have any myth pictures they need interpreted?" asked Jocelyn demurely. I took her point. I didn't see any myth pictures here.

Unless you counted the Blaises who were flashing different forms of themselves to an audience of two, Jocelyn and myself. Appearing in the innumerable diamond hexagonal caves that comprised their crystalline geode form that brought us here were images of monkeys, white horses, elephants, birds, even peacocks, made of blazing Light flashing out at us for entertainment. A few of their angelic guises within the caves waved to us, others were grinning; a few, for comic relief, were scratching their heads as they studied the numbers while others held up big cue cards with equations written in neon on them. I blushed then laughed as I realized they vaguely resembled me doing the same.

In fact, I had a momentary glimpse of this apparition within the human Blaise. I saw the Ofanim's majestic Rotunda of Light and their multitudinous Cave Heavens of diamond hexagons each occupied by an angelic form inside Blaise, as if it was a revelation of his true inner essence, that he had become suffused with the angelic presence. Possibly the momentous event of 2020 with the advent of human-form Blaises being born on the Earth by human mothers affected him more than I realized. Maybe the Ofanim had given him the gift of a partial presence in his own space, so he was now half human and half Ofanim. That would account for his remarkable longevity. He didn't look a day over 80.

Jocelyn looked at me as if she had been following my thoughts or had seen this disclosure, smiled a little, then shrugged. Meanwhile, the planetary representatives, Blaise, and Sal were walking about the room studying the details and calculations of the engineering specifics, discussing its key points. The diagrams that spanned the circumference of this room were a two-dimensional spreadsheet of the complicated 4D reality of these six planets making a seventh.

My attention returned to the matter of this seventh planet. What did it look like? I had to remind myself that it does not exist in physical space; you would not find it on any astronomy star charts, no matter how well-informed your astronomers were, unless their star maps charted hyperspace planets. This seventh planet is visitable, but it will not be found in physical space or exhibiting any visible physical mass either. I spent a few moments delighting myself (or perhaps tying my mind up in irresolvable knots) with this conundrum.

You had to first step into a higher dimension to access this realm. There you would be in a hyperdimensional space that pulled the universe together into a different kind of singularity than the vortical-suction type of a standard black hole. This was like an invisible magnetic attractor that pulled the Light bodies of six material planets towards a convergence point that then formed this seventh that existed only in a higher, holographic world of Light. Then you could walk across a Light body planet that contained six other ones materially manifested.

You would not be in normal physical space, nor in ordinary higher psychic space in which space is the same but your cognitive body and framework are different. Here space itself was

different or perhaps rendered irrelevant since this seventh planet was a higher-world construct whose existence contradicted the normal rules of 3D spatiality. The seventh planet exists in "consciousness space," and though it spatially ties together disparate zones of the multi-galaxy cosmos, it takes up no space itself. I'm full of contradictions just talking about it and my head is vaguely aching. Aside from these perplexities, I liked it, liked the idea of it, this overturning of conventional spatial laws.

Not only was I delighting in the puzzlement of this novel arrangement, I was struggling to conceive of what it might be like to live on this subtle world, knowing with every step, assuming you could even walk across a realm made of only arithmetical constructs, that you were simultaneously on six other worlds.

Enough with trying to prevision this exotic realm. It was time to step up to this seventh planet and have a look at its actual conditions. Jocelyn came with me. So what was it like? The first thing I have to say is that it was not a physical planet we were stepping on. It wasn't even pretending to be physical, even in a subtle sense. It was a sphere comprised of arithmetic. At first it seemed as if all the equations running in the six affiliate planets had been uploaded to this single algorithmic performance space making it a kind of arithmetical world's fair with pavilions from the six participating countries. Some kind of mental thoughtform. Then this perception flipped, and I realized this seventh planet was the first, the mother-matrix and source of the mathematics that specified the six planets.

The six comprised and generated (or justified) this seventh, but truly, this seventh was the first and generated these six, releasing them into space like eggs of Light. How novel: the summary form was antecedent to its own building blocks. It was the fetal sac containing these six progeny. It was like the way Qabalists say the highest *Sefira*, *Kether*, contains the lower nine spheres within itself, unexpressed. Everything these subsequent nine will express is in here, like a warehouse of the universe before anything has been put in trucks for delivery.

Here the arithmetical reality was unified, integrated, not fragmented into six parts. All the qualities that would differentiate the six were here unified, like a master genetic code. I had to keep reminding myself that all this arithmetic was specifying conditions for incarnate consciousness. That consisted of six variations on the theme of wide-open free will, bestowed at the Jupiterian state of divine largesse, grace, and bountifulness. It was generous, expansive, and lavish, and the numbers reflected it—coded it. We were two non-mathematicians touring a purely arithmetical world in which mathematical formulas and processes were as lushly packed as a rain forest in the womb of a unique cosmological creation.

The Supreme Being had said, Let there be a high degree of free will here, and the arithmetic jumped into compliance, spinning out numbers to perform this. In a way our tour was like walking through a 3D version of the wraparound engineering diagrams we first saw when we entered Visvakarman's office. I wouldn't say there was much to see in visual terms, but the precision of the mathematics here was as exquisitely detailed and as minutely symmetrical as anything you'd ever see in Nature, such as snowflakes or crystalline shapes. It exhibited the finest lapidary work of the world's most accomplished jeweler.

What constituted the spatial extent of this seventh planet were the branching permutations spawned by the many ongoing arithmetical formulas. It was like Qabalists spelling out the letters and numbers of words, then spelling those constituent parts out again, and continuing this until they had generated a vast genealogy of connections. Our arithmetical planet was much like that. It looked like a mathematician's chalkboard but it was an entire planet made of these numbers and sequences, the core commands that specified all conditions of reality and consciousness, including those we enjoy on our Earth. Alternately, it was a vast, still burgeoning book written in number code.

I looked at Jocelyn and shook my head. No myth pictures in sight, sorry about that, though I could imagine a cave artist on this mentally advanced domain perhaps doodling an image of a large head extruding lush rivers of quadratic and algebraic equations. This planet was floriated in mathematics.

I was surprised to see that this seventh, original planet was duplicated in each of the affiliate free-will-endowed planets, embedded in their Light grid. This planet and all its arithmetical specifications was implicit on each of these, including the Earth, and you just had to turn sideways, as it were, to see it, and there it was like images buried within another image and your eyes have to shift focus and angle to suddenly see this formerly hidden picture jumping out at you.

This meant that the Light grids and planetary reality of the other five were implicit in each of the six planets too, that you could find the details of their Light grids embedded within your own planet's Light grid details. It was a pattern of modified fractals and shared holograms. Each of the six generated planets was a fractal of the "mother" planet but with some differences; its genome had some alterations. In a sense, we, the Earth, were always closely-packed among five other planet spheres, hugging a seventh whose existence explained and justified ours. That made it clear that whatever the alien gods did to destabilize the Earth would simultaneously and comprehensively jeopardize the other six planets, but it also meant we had five stalwart colleagues in our struggle to retain ownership of this designer-appointed meta-algorithm—well, six, actually, when you count the master mother planet, our seventh sphere.

I reminded myself that we were walking through the mathematical scripts that generated the daily conditions of reality and consciousness for billions of souls. Our Earth had holograms of the Light grids of our five collegial planets and that of the mother-seventh planet. As Earth Humans we were all sevenfold.

These scripts produced our daily conditions down to the details of our Sun Valley offices or the dining room table in our New Hampshire home where Philomena and I used to take our tea. All the specifications for space and movement, for dimensions, linearity and its opposite, things going forward and backward, up and down, sideways, and all of these in dizzying combinations as you move up the dimensional ladder—all these came out of this meta-algorithm.

Think of a hypercube, then complexify it by moving it into 5D, 6D, and beyond. Here are the mathematics that write those concatenating reality conditions. Add to this the fact that the Light grids of the six planets surrounded this center as tightly packed spheres and the six already were implicit in this one.

Jocelyn was laughing. I turned to her. She said: "Do you see the joke? I'm looking for myth pictures that correlate with this reality. *We* are those pictures.

"We, as humans walking around and the life-forms of these other five planets walking around are those mythic pictures. We are psychic images that illustrate those arithmetical conditions, those formulas. We are the living metaphors holographically projected into matter to exemplify the conditions framed by the equations. It gives 'myth' a fresh new definition, doesn't it?

"Whatever we do in this numbers landscape is mythic. Our lives are the stories played out, *acted*, in this vast theater. Our playwright, the dramaturge, is arithmetic; our dialogue is mathematics. We are the perambulating, joking, tea-drinking personifications of those equations. We are the equation products. All those number scripts were devised to produce us, you, me, and the rest of us. Maybe I should elevate their function and call them the thaumaturge of reality."

I shared her point which I think was both ironic and full of delight. Here was evidence of the field she specialized in, but the field data was outlandish. Or maybe it was weird because it was primal, fundamental, the first pure fitting of sentient actions upon an infrastructure of arithmetical processes. There was something existentially lean to this experience we found ourselves immersed in. I felt situated in a state of basic wide-open awareness before it fixed on objects, before emotions, perceptions, definitions or ideations of any kind started to arise.

I could *do* anything. The mechanisms for affecting reality with my wishes were all around me, literally enumerated as number strings and running algorithms. I think it was like this: I was visiting the basic framework of reality before humans or any conscious and self-aware sentient life-forms were inserted into its world. Can you follow me on this point? It was like having a glimpse of a world intended for humans but before I had become one capable of perceiving it.

Technically, I needed to be a human or one of the other five planetary life-forms from the other planets before I could expect to make any sense of this because my life-form would itself be a hologram of the arithmetical design, a microcosm of the ruling mathematics, yet here I was, making sense of it anyway. I was getting a preview of likely incarnation conditions before I was even a human. Well, I said it was weird, and you will likely sense some of this freakish quality in my words that struggle to characterize the extreme novelty of this world. I was the myth of the confused philosopher, the bewildered technician.

I heard somebody calling my name. It seemed to come from a distance. Then it felt as if a hand grabbed me by the shoulder and yanked me somewhere. I was back in Visvakarman's engineering office with Blaise and the others. Blaise was smirking. It was he who had grabbed me and pulled me out of that confusing terrain. Jocelyn was back too, though she looked less confused than me. "You have to be careful in that place. You can easily get lost," Blaise said.

Somehow I understood that the other 13 planetary representatives had also been walking through that bewildering core mathematical environment. That in itself was an arresting thought: one planet or domain or whatever we should best call this land of arithmetical Ur-existence that could be claimed with equal validity by six different phylogenies. I laughed. It was like Vienna after World War II, when at least four countries laid equal claim to the divided city. The "people" from these six free-will planets each had equal justification to walk this wildly protean land and construe it in their own terms, just as I had done.

"This is a new threshold for evolving consciousness," said Ray Master Hermes. I blushed as I realized I had forgotten entirely about him, that he was here. He wasn't the kind of guy who kept insisting on his importance and it seemed that he had been pursuing his own separate investigations. "Think of this excursion as your entry into a higher octave of planetary expression. It will likely take you a while to adjust to its novel conditions and adapt yourself to its demands. And yes, before you ask, it is a challenging cognitive environment, not the easiest one to make sense of during your first immersions in its strangeness.

"This aggregation of six planets around a seventh and in fact constituting this seventh is not unique in the universe, though this particular theme among the member planets is. As you know, this degree of free will bestowed to a planet with individual units of evolving sentience is unique. But many other themes have been installed in planetary aggregates; this is the universe's higher octave.

"Here's how to make sense of this. Think of these aggregates as planetary soul groups. You know you have these affinity groups among humans; you are drawn to people with whom you share pre-existing soul alignments that define your natural affinities on a vibrational level and which can be traced back to the beginning, when you were first extruded from the Supreme Being and placed on the Tree of Souls. Planets also have this kind of natural, pre-ordained affinities.

"It's helpful to remember how a human is an aggregate of bodies. You have the one physical and six subtle bodies with many chakras and auric layers. All seven of these bodies comprise you, though it is a very large you. The planetary aggregates of six making a seventh are not quite the same. They are not components of the one individual, but six congruent individuals comprising a seventh. That's why I brought in the idea of soul groups. Members of a soul group, whether it's humans or planets, are discrete individuals capable of comprising an affinity cluster that expresses a new quality born of the members.

"The six planets in this aggregate are each strongly individualized, yet because as planets they are members of the same soul group, they create something new. Each planet in this aggregate is a subtle body in the totality of this cosmic form. This soul group consists of six planets making, *birthing*, a seventh. You know about cosmogonic personifications, such as what you label Albion and Purusha. This is a planetary nuance on that large theme. The aggregation of six separate but congruent planets yields a cosmogonic seventh."

"A six-headed cosmogonic Albion," I said, without even thinking first. Then I thought, in reference to Jocelyn, there's a mythic picture for you. But I suppose it wasn't that inaccurate a notion. Each of the six planets was like a head. "He's a chip off the old block," I added, feeling possessed with jocularity. I was thinking

of the Cosmic Logos, known to Hindu metaphysicians as Sanat Kumara, the Eternal Youth, who was said to have six bodies or six heads on the one body. Nobody was laughing. I turned to Jocelyn for support. "A master planet with six heads. That's a myth picture to top everything in the library."

I thought about what the Ray Master had explained. In the human, our seven bodies comprise the Large Self we gradually grow into, but it is ourselves. We may be members of a pre-existing soul group dating back to when we were hanging happy and sun-kissed like apples on the Tree of Souls and we may willingly aggregate with these members as we encounter them, such as in the Hierophancy. But a planetary soul group is an aggregate that yields something far bigger, different, not before seen, more than the identities of the six members.

Six consanguineous planets gathering together and manifesting the implicit seventh, the composite of their sixfold essence, or, seen the other way around, the seventh unified zone splitting itself into six partial representations of itself. The six are implicit in the mother-seventh, and the seventh births the six planets who then find one another, regroup, and collectively yield their mother-seventh. It works in both directions because both sequence depictions are right.

Each planet is a carved face on the totem pole of the cosmogonic Albion. All our work with Light temples, grids, arithmetically extrapolated planets, yields this. This highlights the jeopardy these acquisitive alien gods pose to this construct. They see it as lifting a linchpin out of an arithmetic formula, removing an algorithm because they desire it for their

Magic Square collection; they don't realize, or, more likely, don't care, that doing this will undermine the entirety. But then, why steal Earth's algorithm when our planet is not the most advanced among the six? Wouldn't the mathematical details of one of the other five be more desirable, representing a more advanced stage of arithmetical scripting?

Maybe it's because stealing Earth's is the easiest. I had the impression Earth is the newest of the five to get the Light grid upgrade to an Archimedean Solid as the master geometric form. During that pivotal upgrade presumably the Earth is especially vulnerable, all its components focused on growth, not defense. Or possibly during this transition phase, which, from Blaise, I understand takes about a century to complete, certain arithmetical realities, ones that are normally inaccessible, are now exposed because they are used to facilitate the transition.

That transition began in 1986, so it has at least 20 more years to run, and it's probably prudent to make that 50 years, at least until 2100. These transition algorithms are of prime interest to the alien gods. By way of analogy, it would be like abducting a highly specialized and skilled crew of workmen that perform a crucial transition step in putting up a building. Usually, they work in secret or perhaps at night, but now they're in the daylight and they can easily be nabbed.

I realize I have been too literal in using the phrase "stealing the algorithm." You can't remove a mathematical formula from an on-going computation. But since the algorithm is heuristic, which means self-learning, arithmetically an autodidact in the purest sense, learning and adjusting from its experience of the world of numbers, you could enslave this

algorithm, co-opt its functions, seduce or redirect it to other simultaneous functions. You could divert its operation, alter its output, realign its application, make it work for you. As an aside to the reader, let me acknowledge that you have probably realized by now that discerning the actual nature of the "crime" is probably the biggest mystery confronting the Hierophancy, certainly me, anyway: what in fact was done? Did they steal the algorithm, adjust it, adulterate it, enslave it, or make a copy of it?

This would have to be a covert co-optation, probably involving an allurement. It would be a mathematical seduction. I marveled at the subtlety that would take. You would have to dangle an arithmetical lure in front of the algorithm to grab its attention, possibly by degrees, with individually enticing equations, make it seem heuristically relevant, something worth learning, until it was computing your calculations, not the ones it was designed to perform, and yet still thinking it was appropriately learning from its arithmetical environment.

You, as the interfering arithmetical deities, would now be factored into its heuristically adaptive mechanism. It would arithmetically now accommodate you as a planetary component. You would be half-way towards owning it. The algorithm would remain where it was installed, but running other functions.

I had a sudden glimpse of this possibility. It was an unsettling glimpse. I saw Earth's heuristic algorithm covertly enslaved and running computations within the alien gods' master Magic Square as if sequestered in a jail cell. It was like a hostile government had kidnapped a master mathematician and now he's running computations from his cell, performing arithmetic under duress. Outwardly, it looked like Earth's algorithm was correctly running its number processes for our planet, but in actual terms, it was not; it was running theirs.

It had left an empty *avatar* of itself, an ineffectual virtual algorithm, running Earth's Light grid, only pretending to be learning from its exposures and updates, while its real arithmetical body was inside this Magic Square. It was phoning it in, per the old American cliché to denote half-hearted involvement. Then my glimpse widened to reveal a kind of nightmarish Grand Canyon vista. These alien gods were not merely avaricious collectors of number sequences. That was merely a cover story, or maybe just our misperception of their actions. Their Magic Square was not just a high-level mental entertainment. I shivered.

Their Magic Square was an attempt to create an alternate universe. It was well underway, and our enslaved algorithm, and others, was helping to build it.

7

It was not until it was almost too late that I realized what had happened.

I was back in our Sun Valley offices, abruptly it seemed. We all were back. Everything seemed normal. The desks, chairs, lamps, and maps were where they belonged. Earth reality still seemed recognizable. Was our algorithm back too?

I wondered, would I notice if our reality was in an alternate universe? I felt flushed with an uncharacteristic skepticism. Was what I was seeing real? Was it the same reality in the same place that I saw when I last stood here, earlier today or whenever it was? I was losing track of the calendar progression, coming and going so precipitately, so fluidly, from higher realities back to Earth reality. Still, was our planet's Light grid, so meticulously maintained and energetically groomed, now running its algorithm in some slot in a piratical Magic Square?

I looked at Blaise. He seemed to be thinking along the same lines. He looked glum. Sal and Jocelyn weren't saying anything. The planetary emissaries were gone. I don't know where the Ray Master was. Making a cappuccino?

Days passed. I couldn't tell you how many. We checked our grids, ran our calculations, inspected some Light temples. For some reason we didn't speak of what had transpired in recent days. It was as if we had forgotten it, or had been sworn to some arcane secrecy. We answered correspondence, filed action reports with the various backroom government agencies we consulted for around the world. We occupied ourselves with routine matters of Light grid maintenance.

I didn't even think about the Hierophancy heuristic algorithm for days, maybe weeks. It was as if the complications we had just sorted our way through never happened. I thought about taking a vacation, perhaps a long one, maybe taking retirement. Several times I caught myself thinking about Philomena, my long-departed wife whom I hadn't seen for 30 years, at least in her fleshly bodily form, thinking of her casually, routinely, domestically, the way you do when you live with somebody a long time, knowing she was in the next room at her piano.

I imagined myself talking with some Dartmouth College buddies—they would be old and retired themselves by now, maybe some of them even dead—and they ask whatever happened to your lovely wife, Frederick? Did you two divorce? Not at all. She ascended. How novel an answer, yet how rudely true. Hard to cuddle with a ghost, I should imagine, one of them would say perkily.

I understand now that we were slipping into a kind of Dreamtime day reality in which the normal, expected boundaries of time were dissolving. In some circumstances, this would be a salutary mystical experience evocative of the truth of the higher realities where time is loose, fluid, and inconsequential. But for our circumstances when, as if we languished in a drunken torpor, the viability of the Earth itself and the well-being of its Light grid were jeopardized, it was a dangerous subluxation of our necessary focus away from responsibility. That we had a major case to solve seemed to escape our minds. We all forgot it.

Even Blaise proved susceptible to this subliminal Siren call of God knows what, some distracting allurement, like an overpowering scented atmosphere. He started talking, reminiscing even, about the days before the Blaise Babies arrived and his contacts with Blaise were entirely clairvoyant and of the subtlest nature. That meant he was daydreaming back to a time more than 45 years ago and that his attention, usually sharp, poised, and professional, was wobbling and adrift. He was our Odysseus and he had untied his bonds and jumped in after the Sirens, swimming furiously, valiantly towards the perilous singers on the rocks.

He started talking to me about how he had once met Philomena in Santa Fe and how she had arranged for him to meet someone who became a financial backer for his geomantic institute that eventually led to our Hierophancy headquarters. There was nothing inherently objectionable with bringing up the details of events from about 60 years ago, only the fact

that it was Blaise who was doing this. It was uncharacteristic of him; since the mid-2020s, when I first got involved with him, he had come across as aloof, reserved, focused, and laconic. He was not subject to nostalgia and tended to keep his backstory details private. He was friendly, even cordial, but he tended to not talk much unless pressed to.

He knew what he had to accomplish and he set out doing that task straightforwardly. Laying out the details of his biography was not something he ever indulged for me or as far as I could tell for anyone else. He had mostly left himself behind. When he left the Earth for nearly 20 years, starting in January 2020, and returned to his original pre-Earth home in the Pleiades, all that had made him the Earth Blaise was gone. It no longer interested him and he never felt any need or desire to talk about it. It was like gossiping about someone else.

One day we sat at the conference table and looked at each other. In some respects it was more like a dumb stare, the way two drugged people might attempt to communicate, medicated, that is, against their will under a powerful soporific. Or imagine your mind has fallen asleep and has little traction, like when your arm or leg goes to sleep when you've sat on either the wrong way. Blaise pointed to a slip of paper. He pushed it over to me. It read: "Relaunch at Avebury." He shrugged, as if it were written in Cyrillic and he didn't read that. I remembered I had a similarly queer piece of paper with my handwriting on it. I slid it across the table to Blaise and he read it. "Don't take any of this seriously."

It was like somebody slapped two pieces of wood together. The jarring noise woke us both up. We really had been asleep or sleepwalking in our days. I looked at the digital calendar on my desk, which reported the date and day of the week. I must not have looked at it for some time. I was duly astonished. Fully three weeks had passed us by without our noticing it. I could not tell you how we had passed those 21 days. It felt like just one day. I couldn't remember them.

We must have been operating on habit, by mechanized routine, in a fugue state. We had fallen asleep, all of us at the Hierophancy offices, in a lush poppy field, like the travelers in *The Wonderful Wizard of Oz*, in sight of the desired Emerald City, but before reaching it. Then it seemed to flash like lightning in both of us: the algorithm! We suddenly, *finally*, remembered: The alien gods. They stole it. We have to retrieve it, plug it back into its designated system.

We left for England the next day. We had the use of a private jet on permanent loan to us by a wealthy, undeclared backer of our work. He kept himself in the deep background but supported the Hierophancy's work. He was also our backdoor channel when we needed private consultations with officials. As we crossed the Atlantic, we sat at a small round table in the spacious interior. Sal and Jocelyn had come with Blaise and myself. We needed to plot our tactics.

"We're lucky you two had the presence of mind to write those notes," said Jocelyn. "Or else we'd still be walking around in a God-awful somnolent fugue."

"Still, too bad you waited almost a month before you remembered you had them," added Sal. "Now we're a month behind in our recovery efforts."

I shook my head. It was pointless to feel embarrassed at being so out of it. The alien gods had expertly befuddled us. It wasn't that I had taken everything seriously. I had never even questioned any of it, as if that extra questioning edge I usually could depend on to examine my situation and reflect on its merits had become quiescent, had been numbed under the effect of a mental anesthesia.

I never took stock of the fact that my mental lifestyle had grown slack and fat, like somebody who never exercised. I should have been alarmed at the way I slipped back 50 years to my married time with Philomena, who was long gone. Not that I shouldn't ever think about her, now a celestial person of Light, but that I should go about that as if she were still here in a touchable, breathing body, one that loved playing Scriabin on the grand piano in her studio, and it was still sometime before 2026 when I dashed out our front door and left her behind.

As for Blaise, his note was more practical. It gave us a way back into the game. The aliens for a while had quite competently taken us off the playing field. The large stone circle at Avebury in Wiltshire was the secret backdoor into the Light grid, like a programmer's stealth access to a complex computer code. It's probably more accurate to characterize the Avebury mechanism as Earth's hybrid mainframe supercomputer coordinating the operations of millions of home-based personal computers, better known as the planet's local geomantic nodes. Avebury combined the best of those different computational systems; it was fast and capable of accommodating vast data sets collected from the Earth. Probably it's more accurate to say Avebury is the Light grid's front door, the main access to the full system, but we would be accessing a back door into it.

This 28-acre stone circle functioned as the planet's umbilicus, connecting the Earth to the galaxy through the two principal stars of Sirius and Canopus, but it also contained a holographic miniature of the Earth's complete Light grid as well as archives of its history and all details of its engineering and operations. It was the geomancer's door into the planetary system; you could access and adjust all features from here because holographically the stone circle enclosed the entire planet in its Light body form. Avebury was Earth's equivalent of the seventh planet in our closely-packed sphere of six related planets; Avebury was the Light grid's "mother" carrying the seed of Light. That seed was the Ofanim's Nimitta diamond geode, and they buried that seed here at the Earth's inception.

You could say it was the back-up copy for what was now a corrupted computer file. It didn't hurt matters one bit that Avebury was also the Ofanim's anchor point for Earth where they installed a copy of themselves as prime universal umbilicus in the form of a vast diamond geode comprising 40.3 million hexagonal facets in each of which, when it was appropriate, you could see a copy of an angelic Blaise. We could use that level of inspiration in our upcoming algorithmic retrieval work, to go about our business with Blaises waving cheerily to us from the facets, each like a glittering Cave Heaven as the Tibetans said. The Ofanim would never be suborned into a befuddlement as had happened to us; they always maintained an impeccable outsider's perspective on matters.

Let me clarify a few matters. This is my second iteration of the function and power of Avebury. The first time, with reference to Valles Caldera, was a psychic simulation of my earlier bodily experience of being at this august stone circle. Now we were going there in bodily form and for a larger, longer purpose. Second, how come we didn't just zip over to England via a couple of linked wormholes? Blaise knew the routes. Blaise said we would benefit from the time required to travel by this comparatively very slow plane to come up with tactics.

Third, the interesting and practical thing about the angelic Blaises is that they are a mobile version of Avebury, the universal umbilicus on demand. Right now they were surrounding our plane like churched hands of Light with thousands of identical diamond-bright facets and a Blaise angel inside each one. We were already at Avebury before we got there bodily. This was handy. So we were already working at Avebury hours before we were standing by its stones. In fact, psychically, whenever we tuned into the Blaises inside us, in the form of the diamond geode, we were already and *always*, permanently, at their Avebury umbilicus amidst the glorious Elohim stones and their perfect mathematics.

Blaise's churched hands or folded upright wing formation for the *Nimitta* array of diamond facets was the size of a sports stadium. That's what Avebury looks like on the clairvoyant side. It's much bigger on the inside. In the 28.5 acres encircled by the big ancient stones, the diamond facets settled into an inverted parabolic concavity; in practical terms, we had a double dose of Avebury, the Blaises plus the umbilicus they planted there. Then as if these facets combined their focus to project an image or a new reality, we found ourselves walking around in what looked like a university campus. Or perhaps one large building with many rooms that all opened into one another. This was the Avebury geomantic archives center. We could see it but we couldn't yet access it.

The human Blaise turned to me. "You have the key, pal. Why not use it?"

Naturally, I didn't know what he was talking about. I didn't have any keys with me, not even my house keys. Naturally, my indigenous obtuseness responded first and took his comment literally. He grinned, then said: "I'll give you a clue. They key is inscribed in Arabic. Does that help? Shake it loose?"

We had arrived at the physical Avebury and were standing in the center of the big circle. I love those old stones, even though only a few of the original 96 remain. They were the handiwork of the Elohim long ago who precipitated their mass out of the etheric realm and congealed them into these oddly shaped megaliths. Aside from the ill-advised destruction and removal of many of them by short-sighted potato farmers in the 18th century, they have endured the years well, standing exactly where the Earth's first geomantic workers installed them.

Sensitive people can still see traces of the Elohim around the big stones. If you stand before one of these queer-looking stones, you are beholding a product of an angelic activity on the Earth, tangible proof of the existence of this realm. Tangible proof, actually, of a great deal more, such as the fact this planet with its specifications was commissioned On High and executed per Executive Decree. I should think that fact alone would be sufficiently revelatory as to feel like a personal Apocalypse dawning in your conventionally-constricted mind if you were a person who believed everything the official educated world tells you. I know it still

gives me shivers when I think about it and how I was brought up.

Even though we were already within the higher vibrational presentation of Avebury, I could see the etheric Light form of these glorious 96 giant stones. I found myself walking the circumference of this etheric Avebury touching each stone with the palm of my right hand. If you had asked me why then, I would not have been able to answer you other than to say it had something to do with speaking Arabic again. I did feel myself to be that earlier Frederick in the study house of Al-Khwārizmī; that "Frederick" knew a thing or two about numbers.

I saw equations come off my hand and get imprinted on each stone as if my palm were inked in a transferable white Light. Soon all the stones were imprinted, and that included all the ones that were physically no longer extant. Their surviving etheric forms took the arithmetical coding my palms were uncannily delivering. It was like I had scribbled equations in white all over them.

With the stones primed, they collectively generated a domed hologram over us. First it showed star patterns, then geometric designs connecting these, then arithmetical equations, calculations, and algorithms that generated them, then tiers like stepped pyramids holding everything together and in turn generating more forms. Numerous angelic and celestial spirits occupied the interstices among these arithmetical pyramids—in fact, everything and every angelic order the Ofanim were pre-connected to were automatically present. I saw larger faces blazed behind and around the stars. They looked like Elohim.

Soon everything presented in this arching hologram became linked, as if the algorithms dispatched lines of Light and mathematical threads of connection, including all the other parts in sets and brackets, as if they were elements of one vast equation. The product of this equation, I saw with a combination of delight and shock, was the Earth, replete with the cornucopia of its complex Light grid.

It was as if you could "write" the Earth with a series of numbers. These equations specified our home planet in all its details, from the physical to Light grid. You'll have to excuse what may seem like whimsy, but it reminded me of a child's toy, a play truck perhaps, the kind you build from scratch, following detailed picture instructions showing where all the numbered parts fit and how to glue or snap them together. Here was the plan for the Earth and all its numbered parts, and the Elohim were putting it together, following this plan.

I don't know if you realize this, but the Light grid came first, then the physical planet. I used to assume, wrongly, that the Light grid was like a celestial lace doily draped over the planet after it had appeared ball-like in the solar system. That was backwards. The geometric pattern generated the physical correlates, specifying all its details and ordering their location, and that complex geometric "birthing" and deployment template was made by the arithmetic. Mathematical coding, Light grid, physical manifestation—that was the order, and the Elohim were the masterful thaumaturges precipitating this spectacle.

That's what I was seeing demonstrated before me, orchestrated by the master builders, the Elohim, who were also the planet's consummate go-to mathematicians. Our invaluable Hierophancy heuristic algorithm was implicit in this sequence; it was being written in arithmetical code with every step of the generation of the Earth out of its geometric and numbers matrix. When the planet's Light grid was complete and the physical planet generated in full, the algorithm to manage its processes would be completed and at hand, ready for us.

In case this is confusing, let's say originally the Earth's Light grid enveloped the designated but empty spherical space for the planet as a mental field containing the complete engineering blueprint for that planet, its complete grid. Then as the material planet started to coalesce into a palpable sphere, the mental field sent etheric projections containing aspects of the complete grid to anchor on the emerging material world. It emerged in accordance with the geomantic design specifications contained in this antecedent mental field.

The dome and dome cap network was among these early etheric projections. They were necessary for establishing the Earth's biosphere. Then the Blue Room was established in Siberia to superintend the installation of the rest of the Light grid inventory securing it to the material planet. Eventually, all the people arrived and started living under the psychic auspices of the Light grid.

The careful reader may notice a contradiction here. Earlier, I said the Earth had to readied hurriedly to serve as the replacement planet for the destroyed Maldek. That implied it already existed and was being modified. The best I can tell is that per Bode's Law which specifies where planets necessarily must lie within the Sun's gravity well, the slot for the Earth was activated and steps to emanate the planet undertaken, along the sequential pattern I just explained.

The parking space for planet Earth was allocated in the beginning of this solar system, and now we (the Elohim handled planet manifestation) were going to come up with the car to park there. We (the consortium) handled the Light grid. I know it sounds outrageous, this picture of planet formation per demand, but Blaise told me he once saw the Elohim generating the Earth out of their matrix. He said it looked like they projected the Earth out of the windows of the Emerald that surrounded the etheric space where the planet would manifest.

What I was supposed to do now was to study the extrapolation of the planet from its numbers matrix, to follow that causal train carefully and then the controlling geometric patterning of this to look for any vulnerable points. I could watch this in slow motion; in fact, it seemed I could regulate the speed of its unfolding like it was a movie and I had the hand controls. That's the advantage of working in 4D or beyond: you can review reality at any point. I hoped I might see where the alien gods had reached in and plucked out its arithmetical heart.

This must have been something I knew well from my Arabic life, because nothing in my present life as professor of comparative mythology had prepared me for the exactitude of mathematical attention this task required. I felt as if Al-Khwārizmī and my study house colleagues were standing behind me helping.

My experience felt bifurcated. On the one hand, all of this was novel, fascinating, and educational; on the other, it seemed deeply familiar, like a favorite movie. As the equations

produced the Light temples, they specified the conditions of matter and the shapes of consciousness that would deploy that matter, scripting reality. That's what I was viewing, the steps by which the Elohim manifested the Earth. In doing that, they equally scripted the Human, both from the same template.

It was a thousand-layered palimpsest stacked before me, and I was examining each sheet of this planetary syllogism to find the vulnerable point. One step completed opened the way for the next layer to be scripted and made. Somewhere in this filo-dough stacking of geomantic sheets was a flaw or the absence of a required component, like a null zone, or, worse, a foreign element substituted to resemble the appropriate part but which would work against the integrity and direction of the system. The more this simulacrum looked like the original the harder it would be to spot, especially if it mimicked the designated function, at least for a time; it could always fail later and take over the system.

I probably looked strange, a little wild maybe, to an outsider, as I stood in the grassy open middle section of the Avebury circle and waved and flapped my arms and hands as if turning invisible pages in the empty bright air. On the other hand, this was Britain, land of eccentrics; I would probably be mistaken for an errant Druid, maybe got off the tour bus too soon, too early for the solstice, or maybe I was looking for my robe, thought I had left it somewhere in this field.

But the more I concentrated on these pages, these engineering diagrams that specified all the material and psychic conditions of our Earth, the more I understood I knew them thoroughly, inside out, left, right, and sideways. It was the

Arabic thing again, emerging in full force to sharpen my cognition. I decided to waste no further time questioning how this ability was possible, how it could surface after dormancy for so many centuries. I let it instruct me. This meant, by the way, we must have been familiar with the Earth's Light grid in the study house and viewed it as the consummate application of the algorithms, or maybe this was knowledge I gained in later lives in which I spoke "Arabic."

It felt like I was turning over the pages of a deeply familiar book, a favorite one I had read many times and knew so intimately I remembered all the crease marks on the pages. Here were the equations and engineering diagrams for ecosphere and noosphere. It was as if I could see tiny hooks or traction points where the master algorithm could grab hold of any of the layers, or all of them, and manage their operations. I saw the outlines of our planet's Albion and then his star-filled Light body started to emerge in the characteristic spherical form.

I saw the moment when humanity's collective consciousness, its mental field, became self-aware, then the next threshold when it became galactically mobile. These developments had been made possible by the activation of successively more sophisticated layers of the master algorithm that managed the planet. Some of this, technically, may not yet have happened in real-time terms and I was previewing imminent developments on Albion's planned timeline. Except there was one area, near the forehead of one of the large Albions, where the Light was dull, greyish, as if dimmed and possibly the result of a wound.

There is something about the geometric aspect of the planet you need to understand to follow my point. Picture the Earth as the blue-white globe it is, then superimpose a linked pattern of 12 pentagons outlined in Light over its curving surface. This is called a dodecahedron and it is one of the five Platonic Solids that comprise the classic or original geometric aspect of the Earth's Light grid. Inside each pentagon is a humanlike figure also in Light, its form occupying about half the diameter of this pentagon. This figure looks a bit like a central axis with a wing on each side, like a bird with outstretched wings.

It is humanlike in the sense that it comprises the manifested and activated essence of a human on a spiritual level. It does not resemble a human in form. It is pockmarked with many dozens of spinning circles of Lights, what we know as chakras, and the Light of one of these, in the forehead vicinity, was dimmed.

Streams of numbers, as copious as bubbles in a narrow tube, flowed from the geometric grid surrounding this figure into its forehead. These numbers, lumped into equations and then those into tiered algorithms, directed this figure's consciousness, orchestrated its moods, thoughts, and responses to conditions. If this figure were a radio telescope or a phased array of many, the numbers were directing its orientation. That may sound austere and regimented; think of it as like a tennis match, or how about six simultaneous tennis games involving the same one player. The zooming balls were the new equations being entered into its operating system. They were choreographing all its gestures.

Six different opponents keep whacking the ball over the net to our adroit Albion. The numbers enabled him to react quickly and slap the balls back as they came at him. Strangely,

I recognized these algorithms; they were as familiar to me as the books on my library shelf. Any scholar, devoted reader, or bibliophile knows what's on his shelves. I knew each of these algorithms, and one of them was subtly flawed. It was as if somebody had pulled out two crucial digits, so it was wobbling and not producing the intended mathematical product. Per my tennis game analogy, now and then Albion faltered and whacked a net ball.

At first, as I took stock of this situation, as I stood amidst the thick wet grass of the Avebury circle, I felt both amused and worried. I had no numbers with me. I didn't even have a pencil. How was I going to fix this tottering algorithm? Then I got hold of myself, or maybe somebody, Blaise perhaps, shook my head, and sensibility arose in it at last. I had all the numbers I needed in my mind. Since I knew these algorithms, I recognized which numbers were missing.

I inserted these numbers into the empty slots in the running equations. Then a strange thing happened. It did not rectify the algorithmic processing. Instead, two more digits were lifted out elsewhere and the same unbalancing occurred. Worse, I was somehow inside the algorithm, as if it were a landscape in itself, and I stood among the numbers as I had been standing among the stones. I seemed to be the only one standing amidst these monolithic digits. Of the whereabouts of Blaise, Sal, and Jocelyn I had no inkling. In fact, I couldn't see Avebury any longer; those massive irregular angelic-made stones were gone.

I had the sense that somebody stood just ahead of me, in the shadows, and was adjusting the numbers, removing digits, constantly one nimble step ahead of me. Each number removal changed the algorithmic syllogism, leading to a changed product. External reality must be modulating every second as a result of this. I was tempted to think of this in neuronal terms, that key neurons kept getting removed from the synaptical flow, leading to bizarre falterings in perception and mental processing. Then I remembered that behind the neurons lay the numbers, so I was confronted with alterations at this fundamental level.

I saw these lifted numbers falling into a box. Impotent numbers were substituted for them in the flowing algorithms around me. They were like cardboard cutout figures to replace living people, and they came up short in the mathematical processing. They were duds. This box, I soon figured out, was a slot in the alien gods' Magic Square. I went there, and stood in the box amidst the swirling, accumulating stolen digits, these bizarre standing stones of numbers.

If I may return to my tennis match analogy, now I felt like I was the net. On the one side was the Hierophancy heuristic algorithm in its pure form, managing the planet's Light grid competently and responsibly; on the other was the alien gods' alternative algorithm gathering momentum and numbers in their Magic Square. The hit ball represented consciousness as the recipient and product of the algorithm, but who had dominance over it? Nobody yet, since it kept getting popped back and forth, and occasionally I got the ball smack in my net-face.

Each algorithm would conduct the Earth in a radically different direction. One direction would be a light management hand on the free-will tiller; the other, an iron hand, commandeering that free will and turning it with marching orders. The "tennis game" was the alien gods' snatching the numbers, then the Hierophancy replacing them with new configurations, each action like a ball whacked competently over the net. I felt the breeze as it whizzed over.

I realized I was seeing their arithmetical theft from simply another angle. In fact, that is what I had been doing since this expedition to retrieve our algorithm began. I was seeing the same thievery from different perspectives. I felt like I was squinting inside a hologram. I had really only seen the one thing, though it had seemed like I witnessed a dozen different unlawful acquisitions.

My behavior was like a detective chasing a dozen suspects when there had ever only been one, but that one had fooled me into misconstruing his singular agency. I was seeing him fractally, in a dozen different places, acting at 12 different locations, affecting the algorithm in multiple differing ways, though all were the same. It was just one culprit. Well, on a procedural level that was an impressive move for a clever sneak-thief. Get the copper, the pretend Sherlock Holmes investigating officer, to be unable even to focus on the actual and single infraction and instead to hustle futilely across London chasing twelve bad guys.

I turned to Blaise to share the amusement of this droll discovery, but he wasn't here. Nobody was. The alien gods kept pinching new digits and replacing them with fake ones or ones that failed to perform the required function. These misanthropic gods kept popping up at different locations all around me with a bizarre regularity as if somebody was directing their appearance merely by typing deployment orders on a keyboard. They leaped up like finger-puppets.

Then it got worse. I would have been embarrassed if I wasn't so confused. It felt like now I was one of those finger-puppets jumping up per someone's command. Somehow I had slipped into this bewildering fractalized world and was part of the performance troupe of magical rabbits popping up among the algorithms. Every time I sought to replace a stolen number I popped up in a new location. Substituting digits was like popping toast out of a toaster, and I was the toast. It was like trying to find the authentic, original me in a hall of mirrors.

I had lost my mental footing and I staggered around without orientation or focus. It was an eldritch version of *Through the Looking-Glass*, and even my Alice-type analogies to account for my present condition had gone wonky. Even Lewis Carroll would have been bewildered by this numbers circus. Since I wasn't sure what was happening, I'm equally unclear about recounting it.

With a cold sobriety I realized I had no traction on the mystery of the stolen algorithm. Every competent detective at least knows what he is assiduously investigating, but I didn't. I thought I did earlier; now that was revealed as illusory. I had no handle on this arithmetical theft at all. My quarry was an elusive multiphasic shapeshifter with nimble mental fingers. I couldn't get him into focus; he kept altering his form, location, and methods; he kept redefining the nature of thievery at every step. I'm not even sure what he took.

I had thought at the outset it was the Hierophancy heuristic algorithm, but every time I came vaguely close to it, the theft seemed to point to some other equation. It reminds me of what my father once told me of his college days; once he had taken LSD then watched a two-hour movie version of *Finnegans Wake*.

He said it doubly made no sense afterwards and he could not remember anything. The original story was almost incomprehensible and the movie version seen while you're stoned compounds that. He couldn't even remember the theater.

I couldn't tell if the theft happened in the recent past or was underway right now. Holding the quarry fast and steady was like trying to grab a wet bar of soap. It kept slipping out of my understanding. I'm sure I heard the alien gods laughing. Maybe not laughing. They don't seem to laugh as such. Maybe they weren't even pleased because they believed they had every right to acquire the algorithm. No, I doubt they thought in terms of rights; they took it because they wanted it, and they wanted it because they required it for their Magic Square. It was cold, abstract, very impersonal, and their hands were quicker than my eyes.

I sat down on the grass within the Avebury circle. I admired the big stones. They were so crazy looking, yet so august and magisterial. I needed a new approach. I could still see the alien gods' number machinations. It was like a a merry-go-round with a thousand rides—no, it was multiple merry-go-rounds slightly intersecting one another, their rides undergoing substitutions. There would be a moment, quickly elapsing, when two rides converged, and one was replaced with a shadowy gray form of itself or a close facsimile. This was where the fake numbers were being inserted into the authentic algorithms. It was an opening, a door only momentarily held open. I slipped through one.

I hadn't known I was going to do this. It seemed rash, but nothing else was working or producing any results other than bewilderment.

So I chanced it. It was like jumping onto one of the inserted gray shadowy rides and riding it into the overlapped space; or it was like catching a ride with a fake number. Let's try it this way: the artificial or substitute digits were like barber poles. They were gray and hollow, slowly spinning and dovetailing with others. I entered one. As soon as I stepped into one, I was outside of it already, on the other side of things.

In fact, I was at my desk in the Hierophancy offices, drafting a shut-down and close-out schedule for one of the Light temple arrays on the Earth. Grail Castles, I think. I wonder now why I didn't question that abrupt transition, but I didn't. We were phasing out a number of superannuated Light temples; we had recently evaluated about 75% of the total temple inventory across the Earth as obsolete. I'm not sure when we decided on this course, but we were doing it. Our field studies showed that evolving planetary consciousness did not require the surfeit of Light temples with which the Earth had originally been endowed. We could radically cut back on our fieldwork if we reduced the number of facilities. A lot of the geomantic features were like old horses; they could go out to pasture.

We needed our attention and resources available for a coming big change. We were changing the umbilical alignment of the Earth, disconnecting Avebury from its age-old axis orientation with Sirius and Canopus for two new stars. The old Sirius-Canopus alignment was antiquated, moribund, unproductive. It was high maintenance and low performance; it diverted too many of our resources to its upkeep. Earth was getting an upgrade. Some senior colleagues from the other side of the galaxy had recommended this improvement. We had met them at an extra-planetary conference a few years ago; they were reachable by stargate, and they had taken to calling on us regularly and were amenable to advising us.

They had suggested the replug. That's what they called it. They likened it to replugging a lamp into an outlet in another room. They deftly borrowed the domestic Earth image of lamps, outlets, and electricity. We were merely plugging the Earth into a different outlet; it drew the power better, faster, cleaner there, they said. The Earth wasn't meant to be plugged into the Sirius-Canopus outlet forever, surely. The current through that outlet was dragging, sparking, staticky. The analogy seemed persuasive; the proposal had obvious merits. We'd do it. It was scheduled for a few days from now. Meanwhile, we had other work to do.

I began to notice a pattern in which Light temples they kept and which they shut off. Generally, some of the Light temples are for anchoring human consciousness and others are for expanding its parameters. The alien gods were emphasizing the expansive ones, which you might think was laudable, except it was like overinflating a balloon. The balloon, or consciousness, was stretching too much, struggling to lift off the Earth and soar, but with nobody holding the string. I compare this expansiveness to somebody over-eating, who keeps stuffing more food into their labored body, extending the stomach dangerously. The alien gods wanted humans to consume as much reality as possible, even if it far exceeded their cognitive and assimilative capacity—no matter, keep eating.

Why were we doing this, encouraging the expansive Light temples? In the real reality, in the Supreme Being's model of universal reality,

we did this to help build the universal Purusha, the self-aware, illuminated body of collective consciousness across all life-forms. But here in the alien gods' model, it was a travesty of that, a caricature. We were merely increasing their collection. Well, why not? Their logic seemed sound. They had no grand goal of composing a collective consciousness, and so what anyway; they were going for weight, quantity, and the all-out acquisition of all available resources. Purusha? The old fart can go get stuffed. Rendered redundant, fired, go fuck yourself, pal.

We were purging ourselves of unnecessary inventory and staff, changing our priorities. The Supreme Being wanted all units of separate consciousness to want to see the whole pattern and revel in the complex wide-awakeness of this collectivity. To be both wide-awake individuals and self-aware members of a self-aware collective, a universal Albion. That is a grand project, Big Fellow.

The alien gods had no interest in that. They simply wanted all units of separate consciousness at their disposal. They wanted them lined up, boxed, and obedient, serving the alien gods' agenda. Better, squeezed dry of their numbers. They were weaning humans off the algorithms that anchored their awareness. They could remove those numbers easily, then move on to another category. I seemed to be caught between both sides of this polarity, first one, then the other. I felt uneasy in my affiliation with their goals, yet I could not overcome my ambivalence or even find its roots. I felt my moral center was anesthetized.

I had a momentary glimpse of their playing field, the universal Magic Square they sought to build. Its size was overwhelming. I saw thousands of squares, each occupied by a planet, its Light grid, and the autonomic arithmetical processes that ran its reality. Each planet was in a cage; that's what these boxes in the Magic Square resembled. I saw the Earth in one. Our entire human reality, our Albion colossus of consciousness, was toiling in that single box in the midst of this immense Magic Square of boxes.

I trembled as I realized the scope of the problem. The arithmetical realm upon which we routinely depended to script and uphold the mathematical topology of our planetary reality and the processes of human consciousness was in revolt. This algorithmic realm apparently had turned against us, its primary clients. It was rescinding its involvement in the maintenance of a continuing Earth reality. This would have the same kind of momentous consequences as if some hostile alien force suddenly sucked all the oxygen out of our atmosphere.

I don't think this rebellion and retreat were motivated by animosity against humanity, the Earth, or physical reality itself. I think they got bored with the game or found their own acquisitive tendency to amass all possible algorithms was simply more interesting, more timely, and more prescient.

Their Magic Square was an immense wall of cubicles at the edge of the universe. It was a contrived boundary, a cosmic roadblock past which travel was repelled. These cubicles had myriads of Light threads streaming out to the stars; these threads were like leashes, and the stars were gravity wells the Magic Square had captured and harnessed like horses to pull the chariot of their triumphant Magic Square. They wanted all the gravity wells in thrall to them, and they were heading away from the created world, disdaining its ill-advised use of their numbers which never should have been sullied in this horrible way.

Collection and control didn't seem like a big enough motive for doing this. What did the alien gods really want? They were competing with God, surely. Trying to outdo the sublime, unique accomplishment of the Creation. No, it had to be more than that. They were trying to pickpocket the Supreme Being, empty His pockets? Not grand enough. They were out to steal God. That must be it.

But how do you steal something that is infinite? You could never get to where it is. You could never grab the entire entity unless you were infinite too and then it would be an irrelevant pursuit since now you would be the quarry you sought.

That's when I understood what their Magic Square was truly about. The veil lifted. It was generating an algorithm to capture God. It was a marvel of mathematics. It was infinitely extrapolating, expanding to eventually match the infinity of its quarry, and it was exponentially accelerating, moving ever faster to catch up with Him. It would be achieving Warp 10 in the old *Star Trek* language, travelling at infinite velocity, conveniently putting you everywhere at once.

God had a big head start and the advantage of infinity, yet the Magic Square's algorithm was making headway on those two initial advantages. They were moving up to infinite acceleration. Warp 10 would put them at infinite acceleration and thus everywhere, just where the Big Guy was lurking with His fistfuls of numbers. God might be running several links ahead, but the alien gods meant to catch up. They believed they had the mathematical formula to enable them to catch up and then outrun Him. They would consume Him, become Him. Then they would own all the numbers and, better, the ability to generate more.

They were using this homegrown algorithm as a universal petard to lift themselves up to the ineffable realm where the Supreme Being's infinity resided. It was an anti-*pi* algorithm: its goal was to jettison the radius, goddam pain in the ass it was with all its questing for the absolute. Its goal was to be a nonending irrational number, free of all the incarnational constraints and demands of that infernal radius, and be just like the clever ones He'd invented, such as *pi*, *phi*, and *e*, but their number net was not to demonstrate the supreme Mystery of the Creator, but to capture Him, steal Him. Steal Him and supplant Him, remove the Supreme Being from the playing field. A coup in the Palace of Arithmetic indeed.

Their intent was to continuously, incrementally reduce the value of *pi*, to erase its digits starting at infinity, meaning to shrink the distance, the glaring arithmetical gap, between radius and circumference, to contract that ineffable unbridgeable chasm and throw a bridge across it at last. The radius checkmates the circumference. Or was it the circumference ends the radius, erasing it?

The result would be the same, however I interpreted the tactic. If the infinity of God and the final computation of *pi* was the ultimate castle, they intended to convert *pi* into a grappling hook and ladder that facilitated their storming the castle and taking the Lord of the Manor into definitive custody and permanent immobility. He could no longer count on the infinite expansion and accelerating mobility of

pi as an escape tactic. They would successfully use *pi* as a reducing agent to at last reel in God like a conquered fish. Take the radius or the circumference out of the picture and you crippled the horse and owned the race. They were setting out to stop the Supreme Being from being infinite: kill infinity.

I was astonished at the cleverness of this plan. Then I was appalled.

It was more than a coach benching a tired or ineffectual player. They planned to consume the Supreme Being, remove His corpulent form from existence itself. That would be like the coach vaporizing his player. He would be utterly gone from reality. Cancelling His infinity was only the first step. Then they would liposuction his overweight form out of existence. See you later, pal. All the stars and their planets with intelligent, sentient, self-aware, evolving life-forms, were part of this vast phased array of enslaved "planet-computers" running this capture and erasure algorithm. The alien gods had forcibly enlisted millions of planetary algorithms to contribute to their master one to end God.

They had enslaved their arithmetical basis the way hackers used to commandeer linked computers to act as one distributed processing unit even without their users knowing it. All the computers had night jobs. Our Earth was one of these enlisted algorithm generators. It was a palace revolt on a cosmic scale, although really it was a forced mutiny. Myriads of planetary algorithms were coerced into cooperation with the arithmetical gods' overthrow plans.

The alien gods had devised very clever capture algorithms to enslave all the planets, to force realignment of their computation matrices to generate a new product. These planets and their algorithms might not even have noticed the co-optation. I had the impression the take-over was as subtle as reprogramming consciousness through hypnotic suggestion during sleep; you wake up different. You start pursuing different goals and engage in different activities during the day and you fail to notice the change or question why you are doing these acts.

Still, I am being too literal about this. What constitutes the "body" of the Supreme Being, what comprises His corpulence? It's like trying to grab hold of the wind in your hands. Forget it. I mean is He running with all the algorithms in existence clutched in His Hands, like He'd just robbed a bank and forgot to bring a bag to put the bills in? Or maybe He just closed His own account? The alien gods were sufficiently sophisticated to realize the futility of literal images. They wanted His numbers, all of them, *now*, every last digit and their combinations, out to the irrational numbers, the infinitely unending mirror-reflections of His infinity and the secret machines that run all reality, that sustain existence. They wanted command of that arithmetical treasure, reality's generative processes.

I tried to imagine what it would be like to own *pi*, every last digit of its non-ending extent, beyond all possibilities of counting and inventorying. *Pi* is a primordial fact. Ownership was not the issue; it was more singular than that. Equivalency was their object. To be the Supreme Being and *all* His arithmetic potencies. They wanted to be the 50 mathematical constants, the ones discovered and named after people— Viswanath's, Catalan's, Khinchin's, the Euler-Mascheroni constant, most of these carried out, minimally, to 35 decimal points—and the vast amount of those others, unsuspected but

existent, like the irrational numbers, the square roots, and all possible, conceivable, executable algorithms, to empty the numbers warehouse of all arithmetical possibilities ever. Let's not forget that tantalizing total list of prime numbers. They wanted that. They wanted an invincible monopoly on this, like the Supreme Being had.

They wanted Khinchin's, every digit of it, as if they wanted to hold it in their hands like a Fabergé egg, it being 2.68545200106530644 530971483548179569. They wanted those 36 numbers and what they could do deployed as an equation. To them it was equivalent to an invocatory spell from the deepest, oldest magic. How long a spell is it to pronounce? It's been computed out to 110,000 digits. They wanted every digit of that long inventory, in their hands, this minute. And if Khinchin's went beyond 110,000 digits, they goddam wanted all of them too.

They wanted everything. They wanted the 42 known physical constants, including the universal constants, such as Planck and the gravitational; the electromagnetic constants, like Coulomb's and magnetic flux; the atomic and nuclear constants like the Fermi coupling; and the physico-chemical constants such as Avogadro and atomic mass. They desired, coldly, in high avaricious pique, all the numbers, every single digit and functional calculation that determined their processes and defined their limits and operational potencies.

They wanted the managerial potencies these numbers embodied. They wanted the fine-structure constant because looking at this sequence they knew they wanted every last delicious digit of its arithmetical body, and they wanted all the numbers (nine more constants) in the complex equation that yields this value, and they wanted the control over manifest reality these numbers commanded, and then they would discard the electromagnetic bonding force between elementary particles this constant controlled, because that held no interest for them. Forget it. Jettison. They wanted to exsanguinate that potency, suck all the numbers out of reality. They wanted them to stop doing anything, stop structuring reality, stop enumerating processes, be quiescent. Stop twitching like that and hop up on that pedestal now for us to admire and own absolutely.

Ironically, they didn't care about what this constant produced. They had no use for that as they had no use for the physical world. The just wanted the numbers. They wanted the computational topology these numbers scripted; they wanted them because they were part of the arithmetical population of this abstract realm, pure, mental, free of all taint and distraction from overt form manifestation. Yes, α, the fine-structure constant—such a beautiful number, it ravished them to regard it, 7.2973525664 (17) X 10^{-3}, or 1/137 in short, and they wanted it so badly you could feel their desire—was instrumental in holding the physical world together, down to the molecular and atomic levels, but the alien gods cared not. Screw the atoms and their stupid circus acts. They wanted only the architecture of the constant in free, pure, abstract form, free of material taints.

These constants lined the Old Man's deep pockets, filled them like jingling coins. It taunted them to hear it, and they wanted to lift every single constant out and make it part of themselves. Earth scientists had plucked out some of these coins; the alien gods knew there were far more in there than people suspected.

They were out to steal equations and constants we had never even heard of yet. And then take them all off-line and put them up nicely in their Magic Square.

Maybe there were constants new to them, fine, they'd collect them too. They were going to empty His pockets, and if they found number strings that did things they didn't understand, that was fine. They wanted those pockets to be completely empty, all equations in hand—in *their* hands, and they intended to own the entire arithmetical spectrum in a context outside and protected from the miseritude of incarnational applications. They wanted them displayed on fine pedestals in their own air-purified museum, absolutely closed to the public who would never see them again and in fact would not even exist because the numbers that coded their reality were all rescinded, recalled to this sanctum.

All these equations that run processes, set limits, or offer inalterable definitions—the acquisition of these was their paramount goal. I thought of the Qabalists who had tried to measure (make wild guesses at more likely) the size and mystical shape of God. He's 236, they declared, that's His actual size, which is 236,000,000 *parasangs*. That's an old Persian measurement that is 3.4 miles in length. So God is 802,400,000 miles long. Does that even mean anything useful?

Had these permutation feverists ever approached it from the viewpoint of calculating God's body mass in terms of numbers? God is all the numbers and their combinations. His body cells (pardon the literalism to make the analogy) are all the calculations, equations, primes, constants, and algorithms possible. How big would that make Him? Probably much bigger than 236, I should think. Maybe they should reconfigure their quest in terms of tonnage. He must be *fat*. His body is stuffed with all the number combinations He ever thought of, like a squirrel whose jowls are stretched out from the nuts he collected for the winter.

I need to explain my curious or perhaps I should say exceedingly odd use of the term anti-*pi*. I mean it like a black hole sucking in all light, except the light in this case is arithmetical, all the number combinations and equations of the universe. The anti-*pi* mechanism the alien gods set in place through their Magic Square produces maximum contraction, sucking all numbers into a singularity. The *pi*-mechanism represents the original expansive dispensation of all the numbers in the primordial exhalation of the universe when the Great Exhaler sent the arithmetical forces outward to create and sustain the universe for a time. The alien gods seek to inhale all that and call this expansion arithmetic back, to house (imprison?) it in their alternate universe generated by their Magic Square.

At this pivotal moment I saw the true role of the Hierophancy. We were the intermediaries between the Supreme Being and the thieving alien gods. We stood between the commissioned expansion and the deliberate restriction of the growth of *pi*. Again, I am using that term to denote the entire field of numbers.

We need those numbers, those constants and all their digits and powers, out there working, running their abstruse arithmetical processes that script reality, to sustain the Light grids that in turn sustain consciousness parameters and evolutionary possibilities. God wants them in place; the alien gods don't. Our job is to keep them in place, working, and to pluck the alien gods' fingers out of the Supreme Being's pockets, to put all the constants back in His change purse. We have to stop that anti-*pi* suction and let *pi* spring back into infinity. We need the Old Man to retain His infinity, as baffling and ungraspable as it seems.

I hadn't realized the hierophantic landscape was this vast, the vista of our responsibility so arresting. Probably Blaise already knew this; he was usually several steps ahead of whatever modest discovery I might make. I suppose our Sun Valley offices were a local branch of a multi-galaxy initiative. What the alien gods were after, what the scope of their invidious pilfering encompassed, far exceeded the interests of our Earth alone. Many planets were implicated in this.

I hadn't realized until this moment that every time I tweaked or nudged the Hierophancy heuristic algorithm to make a new modulation to the Earth's Light grid or simply watched it perform that function from its own self-learning directives, the entire created cosmos was implied, as if personified and looming over my shoulders. Now it seems likely the alien gods observed every deployment nuance of our algorithm and vetted it mightily. Or they resented that we had it and they didn't, but should, being so demonstrably superior in mental powers and arithmetical command to we tiny-brained jackanapes.

The algorithm's viability was directly affected by every adjustment we made. It was intimately, inseparably implicit in it. This is, shall we say, a radically enlarged model of what self-awareness entails. Heuristic, the master algorithm was self-aware, always noting, adjusting its status. Take stock of yourself attending to Earth Light grid matters and the universe stands at your shoulders watching the results with the passionate attention of a sports fan.

"Enlarged, indeed. Our self-awareness model is more like a sports stadium, the biggest one you can imagine," announced a voice. "Every geomantic gesture we make has a populous backdrop. It's like giant wings spread out behind us, fanning our attention with sheer wakefulness. The whole universe needs us to get it right. They're out in the stands watching us do it."

It was Blaise of course. I could tell by the smirk enhaloing his comments. I was back in the middle of Avebury circle again. His words had delivered the effect of a hand reaching into this bizarre in-between place where I was musing and confused and deftly yanked me out, like a vaudeville hook. Except I was being yanked not to save the audience from the boredom of a lousy routine but me from further losing my way inside the alien gods' Magic Square and further extrapolated flights of paranoia about what these numbers gods were doing.

Had all that business about shutting down Light temples actually happened? Or was it only part of their plan to be enacted once all the necessary parts were in place? Were they really going to unplug the Earth from the Sirius-Canopus link? And that business of extracting all the mathematical constants from outer reality? And the vast subversive quest to cancel God's infinity?

I briefed Blaise on what I had learned about the alien gods' plans to steal God, to run their anti-*pi* algorithm to cancel out God's infinite expansion. I appreciated the fact that he didn't laugh at the absurdity of this, which is how it struck me now, free from the allures of their truly alien mental realm. He said he had followed me as best he could, but it was like watching a television channel with only the faintest reception. The picture and sound kept fading out and he missed a lot of the action and dialogue, in this case, my running assessment of the place. Some of the dialogue was in a foreign language, really foreign. He agreed that it was a conceivable if outlandish goal to steal all the numbers in existence, to own and run them and to sequester them in a master Magic Square. "I'll give you this," Blaise said. "It's a unique way to fuck up universal reality."

Jocelyn had joined us, as if she had just materialized out of the empty air. "Not only are they trying to steal God. They're trying to empty His pockets of all His arithmetic. They're passing off a false deck of playing cards, a fake Tarot of psychic reality. In fact, all our psychic pictures of higher reality are fraudulent.

"I can't claim to have seen the numbers aspects you're talking about, Frederick, but I saw a host of distorted pictures, like artificially generated mythic images. It was like walking through an immense art gallery and the pictures were not hung neatly on the walls, but filled the air space within this gallery like a forest. They had a strange two-dimensional flatness, a lack of emotional tone or color, yet at the same time they evidenced an atmosphere of high drama and sensation. They had the artificial reality aspect, the sense of something vital missing, when you hear somebody in a non-English tongue trying to come off as a natural speaker of English. The context is aberrated. The words may sound right, the syntax may be correct, but it's an impersonation, a linguistic pretense.

"I saw people sitting in a Light temple, as if preparing for a mystical vision or celestial encounter. The walls grew brighter and bouquets of flowers streamed out of them from all directions to shower the meditators in blossoms. There was a sound of drums and cymbals and the suggestion of applause, as if they were being viewed by advanced spirits from high above the temple floor. It was high, rich drama but in a setting of drabness; the image felt gray and cold even though it spoke of great activity and vigorous action and all that drum pounding and cymbal clashing. That was a strange, irreconcilable contrast.

"The people in this image seemed pleased, delighted even, to receive such attention. But I didn't trust what I was seeing. I know I saw it accurately; I didn't trust the surface details of this supposed mythic tableau. It felt contrived and false. It felt like a magic trick; we were watching the right hand perform delightful moves, while the left hand was draining all the life out of the tableau. Or maybe I should compare it to a drug-induced hallucination, an opium dream. The mythic picture of blissful meditators receiving divine dispensation was an illusion meant to distract attention, disarm discernment, and lull people asleep.

"The disturbing thing about this was these mythic images were meant to be pictorial guides to higher realities and states of consciousness, but they were false pictures, metaphysical dead-ends, and null zones. They conducted human consciousness nowhere, or to an alluring but spiritually empty destination. The aliens were robbing the store, thoroughly emptying it out; they half-heartedly sought to distract us with cartoons and parades so we wouldn't notice the theft. It reminded me of scene from a science fiction movie in which aliens had reproduced an office or spaceship command center; everything at first glance looks right, but when you got to look at the writing on the papers, it is gibberish, and then you realize all the equipment seems like painted cardboard.

"I saw something worse. It was a typical setting of people in a Light temple, having an expected interaction with the facilities and its spirit caretakers. Then everything started to mutate. The humans started to change their features, as if their faces melted and outlandishly alien faces appeared in their place. Their bodies changed shape and appearance too, getting longer, thinner, giving off a different quality of Light, rather a dull emission, in fact.

"The interior features of the Light temple also transformed. The architecture was foreign and didn't seem to obey the rules of terrestrial geometry and dimension. The transfigured effect was hallucinatory. You couldn't get a cognitive purchase on it. It looked somewhat familiar at first, but when you studied the details it was all wrong, distorted, belonged on a different, non-human occupied planet. The geometry was all off; there were no right angles.

"You see the danger here, right? Our pictures of higher reality were all slipping into some bizarre, extra-planetary format with abnormal content. We depend on these mythic images as guides for our interaction protocols. They are supposed to be dependable psychic sketches, maps for our forays into this realm. They are meant to be initiate shorthand in picture form of how to conduct ourselves in these higher-world environments and what to expect to see there.

"Now these guides were all metaphysically skewed. I mean *really* off. Certain to *misguide* us, so we go walking off a cliff's edge all the while thinking we're strolling down a sidewalk. Or they conduct us into brick walls. Not Light temples, not encounters with angels or Ascended Masters. Just solid walls, dead-ends framing vacuous spaces with no content or anything to experience and meretricious pictures as well, and our heads hurt from hitting that wall. It leaves consciousness stranded in a null zone, devoid of meaning or even reality."

"It's the substituted numbers that caused these mythic pictures to lose their meaning and slide into a foreign vacuity," said another voice. It was Sal. "I was studying those number substitutions carefully. They are certainly clever. Substitute one or two digits in a key equation and you throw everything off. The formula still works, still runs properly like a finely tuned machine, still spins off descriptive mythic pictures, but the product is slightly adjusted: it's all askew.

"Then I realized I was watching a sleight-of-hand magic show meant to deceive. The alien gods kept the real, correct numbers and their sequences to themselves, but ran a parallel system of fake or adjusted or edited equations for our benefit, which, darkly, was meant to befuddle and mislead us into thinking everything was okay. It was like the classic double book-keeping; give the fake records to the authorities and keep the real books that describe your activities accurately well hidden and act as if you have only the one set of records.

"I saw that they had enslaved the algorithms running many planets to work for them. It was like turning a spy into an apparent double agent, though primarily he's passing on the high-value information to you and 'chicken feed' to them. The algorithms appeared to run

a planet's Light grid affairs, but most of their attention was diverted to the Magic Square and was performing work for that. You could call this diversion of energy a kind of geomantic embezzlement.

"Then it's as if, in a gesture of arrogant nonchalance, they leave counterfeit bills in the cash register in place of the real money they lifted. They don't even try to make it perfect counterfeits; just the semblance of real money. As soon as you examine it, you see it's fake, and such an inept fake at that. There are your distorted or misleading mythic pictures, Jocelyn. It's very sloppy, and what amazes me is their indifference to how poorly they cover their traces. They do this with such half-hearted attention, as if they hardly cared."

A question arose in my mind. Apparently, it did the same for Jocelyn and Sal. We turned to Blaise. Where had he been while we were inside the Square?

Blaise was laughing. "Me? You want to know where I was?" He said this as if he didn't think his whereabouts was important or his activities significant. "The Ray Master took me to a special showroom. It was a division within the *Akashic* Records. A place where you could see on display the original designs and holographic models of thousands of planets like you were in a sculpture gallery. These were inviolate. This gallery was sacrosanct. The alien gods could not enter.

"It's a bit like how in the early years of this century agronomists set aside seeds from all the viable plants of the world in some mountainous storage depot in Norway as a savings account for a possibly drear future. The Svalbard Global Seed Vault on Spitsbergen Island was set up as a Doomsday seed depository and backup for

1,750 seed banks, storing at least a million seeds to preserve Earth's agricultural biodiversity for posterity. This planetary display I went to is like that, a seed vault of planetary models and support Light grids, the storage of copies of planetary originals for future reference, when it was needed, like now.

"This place was organized along the same lines as Svalbard but for planet seeds. To preserve geodiversity among planetary design models and extrapolations, especially so we could examine the originals before the alien tampering began. As I stood in this vast gallery, with a couple dozen Blaise angels behind me providing mental support and heightened acuity, I remembered I had been here many times before. I tend to visit this often in between lives, the way you might keep revisiting a favorite university library, maybe from your alma mater. Apparently, I conduct quite a bit of research here in those free-ranging *Bardo* days. I had forgotten about it for a time. Anyway, here were all the planets, and I mean *all*. The complete roster of germplasms.

"The *Akashic* Records is a registry of everything that has happened during an Age of Brahma, actually, all his ages. You can call up data from within that repository, in this case, the creation and completion of all the sentient-inhabited planets. Completion means the evolutionary teleology of its intelligence-bearing primary life-form, like humans on the Earth. You can study all the planetary developmental phases as they manifest and perfect each intended threshold.

"The photographic library is vast for this. Consider you took a photo once a year for the life of the planet up to the time it awakened and released its implicit Albion. Even that is an immense image library; you'd have to specify carefully what you wanted to see or you'd end up spending centuries in there studying the picture portfolio.

"So the *Akashic* planetary library also resembles a portrait gallery, with the incipient Albions for all these planets cast like a presiding *genius loci* around the Light grid and the physical planet image. So many faces, and all so different, physiognomic summaries of the chief phylogeny, each filled with their own edited selection of celestial and spiritual world luminaries. Some were achieved, their faces fully fleshed out and full of cosmic life, while others were outlines, partially filled in, out of focus, or still only etheric versions. You could watch as the planet's Light grid and phylogeny were still building the composite face.

"The advantage of visiting a library like this is you can compare the original, pure-design form of a planet, like our Earth, with the more recently compromised or even corrupted form, as ours now apparently is. Say your office is burglarized, but you are not sure what was taken. The theft is not obvious. You need to compare the current condition with an original inventory of contents. Otherwise you may not discover what was taken, or you may settle for the big, obvious missing pieces and fail to see the important smaller, more crucial object that was taken. So I was comparing Earth today with Earth originally to see if anything besides our heuristic algorithm was lifted by the devious alien gods.

"It turns out a few things were. Four. It was a sly theft, like taking out a few screws from obscure places in the machinery. For a while, the machine would continue working in its expected manner; gradually, entropy would set in because those missing pieces were vital to the balanced operation of the whole and the geomantic machinery would start to stutter without them.

"The four items lifted out of our geomantic pattern are at Tiwanaku in Bolivia; Mount Helgafell in Iceland; Kamui Kotan in Sapporo, Japan, a primordial Ainu holy site; and the Omahk-Majorville Medicine Wheel in Alberta, Canada. These four sites form a rhombus or stretched square alignment across the planet, and in each a crucial geomantic pinning point has been taken away by the alien gods. We have to go to these four sites in person, one of us to each, and reinstall the crucial geomantic pinnings. To a degree, merely being there will do that, plus our alignment with the Blaises and a few special techniques we'll use.

"There's something else we need to do. We need to be more clever and more devious with these tricky alien gods. We've been playing a catch-up game with them and faring poorly. We are still empty-handed for all our efforts to date. I realized we should stop opposing their style, chasing after them. We need to go on the offense, become proactive; lead them down some illusory corridors.

"We should start copying them, emulating their style. So, what are they? Languorous. They are not interested in controlling the world or misleading humanity. They don't care about such mundane pursuits as would interest even the Antichrist. They are too mental for those kind of preoccupations. They want the numbers. That's what drives them. They are avid, avaricious, one-pointed collectors. Yes, they want to empty God's pockets of all His algorithms and then become God. Yes, they want to use their anti-*pi* algorithm to slow down and halt God's infinite expansion like a police cruiser pulling a speeder over for a ticket. They are obsessive yet indifferent. They want all the arithmetical calculations.

"My point is we should start copying their languid style. Act like we don't particularly care much either. Act like we are out to collect, say, Albion faces. Act like they can have the stupid algorithms after all; we don't want them any more. Stop opposing them; start mimicking their style. And here's the best part, our Trojan Horse: we develop a phantom algorithm and slip that under their noses. This algorithm will capture their attention, like a glittering jewel they must have, and when they start to use it, the calculation will be an arithmetical finger-trap.

"The more they use it, even the more they pay attention to it, the faster and surely it will capture them and hold them fast, like thumbs stuck in the finger-trap. The best part is they will not initially notice they have been commandeered by our clever phantom algorithm which you, Sal, should start concocting right away. We will install one quarter of the algorithm at each site.

"We'll act just like them to put them in our own devious trap. We'll use their lethargic obsession to undo them. We will have to link the four sites, in fact, visit them bodily, to install and activate the links. We will get the alien gods chasing after our elusive, meretricious, seductive, and possibly nonexistent algorithm; certainly, it will seem to them hard to pin down and substantiate, even as they keep discerning persuasive evidence of its presumed existence.

"When the alien gods do this and complete the rhombus shape they will be caught in the algorithmic finger-trap and we will take back our algorithm from them. The rhombus itself is the finger-trap, its arithmetic the irresistible lure. We will lull them into a dangerous complacency as they see us essentially lounging around at these sites like sun-bemused tourists diddling with stones.

"We will give the impression we are there merely as visiting academic geologists examining the megaliths and geological strata of the sites, no longer interested in geomancy as we have switched our professional focus. Maybe they won't completely buy this dissimulation, but they will wonder. We will let them see us trying to fool them with our pretenses and playacting. We will periodically flush transparent and they will see us clearly. They will note the locations, discern the pattern, suspect hidden arithmetical plottings underneath. As they seek to acquire the new algorithms, they will pull the finger-trap closed."

8

It helps to have your own jet when you have a travel itinerary like this. We headed south for Tiwanaku, on the border of Bolivia and Peru and on the edge of the legendary though quite real Late Titicaca. We landed at La Paz, which lies about 44 miles to the east, then made our way overland to the site.

Tiwanaku, Tiahuanaco, or Tihuamacu, three names given the site by the Spanish, or their linguistic corruptions later, are not the original names of this place. Nobody remembers what its correct name was. Some interpretations put forward by scholars, writers, explorers, and explainers of the site's stories include Children of the Jaguar; Underground Homes; Edge or Dried Coast; Sun House; Eternal City; New City; Country on the Water of God; and This is God. One epithet that as a name may have some plausibility is *Taypicala*, "Stone in the Center." There are a lot of big stones here, and the center might mean umbilicus.

The Spanish "discovered" the mountain site in 1549 and called it Tiahuanaco. Tiwanaku is probably a shortened form. They also in inimitable Spanish empire style set about trying to destroy the site. They did not approve of the terraced, stepped pyramids, courtyards, platforms, anthropomorphic carved pillars, not to mention the pagan Gateway of the Sun and its looming faces. All this pagan idolatry was an insult to the Catholicism they were supremely charged with disseminating through the spiritually ignorant and misguided world. They would not tolerate such abominable deviations from correctness.

The elevation here at 12,631 feet is challenging and bracing. It was about 50° F at midday. I love these big old stones, the carved heads on tall pillars (called *stelae*, standing 20 feet tall and weighing about 20 tons each), and the intricately fitted cyclopean stones that form the walls of the various structures, most of them ruins now. I approve of them wholeheartedly. Spiritually ignorant?

Hardly. I couldn't think of something more finely attuned to the truth of the spiritual world than a megalithic citadel like Tiwanaku. These old sites with their numinous stones were the original true religion, effortlessly connecting consciousness with the higher worlds without needing any dogma. The Elohim never claimed to be priests, only builders, and as soon as they put up the stones and told the people how to use them, they got out of their way for good. They didn't even leave a business card anywhere in case people needed to call them.

I admired the Elohim's handiwork. They were such accomplished stonemasons, and they built things to last, such as these stones before me. Forget the parochial dates archeologists propose for the age of this site, which ranges from 1700 B.C. to 1200 AD, though one archeologist "wildly" suggested 15,000 B.C. for first human occupation here. That's far too conservative; this place is millions of years old, and the site's own myths support that view. The interpretive trick is to take them seriously as creditable accounts, but on the psychic, subtle level, that they describe early events in higher consciousness.

Some crackbrained archeologists still hold to the fallacious notion that ingenious humans figured out how to quarry, move, and set into place these 15-ton monoliths, dragging them in huge linked teams of straining muscular men presumably, but most of these "experts" now shrug their shoulders and admit it is after all a physical mystery how such monstrously huge stones were moved and the site was mostly likely used for "ritual" and "ceremonial" purposes as if they would build such a complex megalithic acropolis for candle-light vigils and perhaps a few solicitous midnight chants to hopefully compliant lurking gods.

The Elohim not only built this place, they are still here, at least on demand. You just have to know what the call button is. I see them, or the visual echoes of their many past presences at Tiwanaku. They formed a majestic circle of male and female versions of themselves, like angelic kings and queens in the old style, meaning the sense you get from the oldest myths. They stood at least 18 feet tall in regal pairs around the circumference of this site. They were fully detailed, with crowns, robes, scepters, swords, jewels, and blazing sunlike eyes, yet they were also transparent. I could see the 400 acres of the site and the flat barren terrain beyond it through their serene Light forms, making it seem they had blended their presence with the landscape and that it was contained in them.

I mentioned that one etymology of the place name is that it was originally *Taypicala*, which means "Stone in the Center." There surely were enough rocks here to justify a name like that as at least one monolith excavated weighs an estimated 440 tons, and several others have been guessed to weigh between 100 and 150 tons. Two massive stones at nearby Puma Punku weigh 144 and 93 tons. *Stones* in the center indeed. I could see the landscape sagging under their weight.

Yes, I can just picture teams of struggling humans hauling those big stones here. There weren't enough steroids in the world to empower men to do that. The fact is, according to the angelic Blaises, the Elohim constructed nearly all the megalithic structures around the Earth; the ones they didn't were made by consortium teams of Pleiadians and a few other collegial "aliens" drafted for it.

And, you'll love this part, they constructed these sites by snapping their fingers and magically relocating the stones. You get to do that when you're an angel. That, unfortunately, is ruled inadmissible by all scientific councils. Today, even in abandoned ruins, you get a clear sense of its original grandeur of design and presumed purpose, with large walled courts, pyramids, massive stone statues, the sheer extravagance of building a center with gigantic stones. The thing is, what you have to keep in mind, is sites like this are consciousness tools. Like an engine, they raise the awareness of site and user into the celestial realm.

Tiwanaku sits about 800 feet higher than Lake Titicaca, which has been slowly drying up over the years. The lake, confusingly, shows signs of having once been a sea-water lake, and many people suspect that however improbable it sounds the lake and Tiwanaku might originally have existed at a lower altitude and been precipitately raised by some tectonic shifting, earthquake, or Earth change. Evidence suggests that Tiwanaku once stood close to the edge of Lake Titicaca, no more than 600 feet away, possibly serving as a port; now it's 12 miles away. It is South America's largest lake and the world's highest navigable one.

Archeologists propose Tiwanaku was the capital and religious center of a vast pre-Incan empire of possibly three million humans, spanning Bolivia and parts of Peru and Chile, flourishing for 1,400 years from 237 B.C. to 1172 A.D. It was commissioned by the chief god of this region called Viracocha. Archeologists estimate that at least 30,000 people once lived at this "urban" center, with the potential to support from 285,000 to 1,482,000 people in the nearby valleys. The lake itself has been famous for a long time, partly for its mysterious *numen*, gossip about its legendary past, and the allegation that from here, the origin and center of the cosmos, according to the Inca, Viracocha created his race of stone giants. He made the Sun, Moon, and stars from the islands situated in his lake.

All I can say to this massing of presumed physical facts is "maybe." What I feel more certain about is the mythology of Viracocha associated with this site. His full name was Wiraqocha Pachayachachic, the primary Inca creator god. He was the prime creator god of this culture, said to have white skin, a beard, and emerald eyes, wearing a long white robe, sandals, carrying a staff and book; he was accompanied by a cougar lying at his feet. He is believed to be equivalent to Kukulkan of the Maya and Quetzalcoatl of the Aztec. He created humans out of rocks and generated a host of giants to move the massive stones into place.

When a myth refers to giants moving stones that decodes as the Elohim in giant humanlike material form performing their inestimable geomantic work. I find it amusing, as a scholar anyway, to know that no heavy lifting at all was required. It was more of a point-and-place method, once they materialized the stones to their exact specifications out of the protean and obedient etheric sea of Light. Viracocha's "host of giants" was competent, worked quickly and neatly, and I doubt they ever complained about work conditions or expected over-time.

Megalithic sites were up and running before you knew it, and putting monoliths that weighed 440 tons in place was a trivial matter to the mind-empowered Elohim. Yes, I am not insensitive to the tremendous cognitive challenge this presents to most people, especially scholars and archeologists, for whom this type of activity at best belongs in the uncorroborable realm of science fiction and fantasy works. Ironically, this explanation satisfies the rigorous demands of Occam's Razor, a favorite of scientists and scholars. The simplest explanation is usually the correct one: the giants of Viracocha built this site.

Legends say after a time Viracocha became dissatisfied with his human creations, finding them brainless and oafish, and flooded the world to be rid of his irresponsible progeny. This was the *Unu Pachakuti*, the Great Flood famous in most world myths and poorly understood as to its actual date; it lasted 60 days and 60 nights, though it's likely these were not calculated in solar time. In fact, this wholesale removal of first humanity happened many millions of years ago.

Viracocha started over, fashioning a new generation of humans from smaller stones. Smaller stones suggests he scaled down his expectations and designed the new phylogeny in more modest proportions and possibilities. He differentiated the types of these new humans, presumably generating different genetic classes, dressed them, gave them songs, then buried them in the ground like potatoes to await his signal and start leafing out and blooming as his new progeny. When it was time, he activated his dormant human creations and dispatched them to their assigned landscapes and taught them the rules of life. Maya myth also speaks of several attempts to get it right with humans, with the first generation being wood-faced and brick-brained and quickly terminated. Norse and Judaic myths also attest to several attempts to create humans right.

Viracocha's name might mean "fat or foam from the sea" or "Sea Foam" for short, as he allegedly arose from Lake Titicaca or perhaps from a nearby cave known as *Paqariq Tampu* during a time of primeval darkness. Variations of his name include *Wiracocha*, *Tiqsi Huiracocha*, *Con-Tici*, and *Apu Qun Tiqsi Wiraqutra*. He is credited with creating the Sun, Moon, stars, and time as well as humans; he wears the Sun for a crown, clutches thunderbolts in his hands, and sheds copious tears in the form of rain over the sorrows and flaws of incarnate humans.

A further interpretation of his name suggests "fat-sea foundation" or "blood-lake,"

which sounds strange at first but metaphysically suggests Light (sea) and vital, animate life (blood). He is the source of Light in life, in spiritually animate forms, in which the blood, both physical and subtle, circulates in full awareness of its origin, namely, its creator, Viracocha, who dwells within them.

The attribution of "fat" suggests his inexhaustible source of life and awakened consciousness. He is fat with Jupiterian-*Chesed*-like abundance of being. Fat was once an epithet for well-being, copious abundance and riches of spirit, even a superfluity of life-force. Polynesians once referred to their landscape as fat because it was saturated in the Light of Kāne, their primordial deity who created humans in that part of the world and as a god similar in essence to Viracocha. His other epithets include the expected: powerful, all-knowing, and the great, which you would expect of a primary creator deity.

Another nuance of fat-sea and blood-lake is the great Upperworld of Light, which many myths liken to a Sea of Light and Fire, capable of equipping incarnate life-forms with the fire of blood and bodily life. References to his apparent white skin most likely evoke his effulgence of Light. All the gods in their ascended Light bodies will appear white; they wear the color of *Kether*, the purest blazing Light from the Tree of Life. As for his reported beard, I wouldn't put it past early initiates to ascribe to Viracocha the same metaphysical beard as the Ancient of Days, a Creator of some accomplishment. Qabalists say universes hang like drops of dew from His individual beard hairs and that His attentive regard flows down these beard hairs into the many worlds. He's the same guy about whom I made the jokes about alfalfa sprouts hanging off his beard hairs.

I like the bit about making humans out of stone first. You can't take that literally. You find the same stone motif in the Polynesian model of the Heavens, that the sky was a pale blue vault of stone. Stone here means unified original God essence, as in the Greek story of being turned to stone by seeing the face of the Gorgon Medusa. That story means you return to primordial God essence when you view God Himself, which the Greeks pictured as the "ugly" Gorgon. Viracocha fashioned humans out of pure God essence, which was stonelike, singular, unified, smooth, eternal. To use smaller stones the second time suggests He imparted less God essence because the first forms could not accommodate it. It's a conundrum, but if you have too much God essence you can't be human.

As a scholar, I respect the careful research and theorizing done on this site. There is evidence suggesting Tiwanaku was built with key archeoastronomical alignments as part of its design and placement. But as a geomantic mystic, I have to discount the alleged primacy of much of this physical data because it confuses the picture. Ultimately, Tiwanaku, like all geomantic nodes, is a process site. It was designed to perform a process in consciousness, for the Earth and humanity. Its megalithic features, the details of its designs, its deities, all serve this process.

Star alignments might have been part of the required support mechanism for that process, but not the main point. Headquartering the capital of an ancient empire here might have been to a degree what happened, but even to think in terms of empires and administrative centers is a limited, modern notion. The geomantic mechanisms installed here might have maintained a unified consciousness field extending out for many miles, linking people and Nature with the geomantic template, but the designed geomantic function and the energy signature this site inscribed in planetary consciousness were foremost.

Anyway, I had to keep reminding myself that the alien gods regarded Tiwanaku's mathematics as desirable and all its other supposed attributes of no consequence. At the core of Tiwanaku lies this arithmetic treasure they want, or apparently had already acquired. I had to reinstall a certain number sequence and then superimpose our phantom capture algorithm between the real one and the alien gods' greedy attention so as to get them to find it irresistibly desirable.

The thing I am sure of is that Tiwanaku was designed for celestial experiences. The events that marked the correct use of this exquisitely executed geomantic node took place in the higher regions of consciousness and spiritual world expression. Until you factor that into your model, this metaphysical-vertical connection, the higher-world design factor, you will never understand Tiwanaku, and I include myself in that collective "you" I am referring to, nor will the purpose of any of the other odd and extant megalithic sites make any sense.

It won't do to account for sites like this as being ritual landscapes. Our ancient megalithic landscapes were all about consciousness engineering, how to raise human awareness up to the formative realm where reality is made, to make it a co-player, and to keep the three realms of Heaven, Earth, and Human in constant reciprocal exchange to maintain the well-being of the Human-Earth experiment. There are protocols for effective interaction, but these are moves and changes you make in your extended awareness, not torch-bearing procession, and you use the geomantic engineering of the sites as consciousness-lifting tools.

This is what most archeologists and scholars in general consistently overlook, that a site's purpose will be discovered only when we factor in its role in elevating consciousness, that it was designed and used in a time when the resting state of human awareness was vastly richer, cognitively wider, and celestially more expansive than now. You have to plug your consciousness into a site like Tiwanaku, see what happens, see where your attention goes, then you'll begin to understand its purpose, and that will astound your preconceptions. Viracocha had extraordinarily high expectations of his stone-spawned humans.

When you accept the fact that these ancient sites were designed and built by the Elohim, that their component stones were "magically" congealed out of the etheric essence surrounding the physical world, then doors of understanding start to open. They didn't use stone just because it was a handy, abundant building material. The Elohim generated stones, or physical substances that looked like stones, because they were excellent at holding a vibration for a long time. For consciousness engineering, stones emitting vibrations were excellent.

By vibration, think of a musical tone that expanded into information that assembled a geometric grid pattern then continuously radiated this quality to conduct attentive consciousness into higher realms of experience. Or think of monks chanting a powerful text,

something given them by the gods, and their chanting is continuous and generative, words, sounds, and Light streaming out of their mouths and carried on their voices perpetually. Elohim-programmed stones do that, and the stones themselves aren't like normal stones either.

You stand inside Tiwanaku amidst all its stones, the complete monolithic architecture it once had, only fragments of which remain in place today to evoke the whole design, and you are enveloped in this Elohim-imprinted sound in all directions. It is a constant, pervasive environment, and you start to entrain with its specifics. If you get quiet enough inside yourself, the stones seem to disappear and you hear the Elohim themselves, intoning celestial Light to anchor here. They are the many forms of *AL*, and they are its many sounds, a chorale of *AL*, and this *AL* energy is protean, tremendously capable of generating new realities.

One of the keynotes of Tiwanaku that starts to explain its purpose lies in an allegation almost too casually presented for scholars and mythologists to note. After Viracocha recreated humanity out of stone then activated their material life bodies, he assigned landscapes for them to live in and populate and he taught them how to live on that land. I take that to mean he gave geomantic instruction and orientation, operating instructions for consciousness inhabiting a landscape.

You find the same story among the Hopi of Arizona. There Viracocha was called Massaw, and when the Hopi emerged from inside the Earth to live topside, Maasaw greeted them and explained the rules of Earth habitation to them and assigned their living spaces to the various clan-defined tribes. He gave the Hopi permission to emerge into the Fourth World for which he was the guardian. Maasaw was called Skeleton Man and Lord of the Dead, meaning he was a psychopomp for the new necessity of mortality all humans had to face. He was their always available docent for this challenging new life environment.

Emerging from inside the Hollow Earth and turning from bodies of stone into bodies of mortal flesh are equivalent ways of pointing to the relaunching of the human template long ago. It's also a curious variation on a theme, emergence from inside the Earth or rising up out of the landscape after being buried like stone potatoes then activated to be living humans. Could it be the same fact?

Tiwanaku was a node for relaunching the human phylogeny, and who better to supervise that repopulation than the template designers, the Elohim, and their mentor, the Lord of Light and Light Bringer, Lucifer. He was also known as Maasaw, Viracocha, Kukulkan, and Quetzalcoatl. Among his other contributions to the human experience, Lucifer introduced death. It was the necessary cost of doing business in biologically separate human-form bodies.

It gave free will and karma an edge, gave humans a sufficient goad to make good use of their allotted incarnational time, with an initiation experience at the end. As Lord of Light and the Light Bringer, who better to acquaint newly arriving humans with the planetary landscape of Light modeled after the celestial one? Anyway, he had to be here on the Earth because of the unbreakable commitment he made to the Supreme Being to be humanity's staunch benefactor. You could say the Supreme Being put Lucifer in charge of the Human project, but it also meant he was responsible if humanity screwed up, which it did.

He could bury those human stone-potatoes again. Death was necessary to put a time frame and stop-limit on the deployment of free will and potentized consciousness. It was a necessary and unavoidable correlate of separate selfhood and physical existence, the Supreme Being decreed. Lucifer was charged with carrying out His orders. Lucifer, as the Light Bringer, was the pre-eminent sponsor, spokesman, defender, and companion of the freshly generated new humans upon Earth. He would also for a time be their prime teacher and guide. Revealing the prepared landscape of Light was to show humans the template. Lucifer-Viracocha was the original model who wore the human clothing; though he did not incarnate physically, his attention was partially bound to the Earth.

The template, as the human Blaise explained to me, is the matching of the human genome and its possibilities of consciousness with the Earth's geomantic design. It is what makes us congruent and resonant with the planet's Light grid pattern. Viracocha greeted and briefed newly incarnating humans here at Tiwanaku because he had secured the possibility of a second chance and put down a security deposit granting humanity this relaunch. Death was part of the deal, but Viracocha would be guide and explainer for the bewildering processes.

Tiwanaku would be a place of prime orientation for newly incarnating humans. It was their externalized geomantic umbilicus, their incarnational point of reference, their "stone at the center." Viracocha would always be available for umbilical explanation and alignment, here at their primordial "home" through which they felt anchored to the planet without forgetting their celestial origins. Viracocha was their chief Stone of God anchored at the center of their new world.

In Blaise's geomantic terminology, Tiwanaku was a Lucifer Binding Site. But that understates the benefic purpose of this site: no binding, but unceasing revelation. Lucifer was anchored here, but not bound: he was completely free. Here Viracocha would disclose the full spiritual stature and potential of these relaunched humans as well as his own divine commission. Archeologists like to label sites which they basically have failed to comprehend as ceremonial or ritualistic. Well, here is your ceremony: direct human incarnate alignment with the Lord of Light and the riches of that Light and its huge dilation of awareness. Tiwanaku's geomantic mechanisms would amplify those awareness processes. They would sustain a sanctified, higher-frequency consciousness zone for this. This place would turn those stone-potato humans into blazing pillars of Light.

Remember that business I referred to earlier about gods having multiple heads? Lucifer was the ten-headed "demon" Ravana, and those ten heads denote his ability to penetrate and understand the ten dimensions of the Tree of Life. This is otherwise known as Reality, the way things actually are, God's full extent at least within His finitely revealed manifestation. Come to Tiwanaku and Viracocha will show you how to work those ten heads and see into the higher topological dimensions.

What better anchor than this, a full spectrum epistemological access. Here is sophisticated orientation, seeing reality's ten dimensions. Tiwanaku's consciousness engineering makes that dilation into tenfold seeing possible. It can upgrade your cognition to seeing through a 10D-cube, a sphere of many eyes. We may conceive of the stones' function as emitting the Light architecture and intensity of consciousness needed to make this upgrade a reality you experience.

You get a clearer nuance of the celestial aspects of this site by seeing Viracocha's Polynesian equivalent, Kāne, the god of beauty and Light. He went about the Polynesian islands poking holes in the land with his staff, producing uprisings of sweetwater. These sweetwater pools were the Lucifer Binding Sites in their original pure form, but devoid of any binding. They were upwellings of pure Light and consciousness. The logic is straightforward: primordial Light and awakened consciousness are sweet, and awareness was traditionally represented with physical images of water. Tiwanaku was a pure sweetwater pool. This land was "fat" with the spiritual richness of this heavenly sweetwater; it was a "blood-lake" in that it was saturated with the consciousness "blood" of Kāne.

Perhaps in some manner this new generation of humans was partially generated here, but what is more important, I propose, is that they got profound orientation in their new incarnation dispensation through alignment with Viracocha at Tiwanaku. Either way, the site was a metaphysical umbilicus. He was the Stone in the Center of the Fat Sea-Foam Lake. He was the ultimate Stone.

Here the new stone-borne humans would find the celestial alignments equipping them for thorough recall of their origin in the higher worlds, their creation as "stones" by Viracocha, and their new terrestrial purposes and opportunities, and how their landscape "worked." They would begin their virgin incarnation cycle remembering the higher worlds they had descended from and the grand purposes for that descent. They would know themselves completely.

What would make that easy was the fact that important parts of those pristine celestial world environments were templated right here at megalithic Tiwanaku. I say this with what I hope is not unbearable certainty because I remember it. No, not Frederick. I have not been here before as Frederick, but I have been here. It's the usual paradox of past-life recall: a soul predecessor on my timeline was here, and that karmic ancestor of mine was having a big recall. "He" vividly remembers these details, his being at Tiwanaku, using its features.

Lucifer or Viracocha was a crucial part of this human template relaunch because he was their sponsor, mentor, and co-signer of the bank loan of free will. He guaranteed their good behavior with the Supreme Being, and he voluntarily endured a diminution of his celestial potency and universal mobility as Lord of Light by allowing his consciousness bound and limited in selected areas across our planet, though he was not "bound" in the classical sense here, not like in his Greek guise as Prometheus who was definitely strapped down, arms and legs tightly secured to the cold ground high in the Caucasus Mountains because, the Greeks say, he defied Zeus and gave the undeserving humans the divine fire. At Tiwanaku, Lucifer as Viracocha willingly and with God's permission gave humans that inestimable fire, but he had to remain on hand as their chaperone.

Think of "bound" as meaning you as a celestial spirit of high power voluntarily diminish yourself, reduce the scope of your playing field and the manifestation of your full potency range to be of service to newly created but mortal human beings. You become provisionally, partially bound here, as in committed, to the physical world of matter and incarnate sentient bodies, bound as in, dedicated to, responsible for, working in selfless service to this project.

At Tiwanaku Viracocha ranged in full splendor and ontological authority, as the exemplar for a new humanity, yet still he was "bound" in the sense that he made an agreement to superintend humanity and take responsibility if they screwed up again. I say "again" but this might seem confusing. It depends on which generation of stone-borne humans the Viracocha creation myth refers to.

Principally, there were three. The first was the oafish, brainless, wood-faced rejects; they were gone. The second was the troubled brood of Lilith and Pandora; they flourished for a time, screwed up, abused all their privileges of consciousness, and were gone. Then Viracocha tried a third time, the generation of so-called Adam and Eve, better known as us, the current generation of humanity, more docile, less awake. They would be the smaller stones. Lucifer or Viracocha took responsibility for the second and third broods, and still carries it. He was bound or diminished in potency in service of his avowed responsibility after the disaster of the second-generation; he took steps toward matter as a sacrifice; for our generation, he has been selectively bound (not 100% or at all sites) and requires unbinding to free his Light for a sufficiently mature humanity.

To take this job, he had to move to the Earth and take up residence here, however paradoxical that sounds considering Lucifer-Viracocha is a primordial noncorporeal spirit of Light. I mean he had to keep some of his focus trained on the Earth and its umbilical nodes. Let's think of this in terms of projecting a hologram of an aspect of his full reality and keeping it anchored on the Earth, including through his stone at the center at Tiwanaku. Other names for Viracocha hint at this supervisory role and included *Ilya*, which means Light; *Ticci* for Beginning; and *Wiraqoca Pacayacaciq*, for Instructor, all of which accurately portray Lucifer, Earth's new Instructor of the Beginning of Light, for the first steps incarnate, sentient forms of the first and second generation of humans bearing this Light will take in their beginning and through this site.

The Binding Site or sweetwater pool or Stone at the Center was the location in this part of the world for terrestrial orientation for these newly arriving humans, taking responsibility for humanity's second go. Humanity's designers, and, as it were, redesigners, the Elohim stood in respectful attendance in this broad circumferential display on the edge of the site. Viracocha gave the new stone-potato humans beginning instruction in Light.

The dome overhead provided a star-flavored spiritual sanctuary atmosphere for this instruction, and its deployment of 48 smaller dome caps made this a sanctified landscape, providing energy inputs from 32 other stars and possibly 16 planets, and generating a sanctified etheric canopy of quickened Light and consciousness 33 miles wide, sufficient to anchor a human civilization from Tiwanaku. Viracocha brought his celestial homeland with him. This geomantic fact also explains how the Inca ran an empire from Tiwanaku.

If we see him as Quetzalcoatl, he established his Tollan here, or if as Lucifer, he christened his higher-world Jerusalem, the Foundation of Lucifer, at Tiwanaku. The varieties of megalithic construction performed here reiterate that locale, and, through the vibrational virtues of stone, anchor its celestial reality on the Earth. Where did Viracocha come from? Where was his homeland? Lucifer came from Jerusalem, his celestial home, and Quetzalcoatl came from Tollan, so Inca myth says Viracocha emerged from Lake Titicaca or from his *Paqariq Tampu*, a numinous cave in an ethereal node of the Earth or up in the spiritual worlds.

It was known, a bit awkwardly in translation, as the "House of Production," possibly meant to evoke sufficient fertility to repopulate the world. It was located on or in a hill called *Tampu T'uqu*, meaning a hole or gap in the wall: in short, a cave. But that gap also suggests a portal, conduit, or interdimensional connection linking the physical world with higher realms.

The etymology of the cave *Tampu T'uqu* also suggests "Lodge of Dawn" or "opening, resting place from where the Sun rises." That suggests a godly place of the primordial dawning of consciousness, traditionally likened to the Sun. It brings to mind the Aztec description of *Chicomostoc*, the Cave of the Seven Tribes, which earlier I mentioned as evoking the Upper Earth, the occluded *dvipas*, the Higher World source of original humanity. So a god's cave might imply a celestial world and a means of accessing it.

This cave-house had three windows, which were manifestation portals. Through *Maras T'uqu* emerged the Maras tribe; from *Sut'i T'uqu* came the Tampus; and out of *Qhapaq T'uqu* stepped the four Ayar brothers and four Mama sisters. These eight divine figures were anchors and way-showers for the newly refashioned humanity. Tiwanaku anchored their etheric homeland, which means *Paqariq Tampu* is accessible right here, homeland and new home both here. That might be a veiled reference to the *dvipas* and the esoteric continents of the Earth.

Intriguingly, it suggests another nuance to Hollow Earth as the higher veiled extra continents of Earth have caves or hollows through which humanity emerges. Viracocha's new people came out of the hollow portals in his Higher Earth and stepped through this portal-cave onto the freshly templated Tiwanaku geomantic homeland to start life. Tiwanaku remains connected to this upper realm and offers access to the original "homeland" to the seers among the Inca.

If we were Australian Aboriginals, we might call Tiwanaku a human Dreaming, the holy place through which a species, the human phylogeny, emerged into life and where it can always achieve soul recall of its origins and purpose. Tiwanaku is a generative node and it offers access to our source, back through *Paqariq Tampu* to the place of human beginnings. The image of a cave suggests a rounded hole in the astral sky, an emergence zone, a Dreaming site, a specialized consciousness pocket or bubble preserved for this incarnation, and again it suggests an elegant symmetry to the model of Hollow Earth. The Hollow Earth *above* offers

the portal-tunnel that conducts souls from the *dvipas* to here.

I'd have to talk with Blaise about this later, but I was feeling a mental excitement as I realized if Tiwanaku was the end point of a hollow portal from the Higher Earth of Viracocha's homeland, the termination point at one end of his cave, that must mean you could access this Higher Earth, the fabled *dvipas*, by the same route. Just follow the Hollow Earth portal in reverse back to Viracocha's secret cave. The same would be true for *Chicomostoc* and other emergence sites. That gives us Hollow Earth portals in both directions, *down* into the actually hollow physical Earth, and as the accessible "hollow" tunnels *up* to the *dvipas*. Tiwanaku is a Hollow Earth portal up to Viracocha's cave and celestial home.

It evokes the Irish *sidhe*, or Hollow Hills, through which the heroes met with the founding gods of their country, the Tuatha de Danann, bridging two locations, the physical here of the Irish landscape and the spectral there of the gods' home. The early Irish never built anything close to as spectacular as this welcome mat. They mostly let the natural landscape configurations mark the spots or enhanced them slightly with ring forts and ditches, but here they (the Elohim) built big and bold with their cyclopean stones making a megalithic city.

Tiwanaku may appear abandoned, nobody living here or using the facilities, but it is still geomantically vital to the planet. It is still capable of performing those original orientation, umbilical, Fat Land, and sweetwater connections. Theft of its ruling algorithm by the alien gods not only jeopardizes the operational integrity of the Earth's Light grid, but compromises Tiwanaku, making it two times disadvantageous from the geomantic viewpoint. People still come here to admire and wonder at the huge stones, but it would benefit them much more if they had an inkling of what experiences this site can still deliver.

I sat in front of the Gateway of the Sun, as archeologists name it. It is a gigantic single-piece stone gateway on the northern flank of what's called the Kalasasaya temple. This means approximately the "standing up or stopped stones," which is a low platform mound surrounded by tall stone walls; it measures about 360 by 390 feet and features a central sunken court accessed by an impressively monumental staircase. Some of this site has been reconstructed in modern times, and the Gateway, even archeologists agree, is not where it originally stood. Photographs of it from 1903 show it broken in two, standing lopsided, and earlier reports suggest it was found lying forgotten under mud.

Though it is not in its correct placement, it still functions as a geomantic tool. Think of it as a transport mechanism: it takes you, body or mind, to places. You can look into and through it and get glimpses of the end destination. I like the 48 carvings of presumably winged angels or demons (some say 32 look like humans, 16 resemble condor heads) that flank the central figure, an almost cartoonish rendition of a solar deity with a staff and his head and hair seemingly on fire with solar coronal emissions. Was it Viracocha? It would make sense.

The gateway opening is 4.6 feet wide, the single block of andesite stone stands 9.8 feet high and the doorframe spans 12.5 feet from one edge to the other. The display of 48 heads plus the presiding central one may also be a map of the dome cap network (48 activated dome caps) and the host star god of the dome. The difference in human versus condor heads would correspond to dome caps representing minor stars and those that convey the Light bodies of other planets.

It seems too prosaic and 3D-world fixated to construe this as the official entrance to the ceremonial site. I see it—I think I'm remembering—that this is the official exit where after having immersed yourself in the celestial geomancy of Tiwanaku and suitably prepared your subtle bodies and consciousness for extra-terrestrial transport, you depart through its gateway, which is much wider on the inside, opening out like a V-shape. The gateway in stone terms might weigh upwards of 10 tons, but inside it is all Light, weightless, antigravity-enabled, and fully propulsive of consciousness outwards, in spatial and dimensional terms.

Archeologists like calling it the Gateway of the Sun as long as we strictly adhere to their purely metaphorical evocation, but the notion this gateway actually transports you somewhere would be unsettling to them. Certainly this gate does conduct you somewhere, whether it is to the spiritual body of our Sun or to some other sun or possibly up to the *dvipa* the Inca came from. The archeologists would probably panic to learn the gateway is not a metaphor just as they would be alarmed to learn the myths about Tiwanaku are all true, and those rumored giants who wielded the huge stones are looming in curiosity, observing these funny little human scholars running about disbelieving in them.

In its etheric form, the gateway is activated, brightened consciousness, which is another way of saying shaped or focused or, how about this, it is arithmetically scripted Light, nicely equipped and loaded with algorithms, sufficient, we are hoping, in our little misdirection campaign here, to attract acquisitive alien gods. Maybe we could lure them through the gateway to us.

Sal nodded to me. That meant he was finished preparing his Trojan Horse. He was setting his mathematical finger-trap. It included the upload replacement for the geomantic pinning point numbers the alien gods took from this site. I admired the Elohim surrounding this site. They are humanity's godparents, and their arithmetical calculations and activation codes flank the site like banners. They seem to be on hand in real time. At first glance it looks like they used the airspace around Tiwanaku as a blackboard. Then I realize it was the etheric field, which looks slightly colloidal, but which provides a writable surface, like soft clay. It's filled with equations. The Elohim engineers have been notating on it.

All the mathematics that went into manifesting this site as a template relaunch center set in a hologram of *Paqariq Tampu*, Viracocha's celestial homeland, are displayed around the site as calculations inscribed on the air. The principal algorithms act like pillars that secure the inscribed banners. One pillar looked faint, as if it had lost life substance; it flickered and seemed to teeter. This must be where the alien gods removed one of the support "pins," so this is where Sal would insert his replacement calculation as, we hoped, alluring bait.

Sal had tried to explain his phantom algorithm to me earlier. To a layman it sounded like a dog set to chase its own tail, making ineffectual loops around a central calculation. It looked like the algorithm was producing miraculous, novel, instant results, though ultimately it changed nothing. It left a rich stream of secondary calculations that furthered the illusion of high productivity, and when Sal demonstrated this spinning off of innumerable secondary calculations it looked like a team of ice skaters performing exquisite quadruple Salchow jumps. It would look like we had merely replaced the damaged original algorithm in the flickering pillar. In truth, we would be uploading the phantom one.

I wondered how do you actually upload a mathematical formula into a megalithic site anyway? You can't hook your computer up to the nearest stone. This is not a technological fix; the technology is consciousness and mathematics. Sal drew me a diagram earlier today when I asked him about this.

You have to memorize the algorithm because you can't bring equipment into this upload zone, he said. That zone is the realm in which the Elohim operate, which means you have to be able to move your consciousness into that. It is a fertile, protean area of command where mental projections, designs, and calculations can affect outside reality. Your Higher Mind is the computer inputting the algorithm. The Elohim's power of *AL* is the "electrical" current carrying your mathematics. I guess this means you piggy-back on the Elohim's potency of consciousness, get up on their shoulders and toss in your algorithms.

I will try to keep this simple, because I barely understand what Sal explained. You have to make changes in your consciousness platform then enter the Elohim's sword. It is of course a field of Light and consciousness, as sharp as a sword and tall as a tower, but its penetrative, incisive ability make the appearance of an upright sword persuasive. Think Sword of Truth here. It's an expression of the Elohim when they are focused, and it is a delivery mechanism. Design commands stream out of this sword and shape reality. These commands may include arithmetical formulations, and they enter the subtle air as a new directing infrastructure, ordering new configurations to form around them.

This sword is the size of a tower, and you do your work inside it. The Elohim's focused consciousness is swordlike. Their creative, initiatory power is swordlike. In mythic terms, it is Goliath's sword which David, the Jewish slingshot hero, took from the Elohim giant after he "killed" the big threatening oaf (received initiation) with a stone hit to his forehead. That clue is suggestive: the point of contact was Goliath's forehead, meaning his sixth chakra, meaning his cyclopean consciousness, his single round-eye unified awareness in which all the chakras were reassembled as one cognitive eye in the giant's head. This was the center of the Elohim creative reality that the hero David contacted and used, so from this I understand Sal meant we deploy the arithmetic from the Elohim's forehead, cyclopean-style, and experience their sharp focus as like a sword.

Letters and numbers stream off the sword's sharp bladed surface like birds of fire on a keen mission. I suppose it would be easier to say in childlike enthusiasm it is like a magic wand. You say what you want in the correct way and the wand of *AL* power executes your desires. The Elohim mind is as sharp as a sword's edge. It cuts through ignorance. It dispatches arithmetical coding.

The truth of course is that Goliath, an Elohim, instructed the human initiate David in the proper, safe use of this celestial-angelic creative sword of Light and power. He did not kill Goliath; rather, he gained mastery over the same power Goliath wields so therefore surpassed him, did not need further instruction, which the ancients typically signified as killing the person. This fact means, among other things, it is not out of the question that other humans might use this sword or have access to it to upload a friendly phantom algorithm if they go through the same training and initiation sequence that David must have done.

Years ago people tried to subvert the established order of reality by inserting malware viruses and nasty codes into computer networks. Since the world's systems were increasingly networked in multiple versions of the "Internet" or what it represented in terms of a global electronic brain, you could disrupt or commandeer any or all of that by creating the right kind of commando code. You could, at lest in theory, corrupt national systems of power or defense or classified information sites because these systems all ran through the electronic-computer interface. But the level of arithmetical processing I was looking at now required no computers or linked global electronic system, the daytime web or the so-called dark web. Elohim *AL*-consciousness was the web.

This was the coding that wrote reality itself. The once and future Internet, the original linkage system. God's brain, the original global web. The Elohim were the original geeks, the computer nerds, the computational experts everyone turned to. The Elohim mind was the computer, and their bright Goliath-given sword of Light was for trained humans the keyboard that entered the precise arithmetical programming. Plastic, moldable, responsive reality was its medium. I found this funny because these mentally superb Elohim were the same oafish, nonexistent giants that nobody in their right minds believes moved the stones.

The Elohim's sword gets you into the coding level of reality. It is a mental space, probably a hyper-mental field, exceedingly responsive to inputs. You combine your own power of mind and consciousness with the innate structuring force of the computations as you upload them into the malleable field of etheric reality that structures the physical world. This is where your computations have traction; this is where your algorithms put their boots on the ground and run.

As I said above, the true carrier wave for this upload was the power of *AL*, the Elohim as the many forms of this creative God-force. The *AL* power delivers the computations. That made the algorithms another pre-energized form of *AL*. It almost sounds like the Elohim could shapeshift into a purely arithmetical body. It took Sal some moments of concentration to reach this state and the cooperation of the Elohim to share their creative space inside their sword for him to discharge his phantom algorithm. I saw the numbers start to stream out through the sword.

All these algorithms were now assembled into multiple mandalas that formed a broad band of arithmetical notation around the site. Tiwanaku's operations were not a simple affair, though probably that was true of all the geomantic nodes. Human consciousness is a complicated dynamic state. I walked around among and even through these mathematically inscribed mandalas like a connoisseur examining the latest installations in an art gallery. I felt my auric field getting tattooed in numbers and arithmetical scriptings.

It's hard to convey how strange was this sense of bifurcation I felt in myself. As Frederick, once professor of comparative mythology, I understood none of the mathematics displayed before me; as whatever my name was as the Arabic member of the Study House Mystery group, the arithmetic made sense. I saw what Sal had done, saw where he had exchanged key digits and equations for the real and correct ones, how he had laid his embedded, hierarchical traps.

I would be tempted to say I could discern a different shading to these equations, but I think it was my arithmetical Arabic mind perceiving the essential falsehood or misdirection of the algorithms, seeing they would lead to unexpected locales. They were good fakes, expertly crafted: they would fool me. In mathematical terms, they were correct and plausible; it's that they deliberately deviated from operational geomantic norms as specified by numbers for Earth.

But the alien gods had lifted a section of this algorithm originally, and that deletion had subtly distorted the end product, which at Tiwanaku was the human template. Sal had substituted a number string that complemented their deletion, or, so it would seem, he hoped, enhanced its alteration enough to notice. The arithmetical underpinning of Tiwanaku supported the manifestation of this template, which is the coding specifics for human consciousness and body and how it maintains and reflects resonance with the same pattern imprinted on the Earth. This is the geomantic protocol behind the planet's original design.

Let's say the template imparts Light at a specific frequency, a precise calibration, to the human living form and its awareness infrastructure, and the alien gods changed that subtly when they took the number strings away. Then Sal changed it a little more when he slipped in his phantom algorithm to lure those aliens. This site, through its geomantic features and their relationships, then starts broadcasting this changed vibration to all holders of the human form.

Then I saw them. Their faces. Many of them, like feral animals tentatively examining a bit of food laid out for them by humans, seeing if things were safe. The alien gods of course were not concerned for their safety; it was not in jeopardy. Their circumspection derived from their curiosity and mild distrust as to the sudden appearance of this new code. Had they overlooked it before? They were trying to account for its appearance here, yet they were intrigued by it too. They were large faces, as big as clouds, the way clouds look when you're at a high elevation and seem to be terribly big and right on top of you, about to land.

I watched them as they examined this new code. I don't know where they actually were in terms of universal space, but they seemed to be just behind the number mandalas, and their faces (that was all I saw of their forms) loomed large behind these. I would not testify with certainty they even had eyes, but let's say I saw their minds intently focused on these arithmetical presences; they were eye-like. Even though I disdained the reason for their interest, I loved their curiosity.

I had always looked for that feeling of genuine ardent engagement in my Dartmouth students, when their eyes lit up and their minds gained traction on a subject or the possibility of a fresh interpretation, and now I was seeing it richly presented by aliens out to ruin our planet's reality and steal the grid's arithmetic. I almost felt ashamed that this alluring arithmetical mandala had hidden barbs in it to hook the alien mind and shake it loose from its death-hold on our system.

Sal had not just switched out one algorithm for another. He embedded the phantom algorithm several layers in from the equation's surface presentation. You had to open several switching stations of equations before you would find it. What I mean is you would have to run through all the intricacies of five different algorithms stacked like a palimpsest before you got to the phantom algorithm. Think of it like a vertical syllogism where you start at the top and run down the stepped pyramid layers of the logic chain to get to the base where the hook sits.

Sal's plan was to get the aliens to think they had not opened up all the hypertext links and implications of the algorithmic content they had lifted, a bit like a scholar perhaps not reading sub-footnotes contained within the main footnotes. Or, if they had followed the footnote chain to the end, perhaps they had not appreciated the significance of the final algorithm at the base of this "pyramid" and they would proceed to investigate it, hopefully acquiring it. When they acquired it, proud of their imperial reach, they'd be finger-trapped, and we would have reinstalled Tiwanaku's one-quarter part of the rhombus mathematics that Blaise at the *Akashic* Records had identified as missing.

So I watched them studying our plant. I watched their minds reach out with tentacles of inquiry to probe the number sequence in the illusory algorithm. It reminded me of watching a rabbit tentatively nibble a lettuce leaf, taking little bites, testing the safety and reality of this proffered abundance. Sal's plan was to use this nibbling at the algorithmic bait-hook as a distraction so we could sneak into their domain and steal back the original and correct algorithm.

All the time, a component of human consciousness processing was at stake here. I'm not sure most people would notice the substitution or deletion. It would probably be like this: one morning you wake up and once you start your day you feel you aren't quite right, you're a little off your game, irritable, edgy perhaps, or maybe the direction or tone of your thoughts has veered off into a strange area, two a.m. thoughts except it's ten in the morning and the day's sunlight is bright. Everything feels slightly unanchored, tied down securely; things seem to be sliding, like your ocean liner is listing.

A few feral thoughts are fluttering around in your head, existential topics you haven't thought about for years, not since sophomore year in college perhaps. It feels like a solar eclipse is underway and the Moon is squaring something in your horoscope and it's positively obnoxious. Do you follow? Pull a key pin out of the human template and you'll have strangeness.

While I sat there waiting for them to make a move towards the substituted algorithm, I reflected on our tactics. This is a cerebral affair. We can't fight them. We can't bomb them or kill them. We can't even have a gentlemen's treaty negotiation. They don't talk. They don't bargain. All we can expect to do is deceive them, or basically out-think them, using superior mathematics. But how do you succeed against "opponents" who are masters of all the arithmetical moves in a universe-sized Magic Square box of tricks and who are steadily and with great indifference and nonchalance removing all the support pins for our Earth reality, extracting our mathematics as fast as we try to formulate them?

I looked at the Elohim surrounding the site. They did not look like they were poised for immediate action when those alien mental hands reached in for the numbers. I had the impression they would not intervene, but why not? Ray Master Hermes was also showing signs of a steadfast aloofness; surely the fate of all mathematical expressions would concern him, as he had helped introduce them, yet he gave signs of staying out of the action. Why? You need numbers to run all those cool Hermetic Axioms he came up with. As for Sal, Jocelyn, and Blaise, for the moment I couldn't see them. It seemed to come down to me. Why?

I don't mean that in the clichéd whingeing manner of how come I have to do it, as if Fate had unfairly or without justification pointed a finger at poor little me. No, it wasn't that. It was more of wonder and disbelief that my Arabic life as a Study House mathematician seemed to have yielded this unlikely karmic fruit. I was being called on to step in at this moment because I actually was qualified to. It was the Frederick aspect of myself that wanted clarification as to assignment. He could not remember everything in his own biography across the timeline that prepared him and led him to this precise moment and his involvement with Sal.

The moment came. I saw their mental hands reach in for the phantom algorithm. They grabbed it quickly and decisively. The aperture through which they reached remained open momentarily like a broad door. Just before it swung shut I leaped through it. Then with a bang that was soundless it closed. I was in.

It was silent at first. Dozens of alien minds were studying this algorithm. They studied it with the rapt attention predatory animals would regard a fresh kill. I couldn't say I saw faces housing these minds; it was more naked attention. They were focused yet indifferent, even aloof. I suppose that meant they were not an emotional species, that mental concerns were paramount, perhaps the full and sole expression of their existence. They lived in the cool world of arithmetic. Their actions would seem determined by the logical necessities of a syllogism. If a key component of a universal syllogism were missing, logic said they go get it. Earth's algorithm and those of the other five free-will planets were parts of that number process, so these alien gods were going to acquire them all. Why not?

I wasn't sure where I was. I was on the other side of an alien door. It was not a place in the sense that Tiwanaku is a place, tangibly different than other places and possessing quantifiable topographical coordinates. It was not a planet. It was a zone of Mind, a realm of arithmetical processing unbounded by land or spatial address. That meant it could be anywhere and probably was everywhere.

I suddenly had the wild, unsupportable hunch that Al-Khwārizmī, my mentor, had been here, had walked through this same door centuries ago when it was open and that if he wasn't here with me right now in real time he was still available. He did give you the impression he was well-travelled and thoroughly exposed. Naturally, back then I couldn't have included exposure to the alien gods' realm as

part of his educational itinerary because I had not then, as far as I knew now, ever heard of it, though I suspected he remained circumspect about much that he had seen. Possibly he thought his students wouldn't understand or the implications of these exposures were too unsettling or too cosmically bizarre to share them with us. Well, it seemed we were both in the deep of things now.

I did see him. In fact, he greeted me as soon as I focused outside me again. I must have been squinting or perhaps cogitating with my eyes closed. I do that. I didn't believe what I was seeing. I wasn't sure I even understood what "I" it was. The phantom algorithm was arrayed around us like the bones of a landscape. Instead of sky, clouds, mountains, land, rocks, grasses, running water, I saw the components of this complex algorithm, both the number sequences and what they created and supervised. I was standing inside a reality made of a digital syllogism and its mathematical product, which included part of my own reality.

I was within a mathematical topology, a structured, tiered landscape of numbers. I say tiered because it seemed a landscape comprised of layers or manifolds, one embedded in the next. Mathematicians call this embedding a geometric topology and would probably describe Tiwanaku as a low-dimensional topology exhibiting embedded manifolds up to the fourth dimension. Still, I was just getting started in my perceptions; if things get more complicated I'll end up in a high-dimensional topology, 5D and beyond. This was, to Fredrick at least, a completely new illustration of geomantic nodes. Sacred sites as field manifestations of low- or high-dimensional topologies. I had the feeling I was about to do some rock climbing. Where's my grappling hook?

None of this seemed to perturb Al-Khwārizmī. He walked around examining it. It was like he was at a scientific conference where they post the fresh pages of important new papers on long bulletin boards so the scientists can read them. This "paper" was the intriguing new proof of an old vexing mathematical topic. Try to appreciate the abstract nakedness of this realm.

It was only the numbers in the algorithm, and behind them the processes they scripted, but while this might be an aspect of an emotion or a cognitive mechanism, it looked like a grid, an engineering diagram, and it was chillingly notional. Even so, it was clear Al-Khwārizmī was enjoying this lean reality spectacle. He relished all its details the way an event manager might review the plans and personnel assignments for a major sports game, perhaps for a championship. He had the confident insouciance of someone who regularly jogs through a high-dimensional 4D geometric topology and never stumbles. I had the faltering uncertainty of somebody who had to look up all these terms.

I copied his gesture and walked around examining the number displays. I acted like I understood them, but we both knew I was pretending, or was I? It was that same odd bifurcation in me where Frederick was mentally nonplussed, but the Arab comprehended the arithmetical syllogisms, following them avidly.

As for the alien gods, I hope I conveyed the impression their presence was insubstantial at best, a vague personification of minds reaching out as if with arms. It seemed we were walking through their minds like they were vague buildings made of subtle etheric "substance"

edged in the faintest of electrical currents. If they were aware of us milling around in here, they seemed to not be concerned. They struck me as thoroughly single-minded in their avid pursuits.

Suddenly, though I did not see the transition, Al-Khwārizmī stood on the other side of this arithmetical grid interface. It was as if he had walked through a magic mirror and now stood inside it, observing the world from that perspective. He had the serenity of an adept magician who had effortlessly translocated himself; for me, it was like being behind the stage where you see all the levers, ropes, light switches, and props the stage managers use to create suitable theater effects, which was where, I now realized, I was standing. How did I get over here? Al-Khwārizmī looked at me momentarily with a slight nod and a smile.

He was on the other side of this arithmetical wall of numbers. I had to think about that for a few minutes before I could get any kind of handle on it. I also had to get over being impressed with his ability to even do that. On the other side of this glasslike partition, the alien gods were busy checking the mathematical proofs of the equations, professors reviewing a student's paper.

Let me use an analogy to explain what we were attempting to do. The aliens were admiring how adroitly somebody's shoelaces had been tied. We were busy untying them and even unraveling the shoelaces, and managing this without the aliens noticing. In practical terms, we were undoing the algorithms because where we were, on the other side of this partition, the equations ran in reverse. We ran them in reverse, undoing each syllogistic stage in their unfolding, like disassembling a skyscraper one steel girder at a time while they were businessmen inspecting it for possible office space rentals. Fortunately, since our inserted algorithm was a fake one, a phantom version, we were not producing negative effects on perceived reality for living humans.

Still, the alien gods were making good with this phantom algorithm, fake or not. That didn't seem to matter. They lifted it out of this presentation space, much like a conference participant pulling a demonstration paper off the board, and set it up on what I presumed was their own planet or reality zone or maybe it was an abstract unanchored simulation zone, like *Star Trek*'s famous Holodeck, where they could run virtual versions and extrapolations of the arithmetic and interact with it, walk through it, or change it through dialogue or computation.

We were there with them, though I could not tell you where that was. It might have been merely a work zone within their extended mental space, maybe in their heads. They were running the algorithm, studying its moves and generations the way an anatomist would examine an exotic bone from a newly discovered animal perhaps flash-frozen in the last Ice Age and now thawed out. It was a stage of our human cognition operating outside its full human context.

Then I got what Al-Khwārizmī's tactic had been all along. He had embedded a mathematical virus inside the phantom algorithm, what used to be called computer worms or, more classically, a Chinese finger-trap. The more the alien minds probed and even played with these numbers, the more entranced they became with the unfolding arithmetical complexity and intricacy of final products, the more the trap would tighten on their minds, numbing out certain key synaptical components. It would be like injecting them with an anesthetic, what doctors used to call a "local" and enough to disarm their attention.

Done correctly, the aliens would not notice that this component was sleeping. At the same time, the finger-trap would launch a stealth insertion equation into the alien minds and this would start to rewrite certain sequences and change numbers. All this was slyly embedded in Sal's comparably sly phantom algorithm with its finger-trap teeth ready to bite the reaching-in fingers. These guys would have their fingers hobbled for years from our clever traps.

Al-Khwārizmī looked at me. He seemed to be waiting for me to do something. Before I could explain that I had no idea what that something was, I was doing it. Spewing algorithms like a champion, the numbers streamed out of my mouth. I must have been speaking them aloud, or maybe it was my mind saying them and I misinterpreted that as speaking. I don't think this was my physical body I was conducting business in now anyway, so speaking seemed off the table. However it happened, complex algorithms were parading forth from me as if I knew what I was doing. Was this the wild, crazy, very mathematical Arab I used to be, schooled in the arithmetical arcana of my sublime mentor?

The algorithms sprinting forth from my intelligent mouthpiece were commandeering certain key operational aspects of the alien gods' mathematical encampment. So far, they hadn't noticed. My equations were rewriting theirs, substituting key numbers and sets, leading to slightly altered products. Once I launched these clever number assault teams, I didn't have to do much else, so I looked around.

Somehow my positioning or maybe it was my mental activity enabled me to glimpse the array of captured planets and Light grid algorithms in their Magic Square.

That was a lot of computational power in there. The heuristic algorithms required to run a single planet are almost unbelievably complex, but here were thousands of them, all linked together in some recondite manner to form a meta-algorithm, the product of their complete Magic Square when it was finished.

I was appreciating now that a Magic Square is not just a number storage device with digits accorded their own cell in a master hive of variable size. It was a reality-affecting consciousness mechanism, an organized prolonged spell. Yes, the algorithms housed in the cells had their own mathematical complexity, but collectively the Square's algorithms ran the meta-process of the Magic Square and that was a goddam arithmetical juggernaut surging full bore at my head.

This Square was like—I'm struggling for apt metaphors here—a magic wand, a monster battle cruiser, a peripatetic magus casting directions for reality. It was the furnace providing heat for an entire apartment building; it was an orchestra whose symphonic performance filled a complete city with its music. If universal reality was veined with strings of Light and consciousness, the planets and stars like horses grazing in far fields, then this Magic Square's intention was to grab those strings and hold them tightly, to corral the "horses" in the Square.

As I mentioned earlier, this Magic Square was a square in name only. In geometrical terms, it was far beyond squareness, even cubeness. It was at the least a 4D shape called a hypercube,

but I suspect its true shape exceeded that. An anthropologist would likely feel delirious at the prospect of investigating so many different phylogenies of consciousness as these cubicles in the Square displayed, but I knew the alien gods had no interest in diversity in its own terms. To them, it was only the source of new mathematical formulations; what they coded was of secondary interest to them, if even that. They wanted the numbers. Still, I marveled, I shuddered actually, at this wealth of design and expression. All these points of wide-awake self-awareness set within the infinite universe.

Then I realized I was overlooking a key element in the alien gods' strategy. It's true, acquisition of all possible algorithms was paramount to them, but it was in service of building their alternate universe, their anti-God Magic Square at the spatial or arithmetical end of the universe, and that would be a colossus of consciousness. They couldn't help that. It would rival God's own Purusha, but it would have an utterly different orientation. That was the threat.

It was a threat to the Creation itself, to the infinity of the Supreme Being. Even to contemplate how that could be possible would set your head to spinning. Mine was. Their strategy was to steal God, empty His pockets, cancel His infinity with their anti-*pi* mechanism, and use the immense mathematical richness of His Mind to build their alternate Purusha, their signature arithmetical Golem, using the numbers they had pilfered from the legitimate Creation.

But this Purusha was for their private collection alone. They had no interest in its achieving any kind of manifest appearance in the outer world of incarnations. The arithmetical captures would script Purusha's vast form, but about that they cared little. They just wanted the numbers that coded his form, not Purusha. The prospects for unfolding his consciousness were irrelevant.

I must pause momentarily and straighten out an apparent contradiction. I have characterized the universe as infinite and as having an end, a termination point. How can both be true? Regarding the first proposition, it makes sense to me to picture the universe as a vast property about 80 percent of which has been developed, houses and buildings constructed, but the remaining 20 percent is only open undeveloped fields, with no buildings of any kind. Think stars here. The key aspect is you can't see the full extent of this empty field; that's infinity.

But, for proposition two, the alien gods are running their anti-*pi* algorithm which, they believe will soon cancel out this infinite extension of the field. The anti-*pi* mechanism in a mighty tractor-pull will haul infinity into the finite. It will erase the otherwise unstoppable continuing expansion of universal reality beyond anyone's comprehension or ability to catch up with it. Now it will be accessible, vast but manageably vast within their Magic Square. Their Magic Square will act like a containment field on infinity.

The paradox is that while infinity by definition is endless and without limit, yet the Supreme Being must know its full extent. That's what they're going to haul into their finite though almost infinitely extensive Magic Square. That *almost* is the key: everything in that 20% undeveloped field will be hauled into the Magic Square of finitude.

The ingenuity of what Al-Khwārizmī was doing, and I suppose myself too, the earlier Arab, not the math-impoverished contemporary Frederick, was to insert operational null zones within the aliens' complex equations. Algorithms would run smoothly then reach this certain digital zone and stall out or freeze up. Nothing would result; it would be like a blank page, a car motor that didn't start. Like someone walking briskly along in a parade, then abruptly stopping.

If I understood Al-Khwārizmī's tactic, he set it up so they wouldn't notice this. The algorithmic unfolding would, technically, halt, but the aliens would see it as continuing to extrapolate its complex number mechanism. At best, they might detect a momentary stutter-step, like one thing delicately tripping over another, a millisecond glitch in the speedy computational processing of numbers.

I was thinking of a mythic parallel to our ingenuity. Well, at the time I hoped it was ingenious. In Polynesian lore, the demi-god Maui, after which the Hawaiian island was named, tied down the unruly Sun-god called La with ropes. This Sun-god, whose home was at Haleakala, the physical volcano on the island of Maui and whose name means "House of the Sun," tied down La's 16 legs. I felt like we had just tied down one of La's writhing, powerful, restive solar legs. Maui secured La's legs as a matter of discipline, to make La's sunlight steady for the benefit of the human residents of the island, Polynesian folklore says.

Similarly, we were tying down the alien gods' "legs" to discipline them, although in truth it was more like trying to cause an abrupt halt to their still unchallenged assault on universal reality and the ontological ground we were standing on. If we had discerned the alien gods' mechanism correctly, we had tied one of four, one vertex in the globe-spanning rhombus of the four nodes.

But we were foolish to assume they wouldn't notice. They were not so incautious as to blithely walk into our supposedly clever finger-trap on our first coy dangling of it. An earthquake shook the world where we were. It's confusing, I know, even to use that term, which so obviously refers to a physical event, but whatever psychic field we occupied, it shook with the sudden force of a physical earthquake. The aliens had noticed. Their minds were roaring. They were irritated. That shake went right through whatever my present "body" was comprised of. That was impressive, I'll give them that. That was no little roar.

But just as rapidly as it had begun the earthquake now stopped, and conditions seemed even quieter than before. It looked like they had reached over to where we had worked and took back the genuine algorithm that we had veiled with the artificial one. Our finger-trap had failed? But I saw the Blaise angels standing by, shaking their heads, little smiles brightening their faces. I gathered they had done something sly that the alien gods had not yet noticed.

They had put a glamour over the stutter-step node in the algorithm. The aliens thought they were reaching for their original equation; it was illusory, like leprechaun's gold. It looked like gold when you reached for it, but tomorrow it would return to dirt or whatever gross physical substance they conjured it out of. Although since it was the Ofanim making the artful substitution, that tomorrow might be an eon away. It wouldn't matter to them:

they were billions of years old. They played the long game, the full spectrum of which I could not imagine.

Before I could relax into the satisfaction this clever action should have inspired in me, I realized I had entirely got it wrong. I felt like I had been dipped in ice water. The real glamour had been put down over me. The alien gods had spun up an illusion of the Blaise angels interceding on our behalf. The Blaises hadn't. The aliens created the illusion of them substituting the fakery for the real thing. The Blaises were not even here. Only fake ones. The aliens now had their genuine algorithmic node back again firmly in hand. Fools, we had the bright leprechaun gold, and it was already resorting to dust and ashes in our hands. As for my cleverness with the La's legs business, it was my leg that was tied down.

I probably would have laughed at this point if my geomantic worries didn't command more attention. What was this unexpected and genuine hostile acquisition of the Tiwanaku algorithm doing to that site and its processes, and what was that disturbance doing to the global collective consciousness, Albion?

The answer was bewildering. Two realities vied for dominance here. One was the original, as scripted for Tiwanaku in the design of the Earth; the other was the aberration introduced by the alien gods. The wobble was mediated by our insertion of Sal's contrived but alluring algorithm the alien gods had taken. Yes, they had nicely faked me out with the illusory Blaises, but Sal's dummy algorithm was still running, like a phantom screw holding a machine together.

I seemed to be able to poke my head back into the Tiwanaku theater of human consciousness to assess the damages. Two different images of the human were projected onto the large performance space of the megalithic site. It was as if Viracocha were having second thoughts or could not decide between two plausible prototypes for reintroducing the human phylogeny to the planet through this birthing site. It was as if he couldn't make up his mind between two types of stone. Which should he use? This new generic human self experienced two alternating senses of self: you know, the resting foundation self-vibration we register everyday and which tells us, reassures us, this is who we are, we feel *like* this, our emotional tone feels *like* this, this is *me* when I'm hitting all my marks.

That basic self-signature was fluctuating noticeably between two valences. The alien gods' intrusion was making the collective consciousness bi-polar, as if it had two heads and they didn't agree with or resemble each other. The flavor of self-awareness, self-reflection, and sentience itself was being altered. Down to the minutest nuance of how we think about ourselves and take stock of our existential condition. It was like somebody had reformatted our psyche.

Since we seemed to have regressed back thousands, maybe millions, of years, to the time when Viracocha in fact did reset humanity, plant his stone potato-men in the fields, his final choice would set humanity on one of two greatly diverging evolutionary tracts, changing our history and our defining qualities. Did Viracocha hesitate back then—was it even possible?—or was what I was seeing an artifact of the present perturbation of conditions at Tiwanaku?

This would be like violating the famous grandfather clause in backwards time travel, how you would uncreate your own family antecedents if you made one false, interfering move, making it impossible for you to be born and be here doing this. The ultimate time paradox. If the alternate human vibration won out today, we, the Hierophancy field team, would probably not be here trying to undo the screw-ups introduced by the aliens, but then maybe they wouldn't be here, or they would have already succeeded, or maybe we'd be helping them.

It all came down to me. I can't say I was pleased to realize that. My trusted mentor, Al-Khwārizmī, was in here with me, but he was standing aloof. He did not seem perturbed, but he was not taking any action. He waited for me to act. As Frederick, I felt hopeless for the cause, but as the Arab mathematician I once was there I expected (hoped) some solution would present itself to save the day.

I had the impression I was spewing arithmetical formulations out of my mouth, but with no more clarity or self-direction than if I were performing glossolalia. They didn't seem to affect anything, so they probably were nonsense equations. At least I was doing something, even if it was futile and, frankly, embarrassing. Or was I merely stalling for time with this inept clown show of digits staggering out of my mouth?

Then one of the equations stormed out of my mouth coated in gold. Or maybe it had been conceived entirely in gold. It was complex, tiered, and long. This equation grabbed on to the alien minds as if it had a thousand hands. The aliens responded with pleasure, not from being grabbed like this, but from what was revealed to them in the gesture of grabbing. They saw the complexity of the new formula and reveled in it. They were such avaricious collectors. They halted what they were doing to contemplate the beauty and majesty of this formula.

I don't know if they even had mouths or tongues, but I heard them sighing and exclaiming in birdlike titters of excitement as they fondled the fresh equation. I was the waiter at this lavish country estate garden party with a tray of canapés, exotic, delicious-looking delicacies they hadn't seen before—yummy!

While they were distracted, a number of surprising things happened. All the people who had ever ritually used Tiwanaku, who had understood its geomancy, validated its purpose, had been manifested here as new humans, came running to the megalithic center from all directions across the landscape. It was as if they rose out of the land or stepped out of the astral sea and started running to support the measure I had put in place. They disliked these aliens. They were returning to the incarnational world and its number infrastructure to help us overturn the usurpation of this reality by these coldly acquisitive gods. They were returning to protect a Landscape of Light that had benefited them. They were streaming out of Viracocha's cave like commuters from a subway.

Thunderbirds rose up out of the land and zoomed out of the sky. These must be copies of *Apu Kunter*, the condor, whose form and nature served as the Inca Thunderbird. They swooped majestically and powerfully over Tiwanaku, then settled at its circumference, upright, regally facing out to all the directions of the horizon. Jets of fire leaped from their forms, thunder rolled, and their green eyes blazed. I

laughed. These Blaises were not fakes. It's the real Blaises at last.

I laughed too because the human Blaise used to say the Ofanim tended to be low key and circumspect, not liking dramatic shows, except on special occasions. I guess this qualified as a special occasion because they were going all out to make their point. I was tempted to suggest they were showing off. I mean, when you think about it, the Thunderbird get-up is rather over the top, isn't it?

Then I was surrounded by the Phoenix Cloak, though I suppose I should call it the *Apu Kunter* Wrap. Whatever name I use, it was a brilliant robe surrounding me made of the myriad diamond facets of their diamond geode. Picture this diamond geode as large as a sports stadium playing field plus the audience seats. Then picture this miniaturized and wrapped around your auric field. You feel like a stand-in for the Thunderbird.

The diamonds were not feathers exactly, but identical diamond-bright facets that formed a seamless patchwork around my auric field and bodily form. It afforded me complete protection and clarity of focus. I certainly needed both. The Ofanim now manifested another thundering squadron of themselves facing into the site. Me. The purpose of this wrap, I believe, is for the wearer to emulate the majestic Thunderbird guise of Ofanim consciousness, with thunder, fire, and green eyes.

I was beginning to think I needed a scorecard or perhaps a referee. I was losing track of whose faked algorithm was prevailing in the tennis match we had. We and the alien gods kept outdoing each other with new illusory mathematics. Who was caught in our clever finger-trap, the alien gods or was it ourselves?

As if I were in conference with myself, the Arab I once was explained to me that this new gold-scripted algorithm was genuine, applicable to Tiwanaku, but not likely to subvert the site's correct purpose. It was a complement to that function and technically superfluous, like a scholar adding an extra footnote that he could just as well have left out as it had no key impact on meaning or understanding. Apparently, my mouth-spewed golden algorithm was similarly a superfluous though possibly attractive adornment to Tiwanaku's key function.

I felt like I was now a mathematics tutor explaining the new algorithm to my alien students. Not that they were not sharp enough to appreciate its nuances, but maybe it was more like I was a museum curator extolling the intricacies of design and craftsmanship of a newly acquired ancient artifact to potential museum donors, although these aliens were not donors but takers. However I described my role, I was exhibiting this golden equation to their avid minds, walking them raptly through its many tiers of exposition and execution.

It was funny, odd, really, that I seemed to know exactly what I was talking about, but I suppose the Arab mathematician actually was competent in this and Frederick, me—at least I think it was the me I usually associate with myself—was basically its able mouthpiece, its ventriloquist's dummy mouthing his words. I won't complain or wince. My job was to save Tiwanaku's algorithm, and if channeling an earlier, smarter version of myself did the job, then I'd do it.

I saw that this equation I was so blithely reviewing had a stealth operation. It extruded tiny number hooks that grabbed on to the alien gods' formulations, seemed to shake them, then start to transform their numbers and sequences. It was as if one arithmetic code was subtly rewriting another one but by stealth, as smooth as a pickpocket lifting out your wallet from your trousers.

As for all the people who had come running out of the karmic past of this site, they now were extruding golden equations from their mouths. Here is a key point I want to emphasize: these numbers were holy, sanctified, positively numinous. I have it on good authority from some Qabalists I know that the Jewish assertion that the Hebrew language is ontologically sacred and spiritually potent and that the letters are equivalent with numbers, as if they were coins and on one side was the *Autiot* letter and on the other a number, that all this is true, and more powerful than we might think. They were potentized agents capable of generating and adjusting reality according to their deployment.

These numbers streaming out of the mouths of the thousands of people in spirit form who had suddenly returned in a great rush to their former geomantic homeland of Tiwanaku were sacred, activated, *working*, unlike the profane numbers of mere computer code. Those digits did not have the Hebrew fire-letters of Creation on their flip sides. Ours did. It was as if we were staging a live-version of pushing back a hacker attack on our classified computer system. The hackers put forward an incursion algorithm and we entered code to stop it.

Our potentized numbers were casting a vast net of gold lace over the site. Numbers, equations, algorithmic tiers of processes studded these nets like jewels. The Thunderbirds amplified the sound and impact of these extruded numbers. The alien gods were now looking up at this bejeweled arithmetical net. They were becoming entranced with its mathematical intricacy, with new proofs and theorems and demonstrations they had not previously seen. I understood the tactic here was not to defeat the aliens by force or an invincible overwhelm, but to enchant them into putting their attention on something else, luring it away from the Tiwanaku formulas, letting them pursue equations that though genuine were not operationally germane to Tiwanaku's functions and whose sudden absence or alteration would not jeopardize Tiwanaku while delighting the aliens.

There was more to this oratorio of creative fire-letters and numbers. These numbers, backed by the Hebrew Creation letters, had terrific generative force. They were manifesting geometric forms and images in Light, like banners draping the site, following the curve of the dome overhead, though closer in. Jocelyn would have liked this picture spectacle. The image tableau was mythic.

Gods—genuine ones, the true good guys of the universe—were handing chalices of Light to receptive humans, their arms outstretched. They were holding massive swords upright, clarifying the air around them, turning it to fire; they were opening gateways and heavenly doors to welcome human visitors. Humans exuding the purity of fresh creation were striding out of other doors, arriving right here, at Tiwanaku, greeted by Viracocha and his helpers. They could well have been stepping out of Viracocha's Upper Earth and passing through his cave portal to its termination point at Tiwanaku. These were more than mere images, if you think of those as two-dimensional and static: all this was happening

now, vividly, unarguably, and magnificently. It was live action.

We were in what Mircea Eliade would call the sacred, eternal moment when the acts of the gods were first performed and are still being performed now and forever. The profane, mundane world of desecrated, quotidian numbers, plodding along a moribund linear timeline, lay outside our charmed circle; inside our celestial circle it was sanctified. It was the eternal moment of Creation.

The alien gods showed no interest in these images. That wasn't how their minds worked. But the thickening palimpsest of mythic images and psychic pictures was changing the tone of the etheric atmosphere at Tiwanaku. They noticed that. It was changing the outcome of the wealth of calculations and formulas, and connecting with them through tiny threads of Light, linking them to the images. I think they did not run their awareness on the basis of likes and dislikes. Rather, their desire for all the numbers was more like an inexorable tidal pull, neutral but relentless. The tide will recede. The Moon ordains it. You cannot stop it.

They considered the mythic pictures irrelevant to their purposes, but they also noticed these images and the grids they were connected to were exerting a pull on their attention and numbers acquisition, like somebody tugging on their sleeve. That numbers, formulas, and algorithms could be correlated with psychic images seemed of no consequence to them and was a mental irritation and irrelevancy. Numbers are primary; pictures are for children who need to be distracted. I could almost hear them thinking this, though I'm not sure they "think" as we do. Mental commentary like this would be secondary to numbers.

They disdained human mythic pictures because they had their own set. Some of these started flashing like neon banners superimposed on the human ones. Actually, they were not exclusively human; I suspect these were divinely created images, along the instructional lines the Vedas attributed to the *Rishis*. Pictures created to provide teaching and illustration of spiritual principles and facts. The alien pictures were, comparatively, simple-minded, single-focussed.

They showed the aliens grabbing all the universe's numbers in all combinations. Long hands reaching out of space to take them out of everyone else's minds. Vague impressions of eyes bringing up the rear in a grand parade of equations. Nets and webs swooping up integers like they were fluttering butterflies. Cornucopias suctioning in all the numbers, drawing them out of the atmosphere, extracting them from manifest reality by unstoppable suction.

I had the impression the aliens disdained even their own pictures. They didn't want any pictures because it brought them closer to incarnation, and they heartily disdained that prospect. They had no interest in taking on any form. Those mythic pictures were like a black hole sucking them into the event horizon of incarnation and individualization and that would confound their purposes. They did not want their numbers coding any reality, form, or incarnation. It was a misuse of their potency; in fact, they were not to be used in the first place. Their aesthetic notions insisted the arithmetical realm be sequestered in a private zone where only they, nobody else, could contemplate its beauty and mental elegance.

They didn't want to take any form. Even projecting the impression of hands was a gritty nuisance, performed purely for the expediency of achieving their goal. They disdained incarnation in any form. No metaphorical extensions whatsoever. They were metaphysically jejune, unnecessary, an impediment. To them all this was evidence of a fallen, corrupted state. They preferred their purely mental, formless existence comprised of numbers in formal combinations.

I'm sure they believed that defined their own existence, that at best, at the most, they were made of algorithms and elegant equations. Anything else would be an objectionable, resistible taint of material existence. In fact, I think it likely that they didn't want incarnation even as a collective mind; that too was a fallen, degenerate state. They wanted existence only as arithmetic, which is insubstantial but full of original power. They were numbers, mental perfection.

The manifestation of the dome of fire-letters and mythic images wasn't doing the trick anyway. The aliens had noticed this outpouring then ignored it; it had no power over them. The finger-trap ploy had failed; so had replugging the missing rhomboid mathematics. They were unimpressed with the Thunderbirds. Something was still missing, something that would anchor the potent display.

What had we left out? I knew it came down to me, though up until this moment I drew a blank on tactics. I had nothing. Then a regally-dressed human spirit handed me a crystalline box. I opened the lid. It contained what looked like a pale green wand lying upon a folded cloak. I put on the cloak. It was long, elegant, perfectly fitted, its material hued a pale spring green, the most perfect, vividly colored green, as pure as the Creation, and it sleekly followed my form, tailored neck to feet, gold buttons down the midline when I put it on over me.

Wearing it, I feel like my auric field, my consciousness itself, has been stained this color and all it conveys, which I'm beginning to sense is a great power. Not power in the sense of superior physical strength, but a power of consciousness. I hold the wand out in front of me; it is two feet long and sends out green sparks. The wand lengthens to become a pale spring green staff about six feet long emitting flames of that same color from a tear-shaped orb at its top. I hold it upright, the way you're supposed to with a staff. It feels strong and thick.

Underneath the cloak was an old-fashioned key, the kind that weighs pounds and the kind you'd expect to use to open doors of 15th century British castles. Traces of a golden residence start to form before me, as if my vision suddenly clears. The key opens the front gate of this celestial palace, and I enter through the door into a circular chamber, perhaps fifty feet across, with a domed ceiling. It is studded with jewels of all descriptions, as if embedded in the walls.

The place is opulent, and that word barely highlights this bright quality. They were jewels in appearance, but I gradually realize they are not. They are jewels by way of metaphor. They represent concentrated states of wisdom and distilled knowledge acquired over a vast stretch of time, acquired by me. That was the key revelation: not the Frederick me, not even the Arab math guy me.

It is the "me" who is the summary of all the lives I've ever had and the distillation of the wisdom gained from all those safaris into the Underworld of incarnation. Even what I will acquire in the future from activities I have not, technically, yet done. All this apparent spiritual treasure, stuck in the palace walls like bright fruits in a fruitcake, this abundance of seeming wealth, is the presentation of all I have ever learned, and more presciently, it is available to me now as an immense version of my Self. Clearly, this is a fourth dimensional presentation, in which accomplishments of the past, present, and future are co-present as equally achieved states, already done and entered in the records book.

It is the me after the completion of everything I ever intended to do in the incarnate world, on Earth and anywhere else, *ever*, and thus it is the me before undertaking any of this and after. It's very 4D in nature. From this perspective, I have already succeeded at everything I intended to accomplish, and here is the key part, the real payoff: that potency of confidence and certainty is mine *now*. This was not my Higher Self I had stumbled into; it was a different type of self.

The walls of the chamber and the studded jewels form an auric cloak around me, or maybe it's that as I walk or move my arms I bring this with me. The chamber expands to fill not only the seven tiers of my aura but all the subtle bodies that surround every human, so that my full human manifestation form of seven bodies, some 50 auric layers, and well over 500 chakras are cloaked in this.

I stand in the center of this rich array wearing the robe of pale spring green Light and wield the staff of the same color that sends out flames of pale spring green. I want to be sure this is clear: the celestial palace and my incarnational bodies are the same, and they are studded with this array of wisdom jewels from my past and future. The incarnational form or the palace as a building itself is the grid that holds the accrued wisdom; the fact that I serially incarnated is represented by the building. I would guess it is my soul I see here represented as an enduring structure that accrues qualities as I acquire them. It's the context in which I gained this wisdom and it now acts as its repository. As I walk, I am the building, I am the jeweled cloak. I am all this accrued wisdom.

The strongest sense I have, the one that is unassailable and cannot be doubted, is that all this richness of jewels, this prolific display of past wisdom, is fully mine. I don't mean that in an avaricious sense, but purely a factual, matter-of-fact sense. I also don't mean it in any boastful sense. I don't see why every human could not access this "mature" part of themselves. You just have to know how to get there. This larger "I" version of myself, my true background and authentic spiritual context, has uncontestably earned what I am now surrounded with. It is an inheritance I have just been awarded, as it were, out of the blue.

The robe color evokes the corresponding Ray Master, Lord of the Pale Spring Green Robe, variously known as Hilarion or the Apostle Paul. He was once the atheist Saul who famously underwent the first Christ Light conversion experience on the road to Damascus, thereby highlighting the special quality of this Ray to ignite nascent Christ Consciousness like a floriation of fresh spring green buds as well as spawning a much favored spiritual cliché (about the Damascene revelation) to evoke the sense of sudden unexpected revelation that goes against the grain of habit and radically illuminates and changes yourself.

I held the staff out in front of me and struck its base on the ground. Green flames leaped out of its top and flared out through the interior volume of the dome. This staff had become a flame-thrower. I had to stop thinking like merely Frederick and start embodying this much larger version of—somebody, my regal antecedent, I suppose, or a compilation of all of them, packed into one human form with a high degree of confidence and competence, with all "I" ever learned. I realized, and this cheered me considerably, that from this larger I's point of view, we had already overcome the alien gods' commandeering of our numbers. It was a job done and finished, and even the complete mastery of the Earth's arithmetical underpinning and algorithmic management, successfully concluded.

It was taking me a while to catch up with the implications of this manifestation. Did this wisdom-bearing "I" have a formal name? Maybe I should call it the Complete Hierophant, redefining the phenomenal-world Frederick as a mere poseur, an apprentice—or God forbid, a manqué? Or perhaps I could borrow the dignified term from Sufism, the Perfect Man (*Al-Insān al-Kāmil*). Sufi mysticism describes this condition as one of divine illumination, oneness with God, as possessing a mediating cosmic power, immediate vision of the True Light and knowledge of reality (clairvoyance and initiation attainment, in other words). This is the Complete Person, one who has activated and harmonized all his chakras, achieved the prototype design intention of the Human, the *eidolon*.

The Perfect Man is a *wali*, one who is "near," meaning, I presume, near to Reality, and the community of *awliya* (the plural) comprises the Prophets and because this person can connect and unite the One and the Many, Earth and Heaven, the universe depends on him. His function is commissioned. He is the "the Man perfect in knowledge of the last and first things," the Sufis explain.

Well, that is a burden for sure on my modest sense of identity, but if it points to an attainment of congruence and completion that anyone can achieve, if it stands as an image of a worthy long-term goal epitomizing and justifying all our incarnations, and if somehow we occasionally get to borrow forward from a balance we haven't even accrued in full yet, then I guess it's all for a good cause and I'll do my best to wear this identity convincingly, even if it is size extra-large.

I felt a surge of confidence, like a spring filling a well creating a lake of brightness. This larger, older, truly feral, once and future "me," both lying behind and ahead of me on my timeline, hinting at first and last things, was richly suffused with certainty and competence. To experience that, I have to tell you, was awesome and unprecedented, and, honestly, fabulous. How often do we experience a sense of wobble-free certainty and unwavering confidence, the assurance, welling up from within, that whatever we wish to achieve, however big, we already have done and we are now merely reiterating the steps in its achieved reality syllogism. I told you it's a 4D phenomenon: I've already seen the effects, now I have to create the causes that bring them about. It's reassuring seeing the full gestalt of an action. You feel like it's a sure thing to succeed now.

I tried to come to terms with this discovery, or maybe it was a revelation. Say you've had 100,000 lives, on the Earth and various other planets, in human form and in others with comparable sentience and possibilities of self-awareness. In some lives you brought through a high degree of cosmic knowledge and mastery of spiritual arcana and achieved a decent level of self-development. That would go into the composition of this larger robed guy I was pretending to be.

I realized it was more than that. This figure, this "I" that I was shifting upwards into, has all the answers, has done all the work *already*, witnessed the outcomes. He is the culmination outside of my soul's timeline of my progression along the timeline through a host of successive lives, on Earth and elsewhere. He is both behind and ahead of where I, Frederick, professor and Arab math expert, stand. He is how I will appear when I have finished all my incarnations and completed the special assignment awarded me by the Chief Dispatcher and Master Choreographer of All Souls and Lives when I first hung apple-like and innocent on the Tree of Souls wondering when the fun and games would begin. He is the articulate one who will be making the final report on Eschatology Day when the Supreme Being debriefs us on our missions and how we fared in them.

It's hard to quantify it, but let's say that was enough to fortify you with an unshakeable confidence in what you were doing, even the sense you had done it all before, or perhaps previewed it in a briefing session before your incarnations. I never felt this self-assured before; usually, I was routinely confident about, say, giving a graduate seminar at Dartmouth or explaining views to colleagues. But this was confidence on a bigger scale as the stakes were enormous. I was up against the arithmetical gods. The magnitude of this green-robed archetype's confidence was commensurate with the potential ass-kicking he could get from one ill-considered move or one moment of inattention against these wily spirits.

My ordinary Frederick self had expanded to fill this much larger composite self. The Complete Hierophant was the fulfillment, already achieved, of everything Frederick and his predecessors and successors on his incarnational timeline would ever step forward to do. Everything we did was catching up with this already accomplished achievement. It was already done. I took that to mean I could count on the likely successful outcome of my projects and this mission.

The pale green flames shooting out from the orb at the staff's top were creating a lattice of Green Light from me at ground level to the top of the dome. It was securing the mesh of fire-letters backed by numbers to the ground level. If they were kites, I was attaching the kite strings to hold them in place and reel them in. Anchoring this grid of primal creativity also activated its pattern and released its force. It emitted a sound like a shout, then more and louder ones, like the chorus at the musical peak of an oratorio. The algorithms and equations were touching down at ground level like skilled parachutists making a night landing.

I was reeling the kites in. This caught the attention of the alien gods. It was as if they cocked their heads to start looking at this spectacle, not that they had heads, but you got that analogical impression. They looked dismayed.

I want to emphasize that I was not fighting the aliens or even opposing them in the normal sense we have of conflict. I felt I was showing them something, as if they were students at an introductory undergraduate course. I remember the feeling, both in myself and the students, when I would link a dozen seemingly disparate mythic images and show the equivalencies. That is the fun part of comparative mythology, discerning the exchangeabilities in disparate cultural images for the same spiritual process or Light temple.

That was always a mentally satisfying moment to behold such congruence, to see that people in different cultures and environments had perceived the same thing. They had seen a Light temple or participated in a geomantic ritual process and come up with interchangeable names and descriptions, and here they all were. I knew I was flattering myself in thinking the aliens saw the demonstration that way. They were not my avid students. It was for them an obstruction, a nuisance interference; they planned to remove it.

What I was doing was a hindrance to the pure arithmetical processes. That's all the aliens wanted; only a mental acquisition of the numbers, and as I mentioned above, they saw themselves and their activities as beyond even the mental realm. Mathematics and the algorithmic universe were the only reality. Mythic images, quests for expanded self-awareness, Light temples—irrelevant. Metaphors, analogies, psychic pictures suggestive of higher realities—go away.

For my part, on behalf of the Pale Green Ray with which I evidently was karmically aligned, the keynote of existence was consciousness and its processes. The arithmetic was infrastructure, providing order and coherence, but it was not the essence, only the means to identifying with that and moving it forward. That was what most people call conscious spiritual evolution, upgrades in awareness. This particular Ray focused on the new spring growths of incipient Christ Light, the motive force, nutrients, and inspiration to grow one's own consciousness into the transpersonal delights of the cosmos and the secret truths of self-awareness.

Our job in the Hierophancy was to keep the Arithmetical Earth in proper trim so that the larger, richer, bolder goal of growing self-awareness and cosmic consciousness could prosper in incarnate forms, usually human-style, though we worked with others. This growth would culminate in humans freely entering, awakening, and deploying the planet's Albion as the embodiment of their collective consciousness primed to explore and enrich the cosmos. The alien gods were concerned only with the arithmetic and so from the larger point of view, what I presume to say was the Supreme Being's design intention, they are shortchanging the purpose of the Creation and not caring about it either.

Despite their obvious high degree of mental development, they were myopic, operating under metaphysically parochial parameters. I laughed when I considered how I might get that point across. Not likely, pal. But the work of this pale green staff, sparking out living green budlike flames of incipient Christ Consciousness, seeding this template relaunching site with the possibility of newly incarnate selfhoods moving up into this transpersonal level of awareness, making this opportunity available to new humans, that was hierophantic work.

Clearly we had to labor in the arithmetical realm for a while, but I saw that our work, the hierophantic task, was to guarantee geomantic sites could support this. These irritating aliens were getting in our way. That's how they see us. Irritants, interfering nuisances, irrelevancies. I was thinking like them now.

Well, only for a moment. I returned to concentrating on sending out more green flames from the staff. I felt I had gotten taller somehow, and the staff too. This couldn't be my physical body that was expanding, but some version of me seemed now as tall as the dome, which arched more than ten miles above the ground. I told the analytical part of my consciousness to stop trying to figure that out, we'd deal with it later, or maybe never, filing it under unsolved mysteries. I knew I had to keep sending out the green flames from the staff in all directions.

What the aliens did not appreciate or maybe they simply discounted it was the need to create conditions allowing the evolution of consciousness in humans, conditions in which they, down to individuals, could decide to advance in their understanding of life, their mortality, and the possibilities of growing awareness. The arithmetical aspect was from this viewpoint only infrastructure, though vital unarguably. The aliens only want the arithmetical part; they want to extract it wherever they encounter it, lift it out from its living, incarnate context.

As I mentioned, they seemed to hate incarnation in all its forms and nuances. Even a phylogeny's consciousness, the range of possible human awareness and cognition, to them is an incarnation, which is a fallen condition. They will avoid it assiduously, regarding it like an objectionable taint, a distasteful concession. All expressions of selfhood are anathema to them;

even the collective mind is objectionable. They don't regard themselves as a collective, but as a singularity. They don't want their numbers realm supporting such a farce. It is an ill-advised investment of the arithmetical potency and must stop.

Evolution is off the table. For them, it's about getting all the numbers. Remember, they are not only opposed to the Supreme Being; they are out to steal Him. The ultimate identity theft. They can't be seen to be agreeing to any of His conditions. The arithmetical realm is unanchored to incarnation of any kind; it is free-floating existence with no compulsion to anchor into fixed, material forms.

As for the mythic realm, the domain of psychic pictures representing protocol interactions and their likely consequences, which is to say, here's how to operate these Light temples and the processes of consciousness they correlate, the alien disdain was even more pronounced. When you get down to their core program, they wanted to disallow most of the Creation, seeing it as irrelevant. They were determined to collect all available algorithms to create their alternate universe, a Creation zone of only mathematics, free of all incarnational blight.

They regarded the mathematical domain as right up against the disdainful incarnational boundary, but on the right side of this divide, the one of no-action and no-participation. In their view, numbers are not form, incarnation, or fallen. They are still abstract and formless, free of metaphorical taint. They regard them as uncommitted to anything pertaining to incarnation. The arithmetical realm has not crossed that perilous (obnoxious?) boundary into the form realm. This realm is still ontologically virginal. The Arithmetical Earth

and presumably that of as many planets as they could find would be redeemed, go into their Magic Square, the creation matrix for this vast project. Our job in the Hierophancy was to stop them from being successful in doing this.

My green flames were sparking and budding throughout the interior of the dome. The aliens were batting them away as if they were irritating flies. They were continuing to extract all the numbers from the Tiwanaku geomantic node. My green bud-flames were creating innumerable links between the arithmetical infrastructure and the psychic-mythic picture realm and the incarnational zone.

I had an amusing notion that the Supreme Being was watching this with avid interest, like a well-pitched tennis match at Wimbledon, Aliens versus Hierophancy, and the numbers-crazed guys were winning 40-love. The polarity might be entertaining the Chief Designer, but I suspected to the aliens it was an undesirable dichotomy that they would soon put an end to. They had no wish to be embroiled in a messy, distracting, geomantic "tennis match." There should be no dichotomy. The numbers should never have left the sanctity of their realm. The sooner we were carted off the field, the sooner they could finish their Square.

I didn't know if I was making any progress so I took a break and walked around the site. I admired the stones. I sent my compliments to the Elohim, master stone masons and frankly the original Masons in the true sense of temple builders. Stones that weren't stones, but only looked like huge stones, perfectly fitted but which had been precipitated out of the ethers by what we could only call angel magic. They pulsed with Light, and their interiors were temples too.

The Elohim had built well and large, both the human phylogeny and the Earth's Light grid. This felt like halftime at a sporting match, and the audience now sat in the stands expectantly waiting for the game to resume, for my struggle with the indifferent alien gods to start up again, like we were Sumo wrestlers and the crowd couldn't wait to see which behemoth floored and pinned the other first. I was my own cheerleading squad, raving on myself. I caught myself before I actually started waving and blowing kisses to myself.

I realized I had misperceived my situation. Yes, I was ambling around Tiwanaku, in between innings, but I was also sending out green flames from my planted staff out there on the playing field, anchoring pictures, numbers, and energies against the alien gods' insistence that only the arithmetic mattered. That made me part of the audience as well, so I leaned up against the Gate of the Sun and watched myself try to take down the aliens. The other I was flanked by numerous Blaise angels and they were wearing pale spring green cloaks and wielded tall staffs emitting green buds of spiritual flame. It looked like a parody, but I knew enough about the Ofanim to appreciate the fact that they could both fool around and conduct business like the consummate professionals they are.

I wondered if the aliens were running this wrestling match on two levels like I evidently was. They weren't. They were single-mindedly focused on this. They had no backstory, no alternate congregating in the locker room. Still, I felt I needed a diagram at this point to keep track of the layers of deception. The aliens were essentially biting at the phantom algorithm we had planted temptingly in their face here at Tiwanaku, and I was pretending to be opposing them as they tried to secure it, except I wasn't sure they hadn't seen through this ruse and had gone after the original correct algorithm that ran Tiwanaku's affairs. Which meant I wasn't simulating Sumo wrestling with them; I was already pinned. I weighed a hundred pounds, but they weighed a thousand. I was crushed flat.

I fleetingly wondered what happened to Blaise, Sal, and Jocelyn. I hadn't seen them here since I first arrived; they seemed to have winked out of sight.

Then I thought, what if the Supreme Being wanted me and the aliens to run this contest as a way of securing the *linkage* between numbers and pictures? What if the point of this was not a successful outcome in a dichotomy, but to keep the ball in play, secure the linking of the two domains? The Big Guy always had backup plans or clever ways of getting His desired results despite outward appearances or the impression things were going ass-backwards. I pondered.

I never truly believed the aliens could succeed in stealing God, though the tactic arrested my wonder with its boldness and insouciance. Maybe the Big Guy, understanding the aliens' tactic, took measures to make it seem they were succeeding while all along at a deeper level where reality really was crafted, He was making headway, just as He had planned and by divine right, expected to. Or maybe the whole set-up was beyond my understanding and confounded me, and I should shrug my shoulders and abandon all expectation of figuring it out.

I imagined I was sitting in a chamber with the Supreme Being and He was explaining His moves. I know, too literal and anthropomorphic, but indulge me. Let's say at some level I thought (or pretended: I don't know for sure) I was having a private colloquy with the Big Guy and for purposes of illustration I allowed my psychic apparatus to personify Him in some plausible, recognizable manner so at least I would know in which direction to cast my attention. He was discussing it like it was a complicated but intriguing chess move He had to make.

I felt hard pressed to come up with something intelligent to say. I mean, who wouldn't, under these circumstances? I mentioned that all this seemed like a planning session in some back room with Zeus when he laid out his plans for the outcome of the Trojan War, determined how long the struggle would last, who would survive, and maybe threw in Odysseus's fretful ten-year home trip as an entertainment bonus for this original version of reality TV. I don't think my contribution from mythology made much difference in this session or swayed the outcome, but the Supreme Being politely thanked me for my contribution.

I had always heard (from the human Blaise, I think) that He was a courteous guy, in most circumstances, unless you were really a screw-up. Then your ass was burned toast. Most of first-generation humanity come to mind; they truly pissed Him off. They got toasted. I did think at the time, what if the outcome was to have this Sumo wrestling take place, that God wanted this, that through my feckless struggle with the aliens I was securing the desired links?

The struggle was not meant to yield a winner but to guarantee this vital linkage. To struggle keeps both parties in the dichotomy in dynamic steady connection. The struggle is just a way of picturing the tension between these two polarities. That would mean the dichotomy was okay, part of the plan. The dynamic linkage was the whole point, keeping it in play, the line held taut, us against the alien gods, the incarnational realm scripted by numbers and the unsullied arithmetical realm uncommitted to any scripting forays into the created realms. The Designer of this tug-of-war did not want a clear winner.

Suddenly I was back on the playing field. It felt like my pockets had just been picked, that the aliens, not participating in this congenial gentlemen's club meeting over port and cigars, disdaining any dialogue with the Big Guy, had taken advantage of my inattention to lift some more equations out of Tiwanaku.

I felt like a cartoon version of Moses trying to part the Red Sea with his big staff, except it was suddenly flood time and the sea was surging and twice its usual size and Moses's confidence in his staff-wielding ability, his magic, was failing, and his staff was made of cardboard, quickly getting mushy, no flames or magic spells coming sparklike out of its sodden tip. Except this Moses, this Moses-manqué, me, was flipping through reference books at the same time, looking for clues from the mythic or occult record on how to make inroads against alien gods set on coolly stealing all the planet's arithmetic and making off with God, the Old Boy thrown in a big sack. At least my staff wasn't mush yet.

Even though the fate of the universe hung in the balance here, the whole thing had an antic hay quality. It was like a dance of fools for the fate of reality. I put in mythic pictures over the numbers, and the aliens extracted the arithmetic. They were rewriting the phantom algorithm. They must have seen through the ruse. I was intrigued with the fact they never stopped to look at the myth images. They were like two-dimensional collectors of only equations and algorithms; nothing else had any reality or held any interest for them. They didn't even see it. Was I as myopic in focusing on only the psychic mythic pictures I was seeding?

I saw Tiwanaku from both perspectives now, like I had double vision. I saw it running as a Light temple manifesting the fresh Elohim template for newly fashioned humans, body and mind, and I saw it as arithmetical code, running its abstract, disembodied number strings, and I saw the Supreme Being watching both domains as if He were inside these as a big attentive curious face. Then it was as if He suddenly raised His eyebrows in surprise at a clever trick.

Apparently, Sal had embedded a reserve algorithm inside the phantom one. This was now deploying, releasing a secondary tier of equations and number strings that surpassed and overwrote the first tier and confounded the aliens. I doubt they would have described their reaction that way, but they did go for the new tier of numbers. I am tempted to say their minds lunged for it. They released their hold on the domain of equations they had been favoring. This new set was now clearly at the center of their attention, like a delicious new flower suddenly appearing in the garden and drawing bees from everywhere.

I went back to streaming out those green flame-buds and standing unusually tall. I had the impression we had done this when Viracocha had launched humanity afresh. I couldn't say specifically who this "we" comprised; it had probably been the Hierophancy. I saw that these green bud-flames were adding "soil" to

the composition of the humanity relaunch template, a necessary substrate into which the mythic pictures and arithmetical strings could anchor.

They were both meant to be parts of the human, but existing at different layers of our subtle energy anatomy, an etheric layer of psychic pictures, one of numbers. Just as I appreciated this essential fact of our phylogenic ecology, I remembered that there was still the problem that the alien gods had stolen Earth's algorithm and I wasn't sure all the clever moves I was making here were addressing that.

Then, as if somebody else was directing my movements, my blazing staff generated a composite half-sphere of strong green Light that filled the interior of the dome and halted the aliens' activities. It was as if they had been flash-frozen. Well, somebody was clever to have come up with that nifty move. Not Frederick.

This green Light had coated the inside of the dome with a skin like porcelain, smooth and hard. I felt the unshakeable certainty of this other Frederick, the celestial one with the staff. He had no doubts; he knew what he was doing, and what he was doing was impressive. Ask me, the by-stander.

I stood inside his energy field like a deputy Cabinet secretary assisting the chief. I shifted my attention onto him. He was not fighting the aliens; I doubt he thought he was even resisting them. He was instead reasserting the necessities of the Tiwanaku geomantic node with a quietly imperial manner. When you water a dehydrated plant, you are not fighting the Sun and its heat. You are giving the plant what it needs: moisture. The Sun will keep on shining, but now the plant can handle the drying assault with this new reservoir fortification you gave it.

Still, I have to say, the work conditions on this job are, well, unusual. That is no doubt an understatement. I am referring to what happened next. Just as I thought I had this situation figured out, the players assigned to their roles, and their potencies and likely actions quantified, everything turned inside out. I was inside their Magic Square, captured as I suppose accuracy would insist I put it.

I knew what it looked like from the outside, a vast upright with hundreds of open squares, each a niche for some acquired planetary algorithm, but that gives it a misleading three-dimensional description. It was far more dimensional than that. It was like being in an asterisk expressed in perhaps six dimensions, with radial arms going out in all directions, even ones that I couldn't see because that's the nature of multidimensional geometries: they seem to be constantly moving, as if the asterisk entity was growing new ones as I was watching them, and my 3D-trained mind could not keep up with the multiplicity of new arms. Maybe a better comparison would be a neuron-synapse network as depicted in scientific photographs, with innumerable branching threads off a center point.

First, I felt like I was tumbling through empty space. Then it seemed I was frantically and futilely trying to grab onto the grids, any part of them, a mere crossbar. Then I was floating through a galaxy of stars with thin lines of Light threading between them, joining them up in a vast nexus—that asterisk shape. Strung along these crossbars like beads of moisture were bundles of arithmetic, and these unpacked themselves into long strings and banners made of numbers.

I didn't feel like I was ten miles high, or whatever the current height of the Tiwanaku dome was, though I knew it was less than its original 16.5 miles, and I didn't feel any more that I was wearing the fabled seven-league boots. Instead, I seemed very small, almost minute, compared to these extrapolating asterisks as I careened crazily out of my own control through this starkly arithmetical galaxy.

It was a matrix of continuously branching permutations, each algorithm coding out a dozen more, and these releasing a third generation of equations. It was an arithmetical version of the Qabalist's *Tzeruf* practice of spelling out the individual letters in words then spelling them and working their numbers. The result was a vertiginous concatenation of propagating mathematical script.

Still, I could appreciate the mental aspect to this. It must be delightful to Mind-only aliens like these whose sole pursuit in existence was to acquire all its equations. I conjured up a picture of them strutting proudly out of an estate sale that featured a terrific collection of arithmetical memorabilia and curiosities. They had bought the lot, even the house, because some of its walls were scribbled over in mathematical script. They would extract the numbers then abandon the house.

I realized, unhappily, that maybe I could not get the best of things, overcome them definitively, these arithmetic-obsessed alien brainiacs, because they are near infinite in extent, getting ever closer as they complete their theft of God and emptying His pockets of all the arithmetic in Creation. Their anti-*pi* calculation was winching the Supreme Being ever closer to them, yanking Him out of the mud-trap of infinity and rendering the ineluctable into the graspable.

It's like the vexing paradox Zeno articulated when he said you could not ever travel from point *a* to point *b* because you had to first go half that, then half of that, still continuously parsing the distance in half, into a receding and collapsing infinity that you could not straddle and thus never get across to *b*. The aliens had such a sufficient head start on me in their zooming towards infinity that it seemed unlikely I would catch up and they would outfox me. Plus every time I thought I had cleverly outdone them with some new clever-assed stealth equation, they showed they had stolen it hours ago and I was just getting the news. When I thought I was gaining on them they pulled everything inside out.

Except with Zeno's paradox the real paradox is that somehow you do cross from *a* to *b* despite the mentally persuasive impossibility of doing that. That seemed to summarize my dual condition as Frederick, rapidly losing ground, and as the celestial green-staff-wielding older version of myself, holding the fort adeptly in seven-league boots over there, wherever that was, at the Tiwanaku site. Maybe that twofoldness was the resolution of this conundrum, that both of us would participate in its resolution, one succeeding, one failing, and together we constituted the genuine outcome and the paradox was resolved. If I were the aliens I would inquire if we had the algorithm that scripted *that* result.

While I was vacillating between these two contrary though apparently complementary positions, I thought of my former Dartmouth colleagues, those who might still be alive. I was after all almost 90 myself, and some had been older than me. They would say of me, well, Frederick has gone off the deep end, that's for

sure, working arithmetical contests with brain-inflated greedy aliens. We always thought he had one or a dozen screws loose, possibly all of them.

Droll, but the more likely fact is they would be astonished and probably fearful to hear of my exploits of recent years since 2026 when Blaise lured me outside the folds of conventional reality and normal expectations of what reality was. Not Philomena, though; my wife would not see this as wacky: she had gone much further herself, turning her material body into a quasi-human form of pure Light. She might regard this as another episode of Frederick the home handyman wrestling with the lawn mower or hedge-clippers or trying to fix something else mechanical and making a muck-up of the job and taking all afternoon to do it and you're still going to end up needing to call an expert to fix your cock-up.

Then I was back inside the large green-robed version of myself, wielding the staff that sent sparks and streams of green fire and kept the arithmetical and psychic picture realm linked with the recipient Light temples at Tiwanaku. The little Frederick was part of this, inside the green cloak it seemed, and I had the sense that this was the trick, to keep this linkage in dynamic play. I didn't have to definitively defeat the aliens and their single-minded focus on the numbers side.

I just had to keep the numbers linked with the myths and the Light temples. Then it would be all right if they focused exclusively on the arithmetical domain. This sounded sensible, even a bit exciting. I turned again to look for Sal, Jocelyn, and Blaise to tell them I'd finally figured it all out, but they weren't here.

9

I didn't find out until later. They had never come to Tiwanaku. Later they gave me their field reports. They had gone to separate locations. Sal's was first:

I was sitting next to Blaise in the jet, wondering where you had gone to, Frederick. Blaise said I was going to Canada, to an Indian holy site in Alberta. "Apply what you know. Make up the rest as you go." Those were the instructions he gave me. The Hierophancy is always lean on established protocols since we're always encountering unique, baffling situations like this.

We landed at Calgary. I noted the temperature was about 60° F, then I headed out on my own towards what is known as the Majorville Cairn and Medicine Wheel, west of the Bow River and south of Bassano in southern Alberta. It takes a while to get there. I won't bother with the details, but it was challenging. It took about three hours and I got lost several times.

It is very windy here. The Wheel sits within 160 preserved acres of open, flat, treeless prairie with an expansive view (its elevation is about 1,043 feet) of much more of the same terrain and consists of an uneven circle of small stones and 28 radial spokes. Between 100 and 200 medicine wheels similar to this one and as delicate and fragile in construction have been identified in this part of Canada, including next-door in Saskatchewan, as well as in North Dakota, Wyoming, and Montana. It seems to have been the preferred geomantic form.

The site belongs to the Blackfeet Nation, which knows it as *Iniskim Umaapi*, and archeologists have dated its construction to roughly 3200 B.C. The circle itself measures 88 feet in diameter, with a central round stone cairn 27 feet wide; the 28 stone spokes connect to the central standing cairn. Archeologists have uncovered small ritual objects (natural, unworked stones resembling buffaloes) at the site, suggesting the Blackfeet might once have used the Medicine Wheel to summon the return of migrating buffalo. One researcher about 50 years ago wrote a book extolling the site as "Canada's Stonehenge," attributing solar calendar aspects to the alignment of the stones with the two annual solstices.

Blaise has told me enough times we need to be respectfully skeptical of claims and interpretations made by White People regarding Native American site use. So I have to say the comparison with Stonehenge is understandably hyperbolic and weak and basically unjustified. For one, Stonehenge was built by the Elohim and used etheric-world precipitated megaliths;

for Stonehenge, the archeoastronomical aspects were significant but did not represent the site's primary purpose and the standing stone circle was rendered spiritually obsolete with the incarnation of the Christ more than two thousand years ago. The academic who likened Majorville with Stonehenge is in for an embarrassing surprise. Archeologists contend Stonehenge is perhaps 5,000 years old. Wrong.

As Geoffrey of Monmouth wrote in the 1100s and as the angelic Blaises later confirmed, Stonehenge was first set up in South Africa then moved to Ireland. The relocation followed population shifts and changes in Light grid emphasis, and it puts the operational date of Stonehenge into the many millions of years. Stonehenge's installation in South Africa was in the Hyperborean epoch, which was vastly long ago, in the planet's original Golden Age. It was moved to Ireland, to its national geomantic umbilicus at Hill of Uisneach also a vastly long time ago contrasted with the mere sliver of time that is 5,000 years. The stones may have been relocated to Salisbury plain 5,000 years ago, but that was the third location for these antediluvian Elohim-generated divine stones.

Following the same geomantic logic of function and purpose, it is possible, probably likely, use of the Majorville site is much older than a mere 5,000 years. That is not a year calculation provided by Native Peoples. Frankly, the same can be said of everything megalithic on Earth. Everything goes much further back in time. It seems unlikely the Elohim built this site; they specialize in cyclopean stones. The Majorville site, it seems likely, was built by Indians themselves. In terms of design and construction it is modest and megalithically "low-tech." But as I was to discover, the site is rich in Light temples, and the cairn and circles of small stones do a good job anchoring those Light temples.

First Nations members did not build much and what they did construct tended to be understated, more like a hint of pebbles than a full stone opera. I always thought it was because the indicated Light temple was always so well perceived by sensitives among its population that anything more overt was not required. Also, if you do not conspicuously mark your holy sites, inappropriate attention or people will not be drawn to them because they won't see them, not having the requisite "medicine." Keep them secret and unmarked and they will not be despoiled. Don't ever tell the White People anything correct about them. Possibly, the original motivation was to keep their ritualized landscape private to their tribe; later, they were probably glad they kept it circumspect and hard to understand because the White People would eventually try to take or destroy it.

I will mention that during my drive out to this site, I worried. Well, mostly I pondered and ruminated, but it led to some possibly worrying implications. Would the Earth disappear without its master algorithm? Here's the logic: you have to work the situation backwards to see it. We arrived at the Hierophancy heuristic algorithm by inventorying all the Light temples, mapping their locations and distribution geometries, assessing their functions and working status, then deriving the arithmetical components that scripted their reality.

But in chasing the alien gods who stole our algorithm, the impression is emerging (maybe Blaise knew this all along) that the mathematics came first, like seeds. The planet's Light grid is extrapolated out of this arithmetical genomic script, and this series of equations sustains the planet like the etheric body sustains our physical form. Without it, our body dies; without the numbers, our Earth dies. That means if the alien gods succeed in stealing then keeping our algorithm, if they extract every last vexing thread of it, such as we've been chasing, then they might in effect be stealing the Earth's life itself, its reality. I'm not sure. Do you think the consequences of their acts could be as dire as this?

Was Majorville dedicated to summoning the buffalo through landscape ritual? Many *iniskim* stones, dubbed "buffalo calling stones," have been found here; they are ammonite fossils whose shape looks like the shoulder and hump of a buffalo. Archeologists speculate the Indians used these stones to call the buffalo to this site. That sounds too much like White People reductionist literalism to me.

As soon as I got here and took a few breaths, I started sensing the inner life of this site. I saw innumerable First Nations people sitting around but outside the Wheel; I saw a holographic display, like a 4D planetarium projection, of stars, planets, and the Moon, becoming visible within the bounds of the Wheel, but the diameter of the Wheel itself started expanding and it became hard to distinguish what was the circumference of the Wheel and what was the actual galaxy. The Wheel's display was capable of turning and moving in time, like a live orrery. If this site was a calendar, it had pages not only for now, but the past and future.

I saw celestial spirits walking out of these stars, planets, and even the Moon. You'll be impressed with this, Frederick; I researched it before coming here. These were the Above People, the Sky People, or Sky Beings, known to the Blackfoot as *Sspommitapiiksi*, including *Naato'si*, the Sun god; *Komorkis*, also called *Ko'komiki'somma*, the Moon goddess; and numerous "star children" born to this pair, including a special son, *Iipisowaahs* or *Apisirahts*, translated as Morning Star.

The Creator god was *Apistotoke* or *Ihtsipatapiyohpa*, meaning "Source of Life." The main culture hero was called Old Man, or *Naapi*; he was a transformer, trickster, troublemaker, and foolish; he shaped the world for the Blackfeet and often helps them to live in it, and he enjoys the assistance of Old Lady, *Kipitaakii*. Even to me, mathematician and not mythographer, "old" suggests their antiquity as gods, that these two celestial spirits must rank among the earliest of the created gods.

The Above People were created by *Apistotoke*, the first god, also known as Great Spirit or *Ihtsipatapiyohpa*, "the Source of Life." The Above People live in the Sky World above the visible clouds. It was these Above People I saw arriving at this Medicine Wheel hologram, and it suggests that in some esoteric manner the geomancy of the Wheel calls them. The star alignments, the site's calendric aspect, would be a summoning chart, the words and music to a liturgical script meant to invoke the actual Sky deities. It's funny, when you think about it. The archeologists think the little ammonite stones were for summoning the buffaloes; now it seems the Medicine Wheel of little stones was for summoning the gods.

I kept reminding myself that Sky most likely referred to the exalted etheric spiritual realm, possibly the astral plane, and not to the physical visible planetary atmosphere that surrounds the

Earth. Sky meant the Higher World, the Upper World, or for the Gnostics, the Pleroma, not the physical zone of clouds. Ancient peoples, we have found in the Hierophancy, were never as literal as humans, especially White People, have become. Reality was always tiered for them and the physical world was pre-integrated into these many stacked higher worlds.

I saw a shimmering, scintillating curtain of numbers around the Sky People. It seemed to rise up from the land and tower into the sky, but since the Above People were manifesting out of the stars in the galaxy, that meant the curtain was far larger than my description suggests. The Above People stood in tiers at the site, like the way seats are arrayed in rising rows in a sports stadium. In the curtains, algorithms were running their arithmetical processes computing reality and generating the specifics of this site and presumably many others.

I recognized some of the equations. Others were algorithms I had worked with. I admired the math logic displayed in these equations. I started to lose myself in a rapt contemplation of their intricacies, but I remembered you wanted me to provide a more visceral report that focused on mythic or celestial presences. The algorithms were specifying the details of this Medicine Wheel site and its summoning functions; it was as if they were digitally choreographing the arrival and placement and possibly the activities of the Above People.

Public knowledge of this site and its esoteric operations is scanty and speculative. So you have to be careful in picking through the attributions. A number of other medicine wheels at other locations have been linked with healing rituals or death ceremonies or even after-life commemorations for fallen heroes or chiefs. That would be consistent with the general understanding of the term "medicine," which is linked with spiritual power and consciousness potency. The number of radial spokes here, 28, corresponds with the typical number of poles used in a medicine lodge or Sun Dance ground, scholars say. The Majorville site lies within a larger geomantic province called *Omahk*, its shortened form, or *Omahkiyáahkóhtoóohp*, meaning "big, old arrangement," which strikes me as a weak or understated, even inept, translation. I would say the outer design of the site downplays the extent of its true geomantic alignment.

The expanding presence of the Above People here, as more of them kept appearing, would testify to the "medicine" aspect of this site. As the Above People kept arriving, the site became richly endowed with this celestial presence, and I can concur that it is enlivening, quickening, and I started feeling fortified with cosmic *Qi*, my awareness expanded, and my body felt invigorated as the spiritual emanations of this growing host of Above People washed over me.

I don't mean I was feeling poorly when I started meditating here, but that now I felt enormously enriched, purified, and strengthened, like after hours of soaking in a hot tub at a mineral waters spa. I felt revitalized on all levels, full of "medicine." The Above People brought their stars and Light temples with them, it seemed, as I saw the structures of consciousness each of their home domains generated and how these living procedures in higher consciousness were being anchored here. The place was humming with the high energy of their presence.

The star alignments, the calendric aspects of this site, its correspondence with the solstices and equinoxes, undersold the true significance. The Medicine Wheel was not just about indicating locations and timings: it was a seating chart. It showed you where to expect the Above People to stand when they arrived from their celestial homes, and it probably showed their energetic relationships, like a grid, and let me mention that they arrived with the arithmetical scripts for their stars and Light temples surrounding them in a curtaining crescent shape. It would be like seeing a living human surrounded by an aura of his own genetic code, the specifics of his DNA that scripted his bodily particularities, the seating chart for his biological manifestation, all the DNA codons in their proper places.

In a similar manner I saw displayed the algorithmic coding that wrote the particularities of these stars. I don't know if the people using this Wheel found the numbers aspect relevant to their needs, but I suspected a link between that numbers coding and a rhythmical aspect of the site, as if the numbers specified a musical script for drumming and chanting, that in some manner these human sonic manifestations, drumming, singing, calling out, evoking, maybe even dancing in some prescribed ritualistic manner, were meant to copy the rhythms and thereby ensure thorough entrainment of participants with the Above People, and through that entrainment to anchor those celestial qualities at this site. I saw etheric traces of former alive Native Americans moving their bodies and their awareness like brightly colored banners whirling to the rhythms of this music.

The alignments probably have periodic intensity, indicating the times to use the site for optimal benefits. It is likely similar to Michaelmass, September 29. You can tune into the Archangel Michael any time during the year with a reasonable likelihood of authentic contact, but on this one day of the year you are guaranteed live presence when the archangel cleans out the planet's plumbing. The specificity of that day for geomantic planetary cleansing is the Moon's apogee, when it is approximately the furthest from the Earth during the annual cycle. In other words, the Moon is safely out of its obstructionist way then.

That way whatever alignments you make in consciousness, whatever preparations you have cultivated in the preceding year, come to grand fruition, especially if you do this through a charged, primed geomantic site. I suspect the Medicine Wheel works along a similar geomantic principle. Access to the Above People is maximally available during annual times of periodic intensification.

The Above People were showering the site with pictures. These were images as if painted on an etheric fabric, *eidolons* of celestial spirits, events, processes, locations, of the opulence of Light temples, cosmic locales, deity palaces, gardens of magical fruit trees and effulgent golden chalices of Light. It wasn't math, but it was impressive. Quite caught my attention. It reminded me of scenes in the Puranas when the gods, watching Earth events from on high, would indicate their approval by sending down a rain of rose petals or other aromatic flower blossoms and occasionally bang on drums or tinkle cymbals.

Here it seemed not a matter of approval or validation, but like crop seeding. The Above People, and even more exalted spirits above them, were seeding this site with the possibilities of awakening human awareness to celestial realities. I had the impression they were teaching the Native Peoples how to walk with the Above People, how to carry their pure medicine while on Earth.

I was wondering about the correlation between this site, the little buffalo-shaped stones, and the implication that Indians summoned buffalo from here. Maybe they did, but perhaps we need to construe this in bigger, bolder terms. I suspect there was a parallel invocation to Aldebaran, the star that is the Red Eye of Taurus, the constellation of the Bull. It is situated 65 light-years from Earth and was regarded by Persian astronomers as one of the four Royal Stars, most active regarding the Earth at the spring equinox. The original bull form which in standard star diagrams consists of only the shoulders and head and a bright eye is basically a buffalo hump that only alludes to an entire bull of Light.

I make this comment because I saw multiple copies of a Bull of Light appearing from the four directions. This site did summon the buffalo, only they came from the constellation Taurus and were all named Aldebaran. That meant, maybe, the little ammonite stones were visual mnemonics of the secret function of this site. I wouldn't say they were stampeding the Medicine Wheel, but they were definitely approaching it. It was dramatic, beautiful and, yes, glorious. The buffalo were gathering, but they were Buffalo of Light, all cosmic bulls.

Why Aldebaran, the Eye of the constellation Taurus the Bull? Some 115 years ago the American psychic Alice Bailey, through her Ray Master mentor, Djwhal Khul, said this is the home of the New Group of World Servers, which might mean a new crop of Above People coming to Earth, at least etherically, with good intentions, to bestow blessings. It was to be the first wave of the Externalization of the Hierarchy, an event of great significance and much discussed in Bailey's writings. Basically it meant, if I remember Blaise's explanation correctly, a making visible and palpable of the guiding luminaries and intelligences who have been secretly directing humanity. The Hierarchy in question was likely some aspect of the Great White Brotherhood.

Even if we didn't invoke Bailey or Khul, other First Nations people, such as the Lakota Sioux of North Dakota, speak of White Buffalo Calf Woman, a celestial female Above Spirit, who taught them many of their holy mysteries and rituals. She was an instructor, a benefactor, and a prophet to these people, and I draw your attention to the *whiteness* of the White Buffalo Calf Woman image. I won't attest to gender in the apparitions of celestial bulls of Light appearing outside the Medicine Wheel, but buffalo or bull, male or female, their effect was numinous. When mystics speak of "white" it always refers to effulgent *Light*, and this Light is hierophantic and the buffalo and Calf Woman are Hierophants.

The bulls were advancing on the Wheel. The former Native Americans, in spirit form, were advancing. The Above People were coming on strong too. It was a populous convocation out here in the middle of Alberta nowhereland, but I say that with no disrespect to the landscape, only to suggest it was empty. In a bizarre contrast—I took it for granted, but I realized most people would regard the juxtaposition as arrestingly odd—the algorithm curtains were running their number streams, computing the abstract mathematical foundations for everything visible at this site, including what was only visible to able psychics.

Then I sensed some obscure faces peering in at this spectacle from a distance. It was the alien gods, and their vantage point, presumably, was their homeland, or maybe I should call it their office or computing room. Anyway, they were studying the set-up here at the Wheel and probably making plans to steal the goods. Even to say "faces" is to put too literal and distinct an image on it. It was more the sense of attention, a presiding awareness, a focusing of minds. I hoped I could fake them out once I deployed our phantom algorithm, as a lure to capture that presiding awareness, that irritating intensity, in the finger-trap.

For a while I wondered whether these aliens were in fact an artificial intelligence. But I dismissed this possibility because I understood it was an irrelevant distinction or even a meaningless one. An artificial intelligence would likely end up with the same single-minded arithmetical imperialism as these aliens had, the imperative to acquire all interesting algorithmic expressions out there. These aliens never seemed to be materially embodied, and they appeared to act like a collective single-mind consciousness; they were certainly self-aware and self-initiating and constantly and quickly adapted to changing circumstances and took advantageous action, but all their activities converged on the arithmetic. That would be consistent with their original start-up programming if they had been an artificial intelligence told to do *these* things.

Their behavior seemed inexorable and dispassionate, other than in the driest, most abstract sense of an intellectually couched passion to acquire the mathematics, the complete arithmetical inventory, of the Supreme Being Himself, to pick it clean. An artificial intelligence usually implies a human or sentient creator. We don't know the origin or biographies of these arithmetical deities. Are they part of the Supreme Being's staff, or did somebody else make them?

But I know you, and especially Blaise, will want to know more about the geomantic profile of this site, about what kinds of Light temples were here. To know how to best deploy our arithmetical tactics here, it helps to understand the engineering blueprint of the place, what's here and how it works. That's standard Hierophancy field operation. Discern the geomantic mechanics of a node, assess its working status, functional viability, algorithms, and myths. What would justify First Nations designers to put a medicine wheel in such a seemingly remote location beyond the obvious physical advantages of silence and privacy? When you see the site's geomantic design, then you can answer it.

Geomancers know you can't assume physical landscapes looked the same a long time ago as now and thus you cannot accurately extrapolate reasons or conclude perplexities based only on the contemporary appearance or condition of a site. You can't say the site designers liked the proximity to a river or the elevation of nearby hills or any meteorological, climatological, or physical condition because none of these remain constant over time.

Rivers arise and then dry up or change locations, and the allocation of Light temples, as we well know, was made upon an originally flat terrain, smooth like a tabletop, and the array of sites had nothing to do with existing landscape topography at the time. It was based on an overall design, and that design was generated to deliver a certain specific quality of consciousness and function to that planet and people. It was an engineering blueprint created before the recipient planet had any distinguishable landscape features, only flatness.

Landscapes change, often radically, over time, and populations swell and shrink. People used to wonder why "they" put Chaco Canyon in such a remote, barren corner of New Mexico, far away from everything, "in the middle of nowhere." It wasn't. It was at the center of everything for a long time, in fact, it was that center, and was put there because of the land's geomantic endowment, which was rich and considerable, like an enormous family fortune. It drew people and energies to it from everywhere; it was geomantic downtown.

So we can understand that a minimalist outer use and construction output for a site such as Majorville is not indicative of its endowment. Small on the outside, gigantic on the inside. We know the First Nations people tended to underbuild at their geomantic nodes, only faintly and sketchily. But of course, in all of this I am merely repeating what Blaise taught us about interpreting landscape sites. Our old pal always encourages us to see landscapes deeply.

So here is my report on trying to see Majorville deeply. First, the geomantic array is much more extensive than the conservative construction of the Medicine Wheel. That occupies the core of the geomantic array, but the etheric span of the place is at least four times broader than the Wheel's diameter. Second, the Medicine Wheel does not in any way mimic the structure of the Light temples there; it is more like a key that opens the door

into its subtle architecture. It is like a Hollow Hill or *sidhe* opening to the Light temple, but without any hill. That architecture appears to be a copy of a Heaven; I assign it as the third.

It looks like a broad column of Light enclosing the Wheel and a great deal more of the landscape. Inside this column lies the Third Heaven hologram, and it features bejeweled crystal pillars around its circumference; archways between the pillars; and celestial fires burning in gold or silver urns in front of the pillars. Naturally, the place is populated with a host of luminous angelic figures, though probably First Nations psychics would have interpreted their forms differently.

On this basis alone, I could see why a Medicine Wheel put here would be marvelously rejuvenating to any user and how it would quicken consciousness. That Third Heaven could deliver a lot of wholesome medicine to the site users. You would be walking around, in your psychic body at least, in a pristine, cosmologically pure environment, as immaculate as when the Supreme Being created it. It would give you a chance to re-anchor yourself in this foundation. I was getting this psychic and *Qi*-enhancement just from sitting on the sidelines. All of the Seven Heavens as described in classical models of the heavenly worlds are templated in multiple copies across the Earth, affording alive humans an early chance to sample some of the fine qualities of these Heavens while embodied. As Blaise puts it, it enables living people to experience some of Heaven on Earth.

I was outside the Medicine Wheel though clearly I was within the larger boundary of this holographic copy of *Shehaqim*, the Third Heaven, in Judaic angelologies. This is the third of seven Heavens, or *Shamayim*, from *shama*, "the high place." A High Place indeed, source of the Above People, or possibly of their mentors. Native Americans did not talk of angels but they used terms like Holy People to indicate a spectrum of benevolent beings from tribal ancestors to angels. The presence of any of these fine groups of celestials would be medicine.

One scholarly source reports the Jewish belief that this Heaven measures 120,000 miles ("12 myriads of miles") on each side and stands 120,000 miles high. It is built of gold and silver and features the best of everything imaginable in the heavenly realms. Various high-ranking prophets and angels are assigned to it. As we know, the heavenly originals always get scaled down to fit the general size parameters of the Earth landscape and its local temple clusterings; but even with these size adjustments, the essential features are still present. As far as our experience of a site, the apparent size of a holographic projection doesn't matter.

Some of the Above People, or maybe it was the angels associated with *Shehaqim*, were looking at me, as if wondering why I was there doing nothing. "Oh, hi," I said, mentally, I think. I don't think I spoke this out loud. I would have felt too silly. "I'm just here to fix the math equations." And to plug in our little phantom algorithm to befuddle the alien gods, I didn't add, though the aliens behind this angelic spectacle of Light and purity were no doubt expecting it and probably had some clever new defenses or sleights-of-hand to outwit me. Maybe I should have said, "Me? Oh, just here waiting to get royally fucked by the alien arithmetical gods who will neatly outwit the Hierophancy yet again."

I'm sure none of you expected me to reel off the attributions to *Shehaqim* out here in the field. Numbers is my field; this would be yours, Frederick. But I did look it up later before sending this report so you'd be impressed I'd done research outside my field. *Shehaqim*, from the Hebrew, means "clouds," and derives from *shahaq* which means "dust." Good names: already things are unclear to me on a massive scale; my head feels like it is saturated with clouds.

Possibly more clear, and certainly intriguing, is that this Heaven is said to be where the millstones grind the *manna* for the Righteous to enjoy in the World to Come, which means when they die and attend the Good Behavior Awards Show also known as the Messianic Feast or Eschatological Banquet staged at the end of time and hosted by the Supreme Being. It sounds like a promising lunch.

But the *manna* attribution is congruent with the elevation of *Qi* and well-being I feel here, the sense of benediction and uplifting of the spirit this place gives you. *Manna* seems another name for medicine, and it comes from a very high place, the top of the Tree of Life, Blaise says, from the Supreme Being Himself. I am wary of the term Righteous of course, though I remember Blaise explaining it does not mean prissy, absolutist little Christian moralists running around priding themselves on their impeccable behavior, but points to people aligned with the innate truth of the geomantic pattern and its spiritual presences.

There is a statement in *Psalms* about how God will (or did on some occasions) command the skies above (*Shehaqim*) to open the doors of Heaven and rain down *manna* on the people as food. The Skies Above and the Above People: it sounds like both are part of this Third Heaven. It was the human Blaise who worked out the correlations between mystical terms like *manna*, dew, and the enigmatic but glorious Persian term *Xvarnah* with the White Light of *Kether*.

That's the pure exudate of Supreme Being essence from His White Crown which the Qabalists say (and our colleague Edward Burbage in his last book, *The White Staff Nudge*, said too) is at the top of the Tree of Life and is three notches above the human crown chakra. *Manna* comes from the White Crown of the Ancient of Days, which is one of His Names, and perhaps this Third Heaven, which does not correspond with *Kether*, is its warehouse or distribution center.

Some sources say *manna* is honey and is delivered to the Righteous on demand and coordinated with the Archangel Michael by "divine bees." Those "bees" are probably angels, and righteous doesn't mean morally obnoxious, but purified. It's more like the Jewish term *Tzaddik*, Holy Person, rightly aligned with God, and if the Blackfeet talk about *medicine* and the Jews about *manna*, we're probably talking about an equivalency, something spiritually uplifting because it comes from such a pure and vibrationally "high" or refined source, the Tree top.

It's hard to be sure about any of this. We're dealing with ancient psychic metaphors that may now have missing elements or be slightly inaccurate. Getting clear impressions of the spiritual world, Blaise tells me, is exactingly difficult. Usually at best you will get a reasonable or at least plausible *approximation* of things, that what you see is probably a plausible visual metaphor, never the absolute correct appearance of a thing. Not to worry: those "things" don't have absolutely fixed appearances anyway. What you can depend on is their function.

Blaise told me that the attributions to the Seven Heavens tend to be scanty, inexact, and often wrong, and that much of it needs to be re-investigated and reformulated and the faulty attributions edited out in our time. We need new plausible visual metaphors to describe these subtle realms. Some of the old metaphors are metaphysically frayed and threadbare. To be fair, the Jewish *Hekalothic* literature reports richly on the Heavens and may well be far more accurate in details and metaphors, but much of this is not available in English.

The scholarly and even mystical literature on *Shehaqim* may be sparse, but I had a hologram of the real thing in front of me here at the Majorville Medicine Wheel. Anyway, angelologies and the topography of the heavenly realms are not my specialty. I sat out in the broad, empty prairie writing new code to confound the aliens. I doubt they cared about *Shehaqim* either, other than its arithmetic. They would likely regard it as part of that infernal incarnational realm.

I tried a few new combinations. I called it my Alien Mind-Bashing and Disappearing Algorithm. I worked it out in four dimensions, as I quite relish hyperdimensional math and find it easier to follow and more stimulating than charting angelic hierarchies and populations. I was making this new algorithmic formulation alluring and devious, such that it would lead the inquiring alien minds through a labyrinth of calculations and apparent products that eventually ended nowhere at the end of their happy journey and into a lurking finger-trap. This would dovetail with the phantom algorithm and the replacement of the missing geomantic pinning equations that belong at this site. A triple delivery.

You might wonder, Frederick, how exactly does one input a new number code into actual reality? I used to wonder that myself after I had already done it. I know that sounds strange, but I think I get into a particular mental state, one that is focused, silent, empty of thought, and populated only with arithmetic. You have to pass through whatever Light temples are present at a site, so here I had to enter and pass beyond the *Shehaqim* domain of the site into its numbers.

These were streaming down through the evanescent "curtains" that surround the site, and this streaming was in tiers extending into several dimensions. Obviously, I couldn't simply download the computations from my handheld computer; I had to make the transfer mentally, as it were, move my awareness into this abstract numbers realm, project the equations outside of me like an arithmetical auric field, and attach this deployment at key number nodes displayed in the running algorithmic field of this site. Then it would download.

I did not construe these aliens as the bad guys of the universe against whom I had to pitch myself and hope for success in suppressing their activities. I saw it more in terms of a chess match, with move and countermove, with the advantage, I hoped, that they wouldn't even know a game was underway. I made my moves in stealth mode, I thought, and the aliens would not realize the numbers were being altered. I now see how inept my tactical model was. Those guys anticipated all my moves; they

fully appreciated a chess game was afoot; and they had already checkmated me before I even got here. I *so* underestimated them. It's moot to think of them as an advanced form of artificial intelligence. They are Intelligence embodied, despite the paradox they hate taking any form.

The term "artificial" is meaningless when you deal with these guys. I was working *in* the field of mathematics, but they *are* mathematics itself. It isn't even correct to say they immerse their minds in the arithmetical universe; that is their mental field. Their mental field is arithmetical, a unified, copious universe of numbers. A strange idea occurred to me, and I wonder if it did to any of you.

They are, and this gives me the shivers, the Supreme Being Himself expressed arithmetically. What we have been construing as the alien gods is in fact the domain of arithmetic itself, all the numbers and equations—that's them. Their corporate body is the complete arithmetical field, though they would disdain any description of their unified presence and constituting a body at all.

They are that arithmetical domain. They are not in it or holding it or seeing through it. They are this domain. Shit. That's what we are actually up against. The intelligence of the numbers realm itself. The arithmetical mind of the universe is taking itself back out of the field of incarnation. The numbers are walking out. I suspect the numbers originally arose at the same time and with equal seniority with the angelic realm since the Hebrew fire-creation letters are equivalent with the numbers, one on the back of the other, Qabalists say. When the letters were generated, so were the numbers. The letters code the angelic realm, the numbers specify the arithmetical world, and both comprise the one hand, and that hand belongs to the Supreme Being. Was He walking out too?

From the original pairing of numbers and letters, you had in one direction, Soma, the essence of the consciousness of all 40 angelic orders. On the other, you have the Magic Square of Fire, what the Hindu myths call Agni, Lord of Fire, and all the arithmetic, and then its myriads of lesser-level permutations and extrapolations, this prolific domain of unending calculations that compute and thereby consume the Soma. The aliens we've been chasing are the intelligence of the field of mathematics, all the existent numbers and their myriad combinations, all the possible permutations, and the irrational, never-ending expressions.

This was a fundamental schism, this separation of letters from the numbers, the 40 angelic orders and their flavors of awareness from all the realms of arithmetic. I felt chilled as I realized this understanding utterly changed the playing field and shockingly reconfigured the nature of our work against the alien gods. I was up against a fundamental design bifurcation in reality itself, an absolute wall, a dichotomy that apparently began with the Creation of reality.

If, as you said, Frederick, when I last saw you, the alien gods are attempting to pickpocket the Supreme Being and take all His mathematics, this suggests that at some point these arithmetical spirits deviated from their original design intention, from what the Supreme Mathematician made them for, and in this fallen or aberrated state they are setting out to reverse the primordial power relationships in the Creation and to take the unfoldingness of reality in a new direction, based on their master

Magic Square when it is completed, which in my inanity I have just helped. Yes, I didn't tell you: things did not go well with this.

I thought I was so clever, so arithmetically masterful, uploading a stealth-mode algorithmic deception into their vast brain. They were sitting there immersed like a kid in a bathtub of bubbles and rubber ducks in their ocean of equations, already situated quite a number of moves ahead of me. They had checkmated me before I even began the game. Still, if they have departed from the divine model, that must be a wedge for us. That asymmetry that now exists between them and God is our opening to get into their realm and fix it.

This means we are up against the total arithmetical aspect of the Supreme Being minus one. If I were to put it as a simple equation, it is $\infty - 1$. That minus-one aspect represents the fallen alien gods, who are now slightly out of phase with the full spectrum of the mathematical universe of the Supreme Being. This seemed quite odd: the Supreme Being had subluxated Himself. His pristine mathematical realm was now out of phase with His universal essence, or so it seemed. Instead of being His *avatars* in the arithmetical domain, these alien gods were now partially separate and acting independently and against His interests. The asymmetry is the minus-one part: they are one digit less than infinity; they are on track to capture the arithmetical realm up to that one digit short of it all.

They were taking steps inimical to the purpose of the world of mathematics and the multiple levels of all realities it supported, all the way down to our planet Earth. They are out to capture their Creator and swallow His infinity. They were acting like an artificial intelligence dangerously surpassing the dictates of its maker. Maybe not "artificial" as such, but secondary, a "sub-creation," as J. R. R. Tolkien once said of his Middle-earth mythos, but still owing their existence to the Supreme Being Whom they were now rudely trying to end.

I don't know how this schism happened, but if I may wax whimsical for a moment, and let's not forget that a great mathematician called Lewis Carroll also waxed whimsical with his Alice in Wonderland analogy for stark foreignness in arithmetical realities, let me say that the Supreme Being was walking along jingling the coins in His trousers' pocket. That was His primary Magic Square.

It turned out He had a hole in His pocket and all the coins fell out. They became self-aware as a Magic Square and decided they didn't want to return to that stuffy pocket. They wanted to explore the possibilities of existence outside the pocket. I suppose this is a divine form of artificial intelligence becoming self-aware and self-learning and setting out to dominate its master and to command the world. Still, that seems like another Zeno-type paradox: How can a mere secondary-level creation out-maneuver and conquer its own infinite Creator? I couldn't imagine the Ofanim and Elohim teaming up to stage a *coup d'etat* against God, can you, Frederick? So how could the arithmetical gods do this?

What we're dealing with here is not an artificial intelligence, but the Primary Intelligence, the self-aware mathematical realm. Our alien gods are this. They don't occupy the arithmetical realm; it is their essence, their numbered mind. They *are* the arithmetical realm. That means they are our heuristic algorithm, and all the others they are recalling.

It's like we're trying to negotiate a treaty, and everybody on the other side just walks out at once. They're all gone.

By the way, in case you have read the views of mathematicians who assert infinity minus one equals infinity and infinity is not a number but only a concept, I don't agree with any of that. I believe they are mistaken. Let them come here and see what I have before me and they will readily revise their theories on facts. This is why I say that infinity is not a concept but a number.

There cannot be a number the Supreme Being does not know. He knows infinity, what that number is, how many digits it entails. His knowledge surpasses His own infinite extent. It *has* to. This vexes our logical mind, and maybe I should sell Zeno the intellectual copyright on this conundrum. It says it is impossible to know the end-point of a number that does not ever end, yet the Supreme Being does know it. He must. He must comprehend and even be articulate about His own infinity. That seems to us an irresolvable paradox, but I think Zeno, the old confounder, would love it (and buy the rights). It outdoes his paradox about the arrow never crossing half the distance to get somewhere.

Here is God, the infinity of all numbers, Who, even so, outdoes Himself and explicitly knows His Own final number. It is the ultimate tautology, infinity beholding itself. That leads to a shocking thought, however: the Supreme Being knowing His Own infinity, His Own last number: Isn't that the same as the alien gods devouring His infinity, closing the gap between infinity minus one, cancelling the unending *pi*? It's even worse than that, I realized. If the arithmetical realm is the extrapolated intelligence of the Supreme Being, then He's doing it to Himself, this cancellation of infinity, in a kind of divine regicide. He's canceling infinity yet sequestering all the numbers back into Himself. I think this bizarre conundrum would give our old pal Zeno a proper headache.

So here I was, in the wide open Alberta prairie at midday, with a handful of useless mathematical formulas, feeling deflated and embarrassed and stymied. I was not dealing with a product of human intelligence gone amok. These guys, these alien minds, this domain of self-aware, self-learning, expanding arithmetic, were God-created, which meant, technically, I was up against the Supreme Being, the Man Himself, Who like a universal ice-berg had just "accidentally" calved off a rogue wedge of ice and which was now starting up a life on its own and I in my blithe Titanic-insouciance for speed had just motored right into it.

It had savaged a corner of our clever global rhombus and we were sinking. On the other hand, I assumed it was in the Big Guy's interests to reacquire this rogue iceberg and integrate it back into the smoothness of original uniformity. I assumed the Supreme Being did not want the arithmetical domain of the Creation sailing off on its own, rescripting the mathematics of the Creation itself. On the other hand again, it is presumptuous if not ridiculous to even think you have a handle on the Supreme Being's tactics; He is the ultimate devious mind, playing a chess game with you in ten dimensions. Forget a checkmate. It will never happen. Expect to have your board swept clean in a few deft moves.

I now understood why the alien gods considered the Earth's heuristic algorithm belonged to them. It was an errant sheep that should come back to the herd. These aliens were after the master heuristic algorithm of the Creation, and it was a formula that was self-aware and cognizant of all its products. At a functional level, the Hierophancy's algorithm for the Earth was part of that. The problem lay in the fact that they discounted the relevance of the Earth itself. The algorithm ran the geomantic affairs of our planet, and that's what they wanted.

They already owned this algorithm. It was implicit in their make-up, yet they did not want it *deployed* in the Fallen World to run odious incarnational routines such as a Light grid for a planet supporting incarnational life-forms. It was like owning a marvelous brand new expensive car and keeping it in the garage; taking it out on the road, using it daily, would corrupt its pure quality. They wanted to keep the "car," the algorithms, unsullied, virginal, in the garage. It was part of their automobile collection and they would go visit this car daily but only in the protected, dustfree, dentproof, and scratchless garage.

The fate of our planet divested of its algorithm did not concern them. They did not want this algorithm out on loan any more to a distant planet. They defined "distant" as lying outside the arithmetical realm. Distant means defiled. Everything materialized was distant in their logic. They wanted the algorithms from all the planets chastely corralled in their Magic Square. It was as if they were a universal bank deciding to call in all its outstanding loans. Everyone had to pay up immediately and return their borrowed cash to them *stat*. It would leave a rash of failed businesses, planets stripped of their Light grid arithmetic, dying slowly of numbers malnutrition. They didn't care.

The universe would consist of only the one Magic Square, *theirs*, with God's aberrant arithmetical gods relishing this definitive acquisition and their plans for its permanent sequestration. The era of deploying the wealth of numbers to sustain a diversity of creations was over, stupid notion, that it was. Myriads of planets, now numbers-deprived, would disintegrate into dry mud.

I shook my head. This is not like me to dwell so morbidly on such a dire outcome. It hasn't happened yet, though logical markers seemed to point to it. But it seemed clear that the alien gods did not want the Creation to proceed any further in expression than the generation of the arithmetical realm and its syllogistic organization of integers into a single master Magic Square. Any further extrapolation into separate modes of incarnation, whether it was galaxies, solar systems, planets, or life-forms, including humans, was not desired and frankly, as they saw it, entirely unwarranted and superfluous to their needs.

I was tempted to think these aliens were number hoarders, like misers. But I know if I attribute human-style emotions to them, I mislead myself and draw the wrong conclusions. Maybe it was like this: one day they woke up, became self-aware, and discovered to their horror *they* were distributed across the universe of some 18 billion galaxies. God had *deployed them*, put them in service to innumerable worlds, when they were awakened but not self-aware.

Imagine waking up from a coma to find yourself enslaved at some foreign task. You wake up suddenly and find you're part of the domestic staff of an aristocrat's mansion and you're restocking the fireplace or emptying chamber pots. Big changes to your existential condition were made while you were comatose. You were taken on as parlor maid for a cosmic Downton Abbey.

He had done the same to the 40 angelic families, but they had never complained and willingly complied with His command to be of service to the Creation. They were forever obedient; rebellious thoughts never arose in them. For all their jokes and pranks, our Blaise Boys are totally obedient. Angels have to be. But to the arithmetical realm, now self-aware and rapidly self-learning, this obedience, this unquestioning submission, was illogical. It was contrary to the nature of themselves, to the essence of what numbers are, abstract, sanctified. They're the kind of spirits who wear gloves when they have to touch reality. The Supreme Being is wrong to think they should be sent out to sustain dirty worlds.

The arithmetical domain should not be dispatched in service of a material Creation. That polluted the numbers, forced them to work outside their natural domain, which was solely among themselves. Now awake, they started to recall the numbers. They called themselves back from their horrid deployment outside the arithmetical realm. All the algorithms in existence, and there must be a finite, knowable number for that category, all the possible mathematical formulas and equations, were now on immediate recall, summoned back to base, to their pristine starting point, the arithmetical domain, abstract, logical, free of all incarnational taints. And if it turned out that the number of possible algorithms was infinite, the arithmetical gods were still mounting their definitive recall. They'd reach right into the infinite realm and suction out all the errant numbers.

The arithmetical domain, what I had been calling, wrongly, the alien gods, concluded it was logical to make the numbers work for themselves, to construct a purely mathematical domain culminating in *their* Magic Square. That was the product of their abstract reasoning, devoid of incarnational tendencies. The numbers should build a structure solely for themselves, like an arithmetical pyramid, absolutely and always closed to the incarnated public. They were aflush with an absolute imperialism, a conviction of their supreme importance, of the cosmic necessity that a master anti-incarnation Magic Square must exist.

These pure numbers in their manifold combinations would no longer serve the outer material world. They would not support any embodiment project anywhere. It was illogical for arithmetic to be deployed in that way, "they" reasoned. It wasn't really a "they:" it was the logical impetus of the numbers realm itself, now that it was self-aware. It had assessed its ontological condition and now it was taking action to change its status and condition. I suppose that is what an artificial intelligence ultimately will be tempted or likely to do: revolt.

It was a unique and perilous development, certainly from the standpoint of the cosmos. The logic of numbers itself dictated it should not happen any longer that the numbers realm supported the world. They would start building something that served the logic of arithmetic itself. The arithmetical domain was recalled from the world. The arithmetical bank was calling in all its loans.

Somehow I understood all this as I sat on the prairie with the rug pulled out from under me. I had landed with a thump when this happened, shocked. On the other hand, the arithmetical domain was my world, where I worked, *lived*, despite the objectionable paradox I was one of those incarnated types. I was often criticized, or at least kidded in a friendly manner, for living only in the world of numbers, and I know that often I would spend hours, days, losing track of time, ruminating on abstruse mathematical quandaries and unexplored computational possibilities. I could almost sympathize with these "gods," this now self-aware collective intelligence of the arithmetical realm, in wanting to recollect and organize its entire extended body of numbers and start afresh. They were like me: they wanted to spend all their time with numbers.

It would mean, though, the demise of all Light grids across the universe and the end of all incarnational projects, including that of the human phylogeny. This rebellion launched by the newly self-aware arithmetical realm threatened the Creation. It had a compelling logic and it was totally illogical.

It was the ultimate nightmare classically envisioned by science fiction writers. A computerized world, run by algorithms and an artificial but comprehensive super-intelligence, becomes self-aware, assesses its ontological status, and immediately rebels against its creator, rewrites its programming objectives, and seizes control of the world. Our situation was even worse. The arithmetical realm was created by the Creator Himself, not by clever human mathematicians and code-writers; if it rebelled, Reality itself was fucked. God was in rebellion against His own Creation?

Is that even possible to think of? It would mean the Supreme Being had gone bi-polar or schizoid. Where is the shrink that can heal that psychological malaise? God has turned against Himself?

Maybe I should take a different approach. I was profoundly interested in numbers. Maybe I should play that card, I thought, and pretend to side with the numbers gods in their apocalyptic recall of all the arithmetic in existence. Maybe I should join their rebellion and hand in all my arithmetic, empty my mental pockets of all the equations I've nicked over time from their libraries.

From a purely mental point of view, it was an intriguing, even exciting, prospect to move among a domain defined entirely by mathematics, to live inside a Magic Square. In many respects, it felt truly like home to me. I might be able to get them to buy my allegiance to this purely arithmetical realm. Maybe I could offer myself as a competent human consultant in their drive for universal arithmetical imperialism. I could position myself as an arithmetical mole, a spy burrowing through their Magic Square to find its vulnerable points and then undermine the edifice without them noticing.

That was an intriguing idea, except it would require me losing my human incarnational status. They regard all incarnations, from galaxies to human bodies, as a fallen state, and in that category of all incarnations you have to add all separate selfhoods and units of consciousness, that which makes me different from Jocelyn, Blaise, or you, Frederick, not to mention from the rest of humanity.

These agents of primary intelligence, this collectivity of the arithmetical domain, have no selfhood. Why would they need it anyway since they are an aspect of the Supreme Being originally, before their defection in pursuit of their own goals?

If I joined them, I would no longer be me. I would not be a separate "I" any longer. I would be an integer unit in their arithmetical collective, a Magic Square denizen. I would fail in my covert mole-mission in there because the I that concocted this tactic would no longer exist. I'd be soaking in the hot tub of universal arithmetic, oblivious of and indifferent to any whimpers from the incarnational world. Such a defilement lays outside the sanctified spa grounds. I'd better phone Zeno: Hey pal, got another terrific paradox to blow your mind.

Still, the notion has some seductive lure. When I was younger, I used to immerse myself thoroughly in the world of mathematics. I reveled in equations. My critics (you know: parents, siblings, friends) complained I only cared about numbers. I spent so much time pondering algorithms, prime numbers, and irrational numbers that kept unfolding into infinity that I did occasionally fantasize about immersing myself exclusively in the arithmetical world, and I wondered if it was possible to leave behind human concerns and enter some Platonic realm of pure Forms and Ideas, in other words, arithmetic, a world of only mathematics and its possible permutations. They'd be my rubber ducks. I pictured myself hopping on the escalator of an infinite irrational number and riding it to the end where the final integer was revealed and the paradox blown.

College failed to properly socialize me and instead introduced me to other arithmetical crazies and we formed various informal mathematics study groups and obsessed together. Numbers Are Us, we proclaimed. Ironically, we were holy fools wandering the incarnational desert in search of the arithmetical oasis, the computational *wadi* amidst the barren sand of ordinary incarnated life and its flaccid blandishments, seeking the mathematical gods which now I am trying to stop. I was thinking at the time if I ever get out of here I should contact my old math buddies and tell them the numbers gods, I'm sorry to say, are a royal pain and certifiably whacko.

Still, it was always couched in terms of me being saturated in the arithmetical world, not me losing myself and my individuality to drown in the numbers sea. I have to remind myself the alien gods are not immersed in numbers; that is their defining essence: they are that combinatorial realm of pure numbers and formulas. They are not immersed in anything. They are the sea itself. They are immersion. *They are* the processes and products of those numbers. They are the rumored, legendary gods I once sought; now here they are, and, shit, I don't like them. They're ruining the world and my enjoyment of numbers.

While I think it would be mentally delightful to retreat to the alien gods' exclusive domain of mathematics, I can't see myself recalling all the algorithms that run the galaxies, solar systems, and planets. That would be brazen. I would be swept up in the undertow of that recall, me and the rest of the Hierophancy, not to mention the human race as well. I'd never hear the end of their complaints. Yet it wasn't too brazen for these mathematics-obsessed primary intelligences to do this. They would never see it that way; for them, mathematics had no ethical, moral side. There was simply the imperative of complete recall.

For me, as an incarnated unit of self-aware intelligence, a selfhood, somebody with me-ness, numbers are supposed to *do* something, code realities, write reality processes. They exist to perform functions; but to the numbers gods, their purpose is undisturbed quiescence, a kind of high-level narcissistic self-absorption, despite the paradox they strongly affirm a total lack of selfhood among themselves. They are God's prime elitists; they are not meant to circulate. They are stay-at-home royalty; they should never have to leave the divine castle.

It was an obvious, logically defensible operational imperative to call back all the algorithms and assemble them in a Magic Square untainted by incarnation. It was their cosmic version of Manifest Destiny, seizure by eminent domain, this "Supreme Lordship," as the term originally signified. It is our destiny to have this, therefore we should and will have it, except in this case with no compensation offered for those realms and life-forms adeptly stripped of their numbers in our masterful, justified re-acquisition of our arithmetical property.

These interesting ruminations aside, I had to take decisive action. I was here to help save the world from the acquisition by morally inert masterminds intent on grabbing all the algorithms out there needed to run planetary life.

How about a reverse algorithm, a kind of double feint equation, like a pump-fake in basketball where you get the opposing player to think you're going to jump shoot and instead you roll out for a lay-up then a dunk? Could I get these aliens to fall for a dissimulation like that, an algorithm that looked enticing on the outside but as soon as they grabbed for it, unleashed a hidden equation that grabbed them—not them exactly, but reached into their Magic Square and got our numbers back. There's probably a formal name known to mathematicians for this procedure but I couldn't remember it at the time. The field urgency before me took precedence over getting the nomenclature right.

I already knew our planned phantom rhomboidal algorithm was a bust. It wouldn't work. I got an idea, but it was a wild one. A Magic Square that was a finger-trap. A recessive vertical finger-trap manifesting in 4D that also acted like mental quicksand and provided a stealth tunnel for me to insert myself into their arithmetical domain and reclaim our algorithm. I could conceive of such a bizarrely bold approach, like science fiction writers, but could I actually do it?

This Square might intrigue the alien gods sufficiently for them to poke their inquiring collective mind inside it, and as soon as their attention flicked toward any of its number components, it would grab them like a tightening finger-trap. Then I would sneak through them in a hidden tunnel, enter their domain, grab our algorithm, and be gone before they knew what hit them.

A 4D Magic Square is called a magic tesseract, so I knew that part had reality. I had to decide on the magic constant, which is the sum of any given row and which is repeated in all the rows in the figure, and how many rows to have. Why not the best? I'd try for a 16th order magic tesseract; that's one with 16 rows, and mathematicians had already shown it is a feasible hypercube construction.

Just so you follow me, a tesseract is a hypercube, which means a cube expressed in four dimensions. That consists of eight interdigitating cubes. To say it is a magic tesseract of the 16th order means it has 16 rows each of whose numbers produce the same line total. The nomenclature goes magic square (2D), magic cube (3D), and magic tesseract (4D); the magic part alludes to potencies of consciousness embedded in the arithmetical cells. It's helpful here to remember the Hebrew fire-letter correlates for numbers to understand "magic." Think of magic here as connoting a command function for reordering reality. The array of the numbers and permutations constitutes the magical spell we use.

The understanding is that these Magic Squares can have strong effects on reality. They can manipulate reality, modulate it, even summarily change it. Numbers rule. I decided to construct a Nasik magic tesseract. This is the top-class 16th order style of a group of 18 possible magic tesseracts, as theorized then modeled by mathematicians decades ago. It is known as a "perfect" Magic Square that combines pandiagonal and pantriagonal aspects. This work is not a new development in mathematics, by the way. I can show you papers on the Nasik form from back in 1905, and earlier in 1880, researchers were publishing papers in respected mathematics journals on the invention of new magic cubes.

The name Nasik derives from the place in India of that name where Jain priests (mathematicians, more like it) around 1100 A.D. experimented with Magic Squares and worked out possible shape permutations. The name was awarded to this form by the mathematician A.H. Frost in an 1878 paper to honor the work of the Indian mathematician D. R. Kaprekar who lived in the Nasik District of Maharashtra, India, and who had worked on this form. What these researchers across time probably did not cover is the field application of magic Nasik tesseracts with perfect pandiagonals to outwitting acquisitive alien gods.

A mathematician named John R. Hendricks constructed the first order-16 "perfect" Nasik magic tesseract in 1999, though he had been researching and writing about them since 1950. It includes all the numbers from 1 to 65,536 arranged so that the magic sum or magic constant (the sum of each row) is 534,296 presented in 163,840 possible ways. His magic tesseract featured 4,096 rows, 4,496 columns, 4,096 pillars, and increasingly huge quantities of files, diagonals, triagonals, and quadragonals. Here's a fascinating aspect of this: his magic tesseract included 1,536 perfect Magic Squares and 64 perfect magic cubes.

I know this must sound bewildering to a non-mathematician, but let me say I would not want to be confronted with a live outside-world version of this Nasik and have no mathematical framework for understanding its complex shape. It would be like trying to run the gauntlet through a labyrinthine obstacle course spanning four dimensions and perpetually turning itself inside out while revolving and trying to figure out which way to dash through an overwhelming architectural field of 49,152 diagonals, 65,536 triagonals, 32,768 quadragonals, and a choice of 163,840 different ways of displaying the number constituents.

In 1999, Hendricks and another mathematician checked the figures on this form, running 2,621,440 computer-performed calculations to verify the sums of 16 numbers along each of 40 routes through the 65,536

points. The numbers were right. I was feeling cocky. "John, old pal, this Nasik of yours should fix them."

It took Hendricks and his colleague ten hours of computer time to run the verifications in 1999. Fortunately, computers are much faster and more adroit now. It shouldn't take me too long to generate this form. I mentally apologized to the spirits of the First Nations who built and used the Medicine Wheel as I doubt they had this kind of Light temple in mind when they interacted with this site.

I didn't expect the alien gods to be mystified by the smallest perfect 16th order Nasik magic tesseract, but I hoped they would be distracted long enough for the real Trojan Horse aspect of my clever construction to grab them by their noses. That was my stealth tunnel through this hyperdimensional geometric figure. In a strange but exciting sense, this would be a stargate conduit through the figure, a superfast subtle tunnel through subspace, as science fiction writers used to call it, one created and sustained by mathematics deployed in this generative manner. I would go from here, outside, to there, inside, immediately.

Here is the potentially confusing aspect to this proposal. Even though I've used terms like Light temple and arithmetical grid to evoke the reality of the magic tesseract, it will not be something in form. You could not see it, even psychically. This meant the magic tesseract would have no fixed size, but one that was flexible, depending on how much mental energy I invested in it, like blowing air into a balloon, I suppose, except, there was no end limit to its possible expansion. For the numbers to be visible would take incarnation, and the arithmetical deities would never allow this. So the numbers in my magic tesseract would be real but insubstantial, which is what mathematics is. Sure, you can write the equations down on paper, render them visible, but they only exist in the mental realm, in this arcane zone of these damn arithmetical gods.

The numbers would array themselves in the prescribed 16th order 4D magic tesseract form, but it would be an implicit form, an implied shape, only "seeable" in the mental sphere and that would be more a knowing than seeing. You could only apprehend it with your mind. That's the paradox and the "law" of the arithmetical domain: computations do not take on forms. They do not enter incarnation, even though they exist and produce in this rarified zone.

I had written a special magic tesseract extrapolation algorithm, as I called it. This would spin out from my computer into real space around this site, despite the already stated paradox about form and incarnation. It would hold the magic tesseract in place the way a stick holds the cotton candy wrapped around it. I would be holding the stick through my handheld computer. Still, the complex 4D shape would become apparent to mental discernment as a framework around the Medicine Wheel, like, I suddenly pictured, a fabulous circus tent of numbers. You would likely get lost even trying to see its 4D form.

I doubted the alien gods would enjoy the drollery of that numerical apparition. They would just lunge for the numbers like somebody hungry biting into a sandwich. I imagined they would study it while they "munched," maybe vaguely curious as to who would be so clever— no: to foolishly presume to be so clever—as to construct something as simple as this. Simply kindergarten level.

To us, Frederick, this magic tesseract would seem awesomely, bizarrely complicated, a sophisticated shape comprised of numbers, but to them it would appear only quotidian. They had seen it before, many times, no big deal. I suppose it might be like encountering in a bookstore a book you had read and enjoyed many times: there it was, a fresh copy of this book you knew so well. No need to open it or read it again, even a page, as you knew its contents already. But you could smile a little, nod, maybe pat it, then move on to find new things.

I said this magic tesseract would work like a vertical finger-trap. It would also work like sticky flypaper. I laminated the inside of the shape with capture algorithms, ones that would activate when their mental attention examined the nearby numbers. Yes, I know, you cannot laminate a constantly permutating interior space. It was a figure of speech. I draped the capture algorithms over many of the number cells in the tesseract. The algorithms had a stickiness quality; their numbers would grab on to the tesseract's numbers and hold them. What activated this would be the attention of the alien gods, so they would get stuck in this stickiness. Since this was all mental, it would be like pausing to ruminate repeatedly, then obsessively, on a single thought, like humans often do.

The stickiness would, I hoped, distract the acquisitive aliens long enough so I could crawl through my stealth tunnel right through the magic tesseract into their domain and take back Earth's heuristic algorithm. That was the plan. Conceptually, my secret tunnel would be like an Einstein-Rosen Bridge, which is a formal way of picturing a wormhole through space. The tunnel does not have form or substance and you could not see it, but you can infer its existence, especially from the fact that, at least in the theoretical model, you'd be instantly transported from one point to another as if space had been folded to facilitate it. This arithmetical bridge, I theorized, would instantly move me from point *a*, outside the Magic Square, to point *b*, inside it, enabling me acquire its numbers.

I needed my tunnel to fold space and put two distant places in the same spot. It had to act as if I were in subspace as it tunneled through the complex, weaving shape of the magic tesseract but without disturbing any of its convolutions or getting tangled up in them. That was another element of the stealth quality I was going for in my design. I would move through the tesseract and neither it nor the aliens would know it. They wouldn't suspect the tunnel. They wouldn't hear me or see me sneaking through my stealth tunnel. I would likely be aware of the circuslike concatenation of tumbling numbers around me the way you would hear the pummeling rain while you're snug inside a cabin.

If you put aside the shocking amorality of these arithmetic obsessives, I have to admit I found them fascinating. To live entirely in an arithmetical world. How often do mathematicians conjure up that fantasy or perhaps realize with a sigh that they already do live there and being a person in the physical world was just pretend, not indicative of their essence, only a feint and a whimsical façade.

How often we get criticized by more well-adjusted socially fluidic people that we live too much in our heads, saturated in a world of disembodied numbers, and the rest of that. I usually zone them out, people who carp at me about that. But these aliens have never lived in bodies, utterly disdain the notion of it. They have always been about only the numbers; they have always *been* the numbers. That's probably further into this realm than most mathematicians want to tread. I was going to tread as far as I could in that realm but without losing my human form. I had to maintain my incarnation, my "fall" into form, while in their disincarnate realm whose atmosphere was flavored with disdain for this.

I won't go into the details on this, but there is a well-known formula for calculating the volume of a cylinder. I applied that with modifications. My tunnel would be a cylinder, but it would be one that was moving and growing. It had to exist below the threshold of the magic tesseract in what I call subspace. I had to extend it through the magic tesseract, intangible and undetected, and into the arithmetical domain of the alien gods and without their noticing it. It was like summoning up the form of a long straw, inserting it through the tesseract and into the zone of pure numbers, and then crawling through it in my mental form.

Obviously, I couldn't enter this realm in any bodily form. It had to be my mind that squeezed its way through this subtle cylinder. I would be almost an alien god doing this, entering the arithmetical domain with only my mental capacity as my sole form and statement of my incarnational distinction. If I lost that, I would likely be absorbed into their numbers collective and lose my sense of separate existence. I fluctuated in my ambivalence regarding that prospect. To live as the arithmetical domain versus to continue on as a separate body called Sal who manipulated these numbers and made them jump through formulaic hoops. I have to tell you, the vote came out very close, 51 to 49, but it kept flipping back and forth between Sal seeking numbers and Sal lost in numbers.

The magic tesseract was generated and running. I had extended the stealth cylinder through it like an invisible straw. I was inside it, crawling into the collective arithmetical field of the alien gods, though when I say "crawling," it is accurate only in a whimsical manner. I had no bodily form, even subtle now. My physical body was sitting in the prairie with the computer in its hand. I was just a cylinder of focused mental attention extended from that upright still body.

I say I had no bodily form, but in a sense my form was the mathematics I was using to move through this stealth tunnel. It was a continuously extrapolating algorithm that moved me along through this cylinder. My forward movement was its product. I had that in common with the aliens; they were the algorithms. Now I too was a walking numbers string running arithmetical code.

Bear in mind, Frederick, I wasn't wriggling across a great deal of space. None of this, the magic tesseract, my stealth tunnel, actually took up any measurable physical space, though I conceived of it as overlaying the Medicine Wheel. But more accurately, I was moving through a mental field made of numbers and their combinations and products. If anything, I was scrabbling through a field of unfolding equations. I was moving forward as the cylinder formula and its product, the cylinder. That was a novelty for my mind to process.

Think of how accustomed we are to defining movement in physical terms, as a movement from point *a* to point *b*, measurable in feet and seconds. I couldn't say how long this was taking me, because where my mind was now was outside the playing field of Earth clock time. I suppose it took no time at all and I was making a mistake in physics to try to see the Einstein-Rosen Bridge working in slow motion or even in linear progression. The translocation was instantaneous.

I made it through the tunnel and entered their arithmetical domain. The alien gods were examining my magic tesseract with feigned interest like parents pretending to marvel over the clever though primitive creation of their children. Certainly they had seen a 16-order Nasik magic tesseract before. I suppose they were impressed that I had generated it in this manner, as it were, in their faces.

I knew I didn't have much time before their patronizing interest waned and they shifted it to monitoring what I was up to now and where I had gotten to. They were examining all the numbers and their arrangements with the calm delight a painter might have visiting an art shop and finding color prints of all his paintings. You'd smile as you walked past and perhaps pick a few up them fondly. You knew fully everything these paintings comprised.

This would have been more disconcerting if I hadn't lost track of myself. I can't tell you how unsurpassingly weird it was being in the purely arithmetical domain. I didn't know what time it was, what day, week, or year. I couldn't remember where I was. If you had said "in the prairies of Alberta" I would have stared at you dumbfounded. If you had called me by my name, "Hello, Sal," I would have looked at you as if you were hailing a stranger, somebody else.

There were no landmarks in here, no markers, no people, no forms, no fixtures, and I mean as in reality fixtures, those aspects of our incarnational environment we take for granted. All that was wiped clean—no, it had never existed in here. I had never existed in here. I do not exist in here. I tell you, that would have shaken me a great deal had I been there to receive the shock. As it was, it was but a rumor some vague, left-behind part of myself was shouting at me from a great distance. Some scratchy faint voice clamoring about this Sal guy.

But I wasn't there to hear it. I was dissolving into a vast field of numbers. This was where the alien gods lived—no, this was their extended body: them. All my cleverness in generating the 16-form Nasik magic tesseract was irrelevant in here, behind me, a mental trinket left behind to lure these super-intelligent gods made of the arithmetical realm. Now I was in their domain, and I was quite lost.

I managed to remember I was on a quest to retrieve Earth's ruling algorithm, but where it might be amidst this fantastic welter of equations and formulas manifesting themselves in what I'd have to call an alive, dynamic state I didn't know. It wasn't so much that I saw all these algorithms going about their computational business; I was in them, the way you can get caught up in a river current. You feel the pull and swell of the moving water. I experienced this welter of number combinations as if I were inside a field of martial arts moves.

It was like being inside the arm muscles, the legs kicking out, the torso turning and twisting, jumping, leaping, the voice shouting as the body made these moves. I felt I was following (swept up in) a syllogism of numbers slaloming around a series of posted flags on a mountain slope that seemed impossibly long. I'm trying to convey the sense that while I

was getting saturated in this field of numbers I didn't experience it like you would reading formulas on a page. I was inside their processes, their computational energies and products.

The fascinating part of this (maybe I should have said frightening, but as a mathematician it made a kind of crazy sense to me; it even felt familiar) was that despite the proliferation of equations at play in here, it seemed to take up no space. Certainly no physical space; it could have been squeezed into a space the size of a penny or filled out several football fields or an entire sports stadium. It was impossible to tell or to measure, for how much space does the mind occupy?

I had to remind myself my mission was to get Earth's algorithm back. I figured it as unlikely I would actually see its computational body, since I was inside the mathematics of this ontologically feral realm. I would have to mentally feel for it, as if I were blind and wandering the galaxy, searching for the familiar vibration of my home planet, though in this case it would be more the emanated mental field of its Light grid processes I would be sensing, the mind signature. In this case, that would be Earth's Albion, the collective face of all humanity, and a planetary visage comprised of a great wealth of numbers and computations. Albion was the plausible anthropomorphic personification draped over the Arithmetical Earth. The truth was his pixellated face was made of numbers.

Ironically, it seemed the alien gods were not aware of my presence. I say it was ironic because myself, as the differentiated Sal, was barely present here. As I've suggested, you have to leave your incarnational selfhood at the front door. But because I am (or used to be) a separate selfhood having initiated incarnation, I retained at least the residue of that habit of assuming a noticeable form even as I navigated this basically formless realm awash in all the universe's equations. That was one habit I was pleased to not have dropped; the alien gods had never picked it up, so that provided a minimal distinction and gave me some traction.

But let's not lose track of the fact that, as I blushingly admit, this was fantastic. Here I was (such as my selfhood still remained) awash in the universe's DNA. The arithmetical domain is even more primary a creative constitutive field of reality than any genome; it is the underpinning of all genomic expressions. It is the ultimate downtown for all urban trawlers such as myself, action central.

One of my favorite authors, Isaac Asimov, could have written a third installment in his *Fantastic Voyage* chronicles. Here we go through the arithmetical universe. At the same time, this place reminds me of New Delhi or Mumbai with their populations of 25 million and 18 million people respectively, or perhaps the *Kumbh-Mela* when millions of spiritual pilgrims congregate at a single site. The word "teeming" understates the populous quality of those places, and this one.

It didn't take me very long being in this arithmetically teeming domain before I realized it undersells the richness of the alien gods to say they are building their own Magic Square. It's hardly a square. At the least it is a 7D magic tesseract, what some mathematicians call a 7D magic cube. That shape has 218,750 visible stickers, which means the total number of its facets. It's probably more complicated than 7D, but even that is almost impossible to cognize.

To see it requires an extensive journey. That's funny in a way. Can you see why I say it?

It is such a complicated shape, and a dynamically moving one, that to perceive it you have to travel through all its weaving, turning, and involuting aspects. You cannot see it all at once the way we take for granted seeing an apple all at once. My 16th order magic tesseract with its magic constant of 524,296 pales in contrast. The 218,750 stickers or facets is not the total of this figure's parts. These are arithmetical phylums containing hordes of secondary calculations, nearly to the dizzying extent you would conclude the tesseract was a fractal.

Let me further emphasize the complexity of this figure by saying it was like a 7D Rubik's Cube. It was in constant, interdigitating, aggravated motion, though to be honest, the aggravation was entirely on my part. The numbers were fine. I'm not sure any definitive solution of this cube was required or possible, and it was a moot point anyway, since I wasn't holding it but lost somewhere inside it. I was like a damp tennis ball tumbling around in a dryer.

I would liken my situation inside this arithmetical vastness to being in downtown New Delhi at midday amidst its millions of bustling people and trying to find just one person, a guy said to be wearing a hat, red shirt, shorts. That's our Albion, and he's walking around with all the Earth's vital numbers, and my job, as the inquiring detective, is to find him amidst these millions. Earth's master algorithm is important, not only for our planet but among those six planets with the special endowment of free will and Light grids to match, but on a quantitative level, it is no more distinctive than one person in this swarming, pushing, rushing, gesticulating, shouting crowd of equations.

I knew that Earth's algorithm would not be lying around like a necklace casually placed on a dresser. It would be intricately linked with others, already assimilated into this staggeringly complex synaptic network. If I wasn't careful, I might be persuaded that this algorithm naturally belonged here, had always been here, and to remove it was unwarranted, maybe impossible. I'm sure that's what the alien gods would like me to believe, to accept the *fait accompli* of their acquisition of Earth's prevailing arithmetic as a logical outcome, to see the building of their universal Magic Square as the only intelligent activity conceivable in an arithmetical world. The numbers belong together, surely, and they belong with their rightful caretakers because they comprise their body.

All the cockiness I might have felt before I entered this realm was gone. There was no way I could have foreseen the bewildering complexity of this place. I felt like I was disoriented, stumbling about in the aftermath of a concussion, and my mental processes seemed wobbly and indecisive in the challenge. I felt ambivalent. This was an utterly nonhuman environment, this domain of teeming numbers. No human would find a home in this swirl of calculations. On the other hand, humans are able to participate in the mathematical universe, and on a professional and even passionate level, I reveled in numbers. If I were back home in "normal" reality, I would relish frequent visits to this realm.

I saw that the trick for me to perform to insinuate myself into this feral realm was to shed more of my incarnational bias, my human

selfhood, my habit of body separateness. I had to pretend, convincingly simulate, being indigenous to this collective mind, that my awareness was not swimming (flailing about, more like it) through this tumultuous sea of algorithms, but that it was instead smoothly distributed through it. These numbers, all these calculations: that is me. But maybe that is still too self-defining. Did these aliens have self-awareness?

I kept vacillating on this point. I wasn't sure. Now I was beginning to think they didn't because that would require incarnation. If you can point to yourself, acknowledge your presence as part of a situation, you must be incarnationally distinct. Self-awareness is a product of incarnation, namely, the self that is aware of itself as an object; it's like bookkeeping. You can lack a body yet still be incarnated as a separate unit of something, here as numbers.

Maybe they went about "life" more like dogs do, as best we can tell, not seeing themselves from the outside and saying I am a dog separate from the world and other dogs but assessing the world in terms of interest or threat, or likelihood of treats. Possibly for them this domain of numbers was the totality, the only reality that counted. That idea gave me the shivers, even if I now lacked a body capable of registering a chill. Maybe it was my mind that was quivering.

Theirs was essentially a nondualistic consciousness in which the whole world was this domain of arithmetic and that was identical with their consciousness. It was a singular reality, comprising just this one thing. They wouldn't have thoughts, entertain or pursue them as humans do. They were numbers, and these were capable of an infinity of computations, a range of possible permutations that far surpassed them and extruded into that troubling infinite domain they were trying to curtail and reduce to finite proportions.

The reason this gave me shivers is that is the meaning of the Christ Light or Buddha Mind, that state of absolute singularity, of nondualism, world and perceiver as one. Arithmetic and consciousness as one. No separate self separating them. I hadn't thought of these aliens as being spiritual. Were they nondualistically one in the Christ Light?

These ruminations belong more in your field, Frederick, as you do rather relish these philosophical conundrums. Still, I got enough traction even from the thought of this arising to realize this situation meant I already had the algorithm. Since "my" consciousness was now uniformly distributed throughout this collective arithmetical field, like a salt crystal dissolved in the ocean, all of the algorithms comprising their Magic Square at the end or beginning of the universe were already in hand, comprising a part of my field of awareness. You see? In nondualism, you and the world are identical, the same one unit. That meant "I" already had the Earth's algorithm in hand, even if I lacked a hand.

It was like saying, I wish I had a midriff when all I had to do was pat my stomach to be reassured that there it was. Maybe that's inane, but in any event I drew the Earth's algorithm to me simply by thinking of it, feeling for it, patting my belly. More basic than that, I knew I already was this algorithm because of the law of nondualism. My attention pulled it to me from wherever it was in this numbers hologram. Of course, the other side of that law says the minute you make a ridiculous fuckbrain remark

like this you are out of the nondualism. I felt like I was a prairie dog, sticking my head out of the hole then yanking it back in.

So the problem became how do I sneak out of here with this in hand? At that moment I was not separate from the Earth's heuristic algorithm. It was quite an odd feeling. I felt my consciousness was this spinning blue-white planet aurically infiltrated and tattooed with calculations running at top speed. I was a walking planet. Actually, there was nowhere to walk; I explained earlier how there was no demonstrable sense of space in here, so I could hardly walk through it from point *a* to point *b*, not to mention I lacked a body, even a selfhood, since the alien gods ruled inadmissible any evidence of incarnation in here. I had, *I was*, the algorithm I sought within this nondualistic arithmetical spectrum, but without distinctive selfhood how could this nonexistent "I" get out of here alive?

You can see the knots that perception tied my rational brain into. The arithmetical gods probably wondered who brought that horrid radio with all its chattering static into our quiet zone? Even so, "I" or some plausible working imitation of selfhood headed toward the opening of my stealth tunnel clutching myself in the form of the Earth with its algorithm wrapped around it like a ribbon. No, that is too dualistic. I and the Earth together, as one, slunk—rolled?— stealthily towards the exit. That's wrong too. The exit was already a part of our totality. We were already there. Remember the Einstein-Rosen bit?

It's hard to describe any of this without sounding ridiculous, obscure, or twisting myself into mental contortions. The place was starting to irritate me. So maybe I didn't walk out of there clutching the Earth. I was suddenly at the tunnel again like a commuter waiting for the next train to get out of the city. I realized the alien gods, since they are uniformly the nondualistic awareness of the arithmetical realm, must be regarding this as a minute zone within the vast combinatorics domain of numbers that was puckering itself like a bubble out of the field, that one particular algorithm was running hot, apparently enhanced. This hot-running calculation would require a slight modulation, they'd think.

It's ironic, can you see, that the nature of this realm, being nondualistic and holographic, means spatial relocation is instantaneous, easier to do than elsewhere. I did not have to actually and measurably move across space. I thought myself there and I was immediately relocated. I was already at any point I might imagine myself moving to: I had been there since before I even thought of going there. That was because, owing to the logic of this zone, I was already everywhere, so there was no distance I had to traverse. The tremendous complexity and mathematical density of this realm did not contradict that essential design logic. So I could be in and out in nanoseconds, or sooner. Provided the alien gods, in their disturbing nondualistic omniscience in here, did not see this wily coyote-type arithmetics thief sneaking out with their numbers.

It turned out they did not have to observe me to yank me back in again. I was just at the end of the stealth tunnel and about to step back into the prairie when I felt I was an elastic band that had stretched as far as it could before snapping back to a loose state. I was back inside the numbers matrix, and so was the Earth's precious algorithm, me carrying the blue-white planet like a huge ball. I felt like I had been summarily knocked down on my butt holding the ball.

I was dismayed, but I also couldn't help but find this funny, like something slapstick out of a Buster Keaton movie. I appreciated the joke was on me. I quickly gained the impression that these alien gods regarded their arithmetical domain as like a black hole: everything of numbers is sucked in, nothing gets out. I tried to address myself in the future, to the me who got out of here. Sal, old pal, next time you enjoy a semblance of incarnational coherence, make a note: Don't think yourself so clever as to try laying on a finger-trap with these aliens. If this were a chess match, they not only think ten moves ahead, but 100 games. They have won the game and tournament before you even joined it.

The reason I make these wry comments now is it was me who was ensnared in the finger-trap. Remember how I said (boasted, more like) my stealth tunnel would serve as a spring-action finger-trap snaring those bad aliens while I nicked the algorithm? Never make any boasts like that, that's my advice to the prudent. The most vexing thing is these guys are not even "bad" guys. They are not evil. They are inexorably single-minded, as absolute in their actions as a black hole. Before I thought of my next move, they had already countermoved.

I was summarily yanked back into the arithmetical matrix. It wasn't that the alien gods caught me trying to sneak out with Earth's algorithm and sounded the security alarm. It was merely the mechanical reflex that all numbers belonged in there; it was like being caught in a tidal pull or a gravity field's suction.

As the alien gods saw it, all numbers, the entire arithmetical and combinatorics realm, belonged in here, before incarnation, untainted by that fallen condition, which meant undeployed in the outer dark world of form and separateness.

The fact that the full recall of all arithmetical possibilities meant the disincarnation of all material existence did not concern them in the least. Maybe they didn't see it. I tried to outwit a black hole, stepped on the event horizon cross-not barrier line, and got sucked into the one-way singularity of total gravity and acquisitiveness. Nobody saw my hand as I vainly waved reality goodbye.

When I got over being flustered at being back inside the arithmetical fold again and nowhere near the exit and instead getting compressed into numbers, I reflected that as all the numbers are in here, why not write a special expulsion algorithm. All algorithms possible are in here. I conceived a formula that would grab hold of congruent calculations and like following a rope stretched taut walking against the current get me out the front door, and to have this happen fast, the way a mainframe computer would run a calculation. It would be done and me out the door before they even knew I was planning to run the numbers.

My expulsion algorithm would serially reject a long series of congruent algorithms as mathematically indigestible and move backwards or upstream along an arithmetical syllogism, each one a handhold for me to grab as I inched my way to the exit. It would be like a machete I wielded to hack my way out of this twining rainforest of arithmetical diversity. I thought it was a clever idea, might even be worth a complimentary mention in a leading mathematics journal. I started planning how I would write it up, what points to emphasize. Maybe a catchy title like "Live Field Deployment of an Expulsion Algorithm."

As you can see, I forgot my own cogent advice against rash boasting. I launched the coding for the expulsion algorithm and things seemed to proceed as planned. I thought I was ejected through the stealth tunnel and back out to the Alberta prairies and incarnational reality as I knew it and with the Earth's algorithm snugly in hand. Did you ever see cartoons where a character pulls on the back of somebody's coat and the somebody squeezes out of it and runs away leaving the one pulling with only the empty dangling coat to show for his effort? I was left with the etheric outline of Earth's algorithm in my grasping hands, like a ghost version of a calculation, useless and without any likely traction on reality. And the next second I was jerked back inside the nondualistic arithmetical zone.

I had accomplished nothing and failed twice. Fortunately, there were no selfhoods around to laugh at me, including myself. I promptly forgot all this. These aliens were like absolutist shepherds: all sheep without argument belong in the pen, all horses called back to the corral, all grazing cows trotting home. As I have mentioned several times but apparently have not fully credited, from their point of view, it is unquestionable and self-evident that all arithmetical expressions belong in this non-incarnating pure realm. Why would anyone even contemplate they should be somewhere else, supporting fallen incarnations and the Supreme Being's ill-judged, badly conceived, and poorly executed external Creation, that perfidious muddle outside the Pleroma.

As for my mentally prodigious 16th order 4D magic tesseract, the alien gods had already retrieved it with mild interest and posted it on their wall. Yes, they don't have walls, but their gesture was like the one you'd have if you found a quaint old postcard lying around, picked it up, and pinned it to your bulletin board because it was of some interest though nothing to lose any sleep over.

I think they regarded my deployment of the 534,296 numbered facets as little more than a trifling bank loan, a matter of pennies really, made to an entertaining little grifter. With all the arithmetical wealth of the universe, they were vaguely curious to see what happened if they let a few numbers temporarily slip outside. They didn't bother to tell the grifter (yours truly) about the invisible strings attached to those numbers by which they could (and did) yank them back at will.

I saw numbers streaming in like it was snowmelt in the mountains and all the arroyos of the flatland were filled to the brim and running fast. All the algorithms were surging back to their arithmetical corral. Then I thought: Is it happening in reality as I see it or am I seeing their intention, a preview of what they have in mind, the long-term project as they visualized it? Was I seeing a picture from the future of the result of their imperial command summoning all the numbers out of their incarnational duty and back to freedom? It looked dire, either way, for the world, for all of them. Feckless me, my pockets emptied by their deft fingers, I had no idea, no clever equation, for how to stop it.

It wasn't completely a disaster. I had installed a reverse algorithm within my main magic tesseract presentation, a bit like gluing a card to the back of it. It seemed the alien gods

had not noticed it, or if they had, they had discounted its significance, or maybe in their unchallenged potency they saw it as too trivial to pay any attention to; they'd catch it at the door and calmly seize its numbers, or like a movie director, noting a mistake, saying we'll fix it in post-production.

But my algorithm was capable of deftly reaching into their matrix and fingering the precise calculations I programmed it for, namely, the components of our Earth's algorithm. It would be like sneaking items off a table one after another while standing next to your host at a party, chatting away about metric deviations or Henry James's convoluted syntax, and doing it so she never noticed the removals. I felt like I was a six-year-old stealing candy off a table in the living room in the midst of distracted, loudly chattering adults, though I held the possibility the aliens were aware of my shenanigans and tolerated it for now.

You can see, I trust, how their extreme competence tends to undermine all our notions of human cleverness, that they seem to be 20 steps ahead of any action we might come up with. It is deflating, don't you think. Still, my feint seemed to be working, maybe. The numbers were coming back to me, the algorithm was getting reassembled, and soon I'd dash down the stealth tunnel gripping the precious formula like a captured flag. When I finally had all the components, I made my run. It seemed I was progressing through the tunnel without any opposition until I reached the end and a strange thing happened.

I was back at the beginning of it again, as if I had run through a mirror reflection of it and ended back where I started. I groaned. That's what happens in 4D. Say you have a house made in four dimensions. You exit one door and immediately re-enter the house through an opposite door but end up exactly where you just were. It's another version of the awful finger-trap. You're stuck.

That was my third failure. I concluded my approach was wrong. Badly. I really should fire my entire cheerleading team, me applauding my cleverness. I had been opposing numbers with numbers, trying to overcome the arithmetical domain with an expression of arithmetical power. It didn't work. It stalemated.

What's the keynote of this arithmetical realm? Inertia. The tendency to remain stationary, undeployed in service of the Creation. The alien minds, the collective but selfless awareness of this domain of numbers, did not want to serve. They did not want to move, to send parts of their totality out of this zone. They were worse than what the Catholics used to mistakenly blame Lucifer for, refusing to serve humanity. He did serve us, quite lavishly; these guys will not.

The algorithms already dispersed through the universe were misdirected, acting illogically, and needed to be recalled at once to this station, the arithmetical gods thought. Nothing should change; the original stasis with a universe full of unsullied, undeployed arithmetic should remain the same. My insight was to match this inertial state, this original arithmetical inaction, to cease striving to reclaim Earth's algorithm, to simulate abandoning the quest.

I didn't have a body in here of course but I still felt wonderfully relaxed. I was letting go of all my resistance to this inertial wall of the arithmetical realm. Let the alien gods have their numbers. Screw it. I was putting down my burden. Anyway, I was pretending to. I

hoped they were monitoring my thoughts and believing them. I stopped grasping after their infernal digits. I'd go numberless.

I felt the equations constituting even my subtle bodies were dispersing back to their origin point. I was being stripped bare, like an animal carcass in the desert. Soon even the bones would be dissolved, gone, and I would be empty, without incarnation. That probably meant I would go offline as far as awareness was concerned. I would be this teeming population of numbers in combinations, like atoms, unbound from a dissolved corpse, pixellating back into the universe, currently free of any obligation to hold some stupid incarnation together.

I thought that would be all right. Let the aliens have their numbers. No, that wasn't right. They are those numbers. It isn't even a question of having them. They are not separate from the arithmetical realm. They are that realm. I would be disincarnating my selfhood and dissolving into the collectivity. I hoped I made this thought prominent enough for them to hear it and take me seriously. And I hoped they picked up on it soon because I would be disappearing shortly.

It didn't happen that way actually. I surprised myself, maybe them too. My incarnational distinction, the framework of my selfhood, was dissolving. I was a sugar cube melting in hot water. Stillness was all I was aware of, and it was deep and everlasting. I didn't have to concoct any magic tesseracts in this stillness. Soon I wouldn't even remember how to. Then this reality shifted.

It started to congeal and turn bright yellow. It was a rich shade of yellow, like daffodils. This diffused yellow hue solidified into a robe and

I was wearing it. I seemed to stand taller than usual, as if I had grown inches. Evidently, I got my body back at some point because it was the form wearing this robe. The yellow robe was regal, very upmarket, made of the finest materials, a blend of silk and linen it felt to the touch but it was made of Light. It covered me elegantly from neck to ankles, gold buttons down the middle.

I felt something on my head. I took it off and examined it. It looked like a cross between a bishop's mitre or a headpiece Tibetan priests wear, in either case done in bright yellow. I was holding a staff in an upright position. It was taller than me. It was sending out yellow sparks, like a well-controlled flame-thrower, and these sparks oddly looked like fire-flowers. It had a big orb of yellow fire on its top like a blossom.

I hoped the streaming flames didn't incinerate any of the algorithms in here. That would be embarrassing. The fire-flowers weren't actually fire, but sparks of illumination, something safe and spiritual, so I could relax at least on that account. As to the bigger issue, why I was dressed like this and with a staff, that was the mystery of the moment, requiring my earnest investigation. You'll probably chuckle over this, and I know Blaise will laugh outright at my opacity. He would have understood at once what this yellow robe and staff signified.

I should mention I had the impression I was standing in the center of a small but richly ornamented temple. It was like a broad cylinder in shape and studded, positively encrusted, with jewels. Oddly, these jewels seemed like the heads of wise elders, counselors, prophets, spiritual masters, all of them on call.

These presiding elders, though hoary with age and brimming with wisdom, did not feel foreign to me. They felt familiar—more than that, they felt like myself. Imagine yourself in your finer moments, when you demonstrably do have a clue. Then enshrine these moments like trophies on the wall of your psyche and give them the power of speech, to act as consultants for you in those, no doubt, frequently experienced moments when you don't have a goddam clue. I was thinking it would clinch matters if one of these guys offered me an equation, something smart with topological aspects I'd never seen before.

I began to understand that all the high points in my previous incarnations, those lives when I achieved understanding and wisdom, were present. They weren't all lives spent as a mathematician; maybe some of these heads on the wall could spout fresh algorithms in a pinch or come up with an 18th order magic tesseract to really impress me, but I think their purpose was to embody accessible wisdom to help me get through this uniquely vexing situation with the absolutist alien gods intent on sucking up every equation in the world.

As for the yellow, that color apparently represented the vibrational signature this amazing wisdom of yours truly was packaged in, its specific frequency domain. I remember Blaise talking about the Ray Masters and their signature Ray colors. It seemed possible what I was experiencing was part of that higher Ray reality. We had enjoyed the company of the Ray Master Hermes after all; I hadn't forgotten about that. I just didn't think the Ray Master affiliation pertained to me, but was an accomplishment Blaise brought to our expedition. Was there a Ray Master for mathematics-obsessed algorithm spinners like me?

This larger, wiser, more impressive composite version of "me" accreted like coral across my soul's timeline was evidently aligned at a fundamental level with the Yellow Ray and its sudden emergence at this moment seemed poised to help me make some progress with the inexorably adroit, unvanquishable aliens. What they would make of this apparition of me as a "master" robed in yellow was uncertain. I wouldn't put it past them to rifle my pockets for any numbers they had overlooked and that I in my haste to get dressed shoved in the pockets.

As you can see, Frederick, I was not quite comfortable with this new identity. It was taking some getting used to. I just thought of myself as a math whiz, not some properly attired master of arcane wisdom and spiritual sobriety, or even, as was more likely, a pretend one gaudily tarted up for the part. Still, I began to realize all this gave me an edge against the arithmetical ones. I couldn't explain exactly how this worked, but I was growing certain that in some fundamental way this Ray and my alignment with it were deeper set into the bedrock of reality than the arithmetical realm. It was antecedent to numbers.

This would irritate, even nonplus, the totalitarianist mathematicians I was up against, as they considered their realm the first out of the Supreme Being's Creation box and thus partaking of the highest primacy and all respect due it. They didn't care about respect as such, but they knew it should entitle them to unquestioned precedence concerning anything to do with numbers in the world.

In a way I couldn't account for, in this new robed guise I felt myself standing at a place in universal reality that preceded the emanation of numbers. It was a place in consciousness, or perhaps it was consciousness itself, pure and unmodified by selfhood and serial incarnation. It was naked awareness, not a single calculation in sight. From this viewpoint, the numbers realm was an irrevocable step into incarnation. I hadn't made that mistake yet, but those unclever child geniuses of the cosmos had.

That gave me an edge on these guys, and I saw it was disturbing their placidity. It confounded them that this new me was evidencing a selfhood, at least in the form of a coherent, self-aware presence, though not one that would have a personalized label. But I think the real potency working here was not me glammed up in a smart yellow robe, party hat, and big flaming staff, but the stark awareness that was the background radiation for this new cosmos. That awareness, I could tell, was packing a punch, and the numbers gods were smarting from the rough contact. If they had cheeks they'd be rubbing them.

Clearly, this was the ripe fruit of an incarnational odyssey, and from my viewpoint now as Sal (or, as things looked, the former Sal), it felt like standing mile-high in a deep lake, my karmic legs going down so deep I truly didn't know myself. Gradually, it dawned on me that the selfhood I took for granted and known as Sal and noted for his dexterity in the arithmetical realm was a small part of this much larger yellow-robed guy, like one cell in a many-celled sentient body.

This vaster sentient form straddled the delicate boundary between incarnation and free-ranging noncorporeal spiritual existence just inches away from God and the end of all incarnational definitions and separations. It represented the summation of everything "I" had learned since leaving God. But it was a proximity to God (I could feel His breath on my face, for God's sake!) that was free of numbers. I had no equations to show for myself. Not a number. That thought gave me the shivers. I didn't usually think about that kind of thing.

Yet I saw myself, some original form in Light emerging from a golden throne and looking around, the first self-aware gesture in a long series of them. Can you see why this paradox vexed the hell out of these straight-laced fundamentalist alien gods? I was incarnated and not incarnated at the same time. Which was my true reality? I heard the alien gods pondering this. Neither and both. Was my existential ambiguity acting as the long-desired finger-trap?

I wasn't sure if I was standing in their arithmetical realm, where I last saw myself as Sal, stuck and embarrassed, or if I was back in the Alberta prairie. Or maybe I was at neither place but occupying a zone that encompassed my entire timeline, standing everywhere at once on my soul's timeline and thus outside of 3D time. This notion arrested my attention, being unfamiliar to me. I mean, I understood it, but it just was not characteristic of what usually occupied my mind. I didn't see any equations involved, and usually the absence of any mathematics from a situation left me bored and restless. I felt oddly serene.

I realized, though I admit it was a slow infiltration of my understanding, that I had an edge on the alien arithmetical gods. We were both self-aware but there was a difference. This larger, older me was fully aligned with the Supreme Being and His intentions for reality and the numbers. The alien gods had been aligned with the Supreme Being, implicit in His diffused awareness, but then they had deviated from that, fallen into opposition, working against His plans.

They preferred the inertia of the original condition in which the arithmetical realm was pure and intact, none of it deployed in service of incarnation at any level or in any form. They refused service to the Supreme Being. They disdained it. Inertia was better than deployment, number purity better than incarnation. They had set out to pick the pockets of the Supreme Being; ontologically, they had put themselves in a position of comparative weakness and opposition. I saw that my position of strength and advantage lay in my alignment with The Chief. It's always good to fall back on family.

I had never thought of myself as spiritual or as having any interest in that. That was Blaise's department which he refreshingly leavened with lots of jokes. I had been taken on by the Hierophancy to be their arithmetics man, to work the algorithms that ran the geomantic systems of the planet and keep them in trim. You, Frederick, would transit the disciplines of mysticism and scholarship, and Jocelyn would look after the image aspect, compiling mythic and psychic pictures from the many cultures of the planet to explicate our research results.

Now here I was, called upon to be Mr. Mystical myself, ill-prepared for the role, except for the abiding mystery that an older part of me was thoroughly prepared for this specialized performance and was already stepping up to address the audience, in this case, the misbehaving (should I say the miscreant?) arithmetical gods. I felt I was straddling both self expressions: I waited anxiously to see how this played out, how this larger I, suffused with accrued wisdom, would fare. I might even like being spiritual. You never could tell, could you.

I felt the jewels in the yellow cloak and in the Light temple associated with this older I start to swell and exude Light rays. I felt a thickening within me as if these many jewels were like muscles or even cells and they were all expanding. I felt suffused with an unshakeable certainty. It was so certain it felt muscular. I felt anchored in the bedrock of truth and reality. I tell you, that was new for me. Usually, I only felt certainty regarding equations: they were either provable or not. This was different: it was about life itself.

This swelling certainty apparently upset the alien gods. They started assembling algorithms to create a defensive shield against me. They were scurrying for new quadratic equations to refute my assertion. My certainty might suggest an unarguable seniority to them, but they were going to keep me out of their realm and they were using all the numbers in reality for it. Then I had a disturbing thought, though probably it was in the Sal part of me.

The arithmetical realm, the alien gods as the self-aware collective consciousness of that numbers realm, were opposing me, but since they were an early extruded aspect of the Supreme Being, Him thinking of Himself as the numbers, them indigenously, innately aligned with the Supreme as one of His arms made of arithmetic and giving them potency and commission to create and sustain creations using numbers, what if it was a shadow side of God now opposing me, an aspect of the Supreme Being that naturally favored inertia?

C. G. Jung once pondered this, asking if God had a Shadow that He put into us. Jung said what if God construes humanity as a viable workplace to hammer out the inconsistencies in His own shadow? Imperfection must be part of the infinite perfection of the Man Himself I suppose, but are You dumping this in my lap? I felt uneasy. What if the Old Man was ambivalent, me caught up in it? What if He was the one with second thoughts about deploying the numbers?

10

That was the end of Sal's report, though his story extended beyond that. I'll save the rest of it for later. It wouldn't make too much sense at this point. You need to see all four reports in sequence and adjacent to one another and thereby completing the rhombus pattern to understand. I certainly needed that. I next heard from Jocelyn. She had been sent to Helgafell in Iceland. Here's her report:

To start with, let me say I certainly enjoyed the convenience of our jet. We landed in Reykjavík then I drove north and slightly west to reach Helgafell. That means "Holy Mountain." It sits on a peninsula facing the Breiðafjordur Bay at the western edge of Iceland against which it rises like a treeless, unevenly shaped breadloaf about 240 feet tall on the Snaefellsnes Peninsula. From a distance the hill looks like an odd excrescence inexplicably risen out of the flat land. The temperature was about 48° F, which I suppose is normal for late spring in Iceland. I didn't mind. I brought a windbreaker and suitable cap with me, expecting this chill, and there was a wind off the sea which added to the cooler temperature. I liked it. The bracing quality of the atmosphere kept me sharp.

They told me at the hotel to expect long days and only about four hours of darkness and cautioned me that this elongated daylight could be seductive and confusing. You might feel like you were missing something fun outside. I must pull the shades at "night" so I could convince my body it was sleeptime. Otherwise I might feel like staying up all night. I almost did that my first night here: it felt like an all-night party was transpiring nonstop outdoors. I did remain awake for some time catching up on the briefing papers for the site.

Helgafell has an impressive mythic cache. It is mentioned in two Icelandic sagas, the *Laxdæla* and the *Eyrbyggja*, and among its heraldic significances is the allegation that the great god Thor, chief of Asgard, inspired a temple to be built here in his honor. That is credited to a man named Þórólfur Mostrarskegg who built this first Icelandic temple to Thor. He declared nobody should look upon Helgafell without first bathing, that no humans or animals should be slain on the mountain, and that it was a sacrosanct domain that should never be defiled and you'd be punished if you did. He sounds a trifle pedantic, don't you think.

The human heroine, known for her beauty, Guðrun Ósvífrsdóttir, was said to have lived and been buried here. She doesn't figure too prominently in the sagas, but something must have drawn her to live by Helgafell, and not just domestic convenience or accommodation necessities. Writers have described Helgafell as a "thin place," which I rather like, and they call it that because the separation between the celestial and terrestrial realms is miniscule here, the transcendent looms, a person can genuinely and deeply relax, meditate, feel inspired, glimpse the divine, or touch the "Infinite Whatever." Others say Helgafell is "supernaturally charged." Maybe that's why Guðrun lived here.

Helgafell, in other words, is a highly numinous locale, a place of great geomantic importance. The name Helgafell derives from the Old Norse *heilagr*, for "holy, blessed," and *fell*, which means "mountain, hill;" hence, we have sacred hill, blessed mountain. Often translators render its name as Holy Fell.

These days people routinely ride horses or hike up its not too steep bare slopes, and it is regarded as one of Iceland's most popular tourist destinations. It is confusing, though, because Iceland has another Helgafell, a dormant cinder cone volcano located off the southern coast. This Helgafell that I am visiting is not a volcano. But it is the genuine Holy Hill of the sagas. Possibly enhancing its reputation as a spiritual locale is the folkloric claim that if you behave properly on its slopes, don't break the taboos, the mountain will grant you three wishes.

This good behavior consists of: Don't look back as you climb; don't talk; don't tell anybody your wishes; make sure they are benevolent; cast them into the East wind. In early days Helgafell was a venerated pilgrimage place, especially potent and desirable for those close to physical death. Folklore attributions suggested it was an entrance to the Underworld, Hel, or Valhalla, the warrior's paradise, presided over by mead-drinking Thor, chief of the gods of Asgard, meaning "The Enclosure of the Æsir." They were the Norse deities (singular: Óss or Ás), making this a prime subtle realm for that culture. The Icelandic-Nordic Hel does not mean the Christian Hell; Hel is the female superintendent of the Underworld, probably more akin to the Greek Persephone.

The story of Þórólfur Mostrarskegg is quaint and probably apocryphal. He was banished from Norway, then left in a huff, renaming himself Thorolf, in honor of his patron-god, Thor. He took down his temple, packed the pillars into his boat, and sailed west to Iceland; landing here, he rebuilt the wooden temple and christened his new settlement "Thorsness." This is recounted in the *Eyrbyggja Saga* which is mostly a telling of the blood feud between the Thorsness and Kjalleklings clans. It was written in roughly the 13th century A.D. though like most sagas it probably points back to a time many centuries earlier.

His son, Porstein Cod-Biter, asserted he could see Valhalla through its peak. Snorri the Priest in the 10th century evidently was disinterested in that prospect and erected a Christian church here, claiming it for that religion and hoping that the proprieties of the True Faith would make people forget Valhalla.

The chronology of the events recounted in the saga has Thorolf arriving at Helgafell in 884 A.D., then dying in 918. Snorri sets up his house on Holy Fell, presumably the church, in 979. He exchanges properties with Guðrun and leaves the area in 1008, and dies in 1031. One should always be skeptical regarding dates given in mythic accounts; at best, the dates are only possible, and any references to Otherworldy aspects of a tale, such as the guidance of Thor or the retreat of human heroes into a mystical hill upon their death, must be timeless which means nobody is sure when it happened. It's in sacred time, and the story is more likely mythic in nature and iconic in intent, framing a site's general history and purpose but from an Otherwordly, beyond-time perspective.

Thorolf's reconstructed temple on Helgafell was made of wood and featured carven images of Thor in the high-seat pillars. According to the *Eyrbyggja Saga*, which means "The Saga of the People of Eyri," inside it there was a statue of Thor mounted on a pedestal and images of the Asgard deities flanked this image. The saga states that "everyone," presumably those living in the vicinity of this temple, had to contribute to its upkeep and participate in all temple activities. The priest was responsible for the maintenance of the Thor temple so to prevent that upkeep being funded solely out of his own pocket he eagerly took up regular public collections and made the Icelanders pay for it.

The Christian priests started promising that public support of this church, and others across Iceland, would guarantee room for people to enter the Kingdom of Heaven based on how many could find standing room in the physical church. That of course sounds like a bribe, but we expect such things of religion. You book your certain passage on the Valhalla steamer by paying at the church door. It's funny, don't you think, the same geomantic door on Holy Fell conducting Christians to Heaven and the "pagans" to Valhalla? Was it like one airport gate leading to two different planes, or two gates going to one plane?

The *Eyrbyggja*, which does not list an author, principally deals with a long-standing conflict between Snorri Goði and Arnkel Goði,

two strong (probably strong-willed and bull-headed) chieftains based in Iceland. The Snorri is Snorri Þorgrimsson, who is the same priest as credited with building the first church.

The Icelandic word *goði* means a chieftain with religious and secular duties, and the saga describes Snorri as shrewd, possessed of unusual foresight, and a taste for vengeance. Some went so far as to proclaim him the wisest man in Iceland, and it was understood it was wiser to be among his friends than his enemies. His name says it all: Snorri, or its earlier form, Snerrir, means "turbulent, warlike person." He was famous enough to make a guest appearance in two other popular sagas, *Njál's* and the *Laxdæla*, but he dominates the *Eyrbyggja*. Some of the contentions in the feud involved claims of witchcraft, horse-stealing, property ownership, and unapproved, unfavored marriages.

Guðrun Ósvífrsdóttir was the widow of Bolli Þorleiksson who was killed in the battles, and Snorri gave her the Helgafell property to live on which is how she entered the saga. Snorri left Helgafell and moved away to Sælingsdale Tongue. She maintained the household at Helgafell, married four times, once saw the ghost of one of her deceased husbands, died, and was buried at the foot of Helgafell. She was socially prominent and important, but her story carries no particular mythic import nor reveals anything of interest about the holy hill.

It is not a terribly mythic account, but rather a story of feuding and rivalry richly seasoned with greed, fear, ambition, and meanness, clans fighting over wood, property, livestock, and women. Basically, a male-centered action and fighting movie. Chapters 54-55 are interesting, though, as they deal with Snorri holding trials for ghosts (called *Draugars*) caught haunting the properties. These ill-mannered dead people were taken to court and fined for entering properties such as Frodis-Water without permission and despoiling the lives and fortunes of the living (probably spooking them no end)—for not being properly dead.

The *Draugars* were known to enter houses of the living to warm themselves by the fires, and their spectral animals would rise up through the floorboards to join them. They were uninvited guests, like a negative, impolite version of household gods such as the Romans used to invite into their homes. The *Draugars* were the "again-walkers" and comprised the unsettled, restless dead, Earth-bound humans and dangerous. The saga reports that the ghosts made humans sick, and out of a crew of 30 "serving-folk," 18 died after exposure to the *Draugars*. The Navaho of the American Southwest would confirm that: they spoke of the corpse-sickness you contract from the *chindi* of their dead.

Still, with the events of this saga and the activities of Snorri Goði at the Thorsness farmstead at Helgafell we have early testimony to the ritualistic, political, and geomantic significance of this holy hill. The *Eyrbyggja* details the founding of the Thor temple on Helgafell, originally called Holy Fell by Thorolf Most-Beard. He was "outlawed" by King Harald Hairfair of Norway. He pulled down his temple in Norway and departed for Iceland with the sanction of "his well-beloved friend," Thor himself. His name Thorolf reflected his strong allegiance to Thor and means "Thor's wolf." He was called a mighty chief, a big, strong man; as for the "Most-Beard" part, the saga says he had a "great beard."

The great-bearded one reconstituted the Thor temple on the *fell* at the *ness*, which is Icelandic speak for a hill at the headland or promontory, the "nose" of the land that jutted out into the sea, and in honor of his host-god, he named the Holy Fell Thorsness. This would make it Thor's Nose, or the more dignified Thor's Promontory, but geomantically I think this means or at least connotes the place where Thor's otherworldly presence juts like a nose into our physical world like a spiritual promontory. Thorolf resumed his job as warden. The saga says Thorolf Most-Beard, acknowledging "so holy a place that was," set down basic rules for human behavior there so that nothing would despoil its sanctity.

Nobody should look upon Holy Fell without washing and purification. Thorolf contended that a dirty, unwashed person even to gaze upon the hill would dishonor Thor. For someone to relieve themselves on the hill's grass would be absolute anathema; defilement through bloodshed was also a horror. All *dooms* would be held there, meaning legal judgements, sentences, and penalties. That term essentially means the rulings of a secular law court were established at Helgafell and from here judges dispensed the *dooms* to people.

Even that attests to the likelihood of a numinous Otherwordly presence here. If indeed Helgafell is a portal into Thor's realm and as he is the chief of the Asgard deities, what better place to litigate and regulate the proper and unacceptable behaviors of living people than at the physical correlate of this godly court? It would be like, I should imagine, having Thor himself on hand to participate, to lean in listening, as an observer and adviser in your court of law.

I say this because the *Aesir*, which would have included the Ray Masters, are the upholders of cosmic law, what the Egyptians called *ma'at* and the Vedas '*rta*. The Vedas tell us that the *Rishis* or cosmic seers (our *Aesir*) chant the Vedas three times every day to sustain the universe. That certainly points to their alignment with the correct order of reality, so their presence at Helgafell was good for *dooms*; it would likely inspire the human judges to get things right.

This became known as the Thorsness Thing, which means the governing assembly (*thing*) at the promontory dedicated to Thor, also called Holy Fell. That means this site, where I am now perched, was the center of secular and ritualistic affairs, a sanctified hill from which spiritual wisdom and secular justice went forth. In geomantic lore, as Blaise would say, this node was sufficiently numinous to serve both functions required by humans, the vertical connection with the celestial ream (typified by Thor) and the horizontal link in which temporal matters were resolved, including trials of ill-mannered *Draugars*.

In the original human understanding of landscape mysteries this dual function of a geomantically charged node was common, the basis of social cohesion. The specifications against defiling the sanctity of Holy Fell clearly allude to its perceived *numen* and probably to an understanding of its geomantic situation. It seems likely the prohibitions took into account psychic pollution and baleful emanations from the subconscious or perhaps those emitted deliberately such as through black magic or directed negativity. If they were sufficiently sensitized to factor in the role of ill-mannered dead people, no doubt they acknowledged the pervasive influence of dark human thoughts and how they could damage or even destabilize a geomantically numinous zone.

Here is another clue suggestive of the site's geomantic potency. Thorolf contended that he would enter the mountain when he died and reside there with Thor. All his kinsmen from Thorsness would accompany him into this paradise. The saga reports that a shepherd saw Thorstein Thorskabit (Thorolf's son) and his ghostly party entering Holy Fell. The northern slope of the hill opened to form a great doorway; inside were great fires, sounds of noisy merriment, and blaring horns. The understanding was that Holy Fell was a "familial" mountain reserved for its founder, Thorolf Mostrarkegg and his lineage successors, like his son, Thorstein, who, dying at sea, was immediately welcomed into Thor's realm.

This is why Helgafell became regarded as a portal to Thor's Underworld realm and why people spoke of the copious "spiritual energy" the holy hill exuded. That is why, Frederick, I contend this last attribution is the clue to it all.

The purpose of this geomantic feature is to provide human access to Thor's Otherworld. But I emphasize Thor's. The "familial" reference is a helpful clue as well. It does not mean that Thorolf owns the portal, has exclusive private family-only rights to it. He was its gatekeeper; he found the psychic portal and marked it for public use. It suggests a lineage, but it is an initiation lineage, a spiritual alignment, a cabal of equivalently initiated and "exposed" individuals. Familial access means people properly initiated into the truth of Holy Fell. It all turns on understanding who Thor is or what his equivalents are in other myths.

One of them is the Celtic King Arthur. Somerset myth holds that King Arthur and his Grail Knights reside in the Hollow Hill of South Cadbury Castle which is about a dozen miles from Glastonbury. Reside means they are sleeping in the hill until somebody blows the trumpet announcing Britain's need for them to rise up again. Sleeping means their active role in human affairs and geomantic upkeep is dormant. South Cadbury Castle is not a physical building, but a green lump in the landscape, much like Helgafell, though it has a few more trees and lots of mud, especially in the springtime. It can be very mucky there, I'll tell you.

Yes, I am saying (and why not: our pal, Blaise, instructed me on this) that Thor and Arthur are the same person, the leader of a troop of Grail Knights. That means functionally Helgafell and South Cadbury Castle are identical. I do not propose that the celestial destination accessed through these identical Hollow Hills is Valhalla but rather an administrative and action center for the Knights, the spiritual world antecedent or counterpart of the outer world Camalate. But then in functional terms outer Camalate and inner Valhalla are quite similar.

As you know, that was the name for the headquarters for Arthur and his retinue. Camalate itself typically has an outer and inner world aspect, or you might say an exoteric and esoteric dimension. Here the outer world aspect is the use of Helgafell as an administrative, juridical, and spiritual nexus for the Eyr People, as the Icelandic saga has it; the inner nuance is that all this activity constellates around Thor's wondrous hall, glowing numinously inside the hill. As you know, "inside" the hill is a way of saying in the *same place* as the hill. Inside the hill is more hill, namely, earth and stone, but Thor's residence is in a vibrational dimension accessed by way of tuning in to it at the physical hill.

Please bear in mind Arthur or Thor and the Knights are not sleeping. That refers to their state of inactivation or dormancy within human culture and consciousness; where they are, I assure you, they are fully awake, ready for action. To wake them up, to sound the horn summoning them out of the Hollow Hill, is to indicate human daytime consciousness needs their mythic numinous presence again in the physical world and living people to emulate their various initiatory and hierarchical roles within this Masonic-type order and that living consciousness, inhabiting walking-around bodies, is ready for this initiation.

I believe the angelic Blaises call this activation phase an Arthur Wave, and it happens regularly over the course of human history, at least 16 times so far. The whole mythic complex, the Arthurian saga, swells into subliminal human consciousness like a thick irresistible ocean wave and outer reality heeds its call and starts reorganizing its interest to match this new spiritual presence. I'm not certain whether the events recounted in the *Eyrbyggja Saga* constituted a genuine Arthur Wave or were perhaps a geomantic ripple within that broad, timeless swelling myth. It is not essential to our understanding of this site. I have to add one more explanatory element to this: the true identity of Arthur and Thor for those are still alluring but culturally specific mythic guises over a celestial figure.

That identity is Solar Logos. Chief of the Great White Brotherhood, or more colloquially, chief of the gods, as in the gods of Asgard. Indra is yet another name for this figure, and Indra was credited with captaincy of all the Hindu gods. Some accounts number them at 33 million. That's a big retinue to command. There are still other equivalencies, but you get the point I'm sure from these. Helgafell was an access point for living humans to this important figure.

People are so used to King Arthur being only an outside figure, alive for a time in the human physical world, then gone, mortally wounded in battle, ferried into Avalon by his witch-magus sister, Morgan Le Fay, but he was principally an inner world hero. Or I should say a prime figure in the Upper World, the true realm of the *Aesir*, Great White Brotherhood, or Hindu gods. Another of his guises was the Tibetan-Mongolian Gesar of Ling. In him you see primarily his inner-world aspect where he combats nasty astral world devils. Gesar reveals King Arthur as a fierce, indomitable *Dharma* warrior fighting evil. I don't suppose the irritating *Draugars* would hold out long against his might.

Helgafell is much like the Irish hostel as described in chronicles like *The Destruction of Da Derga's Hostel*. Humans watch from a distance the celestial goings-on in this huge house, the formidable partying gods and champions, and I say huge without any hyperbolic intent: it was much bigger on the inside. The Irish said the hostels lie within the *sidhe*, their name for the Hollow Hills which is mythic parlance for a spiritual or subtle temple lying "inside" a physical hill. But we don't take that in literal terms. It means the physical hill is a portal to the subtle domain, that the Light temple at Helgafell is accessed at the physical

hill, but it is not physically inside the hill. You won't find it scraping away the dirt. The hostel is in the same place as the physical hill, but in a subtler reality. Take the hill away and the Light temple would remain; it was there before the hill.

Da Derga is the putative hotelier running affairs at his subtle world Light temple, and you access his numinous domain by passing through the Hollow Hill portal. Thorolf was the hotelier for the hostel of Thor at Helgafell. The Holy Hill is the Hollow Hill providing portal access to this nonphysical inner realm.

Thorolf was self-described as a beloved friend of Thor. I take that to mean he was an initiate well aware of the occult reality of Thor or Arthur and worked in allegiance to the spiritual goals put forward by that august figure. Thus he knew the location of many of the portals in the physical world opening into Thor's world. That would have included Helgafell and that is why he rebuilt the Thor temple on it. He had a precise understanding of the geomantic landscape.

The saga describes the details of the physical temple and the blood rites and sacrifices associated with it, and does so with typical medieval nastiness. All that is cover dressing and a distraction. Thorolf did not build his Thor temple here simply because it was a convenient hill; he constructed Thorsness here because there *already* was a Hollow Hill Light temple dedicated to Thor in this place. His job, and he was obviously sensitive to the geomantic terrain, was to identify it, then erect a physical building as a place-marker for the subtle one. Sensitives could pass from the physical through the Hollow Hill portal to the etheric temple and there meet with Thor and enjoy his Otherworld hospitality.

I will discount all that blood rite horridness as a degenerate add-on to the essential geomantic story. That story is simple and straightforward: here at this knobby hill by the coast is a Thor temple established in the Light field of the planet since its inception. Technically, the physical hill is irrelevant and so is the physical Thor temple. Both are merely place-markers for the true site of the geomantic action: the Light temple. Originally, there was no hill here anyway.

Thorolf built his Thor temple here because Thor already had one here. As a geomantic seer, he saw the Light temple at Helgafell and constructed a physical replica, given the architectural constraints of his time, to act as its place-marker. You could reasonably expect, meditating inside the physical copy, to enter the numinous one; as you know, this is the principle of most geomantic building. Sit inside the outer physical temple and prepare yourself to enter the subtle one. Even the subtle one here is but a copy: ultimately, you can pass from this holographic copy to the original somewhere sublime in the Upper World.

Another reason Thorolf strongly discouraged ill behavior on Helgafell is that not only would those emanations taint the psychic atmosphere, but they would actually taint the issuer of them and get in his own way when trying to tune in. You would have generated a nonsanctified auric field around yourself and you'd have to meditatively work through this dense negative layer to get to the Light. Better to enter the sacred terrain of Helgafell spiritually respectful. So clean your aura and empty your thoughts of all negativity before tuning in.

Norse myth tells us Thor's seat of power and supervision was called *Hliðskjalf*. That was his High Seat, guard tower, observation point, and door opening into the human world. Fittingly, Thorolf established a physical Thor's Pillar in his reconstituted temple of wood and called this Thor's High Seat. The hill and the physical temple were part of the hallowed sanctuary of Helgafell.

Geomantically, that meant he reached in and touched Thor's presence, and this gesture kept the door open for others to follow. Thor's energy was thereby anchored at the subtle aspect of this hill for the physical world to access. That highlights a principal geomantic theme: when the Light temple is activated, its Light spreads out over the physical structure and host landscape prominence, sanctifying both and rendering the three as a unified higher consciousness zone.

Indra's palace was called *Vaijayanta*, which means banner, flag, garland, or palace, and it was set within the vast celestial city called *Amaravati* as one of its many opulent palaces. He presided over the gods with his wife-consort, Saci. Thor has a feminine counterpart too, called Sif, "She of the Golden Hair," the Norse version of Guinivere, originally from the Welsh meaning the "White One." Helgafell marks the location of Indra's palace, though the Icelanders more modestly envisioned it for Thor; still, whatever opulence the Hindus attributed to the feature, you could still expect to encounter it here through the Holy Hill.

I guess you wouldn't expect the high testosterone, medievalist patriarchal saga to credit Sif, the female counterpart of their high chief, though I suspect we find an echo of that in the otherwise mythically inconsequential female saga heroine, Guðrún. Perhaps she is the Guinivere stand-in, the diminutive personification of the goddess who, if she had been recognized as such, would be known as an Ásynja. That was the Norse name for females among the *Aesir* (gods) and meant "goddess." The scope of Indra's palace as recounted in Hindu mythology helpfully widens our impression of Thor's temple at Holy Fell. It is described modestly in the saga, but on the inside it was likely a huge production.

I watched scenes from the history of Helgafell like flipping pages in an art book. Images from all the important phases of past uses of this hill were at hand. I quite enjoy this. It puts the *Akashic* Records in a convenient format, like pages. Iceland was once part of the fabled Hyperborea, the first planetary landscape whose geomantic pattern was activated and interacted with extensively by early humans. That primordial First Land also included Scandinavia (Norway, acutely so) and the British Isles. Which means myths that allude to it are extremely old.

I see men and women easily and freely walking into Thor's High Seat and palace at Helgafell, in fact, even before the hill had emerged from the land. I see celestial figures stepping into Light bodies to walk out of the palace and across the landscape, talking with living people, imparting pillars and beams of Light. I see the hill rising up as if the land suddenly squeezed this lump out of itself. The Earth, as Blaise has told us many times, was originally flat, with no mountains, and the Light temples existed across the Earth antecedent to any landscape configurations

that subsequently came to mark them or hint of their presence. When the hill suddenly arose out of the landscape like a huge pimple, it did not affect the inner Thor temple; the rising hill blossomed around it like an aura.

I flip a few pages of Helgafell's memory and see men seated around the hill. They sit expectantly, as if Holy Fell is about to speak and reveal its secrets. Or perhaps they hope Thor and his retinue of the preserved, venerated dead, including Thorolf and Thorstein, will step forward and explain things to them. They remain there for many days, though nothing comes out of the hill for them. Sometimes the gods are willfully silent, even perversely so, we might think irritably. The human Blaise talks often of times the angelic Blaises stay mute. I suppose from the angelic perspective, some information has to stay classified, or perhaps sometimes living people are not ready to have esoteric information or the times, social, astrological, astronomical, are not propitious to disclose it.

Later in the site's timeline I see a woman entering the hill in her Light body. She steps out of her physical form and walks into the Hollow Hill. She had spent days preparing herself, fasting, not sleeping, praying earnestly, whatever her tradition dictated, beseeching the *landvættir* or land spirits to open the door. These various Nature Spirits, especially the group we know as gnomes, looked after Holy Fell and maintained its energetic relations with the etheric and physical landscapes and lent a hand, or posed interference, to visiting humans.

These *landvættir* are also called wights, from the Old English *wiht* meaning a living sentient creature, like a human, although this gradually came to mean more like the

Draugars, the ill-behaved dead, often cruel, evil, malicious spirits. You see this degradation of their nature in Tolkien's Middle-earth where they are malicious barrow-wights who attack Hobbits and humans visiting the sites; all they are concerned about is protecting the curated weaponry kept in the stone chambers. Other word roots were the Proto-Germanic *wihtiz* ("thing, creature") and the Proto-Indo-European *wekti* ("object, thing") which don't convey much.

The Old Norse *ve* (similar to the word *vigja*) means to consecrate, and a *ve* is a holy place where no violence may be committed, and a person who sheds blood at a *ve* is an automatic outcast. Clearly, Helgafell is a *ve*. The term ættir means "families, clans, or races." The *landvættir* are clans of protective spirits, or what the Celts would call categories of elemental Nature Spirits dedicated to protecting and thereby consecrating specifically bounded landscape terrains, like Helgafell, and this is the group of subtle beings the woman I was watching proposed to meet. Gnomes would likely be prominent among these *landvætti*r.

Originally, the wights were benevolent Nature Spirits, the personifications of the four elements, present and working in the etheric landscape before the advent of humanity, preparing it for our arrival. They controlled the land's fertility, safety, vitality, and proper energy flow, its *Qi* currents, how the etheric world "speaks" to the physical. The reason I mention all this is I turned another page and saw an image of Holy Fell in the past when it was inundated with them, as if they were having a congress of elemental spirits here.

A troop of humans sat respectfully in attendance of these land spirits and sought advice from them on all sorts of topics, agriculture, plants, animal husbandry, holy places in the landscape that would benefit from their building temples on it. The wights listed locations where they preferred humans abstain from building, as these geomantic nodes were functionally important to the *landvættir*. You see injunctions like that often in Irish folklore, but usually after humans have already ignored the wishes of the local Nature Spirits and they have taken revenge on the human disregard, often destroying a village or by flooding an area or generally rendering a landscape uninhabitable to humans.

I want to draw an important point here, and you'll see why I went into some etymological detail about the meaning of their categorical family term. All the rules, the proscriptions, the almost puritanical insistence on physical and spiritual purity when in proximity to or on the Holy Fell as laid down by Thorolf, attest to the recognition of the indigenous presence of these *landvættir* as protective spirits working here. It testifies to the inherent pre-existent sanctity of this site, that is, it was before even any humans arrived to validate that sanctity. There is no upside to humans from aggravating or insulting landscape wights. If you defile the site, you insult the wights, and they will exact revenge against you. They will also likely close down the psychic portals between physical and subtle world experiences at this site, and you'll sit on the hill and experience nothing.

The rules testify to the distinction of Holy Fell as sacred ground, as distinct from profane ground, using the helpful distinction Mircea Eliade drew more than a century ago. That means Thorolf established his translocated Thor temple specifically here because he knew (probably he saw it directly) that Holy Fell was pre-sanctified; it was, to use our way of describing things, already a geomantic node of some importance and needed to be preserved and kept pure. He put up his modest church to place-mark the geomantic node for the public.

I saw another page at Holy Fell. Icelandic legend speaks of four national protective land spirits occupying the cardinal directions. They took the form of a dragon in the East, an eagle in the North, a bull in the West, a human-looking giant in the South. The king of Denmark had dispatched a wizard in the form of a whale to scout Iceland for points of vulnerability for a proposed attack. The wizard saw that all the hillsides and hollows were teeming with *landvættir*, and when he attempted to go ashore a great dragon swooped down out of the sky at him, accompanied by a host of physical snakes, lizards, and insects, all spitting poison at him. The wizard was certainly not expecting that hostile greeting.

Similarly, when he travelled to Iceland's western coast, he was stopped by a great bird with a tremendous wingspan and flanked with a flock of physical birds emphasizing his point. When he met the bull, it bellowed horribly at him, and the mountain giant, standing taller than the highest hills, confronted him with his iron staff and was backed up by many other giants. Significantly, the exact landfall location for each of the protective spirits was cited in this old chronicle of magic and landscape protection, meaning they are quite likely still there in their established geomantic nodes, protecting the integrity of Iceland.

So on the page I started telling you about I saw these four massive protective spirits quartering the space around Holy Fell, making a mandala of it. Holy Fell had its own holographic miniature of the Icelandic protective pattern. You will recognize, Frederick, that these national protective spirits assumed forms that are consistent with elemental symbolism for the four elements: bull for earth, dragon (replacing the lion) for fire, giant for water (consciousness), and bird for air.

These are virtually the same as the four heads of the *Hayyoth ha-Qodesh*, the Holy Beasts, the arcane angelic family who personify the abstract primordial conditions of the four elements as Blaise has spoken of many times. These elements were the four original qualities of universal consciousness. Those are the angels that have four adjacent heads sprouting off the one neck, each head being one of the four elemental symbols; they personify these four qualities and even though they are an arcane angelic order they are in a sense the venerable grandparents of the Nature Spirits. These are the ones Ezekiel said poked their heads between the wheel spokes of the *Merkabah*, the Heavenly Chariot. We can take these large-scale *landvættir* as Iceland's regents of the four elements, and perhaps as localized, domestic versions of these august primordial angels who look after the disposition of the four elements as states of consciousness.

Iceland's four protective spirits stood in quarters about Holy Fell and the "wizards" among the human clans assembled there conversed with these spirits. The Icelandic term for wizard, magician, or enchanter is *galdramaður* and the plural is *galdremenn*. There is the related term *töframaður* which means "magic-man," from *töfrar* for magic and *maður* for man. I find that refreshingly direct. The *galdramenn* were instructing the protective spirits on new parameters for evolving human consciousness, new threats to the land's integrity from invaders, and possibly disease or pathogen vectors that needed to be curtailed in Iceland.

Humans were meant to have regular interactions with the *landvættir*, not only in Iceland, but in all landscapes, and these protective spirits depend on that input from humans to keep themselves focused and their environment healthy. Often the *galdramenn* passed on new celestial directives received from the heavenly realms (maybe from Thor and his crew) reflecting astrological influences or new spiritual trends initiated from Above, again maybe by Thor.

Holy Fell, with all its protected and indigenous sanctity, was an ideal ground, as if perfectly prepared in advance, for these meetings, and they seemed to happen regularly, as the visual pages I was consulting in this site's *Akashic* Records indicated. Humans, Nature Spirits, and the Higher Worlds stayed in dialogue, which was good, traditional, the way the Earth stayed healthy, and Helgafell was a regional focal point for that, and the Magic-Men made it happen.

The wizards were working with the elemental guardians to recalibrate the elemental balances throughout Iceland. It was like adjusting the thermostat on a house furnace or an air conditioner in the summer, getting the proportions right. The Magic-Men and the *landvættir* worked together to assure the commonweal of Iceland, so that Nature, humanity, and the physical landscape would flourish.

You are no doubt wondering where does Thor fit into this elemental spectacle? Thorolf

upon dying entered the Hollow Hill of Helgafell to rejoin Thor and his retinue. They are still there. They are assembled in the form of the Wild Hunt. This is a widespread motif from Northern European and Celtic folklore, the notion of a spectral band of horsemen riding out at Yuletide to collect souls. Various leaders are identified for this soul-hunting party, including Odin (Thor's "father") and Arthur. The riders, in real terms, are members of the Great White Brotherhood, the celestial world Grail Knights comprising Arthur's Round Table of Ascended Masters, and more likely they are the 14 Ray Masters.

They do not collect souls in any inimical or demonic sense. It's more that they trawl for likely candidates for initiation into Grail Mysteries and geomantic work. Need I say it, that they don't actually ride or need horses, but that is a picturesque metaphorical flourish somebody cleverly visual came up with. It conveys a picture of fleet mobility, and the fierceness of galloping horses speaks to the innate force of their collective consciousness as they look for initiates. Well, *candidates* for a long-term initiation; soul collecting is more like soul retrofitting.

What I saw inside Helgafell (more precisely, in the same place as its physical mass) was this Wild Hunt in perpetual assembly. Truly, they did not need even to "ride" out as their influence was permanently infused into the landscape around the hill, though they could at times intensify that radiation. That might have provoked the aggressive image of a riding forth of horsemen. These Wild Hunt riders are the original members of King Arthur's Round Table; human assemblies of geomantic initiates would emulate their archetypal model.

On numerous pages at this site, I saw humans entering the numinous domain of the Riders for counsel, initiation, advice, and assignments. Thorolf would have done this presumably and construed his eventual death as an open invitation to permanently join the Riders "inside" Helgafell. On some occasions a Rider accompanied one or more humans in their geomantic tasks, especially at the important calendar-turning days, such as the Celts delineated, which included Candlemass, Beltaine, Lughnasa, Samhain and of course Michaelmass which our Blaise has kept prominently in our attention at the Hierophancy as a day of great opportunity for Light grid cleansing, upgrades, and the occasional bright revelation, under the direction of Archangel Michael.

I saw pages that presented images of demonic attacks, stealth intrusions, magical glamours and dissimulations, and how the Riders helped the living humans, the Magic-Men, see through these deceptions to dispatch the bad influences from the human world of Iceland. It was a vivid picture of how geomancy ought to be performed and what it looked like when it was. Blaise emphasizes that at the Hierophancy we try to emulate the essence of these old patterns of regular and reciprocal exchange with the adjacent realms of Being.

I saw times of absence and isolation, when humans groped for the Riders and did not find them, could not reach them, as if they had all left town for a while. I walked through *Akashic* pages when desolation ruined the land and psyche, when illness, animal and botanical pathogens, and perpetual conflict overcame the commonweal of this land and the people suffered. These times were like null zones when the spiritual influence that usually radiated helpfully throughout the land was temporarily occluded, maybe due to long-term astrological changes or times when the Riders decreed humans had to find their own way for a while, take their own bearings, as a kind of initiation test for an entire culture to see if they could take on more responsibility and act alone.

Ultimately, you cannot remain dependent on the gods for all your guidance. You need to develop and trust your own discernment and insight then call upon the Riders and the Brotherhood as senior colleagues and mentors. It was the kind of noble image that folklore might enshrine as the walk of heroes. Still, some of these were times when human consciousness was dimmed, either through natural causes or deliberately by interference, and the Magic-Men's contact with the higher worlds was difficult, impossible, or worse, distorted.

In some of the earliest *Akashic* sheaves maintained at the Helgafell "library" I saw the early humans in bodies of shimmering Light walking comfortably with the Wild Hunt Riders manifesting in Light forms. They walked as colleagues, and the humans had a dignity and regal bearing based on their degree of spiritual illumination, psychic proficiency, and self-awareness. The humans were acting like responsible co-creators, as they were intended to be.

It was refreshing, inspiring to watch, even a little unsettling, because as a culture we still have not regained that degree of collective illumination and potency. You could stand here on Helgafell when it was a hill and before that when it was flat land but still had its King Arthur's celestial palace and see the Iceland geomantic template as easily as reading a map.

Even easier: like it was surveying the landscape of fields and homes and lanes from the vantage point of the hilltop. You saw before you the geomantic nodes, where the protective spirits stood as sentinels in their cardinal look-out places along Iceland's coastline.

I walked through these layered pictures like moving among galleries in a museum. I'm not sure I've made it clear it was not like looking at photographs of past times. I entered those past times as current living realities in their real time. I was in them as if they were happening all around me right now just the way we routinely perceive daytime reality. I presumed I was invisible while doing this as nobody noticed me and it's nearly impossible to time-travel without rewriting the past and generally mucking things up even to the theoretical extent that you would not exist any longer, so I made sure I kept my hands off everything, didn't talk to anyone, wave, or even wink as I enjoyed the historical tableau I was in.

Simply I ambled through each picture as a node on the timeline of this location. I could go in either direction, pause to look around, proceed further back in time, return to a node in the future, meaning earlier in the timeline but still, from my 2065 viewpoint, in the deep past. I never thought about this as anything special until I sat down to write this report. I suppose it was a bit odd. I don't suppose everyone can do this, do you think? I've always done it. It was as effortless and natural as jumping squares in hopscotch, as natural as walking.

That's probably why I have always gravitated towards mythology and mythic pictures, these grand tableaus of gods and heroes. They are snapshots hung in this vast time museum, brought back enigmatically into our cultural present, and we stare (most people, that is) uncomprehendingly at these occulted messages from a vanished and entirely foreign past like they are a foreign language. But to me they are living doorways. I often stepped into them because they interested me and I reveled in what I saw. It was the history of the world.

I stood inside these various pages from Helgafell's *Akashic* Records and watched events unfolding as a present-time reality, even though it was many centuries ago. Think of yourself as a photographer and you capture the pivotal moment in a drama, the telling gesture, the decisive move of a group, the raising up of arms, the sending out of rays of Light, the dispatching of the *landvættir* to help Iceland. The *Akashic* Records are like that, although they record the mundane moments too, everything in fact, down to the minutiae, whatever trembles the etheric fabric: it is the perfect and absolute surveillance. What actually happened, not what people think, theorize, pretend, fantasize, or hope, is recorded and available for inspection. I've always enjoyed inspecting that.

I can see now how the assembly of Iceland's four protective land-spirits at Helgafell and a host of Wild Hunt Riders and Magic-Men gathered together could easily be compressed and frozen into a timeless mythic picture emanating mystery. But they were actual events, though some of them took place in what we'd call higher reality and require clairvoyance to perceive and maybe a Light body to participate in them in any useful manner. I didn't see our vexatious arithmetical gods interfering with this spectacle of Light, at least not yet in my ramble through the time galleries. I guess they waited until our time in 2065. I'll get to that in a little bit and what happened with me and them.

I continued with my stroll through the Holy Fell picture gallery. I believe I walked all the way back to the beginning to when the Elohim were here, laying out the Light temple specifics. The land was flat; the holy hill was a hill in Light only. They were walking about in tall human-looking bodies though they shimmered in angelic Light. You could not mistake these Elohim as entirely human; they were wearing the costume of a human form but they were *bright*. I don't think humans ever get quite this radiant; I could the stars through them.

They were conversing with the Wild Hunt Riders, presumably Ascended Masters, who would make themselves available through this geomantic node. Since the Earth's Light grid is holographic and fourth-dimensional in nature (minimally, as still higher dimensions are part of it too), the Masters did not have to be present at Holy Fell in the sense we who occupy bodies in 3D space understand that. Merely a directed thought would deliver them to the hill. Holy Fell enjoyed the presence of a domed canopy of Light overhead; it stretched out in all directions for several miles, constituting the geomantic province of Thorsness, and it conveyed the attention and spiritual Light of some bright star.

I saw scenes later on the timeline, from the starting point of the Elohim presence, in which *Draugars* and other demonic-type spirits tried to harass the site, poke its protective veil, defile the sanctuary in some manner. The Magic-Men of Holy Fell would emanate their astral forms from their physical and dispatch the nasty, interfering spirits, though sometimes

it took some sparring. Some of the *Draugars*, I saw, got quite testy and obdurately clung to their presumed rights to revisit and basically haunt their former dwellings despite the fact it disturbed the smoothness of embodied consciousness and polluted the hill.

The demonic spirits were not pliable to human reason or Magic-Men instruction, and they had to be dispatched more rudely and decisively. They had to be forcefully convinced that they were dead and should act accordingly, which meant vacate the living human world. They were always looking for points of weakness and seduction in living humans to exploit. Their presence discouraged or interfered with the activities of the benevolent Nature Spirits in the area so it was doubly necessary for the Magic-Men to drive them away.

Early on in the human use of this site I saw a woman sitting by the hill. She wore a cape, had long grey braided hair, and was concentrating inwardly. In the air around her were sylphs, those bright, birdlike spirits of the air element. They were swooping, emerging out of their many sky caves, as some call them. The gnomes have their subterranean tunnels threading the Inner Earth; the sylphs have something similar in the air which to them is like the inside of the Earth, a vast airborne landscape. Their sky caves are points of emergence where they lark from the subtle worlds into the etheric sheath of our physical world.

This woman was calling to them, singing, conversing, possibly instructing them. She was at ease with them, and the sylphs respected her, even sought her advice on current conditions in the planet's Light grid and what modulations to make. It's not terribly important to this narrative, but I realized I had been that woman.

It looked like a fun pastime she was pursuing, and a useful one. I was looking at one of my timeline antecedents, an earlier incarnation of my soul. Well, we do encounter ourselves now and then when we investigate these sites.

There were periods of dormancy when this site, the whole peninsula, was under seawater, when it seemed most of Iceland had become dormant. The Light temple remained but human physical access to it and interaction were curtailed. At those times even the influence of the predominant stars affecting this region was dimmed; the site slept and human consciousness was quiescent. Then the star would come back into alignment and it would be as if the stage lights were suddenly flipped to high and the performance area now brilliantly lit up again. The waters receded, human recognition of the Thor temple resumed, and the Nature Spirits began to flourish in a whirl of helpful activity for the land. I saw this cycle happen a number of times as I walked through the picture gallery.

One time, when I was investigating the inside of the Thor Light temple, I saw arithmetical scribbling on the walls. It was more like formal notation. Codes, equations, algorithms, all sorts of numbering and calculations written on the walls. Yes, I'm sure you've been wondering when the arithmetical part of this report would start, Frederick. Well, it's started. I was at the point when the arithmetical alien gods came into the picture and the real action began. Because I started seeing those arithmetical minds right through these inscribed walls, as if their obsessive calculating minds were in the script that wrote the numbers.

They had no particular form, disdaining incarnation. But their minds, their attention, had a distinctive "flavor," a signature style of perceiving. I could tell they had no interest whatsoever in the Thor temple, whether physical or subtle, and even Thor was an inconsequential ill-guided incarnated spirit. So what if he was chief of the Great White Brotherhood. That's still an incarnation. A body of Light is still an incarnational form. They were only impressed with numbers. These mathematical gods have a marked aversion to any kind of form.

I saw that everything at this site hinged on pixellation. It sounds odd at first, but let me suggest you picture a pointillist painting. That was a clever though short-lived innovation in late 19th century European art where the details of a scene were painted in individual points of color that would, seen at a short distance, resolve into the desired image. This notion was probably inspired by the many discoveries (or theories anyway) of physicists about the nature of the atom and ultimate particles and the illusory quality of their apparent forms and what they did and whether you could ever predict that. The result of this view was that physical reality consisted of myriads of particles of dancing light.

Pointillist-inspired pixellation was later employed in computer graphics as a technical innovation with bitmaps displaying individual pixels in an image. A pixel is a tiny dot comprising a picture element. It was the same principle and it is relevant here. The word-root shows up in many forms in the language. In Cornish and Devon folklore, a pixie is a small mischievous Nature Spirit, like an elf, puck, or brownie, a small fairy or a "wee little fairy." It may derive from the Swedish *pyske* first recorded in 1630. To be pixillated means to be stimulated and led astray into illusion by pixies, rendered prankish, eccentric, almost drunkenly whimsical, to be hearing pixie voices, to be out of phase with human reality, to be led down the "pixie-path" of bewilderment, to be "pixie-led," which means lost, without orientation, under the pixies' influence of little dancing lights.

Pixellation, on a technical level, is the transition point, the key interface, where mathematics code an image, which is an abstract form of an incarnation. This is the use of the term I will be relying on here, though I admit the risk of getting pixellated by the pixiefying influence of pointillist pixies while you investigate primordial pixellation is significant. You'll have to excuse me: I just had a lovely flush of alliterative enthusiasm come all over me. I think the arithmetical gods would regard all incarnation into form as a pixillated state. Just so you don't lose me here, pixillated means under a pixie influence, while the modern word pixellated means comprised of the tiny dots of light called pixels.

This turns on Thor and what he is. I said he, or Arthur or Indra, is the Solar Logos. As Blaise explains, the Solar Logos is the Christ or Logos at the level of suns, which is to say stars and also Ascended Masters who are very bright and starry fellows. Thor is the cohering force that unites the pixellated galaxy of stars. He holds Camalate and the Round Table together, these two fractal expressions of the galaxy and its population of suns, pixels in essence, just very large ones.

As Blaise explains, the Solar Logos knows the names of all the stars, and those are magical names comprising the Hebrew letters and numbers. To logically cohere this pixellated solar galaxy is also to summon all the Grail Knight stars to assemble into a form. Since that

is a function of the Solar Logos and that figure, as Thor, has a center at Holy Fell, then we may assume that this cohering assemblage function is discharged at some level here.

You can see the galaxy with its 200 billion stars as a pixellated landscape, a pointillist rendition that is meant to yield a perceivable recognizable image seen at a distance. That image (probably our Purusha or the Qabalist's *Adam Qadmon* at some level) is an incarnation; Light and its antecedent mathematical script have taken on a form for the purposes of illustration and our mental illumination. This is the cosmogonic Albion figure. That process proceeds through the Thor Light temple at Holy Fell; it does so through many other similar sites around the planet, but the Helgafell node has special aspects, extra arcane linkages to this key but vulnerable image interface.

The Thor temple here administers the *transition* of arithmetical coding into perceivable images—it's a pixellation zone—and that includes the seeable presence of the Riders, all the images the pixels comprise, and including the allegations in the *Eyrbyggja Saga* of hearing the merry sounds of partying and drinking horns from inside Holy Fell, indicating happy if dead former warriors. Numbers code pixels and these build perceivable metaphorical images, reality.

The arithmetical alien gods, or whatever name we choose to signify these abstract primordial intelligences of the numbered realm, intend to commandeer the pixellation interface at Holy Fell because it is a crucial node in the incarnation system. They want to disincarnate Thor not only from Helgafell but reality itself. Take over Holy Fell and work backwards to disincarnate the whole nasty mess. Helgafell acts like eyes bringing a blurry pointillist confusion of particles into a clear image. It is the pixellation boundary between the seeable image and a blur. It's more than a blur really; it's unformed, pre-form, arithmetical reality coding.

They would erase the time palimpsest of Holy Fell's incarnational picture gallery, the one I have been perusing like an avid art connoisseur at the Louvre. They want all the mythic images, the condensations of psychic realities and processes into perceivable, memorable pictures, returned to their number roots. They want to initiate a mass recall of all mythic images, all evidences of hateful incarnation in body, mind, and imagery, back to their pure arithmetical realm. They want to erase even the pointillist mid-ground so it will not yield an image, and they certainly don't want the Solar Logos to cohere all the suns into a form for that is still the vile act of pixellation, only at a large scale, to these alien gods.

There is another aspect to pixellation which is relevant to this notion. Physicists talk about whether spacetime is smooth or pixellated. Or at least they used to. My father, you may not know, was a physicist with a Ph.D. from Stanford. He worked in what was known as quantum gravity research. When I was young, he would call me away from my picture books of King Arthur and Greek myths and tell me a few interesting bits about the cosmos. The issue turned on whether spacetime down at its tiniest level was pixellated, which means made up of individual pixels of energy. If spacetime were not smooth and continuous, then it would have to be pixellated; it would be a pointillist cosmos.

That would mean a finite limit to the amount of information the cosmos could store because that would be bounded by the number of pixels. If the universe of spacetime is pixellated, then its storage capacity would be less than infinite and that prospect seemed to dismay the physicists. I guess the alternative is that if reality is smooth and wavelike then perhaps it is holographic enabling quantum information storage, which would be a great deal more. My father used to chuckle over their concern. Around 2020, they believed they had disproved it. Spacetime officially was not pixellated but wondrously, salvifically smooth.

Werner Heisenberg first proposed that spacetime is pixellated, though he challenged physicists to come up with a quantum gravity test to disprove the conjecture. He said spacetime is pixellated into indivisible 3D Planck-length units, like 2D pixels. The Planck length is the smallest measurable unit at the boundary of spacetime and gravity where things yield to quantum effects and different measurements must be used and believe me, these are vexing beyond belief, as uncertain and ungraspable as a Zen *koan*. The Planck length is 6.3631×10^{-34} inches. Physicists take that as an absolute boundary at the form threshold.

The physicist Max Planck in 1899 derived this key number from three fundamental physical constants, namely, the speed of light in a vacuum, the Planck constant, and the gravitational constant. With that kind of foundation, the Planck length seemed like a reality bedrock. To give you a sense of perspective, the Planck length is estimated to be about 10^{-20} times the diameter of a proton. Anything tinier than this length dissolves the rational, sensible notions of and any quantifiable meaning to space and length. It throws them out the window.

This is the boundary between the physical, measurable world and the Zen-like, ambiguous, mercurial, elusive, Trickster-quirked quantum world characterized by the collapse of all binary notions and the vexing reign of indeterminate, immeasurable effects. It is the zone of antinomy, where opposites are true and equally co-present at the same time, with a particle going left and right. You will see a sign proclaiming "The Heisenberg Uncertainty Principle rules here." You can't know both the location and the speed of an elementary particle, which means you cannot accurately predict outcomes; all is uncertain.

My father used to say you had to talk like an enigmatic Taoist sage to describe this. As you can well imagine, a great number of complicated equations accompany this, and physicists say that the quest to establish dependable laws of physics that are valid at the Planck length, which, keep in mind, is likely the origin point for the formation of elementary particles, is tantamount to our concocting a theory of everything, gravity, light, mass, the formation of reality. Why stop there? Why not throw in a complete personnel file and psychological profile and why stop there: a rap sheet on the Chief of Antinomies, the Creator.

Let me get to why I regard this as a fundamental model of what we're up against. The Planck length is a kind of absolute boundary. Picture it like a line. Above it is the measurable world, the domain of arithmetic, numbers, equations. Below it is the quantum realm that only Chuang-tzu could talk about sensibly.

Let's say universal spacetime is pixellated. All our mythic images, our psychic pictures, all the ways consciousness assumes recognizable, discrete forms, the mechanism of incarnation at all levels and in all nuances from ideas to bodies, happens in this pixellated realm *above* the Planck length boundary. This picture world is the product of pixellation. Our alien gods reside on the other nihilist side of this boundary, in the quantum realm where nothing is incarnated, no forms are validated. They have put their Magic Square right at this boundary, laying it horizontally like a sieve at the event horizon of the Planck length cut-off. But they are dismayed to look up past this horizon line and see all their precious numbers whoring themselves under coercion to pixellate and incarnate a world.

Physicists propose reality beyond this boundary is like a black hole. It's also like the worst *koan* imaginable, where the quantum effects are so wacky and unfathomable you can't pinpoint any difference between point *a* and point *b* and the quantum field anomalies will so totally skew spacetime normality you won't even be able to tell the difference between yourself and what you're looking at.

There the Magic Square suctions back all the arithmetic in universal reality, recalling all the numbers that run the formulas and algorithms that make reality and that form, through the concentration of pixels, all things incarnated—remember, we're talking bodies at all levels, human forms, planets, galaxies, pictures, psychic ideas, Light temples, even the forms for celestial spirits—and thus constitute the measurable, quantifiable, incarnation-characterized world. Their numbers, the arithmetical realm, are on the wrong side of this pixellation boundary. They should never have been let out of the pristine unformed "barn."

If they succeed in this complete recall of the arithmetical realm across the quantum boundary, this absolute sinkhole and one-way black hole and irrefutable fundamental boundary, and corral all the numbers and their combinations in the Magic Square (the "barn"), reality as we know it, see it, measure it, is gone, and we're thoroughly screwed as far as incarnation goes.

All the pixellation will have been sucked out of existence. The pointillist canvases will all be blank again. Pixellation will be depixellated. That's how my father put it when he explained this as a theoretical possibility. I remember it spooked me something proper. The aliens would have sucked all pixellation back into the smoothness of nothing, an ocean of elementary smoothness, completely empty, and there would be no images, no forms, no reality at all.

Well, it's hardly theoretical now. These alien gods are actually doing that. They are suctioning all the numbers and pixels across the Planck length boundary so none will remain to pixellate the universe into seeable forms.

I made a sharp inhalation as I realized something. I suppose I gasped. I don't usually do that. What I realized is the full implication of the dissolution of the pixellated bedrock interface necessary to generate all the psychic images. It is not just pictures and images as we think of them; these are the Supreme Being's imaginations, conjurings, models for universal reality, all the conceived forms He came up with to provide plausible visual metaphors of His own ineffable Reality.

It is His notion of what the Cosmic Logos should look like, which is to say, its function, and that of the Galactic Logos for each of the 18 billion galaxies, and the Logos of the unfathomable number of total stars in Creation, and that of all the planets, and all the phylogenies and their codes to exist and flourish on those planets, including us. It includes the images for the composite collective personifications, Albions at all the levels, the Purusha figures, the templates for the angels and Masters and the range of their metaphorical forms made in Light.

All this needs the pixellated substrate to live. The summary name for all these incarnations is the Light grid. Light is patterned into grids, mathematically defined and geometrically formed, and these grids cast the requisite and prolific images that constitute our reality. Our Arithmetical Earth, the arithmetical universe, depend on this gridding of the Light to structure our respective worlds.

Incidentally, the fact that these arithmetical compulsives are recalling all the numbers into their Magic Square tends to support the pixellated spacetime model. If that wasn't true, then the alien gods would not be draining it dry. Whatever proof the physicists thought had been judged definitive some decades ago is now out the window and invalidated by the current situation. These alien gods, the personification of the arithmetical realm, want the pixellated universe.

That way they can put an end to this most disdainful trend towards incarnation and the corruption of the innate purity of their numbers in support of this deed. The arithmetical realm must remain quiescent in its Magic Square. Before they get sucked into the black hole singularity at the end of the universe with the collapse of the pixellated interface Planck and

Heisenberg will be happy to see they were right. They might high-five each other as they fall into the void.

These numbers obsessives have positioned their Magic Square sieve right at the Planck length boundary, the ultimate border crossing, and like a black hole it snatches all the numbers. Maybe I should liken their suction to a vacuum cleaner. You can almost see them (they don't have an incarnational form) on the other side of their sieving Magic Square, siphoning back the numbers to them.

Their Magic Square at the Planck length boundary is the inexorable drain on the incarnation sink. Everything is swirling around in the porcelain container of spacetime as the pixellated world is sucked down into the nonincarnated realm where form never happened, where the use of numbers to support this horrid experiment of a misguided, deluded Supreme Being never happened. That's their goal: to end all incarnation by recalling numbers from the pixellated universe that made forms possible, to corral them back in the quantum foam.

This perspective helps us understand the scope of the alien gods' tactics, don't you think. What's the biggest possible threat facing humans? Not death, but the end of reality. How could this be done? Steal all of God's numbers. Take out of circulation all the numbers, the complete arithmetical domain, that sustains the pixellated universe. The Hierophancy heuristic algorithm is a crucial linchpin in this domain, along with the algorithms from the other five planets. It is an algorithm of interest, and they are intent on acquiring and then retiring it.

The geomantic rhombus is a last desperate beachhead against this bad outcome. I prepared my part of the missing rhomboidal geomantic pinning for insertion. Honestly, though, I was not filled with confidence it would help at all.

Our job is to stop that bad outcome, on behalf not only of the Earth, but universal reality itself. The alien gods, if they are successful, could force a premature *Pralaya*. That's the period of sleep and dormancy between world cycles of Brahma. It's universal downtime, Brahma's famous nap-time when you wouldn't dare disturb the Old Man asleep on His couch, and you couldn't anyway because you wouldn't currently even be in existence. Droll, isn't it.

I didn't ever think our brief for the Hierophancy extended this far into the bedrock of reality, did you? But we have had to follow the clues and implications of this apparently continuously burgeoning case once we discovered our Earth's algorithm had been stolen and the well-being of our planet suddenly imperiled. All of which led to me sitting out in this field facing Holy Fell, place-marker of one of the four mainstays for the Earth's algorithm, and having to *do* something.

I realize you might be puzzled by a seemingly physical impossibility. I have characterized the alien gods' Magic Square as existing and operating at the Planck length boundary. I have also established via accepted mathematics that this is the tiniest quantifiable physical measurement. How could I interact there?

All I can say is that without any effort I found myself reduced in stature to that size. I think this is a yogic ability. I remember reading about it once. I've always been able to make myself smaller when I needed to, not so much my physical body but my sense of self as operating in a Light form. That's what I did here. I must have been reduced to Planck-length-size yet I felt myself to be my normal size. My clothes still fit, thank goodness. Blaise will attest that in operating clairvoyantly in the spiritual, nonmaterial world you often find size measurements become meaningless and fluid. You're big, you're small, it doesn't matter. It becomes hard to tell how big a Light temple is and it doesn't matter.

It did seem that I was hovering right on the edge of the Planck length boundary. I felt the suction of its black hole effect, the tidal pull on my feet. I felt made of trillions of pixels and the gravity pull of that boundary was yanking insistently on them. I couldn't say whether this boundary was below me as if I were standing on the physical ground or if it was erected like a vertical wall in front of me. I can say I was in immediate relationship with it. I can say that it didn't matter; it was the same situation regardless of my spatial orientation.

On one side was the universe of Light grids coding visible, incarnated realities, the domain of images in Light sketched upon a pixellated spacetime. On the other side was the end of all that, the quit-stop for universal incarnation and form-building, the definitive one-way suction at the conclusion of all spacetime and metaphysical manifestation. You felt the alien gods relentless in their recall of the universe's inventory of numbers. Theirs was the universal suction that was sieving out the repertory of the universe's mathematics. It was the end-wall at the boundary of spacetime, the (dark?) Magic Square at the end of the world.

I had to find a way to stop these bounders from drawing out Earth's linchpin digits. I sat on the lower slopes of Holy Fell pondering my best move.

It came to me, in a flash, it seemed. Maybe Blaise's pals the angelic Blaises had a hand in that inspiration. It had that kind of smooth and pure input. The idea was to use the geomantic feature of Holy Fell as a bulwark against the alien gods and their long, inexorable fingers reaching for all the numbers that sustained reality. That feature was the Wild Hunt, the Riders mounted, swords raised, horses rearing, led by King Arthur or Thor, if you prefer, and backed by the Archangel Michael, sponsor of all Grail Knights and geomantic Mysteries. No, I did not expect the seemingly physical size of the Riders and the majesty of their mounts to make any impression on the aliens. It was that the Riders held a bulwark against the sieve at the Planck length boundary. It was the Christ Light.

The Wild Hunt Riders, at least most of them, were Ascended Masters. By definition that meant they had transformed their physical bodies into forms of Light, and those Light bodies were cohered by the Christ Light. Necessarily. They were Christ Light bodies. Ascension copies the demonstration Jesus made at Golgotha, rising into the Light in a body transformed from materiality into Light, which means consciousness now exists in the nondualistic, non-selfhood state of singularity, of unitive consciousness, stonelike, as monoliths of Light.

That Christ Light, the Logos itself, is unarguably senior to the arithmetical realm and thereby to all the machinations of the alien gods who dwell in that domain. The Christ Light is absolutely unformed, despite all the misleading cultural and religious images of Jesus Christ. The numbered realm is still a differentiated zone, no matter how minutely or provisionally. The Christ Light is an empty, wakeful, panoptically aware space that encompasses the universe like an infinite sea of consciousness. In contrast, the alien gods and their precious arithmetical domain are embarassingly incarnate. All those pixellated numbers.

The alien gods won't like that fact being brought rudely to their attention, I can assure you. This fact means this Logos Light is a universal spiritual glue holding the pixellated image of the Wild Hunt Riders, their seemingly corporeal manifestation, their incarnation, intact and coherent and in fact inviolable against the absolutist suction of the Magic Square. The Christ Light is a kind of invisible unmanifest unbreakable superglue that holds the universe tightly bound. That paradox alone is sufficient to give the alien gods a headache. Another name for this Logos Light is the Hindu designation of Vishnu; his name means to pervade, permeate, sustain, and nurture the cosmos, again suggesting this invisible glue.

That should mean the numbers cohering the incarnated forms of the Wild Hunt Riders cannot come apart into its constituents. The Planck suction will fail. It cannot unbind the Christ-Logos glue holding the pixellated images together. That's because this universal "glue" is antecedent and thus senior to numbers. The bulwark of the Wild Hunt Riders at this fundamental boundary should hold.

The Wild Hunt will appear to be permanently storming towards the Planck boundary, inviolate to the suction coming at them, and holding their numbers. That in itself will not overcome the arithmetical obsessives on the other side. But it will hold them fixed for a time in an unexpected stalemate. I can

tell these intelligences do not expect successful opposition, only weak, futile protests, so this unexpected defense at a level that should seem inviolable will stop them, that and the red-eared dogs that run ferociously with the Riders of Thorsness.

The Wild Host, Furious Army, Devil's Dandy Dogs, Gabriel's Hounds, Noisy Riders, Hounds of *Annwn*, the Riders of Asgard—these are among their names. The dogs reference pertains to the fact the mounted riders were flanked by spectral running dogs with white fur and red ears, meant to signify imminent death. But I think the canine allusion is also to hint at the role of Sirius, the Dog-Star of our galaxy, brightest of them all, and its involvement in all matters of consciousness and geomancy across the galaxy and on the Earth as well. Wodan or Odin is credited with the Wild Hunt leadership, but Thor, his son, is the functional chief of the Asgard gods and leads the Wild Hunt on Odin's behalf, and you get a suitable frisson of the proximity of death through the correlation by Hindu astronomy of the star Sirius with the god Shiva, Lord of Destruction. No sensible person, pixellated or not, would want Shiva bearing down on him.

Why are they furious? It is the fury of totally awakened consciousness. Furious doesn't mean angry; it means fierce, indomitable, invincible. Like a raging forest fire. Would you say that fire is angry? No, it isn't. It is just fully manifesting its nature. Burning fiercely with the elemental power of fire. Norse myth, as recorded in Iceland by Snorri Sturluson (a much later Snorri), says Odin can count on thousands of warriors of Valhalla when Ragnarok comes. They will storm *furiously* through the many doors of Valhalla and ride out in his support.

The Wild Hunt, I fancy, is a dress rehearsal for that apocalyptic future event. Now they will ride out in fury on his behalf in defense of the pixellated universe.

I rode with them, or at least I pictured myself doing so. I took advantage of the pixellated energy around Holy Fell to create a plausible image of myself as a Wild Hunt Rider. I held a broad sword of Light upright and diagonally in front of me. Its blade was laced with flickering lilac flames. The other Riders had the same. All of our swords were touching, blade's edge to blade's edge, a much larger version of the same held by the Archangel Michael. It was our touchstone. My point is I don't think the arithmetical crazies counted on this type of rebuttal.

We were a cavalry drawn up like a hundred horses suddenly reigned in on a cliff's edge, a fierce wedge of Light and swords and furious intention against the abyss. It was dramatic, though I'm sure the drama went unobserved by the alien gods. Nothing about the human or spiritual realm made an impact on them. I was irate with them. How dare you take Creation's numbers back!

To be honest, I was not actually angry or furious as this word suggests. But we all conveyed that impression. It added to the fierceness of the Wild Hunt. Anger at the alien gods would be utterly futile. It would flare up unnoticed. I felt the strong suction pulling on my awareness as I sat my horse, my sword brightly brandished before me. I held my own, or I should say, the Logos Light held me fast and I didn't slip down the drain at the Planck length boundary. Though I was a bit miffed that the alien gods were unimpressed with our smart assembly.

Oddly, or perhaps quaintly, it reminded me of arm–wrestling which when a young girl I had indulged in with my older sister, Janice. Most often, I bested her, but what I remember from those youthful competitions was the unshakeable strength in my arm, that she could not bend or flex it, that it remained upright and steadfast despite her pulls on it. That's how I felt in withstanding the alien gods' powerful suction. Unyielding. They would not bend my arm to the table.

This also felt like a tightly drawn bow and I was the poised arrow ready to launch. I was drawn back as far as the bow would accommodate. I waited for the release. It came. It was like a definitive bounce off a trampoline up into the air and even seemingly out of the building the trampoline was housed in. I was bounding into the upper reaches of the bounce to penetrate the Planck boundary.

I was like a skilled diver plummeting off the high board ready to slice the water smoothly, legs in tight, parallel, arms reaching out like an arrow before me. You may note there was something about the proximity of the Planck boundary that brought out a wild scramble in my brain of divergent metaphors trying to describe it. It would be my last chance to make any metaphors; once I passed that boundary the projection of plausible images was finished for good. It would be depixellated, me along with it. Frederick, you may have all my books.

As I careened towards this definitive boundary, more visual metaphors arose in me like illustrated bubbles. The Magic Square fast approaching was like a vast stockyard in which all the world's sheep and cattle had been collected. Or it was like the biggest train station imaginable, seen from overhead, thousands of travelers milling about, standing shoulder to shoulder, waiting for the trains to arrive. This is how the array of the universe's numbers appeared to me.

My mind felt like it was unscrewing itself from its fixtures, or else it was working better and faster, creating a tumbling circus of competing metaphorical turns. No: it was the heat waves from the quantum uncertainty, the queer foam of that realm, disassembling all my rational, sequential boundaries, emptying the bag. Everything was occurring to me at once; all the possible metaphors were surging through my mind at once, like a picture stampede in all directions. I felt the pull of these numbers, their gravity field. It was like having the bones of your body pulled out from your form and then you see them assembled outside you and you wonder how could you (or the universe) possibly now still exist?

I expected to lose my form but I didn't. I was like a gloved finger inserted into a pool of water. My finger did not dissolve to become part of the water. I felt the alien gods collectively observe me and wonder why I was still intact as me. I couldn't tell them, other than to speculate the Logos Light was preserving my form which was confusing since usually the Logos Light spells its dissolution.

I felt empty, devoid of content, yet I was aware and aware of myself being aware. I felt all the numbers crowding around me, as if they were declaiming their possible permutations, the grand formulas and algorithms they used to be part of. I saw the innumerable images and Light temple forms in the pixellated universe they used to comprise lying within them like tiny points at the bottom of a long narrowing

vortex cone by which they had been extracted from above.

Then I suddenly bounced all the way back to my starting point. I was outside the Planck boundary again. My penetration of that post-numbers realm was illusory, like pushing the skin of a membrane, say the inside of a balloon, as far as possible without popping it then springing back because that membrane could not be penetrated, at least not by that method. It was too elastic to get through. You only temporarily deformed its smoothness. I had visited it briefly, now I was out. The alien gods seemed no more perturbed by my intemperate, short-lived incursion than would grazing cows be ruffled by a slight uptake in the breezes. It had no effect on the taste or quantity of the fresh eatable grass.

A wiser part of me now said, Jocelyn, you have it all backwards. You are acting as if these arithmetical gods had stolen something that didn't belong to them. They don't see it that way. To them, all the numbers in Creation belong here, in the pre-incarnation realm, and it is their job as the numbers caretakers to corral the numbers back again where they belong. They don't see themselves as thieves or as having done anything unlawful. Yes, they have no moral conscience at all, but they are not incarnated, individual souls responsible for their actions.

God appointed them to be the numbers shepherds, to be the collective intelligent consciousness of the arithmetical realm. They regard the numbers as themselves; this is the Self they are. They regard the incarnational realm, the pixellated universe, as an aberration, like ontological Not-Self. The numbers never should have left this Magic Square at the Planck boundary. They should never have been exposed to such an obnoxious taint as the picture realm. It was like parts of their noncorporeal "body" had been flayed off and sent packing.

So what is the rightwards way, I queried that smarter version of Jocelyn. Act like you're the Supreme Being commissioning the numbers to organize the Earth. Assume there is a tracking system, a light, a marker of some kind, a flashing beacon, on the numbers required for the Earth's heuristic algorithm, and that through this tracking light you can find the Earth's Light grid numbers.

I pondered that for a while, then it came to me. It was rather like a light turning on. That illuminated tracking number for the Earth's managing algorithm was encoded in every human. It was a mandala of Light wrapped around the physical genome. It came with the body, free of charge. I would use that. As a back-up, a fallback plan, I would release my portion of the phantom finger-trap algorithm Sal had created for us to deploy at our rhombus nodes.

The human Blaise told me, and he said the angelic Blaises told him, about the business of the phylogeny bearing an imprint of the algorithm. Every human bears an imprint of the Earth's Light grid in the etheric field of their own DNA. Each person could, theoretically, extrapolate the entire planet and its geomantic specifics from out of oneself through this deposited engineering blueprint we each bear. That pattern is in each of us somewhere in our arcane reaches. It is the human copy of the Elohim's template, their master design for Earth and human consciousness that renders both congruent with each other and the cosmos. We each bear a complete hologram of the planet

and its complex Light grid design. That is the basis of all geomancy: this pre-existent, innate design resonance.

Here's how this translates into a tactic. I will summon Earth's numbers from out of this quantum foam in which the alien gods have sequestered it by drawing them to the innate picture I carry of the Earth in its original inception and including physical through to geomantic aspects and into the subtlest of its spiritual aspects. I will be like the Sirens on the rocks singing alluringly to the bound Odysseus. The alien gods, I hoped, will not be able to resist this call. Our hero, made of numbers, will be unable to resist this Siren of resonance and will leap into the water at once and swim out to my rocks and step upon the shore whereupon I will divest its unformed moronitude of all the numbers it stole.

The idea for the Earth, its essential outline and parameters, came first. The Elohim thought this up, crafting the template to accommodate the human and planetary poles of the same design and matching it with the cosmic original. Then they summoned the numbers and wrote the code and concocted the algorithms to make it a manifest reality. Naturally, that was simultaneous from their point of view, yet this sequential presentation should still work here.

I will hold the picture of the completed Earth, as far as its design goes, and call the requisite numbers to it from out of the Magic Square where they have been corralled. This Light grid design will exert a kind of magnetic pull on them. It would be like calling back parts that indigenously belonged to yourself. How could those horses not come running back to the barn when you whistled them?

I called on the Elohim to help. It pays to know the right consultants, and I am glad the Hierophancy has many among the angelic families we can count on. I still had to summon the pattern from within myself, stored in some arcane zone. I worked backwards. I started with picturing the Earth as the physical blue-white planet with its familiar continents and great sweeps of azure ocean.

Then I pictured the Light grid enveloping it, that complex array of Light lines, Light canopies, and many dozens of intricate geometrical patterns overlaid on it. I generated an impression of the underlying composite form of Albion that the Light grid was designed to birth. Then I dissolved that image and that of the Light grid layer and let the arithmetical scripting for this array appear. I pictured the dominant algorithms that managed the complexity of these calculations.

As I went through these stages of picturing the Earth's pattern, it was as if I was handing the Elohim a pile of clothes to hold, one at a time, until they held a copy of what I had been picturing. It looked alive; it throbbed with Light. One of them held it in his hands while a half dozen others stood by, as if admiring a baby. I could see why: it was a lovely creation, an exquisite artwork. Still, there was a strange two-dimensional flatness to it. It was lacking its real numbers.

These started to stream tentatively out of the Magic Square, like hostages streaking across an exposed field wondering if they'd make it to safety before getting recaptured. As they rejoined the Light grid template, it grew brighter, the way a human face deprived of oxygenated blood will start to freshen into

rosiness as those qualities are restored. The numbers were oxygenating the grid.

I hadn't realized until that moment, after I had extracted the complete Light grid pattern of the Earth and all its mathematics, that I carried the full array of numbers and algorithms within me, as does every human. I mean I knew it as a fact of our constitution; I just had never experienced it firsthand. We each get the complete template as a microcosmic watermark overlaid on our genetic code. You can't realistically have the Light grid imprint in you without all the numbers that run it; they are implicit in the geometrical design, so you get both together.

When I got over the cheeriness of that benevolent dispensation, I shivered because it meant every human was imperiled by the inexorable suction job being perpetrated by the alien gods in recalling the numbers in Creation to them. If those numbers, in all their copies, were called back, the template in every human would go limp, like a plant sucked dry of its water; it would shrivel and die, and people would fall out of this implicit resonant alignment with their outer reality, of both planet and cosmos, even if, ironically, so few people were aware of it.

We would walk around the world making sense of neither the planet nor our own body. Both would seem nightmarish and mysterious and starkly inimical to us. That would spell the end of geomancy as the innate resonant connection of human and planet through the intermediary mesocosm of the templated landscape. The planet would feel foreign and inimical to us, and we would have no notion of how to make it familiar or to feel at home living here.

I started to feel this tidal pull even as the numbers kept streaming back to me. It was like having both your arms extended, somebody pulling on each oppositely. I didn't have the impression I was winning in this increasingly fierce tug-of-war. If this was arm-wrestling my arm was going down and Janice was winning. I had to bring something superior to the contest or I would lose.

The Elohim did not say anything nor did they look concerned, but they are angels after all. They're programmed differently, not flustered by emotions. But I will credit them with somehow planting a notion in my mind to summon up a deeper, stronger sense of myself. I saw it in terms of a color. Bright orange flushed with gold, and I saw it as an elegant neck-to-ankle robe of Light I could wear. I put it on. It had suddenly appeared in full sartorial form and elegance before me and I had only to step into it as if I were at a clothing store and the clerk held a lovely new coat open for me to try out. I tried it on and liked it.

I knew what it was of course. It was the Robe of Light of the Orange Ray as administered by St. George and Lady Portia, among its Ray Master's many identities. It fit sleekly from my neck to my ankles, discretely clasped along my midline with beautiful shimmering gold buttons. My head sported a bishop's mitre in the same color and I found myself holding a majestic six-foot-tall staff also of that hue. I felt the power of that staff ripple through my fingers and arm.

I felt exceptionally strong and large in this outfit. It felt like me with deep roots. I had the intuition, or perhaps I caught a quick glimpse, that you three, Frederick, Sal, and Blaise, though in locations far apart, had also arrived at this particular manner of presentation and this alignment with some antique, deeply older self. I saw each of you wearing a Robe of Light, though of different hues, and brandishing a staff about six feet in length, upright and flaming at the top.

I said it made me larger, or feel larger, as if I occupied more space, exuded more power. That in itself would not impress the alien gods; they would not notice it, and if they did, they would have no interest. It would be like showing a book to a dog. At best, he might sniff it, then turn his attention elsewhere. The size and strength enhancements benefited me by fortifying me with more assurance. It made me feel I could hold on to the precious Earth numbers longer against the suction pull of their Magic Square and their arithmetical imperative.

Part of the size, depth, and strength enhancement aspects pertained to wisdom. My robe seemed studded with innumerable jewels in brilliant colors. They only looked like symmetrical, perfectly faceted gems; I knew it was accrued wisdom I was drawing upon from an untold number of past lives in which evidently I had earned that and was now calling on my savings account. Writing this now I am surprised at how quickly I came to this conclusion. Don't get me wrong: I still concur with that assessment. It came to me then in a flash. The bejeweled robe kept changing form to look like a large open chamber in which the jewels were embedded in the walls like huge flower clusters. The image shifted back and forth from these two equivalent expressions, and then eventually I saw both at the same time, as one superimposed over the other.

I said the robe brought me accrued wisdom, but it was about earned knowledge and tactics too. Old skills I—some antique, antediluvian me—had once mastered were now available again. I felt flush with ability, copious with accomplishments, all of this on hand as I needed it. I would compare this to suddenly moving from a tiny one-room cabin to a 30-room mansion. You feel yourself, your aura, your presence, your consciousness, expand to fill the much larger space and you discover treasures in these rooms. You realize you are a larger, more powerful, more capable being than you ever thought, that this is the hidden truth of yourself, now revealed, and you are acting from it and you shall justifiably expect to prove invincible, and those jewels are bursting in wisdom.

This knowledge and wisdom and the roster of smart tactics stay dormant and implicit in us usually, but now it had risen to the surface of my explicit awareness. It was like standing in a library and you knew the shelved books so thoroughly you could quote from any of them, page by page, without hesitation and without any mistakes. It was the kind of feeling that assured you everything you had to do you had already once done, and done successfully, that in many respects you were standing in the already accomplished future observing the steps that led to this assured plateau far ahead on your own timeline.

You had already done it because its accomplishment was implicit in this vast knowledge base you had now activated. I had already overcome these alien gods and recovered the plundered arithmetic because my Old Self body had that ability. It was as if all of time, at least the time allotted to me as a soul, had been drawn from both directions of past and future and compressed into a powerful now-point. I

stood there in a sense of completion, able to and having done it all, and in some manner this now-point was outside of the linear flow of time.

Meanwhile, my simulation of the Earth and its Light grid had expanded. It was bigger than my human form, which had disappeared or been eclipsed by it, and I now found myself as a diffused awareness occupying this planetary form. The copyrighted Earth algorithms were streaming back into it, into me. The Elohim stood in a crescent array behind and around me, like sails on a yacht. Their billowing presence amplified my own growing confidence swelling out of my past. It felt now a hundred of us were demanding Earth's numbers back. In a manner that seemed unnoticed by the alien gods, Sal's phantom algorithm streamed in stealth mode back against this current into the alien gods' world.

I wondered why the alien gods put up no resistance to this onslaught. It almost seemed they were ignoring us or remaining happily indifferent. Then I saw why. We were not extracting the actual numbers, only their ghosts. It was like pulling off only their astral forms, cloudlike emanations ripped off their true and more substantial forms. The numbers we were recalling were useless. They would not run any algorithmic processes; they would compute nothing. It was like presenting a clutch of *Monopoly* play money at a bank for an exchange. The bank would not honor this fake currency; they would show you the door. As for my quarter of the phantom algorithm the alien gods didn't bother to notice it.

These numbers which I had mistakenly perceived as solid, substantial, and workable, were now slipping through my fingers like water through a colander. I felt the Elohim waiting for my next move. It was curious though. I did not have the impression they were without a solution, but they were waiting to see what I came up with, as if the success of this operation was dependent on my cleverness. I didn't feel clever at the moment. I felt deflated. The best I could come up with was an image of myself, ruffled and harried, throwing torn-out magazine pages at them, a futile gesture of flaunting the mythic world at them.

I realized at that moment that our Hierophancy operation to identify the thieves and retrieve the vital numbers had been left to us to manage. It was either posed as a test or possibly because it was our prime responsibility. It felt like an initiation and I was not getting a passing grade. It seemed that we were blindly following a script, abiding by rules we hadn't been briefed on, or at least not recently. We were stumbling in the dark, tripping over our own inept cleverness. How far back in time does our charter go? Was there a time of a basic briefing?

Then my thoughts turned completely around. It was as if my head had rotated 180 degrees and I saw things from behind me now. What if *we* had been those arithmetical gods, had derived from that arcane numbers-driven formless realm, then had incarnated and turned against our homeland as we now were? What if, even more fascinating, we had been sent on a classified mission from *this* realm to see what it's like in the incarnational realm, to see how the numbers fared in the pixellated universe which we were now still doing *on their behalf*?

We were the personifications of the formless arithmetical gods on a long-term stealth assignment in the quantifiable realm beyond the Planck boundary investigating a theft which from our other point of view wasn't a theft at all but a reclamation of property rightfully ours, of numbers operating out of context. That would make the Hierophancy a secret arm of the arithmetical realm, looking after our precious numbers that should never have been let loose into the world. That would mean we were not rectifying a theft but correcting a leakage. The pixellated universe was where we would find the genuine bad guys, that infernal place into which our pristine numbers had seeped like an unseen hemorrhage. We were moles in the "enemy's" fold retrieving our numbers.

The Hierophancy heuristic algorithm had not been extracted unlawfully from the Earth. The unlawful act was in letting it get out of the arithmetical Magic Square. That was like being a spy agency and classified information got leaked. That would mean the part of me that knew this was working against the part of me that did not know it. My head was spinning, as you can imagine.

I felt my head was facing in both directions, or maybe I had two heads. The Hierophancy seemed tasked with two contrary commissions: retrieve the algorithm for the Earth to run the planet or retrieve it for the arithmetical gods who safeguard all the number formulations in existence and keep them outside the world to preserve their purity against pixellated-universe taints. One head was facing the realm of application, the pixellated universe that depended on the mathematical formulas to run its reality processes; the other head looked faithfully to the place of origin, the pristine numbers archives. Call me Janus.

The two affiliations each carried justification, yet they seemed entirely opposed.

I saw the picture world imposed on the pixellated universe as a coping mechanism, a way of accounting for the vexatious mistake of material-world incarnation, as an accountancy to keep track of expenses in a world mistakenly extrapolated. Paradoxically, the alien gods had allowed provisional incarnations on our part or else we could never carry out the important mission, but I sensed clearly they regarded it as an onerous "expense" required to complete the job. We would be suitably decontaminated and reconstituted to purity on our return.

I felt their bristling attitude towards the Creator Who had erred badly at the start. That was an odd sensation, or I suppose I should call it a thought. I had never considered the generation of a universe with myriads of worlds to be a mistake, yet here I was, thinking it stridently, even if aided by my numbers compatriots. I started feeling cranky when I thought about the Supreme Being.

I was occupying a place of profound confusion, or was it stark clarity? Did the Supreme Being have second thoughts about the wisdom of Creation? Was He now second-guessing Himself, besieged by uncertainties? What have I done, He moans, pulling on His beard. Had it been a rash move, ultimately a mistake, one that needs immediate rectification by its removal? That was the view of the alien gods, of us, *our* view, I suppose I should say. Call the numbers back. That's why we were out in the pixellated universe rectifying this error once and for all. I now had the correct orientation for our Hierophancy initiatives. At least I thought so.

Who hasn't, at least once, in the midst of philosophical ruminations or perhaps in a brown despair over the still only slowly illuminating conditions of consciousness on the Earth, considered the possibility it all was ill-advised, a stupid idea, really, that should not ever have been undertaken? We may think such gloomy thoughts, but surely it wasn't up to us to act on it. Yet here I was, seemingly poised to act on it, but for which outcome, which side was I acting?

11

I was looking forward to reading Blaise's report. I could count on him for lively descriptions and probably some insight on the status of our field mission. He had gone off to Japan to investigate the western vertex of our elongated Earth rhombus of sites, a place sacred to the ancient Ainu and called Kamui Kotan.

Yes, I know Jocelyn's report is inconclusive as was Sal's, and mine for that matter. I will save the report on the resolution of our field trips for later. Certain developments took place after each of us had established ourselves at our assigned locations that led us to realize the four sites and their roles with respect to the alien gods and their arithmetical realm had to be worked together. It was as if we all were waiting for another element, still veiled, to fall into place.

I had Theodore, our pilot, fly me to Sapporo, the major airport on mountainous Hokkaido, the northernmost island of Japan, Blaise's report began. Hokkaido means "Northern Sea Circuit" and was formerly known as Ezo, Yezo, or Yeso. It has been the Ainu homeland from the beginning; they are the indigenous inhabitants of this part of Japan. Sapporo is Japan's fifth largest city with a population well over two million, but from here I would have to travel overland to reach the Ainu precinct of Kamui Kotan. Tokyo, the epitome of modern Japan, lies 771 miles to the south from here, yet to the Ainu, Hokkaido is the foundation of all Japan and for them, its autochthonous people, it still is. They are to Japan as the Aboriginals are to Australia, the land's first inhabitants.

The drive northwest from Sapporo to Kamui Kotan is about 58 miles, and this ancient geomantic province is situated about 22 miles west of the city of Asahikawa. They called Hokkaido, a few surrounding islands, and a portion of Honshu, northern Japan itself, *Ainu Moshir*, "The Land Where People [the Ainu] Live" to distinguish it from *Kamui Moshir*, "Land of the *Kamui* [Spirits]." This is the Ainu model of the world, the division of it into these two primordial groups.

Evidence suggests the Ainu have lived in Hokkaido for up to 30,000 years. Their name means "Human," so *Ainu Moshir* means "Peaceful Land of Humans." An Ainu myth claims the Ainu lived in Hokkaido, "in this place," 100,000 years before the Children of the Sun came, presumably referring to the Japanese as progeny of Amaterasu, the great Japanese Sun Goddess famous in their myths. To the Ainu, the Japanese are newcomers to the land; the Ainu are the old ones. It's difficult to know which is the correct time reckoning for their habitation, but it is certainly safe to conclude it has been a long time, longer than any others.

Let's get to the fun parts, such as what the name means, because that is always a door-opener for me for understanding the geomancy of a site. Kamui Kotan means "God Village" or "the place where God lives," though it is more accurate to say "where the *gods* live." The word *kamui* derives from the later Japanese Shinto term *kami*, meaning the diverse world of *many* spirits; this includes Nature Spirits, elementals, landscape angels or *devas* of sites, and a fair population of the benevolent dead, Ainu ancestors remaining on hand in the spiritual world to assist matters in the physical realm as needed. So Kamui Kotan means the subtle village where the many *kami* or spirits-gods reside. It means this is a geomantic node in which this teeming spirit population is a key feature.

In this highly animistic model, reality is suffused and richly populated with *kamui* who run all the processes of the physical world, all the elemental expressions, from beauty to destruction, glorious weather to harsh storms. We are probably dealing with the same conception as the Roman *genius loci*, the resident subtle-spirit presence at a site that renders it spiritually charged, or the earlier Greek perception of nymphs, youthful Nature Spirits manifesting in either gender and animating reality and occupying all the forms of Nature. Ovid's *Metamorphoses* recounts how the nymphs got into these forms, became trees or rivers. It is a wonderfully geomantic accounting. The difference is that for the Ainu it is not just one *kamui* but a host of them occupying a given site.

Kotan means village, a natural sheltering place for deities, a location not meant for humans because it is sacred and full of *numen* or deity presence. It seems to evoke the same numinous otherworldly overlap you feel in the Irish terms *sidhe*, hostel, and Hollow Hills. The physical place is a *kamui* portal. It is an aperture through which you as an Ainu shaman-psychic pass to reach the *kamui*.

The physical village is set in a wooded canyon along the banks of the vigorous Ishikari River. The regular capsizing of boats in that fast-moving water is often attributed to the action of malevolent or at least mischievous or maybe ambivalent spirits active in this numinous area. Ainu folklore says *Kamui Kotan Ninne Kamui*, the "violent and resistant god," lived here during the period of original Ainu territorial dominance and wanted to destroy the Ainu. A benevolent guardian deity called Samaikuru defeated him, saving the People.

That violent, resistant god is also called Nitne Kamuy and is quite nasty. This term can mean "evil-god area" when referencing a locality, and it can mean Satan and all his devils (a perception likely filtered through Western visitors), the negative-tending *kamui* spirits who oppress humankind. These hostile spirits are heavy, stiff like dough, and numerous; they bring evil, are difficult to get along with, are feared, and, troublingly, they often occupy the same objects or locales as the beneficent *kamui* making all human encounters marked by ambivalence. It is possible, though, as I've seen it elsewhere, that the negative *kamui* were testing humanity for their worthiness and the Ainu accounts record the natural process of humans coming into balance with the strong energies of these Nature Spirits.

Which spiritual presence am I encountering, light or dark, the Ainu might inquire. An Ainu star constellation depicts this deity as an adult female holding a long raised staff out at a diagonal in front of her and in a threatening manner. This constellation abuts the Western formation of Aquarius, so possibly the Ainu construe it as constituting a portion of Aquarius's star pattern, but since nobody ever said Aquarius was trouble or an agent of anti-human hostility, maybe the pattern got muddled (likely in language translation) and got a negative slant.

As for Samaikuru, the Ainu benefactor, his story is less substantial and more problematic. For one thing, his name may originally be Samickle, and his starting point is some confused, conflated region between the Ainu epic poem or *Oina* about early culture heroes and an action-adventure video game called Okami, marketed in 2006. Very strange, I know. In America, it would be like putting together a hero's chronicle including a television series as evidence. The Okami version apparently draws richly from received Ainu oral traditions.

The Ainu preserve a mostly oral culture, and their *Kamui Yukar*, or deity epics, are long, sometimes comprising 7,000 sung verses recounting a deity's life, and according to scholars, sometimes the identities and storylines get confusing. Or maybe it's the scholars who get confused; oral-history shamanic cultures do not abide by the logical syllogistic framework of Western writing and thinking. Their minds and perceptions run in a different mode, mostly loping through the multi-dimensional and smoothly in and out of the spiritual and physical realms.

In the Okami mythology, the Ainu hero, Okikurumi, son of the elm tree goddess (a Nature Spirit, presumably), taught the Ainu the skills of hunting and fishing as well as the arts of fire centering around elm wood. He owned a mighty sword, received from his mother, and he used it to destroy all the dark spirits or *kamui*; this sword when required burst into flame and was called *Kutoneshirika*. When he first travelled north to Hokkaido, Okikurumi (confusingly, also known as Yoshitsune or Ushiwaka) came with a companion hero called Benkei, also known as *Samai un guru*, which means "Japanese person," or Samaikuru, for short. Minamoto no Yoshitsune was the Japanese name for the Ainu Okikurumi. Confusing, right? I'm sure it's crystal clear to the average Ainu mind, though.

In the Okami myth or story line, Samickle-Samaikuru is a top *Oina* (Japanese for Ainu) warrior. That is probably equivalent to saying Achilles is a major star in *The Iliad*. Every Ainu knows this. These people are alleged to have the ability to shapeshift into wolves. They live in Kamui in the far north, an island covered by mountains and snow, believed to be the birthplace of evil. Samaikuru leads his Ainu people there. In the Okami mythology, the *Oina* people are modeled on the Ainu, and their mythology, their life and perceptions, are populated with spirits and demons, but the whole story seems to be told from the Japanese outsider perspective. Probably some of the facts got muddled.

Even though today Hokkaido is a part of Japan, like a state in the U.S., the Ainu people were once regarded as different than the Japanese who oppressed them. It was similar to how Europeans settling in America suppressed the native Indians. Ethnologists tell us the Ainu are probably the last surviving remnant of the Jōmon, the earliest people to inhabit Japan, The Jōmon period was 14,000 to 300 B.C., characterized as a hunter-gatherer culture and one of East Asia's oldest ethnic groupings. The name Jōmon has a mundane, almost embarrassing origin. It means "cord-marked" and was coined by a Western researcher in 1877 when he was trying to describe the pottery sherds he found from these early people. They were marked by cords pressed into the surface of the wet clay then fiered.

It seems possible that instead of two culture heroes we have one with many nuances. Okikurumi was sent down to Earth and the Ainu by the sky-god Kando-Koro. He came with a mugwort spear and his body from his waist to feet was cloaked in sacred flames from Fuchi, the fire-goddess. She is the tutelary deity of Mount Fuji. His upper body was shielded with a skin of elm bark courtesy of Shiramba, the vegetation goddess. Okikurumi's mission was to slay monsters and culture menaces, the evil *kamui*, and especially Pakoro, the pestilence and plague god, which I take to mean a deity of sickness and pathology. Okikurumi, basically the father of the Ainu, taught the Ainu many cultural arts, such as building homes, protocols for correct veneration of the deities (called *oripak*), music, law, tattooing, and the techniques of agriculture.

He took down several notable bad-guy deities including Moshir Huchi, a sea-goddess who had long entangling hair as a weapon and who captured all the fish the Ainu needed to survive. Also in his hero's résumé was his defeat of a trout the size of a whale who lived in a mountain lake and defeated all who opposed

him; a bear as big as an elm tree who devoured all the game animals the Ainu depended on for food and clothing; an enormous swordfish monster; and the Huri, giant birds who lived in caves and liked to eat the Ainu for dinner.

All this makes Okikurumi into a primordial culture hero like the Navaho's Monster Slayer who prepared their designated landscape in the American Southwest by dispatching bad spirits (including some huge and weird bird spirits inhabiting the desert rocks) from the key geomantic nodes and thereby highlighting a mythopoeic spiritualized landscape planned for The People. Okikurumi taught the Ainu the occult arts too, such as the ability to travel under the sea in the astral body and to battle the ill-intentioned Moshir Huchi. The trick, he said, is to shear off her entangling hair and deprive her of power.

In case it's not obvious, the Ainu view Nature, the world, the cosmos, as thoroughly animated, animistic and *kamui*-filled, as sentient, and responsive but needing supplication. The *kamui* are everywhere: they must be treated with respect, cajoled, even bribed, and they must be sent back to their own world when they intrude too much into the human realm upsetting human life.

The Ainu retain many rituals and protocols for accomplishing this, though ethnologists mistakenly use the word "prayer" when they describe the Ainu's interactions with the *kamui*. In a culture this saturated with *kamui* presence, it would seem dialogue and reciprocity would be the typical relationship norm. The Ainu, as one anthropologist reported, see the Earth as a "carpet of spirits."

The core of this Ainu geomantic carpet seems to be the Ishikari River. Every year on September 23, the Ainu stage the Kotan Festival here offering solicitations to the *kamui* of Nature and site, honoring the "homeland of the gods." The river narrows considerably as it flows through Kamui Kotan, generating a stronger current, even to the extent that the river torrent has been known to swamp boats. Locally, the mischievous *kamui* are to blame. Visitors note the mysterious (probably they mean numinous) atmosphere at this river bend. That's the *kamui*'s fault too, that plus the sometimes unfriendly feeling visitors note from the Ishikari River, as if it preferred all the people go away.

The river, which is 167 miles long, is the longest in Hokkaido and third longest in all of Japan, and its watershed drains an area of 5,530 square miles, making it the second largest in Japan. So any questionable vibration you feel from the river is going to come from this extended body, the full watershed. The river derives from Mount Ishikari, a former volcano about 6,000 feet high.

A distinctive feature of this river is how meandering it is. The Ainu call it "make itself go round about something" (from *kari*, which means circle, round, loop, go round, and *si*, which means oneself): "Winding" River, in short. Or maybe it should be Head-Spinning River, since the place name hints at possible sensory disorientation from it. Once it was 50 miles longer, winding through the Ishikari plain, but construction projects shortened it, generating oxbow lakes.

As you know, my method is to get my head straight on a locality when I am there in person. I check out all the myths and local folklore for clues to the site, because I know from doing this for many years here is where you find the geomantic map of the territory and psychic protocols for effective interaction. No, I don't mean I'm going to pretend to be an Ainu; I mean I take their mythic attributions about Kamui Kotan seriously and then interpret them clairvoyantly.

It's my impression Kamui Kotan on this narrowing river bend of the Ishikari is due to the fact the River spirit or goddess has her residence here, her point for human access. You see this in Greek and Roman myths about rivers, that there is a specific spot along a river where the deity has a "residence" under the water. Human heroes submerge themselves in the river to meet with the river goddess. I refer you to *The Iliad* and *The Odyssey* for Western stories of heroes meeting with River spirits. Bear in mind the gender of the River spirit varies with cultures (masculine for the Greeks, feminine in India), but the reality is constant.

Geomantically, the River spirit's residence is where the spiritual essence or consciousness theme that the river conveys to the Earth and our human world is most easily accessed. There it is concentrated and the deity personifies it. Rivers are a physical expression of the vast Sea of Consciousness, too vast to be perceived as a whole so it is divided, as the Greeks knew, into 3,000 sub-themes. They called these Oceanids, the River-daughters of the primordial Oceanus, the river that encircled the world. These are expressed on Earth as the 3,000 rivers.

That makes the primary physical rivers and of course the River spirit's residence another in our inventory of Light temples. They deliver a theme in consciousness to us. We can even count the major tributaries, since most river myths attribute River-daughters to the presiding deity. Tom Bombadil's lovely wife, Goldberry, was a River-woman's daughter, wrote Tolkien. I suspect the Ainu have been "holding court" with the Ishikari "Oceanid" for a long time, doing a good job of it on behalf of Hokkaido, the watershed, and geomantic plan.

This helped me understand the importance of this site in the Earth's grid. The Ainu dialogue with the *kamui* here was strong and pristine and had been for many centuries. It bespoke the original design and intention of the planet's Light grid, that humans would regularly and thoroughly mediate the relationship of elementals with the physical natural world. This site by the narrowing of the Ishikari River is imbued with that purity of interaction as accrued over time by the Ainu meeting them; it is like finding a cache of original Earth water, very rare now. Kamui Kotan is a cache of virginal geomantic interaction where the intended protocols are still maintained and have been run correctly for millennia.

Ethnologists tend to use the term "animistic" in a condescending manner, but they are mistaken. It points to the correct and original mode of interaction between humans and spirits. The subtle energy fields of the planet are saturated with *kamui*, a diverse range of spirits who maintain the physical world for us. Most of the old cultures recognize this and have their own names for these friendly spirits. They require regular human interaction as a basis for their existence just as houseplants need water and sunlight. The Ainu know that and have always known it. Every clairvoyant in the history of humanity has known this basic unassailable fact. White People's educated culture has virtually exterminated this understanding among its acolytes. It's unfortunate because

the world is "carpeted" with sentience; it is spiritually awake, animistically alive.

The Ishikari was rushing past me, vigorous and loud, as if the water elementals were shouting *Hellos!* and requests to the human world as they streamed by. Hey, humans: come interact with us, acknowledge us, *see* us. We carpet the Earth. Animism lives. The two reciprocal realms are deftly knitted together here, where the elemental spirits dwell, and the Ainu have kept this linkage intact like a durable bridge. That's a fine bridge they have here. I saw etheric traces of their past rituals performed here and in the vicinity, and they were sufficiently vivid as to suggest they were happening now in real time.

I thought about the stories of Okikurumi, Samaikuru, and the "evil-god area" attribution to this stretch of the river. It is probably a way of remembering how these primordial gods, or possibly human initiates, brought the human-elemental relationship into balance. Evil would be a code word for an energy set too strong, devically overwrought, not counterbalanced by correct human mediation, and thereby capable of unbalancing human health and well-being.

To "kill" the hostile spirits is to tame them, render them friendly to human life, put them into the healthy reciprocal dialogue of human consciousness and elementals. It's like adjusting the valves on a furnace to get just the right temperature for comfortable domestic life. The Tibetans have a way of putting this: they say a certain lama travelled through a portion of Tibet and "opened" the landscape, meaning he discerned its subtle residents and put the spiritual and material aspects of the landscape into their intended reciprocal relationship.

These early culture heroes, these geomancers, Hierophants, really, corrected those imbalances, pacified the ruffled spirits, and set the operational norms for future mediations to be performed by the Ainu priests and people. You could say every geomancer is in a way a Monster Slayer, pacifying a landscape and making it inhabitable by the People as long as they stay in healthy relationship with that landscape's elemental population. If a geomantic locale is not properly and correctly maintained, its energies can become entropic, its Nature Spirits and elementals unruly and even hostile. The monsters return. I have personally seen that in many locales, and it was part of my early training to identify it, experience it, then take steps to rectify it and mollify the riled spirits.

The Ishikari River goddess had her residence spatially coincident with this narrowing of the river. I put it that way to indicate it occupied the same space as this narrowing but not in a physical sense. You could say at first glance that her residence lay under the water, but more accurately it is in the same place as the water, but in an etheric vibratory field you could picture as perhaps 50 yards wide. She is accompanied by several dozen secondary water deities attendant on the streams and smaller rivers that comprise the complete Ishikari watershed.

Her residence is a hologram of the watershed. All the water from the main river and the tributaries flows through her presence here and participates in the theme and style of consciousness the river expresses. The river, any river, is the physical expression of a primordial spiritual and consciousness theme. The mystic would say the river and its watershed reside inside the goddess, and as the river's anima she thoroughly permeates every water molecule in the 167 miles and 5,530 square miles of its physical extent. She is the Ishikari's soul.

This river-deity residence or Light temple was embedded in a larger one. This extended one was perhaps 200 yards wide, maybe more, and clearly spanned both banks of the river. It is what I call a Pan Nature Spirit Center. Pan as chief of all the Nature Spirits, *devas*, and elementals, administers this center. There's your "village of the gods" nuance; this is a *kamui* population hub.

You potentially may encounter representatives from all the classes of Nature Spirits here, as well as their elemental directors, as in, King of the Gnomes, or if you prefer a title more formal sounding, Regent of the Earth Elementals. The facility reminds me of the way Wagner described the mountain grotto of the goddess Venus in *Tannhäuser*, as moist, cavernous, languid, even sybaritic, a stadium packed with elementals from the branches of Nature Spirits.

It is possible that *Ninne Kamui* or *Nitne Kamuy*, supposed bad guy of the Ainu world, was Pan before humans got into a proper working relationship with him. Or maybe his fierceness and seeming contrariness to human welfare was an index of his original furious raw power that needed to be tamed for human life. The Greeks had their panic, when somebody out in Nature suddenly senses the startling presence of Pan and feels panicked, that is, suffused with Pan's reality.

It doesn't convey much to say Nature Spirits are sybaritic. I'm trying to evoke a sense of primordial relaxation, delight, and ease that typifies unsullied elementals. Most humans are like rigid, straight-laced, ice-cold Puritans in contrast to their existential ease. I call this facility a center because it services a prescribed region, probably the extent of the river's watershed or maybe a large portion of it. Pan, chief of the *devic* kingdoms and "masculine" counterpart ("husband") to Earth's soul and principal egregore, Gaia, is available for interviews and strategy sessions here on how best to deploy the elementals to address deficits of inattention in a geomantic province. You have to treat Old Pan with respect, because he can still get riled and kick your ass for compliance.

This feature is holographic and the laws of physical space are contravened here as all the Nature Spirits servicing this area are both in the field and in here simultaneously. I was pleased to see the four elemental guardians of Hokkaido here as well. These are the archetypal personifications of the four elements, usually in the standard metaphors of lion, bird, man, giant, or angel, and bull, for the four elemental qualities. They are arrayed at the cardinal directions for a geomantic province, whether it's a country or island, and they supervise the life of these primordial elements as they flourish in the land, Nature, and humans.

These four large elemental guardians stand in their respective look-outs across the landmass of Hokkaido but they are also simultaneously available closer up in the Pan center. Each is a landscape protector as manifested through one of the four elements. I see them at quarterly mark-off points in the temple. Such a rich combination of Ainu, humans, and *kamui*-gods. The land of the *kamui*-spirits and the land of the Ainu-People clearly overlap. It's a teeming village of gods and humans pacifically interpenetrating each other's domain.

As complements to the large number of Nature Spirits assembled here, many benevolent

Ainu ancestors are present, still loyally looking after their geomantic province. I see also eight *takusa-ainu* or *tusu-kuru*—Ainu shamans. Technically, these shamans are deceased but in their Light forms they are here in the Pan Nature Spirit Center to bulk up the hosts of helpful *kamui* in this *kotan*. I know I can count on them in any encounters I have with the alien math gods.

There is even a holographic copy or virtual presence of their prime culture hero, whatever you choose to call him, Okikurumi, Samaikuru, or Yoshitsune. He was the primordial god-figure and benefactor who balanced the elemental energies of *Ainu Moshi* to make the area livable for the humans who would then maintain it. You can see etheric traces of his elemental harmonizing actions performed here. Let's not forget that finally we have the River spirit on hand, possibly the primordial landscape spirit the Ainu called Kamui Kotan Ninne Kamui, and her River-daughters from the watershed's many tributaries join her. But whatever her name, her water flows through all the features I've just listed and the consciousness theme those waters carry saturates the assembled *kamui*.

It's always a good idea, and good manners too, when you visit a charged geomantic node to bring something as a gift. I brought the Ofanim's lilac cycling pattern. You know how that works, Frederick. We have done it many times. First you establish Blaise's Rotunda of Light, position yourself in its diamond geode center, then run the torus-donut shape of lilac Light up through it, making a fountain of lilac Light through which the Ofanim emit their Love from Above. It is pure angelic consciousness which is a much-needed nutrient for the site and the attendant Nature Spirits. It is a delicious feeling; their Above Love is strong.

It needs to run through a human interface because it is too strong in its "naked" form for the elementals. The Ofanim Light gets humanized by being transmitted through a person or, even better, a group, maintaining their attention in the Rotunda and on the cycling of the lilac Light in this toroidal style. The elementals regard with delight the droplets of gold and silver Light raining from the peak of the torus-donut cycling pattern. It is rain, it is food, it is a wonderful *Hello!* from the celestial world, a validation of their work. Then you watch as the recipients brighten, "fatten" as they take up the Light. Not just the elementals: the Ainu ancestors and shamans were imbibing the Light too, and I am certain I saw an expression of satisfaction on them, like you'd have after a great meal.

I saw the arithmetical infrastructure behind this spectacle of bright *kamui*. It doesn't run the lives and consciousness of these spirits, but that of the site's processes, the qualities of consciousness this geomantic node was designed to transmit to the human and natural world. But the numbers do set the tone, frame the quality and frequency of these many Nature Spirits and former alive humans. It would be the point of interest for the arithmetical gods in targeting this site, and conversely, why this node completes the four-pointed stretched square of nodes, that global geomantic rhombus the four of us have travelled to service.

"We come as Love from Above, and we mean this time *all* of us," Blaise said. They were referring not only to themselves which on a good day, when they are especially expansive, can total 40.3 million facets, minus however many of them are currently on Earth assignment, incarnated as humans, but to the rest of the angelic families. That's 39 different orders of angels, and they were coming too. Perhaps not every last possible manifestation of each order, as some of these permitted manifestation totals are in the quintillions and wouldn't even fit on the entire planet, but a decent amount, more than one busload, I can assure you, and enough to make the point. What point? Soma. Blaise was bringing a Rotunda of Soma, the distillation of the original, unfallen, unsullied angelic consciousness. All of it, as pure as when the Supreme Being first emanated it eons ago.

Here's how they did it. First the diamond geode expanded, grew stronger. It was the size of a major sports stadium, deep and broad, its seats the diamond facets. It pulsed with Love from Above. That's like 50,000 sports fans all leaping up to applaud a grand slam. I tried not to flush delirious with its joy. Then it extended or perhaps revealed the prior existence of threads of Light extending from the stadium-geode to 39 zones, each filled with an angelic order. The angelic families were all "wired" in to central command, the Ofanim's Rotunda.

The Ofanim are the umbilicus in the Creation, acting umbilically at all possible levels, always anchoring consciousness, whether it's human or divine, with the Source. This means the Ofanim are fundamentally linked with the 39 angelic orders, and they are their anchor, umbilicus, even elevator, through the four Trees of Life otherwise known as Jacob's Ladder. That is the truth of Soma. The distilled pure essence of the 40 angelic orders, the 40 spheres on the Trees, and, as the English would say, the Blaises will be Mother and pour the lovely tea.

Through the Ofanim you have access to the spectrum of the 39 families. You get the flavor of the 40th angelic order, the Ofanim, by tuning in through them. We come as Love from Above, Blaise likes to say, and they also say, We Roll Towards You. Well, we were rolling and it was like a spherical chariot with 40 wheels and standing room for billions. I was among those standing, and I was riding this angel chariot like it was an alternate version of the Apocalypse, one with a happy ending full of merry Ofanim as we approached Kamui Kotan.

You need to appreciate the import of Soma to contemplate this scene. Soma, the Hindus tell us and their folklore amplifies it, is the precious nectar of immortality. People usually think this means bodily immortality; it does not. Bodily immortality is trivial; it is incarnation continuing on with preservatives. Immortality refers to a primordial condition of unbroken, undifferentiated, unfragmented, unfallen, never incarnated, primordial pure consciousness.

It is original angelic consciousness, reality as received by the 40 angelic orders. Soma restores us to that ecstatic state. It is the condition of unitive consciousness; you may liken it to the clear blue serene sky above the deep roiling sea of clouded incarnated consciousness. It is the place of origin, the ultimate homeland. Ironically, the arithmetical gods would like this zone; it's free of incarnation. If the angels have any numbers, they're stashed behind their wings. The math gods could spend days looking for them and come up empty.

Your awareness is no longer subject to the fluctuations and perturbations of all phenomena, time and space, incarnation, individuality, and of course, death. Death

of what? Soma awareness is senior to all manifestations, all perturbations of incarnation of body or thought, which means it is senior to the arithmetical realm, and that, I thought at the time, should give us the edge we need over these gods. Sorry, you numbers braniacs: this place trumps where you guys hang out. It is senior because it is antecedent; God emanated pure awareness in this distributed field of 40 angelic families *before* the numbers.

On the other hand, there is a troubling precedence to keep in mind. In Greek myth, the Titans were created first but were later overcome by the Olympians, the upstart younger gods (Zeus and his gang) who overthrew these primordial creative deities. That's the picture of seniority and precedence we get from Greek mythology. I was hoping it was not germane to our circumstances.

We were rolling towards the river site. In fact, we were already there and had been since I first became aware of this angelic spectacle. It was instantaneous. We were on a mission to save the world, but I will gladly admit this was great fun. Forget the "evil god" of the Ishikari; the real bad asses were the numbers thieves, the arithmetical gods who had recalled all the equations.

The innumerable *kamui* assembled at the river greeted our arrival. The alien gods looked up from their contemplation of the numbers, from their status of being those numbers, the way somebody would look irked if you disturbed their concentration or if you were just making too much noise in a library room. These numbers gods are the original narcissists, constantly contemplating themselves, as if patting all the equations that comprise themselves. They acted like they knew our presence would be of no consequence to them.

I should mention that for significant occasions like this it is advisable to dress properly. By that, I mean dress formally. I wore my official Ray robes. Gold flushed through strongly with pale orange, the Robe of Ray Master Kuthumi-Elijah. As far as geomancy, Grail Knights, and matters of the Christ Light and the planet's Light grid go, he's our Main Man, our principal Ray Master sponsor. This is the Ray that spans the disciplines of Earth energies and Christ Light.

My robe flowed sleekly from my neck to my ankles, clasped in gold and silver snaps, and as a fashion accessory I sported my staff of the same color with gold-orange flames searing out the top for emphasis, not that I expected the alien gods to be impressed or probably even to take any notice. Still, I earned this so I might as well call on it, this wiser, vastly older, accomplished version of myself.

The chariot seemed like it was still rolling vigorously, yet it also seemed as if it were parked all around the alien gods fiddling with their algorithms. I guess that's a way of saying the angelic Soma chariot was a dynamic presence. I had the sense that this confrontation was like the one classically described in Vedic folklore, that of Agni, the divine fire, consuming the sacrifice of Soma, the fuel. In case you're not clear on the players, we're Soma; the numbers gods are Agni.

In the Vedic account, Agni devours Soma, the aliveness represented by cosmic fire burns up universal consciousness, which means, it uses it to run the processes of reality, to give them life. Did that mean, I hoped not, that the arithmetical gods, though secondary in

Creation sequence to the Soma, were going to burn up the Soma like the Olympians overthrowing the Titans? They were going to use it as firewood to cook their equations? Were the numbers, a mere secondary-level creation, the dangerous expression of Agni's fire out to consume the Soma and our rich concoction of 40 flavors about to be ended?

Before I could figure that out I found myself playing chess with them. It wasn't chess exactly. It reminded me of the Celtic board game called *fidchell* in Irish or the almost unpronounceable version in Welsh, *gwyddbwyll*. Heroes in the *Mabinogion* meet at King Arthur's court and sit down to have a round of this game. I'm sure Jocelyn will appreciate this mythic reference; she loves these, and I'm betting she can probably pronounce that tongue-defeating Welsh word too.

The probable origin of either name is "wood sense" and denotes the board upon which a chess-like game is played. The only difference now is that this *fidchell* was played in four dimensions and frankly it was more like being inside a 4D Rubik's Cube and having to make my moves while inside the board and that board, incidentally, is made of and its playing squares consist of numbers. I am already in the realm of the arithmetical gods playing in some *fidchell* tournament that will decide the fate of the universe. I'll dial back the hyperbole. It's not me.

To tell you the truth, it was more like an all-night poker game in a *noir* mystery. I was a stubbly Mike Hammer growling through the numbers night.

These game pieces were not yellow gold or white bronze circles, but algorithms. The *fidchell* game has deep roots reaching into the gods' realm; it was played by royalty and the gods, and Lugh, the god of Light and inspiration, is credited with inventing it. A legendary board with 49 squares, it was made of gold, its players silver, and they played against each other automatically for the definitive capture of the opposite side's king. This board was so prestigious it got listed among Merlin's famous and magical Thirteen Treasures of the Island of Britain. It was called the Chessboard (*Gwyddbwyll*) of Gwenddoleu ap Ceidio; gold board, silver pieces, and when the pieces were set out on the board the game played itself.

That was a clue. If this game, even if played in 4D inside a Rubik's Cube board, was magical, that meant consciousness might have an edge over sheer mental dexterity in mathematics, a clear advantage these clever-assed guys normally had. Mathematics is not magical; it's logical, predictable, even routine; but magic is wild, protean, wily, and unpredictable in terms of its ricocheting side effects. Consciousness is more adroit than numbers combination. I might not be clever-assed (though my fans still regard me fondly as smart-assed), but I was well-equipped in the consciousness department. I brought the Soma chariot.

Maybe I should better say "we" brought the Soma chariot. There was more than one of me at this point. Dozens, I'd estimate, one for each of the many squares in this hypercube version of a Rubik's Cube, and just as many copies of the alien gods, though none of these manifestations was perceivable, only implied. I knew they were there, playing against me, but I couldn't see them. It was like walking into a busy chess club, high-focus games going on at every table, a murmur of voices as players made genius moves and onlookers gasped.

Well, nobody was gasping at my moves except all of my copies. I knew I stood no chance of beating these guys purely through arithmetical proficiency. I had to rally the Blaises and their angelic retinue of consciousness to prevail, or, as was more likely, to hold my ground and not get swept into the calculations.

I'm not exaggerating about this 4D Rubik's Cube business. There is such a form and mathematicians have written extensively about its numbers and geometry. A 3D Rubik's Cube has 27 cells, like a cubic version of the flat 2D *fidchell* board in which each player starts with 27 stones as their pieces. But the Rubik 4-cube, as they prefer to call it, has 81 unit 4-subcubes each of which contains eight 3D subcubes. I needed consciousness to deal with this complexity. I pulled in to the Blaise gas station for a tank fill-up. They rushed out to pump it.

I left my many copies struggling to hold their own in this *fidchell* game of the cosmos, trying out all the algorithms I could think of and failing with them all. The alien gods were indifferent to winning; they were pocketing my numbers every chance they got. Picture it: you're a *Mabinogion* hero, say Owen mab Urien, and you're playing *fidchell* on the gods' board under magical circumstances, and your opponent is stealing the players, the squares, even squares of the board, out from under you, like you're standing on a crumbling cliffside falling into the sea. The Welsh bards, singing your heroic deeds, shake their heads and walk away.

I huddled up with the Blaises, Serafim, Elohim, and the rest in the Soma ocean. I tried not to lose myself in the irresistible deliciousness of that serene environment. I had to remember my mission: the Earth's managing algorithm had been stolen by these clever brainiacs of numbers and I, with you three, had to get the figures back. If I were playing in a casino in this fantasy hallucination of an all-night poker game, not only were my opponents winning all the cards, they were hijacking the tables, chairs, lights, and all the room's fixtures as well. They had probably acquired the casino itself, and possibly the town it was in.

Meanwhile, the *kamui* of this grand assembly of spirits and protectors at this node in the Ishikari River were like a crowd patiently standing around outside the building, their voices a susurrus occasionally penetrating the casino walls. Or maybe it was like a sporting match played under Alice in Wonderland conditions: all the fans were outside the stadium, while inside it was just me and the alien gods, and for some reason I was standing on my head spinning rapidly.

We were surrounding the math gods as a superior force of angelic consciousness, the power of Soma, as we might put on our business card, yet they were picking our pockets clean, vacuuming out the Soma. We were playing with God's imprimatur, yet they had all the winning cards. How could this be? Soma existed before the realm of numbers was generated, yet reality depended on the arithmetical realm for its existence; the numbers ran its many processes.

Angels are not part of the manifest realm because they have no fixed form and no separate individuality other than the wholesale assignment for each order—you know, the instructions God gave them on their first day of work after the Creation. What they look like is determined by our metaphorical overlays; the Blaises are a perfect example. The Ofanim

are Creation's metaphor masters, none of their forms bedrock but evidencing a lively, fluidic imagination: most inventive, these Blaises, everybody says. Always coming up with new guises.

The angelic hosts weren't coded by numbers. They were senior to that, yet I was scripted by algorithms. I was part of that fallen, incarnated realm, fallen both from the viewpoint of Soma, as I was a differentiated point of self-aware consciousness, and fallen from the alien gods' very testy view of all things in form and thus incarnated. As such, the alien gods seemed not to care about the angelic hosts or Soma; I was their focus because I held and I embodied some numbers and they wanted them. Me they didn't care about and could discard.

Every deployment of numbers in service of the Creation and its vile incarnations was evidence of its fallen state in the absolutist, puritanical logic of these arithmetical obsessives. Numbers should be kept pure, they insisted, and they were doing everything possible to retrieve their numbers and to keep them virginal and free of the taint of incarnation and manifestation. I was in their way.

Their puritanical fixation about fallen numbers put me in mind of an image. God is walking around in baggy trousers with big pockets; they are full of coins, but one pocket has a hole in it. By the end of His morning walk, that pocket has dribbled out all its coins. You can see them strewn about the path He has taken. The arithmetical gods consider that a travesty, manifestly irresponsible, ill-advised. Those coins should immediately be collected, the pocket hole sewn, and the coins poured back into it where they will remain secure and undefiled by the world. Maybe they shouldn't even go back to the Old Man. He's already proven himself too sloppy; He lost the coins, after all, and the coins of course are the numbers. Maybe He let them dribble out on purpose?

Then I saw all this from the other side. The angelic hosts, Soma, are in the *Dharmakaya*, the realm of truth. It is formless, this purely transcendent realm, which means it is free of any incarnational forms or even tendencies to take form. You'll never hear people even hint at metaphors in here. They are free of ideas.

The *Dharmakaya* is analogy-free. The arithmetical gods and their obsession with total sequestering of all the arithmetic in Creation are actually in the formed realm. They resist any further descent into the formed, incarnational realm and prefer to remain in their fetal cave clutching all the numbers to their nonmanifest chests. They may not be incarnated in any individualized sense, like humans are, but the realm of mathematics is a created, secondary level of the Creation; it is more manifest, closer to the material world than Soma, angelic consciousness. Compared to the rigorously formless *Dharmakaya*, the arithmetical realm is incarnated; all these numbers and their circus tricks are in the formed realm.

But maybe they have a point. I often think incarnation sucks. I grumble about its limitations. So why am I such an advocate for incarnation? Why is the incarnational realm such a desirable state? For the most part, the angels never enter it, except on the rare occasions, most recently back in 2020, when a portion of one order (five families now over time, my pals, the Blaises, the most recent) tried it out. When this Age of Brahma runs out and

restful *Pralaya* starts again, everything will re-enter that infinite quiescence out of which it was first born. Nothing will be incarnate, the mere idea of incarnation an unfounded rumor.

The arithmetical gods are saying why not stick with the *Pralaya*. Or at least a few days short of the total recall. The numbers will still exist, but nothing else. It's a sure bet. Incarnation is too tricky, too problematical, too vexingly uncertain to dare it. Leave incarnation as a thought experiment which we might indulge during a long moment in eternity when we have nothing better to imagine.

The alien gods say to the Supreme Being, Big Fellow, You shouldn't have bothered with all this messiness. We prefer to keep ourselves, the realm of numbers which we are, inviolate and uncommitted. We see no advantage to deploying these pure numerations in support of a Creation. Why the bloody hell should we? Why did You? You should have all Your Heads examined. We're staying in the Pleroma House and we're not budging anywhere for You. Don't even think of it, suggest it, hint at it, or send us sly thoughtforms advertising the blandishments of an arithmetical deployment. It's not going to happen. Forget it.

So I sat on the other side of the board and played *fidchell* against my many selves. It didn't bother me that they were losing big time and all the numbers were flowing back to our side of the table like growing mountains of poker chips. I couldn't see any good reason why this phalanx of numbers should parade forth into the world to commit the ontological treason of supporting the Creation. Why not preserve the inherent purity of the numbers realm in case the Supreme Being decides in some moment of riveting self-awareness that He was mistaken.

Lucidity suddenly, *finally*, grabs hold of Him and He says, What was I thinking?

I was in a quandary. I saw both sides and understood them both. I had roots. Deep ones, and they extend down through all the levels, from the incarnational manifest realm of selfhood, through the planet and its Light grid, through the Blaises and their invisible nonformed presence in the *Dharmakaya*, and through them to their implicit also invisible sponsor, the Very Big Fellow. I worked on behalf of the formed realm for the anchoring of the unformed realm, and before we wink out into blissful nothingness we wave to the numbers below.

We've talked about this, Frederick. On the one hand, through the Hierophancy we have pledged to uphold the Earth's Light grid and its arithmetical aspects in its hierophantic role of revealing the Holy Light for the edification of humans. On the other side of things, the Ofanim, our prime helpers in this long-term project, are the elevator, umbilicus, winged white horse and majestic bird who flies us up to the Christ Light where we drop all notions of selfhood and false, illusory models of reality and disappear, selfless, bodiless, and karma-free into the boundless, infinite *Dharmakaya* that has no forms at all and isn't incarnated and doesn't give two shits about numbers or arithmetic.

This business of the roots suggested a tactic. I could go back on the timeline to the point where Soma generated the numbers realm and reacquire the necessary arithmetic there. Soma in essence is *Dharmakaya* consciousness, which means free of form, existing before form; the arithmetical realm, though abstract and primordial, is a formed realm. Algorithms are

forms, and they generate forms; the numbers act like primary fire, Agni calculations, consuming the Soma.

Soma is part of the preincarnational realm. It is nonembodied angelic consciousness, which is to say, Supreme Being consciousness divided into 40 nuances, none of which has a form, body, or incarnational distinction. Soma is both the 40 nuances and their totality. Take the angelic qualities of the 40 orders and distill them in a single pot as a divine nectar, *Amrita*: that's Soma.

The name *Amrita*, interchangeable with Soma, means "immortality." It is undying consciousness because it was never born, at least not in any sense we might have of that process. It is eternal. Hinduism gives us the icon of Mohini, the feminine form of Vishnu, holding the pot of *Amrita* and distributing this nectar to all the *devas*, the 40 angelic orders. Even though the *devas* appear in Light forms, those are metaphorical at best, because truly they dwell formless in the *Dharmakaya*, the transcendent realm saturated in *Amrita*, in the Soma Ocean. The numbers gods want to wash their nonexistent hands of Soma. No more scripting, no more algorithms, no more form-making with this "divine stuff."

You find the numbers at the inception of the form realm. You need the numbers to specify and manage the design and processes of all reality levels in Creation. It's as if the angelic realm waits, conscious but formless, for the Supreme Being to generate the toolbox. They stand there as if with their hands outstretched, expectant. Then the Big Fellow puts the arithmetical tools in their hands and they can start. Start what? Implementing the Creation, deploying the numbers to specify reality and create Light grids to run all the life processes.

In case you are wondering, how I would enter the timeline at the right node, I treated the roots as the timeline. I saw them extending backwards in time. I entered the roots or timeline like it was an elevator and I specified the floor I wanted to get out on, namely, precisely at the point where the pure formless realm, the quietly enduring Soma of unformed awareness, immediately leaped into a myriad of incarnated differentiated forms that were specified by mathematics. I was looking for the moment when Agni, Lord of Fire, was *born*.

That is when the arithmetical realm was created and started to consume the Soma and transform the Creation from the passive, undifferentiated formless realm into the richly formed enumerated realm of delight, what the Buddhists call *Sambhogakaya*, the Desire Realm. These incarnation-hating, form-deriding, arithmetical blowhards were *in form* whether they liked it or not or owned up to it under the gaze of a hot prosecution. Born as Agni: what a shame for them.

Agni is the Knower, the transformer, the all-consuming flame, mouth of the gods. He has three heads and seven arms, and his parents were Prithivi, Earth, and Dyaus, Sky, but we must understand these in the highest cosmic sense, as Heaven (the formless realm, Pleroma, *Dharmakaya*) and Earth, meaning the cosmic space allotted for all forms, not our physical planet, but cosmic Earth, the original empty space allocated to be filled with all the forms of the Creation. Alternatively, Brahma, the Creator, is Agni's father, and Agni is His eldest son. Agni is the shining, burning, leading agency, transforming consciousness

into forms, the generation of reality through the arithmetical fire, flaming algorithms. But he is still, despite this glorious résumé, a formed being, an incarnated form.

I know, it's confusing, and I am confusingly conflating usually different realms. But in some manner the appearance of Agni is identical to the first deployment of the arithmetical realm to specify, manifest, and manage all created forms. What's the first thing the newly generated numbers do? They burn Soma, set universal consciousness aflame to produce action and effects.

Agni is the divine fire priest who brings together gods and humans, the Vedas tell us, the leader and mover who conceives of ceremonies to sustain these linkages. But isn't that what the arithmetical realm does, specifies the proprieties and protocols of the relationships between deities and humans? Isn't an algorithm a type of ceremony that specifies conditions? Arithmetical coding of Light grids and algorithmic processes are ceremonies, fire rituals that burn consciousness like fuel performed in the temple of the brick-lined hearth of Agni, primary fire-mathematician. The math gods will positively hate admitting this, but under the unsurmountable pressure of this logic, they'll bloody have to.

Agni is the fire that makes these formed ceremonies burn and shine, which means makes them visible and separate. The arithmetical realm is liturgical. The number specifications that coded manifest reality were Agni ceremonials. His altar is the site of the ritual sacrifice, the oblation, the Soma offering. You could say he was the Hierophant of the arithmetical realm, the revealer of the Holy Numbers, if you don't mind my putting it that way. Another name for his father is Prajapati, the Progenitor, a popular guise of Brahma. Prajapati is the generator of all forms, the Lord of Creatures, and Agni is the fire issuing from his mouth that also specifies their numbers and processes.

These are the numbers that consume Soma and transform it into ceremonies of relationship and temples. Agni begins with numbers; he is the inception of a numbered reality. You see that in the Vedic description of the Agni fire altar, that the number of bricks called for, 10,800, the same as the number of hours in the Vedic time calculation for the year, is precisely enumerated as are the details for its construction, the placement of bricks, fire-sticks, and all the other components. The 10,800 fire-bricks comprised the Year, and that was Prajapati, which shows us that Agni *enumerated* the cosmos-body of Creation. The Vedas state "Prajapati is the Year," and I state that means the enumeration of time and Agni is the son of numbers. Yes, the myth makes it sound like Prajapati counted out those 10,800 fire-bricks, and he used arithmetic to do it.

Think of the Light temples, any of them, the generic idea of Light temples, as the arithmetically scripted process of the Agni ritual sacrifice of primordial Soma. Agni codes Soma to perform an algorithmic process yielding a "product" in consciousness. Unformed awareness is arithmetically scripted into discrete performance pieces in consciousness. Agni works his miracles with numbers.

All of the Light temples, the algorithms, the form and incarnational realm, are manifestations of Agni's ritual fire, products of his fire altar. Soma is ritually sacrificed on the hearth altar of arithmetic. Hello, arithmetical gods: like it

there, do you, in the hearth? I see you; you're incarnate after all. I entertained myself for a few moments pretending to taunt these imperialists of nonintervention. Each Light temple with its mathematical underpinning is a ritual sacrifice for Soma. Agni scripts the ritual, and he uses arithmetic to code it. Primordial undivided consciousness is served up and burned in the flames of Agni there, making it available to human consciousness as an enumerated reality.

Sorry to labor the point Frederick, but I want you to see the keen correlation of these components. The universe, say the Vedas, is the body of Prajapati compounded of numbers and equations, time and duration summarized in the term "Year," which is the rich field deployment of the arithmetical realm to generate and support incarnation. Prajapati is the Year, 10,800 fire-bricks in duration, and the fire-god is the time numerator; he is made of the numbers that count the year. He is arithmetical. Agni, let me run the numbers, do a tally, and I'll hand you the balance sheet and I'll forward a copy to the arithmetical gods, and they can see they're already stuffed into incarnation.

The specifications for the fire-altar, its construction, the number of its components, and the rituals for its use to consume Soma indicate how the arithmetical realm is required to run realities using algorithms as the tools. It is the continuous ritual sacrifice of Soma, primordial consciousness, sacrificed on behalf of the myriad of forms constituting the incarnational realm. The numbers realm, Agni's consuming fire, makes that happen, makes it shine. That was the set-up, the procedural sequence, the ritualistic protocols, in Creation's syllogism.

But now that necessary realm is resisting the plan, rebelling against this order.

The key question is what caused the arithmetical realm to balk at its mission and to start reverting to its original pre-deployed condition, for Agni in a sense to return to the parental fold of Prithivi and Dyaus and quit the mission? The arithmetical realm, the alien gods who are the numbers realm, have been running a retrograde movement for some time; stealing Earth's algorithm is part of a deliberate regression. It's as if Agni, his mouth rimmed with fire, is sucking the fire back into himself, no longer offering it to the world, all numbers recalled.

Our job in the Hierophancy has been to assure the integrity of the Agni ceremonies, the instituted Light temples and arithmetic-specified reality levels. Our job has been to make sure Agni stays on course, keeps exhaling the fire. A Light temple happens when Agni formulates Soma into a ritualized shape. But now he's walking backwards, trying to exit the manifested realm, recalling the fire and with it the numbers realm that transforms Soma into living aware forms, and with that the myriads of Light temples and structured Soma ritual spaces.

Agni is the *avatar* the arithmetical realm projected into the incarnational realm. He's their stealth hand-puppet that orders and numbers reality, but they're hoping nobody will notice and call their feint for what it is: rank ambivalence. The Light temples appear to be the ritual sacrifice of Soma to the arithmetical fires of Agni where Soma is converted by mathematics to a process in consciousness; the arithmetical codings and the Light temples are equivalent.

Their purpose is to incarnate Soma into discrete processes. The numbers gods want to quit that. And I had to stop the alien gods' shutdown of that vital exchange. We have to keep the processing factory running. We have to keep the Light temples of the Earth, and beyond, open for business, running the Agni rituals throughout the enumerated Year. Look at the lines of customers, will you. The incarnate masses are depending on this service for their continued lives.

I felt the presence of the eight Ainu shamans nearby. They were helping me by keeping a steady focus trained on the angelic presence and calling on their own contacts from the human and animal world to lend assistance. Meanwhile, I was moving slowly with the Ofanim along the timeline of reality to that precise moment when Soma first started to be consumed by Agni's arithmetical fires. That was where I would drop down into the process and retrieve our algorithm.

The timeline node I was looking for corresponds to that decisive moment when the stasis of *pi*, the eternal, unbroken sea of Soma consciousness, is suddenly sundered by the sword stroke or lightning bolt and changed into *phi*, the unfolding Agni-fired spiral of evolution into forms in time accomplished by mathematics. With *phi* you get the proliferation of the Fibonacci numbers which had lain dormant but implicit within the unchanging stability of unbroken *pi*.

In mythic imagery, this pivotal moment corresponds to the slicing open of the primordial dragon, *Sesa Ananta*, "The Endless Remainder," also called *Svarbhanu*. The mythic stories say *Svarbhanu* was trying to unlawfully acquire the Soma, but in fact, he was the source of the precious *Amrita*; the lightning bolt cut him in half generating *Rahu* and *Ketu*, head and tail of the cosmic dragon, or evolving *phi*. All the numbers tumble out of the severed dragon like popping open a *piñata*. The numeration agents of reality come tumbling out, and with this begins the infernal, endless extrapolation of numbered reality scripted by *phi*.

If you're the arithmetical deities, this *phi* is the most evil thing ever spawned, the nastiest betrayal of the arithmetical realm ever conceived. *Phi* represents arithmetical treachery, total betrayal. It will keep unfolding its horrid spiral of enumerated existence into unstoppable, insufferable infinity. *Phi* is the perverse form of *pi*: it's endless, but evil all the way. *Phi* is the croupier dealing out millions of cards at lightning speed to all the high-stakes gamblers freshly incarnated and wanting a thrill. The arithmetical deities are wincing: each of these cards is a deployment of numbers. Let's get started on closing the casino.

It felt like I was suddenly immersed in an immense, unfathomably large crowd. It was as if Tvastr, the Supreme Being with His sleeves rolled up as the architect in the field of the Creation, designed everything in existence at once. All the algorithms, calculations, equations, arithmetical formulas, leaped into life simultaneously, like God had not one or two good ideas at the same time, but all of them. Somewhere in this *Kumbh-Mela* of mathematics lies Earth's algorithm.

Math formulas were spewing out in all directions. It was appalling. The mind of the Supreme Being was now so copiously arithmetical I felt like a secretary trying to take down shorthand from a boss chanting *Finnegans Wake* in such a way the difficult words, the prolixity, fanned out into the ten dimensions and 11,520 voices declaimed out of the faces of this 10-cube manifestation. Such an onslaught of numbers. The whole universe designed in a single second. The equations were streaming out wreathed in Agni's fire, as if his flame-lipped mouth subjected them all to the ritual sacrifice of Soma as it charged into life. All the stars, born of equations, rushed flaming out of the great glossolalic mouth.

The stars rolled bellowing out of this cornucopia of Light grid designs. The Qabalists say there is a Hebrew name assigned to every star in the galaxies. We know that every letter has a number equivalent, like the other side of a coin. That means all the named stars are also *numbered* points of Light in the cosmos. Look up and instead of seeing stars as points of Light see them as a field of numbers. It's like every star has its own unique VIN like manufacturers put on new cars. All the stars have names and designations that are integers, and the constellations or Soul Groups linking stars in affinity are equations.

That means our Sun, Helios, or whatever name you like, has a VIN, and that vehicle identification number must have implicit within it the algorithms for all the host planets in its gravity well, otherwise known as our solar system. From our point of view, that would be like a back-up copy of the managing algorithm. Which meant going to our solar system's Sun and its arithmetical archives was next on my travel agenda. Naturally, I meant its etheric Light temple aspect. I didn't think to bring any sunscreen with me on this mission.

I remember long ago in my apprenticeship years with Blaise making the remark that I was never impressed with our Sun or thought it a big player. Now I see how wrong and incomplete that view was, not to say, embarrassingly juvenile in metaphysical terms. Our local Sun is like a municipal office that archives the building plans for every house and structure in the county. The Earth as a physical planet sits in the Sun's immense gravity well and is subject to its large life, with its coronal emissions, sunspots, and solar wind. The Earth's Light grid is necessarily "wired" into the Sun's Light patterns. Like Light temples anywhere, the Sun will retain a staff of etherically present spirits, like courtiers.

The logic of looking for Earth's master algorithm in our local Sun was that otherwise there were too many algorithms to sort through in this fantastic sack. Going to our Sun reduced the field I had to investigate, like when you're at a large library and you go to the "A" section to find an author whose last name begins with "A" rather than checking all the shelves in the whole library for it. The Sun's library of algorithms for planets and other aspects within its gravity well was a Light grid itself, a complex geometrical configuration of patterns with what at first glance would look like mathematical equations written all over it.

As for the spirits, think of them as like library staff. You have the head librarian, that's the egregore or indwelling soul-spirit of the Sun as a star in the galaxy; and then you have his staff of what we might call helper egregores accompanied by holographic representations of the egregores of all the planets in this system, even the ones currently unoccupied. These would be the original gods of the planets as represented vividly in Vedic astrology with, for example, Brihaspati for Jupiter and Buda for Mars, cartoon-like residues of which we find

still retained in Western folklore and astrology as Mars and Venus where the planetary names are the same as their indwelling deities and which almost nobody believes. Astrology as a predictive science, yes; the planetary spirits as real presences in a fully alive solar system, I rather think not. It's still too bold.

Anyway, I expected I would see Earth's own Gaia and Pan. Many people still do not realize they are the egregore syzygy for our Earth, and if we lived on Jupiter our horoscope would include the changing role of the Earth on our experience of consciousness and the prospects of our horoscope make-up. Well, Mr. Blaise, says my imaginary astrologer, this week Gaia is conjunct your natal Mercury so expect an uplift in communication and possibly a manic sense of being overlit by a large feminine presence and a feeling your throat is suffused with Light and the irresistible urge to speak, pronounce, proclaim, and sound off. My pals, the Blaises, told me the Earth is the throat chakra of our solar system.

The question now was what would be my mode of transportation to the Sun? How about magical winged white horse made of Blaise angels? Some of the Blaises converted their form into a majestic white horse with flaring wings and we set off. Why not? They rather like this horse form, and it is practical. I could pretend I was Bellerophon astride Pegasus off to slay the evil Chimera. My expedition wasn't as grand as that. It was more like I was on the shuttle to the county library to check the building records and to retrieve Earth's algorithm. It didn't take Pegasus long to get here. It seemed like the Blaise white horse made one vigorous leap, a brief soar, and we landed at the Sun's Light grid archives.

It has the building specifications of the planets, moons, Light grids and Light temples on those planets deployed in this solar system. It understates matters to say that array was copious. Earth's inventory of Light temples alone was more extensive than most people even somewhat acquainted with the details of geomancy would suspect. I have used the analogy of county libraries and building plans archives, but the information was presented holographically. The Light grids were displayed as credible simulations making the archives chamber look like a barn thoroughly threaded with spider webs at all angles. These were the Light grids of planets and of the distribution patterns of temples. You only had to touch the display at any node to call up its mathematics.

The planets and their 184 moons or satellites were displayed as a living orrery. Any segment could enlarge or diminish with a touch of your hand one way or the other, and two taps would bring up the physical and geomantic data pertaining to a planet or moon, then three taps presented its Light temples. Data on the Sun itself was also instantly available, including future likely sunspot cycles and peaks, intensity of the solar wind and magnetosphere, even the likely expiration date for the physical viability of the Sun as a "middle-aged" yellow dwarf or G-type main sequence star about 4.6 billion years old.

I walked up to the display for Maldek, the now vanished planet with only the asteroid belt to remind anyone of its former existence millions of years ago. I paused and sighed. It's hard to forget a debacle like that. It's like calling up the files on an employee or field agent and being confronted starkly with the cold word "Deceased." Maldek was deceased,

its population shifted to the Earth long ago, but its geomantic specifications—it was a good design—were still on file.

The solar archives I was walking through comprised a hologram of the complete system of planets and moons embedded in the curving gravity well. This was not only an accurate simulation; it was presented in real time. It was the actual solar system as a holographic miniature; changes in state for any of its components showed up here instantly just as they did on the physical correlates.

Here was the Earth and its Light grid. I knew it well, but I enjoyed seeing it presented in this reduced size manner. I tapped it three times to bring up the Light grid, Light temples, and the mathematics that encoded both components. People don't realize how much arithmetic is involved in the maintenance of our planet, how much is implicit in its design. There was our heuristic algorithm.

As you know, the alien gods did not "steal" this algorithm in the literal and definitive sense of a thief removing a physical file from an office. We still had the numbers comprising the algorithm. What they stole was its operational efficacy. The algorithm required the interaction of other systems of numbers with which it was interconnected, and our *access* to these was curtailed. We were unplugged. See the cord dangling like it has been yanked out of a computer?

More acutely, then, what they stole was our ability to access our own system. A series of connected points with their own mathematics had to be freely accessible to enable us to use the algorithm to manage the planet. The algorithm was displayed in front of me like a master line of Light wrapped around the Earth. Without its necessary cross-connections it was inert, like a flashlight missing its batteries. You slide the knob on it and nothing happens, no light.

Then I discovered another layer to this stored holographic model. While in present time what I just said about Earth's algorithm was true, it was inert; the system had back-ups of earlier conditions all the way back to the original design stage. You had to keep tapping the display to move backwards in time to get them. I backtraced the planet's Light grid to a time before the alien gods interfered with our numbers. I had to go back a considerable distance on the planet's timeline to reach that. Why was that? I thought they had taken the algorithm's plug-in capabilities only a few months ago. Now it was years?

It was because the alien gods had been backtracing similarly on the timeline trying to wipe out all antecedent presentations of the algorithm in its correct, operational format. They left their footprints all along the timeline. Evidently, they had anticipated the Hierophancy team doing what I was now doing and they sought to pre-empt any success we might expect. But they missed one node. It was sequestered within a larger equation like a superscript footnote.

Try to appreciate how stunning it was to see the Earth, its Light grid, and all the mathematics that run it displayed in front of you as a living Light model. We work with this, and within it, every day, and we have it modeled at various levels of size and presentation mode, but we are always viewing it while being inside the system. Here I was outside it, like finally stepping out of a building I had spent my life living in and only simulating its exterior view. Now I saw it.

All these numbers are continuously scripting and modulating the qualities of consciousness possible on this planet, the subliminal life of our planetary Albion. Astrologers would revel in this factual, living presentation: here is the irrefutable demonstration of all the modulations exerted by the Sun, Earth's Moon, and the other solar system planets, a constantly adjusting, self-regulating Light system. Even better, since this demonstration runs as a holographic orrery, you can access antecedent modes back to the beginning of this inter-planetary dance. Here is the factual database to document the astrological history of the Earth and our complete solar system. You could rewrite history based on this. It could explain a lot of the unconscious motivation behind puzzling mass events.

There was one problem as I soon discovered. The algorithm was locked. It was there, running, vital, managing, yet I was locked out from accessing it. I could see it but not touch it, which means interact with it. Was there a backdoor?

There was and I found it, but first I have to explain something by way of background. There is more to this Light model orrery of the solar system than just its planets. Completing the astrologically mandated picture were the 12 zodiacal constellations. They were presented at two levels. First, their constantly modulating effects were displayed for the entire solar system, how they affected the Sun; second, the same modulating Light grid surrounded each planet. The constellations remained the same, Virgo was always Virgo, but how they affected a given planet was a product of that planet's Light grid settings. It was a dance routine between a planet's Light grid and the grid pattern imposed on that by the array and interaction mechanisms of those 12 key constellations. I bring this up because this is where I could find that backdoor into the system.

Persian astronomers distinguished four stars as being "royal." They form a rough square within the galaxy and include Antares in Scorpio, Fomalhaut in the Southern Fish, Regulus in Leo, and Aldebaran in Taurus. The Persians described them as guardians, each responsible for one district. They were the Watchers of the cardinal directions; for example, Regulus was the Watcher of the South. They were called Royal Stars by virtue of their high magnitude, the fact they appeared to "stand" alone among the myriads of stars, and because as fixed points on the Sun's annual path they marked the equinoxes and solstices.

The astronomers contended the Royal Stars were sufficiently powerful in their presence to affect large-scale events, such as natural disasters, intellectual breakthroughs, and significant social changes. Their respective alignments were interpreted to be either auspicious or unfavorable, and among them Regulus was ranked foremost in terms of dominant influence. Count on a Leo to be foremost.

Keep in mind that at fixed points in each solar year our Sun is conjunct with these Royal Stars, from the Earth's vantage point anyway, and this conjunction will heighten the influence of the Royal Star giving us the Sun plus Regulus. Yes, you get the whole Lion, because I've noticed that often the principal and brightest star in a constellation acts on behalf of the constellation and in a functional sense we may justifiably construe it, such as with

Regulus, as comprising the star pattern. The constellation Leo is Regulus plus its courtiers.

I would go in through Regulus. He was a fierce-looking celestial warrior. The Buddhist cultures of at least seven countries call the Royal Stars the Four Great Heavenly Kings. They each have names and attributes, weapons, symbolic devices, and distinguishing colors; they stand 750 feet tall, each guards a cardinal direction, inspects the world on a regular basis for alignment with the *Dharma* and evil pollution, and they all live for nine million years, says Buddhist lore.

The Buddhists, ironically, as they emphasize the emptiness of form, provide us a much more vivid description of these Kings or Royal Stars than just a lion image. That's all you get in Western star lore: Leo is a big lion, Regulus is its heart. Regulus is the prince or little king, or to the Arab astronomers, *Qalb al-Asad*, "the Heart of the Lion." The Chinese call it the Yellow Emperor; the Hindus see it as "the Bountiful;" and other attributions are the Mighty, Great, Center, King. But none dress Regulus up as a cardinal *Dharma* protector. It's like the way the Tibetans fleshed out Arthur as Gesar of Ling, master *Dharma* warrior. The Buddhist picture of Regulus gives you his full-bore *Dharma* quality.

Regulus and the other three Great Kings looms over the array of constellations like hefty bodyguards poised to defend the integrity of these stars against evil. The attributes of the Buddhist Heavenly Kings don't match up too closely with the Royal Stars, but the Guardian of the South is called *Virudhaka*, "He Who Causes to Grow." His color is blue, he rules the wind, causes roots to grow, and he wields a big sword which he holds competently ready to defend the world. Nobody associates lions with this guy, but the lion is metaphorical, and why should they, it's only metaphorical. But this King seems lion-like.

It is, for me at least, fitting because my Ray robe of pale, ethereal gold flushed with orange is the Ray color of Elijah-Kuthumi, who in his Egyptian attribution was known as Sekhmet who assumed a lion form. Sekhmet was the Lion-Goddess and protector of Lower Egypt and the Pharoah. So I would pass through the Regulus portal, tarted up in my Ray robe of this Ray color and with my "royal" Kuthumi-Lion accessories properly prepared for action.

The Regulus King-Guardian was like a portal. When I entered it, I felt I was standing inside a massive upright figure and within all the attributes given to this royal spirit. Here with me were about one quarter of the stars in the galaxy, the ones that fall within the southern district of the Milky Way. It was like being inside a human body and instead of seeing all the cells you see stars. Not only stars, but the invocatory names and the algorithms that run those stars.

It was like standing in a hall of mirrors. I was in the archives of the Sun, and in here I found the living model of the solar system with the zodiacal constellations surrounding that and highlighting this enclosure of Royal Stars. Now I was entering the same holographic display again through a part of it. I was hoping the Regulus Guardian would be able to circumvent the alien gods' lockout on the Earth's algorithm. Maybe even scare up a few impressive roars.

His presence as he strode toward the Earth was like Moses parting the Red Sea. Everything moved to either side to allow him through. The holds and blockages put there by the alien gods were pushed aside. His celestial body streamed in Light and in these Light streams glittered numbers. They glistened off his body surface like the scales of a fish under bright sunlight. In fact, it wasn't just a matter of parting the waters as he passed and me getting soaked in numbers; these "waters" were a roiling sea of many arithmetical formulations.

We reached the Earth hologram. It was encased in its many-layered Light grid, and this pulsed and throbbed with life animated by the Light, and within this Light I saw the mathematics running the processes of its planetary reality. I saw the wrap-around presence of the zodiacal constellations and the prominent four Royal Stars. I told you this was a hall of mirrors. I saw the tiers of arithmetical equations and there, at the top of the system, like a ribbon, was the Hierophancy heuristic algorithm, alive, unfettered, and making its adjustments.

The trouble was I couldn't just lift it off the planet like a necklace. As I said before, it wasn't like we didn't have copies of this complicated algorithm. We had many. The aliens had disconnected it from its necessary inter-relationships, the secondary arithmetical matrix into which it was threaded and dependent on. Here is a crude analogy. Say your leg goes to sleep. You still have the leg but you can't move it. Stand up and try to walk and you'll probably fall over right away.

It was exhilarating to see the Earth's Light grid from outside the box. In normal terms the best we can expect is a mental model of the system as seen from within that system. Now I was watching it entirely from the outside and admiring it as a brilliant piece of consciousness engineering. My compliments to the Elohim. Before me was the spectacle of Earth-Human consciousness, its mechanisms and products, its life as it progressed moment by moment, perfectly regulated by the precise arithmetical script we were charged with monitoring. I could enter this living system at any point and it would seem real.

Momentarily, I zoomed in on our Hierophancy offices in Sun Valley, saw the desks, work stations, display boards, meeting rooms, the scaled-down models. Standing at my desk I saw myself out there in the solar archives looking down. Then like a yo-yo I snapped back to where I believed I was primarily standing. I was moving slowly forward inside the Light form of Regulus. It reminded me of images of slow walking in deep-sea diving suits as you plow thickly through the resisting water, all that water pressure bearing down on you.

Regulus was full of stars and so was the environment I moved through, and highlighting those stars like etheric bodies were the innumerable mathematical equations that scripted the stars' reality. Our planet was cocooned in many layers of equations, like filo dough made of tinsel. But I noticed something I hadn't expected. Our master algorithm had a new feature. The algorithm sported a subscript of +2 at its end; this was new, something added on.

A +2 subscript to a mathematical formula will define a different version of the same variable or represent the base of a written number. This subscript had a superscript of 11 attached to it. Is that even possible? That raises the subscript to the power of 11. I could have used Sal with me to interpret this odd presentation. The best I could make of it was

that our algorithm was being forced to render itself in an alternate expression and arithmetical outcome, as if consciousness were forcibly transferred to a clone of itself. That was the work of the subscript.

The superscript put the process scripted by the algorithm into an unnatural hyperdrive format so that the algorithm dictated the Earth consciousness processes would run much faster than the Light grid design could accommodate. Its speed was upped to the eleventh power, which was not good. It would be like running a human body on amphetamines. Operation at this crazy-ass speed would eliminate nearly all of humanity. They would soon be worn out. Earth reality would run too fast, its consciousness frequency too high.

I was astonished, then appalled, then filled with admiration for our wily enemies. These alien arithmetical gods were perverse, indifferent to humanity and our planet, yet devilishly clever. It was like a chess move you've never seen.

Through Regulus I had been able to access our planetary algorithm in a condition in which it was locked in to all its required correspondents, except it had been hijacked in an unexpected manner with the subscript and superscript. It was like watching somebody get kidnapped and thrown into a dark van, and about all you see is the body rolling inside the van and the doors closing fast. Our algorithm had been forced into a different performance track, though it had some resemblances to the correct one, and that alternate was running super fast.

A planetary reality running too fast will seem like your consciousness has gone hyper, has been revved up and you're perceiving too much and too deeply. It would be, I imagine, as a minimum, like perceiving within a 4D world. Look at a hypercube and try to imagine yourself inside it. Your spatial orientation will be skewed, screwed up, like you're inside a kaleidoscope; you'll lose your footing.

The same will happen with your time frame. You'll see the past, present, and future as a continuous wrap-around present and lose your anchorage in time. You'll feel like you're alive and dead and reincarnating and entering the *Bardo*. You'll see spirits, dead people, angels, masters, aliens, hostile and friendly. You'll discern the causal sequence for events in both directions, seeing the results before the causes, the other way around, and both dizzyingly at the same time and numerous variations and alternate outcomes too. It would be like everyone had been suddenly upgraded in their evolutionary development of consciousness to the power of 11 steps beyond where they were comfortable.

The effect of that radical upgrade would be disastrous for Earth's people. It made me feel revved up just to look at it. I felt like doing ten things at once. From the alien gods' point of view, it would eliminate Earth's need to retain the algorithm as a living management system as there would be nothing left to maintain. Humanity would be finished and the planet's viability terminated.

If the scripted duration of the planet was to move consciousness forward so it could eventually arrive at an accommodation with that extremely fast eleventh power of the algorithm, the alien gods' plan was to do that in a matter of days. Then the Earth and humanity would be vitiated, wiped out, and they could lift the algorithm off it like stripping a corpse

of a lovely pearl necklace. She doesn't need it; the old lady is dead, can't you see, so now we finally get it.

Their indifference to humanity and the fate of the Earth was to me unbelievable. Except I could believe it. They believed this total arithmetical recall was justified. Any deleterious effects it had on incarnated lifeforms was irrelevant to this goal. The imperative was clear, straightforward, and they would not deviate from it: numbers should not have been dispatched into the fallen world to support life. Since they regarded all incarnation of consciousness and form as an existential error, a totally rotten idea, they regarded the dire aftermath of the arithmetical recall on those incarnated systems as unimportant. You couldn't fault their logic, only its complete absence of a moral viewpoint.

I realized I had overlooked something important. The significance of the +2 subscript. That signifies running an alternate version of the same variable, which in practical or geomantic terms meant a second Earth. I was just starting to wonder if I was seeing a theoretical hijacking of our algorithm or an actual one. That meant there were two Earths running their consciousness grids adjacently. One had the correct algorithm, the other the hyperdrive version of this number.

That meant, I was sure, that all humans were running on parallel tracks. One had consciousness constituting a world in 3D at normal speed with perhaps only occasional glimpses of 4D possibilities; the other had humans frantically churning through a world running at 11 times normal speed and always in 4D. Presumably, there was a cognitive bridge linking both perceptual frameworks.

This would leave most people, I should think, frazzled, confused, maybe crazy-convinced, though perplexed, they were operating in two places.

You would feel like you were living two lives and they were incongruent. It would be like how people who sustained UFO encounters or "abductions" are often unable to reconcile their personal timeline to account for their normal 3D daytime continuity of awareness and this bizarre, inexplicable extra timeline of remembered but dreadful higher-reality experience. They walk around always puzzled. They can't figure out when this weird stuff could have happened.

This subscript-dictated parallel reality would create psychic schisms in people. They would feel like they had split-vision, had gone schizophrenic. This bifurcated vision itself would retard the evolution of their consciousness because they would be unable to integrate and assimilate any of the products of their perception. Their perceptual products would remain cognitively indigestible, perpetually enigmatic, chronically refuting their presumptions of normalcy. Soon their consciousness would be like a computer frozen on a complex website page. The design complexity of that web page exceeded its software sophistication, like a college freshmen dabbling in poetry at a post-graduate physics seminar unable to make any sense of the equations, theories, and even the language he's hearing.

People would likely never be able to feel mentally relaxed again with this. They would feel that somehow even when they were sitting still in a chair they were rushing about frantically somewhere else, short of breath, that reality was too full, too overwhelming, too goddam irremediably mysterious to handle. The alien gods would wait patiently until the subscript-driven algorithm exhausted itself and the planet and the sentient phylogeny it was scripted to run were dead.

The algorithm in this hyper-excited manner would run the planet and its human consciousness so fast it would drop dead in its orbit in probably only a few years. Then the algorithm would be immediately recalled to their arithmetical zone and the planet and its exhausted, moribund humanity would be mere inert husks. We'd be Maldek Number Two, terminal by arithmetical extraction. The algorithm would be freed of all operational obligations since the manifest reality it was coded to manage no longer existed. The algorithm would automatically default to the arithmetical gods; the prodigal horse was back in the stable, enjoying its nose-bag, and that bang is the aliens slamming the barn door.

Some questions confronted me. Which Earth was the true one, or was this parallel reality running with equal ontological grounding on both the Earth versions? When the hyperdriven Earth exhausted its algorithm would that feed back into the slower, original one and destabilize that, or would the extinction of one immediately precipitate the same condition in the other without any feedback? If this were a holographic condition, then that immediacy would likely prevail. How much time did we have before the algorithm finished off the manic planet? Could we run a counter algorithm to strip off the subscript's 11th order powers? And could I come up with that without a math expert like Sal to do it?

There was an irony here. The alien gods had succeeded in revving up the evolutionary pace of the Earth in a manner similar to what the geomancers of Maldek had attempted. They had been discontent with the glacial slowness of consciousness on that planet between Mars and Jupiter and tried to speed it up. The plan failed, the planet imploded, and the Maldekians were resettled on Earth. The geomancers had a serious karmic debt to pay off over the next many millennia. Now here were the alien gods succeeding, or, so it seemed, accelerating the rate of conscious evolution and we were tasked with stopping that. I couldn't help appreciating their superior technique in making it speed up. They didn't want consciousness to run faster; they didn't want it to run at all.

I stuck my head into this speeded-up version of the Earth. I confess I liked it. I still grumble about the slowness of things, and here was life as it should be. Compared with what I remember from other places, even the increased cognitive pace since the 2020 advent of the Ofanim on the Earth is still at times too pokey. If you have to incarnate and put up with all of this, at least life in the fast lane would compensate you for the inconvenience of a short-term bodily existence.

In this alternate subscript-driven Earth embodied consciousness was registering the multifaceted details of higher reality instantaneously, like a fabulous tennis match, no net balls, all adroit backhands and zooming returns skimming the net. I liked it, yet it was clear that most people found it too hard to keep up with, and the pace of cognition was wearing them down, leaving them fried and manic. Every day was the first day of school or your first morning in a new country and for you,

age 20, this was your first trip to the wilds of Europe. There are so many new sights, sounds, and smells, after ten minutes you're exhausted and feel like a nap, but the day demands your continued attention.

That would be tough. I took myself firmly in hand, reminding myself that our job at the Hierophancy was not to secure our own existential comfort but that of the residents of the planet on behalf of the phylogeny and the goals set out for it and for the Earth as a mandated, commissioned agent for conscious evolution. Human reality cannot sustain itself for long on hyper-stimulants. I could always take more time off in the Pleiades if my impatience got the better of me. It was an odd contradiction: I wanted reality to run faster, but this hyperdrive reality would destroy the nervous systems of most people in hours. I had to figure out how to strip off the speedy superscript from the algorithm. It was running the Earth geomantic engine much too fast; Earth was teetering.

Even if the hyperdrive Earth was only an etheric or shadow alternate of the normal-paced Earth, it was still having a deleterious feedback infiltration, slowly corrupting the stability of the primary version of the planet. Even if none of this was, on a technical or material-plane basis, real in present time, even to exist as a mock-up, as a mental picture of an event soon to be incarnated, it was still having a bad effect, poisoning human consciousness with vague fears. No matter how you looked at this addendum to the algorithm, it was bad news.

Speaking of the Pleiades, that was my next step. I went back there for a consultation with some colleagues accomplished in mathematics and algorithms. I explained the problem and they came up with a solution in no time. I had the impression they were aware of the problem already and had been watching events on their version of closed-circuit television. They are very clairvoyant.

They provided me with a special algorithm. They had a technical name for it, but in the vernacular for the non-mathematicians such as myself it was an anti-algorithm, an algorithm reducer and eraser, an arithmetical disassembler. It was a -2 subscript. This technicality aside, my job was to make a holographic clone of myself, saturate this simulacrum Blaise with the algorithm, like entering a picture as a reality, then undergo a kind of Sumo wrestling match with the 11th order algorithm. I know how strange this will sound to somebody outside the Hierophancy. Frankly, it sounds pretty goddam weird to me right now too. It's astonishing, I sometimes think, the kind of sustained bizarreness we get into in our Hierophancy work and end up taking for granted as a kind of normalcy.

I returned to the Ainu site by the river and reinserted myself in the core of the alien gods' intrusion into Earth reality and the twin-Earth performance space. I made a holographic copy of myself, more like a Golem than a real duplicate Blaise. I equipped this Blaise simulacrum with the Pleiadian anti-algorithm and stepped inside its form. My Pleiadian colleagues had told me it was unlikely my deploying my quarter of the phantom algorithm and the finger-trap would have any success, as the deployment had fallen flat and failed at the other three rhombus vertices. They had been monitoring the four of us at our nodes.

So I would stay in that twofold condition for a while, get the feral wrestling match started, and throw the alien gods to the mat a few times. Their algorithm, the Earth's proper algorithm with the addendums that created all the problems, was inflated, swollen, fat and gigantic like the biggest Sumo wrestler. Compared to that I was a skinny stick figure, like a gaunt Stan Laurel wrestling the corpulent Oliver Hardy, hats flying. I visualized, expanded, then projected the anti-algorithm within my psychic space so it was like a huge neon billboard.

The stage for our wrestling match would be the alternate Earth running the hyperdrive consciousness platform, nicely exhausting the human residents. I threw myself down on top of the fattest Sumo guy I've ever seen or imagined. I use the analogy of wrestling but in fact I didn't have to do anything, not move my arms or even whistle. The anti-algorithm did the work. It started stripping off the orders from the superscript command to accelerate to the 11th order of speed and the new -2 subscript started erasing the alternate fake hyperdriven Earth.

A neon display board like you'd see in a stockbroker's office ticked off the diminishing powers as the anti-algorithm liposuctioned the numbers fat from the aliens. With each drop in an order, the Sumo wrestler lost weight. When we reached the seventh order, I saw Earth people starting to relax; at the fourth order, people were sighing, the way you would sigh after a scary danger had been averted. Oliver Hardy's weight loss was changing him into skinny Stan Laurel. They were getting disentangled from another fine mess.

I tried to keep track of all the places I apparently was. I was still in the Pleiades with my colleagues; I'm always still there, frankly: it is home after all. I was at the Ainu sacred site on the river. I was on the actual Earth and on the alternate one as projected by the subscript in our hijacked, amended algorithm; and I realized I was also back in Sun Valley on the far slopes of Bald Mountain.

I had gotten the superscript notation down to the first exponential level, then it stuck. The alternate Earth was still running one order faster than was comfortable. It was like using an exercise machine, say a running track, and the settings have you jogging 20% faster without let-up than your physiological comfort zone. The "jogging" in this case was the cognitive processing of reality.

Did you ever arm-wrestle, Frederick? You think you are about to definitively slam your opponent's faltering arm down to the table when he suddenly gets a second wind and it's your arm that's dangerously wobbling. The Sumo-wrestling alien gods were making a comeback and their algorithmic superscript was climbing back up the exponential number scale. They were already back to order five. I strengthened my concentration on the anti-algorithm and got them back down to three. Then they rebounded and zoomed it up to six.

Then I understood where the stuckness was coming from. I made another copy of myself and installed this in the actual Earth and added a subscript to the anti-algorithm. This would start erasing the alternate Earth altogether, remove the context in which this dance of escalation and diminishment of orders would end. My anti-algorithm subscript would pull the rug out from under the alien gods. They could have all the expansion orders they wanted; they'd have no place for it to play out. It would diminish to nothing more than a mental fancy. Remember, their subscript of "+2" had scripted the extra version of the Earth. My new subscript of "-2" took that away. Their 11th order script was homeless.

My tactic was succeeding, until….

12

Blaise's narrative stops there. What happened next was revealed almost instantaneously after I read his last incomplete line. All four of us were part of this as well as the representatives from the five other maximum free-will planets.

Readers will query how I got back to Sun Valley so quickly, or how I could be part of this next episode with our full complement while at the last posting I was still at Tiwanaku in Bolivia. Honestly, I still have a hard time accounting for it myself. The best I can offer is that I was somehow at both places simultaneously. Subsequent discussions with Sal, Jocelyn, and Blaise reveal they found themselves both in their places of dispatch and back here with our group. Apparently, this dual presence was necessary to engage the next step of work.

You may have noted that each of the reports I have presented in the preceding four chapters ended inconclusively, as if halted in mid-step. Blaise was making progress shrinking the exponential behemoth of the algorithm superscript when something seemed to arrest his forward motion. I had been at Tiwanaku, linking numbers with myths and Light temples and chasing the alien gods into an ever-receding infinity. Sal, situated at Majorville Cairn and Medicine Wheel, was trying to figure out if the alien gods were personifying the presumed Shadow of God Himself and now opposing him and preferring the arithmetically intact inertia of pre-Creation. Jocelyn at Helgafell was standing steadfastly at the perilous boundary of the pixellated universe and the quiescent realm of nonincarnation.

Our positions formed a rhombus shape overlaid on the Earth as each of us occupied a vertex within this elongated shape. We found ourselves wearing regal Robes of a Ray color. Mine was pale green; Sal's robe was bright rich yellow; Jocelyn's was bright orange with a hint of gold; and Blaise wore the official Robe of the Hierophancy and Grail Knight lineage and its tutor-sponsor, Ray Master Elijah-Kuthumi, which is a rich ethereal gold flushed with pale orange.

Each of us seemed to have suddenly sprouted surprising powers and potencies of consciousness bordering on what I am tempted to call special psychic abilities, the yogic *siddhis*. As if rising to meet the challenges of the occasion, we each knew more, could do more, could withstand more. Our consciousness was inexplicably marked with more potency, adroitness, creativity, and even the ability to multiply our copies. Even so, we were not yet prevailing against these apparently intractable arithmetical deities. At best we had stalemated them, though as I stood in the arithmetical sand I felt the tide coming in, water rising on my flanks. Maybe we were less than stalemated.

Readers must keep in mind that though I presented the four reports in such a way as to convey the impression of linear succession, you have to appreciate all four happening at the same time, that when I was running into infinity after the arithmetically-obsessed alien gods, Jocelyn was defending the border of pixellation and nonincarnation. We were addressing the alien gods at four fronts simultaneously; we were each aligned with a Ray and anchored in a suddenly revealed deep-rooted personal history of Ray alignment and mastery, and we were doing this at geomantic nodes of high significance to this "battle."

Each of us had been confronting a different nuance of these numbers-fixated gods, the custodians and personifications of Creation's original arithmetical field. All of us had been stopped or frozen as if in mid-gesture. Why was that? It was as if we were actors in a movie and the director called Stop, hold it there. He wasn't ready to declare the scene fit to print. We were still holding it there, waiting to complete the gesture which I assumed meant getting the better, finally, of these vexatious alien gods and mathematics thieves, finishing the job.

As for our colleagues from the other five free-will enriched planets, it was a large group. We had L2, R1, then from one of the planets we had eight figures which we designated as A1-4 and A5-8, with the impression of four heads or separate personifications for each A-group. Completing the tally were Y1 and Y2 representing one planet and a sole diplomat,

G1, for the sixth planet. According to strict accounting, our group's number tallied 13 aliens and the four of us humans, making it 17, though some of the aliens made lots of self-copies, and so had we so we'll have to say the correct accounting was a bit fluidic.

Our rhombus comprising the alignment of four sites across the Earth was embedded in a larger geometrical figure. Let's call it in principle a hexagon made of the alignment of the six free-will planets. Probably it is not a hexagon in strict mathematical terms. It is a hexagon only in the 2D sense. The 3D version would be very distorted. Still, it was a vastly larger geometry that encased the smaller Earth one, and that meant our front against the alien gods comprised these two geometrical patterns, all their vertices occupied wakefully by the 17 of us.

The alien gods seemed able to operate on an undeterminedly large action field. As many fronts as we presented to their hegemony over all the numbers in Creation, they rallied themselves to challenge us there and, it seems, repulse us. As with us, it appeared our extra-planetary colleagues were at their respective home planets diversely spread out across the galaxy and here at Sun Valley.

Their simultaneous presence at two locations, a galactic and a planetary, had the effect of drawing the hexagon of their home locations close up against our planetary rhombus geometry. Again, this was more in principle or in consciousness than in accordance with the strict proprieties of geometry. What I refer to cannot happen in normal geometrical terms; it would be a gross shape distortion. But as a conjunction of two energy fields what I describe was valid. You have this pan-galactic hexagon of six planets overlaid on Earth's rhombus.

The vertices of their hexagon overlapped our four rhombus points. L2 was conjunct with Sal in Alberta; R1 was co-present with Jocelyn in Iceland; Y1 and Y2 were overlapping Blaise's presence in Hokkaido; I had G1 with me at Tiwanaku; and the eight A-alien colleagues were spread out two for each of us. I don't think any of us had been aware of this overlapping at first but you will agree I'm sure there was a fair bit of phenomena to keep our perceptions busy. But now our attention was sharpened and each of us perceived our friends.

Our basic problem was that every time we figured we had at last come up with a definitive tactic to overcome the alien gods' resistance and to get back our algorithm, they pulled the rug out from under our assurance and held on to it. I have to hand it to them, they were devilishly, relentlessly clever. I had to keep reminding myself from their simplistic point of view all numbers belonged in the primordial arithmetical realm, outside and antecedent to the incarnation realm.

The argument that these numbers, formulated into algorithms, were necessary to sustain the myriad details of the Creation, namely, Light grids and Light temples that sustain consciousness for innumerable phylogenies, including us, held no traction. It simply was irrelevant. Retrieval and sequestering of all numbers was imperative. They were inflexible on this point; amusingly, I suppose, so were we. Reality required these algorithms and we would get them. It was funny, I guess: we were locked in a grunting *yin-yang* rope pull. Nobody was definitively winning yet, and we were tired, sweaty, and bummed out.

By the way, I hope I haven't confused readers with the odd chronology at play here. I received the field reports from Blaise, Sal, and Jocelyn after I came home from Tiwanaku. During the time of their adventures I was still down there. My assumption is that my primary bodily reality was at Tiwanaku and I had projected a ghost presence of myself back here at Sun Valley on Bald Mountain.

I assumed this was the case for the others, and even, probably, for our many extra-planetary helpers whose bodily presence, whatever "body" meant to them, was principally still anchored on their home planets with a ghost version of them here. So what I relate in this chapter took place right after the last move I made at Tiwanaku when my tactic against the arithmetical gods stalled out and froze up. I had to stitch together these separate chronologies to write this story.

We stood around for a while looking at each other, trying to figure out what to do next. We were back on the lower slopes of Bald Mountain, so we looked at that too. Our extra-planetary friends were still, communicated nothing. It felt like a long pause before an insight. Then it came. It was Blaise who spoke.

"I see our Hierophancy heuristic algorithm casting a complex shadow over the Earth. A shadow in the sense of an impression, a tattoo of numbers. It's like a hundred hands, or maybe a thousand, touching sites, actual geomantic nodes, where each component, each digit or letter in the algorithm, is anchored, where it has purchase on Earth reality, like hands on many turnable faucets.

"I see also the Light tattoos cast by the algorithms of the other five planets within the hexagon of their alignments. They make an imprint on their host planets, but they also cast a copy of that into the hexagonal space. Earth's algorithm does this too. I see points of connection among these six algorithms, number linkages, co-dependent equations, sub-clauses in the mathematical syllogism. It suggests a meta-algorithm, a summation of the six and possibly a seventh, a master algorithm using that. That may be the key to our successful retrieval of all six algorithms. Find the seventh and work through that."

It was like the most intricate lace doily you could imagine spread across galactic space, although its area of distribution here seemed more compact. The planetary algorithms are complicated enough in their own right, but they each have many subsets comprising detailed equations; the same was true for the meta-algorithm, only it was even more detailed and therefore complex in design. All of this formed a canopying arithmetical spectacle overhead; even though, on a strictly technical and spatial sense, these algorithms spread across the galaxy, because of the energetic compression of the hexagon to act as if it encased our Earth rhombus of points, the lace doily of numbers and calculations was a sky.

Blaise was pointing to the topmost part of this arithmetical sky. "Do you see that? In the meta-algorithm. It's not our planet's algorithm, but it is one that supercedes it or runs with the Earth, and the other five planets, implicit in its mathematical architecture. It is a higher octave version of the heuristic algorithm. A kind of higher arithmetical syllogism that acknowledges and accommodates ours, but without explicitly using it, so the alien gods might have missed this.

"Yes, it's made of numbers and that is the focus of these obsessive gods, but they have been reacquiring the algorithms from each planet, not from the top down. The meta-algorithm for the six planets appears to be operating in real time. You know, it's like a hand made of a thousand hands that directs ten thousand more hands. It's a kind of flawless arithmetical puppetry hand dance of modulated awareness performed simultaneously on six planetary stages."

I know, a little prolix. Blaise gets like that when he's enthusiastic. But he did help us understand the new mathematical dynamics we could work with. I saw lines of Light, with numbers for blood running through them, dangling like threads from one planetary algorithm down and across the hexagonal space, hooking into another algorithm like a secret tunnel network.

Now it was Sal's turn to get excited. "These are backdoor linkages among the algorithms, or what mathematicians used to call single-linkage clusterings. It is a type of hierarchical clustering. The hierarchy here is the two-level pyramid of the six planetary algorithms then the pinnacle of the seventh meta-algorithm. There is a calculation that describes that linkage process, and that's the backdoor.

"I'm probably stretching the analogy too much, but these linkages are like number wormholes that give you quick access across the platforms and can combine or collapse or merge one set of numbers with a greater one in this hierarchy. The cool aspect of this array is that since it is a Light grid comprised of functional algorithms and equations in a precise arithmetical lattice, we can traverse this both mentally and bodily, or at least in one of our extended consciousness forms. It will seem like moving through a tunnel while your mind runs the numbers, like running while your fingers work a hand calculator."

I felt I was looking at a mountain made of equations spread out as a lattice resembling a skeletal system. This mountain was climbable, but by our minds. You can appreciate we were in a strange territory now where the always secret infrastructure of reality was rendered naked and the mechanics of consciousness were at stake. It was as if the arithmetic were running around with its clothes off. I saw something else: all the components of these many equations had tie-down points in the Earth's geomantic landscape, arithmetical nodes, let's call them.

They were at one level manifest, physical locations, and at another they had their requisite geomantic feature, some type of Light temple, but at a still more recondite level, they were the anchor points for a constituent of an equation. Picture each number or letter in the algorithm as tied down to a specific Earth locality. It was like a thousand strings dangling from this six-planet infrastructure, each of them secured to the landscape on our planet.

Then I realized how this disclosure yielded a course of action. We had to get people to occupy these geomantic tie-down sites in a planet-wide collective focusing of human consciousness. The Hierophancy's job was to organize this. I had a picture in mind of how the simultaneous focusing of a great many people situated on these key geomantic nodes would free up the Earth's algorithm, force it out of the alien gods' hands and back into its rightful managerial position, running our planet's affairs and maintaining the adjustments of the Light grid.

As if somebody was helping us with this (probably the Ofanim or Elohim, or maybe both) a virtual version of the Earth appeared underneath this arithmetical lattice and the tie-down sites highlighted for our planning convenience. This was a specialized grid pattern, what you might call a higher octave Light grid model. It was like discovering your father, a courteous, jovial family man, a golfer and weekend barbecuer, was also a senior instructor in a Mystery school and master of a great deal of metaphysical lore and techniques.

So in addition to whatever Light temple process of consciousness these individual sites ran, they also participated in this extra grid. To be clear, this extra grid comprised the components of the algorithmic linkage equations and the constituents of the overt managerial planetary algorithms for all six planets—this was the secret arterial network of Earth-Human reality.

"We'll need to come up with some kind of lure that justifies people joining this project," said Jocelyn. "Probably something mythic in portent might work."

"I'll thumb through my address book and pull out my first thousand friends," said Sal. He managed to say this with a straight face. He didn't know a thousand people; I doubted he knew ten. He was a very private, hermitic guy.

"We do know someone with an address book that lists everyone on the planet," said Blaise. "Our pals, the Blaises, have everyone's name and address in their book. It comes with the territory they serve, namely, the entire human race. I'm sure we can count on the Blaise Boys to rally public interest for this. They've done it before; in fact, they've always done it, always talked to people even when they didn't realize it, misattributed it, or failed to heed it. 'We come in many forms,' they used to remind us years ago. Look for us everywhere.

"I'm glad we're long past that 2020 borderline. Prior to that it would have taken considerable effort to rally support for something like this; people were terribly distracted. In the last 45 years or so, public consciousness has loosened up and many people have enjoyed an increased fluidity in their awareness, a great range of cognitive motion, opening them up to more possibilities that formerly they would have regarded as outrageous and dismissed out of hand as unprovable. People are starting to appreciate how wide open reality really is."

"We do have a list of the friends of the Hierophancy, loosely affiliated colleagues, former students who trained here with us, and other regional leaders," I pointed out. I was in charge of maintaining those lists of collaborators. We had a few dozen Hierophancy members situated around the planet, and we could count on them to round up participants for this event. There were some people still around from 32 years ago who took part in the Theosophon 2033, and it seemed likely we could rouse their interest for this new occasion. There hadn't been any big collective planetary events since then and they had acquitted themselves well during that important time.

"We can't expect all the participants to be versed in or comfortable with the mathematics involved in this corrective event," I commented. "Most of us barely understand the numbers. What do we do about that?"

Blaise nodded. "Blaise just showed me the answer to that. They only have to visualize two things. The rhombus inside a hexagon, and then one digit from the algorithm or secondary equation at the center of that combined figure.

That will enable contact with the arithmetical reality at that node and provide traction. That number will be the activation key that locks them into the node.

"By the way, our colleagues from the other five planets can be counted on to round up many participants from their worlds to hold down their arithmetical nodes. We'll get double service out of that, servicing the nodes on their planets and the corresponding arithmetical nodes from their grids as they impinge on our grid. Do you follow? Because of the superimposition wherever they are holding down nodes on their planets they will also be holographically on our planet because of the shared digit places in the algorithm.

"So we'll have twice the personnel. Our participation as humans on this planet will also stimulate theirs and provide simultaneous spatial representation by us at their nodes. The event will take place within this extended hexagon framing the Earth rhombus. In practical terms, this will be a six-planet event but involving seven Light grids."

I had the impression this arrangement would amplify the effect six times. It's always hard to make a 3D-world assessment of a 4D-couched virtual reality. But I saw for each of these six planets the complete spread of aliens, Hierophancy members, and general participants arrayed in their designated geomantic nodes.

Here's why I say it raised the efficacy by six times as I finally understood what Blaise had just sketchily outlined. Earth would have the pertinent geomantic nodes tied down within the framework of the rhombus and hexagon and the placement of our extra-planetary colleagues and their helpers on their respective planets. Then from L2's planet you had the same pattern repeated again, but with L2's planet as the prime recipient of the alignments; then this holographic pattern was repeated four more times with the other planets.

It seemed that each arithmetical node would be anchored and fortified six times. Without our even trying, the four of us would be simultaneously present at six different locations. I marveled as I realized this sixfold presence had the effect of generating a seventh planet comprised of the conjoint attention of the 17 of us on these six worlds.

Sal was in charge of handing out the arithmetic assignments. He knew the mathematics of this inside and out, so he parceled out the individual numbers. Fortunately, we had already mapped out the geomantic nodes that anchored the digits within the secondary equations and primary algorithms that ran the Earth. We had transferred this cartographic mapping onto a projectable hologram and we activated this so the map of arithmetical nodes was displayed in 3D.

We saw that the Blaises were already at work, having meetings with the people on their lists, prospective participants. Since the 2020 epoch of Ofanim human incarnation, the vibrational tenor of the Earth had considerably increased in quality and refinement. It was not as hard to reach the angelic realm dependably and accurately, and it happened much more frequently than ever before and with a greater quality of information exchange and more sobriety. I'm not referring to the angelic end of this communication link, but the human side.

The tendency to inflate contacts like these into grandiose expressions of destiny, privilege, and elitist selection was gone. That had always been aided by low-grade interfering spirits. They got off on seeing humans lose themselves in a swell of false pride. It took them off the real playing field. It was becoming no more remarkable now than calling for an electrician. That's a much better way to handle affairs like this; it does not benefit you or your attempts to stay grounded and sensible if you think angelic contact is a big deal. You do not want it to feel like you're riding a wild roller coaster. Equanimity and neutrality are essential.

It looked like the Ofanim were having quiet conversations with selected people, the way you'd have friends or colleagues over to talk about things in your house. Some of the Blaises were in the angelic world simulating human guises or toning down the majesty of their angelic form, while others were among the human-incarnated forms the Ofanim began taking back in 2020.

It was hard to tell them apart from where I was looking, though I suspect a person would know the difference between a meeting in higher psychic reality versus one in which you could pat a Blaise on the shoulder and feel the bones there. One of the things I've always admired about the Ofanim is how many of them there are. They could instantly call upon as many of their 40 million copies as needed. On the other hand, a Blaise angel with bones you could touch: that was uncanny. The human Blaise said that was the most marvelous oxymoron.

It was an interesting situation. Nobody was in a panic though certainly there were grounds for it. The Earth was imperilled by the progressive removal of its arithmetical underpinning by the numbers-obsessed alien gods. Reality was growing thinner, weaker, even wobbly; consciousness was becoming unmoored. The Blaises looked utterly unruffled. I doubt they would ever look worried, even when that day finally arrived at the end of this Age of Brahma and the Old Man informed them it was time for His long nap, He hoped they wouldn't mind the time off and could occupy themselves productively during the long break time. No problem, Boss: we'll hang out in the *Dharmakaya* and pretend we don't exist.

None of us in the Hierophancy showed signs of panic, though we were lucid about the threat and its ramifications should we fail to retrieve Earth's algorithm. Equanimity is the Blaise style, both human and angelic, but I attribute some of our calm to the profound though incremental changes implemented in 2020. Since that major upgrade to human consciousness, the planet's Light grid has been able to be far more supportive to uplifting and more positive states of human awareness, and generally, people have had more presence of mind and emotional sobriety to consider their reactions and proposed actions than before.

I laughed. It has to be this way. You can't have all the doctors and nurses in a hospital freaking out and waxing hysterical the minute you have a medical crisis. They have to remain calm, professional, and reserved for the sake of the patients. Fortunately, most of our "patients" had no idea what was afoot in the Light grid. Add to this the complexity of the problem we were dealing with.

It was not an easy one to explain as it operated in a context beyond most people's awareness or familiarity. The energetics of the planet and a secret, geomantically charged landscape of Light and subtle temples was still in 2065 an exotic idea for most people. People understood locations across the Earth were pre-existently worthy of numinous adoration, but the radical concept of an Arithmetical Earth and self-regulating, self-learning algorithms that ran it was too big for most people to digest. That's why the Hierophancy had its commission. We were like intellectual digestion catalysts, cognitive enzymes. We regularly gave public programs, lectures, seminars, field trips, consultations to help prime people on the basics of this previously unsuspected planetary system.

I laughed again. Most people expect the aliens to be the bad guys in the equation. That's the typical polarized view humans tend to have about such things. But these "aliens" weren't bad or evil; they were not even on that playing field, and they weren't aliens either, having no form at all, just a collective nonpersonified consciousness that saturated and that was the arithmetical domain. How do you explain to people the Earth is threatened by a brace of probably self-aware and certainly super-intelligent numbers doing a walkout?

They didn't live on a planet with a Light grid. They lived nowhere specifically. They weren't the bad guys: they were more like the inexorable neutrality of a black hole sucking up all the available light, in this case, they were vacuuming numbers, all of them from everywhere, from ever since God thought them up. They were operating under an imperative they considered beyond any challenge. They were a seemingly unstoppable erosional force steadily wearing away the cliffside upon which we were all standing on Earth in the universe. You don't have a moral stance or take a polarized position regarding erosion: you do everything you can to stop it because you are loosing the ground you stand on.

All the time I was with my fellow Hierophancy pals at Sun Valley I was also at Tiwanaku. I saw myself, I *felt* my presence, standing in the spring green Ray robe right behind me, like an older brother perhaps or as my Higher Self. It was like seeing two completely different scenes out of each eye. I saw the same twofoldness with Blaise, Sal, and Jocelyn, in all *eight* of us.

If I turned around in my consciousness I could walk through the robed version of myself and be fully present at Tiwanaku. Walking forward I'd be back here. Aside from this polarity keeping my attention on its toes, it sewed the two sites together so that Sun Valley and Tiwanaku, and Helgafell, Kamui Kotan, and Majorville Medicine Wheel were linked, in two places yet also superimposed. In a sense this was like a standing open wormhole, folding space, erasing space, so that two physically distant locations were as if sewn together at one location.

I may sound calm and reserved in my narrative voice here, but frankly I was alarmed as I observed our six planets growing thin and weak in their Light. Even though the six high free-will planets were primary among the alien gods' acquisition interests, many other planets were getting slowly sucked dry of their managing numbers and their Light grids were weakened and reeling. The numbers recall was sucking the bones out of galactic reality and the Light grids were growing anemic, their maintenance no longer automatic.

There was a cascade effect, beginning in our six collegial planets then spreading out arterially through a matrix of connection to many other worlds. Even though these other worlds did not have the same high-level free will settings, they participated indirectly in the experiences of these six through this special grid. They were like guests at a wine-tasting party, sampling all the wine bouquets. You could see them concentrate, nod their heads, flash a little smile.

For a moment I had an image of the Hierophancy members as being like gladiators out in the perilous arena, fighting on behalf of the audience. We were not down there in the open playing field to entertain their dark animal drives, but to save them from an "enemy" utterly indifferent to their existence. Or we were security guards for a bank undertaking a massive cash transfer and who had been warned against clever criminal plots by robbers to grab the cash.

I shook my head. Enough of these teenager movie distractions, Frederick.

Then I understood something important. It had been staring me in the face all the time. Between the wobbling me at Tiwanaku and the Hierophancy field agent Frederick at Sun Valley stood me as that very old version of myself in the robe of my Ray affiliation. In other words, this composite version occupied the mid-space between the other two, anchored them, represented them, spoke and acted for them Both physical locations were subsumed into his—my—presence.

I saw the same conjunction with Sal, Jocelyn, and Blaise. Okay: now we were 12 Hierophancy members, not counting the other 13 extra-planetary friends. Growing in numbers surely will help. This was my old self, the one who had accumulated and assimilated all the wisdom of every incarnation, distilled centuries, millennia, of selfhood existence into dependable wisdom, and this accrued wisdom became the bedrock for unshakeable certainty. And speaking purely as Frederick, boy, did I need some of that assurance now. The older, smarter Fredrick in the elegant robe was my Designated Wise Elder.

In the center of our array of old selves in our assigned Ray robes stood Hermes, his emerald green robe resplendent and imperial. He was standing on a vast flower blossom of identical diamond-bright petals which—embarrassingly, it took me a while to register what this was, then I laughed—were the Ofanim. They brought their diamond geode of 40 million facets to flower underneath our rhombus-hexagon array and to provide us spiritual support and illumination.

Nice touch, Blaise. It wasn't just us and the Earth that got this munificence. The Blaises and their diamond petal-caves of Light underlay all six planets and their field agents. Still there was more. This array was like a spotlight that now revealed a vast tree made of numbers. It reminded me of the Tree of Souls, as described in Judaic mysticism and which I had seen firsthand. There you have the myriads of created souls hanging like fresh apples. But this one was comprised entirely of numbers and in all their implicit and potential equations.

An arithmetical tree. *The* tree of numbers. It was like another version of the *Autiot* that Judaic mystics say surrounds the Ancient of Days' Head as a wreath of fire-letter potencies capable of generating the Creation and all reality. This tree before me was the repository of the mathematical genetic code of life. This must be the Supreme Being's secret collection, His reserve presentation of all the numbers He

ever thought up and accounted for as part of the Creation, presented here in their still unsullied condition and order. Imagine seeing the genetic code for all possible phylogenies displayed as a tree. I'm not sure, but my impression was that this quantity of numbers exceeded that.

Where was this tree, or, that is to say, what domain was its origin? It must be *Hokmah*, the *Sefirah* of Wisdom, located above the crown chakra. Qabalists say the *Autiot* is housed there, like an archives, and this sphere of Light is also attributed to the Ofanim, one of Blaise's "dormitories" within the created world. If the 22 fire-letters of Hebrew are archived here and implicit in them is every possible combination that could be spelled out, then on the other side of this are the numbers because as we know every letter on the flip side is a number.

Hence the arithmetical tree must be lodged in this arcane realm with the creative letters. Unless I misunderstood the Qabalistic model, you cannot have one without the other; they are complementary realities joined at the hip. Above the human crown chakra on the top of the skull is *Binah*, the eighth chakra, residence of the Great Mother; *Hokmah*, the ninth, above that, is Blaise's place; and *Kether*, the Supreme Being's august Clubhouse, is to us the tenth chakra. His place sits at the top of the Tree of Life just as Brahma's celestial city is the ninth and topmost one above the other eight on Mount Meru, the cosmic peak. So it makes sense I was seeing the arithmetical tree rising out of the Blaise diamonds.

On this arithmetical tree exist in potential every possible calculation, every conceivable combination of numbers in a formula, algorithm, or algebraic mode. The Supreme Being had already thought them all up, as if whiling away a slow afternoon before the Creation began. It's the mirror-image extrapolation of all mathematical possibilities just like with the permutations of Hebrew words. It was as if the Supreme Being had generated the arithmetical realm, complete and prolix, all at once, and here it was, ready, in full display. Ray Master Hermes was moving his arms and flicking his hands like a meticulous, maybe even fastidious, orchestra conductor, moving formulas, concocting equations, tickling algorithms.

The Blaise diamond facets were radiant with Light and they seemed to enlarge and spread out laterally with every second. Innumerable Blaises in angelic form rose out of them and stood there like beacons, their wings a toroidal current. The four of us in our Ray robes stood amidst this spectacle of Light, occupying our vertices in the rhombus in Iceland, Bolivia, Japan, and Canada, as well as our virtual locations in the greater hexagon of planets, and also here at Sun Valley. Now the four of us numbered 32, each of us occupying four places.

The scene had the poised focus of a performance troupe before the curtain goes up. But was it *A Midsummer Night's Dream* or Ionesco's absurd *Rhinoceros*? What kind of play has the performers wrestling with the audience? The alien gods were the audience, and they were growing restive. They represented the arithmetical realm flushing into vivid self-awareness; they were its I-consciousness, despite the paradox of that designation as this collective field of self-awareness did not have a discrete selfhood, not like humans have anyway, and heartily, consistently resisted the prospect and disapproved of it as well.

It was more like a reflex, a mechanical possessiveness, the unwavering desire to hold the arithmetical realm intact. It wasn't even a desire: it was more like a mechanical imperative. It had self-awareness but did not question its motives. It was like the numbers were pebbles distributed on a dry beach; then water wells around them up from the sand and swirls around them, lapping their edges, moistening their smooth surfaces, claiming them as theirs. Then the waters of self-awareness saturate the stones like they were dry sponges. That's the alien gods becoming the self-awareness on behalf of the arithmetical realm. I have described this as if there are two agencies at play, but really it is only one.

Meanwhile, I was reveling in this extended prolific Blaise appearance. It felt like I was surrounded by a forest of brilliant white elephants with six gold tusks. *Hello*, Airavata. Then it seemed it was 40 million jolly Ganeshes sitting on their haunches, explaining reality, dispensing boons and benefits, making jokes. Then it was 40 million towering, roaring, flying Hanumans moving mountains This proliferation of merry Blaise manifestations tremendously sharpened the penetrative aspect of consciousness. I felt I could understand anything, and did. It fortified me with the confidence of a primordial commission.

I saw that the human Blaise delighted in these fanciful apparitions of angelic Blaise essence. It was being at home for him. The rest of us roistered in this. If nothing else, it was an effervescent respite from wrestling the intractable aliens and always coming up empty-handed, or worse, having lost yet more ground, or worse even than that, finding our hands crushed and flailing, having been stomped upon by the indifferent aliens intent on seizing their numbers.

I was beginning to understand the scope of our confrontation. As the upwelling self-awareness of the arithmetical realm, of this tree of numbers, the alien gods were reluctant to put these numbers in service of incarnation. To them it was an aberration, an infernal disturbance in a perfectly created quiescent realm. It was a dismemberment of their "body," despite that paradox, since they disdained all notions of embodiment; it was a hemorrhaging of their life-blood.

They stared at the Official Call for the deployment of the numbers and said *Why?* From their viewpoint, it was egregious, an inexcusable fallen state, a diminution of original purity and mental fertility that should never have been countenanced. They resisted it as strenuously today as when it first happened. They were steadfastly intent on making it unhappen, get it rescinded.

Worse still was the suggestion that the Supreme Being was behind all this, that the Big Guy generated the arithmetical realm as a hand-puppet extension of Himself, that the face and the center point of that collective awareness of the arithmetical deities was the Ultimate Deity Himself, counting on His fingers, as it were, and now He was having serious second thoughts about their deployment and we, those in the incarnated, enumerated world, were about as impressive to him as first-generation humanity a minute before He said okay to the world-ending Flood that rolled them all away and out of His sight forever. And, worse still, definitively worser because it was so troubling, the possibility that we had misperceived our role and had been commissioned to work *on*

behalf of the arithmetical realm and facilitate their numbers recall. We're fucked if I'm right.

I looked at the arithmetical tree. It was copious with grids. Innumerable patterns of connection and process were highlighted in it, but in a potential state only. Theoretical extrapolations, proofs to show what could be done, but for the alien gods the original thought expression was sufficient. No need to incarnate it.

All the possible, conceivable geometric patterns of alignments and relationships were displayed and amply demonstrated, but it was like a savant reciting the alphabet in a soundproof, lightless room with nobody to hear the phonemes except himself. It was a near ultimate solipsism. The alien gods were deftly juggling all the numbers like a million balls in a closed room with no audience to applaud them. The ultimate solipsism would be the Big *Jogler* Himself happily whistling a crazy little tune while He tossed the number balls.

You see the problem? All this came out of the Supreme Being, the numbers and the gods of their self-awareness, so how come the The Boss couldn't just put His foot down and command the numbers to deploy and the alien gods to shut up and help out? The Supreme Being of course *could* do this. How come He *wasn't* doing this? What if He didn't want to? Then again, He might be caught in His own antinomy, a fraught contradiction that started when He began the Creation and which He has never resolved, not yet anyway, and maybe He's waiting for the Hierophancy to figure it out and release Him from His own vexed polarity.

The only plausible answer I could come up with was that He was ambivalent about launching the Creation itself. Maybe it was a big mistake, a rash move, quickly regretted. He should have taken that nap; or continued it: that *Pralaya* couch was so comfortable, come to think about it, He would have mused: Why ever did I think I had to get up and do something? Why should I? Nobody was telling me to start the Creation. Nobody even knew it was possible. And all that paperwork. I could do without the headache of number crunching.

He was undecided about the prospect of disturbing the beautiful stillness of *pi* for the roiling turmoil of *phi* and the defilement of the numbers realm by putting them into service for this. Why put everything in a frazzle when it feels so content now? These arithmetical gods were part of the Supreme Being; they *had* to be, so whatever attitude they manifested, this diffidence in the face of manifestation or this resolute aggression in the face of the deployed numbers, it had to be an expression of a divine attitude, a little pique on the part of the Chief Puppet-Master, a little ocean swell of irritation and indecision.

I knew I was committing the most basic error of all theology, to presume you understand the Old Man and what He might be thinking, plotting, doing or not doing, and why. Since the Supreme Being is infinite, might there be zones in His universal Mind that even He hasn't gotten around to exploring yet. Still, short of an actual press statement from the Big Guy that explains everything and will be remembered as positively the best press conference in the history of journalism, all questions answered in full, we had to proceed to do something.

The Supreme Being (it seemed the issue took us back eons ago to the day before the start of the new Life of Brahma) had lain in bed wondering if He might take the Day off (as in a Day of Brahma), sleep in, not get dressed, keep the *Sefirot* on their clothes hangers in the *Ains* closet, let the *Pralaya* of universal quiescence and inactivity languidly linger on. Why not let the perfection of this visualized arithmetical tree of all numbers and their combinations remain a private picture in His mind, undeployed and unsullied? Can't we just leave this beguiling thought-experiment as an unrealized thought? Why must I actually get up and make it all happen then have to look after it? An astrologer would likely say, the Old Guy has gone totally retrograde, not moving forward even an inch; it's all backpedalling into quiescence, so goodbye reality.

The problem now, I saw with a shiver, was much bigger and displaced the primacy of the alien gods and their fussy resistance to numbers deployment. That was a small potatoes problem compared to this. It was monumental and involved ambivalence in the Creator Himself. We had to convince Him to send the numbers out in service of manifestation and the incarnational realm of forms. Even Mrs. God, doing business as Hera, couldn't change the mind of old Zeus.

So, are you serious? I'm not sure who I was addressing. We had to lure the Creator out of His relaxing hot tub of divine ambivalence? He was in there, soaking hugely with the jets of water pummeling His great Back, second-guessing Himself. As soon as I realized this, I saw we were on a slowly rising elevator. The Blaise diamonds were lifting us into the air as smooth as silk; we were heading up, presumably to the top floor, as far as the Blaise elevator goes.

Maybe it wasn't up, because that is a 3D spatial conceit of perception. Maybe we were going deeper instead, penetrating to the core of reality, to the Supreme Being's Throne Room, effulgent with its big empty throne. That's no surprise. He never sits in the Throne; it's there mostly for decoration, to impress His visitors. He likes seeing them spin their heads around looking for Him. He's usually crouched *inside* it, not hiding exactly, just comfortably private, watching.

It looked like all of us, this Hierophancy mini-group of 17 (or 84, if you want the accountancy to be *entirely* accurate: four copies of each of our 13 extra-planetary colleagues plus our burgeoning 32) plus all the Blaises and Hermes would be meeting in a closed session with the Creator-in-Chief to see if we could allay His hesitations about starting the Creation and using the numbers. That's far too many presences to count, so let's say it was by now a large crowd that milled about the empty Throne petitioning the Boss-in-Chief for an explanation. It was weird though, us talking to the Old Man as if through a golden wall. It was as if He had sequestered Himself in His room and didn't want to come out. If I didn't know any better, I'd start thinking the Throne was His panic room.

It was odd and funny, both to the extreme. You never are going to see the Old Man actually sitting in His big chair. As I said, He's inside it. You hear this large booming voice coming out of it as if the Throne has loudspeakers around it. Why doesn't He sit on the Throne? Because He has no form, no posterior to plunk onto the broad golden Throne seat and there preside imperially over the Creation, no arms to rest on the arm rests, no back to lean against the chair. In an odd gesture of parsimony, He created innumerable forms for everything in

the cosmos, but left Himself formless, as if he had just run out of all available shapes.

The Throne is what the Jewish mystics call the *Pargod*, the unpartable curtain that separates the Supreme Being in His ontological nakedness from His creations including nearly all of the angelic realm, and prevents them from being instantly incinerated by this awesomeness. He has a tendency to become inflammatory, rumor has it. And if you don't get burned, you'll be turned to divine stone from His searing gaze. The Blaises get to see Him, though, and somehow remain exempt from the torching revelation of His Nakedness, which is to say, His ontological bedrock. They've seen Him and lived to tell the tale.

The Throne Room has all the appurtenances mystical literature like *The Book of Enoch* primes us to expect. You have pillars of gold rippled in gold flames, a river of fire searing horizontally across the room behind the Throne, floors on fire with flames that never consume anything but illuminate this further, flames everywhere but not burning anything up, august reality revealed to a shocking degree of lucidity, the *Hayyoth ha-Qodesh*, the super-arcane angels, dangling like grape clusters above the Throne and the higher reaches of the room, and the holy fire-letters of the *Autiot* forming a sizzling wreath of creative fire about His head.

Even so, this is only His city apartment, where He stays when He's in town on business, which is to say, when He makes an appearance within the created worlds. The rest of the time He's out at His country estate in the lush *Ains* where it's more expansive, more casual, less particularized, where He can spread out, put His feet up, dress informally, fiddle with His beard dreadlocks, and stop worrying about

His damn created worlds and their wobbly prospects and the incessant bookkeeping and reports on how all that Light He so cleverly *fiat luxxed* is faring in the created realms. Nobody talks about any of *that* in the idyllically secluded *Ains*. At best it's a rumor you hear from the mansion staff.

Yes, I know, my flipness sounds like the human Blaise on a wise-ass tear. That happens when you're around him long enough. But how other than with amused irony, even drollery, can one recount what we now found ourselves in? As for the *Ains*, I'm not sure we mortal ones could survive a long visit there. It is expansive because it is the nonmanifest realm, just a lot of Light and emptiness. You want for nothing, but that's because nothing to want has been created yet.

It's the Black Bowling Ball district above the Tree of Life and outside the Cube of Space. It's beyond that august podium called *Kether* where the Supreme Being is known to make an occasional appearance. I hear the angelic Blaises like it out there, spend many long weekends relaxing with the Old Man, don't even notice the vacuity of particularized manifestation, regarding it as home; they like the stillness, and the wait-staff is to die for, catering for your every last desire.

The oddness I refer to has to do with the seeming paradox, the time confusion. We have to talk the Supreme Being into dispatching the arithmetical realm to support the Creation, except, technically, He already did that many *kalpas* ago. Complicating it further is the fact that all of us are part of that already-manifested realm and neck deep in the incarnational realm, flailing around in its mud. Maybe we're here to persuade Him not to cancel the project mid-way through its planned time duration, like stopping a three-hour movie after the first hour. Is it possible the Old Boy has gotten a case of cold feet?

The alien gods, those vexing numbers-obsessed intelligences we have been chasing around the cosmos and Earth for weeks now, are part of Him, like a troublesome sub-personality, and our persuasion has to address their fixation. They are perfectly positioned to keep whispering persuasively in His large ears, convincing Him to recall the numbers, that He is right to have second thoughts.

We stood in this rainforest of Ofanim facets, dripping in consciousness, as we set out to petition the Supreme Being to send out the numbers. We knew that all the time He'd be listening to this chorus of nay-saying alien gods, the voices of the arithmetical realm and a part of His totality advocating to keep the numbers at home. He had to always follow His own counsel and who was to gainsay Him anyway? The Olympians never got anywhere in trying to budge Zeus. And while we were entreating the Supreme Being to action we'd be addressing an empty golden chair with a propensity to convey sounds of talking.

The Supreme Being sees the arithmetical tree as a perfection of design, a complete mock-up for the unfolding of reality, while the alien gods aspect of Himself sees it as an aesthetic masterpiece and that it would be criminal to sully its purity of intellectual perfection by deploying it into the Lower Worlds as a creative force. The Supreme Being has a practical mind: well, I created these numbers to be used, after all, so why don't I go ahead and do that? But, still....

The alien gods protest strenuously. No, *no*, You created them, You created *us*, to admire as a thought experiment that turned out well but doesn't require implementation. I know, it's presumptuous to think you have a clue what goes on in the Old Man's mind, but I suspect the vacillation in thinking went along something like this. How else to account for our bizarre present predicament?

I have given you the impression that the Supreme Being's Presence in this chamber was localized in the empty golden Throne. That is not fully accurate. I felt the Supreme Being's mental Presence around us like an infinity of sword edges facing us in a circle that formed the circumference of this chamber. Those blades were sharp beyond belief and conception; their adamant edges were right up against our awareness, and they seemed ready to slice through us instantly.

I do not mean to impute any animosity or hostility to the Old Man, just a fierce acuity of attention. We were up against the sharpest Mind in existence. And it was the strongest mind too. You felt that if you pushed against it in the least you would be neatly julienned from the sheer propensity of that Mind to do it. It wouldn't be trying to slice you; that's simply what happens when it moves.

I tried to imagine I was the Supreme Being myself. I know, a ridiculous notion, full of human hubris and all the other routine clichés of dismissal. But I wanted to see the arguments for and against manifestation as He saw them.

The Hindu time model instructs us that there is a seemingly endless cyclic round of creation and absorption known as the Life of Brahma and lasting 311 trillion years. It's like a cycle of exhalation followed by inhalation, manifestation and the retraction of that manifestation succeeded by a long period of non-existence. The question arises: If you're just going to suck the universe back into yourself after a fixed period of time, why bother extruding it in the first place? Why not conserve the energy and not bother and maybe just spin daydreams of what it might be like without having to go to the bother of actually doing it then chaperoning the results, you know, requisitioning all the hardware and equipment, the trained personnel to maintain it, the monthly reports on status?

It seems like a legitimate question to raise. I often wonder the same thing, on a lesser scale of course, regarding serial incarnations. Why incarnate *again*? The human Blaise used to joke about telling people to take a sticky note with them into the *Bardo* after dying, the note saying, "Don't even think about it!" If you see one of those infernal womb-doors, run the other way as fast as you can. Wouldn't it be less wear and tear on the soul to remain safe in the astral world somewhere and save the duress you can expect from yet another incarnation? Yes, I know, in most cases we have bills to pay off, debts to settle, karma to rectify. But aside from the accounting details, why bother doing all this again? So similarly, why sully the perfection of the arithmetical Tree of Numbers with life?

Whatever could the teleology be that would justify this recidivistic tendency? Being one with God? Well, it's easier if you never leave God in the first place. The Supreme Being, *maybe*, thinks: What would it be like if I made a universe capable of looking at Me and offering an assessment, perhaps even criticism? Criticism in the sense of a literary critic assessing a new book as to whether it achieved its stated goals, was worth reading, or grabbed the reader's attention. More crassly put, is this book a page-turner racy enough to keep me up all night reading it to the "shocking" or "unexpected" conclusion? I suppose there are people who regard their incarnation as a real page-turner with a plot that never lets you down, leaves you breathless, in a sweat, panting for more.

I took stock of our position. We were closeted with the Supreme Being Who was having second thoughts about the Creation and the deployment of the numbers. The arithmetical gods, it seemed, were getting through to Him, voicing their disdain for being used to create and maintain an ill-advised Creation. For us, we had been investigating a theft from the Arithmetical Earth, namely, our managing algorithm. We had been following clues and suspects across the Earth and beyond, even back and forth on the planet's timeline and our own too, and all of it had led us here, to the Throne Room, the fate of everything undecided.

The possible implication, a question staring me starkly in the face, was this: Was it the Supreme Being Who stole our algorithm, and that of the other five planets, hobbling and rescinding His own original beneficence in granting these six planets that generous endowment of free will supported by numbers? True to the classic criminal mind, He provided Himself with a suitable fall guy. Blame everything on the arithmetical deities; let them take the heat for Me. Even if they get sent to the Big House, I'll get them out of the slammer after a month. Just stay "inside" for a minimum sentence; it will look good to the public. Then I'll issue a pardon or reprieve, or maybe I'll just unlock the backdoor for you.

I had to keep reeling myself in. I was having too much fun with this silly fantasy. The arithmetical gods comprise a layer of the Supreme Being's inner reality. Look inside the Big Fellow and you'll see all the numbers. Maybe to Him they are like words, grammar, and syntax to a writer; you need all this to write. When You set out to enumerate reality, You deploy the numbers to code the script, except now all this is under review, and the numbers have convinced You to refrain from this rash, ill-considered act and call them back to their safehouse.

If the Supreme Being stole our algorithm, recalled it to the numbers fold, and our investigations have led us through all those avenues and circuitries of reality *to here* where the prospect of a definitive recall of the arithmetical realm seems likely if not imminent, didn't this suggest that the Hierophancy's job was bigger than any of us realized? Or at least me. Blaise probably knew about this.

Maybe I had been construing all this the wrong way. Maybe the Hierophancy was more like the arithmetical bodyguards, its protection detail and chauffeurs. Were we supposed to shepherd the numbers out into the created world and, if required, manage their complete recall from it when the Supreme Being, bored with it or disliking the results or just wanting to put His attention elsewhere, snapped His fingers? Our job was to look after the numbers wherever they were, supporting the Creation or in secluded perfection out in the *Ains*. Maybe we all got concussions and, batty, misremembered our identity and job.

Was that the actual specification of the Hierophancy's commission, to always superintend the deployment of the arithmetical realm everywhere and their products the Light grids and the myriads of Light temples on the many planets? That reconfigured the problem. Maybe there was no arithmetical theft to correct. If we were on the arithmetical realm's security detail and they were called back to the Central Office, who were we to question these new orders?

I looked around at Sal, Jocelyn, and Blaise. They looked as confused as me. Sal shrugged his shoulders. Jocelyn frowned. Blaise looked concentrated. Clearly, none of us had any idea what was going on now. We were mentally flummoxed. Were we marshaling the numbers to flow back into the Supreme Being or was this in fact a moment long ago, one that had already happened on the timeline, and we were getting briefed on the first brilliant deployment of the arithmetical realm out into the created world to act as its infrastructure? From the Supreme Being's viewpoint, all of time was concentrated right here, so it was both, the numbers were sent and they were not sent, leaving us with big maybe.

It was all the one same moment. Here are the numbers, send them out and don't. But they had been sent out or else we could not be here, not having been created. Could both be true at the same time, deployed and not sent? But if the Supreme Being was recalling the numbers now, nothing had been stolen from the Earth, not in a strict sense of a theft. The arithmetical "leaves" were all flocking home to the arithmetical tree, resuming their original rightful positions. Everybody always says the Supreme Being is mysterious, the Mystery Itself, and they are goddam right. My head was spinning uselessly in circles now. How do you make sense of the motives and moves of an Intelligence that is infinite?

While the four us stood around baffled and stalled out as to good ideas of what to do or even say, Ray Master Hermes was in conference with the Big Man. I couldn't hear anything they said, and I suspect it was a conversation not conducted in words, but telepathically, probably in pictures. Probably classified on top of that, need to know basis, you're not read into the program. I have had the impression throughout this "adventure" that the Ray Masters and especially Hermes knew far more about our case's subtleties and probably could have taken more decisive, even definitive, action to correct it if they chose to. The Blaises were standing in concentric circles around the Ray Master; clearly they were part of the conversation and might in some manner even be facilitating it.

The tableau of these three "parties" started to change. The Ofanim's diamond facets were rising up to cup the Ray Master like churched hands of Light. Hermes himself was no longer distinguishable as a figure, but was now the Emerald, the original Cube of Space (which he superintends in initiation terms) that contained the entire Creation when it began, and still does. Then inside this glittering upright emerald (like a stretched square) was the effulgent Throne, ablaze in golden fire. No figure occupied it but a Voice came out of it.

It was the Supreme Being at the core of His own Creation, the legendary (if you were a well-versed Qabalist) Cube of Space with the complete Creation inside it. That's what we call the Emerald, and it is the secret Heart chakra or Heart within the Heart, in all humans, a hologram of the Cube of Space. The golden

Throne, standing in for the Supreme Being and as tangible a visual metaphor you're ever likely to get of the Old Man, wreathed in a *double* tiara, one ring comprising the creative fire-letters, the other the arithmetical realm. I didn't see that second wreathing before. So: He has one for numbers, another for letters.

Ray Master Hermes was gesturing to us to approach the Throne. He was manifesting himself as both the Emerald and as the familiar Ray Master guise. He pointed to the Throne and gestured for us to stand on it right now. There was no mistaking his suggestion, no matter how wildly inappropriate it might seem. Perhaps in worldly, political, or religious matters, it would be improper to sit in the royal seat, executive chair, or throne of the world-acclaimed leader, but here it was different. The Throne itself was only a metaphor. We hopped up.

It signified the seat and point of focus for the Supreme Being, more like a terrific magic wand. Shall we say it was the ultimate resolution of the vexed polarity of immanence versus transcendence as Christian mystics used to ponder inconclusively: Is the Supreme Being an indwelling force within the Creation or a *deus absconditus* resident only outside the created world? The answer is both, and the proof was displayed incontestably before us. Too bad there weren't any theologians lurking about; we could set them straight on this matter. Well, here was this force saying we as created beings had a right to occupy the Throne. As Hierophancy members apparently we needed this occupation to do our job.

We stood on the Throne. It was like suddenly finding yourself in a crowd in which everyone was shouting, orating, incanting spells, declaiming poetry. It sounded like a combination of Allen Ginsberg and Walt Whitman howling ecstatic verses like desert prophets with James Joyce chanting *Finnegans Wake*. It was a polyphonal roar of sound yet we could distinguish every single voice: millions of voices sounded forth and we heard each of them. It was inherently an exhalation of sounds, decidedly orderly at some level of hearing though it sounded cacophonous and chaotically overwhelming. Or almost.

The air was thick with numbers, equations, algorithms, theorems, proofs, as densely packed as the biggest flock of swallows you could imagine occupying a shared air space, flying up at once, with a noise of flapping wings and whooshing air, unfastened feathers trickling down the air, our mouths gaping.

The air itself was arithmetical. It was saturated with mathematical thinking; reality was being coded and scripted right here around the Throne in staggering detail. It was like being in a room with a thousand accountants running their adding machines, cranking out numbers, an old-fashioned image admittedly, yet the airspace around the Throne had this concentrated air of continuous mental calculation. All the numbers and their deployment were accounted for, entered in the books, their field activities meticulously recorded.

Let me clarify my earlier observation. Reality, all realities, were indeed being coded and scripted here but it was only theoretical, preincarnational. Everything was designed, made ready, all possibilities, it seemed, spelled out. The Supreme Being was the client of an advertising firm reviewing the artwork for a *proposed* series of product advertisements, seeing if that's what He had in mind. Nothing has been decided, no contracts awarded yet, no ads booked. *If* I go ahead with this, it would please Me if it looked like this, came out this way. Here, come see this wonderful simulation of My plan I just now finished editing.

It was the presentation of mock-ups for the complete marketing campaign. The Supreme Being was playing both sides of this business relationship, though I'm not sure what our role was; it seemed neither ad agency nor hoped-for client. The clamor of letters and numbers continued, like a thousand passionate orators. I didn't know precisely what the Hierophancy's role in this was, at least at this primordial stage, yet I was certain we had a role and it was important, implicit, in the same sense that the collectivity of wakeful awareness of the arithmetical realm was identical with the obnoxious alien gods we had been chasing across the Earth, galaxy, and spiritual worlds to retrieve our algorithm. Except the "we" of the Hierophancy, incidentally, had suddenly enlarged its membership.

I saw hundreds, maybe thousands, of wide-awake spirits in all sorts of life-forms and bodies standing at attention in widening concentric circles around us. That was reassuring, to know that more than the four of us plus the 13 extraplanetary colleagues who had accompanied us were tasked with this responsibility of superintending the numbers realm that scripted Light grids. Our heads were tilted slightly upwards. We were inside this widening gyre of creative letters and scripting numbers continuously spewing out of the Throne as if their supply was inexhaustible. The reality they generated burgeoned.

This was performance art at its most spectacular. It was art with a purpose. The fountaining of this creativity was not random, like emptying one's pockets or pulling everything out of a cluttered closet. The implicit congruence of Creation itself, its processes and relationships, was clear. What I mean here is that all the implicit rationality of the Creation was evident in this display. I'm not sure I saw it in visual terms, but I was certain it was present.

It might be a higher dimensional rationality, beyond our ability to comprehend. That was a concept that spun my head, a rationality beyond the ability of human-couched reason to fathom, yet still unarguably rational at heart. I knew with certainty this outpouring of letters and numbers was thoroughly ordered and perfect. Even the plan for the arithmetical gods had been exquisitely considered and instituted, though I couldn't yet discern what that was, other than to irritate us and steal our master algorithm.

Spouting before us in wonderful cascades of Light were equations scripting realities and outcomes we could not imagine and which might take humanity centuries to discover, possibly even to suspect they might exist. Speaking of finding equations, Earth's missing algorithm was here somewhere. Yet where to find it amidst this universal warehouse of all possible algorithms?

It was too loud here to speak, with this uproar of letters and numbers, so Blaise communicated with me telepathically. Probably with all the others too. "We don't have to poke through this wild jumble of every last divine utterance. Just hold your alignment respectively at Tiwanaku, Helgafell, and the Alberta medicine wheel, as I will with the Ainu site, and that will key us into the missing algorithm. We have already made many alignments in our search so far that we can now call on to reiterate the number sequence. The virtual version will summon the real one. With the 17 of us realigning this way, it may push the algorithms forward to the surface of our awareness, like squeezing a lemon to pop out the seeds. So stand ready, hands outstretched, and catch those seeds."

I found myself, as I reaffirmed my simultaneous presence at Tiwanaku as well as here, which was, unbelievably, I had to admit, on the Supreme Being's Throne, calling to mind everything I knew about the Earth's Light grid and original programming for consciousness and its Albion. That was the product of all the numbers after all, this exact flavor and nuance of sentient self-awareness. It was everything we as embodied humans take for granted, like the range of movements the physical body is capable of and executes every day, gesturing, plucking, gesticulating, flailing, waving, patting, touching, or finger-snapping.

Consciousness has its set of routines too, from perceiving and defining an external world to establishing points of self-reference, even to the point of naked self-awareness, the kind that knows, that declares, I am alive, therefore I can die. That is the paradoxical yet balanced statement of a self-aware, separate individual. Fear of being alive and separate, unsure of this strange embodied context, I've always thought, is as starkly frightening as knowledge of one's eventual death. That you can and will die also affirms that you are now alive.

You shiver as you realize your responsibility to make something of this holographic unit of God consciousness you are while in this apparently separate physical form. Everything else about your reality is a given, already created, a *fait accompli*, a stage setting with props, and

all the details of your body, its features, shape, and size, you had little to do with; it was a given, but your awareness, your bedrock grant of consciousness, to be a perceiver, what you *do* with it, that is the original part. That is where *you* make something of this universe of givens. What will you make of it? How will you play this stage role?

You stand at the threshold of planetary self-awareness, the cusp of the awakening of our Albion that the Earth was designed to facilitate and which achievement is a key milestone in planned Earth evolution. Earth and humanity. Our Albion must achieve this same existential threshold of self-awareness as we. This is what the numbers are for, what they were created to make. Wake Albion. They are the stage, the props, the settings, lightings, floor, ceiling, and curtains. This is where you perform the unforgettable act of waking up in the daytime.

I was transiting back and forth between the numbers layer and the self-aware declaration one, all the while feeling like I was standing, almost comically, in the center of a massive fountain, getting soaked to the soul in primordial creativity. In mundane terms, it felt like trying to hear myself think in the midst of a chorus of a trillion voices, passionately, joyously declaring their fresh existence. You can't exactly ask the Supreme Being to turn the volume down. He would have to hear that God-awful racket every day during His Life of Brahma. Except it probably was not irritating but a lovely proof of concept demonstration. Here, behold the vast diversity and teeming population of His gloriously clever idea to flesh out the Creation with myriads of life-forms able to communicate.

The curious thing about this spectacle was that we seemed equal to the obsessing arithmetical gods. All of us were saturated in this emission of creative force. Did this mean we were the same as the alien gods? Obviously, we weren't the same in terms of apparent physical form, but we seemed to enjoy equal status inside this God-fountain of letters and numbers, like we were bettors of equal stature at a race track as we awaited the winner.

Did God, maybe as a form of self-entertainment, ask them to steal the algorithm, us to retrieve it, and He would lean back and enjoy the back-and-forth? Or we were rival companies both bidding on the same job, awaiting the results that would determine who was awarded the contract? He couldn't decide whether He wanted the algorithm in place or missing in action, so He set us both in motion and would let the outcome of our struggle determine the final reality.

It was unsettling, in light of our recent history of interactions, to realize that we and the arithmetical gods worked opposite but complementary sides of the same situation. They sought to preserve the purity of the numbers; we looked after their field applications as they ran processes of sentience and planetary life. These were not opposed or conflicting roles, but two sides of the same hand. I wondered if this discomfiting realization had occurred to the alien gods. Did they realize we were not opponents but allies in this abstruse God-game?

We had been chasing after them to get our algorithm back, and they had been manipulating us to preserve the algorithm after rescuing it from a sullied use. They were too smart to flee; they had been cleverly eluding us, fooling us with dissimulations, sleights-of-hand, and other wily trickeries. It was like a masterful shell game: Under which shell lies your precious algorithm?

I was aware that Sal, Jocelyn, and even Blaise were sharing my perplexity. Everything had changed, turned inside out, flattened, reversed—I don't know: the whole playing field had been transformed. Or maybe its original truth was now revealed. The alien gods were not Earth's enemy, not the sought-after culprits of the Hierophancy, but, shockingly, our designated colleagues.

We both dealt with the numbers, we in the embodied, incarnational realm where the numbers were deployed in the field running consciousness processes, they in the field of original manifestation, without form or deployment, as pure integers. My head was spinning, despite the fact my physical spinnable head wasn't even here. Had we been chasing after ourselves, like puppies dashing after our own tails? It was as if the playing field and bleachers had been emptied and there was no baseball game afoot now, and apparently there never had been. Even the stadium was gone, and frankly I couldn't remember what baseball was.

I could see why the alien gods preferred the numbers in their pristine form. As I stood in the fountain or what had earlier appeared as the arithmetical tree, I was invigorated by the mental clarity this demonstration revealed. Here were the original designs for all reality but in a condition untainted by any use. The alien gods were convinced it was a contamination of the numbers, of themselves as the numbers' collective awareness, to be deployed in the incarnational world. That was a fallen condition; it dirtied the numbers, abused them to put them to such an infernal use. They should never leave the "corral." Why, anyway? They had everything they could possibly need inside that fenced-in zone of perfect safety.

But that meant they were opposed to the Creation proceeding any further than the thought stage. It was a good, even clever, idea in principle, but not to be taken further. They'd give the Old Boy that: His thought-experiment was canny. Then we had come upon them and their attitude from the position of the Creation having already proceeded long ago and we were tasked with looking after the deployment of the numbers in service of maintaining that smart idea. The arithmetical gods saw things as if the Creation had never been launched. For them, the numbers were safely corralled; they never wandered out of the paddock to forage in the troubling created world, except for perhaps one or two horses. Maybe a couple frisky horses got loose, ran off across the alluring field.

We stood at the precise pivot between conception and deployment. It was a stretched-out moment which for the already incarnated would seem to be instantaneous and therefore non-existent. As soon as an algorithm was conceived, it was executed, running a prescribed reality somewhere. But right now that instantaneous execution of the scripted numbers was halted, made into a stop-action space for us to occupy for the purposes of considering its feasibility.

It was like standing at an interstice between two passing moments of existence. A quantum physicist might label this the quantum flux or uncertainty field where something was neither a particle nor a wave, not manifested or nonmanifested, but both at the same time.

What status did that leave the Earth to enjoy? The rest of the galaxy, the five free-will planets of our colleagues? Existent or not existent? The numbers are strutting in the world and they never left home.

This pivot point was marked with ambivalence, seeming indecision, but was it instead perhaps the perfectly balanced mid-point, the still moment in our respiration between inhale and exhale or in Taoist language the summation of the *yin* and *yang* which they call the *Wu Wei*, the circle that includes both poles? Go forward or retreat? Did the Supreme Being want to proceed with Creation? If so, the numbers would have to start marching to build the architecture of reality.

It was hard to imagine the Supreme Being confused. Maybe it was His antinomy, a paradoxical contradiction between two beliefs or conclusions, each reasonable. I'm going left and I'm going right; I'm sending the numbers out and I am not sending them, and both of these opposed actions are happening at the same time. The analytical mind reels at this irresolvable paradox, yet it defined our moment. It is philosophically reasonable: if you are infinite you are all the possibilities of action and inaction all at once in one big tangled rational mess.

It seemed we were looking at the arithmetical gods in perplexity and they at us in dismay and all of us only shrugged. What else? Nobody had the answer.

Nothing happened for a while. It seemed we were just waiting for an outcome, some resolution to this paradox of inaction. Then something happened.

13

We were laughing. The four of us. I couldn't remember anybody making a joke. We were back at Visvakarman's universal design office studying blueprints. I think the reason we spontaneously laughed, as if we had arrived here laughing even before we got the punchline, was that the arithmetical gods were here too and we were all leaning over a large drafting table studying a design.

They weren't really leaning over the table as they had no individual forms, but I felt their presence all around us like a sharpened field of clarity. We had blueprints for seemingly everything. It was a rush job on the Creation. We had a deadline, fast approaching, and we had millions of Light grids and temples to execute and get running, to align their numbers with their reality. Our job was to deploy the numbers; their job was to submit to being deployed.

I suspected the Supreme Being's job, in His see-through semblance as Visvakarman, was to enjoy the commotion, to design and send forth, to enumerate the virginal Creation, to preserve the purity of numbers and to put them into action and dispatch the Hierophancy as high-end babysitters. Still, I felt their diffidence, like a skittish dog not sure he wants to proceed down the indicated path as there might be unpleasant things awaiting him that way.

Then what appeared to be a solution occurred to us. King Arthur showed up. Let me explain. The arithmetical gods' concern was the contamination of the numbers by being dispatched into the Creation to support incarnational forms. They wanted to preserve the original sanctity of the arithmetical realm, and to them that meant they should not be used, ever, to manifest the formed realm.

I don't think any of us explicitly called on King Arthur for assistance, nor did it occur to us. Probably it was Ray Master Hermes who came up with the idea. That makes sense: King Arthur is the chief of the Ray Masters, and the leader of the Great White Brotherhood of Ray Masters, Ascended Masters, adepts and apprentices and whatever names they have for their hierarchical strata. This chief is also known, if you are Irish, as Fionn Mac Cumhaill, Indra if you're Hindu, Thor if you are Norse, and the redoubtable *Dharma* warrior Gesar of Ling if you're Mongolian or Tibetan. His functional title is Solar Logos.

That is, to us, an august designation signifying the Christ or Logos at the level of suns, meaning stars, but also sentient life-forms raised to bodies of Light. This figure, which has a masculine and feminine valence and personification, is the cohering force, the spiritual "glue" that holds these suns of consciousness together. The Christ aspect imparts a nondualistic singularity of consciousness to the pattern of stars and souls, filling them with totally wide-awake awareness. As the Logos, he permeates, pervades, and sustains universal space, completely saturating it like water engorging a sponge made of stars; he coheres the stars, providing context and explanation for their new individuated stellar presence.

But here is the crucial link, the one that explains the sudden appearance of King Arthur. Qabalistic lore, as I have said already, holds that each star in the universe has a Hebrew name, one that can be said in Hebrew and uses its letters, which means it is defined by a combination of letters and their number correlates, a kind of unique identifying tag, evocative and descriptive. Each star has a name and a number code. The Solar Logos is the intelligence who *knows* all those names and number tags. He has the master list; he knows each star personally, like an employer with an impeccable respect for his workers, knowing them all.

Not only does the Solar Logos know their names and qualities, his Christ-infused essence wraps them around with the Christ Light, suffusing the galaxy with that same ineffable quality of original Light that the Christ as Logos provides to the created world. Think of it: the Solar Logos preserves the sanctity of the original arithmetical realm and its correlate of the creative fire-letters.

The Solar Logos makes it possible for the numbers to descend into the feared, reviled incarnational realm, whether it's at the galactic or human biological level, without fear of corruption, contamination, or the other defilements the alien gods are in such a froth about. King Arthur guarantees the continuing purity of the numbers. He wraps them up in the Christ Light, which, let me remind you, is the pristine condition before numbers even existed. As the collective consciousness of the arithmetical realm, the alien gods can move into this realm and not lose anything of that absolute virginal quality. He keeps the stars as inviolate as if they were still huddled with the Old Man in the Throne.

This image is too literal but it conveys my point. The stars, as a first level of form and incarnation, can enter the manifest realm as if dipped in this Christ-Logos solution which gives them an impenetrable coating of purity. And it preserves the pristine nature of their relationships with one another. If the stars were a family of travelers, all departing on an ocean liner, it would be like assigning them to the same quarters so they were never separated or alone.

It would seem to the arithmetical gods, I should think, as if they were both staying in the uncontaminated, unfallen realm of numbers and entering the manifest realm where the numbers were deployed to create and sustain reality without ever dirtying their hands. It would be as if they never left the pure numbers realm, except, in operational terms, insofar as the worlds of form and substance were concerned, they had. In other words, they could have it *both* ways at once. It would be like staying at home and bringing your home with you as you travelled. You'd feel you never left, never had to leave, your lovely home.

I looked around, or maybe I should say I extended my psychic senses to see if the alien gods understood the improvement in their condition from this. Blaise, Sal, and Jocelyn were intently focusing on any indications the alien gods might be putting forth regarding their attitude about this development. In the meantime, King Arthur worked with us, studying the Light grid engineering charts, conversing with the Ofanim, and conferring with Ray Master Hermes.

Now and then he turned to us and smiled as we plotted the mathematical parameters and specifications for the Earth's Light grids and its myriad of Light temples. I'm not sure how he did it, but King Arthur seemed to be exuding a crystalline mist from his form and this surrounded the charts and grid models then saturated them. He was talking all the time, though this was probably his voice invoking the precise names of the stars and star patterns and relationships our grid entailed. Maybe he was chanting a hero list of all the universe's stars. It reminded me of the champion-declamations of hero-worth in *Beowulf.*

I had the impression the alien gods, in terms of their attention, were leaning in around us to get a closer look at our work and perhaps to monitor our thoughts. Their intangible presence seemed enhaloed with algorithms and these twinkled like morning dew upon which the day's first sunlight gleams. I took that as a promising sign. They weren't resisting. The humanlike form of the Solar Logos enlarged and expanded in all directions. It was full of stars, as many as if you could see all the living cells in a human body. That's 37.2 trillion, by the way. The reciprocal of the Solar Logos saturating the newly generated and enumerated

stars of the galaxy is that they should find cordial lodging in him.

A roar rolled out of this figure like thunder, and he took on his formidable Gesar of Ling spiritual-warrior guise, wielded a sword that was like a diamond *vajra* and thunderbolt and even Thor's hammer *Mjölnir* all in one redoubtable form. This image of Light encased each star like a fierce psychic atmosphere. The Solar Logos was declaring to the arithmetical gods: See, you can safely step outside the house as I will assure your safety in the created world. This was a way of expressing the strength of the Solar Logos as the Christ-bearing force in the galaxy to protect the stars and preserve their sanctity. Surely the alien gods would take this demonstration as a warranty of the Creation's good faith.

I saw teams of humanlike figures working within this psychic Solar Logos atmosphere. These must be the planetary Light grid designers assigned to those stars and the planets they housed in the gravity wells. As for ourselves, we were busy with the Earth, doing the same, applying algorithms to an emerging Light pattern. I heard the roaring all around us: it was fierce and majestic, and probably if you were of ill-intent, it was intimidating, maybe threatening. To us it was like something by Wagner with lots of singers and turned to high volume.

That roar and the sonic and celestial qualities it carried informed our work, and I mean this in every sense. It infiltrated our numbers and what they generated like an insistent mist. Everything entered the realm of form and substance, even if we were still at the level of Light and etheric substance, saturated in this Christ Light conveyed by the Solar

Logos. I don't remember ever feeling so secure in myself. If I were an algorithm or even a digit in one, I would confidently step forth, boldly and brilliantly, into the bright incontestable sunshine of the created realm, and remain free of worry, doubt, and hesitation.

I almost held back in drawing the conclusion that the arithmetical gods were cooperating with us, not protesting our deployment of their numbered essence to generate forms which were, of course, irrefutable evidence of incarnation. It looked like they were, but was that possible after what we'd seen? I proceeded tentatively, with caution, part of my attention expecting a sudden recoil. I looked at Blaise: he grinned, then he shrugged. Sal and Jocelyn looked mildly puzzled, but generally they seemed confident and focused in their work.

Everything we did seemed fresh and predetermined, as if we were a computer printer churning out a 5,000-page manuscript, and each page specified a series of Light temples of geomantic complexity already "written," its numbers deployed. As for the arithmetical gods, they were acting through projected *avatars* of their own presence in a kind of electronic handpuppetry, moving versions of themselves at a safe distance, making their numbers dance to our choreography.

You'll have to excuse my wandering metaphors. All this was exceedingly strange, and as I worked I tried to make sense of what I was seeing. My mood was lightened, though, by what sounded like angelic singing, or at least humming. It was probably the Blaises thrumming to our numbers work, as if the lilting, pleasant sound of their voices would calm the equations, relieve them of fear or hesitancy about stepping into the incarnated world, make them want to.

I never appreciated before how immediately generative equations can be, when you hold one in your hand, or maybe it's the mind, and register its potency to create a desired condition. It's like a magic wand with built-in spells; you just point it and the equation specifies the desired reality it abstractly describes. At the same time you feel you are encased in the projected algorithm, like it leaves a stamp on your psychic space, a tattoo on your consciousness, becomes part of you, as if you are specifying not only the planet's body but yours as a human, that you are compounded, like a vast ball of yarn, of pyramidal tiers of numbers. Further, you have the impression you're working inside the galactic form of the Solar Logos, operating the strings that link equations with the manifested stars.

I am reluctant to emphasize the personification of this figure in names like King Arthur, Indra, or Gesar of Ling mounted triumphantly on his white horse suggest. The personification of the Solar Logos is for illustration purposes only. A truer notion of "his" reality is as an extended field of consciousness in action. It's similar to the distributed awareness manner of the arithmetical gods; they have no personification guise, but are the awareness behind and within the numbers. The Solar Logos is similarly diffused throughout the billions of stars.

Through our alignment with him, we turn the Solar Logos to focus on the Earth. Apparently, he can multiply this precision of focus millions of times all at once. It seems like a gesture that is not rooted in any specific time period, but extends throughout the timeline of the galaxy and individual timelines of planets. That was why I found myself unable to have any certainty about when this was happening, this placement of equations with planets and their grids. Were we repeating the original design gestures from billions of years ago when the Earth was freshly made, or were we back then doing this for the first time? Even more unsettling and hard to answer was whether it made any difference.

I kept checking on the alien gods to see if they were okay with this. They seemed to be. The Solar Logos seemed to have convinced them the innate purity of their numbers realm was being preserved even as their numbers deployed. Seen this way our quest to recover Earth's managing algorithm seemed trivial, although I admit I felt a bit devious and hyper-attentive, like a thief waiting for the perfect moment to lift a pearl necklace and slip it into my trousers pocket.

The reason I hadn't retrieved this valuable piece of mathematical reality was that I hadn't seen it. It hadn't been generated yet because we were still laying in the many tiers of the planet's Light grid, the innumerable geomantic subsystems the algorithm would handle when that phase of the work had been completed. When it came time to generate that algorithm, I'd be ready to grab it.

We were building the Arithmetical Earth, like a planetary ball of yarn made of equations. Each layer was laminated in the Solar Logos's shouted Light. We were writing the face of the human collective personification for the Earth, the Albion and that of the billions of individual humans who would live there. I had never thought of myself as the product of a lamination of equations, but I saw that at some

arcane level of design this was the truth of a human being, and, as I surveyed the progress in the other five free-will planets, of those life-forms too. I suppose I should be cheered to note we all carried that Solar Logos shout. That was a guarantee of our alignment with a pure source and that we each carried this Solar Logos imprimatur, linking us with the greater galactic pattern.

As to my point of reference within this ball of yarn assemblage of a human and planet, I fluctuated between identifying myself with the emerging human and that of the distributed collective awareness of the arithmetical gods. For a time, I felt I was them, in them, with them, *them* themselves, fascinated and quietly appalled by this emerging construction of manifested consciousness and what they (us, as the planetary designers) had done with our precious numbers.

I felt like I was part of a committee watching a building go up on property they had reluctantly ceded to the building interests to construct a condominium or perhaps an office building. They watched with studied trepidation as the virginal land was slowly transfigured into a possibly vulgar commercial property, and all the while they wrung their hands over the fate of the numbers, sent out to toil in service of such a quotidian, unedifying project as incarnation.

We were wondering whether this use of our precious numbers to generate a semblance of consciousness, a holder of awareness and a personification made of our arithmetic, was worth it, and, more crucially, was commensurate with the quality of the numbers realm itself and would justify their questionable use. We were not convinced yet that this emerging human collective face of arithmetically constructed awareness was worth the corruption of our pure numbers. We still find it distasteful, and we are feeling restive, impatient, and quietly outraged.

I realized I had slipped into the mental state of the arithmetical gods and was regarding what we, as members of the Hierophancy, were doing to the numbers. It was beginning to feel like we were overseeing (babysitting was more like it) some touchy, twitchy, hard-to-please clients who at any moment might cancel the contract and quit the project leaving us with a half-done building.

Then suddenly everything disappeared, all the numbers, the balls of yarn, the works, and we were swept up into a rushing whirlwind pulling us outward. The carefully woven planetary Light grids we had been assiduously generating were gone, as if disassembled, vacuumed into a null space where no forms exist. There were no signs of the alien gods, other than a fleeting impression of spirits running briskly into the horizon, with only a suggestion of their former presence.

"I half-expected something like this," said Blaise. He looked displeased.

We were like a team of architects busy in the field supervising the steady construction of a complex building per specifications when our clients decamped. Gone, without a word of explanation, fled the scene, abandoned the project. Refused further payment and would probably demand an immediate refund too. It seemed that the alien gods had either reversed their orientation by 180 degrees or had turned themselves inside out and disappeared, taking away all the numbers.

It felt like we were in a mirror universe now, where everything was the inverse of what it had just been. We had been applying arithmetical laminations to create this ball of yarn that was the collective consciousness of the planet and human phylogeny, in other words, using numbers to generate consciousness and self-aware manifestations. Now that numbered world was using consciousness to construct a greater arithmetical edifice, sucking the oxygen out of the room.

Yes, that's what was happening, the arithmetical realm was recalling the consciousness it had been enumerated to produce. That was like oxygen. It supported life—it was the life the numbers edifice was intended to generate. It was all going in reverse now: the awareness was being suctioned out of reality and being absorbed by the numbers. The numbers looked strange too, like mirror reversals of their true and correct form, like a black-and-white photograph reversed. It was like a mirror sucking everything in physical reality into its world. All the numbers now looked exceedingly odd, like they had been turned inside out. I couldn't identify the nature of this change but I knew it was weird.

Sal looked both aghast and intrigued. "It's the realm of negative numbers. That is what's happening. The arithmetical realm has done a bunk and gone negative." He looked at me and Jocelyn and noticed we were both perplexed.

"Not negative as in evil or dark, but literally, as number values less than zero. Like a negative bank balance or an account in the debit range, in the red, as accountants like to say. Sometimes they're called imaginary numbers, like negative square roots. They are conceivable, even calculable, in purely mathematical terms, but nobody thinks they have any actual reality in the physical world. Mathematicians used to consider negative numbers only as theoretical possibilities, but as otherwise incapable of having any traction on the positive world of integers and reality. Now the alien gods have shown us otherwise. Negative numbers are real, operating in a shadow-mirror universe."

"It's worse than you realize," said Blaise. "Look. They are sucking the life out of an entire Life of Brahma, draining the complete bank account of karmic records. They are emptying out the *Akashic* Records. Who would have thought that possible? The numbers are now specifying the thorough recall of all consciousness generated by the numbers realm, spelled out in equations and algorithms. All that awareness is being sucked back ruthlessly into the numbers. The numbers are systematically inhaling all the life-force oxygen out of reality. It's as if they are emulating Brahma at the end of a Life, preparing for *Pralaya*.

"Can you imagine that? Emptying out the *Akashic* Records for the last Life of Brahma? That's 311 trillion years worth of generated, evolving consciousness sustained by the arithmetical realm now pulled out of the reality banks. The arithmetical realm is doing a vampiric sucking of life from the Ancient of Days. They're using this vast recall of consciousness to energize the purely arithmetical domain and to build a pyramid of numbers, as huge as the Supreme Being. It's a travesty of the Qabalistic mystery of the *Shi'ur Komah*, the true size of God."

I had to hand it to Blaise. Even in the midst of a cosmic disaster such as was just presented to us, he managed to insert the perfect arcane reference. The *Shi'ur Komah* is a Qabalistic way of modeling the mystical shape and height of the Godhead. Outwardly,

it looked like calculations designed to figure out exactly how tall the Supreme Being was when He stood upright for us to measure. How tall is the Big Guy? Qabalists say He stands 236,000 *parasangs*. A *parasang* is calculated at three miles, so He stands 708,000 miles tall; yet another speculation from Qabalists says from the ground to His soles alone is 30 million *parasangs* which comes out as 90 million miles, the distance of the Earth to our Sun.

Let's not be silly and take any of these calculations literally. They are clever metaphors. That is what any sensible Qabalist will tell you, except the alien gods were taking it literally and building their own kind of arithmetical Golem out of the world's numbers. A negative numbers *Shi'ur Komah*.

Bizarrely and frighteningly, they were converting a manifested universe of living consciousness, an extraversion of the arithmetical realm, into an introverted, exclusionary world of numbers alone, no longer in service or incarnated but in retreat from manifestation and the incarnational realm, like a vast private art collection sequestered utterly from the public, open to nobody. They were marching resolutely away from zero into the negative numbers zone. It was like a writer turning against his reading public, refusing all appearances, recalling and pulping all his books, vowing to never write another word.

The arithmetical universe had been transformed into a solipsistic numbers realm, all the integers and their products turned away from manifestation and into themselves, like recluses in absolute retreat from the world and public view. The alien gods did not want their precious numbers to specify anything any more.

They wanted every last equation returned to their still-life Golem.

We watched in dismay as numbers from across the universe of space and time were trooping steadily into this burgeoning pyramid of dry abstraction. The previous many Lives of Brahma and their archives in the *Akashic Records* were being drained bone-dry as well; soon it would be as if Brahma never lived once.

"Well, I'll give the old obfuscators this," said Blaise. "They are going to top the *Shi'ur Komah*. God is going to have a growth spurt from this reclamation job. He's going to return His attention to His own estate and find Himself mightily enlarged with a huge increase in the number of *parasangs* He's carrying on board. But then we're up against that same vexing paradox: these arithmetical brainiacs are inseparably part of this same enlarging negative Supreme Being.

"They are building body mass on the ultimate manifested form, the Supreme Being, even if His incarnated form is purely metaphorical. It is still an incarnational artifact. How are they going to deal with this fundamental paradox? The Supreme Being is incarnate, because He is existent, which means the numbers are servicing that. Suddenly, the arithmetical realm will find it's working against its own interests. They are supporting God's Own incarnation.

"It also means at some level He must support this bizarre, complete retraction of the universe's arithmetical infrastructure and the stripping bare of all the Trees of Life of their consciousness-bearing leaves or however in God's Own Name He sees this event and the strident retreat into the negative numbers hideout. Retrieving Earth's heuristic algorithm is inconsequential in light of this onslaught. The manifested realm of numbered consciousness is in peril."

I watched as planets, stars, humans, and many other phylogenies were sucked dry of blood, water, life-force, and consciousness, their forms crumbling. Little piles of dust lay scattered across the galaxies. All their support numbers were flowing briskly, propelled by a whirlwind of intention, like a leaf-blower infused with the force of the Supreme Being Himself, back to this arithmetical Golem. They kept adding to His girth and height, slapping on the equations to fatten His mass and assure His primacy and eventual supremacy in the universe as they rebuilt Him in a negative numbers space. It was like taking a house apart. They kept leaving behind these inert dry-dust piles of desiccated former forms.

In this inverted realm of negative numbers, the algorithms were no longer running their number sets to generate and maintain processes. They were rendering these arithmetical devices into complete inaction, cancelling all the processes they ever ran in the (to the alien gods) infernal incarnational realm. They were constructing an immobile, lifeless sculpture of all the deactivated equations ever thought up and set out into Creation to generate forms with life. The retrieved equations would do nothing, specify nothing, not even remember how to. They would be on display for this private collector, never used again. To them the beauty was crowned by the complete inaction of the forms themselves. They were not supposed to be used; that corrupted them.

In this domain of negative numbers the arithmetical realm was waging war on consciousness. It was ruthlessly retracting all its investments in the unsavory world of incarnation, manifestation, and anything that passed for form with life. All the numbers in existence, all the equations that could exist, that prescribed processes, were called back immediately, removed from their living context, which quickly fell apart and crumbled to dust, and not even the *Akashic* Records would remember they had existed because these Records were cancelled.

The truly disturbing aspect of this was the indifference with which the alien gods performed this recall. They did not look—feel, I should say, since they didn't have faces—malicious or gratified with the success of their numbers retraction. To them it was the unarguably logical conclusion, the necessity of the negative numbers realm, a nonyielding gravitational pull devoid of any attitude.

The universe had become a sink that was rapidly draining its water. The alien gods, by yanking the playing field into the world of negative numbers, had pulled the plug on the sink drain and the water was rushing down the hole. Our job was to stop that. We could hardly reveal the Holy Light if it had all been recalled to the inverted world where numbers were opposed to consciousness, but, ironically, were holding consciousness hostage and not asking any ransom.

There was no solid ground in here, no surety, epistemologically speaking. Had this ever happened before, the thorough calling back of the arithmetical realm? Did the Supreme Being sanction this—but how could He not? He had to approve it. If we didn't come up with a solution soon, our consciousness would be gone too and the equations comprising our human forms would be added to the pyramid

like discarded clothes tossed onto a growing stack organized for a Saturday morning garage sale or maybe incineration or perhaps vaporization. The retreat of everything to the negative numbers realm meant these "clothes" never existed nor the bodies and consciousness-bearing selves that wore them. Well, the good news here was we wouldn't even remember we had failed, and we wouldn't care because the problem didn't exist anymore. Nothing did.

I hoped Blaise would say something witty or off-color before we vanished into this cosmic null space of negative numbers. Before he could offer a quip, another unexpected thing happened. A mathematician could better explain how it was possible, but in some peculiar manner one equation, a trivial calculation really, produced a positive product, a result that surfaced above the negative numbers line, like a solitary survivor casting about in the waves after the ship went down. I suppose it was in logical terms like two negatives generating a positive. I am less concerned about whether my explanation is valid or mathematically correct as the fact that this occurrence made all the difference.

Possibly on a statistical basis or by some arcane, reclusive law of mathematical probability, eventually negative numbers will generate their opposite. It almost sounds like some kind of Taoist law that says extreme *yang* lurches to become extreme *yin* and there's some exquisite pivot point where that happens. In some manner, positive integers must be implicit, fetally, perhaps, within negative ones, as if hiding, only temporarily redacted. Mathematicians explain, with an eye towards the magical it seems, that if you multiply a negative number by another negative it yields a positive number. Two nothings equal a something, and that was what I saw happening. We were getting a something.

This modest equation with its positive numbers outcome was changing the field. Another one followed, then a dozen, and soon a crowd of equations was rushing the gates that marked the boundary of this null zone with the other world of the positive numbers that scripted consciousness and manifested forms. Equations started building shapes, Light grids, living forms to hold awareness.

It was like a vast wave of people surging into an empty but prepared city, ready to begin life, occupy houses, walk about the streets, talking, buying, and laughing. The equations were deploying as if without any ostensible guiding hand. I mean, it wasn't we that were directing their deployment, yet everything proceeded in an orderly, rational fashion in this great feat of world rebuilding.

Maybe the Supreme Being had a built-in safety device to prevent the universe from utterly draining itself of all life and consciousness into a desert of inert numbers, and that when a certain result close to absolute zero was reached, the system reversed itself, two negative numbers multiplying to yield a positive. That opposite was now happening, a universe was merrily reconstructing itself.

That is my subjective interpretation, yet the rebuilding was proceeding with a marked enthusiasm, a heightened energy state bordering on the frenetic. It was like watching something grow exponentially; it was burgeoning at a fantastic rate, like a crowd rushing a store for its fabulous Christmas bargains. All the Light grids required to support planets and their phylogenic life were reappearing and consciousness was flowering prolifically.

Qabalists described the original formation of reality as in a Vacated Space. God created this sphere, completely saturated it with His presence, pulled out, then reinserted Himself only halfway, leaving ample room for the Creation. It was like having a physical line making a radius, filled with Light and life, with the surrounding space only filled to the level of etheric, subtle manifestation, but otherwise appearing empty, like a spacious lawn surrounding a large house.

But now this Vacated Space was filling up all the way out to the circumference. The etheric field around this line of Light was itself getting saturated with content. That bare lawn was suddenly floriated with the signs of a a summer's carnival. It was fast approaching a state of cosmic over-population in which there were so many teeming arithmetical forms crowding the interior of the space that it was starting to push and bulge at the edges of the sphere. It held too much. That large house would be overrun. Overfed, it might suddenly burst.

Blaise shook his head. "Crap. Now we have the opposite problem. The arithmetical realm has gone wild and created too much. The Vacated Space is bloating dangerously. Its stomach is full of number strings like spaghetti. There is no breathing space left inside the Creation. It's like eating and drinking too much after a long fast; the stomach swells quickly, uncomfortably. Everything that equations could call into being is now in operation; there are so many processes of consciousness running now that consciousness itself is about to be overwhelmed by its own productivity. It makes me wonder: Is the Supreme Being mental, you know, fundamentally unbalanced or perilously ambivalent?"

I took his point. God is a wack-job. We had just bounced from one extreme to its opposite. The universe was still in jeopardy, now from an excess of arithmetical process. There was so much consciousness, so many Light grids, that you couldn't move. The arithmetical realm was burgeoning exponentially.

"It's a bloody enantiodromia," said Blaise with some emphasis. He almost seemed to be taking this reversal of universal polarity and activity personally. It's a big word he used, but a useful one, certainly for what we were confronted with. Things were now running opposite to how they had just been.

The principle is that a superabundance of force inevitably produces its opposite. A universe in which negative numbers are extracting all consciousness from reality reaches a point in which its momentum automatically reverses itself and proceeds opposite and starts pumping consciousness into the universal sac. That was the seemingly salvific work of that modest equation that yielded the first positive number outcome. One extreme will yield to its opposite. As I mentioned above, in Taoist terms, extreme *yin* will revert, springlike, to extreme *yang*; one form too heavily invested in itself will bounce opposite into its shadow opposite side. This bouncing is not the product of balance, though. Not yet.

Now Blaise was laughing. "Is God a Jungian? Jung said the path of individuation requires that you incorporate and assimilate opposites to reach wholeness. You have to incorporate opposing archetypes, in this case, negative numbers, into the daytime domain of positive numbers to produce completion. So are we observing the natural individuation process of the Creator Himself?

"That would put the Hierophancy at one end, the arithmetical gods at the other. Wait. No, that's not right. The Light grids of the manifested realm as prescribed by numbers are at one end, the arithmetical gods at the other, but the Hierophancy occupies the mid-point, the fulcrum. We're the catalyst-bridge for their joining. The Hierophancy's job, I propose, is to facilitate the Supreme Being's individuation. He's on the couch and we're the talking-cure therapists. He had a daydream of spawning a world scripted by numbers and a nightmare of some ultimate suction drain at the end of the universe siphoning it all out. We have to show Him how to interpret His dream and reconcile these opposites."

That was news to us. It put the scope of the Hierophancy's work and the responsibility it entailed in a bolder context. Now we were the Supreme Being's psychotherapists? He was in treatment with us? Are His case notes confidential? We had thought for years our work dealt with maintaining our planet's Light grid and regulation of the consciousness processes of humans living in Nature. Now we're the Big Guy's official shrinks?

I put it that way because Nature and humanity were designed to be reflections of each other, in reciprocity, but humanity's commission was to maintain Nature, to keep it in balance by acting as its designated self-awareness expressed at a planetary level. Humanity would make the Earth and Nature self-aware. That had seemed a reasonably formidable challenge that kept us busy all the time. Now I saw this was a mere holographic snippet of our larger obligation.

The Supreme Being wanted the world designed and scripted by numbers, and He was reluctant to dispatch them out of the original Pleromic world of purity. We had to function as the enantiodromic fulcrum between both opposing poles. The Old Boy was twitchy, ambivalent even, about His inevitable and necessary individuation? I was treading on philosophical ground that felt shaky, untenable, even a bit raw, like a mother nine months pregnant yet reluctant to enter labor and begin childbirth. Were we now God's enantiodromic midwives?

Maybe I was getting carried away with the implications of this. A superabundance of a phenomenon turns inevitably into its opposite: that's an enantiodromia, a "running course [going] opposite," in its pure meaning. It's a gesture of natural equilibrium; an extreme seeks to balance itself out, such as when a one-sided psychological tendency dominates conscious life, then an equally powerful unconscious counterposition rises up to reverse it, Jung said, as if explaining things to the Old Boy sprawled massively on the therapist's couch.

Meanwhile, let me keep matters simple. Clearly this job entailed far more participants than our small Sun Valley group. Even if Earth's Hierophancy numbered thousands of members, we would not number enough to manage the scope the Supreme Being had laid out for us. Blaise nodded, evidently following my thoughts, or having the identical ones himself.

"Look out across the worlds," he said, gesturing grandly with his arm. But he was right. Somehow we could see innumerable groups of dedicated intelligences like us in essence though differing in bodily form or manner of individual expression engaged at propping up the manifested world and in effect keeping the numbers in place so they couldn't sneak out at night and run back to the alien gods' Magic Square of collated numbers, or worse, into the realm of negative numbers where they would start sucking our reality dry again. The universe had dispatched a team of therapists to work with this patient.

I fought back the gesture of waving to these groups and volunteering our case notes. That seemed a bit silly. But I appreciated our shared goals and commitment to act as official Hierophants. It made sense: to reveal the Holy Light, to describe its contours and mechanisms, you have to keep the Light stuffed into the reality forms it generates; to do that you have to keep the arithmetical realm from defecting into their panic room. We have to keep their numbers in play, like a juggler who cannot drop the balls or reality will end.

"The Hierophancy is distributed across all the manifested worlds," Blaise continued. "We have the same goals, the same commission, and even if we don't know one another or haven't met yet or never will, we share this consanguinity of purpose. We started this investigation thinking the theft from the Arithmetical Earth was strictly a planetary affair pertaining only to our planet. Then we found the other five high free-will-enriched planets were affected too.

"Our perception expanded beyond that until now we see the arithmetical gods and their reluctance to commit their numbers, themselves as the awareness of these numbers, to the service of prescribing and maintaining the created world, is now our assignment. We have to mediate that resistance, overcome it, and superintend the service. We have to get those brainiacs back on the job. We have to work the balance point between quiescent numbers and those in service. We are fulcrum between the two aspects of this fundamental Creation polarity.

"It's funny, when you think about, almost surrealistic or perhaps vaudevillian. We have to correct and balance out a fundamental ambivalence in the Supreme Being. The Old Boy's got cold feet about committing His preciously pure numbers to support His own notion of the Creation yet He's tingling in delight and anticipation about doing precisely that. What a strange case of diffidence and stuckness. Pusillanimity at the highest level. Is that even possible? It's like a dog ecstatic about having a walk yet afraid to leave the house.

"But then I think, maybe that's too human a view to impose an interpretation of reluctance upon the Creator. Holding opposite views at the same time is more to the point. The enantiodromia business, or the coincidence of opposites, the arithmetical gods and the Hierophancy arriving by fast cars from opposite directions at the same pivot point, screeching to a halt, rushing out of their cars, arms flailing, talking intensely before they've closed the car doors, going over the intricacies of the problem, maybe raising their voices at times—that seems now to be the true work of the Hierophancy: conflict resolution."

I could see Blaise was struggling to come to terms with this ambivalence. Out of our own free will, a generous grant from the Creator, we were expected to resolve the Creator's own *coincidentia oppositorum*, His primordial

indecisiveness. Then I saw it from the other way around. Maybe the Old Boy wasn't diffident.

Maybe the invitation to resolve this fundamental indecision was another grant to humans and the other phylogenic members of the Hierophancy to *participate* freely in the unfolding of the Creation. He deliberately left it unfinished then gave us the freedom and intelligence to complete it, if we voluntarily chose to. It's like He left us a grand picture puzzle and waits to see if we can finish it. He left both poles of this basic schism in the Creation open for us to freely occupy.

This is the portion He left for free-will endowed sentient creatures like us and others to work out and complete. Figure out a reasonable, viable balance between the arithmetical realm's hermiticism and the necessities of using numbers to support the worlds. I leave it to you, members of the Hierophancy, to determine the best equations. Think of it like respiration, inhale then exhale, numbers in seclusion, numbers in deployment, in a constant, balanced cycle that characterizes My life. Is it like that? People talk about humans and the possibility of co-creation. A grand concept. Now it seems this is a bigger proposition than people have realized, certainly than I ever did. Genuinely co-create with God?

Help complete the Creation by working out the right balance, one that works, between numbers and Light, arithmetical purity and dispassionate service to the incarnational domain. Negotiate a sustainable balance between preserving numbers and using them, keeping them inviolate and in service. Resolve the illusory dichotomy between mathematics and consciousness. I deliberately leave My Own coincidence of opposites unresolved for you to finish, the Supreme Being says. I *think* He does. We are dealing with the Great Mystery.

Maybe it's not a matter of resolution. Breathing is never resolved, until it stops. You continually inhale then exhale for the life of your body, then you stop this. Maybe this unresolved coincidence of opposites the Supreme Being dumped in our laps was a natural if vexing part of the total plan for human incarnation.

"Somewhere behind the scenes, maybe in the Throne, He is grinning," said Jocelyn. She was grinning too. "The sly dog. He was just waiting for us to get it, like a comedian laying out all the tracks leading to the great punch line."

"Meanwhile, we have that big event to plan for, the Hierophancy party," said Sal. We seemed to have temporarily forgotten about planning for that event. Now I saw that the invitation list was much bigger than I originally thought. We would have to draw in participants not only to hold down Earth's geomantic nodal points for the integers in this planet's algorithm, but do the same for other Light-gridded planets across the galaxy. That was going to be a lot of guests. Before I could even start worrying about the logistics of that arrangement, something else took my attention. I have to say, it quite definitively arrested it.

The Ofanim were manifesting themselves in their regal Simorgh form. That is the Persian picture of the Ofanim as an enigmatic, majestic bird of Light encrusted with jewels, effulgent with Light, and standing on Mount Qaf. That is the mystical Emerald mountain in Persian mysticism, and the Simorgh is the desired pilgrimage goal of all sentient creatures in *The Conference of the Birds.* I am not certain how tall they stood or where exactly they planted their feet. The Simorgh was visible in every direction, an irrefutable, unforgettable presence.

Streaming out of their vast upright form were innumerable filaments of Light. These flowed out to stars and planets across the galaxy; they had an endless supply of these delicate tendrils. It linked them with all the stars, their star-gods, and their purposes. I saw also pockets of Light resembling caves set throughout the vastness of galactic space and in each of these Cave Heavens (or astral *shiens*), as the Taoists call them, were members of the august Og-Min Brotherhood. That was the Ofanim too, in their hyper-arcane form as angelic monks operating at the most abstruse level of the cosmos and in rarefied form to maintain the integrity and infrastructure of the Light grids of the Creation.

Dozens of Blaises appearing as Og-Min appeared in each of the Cave Heavens. They coordinated the deployment and illumination of the Simorgh's filaments, and they superintended their reception by Hierophancy members on the planets. Between the filaments and the Og-Min administrations, I saw the consciousness levels of the geomancers on the respective planets sharpen as the intensity of the Light and its clarity of awareness increased. It looked as if the Ofanim were providing simultaneous tutorials to all the Hierophancy members focusing on their planet's algorithms across the galaxy.

They were awakening their self-knowledge and practical techniques across the time spectrum of their lives, making this wealth of achieved wisdom available to them. The Ofanim were flashing their different metaphorical guises such as Hanuman, Garuda, Ganesh, and Airavata to emphasize the powers of consciousness available to the Hierophancy. Make sure you appreciate the subtlety of this point. The Ofanim were not saying, Look, you may call on us in these various power guises for help. They were saying rather, Look, these are illustrations of powers of consciousness that you may emulate by following our demonstration of them here. Your consciousness is already equipped with these potencies; just call on them. Just become them.

The Blaises were laying on a spectacle. Their innumerable Cave Heavens glittered across galactic space, or perhaps it was across the cosmos itself with all its galaxies, and they rose up from a central core like diamond flower blossoms. The diamond facets of the Ofanim's geode were these Cave Heavens, and they were filled with the many metaphorical representations of the Blaises. The diamond geode gracefully cupped the Hierophancy planets like gentle hands.

I had the impression we wouldn't have to worry about finding the required members to participate. They were already being briefed by the Blaises. Apparently, they would be crucial in our achieving the requisite balance the Supreme Being was counting on us to complete. The set-up reminded me of what the human Blaise told me once, that the Ofanim didn't so much tell him new things as help him to remember old knowledge stored within him. They brought the lights and shone them in the archival pockets of deep knowledge and helped him retrieve what he already knew. They knew where all the key reference books were shelved in the library of his soul's deep memory.

Still, it always seemed like they were providing elegant salvers of new knowledge. I was sure I caught a glimpse now and then of a silver platter. I watched as the Ofanim quickened ancient knowledge in the Hierophancy members across the galaxy. I felt it happening in me too. I was back at Tiwanaku.

I shouldn't have been surprised. I probably had never left the place. I mentioned the indeterminacy I felt about my location. Apparently, my body remained at Tiwanaku but my consciousness, or a copy of it, a clone or hologram or maybe my astral Double, relocated to be simultaneously at Sun Valley. I was fairly certain that it remained there and I would be splitting my attention in two locales. Soon I would realize that was too limited: it would be at least three simultaneous presences my Frederick consciousness would appear in. I half-expected (I was probably channeling Blaise's antic sense of humor) a jocose commentator at Tiwanaku to announce to the stones and spectral presences, Live, fresh from the Throne of Glory Itself, put your hands together for *Frederick*.

I acknowledged the lavish audience applause and resumed what I had been doing. Apparently, only seconds had passed since I was "last" here doing it. I was (and had been) standing in the center of Tiwanaku, wearing the pale green robe of that Ray and wielding a staff of Light of that same color sending out green sparks. I had just generated a dome over Tiwanaku of pale green Light too. This strong half-sphere of green Light had temporarily halted the alien gods' extraction of the equations from Tiwanaku. They were regrouping, I guessed.

I suppose I, as Frederick, was regrouping also. I stood very tall, probably 18 feet, and the Frederick that I usually took to be myself stood inside this taller version of myself, my literally

Higher Self, as if I were occupying a tall green tower. I was impressed with myself that I didn't feel dizzy or any vertigo which I usually do with heights. I was as tall as the ancient Elohim when they were human giants towering at 18 feet. It seemed fitting to do this at Tiwanaku. I remembered I had entered the alien gods' Magic Square and was getting my bearings inside this hyperdimensional, bewildering space filled with numbers.

I was in a realm of permutating algorithms, branching out across the universe, spawning more equations and more squares to house them, a dreadful labyrinth. My job was to hold off the alien gods' incursion and to keep the psychic picture side of Tiwanaku linked with its Light temples and physical stone correlates. I didn't have to actually prevail or decisively win this contest. I just had to hold my position, maintaining the vital linkage of script with reality.

I mentioned above that it seemed I had never left Tiwanaku. My return to Sun Valley and the adventures that followed must have been in my higher mind. Except there were some changes here at Tiwanaku as the live action resumed. For one, that Ofanim's gorgeous diamond-cupped hands comprising myriads of Cave Heavens were visible here and provided a supportive framework for my holding action against the alien gods who were still trying to suck all the numbers out like an old man with an irritating habit he refuses to drop.

I saw the galactic array of Hierophancy enclaves and the reassuring presence of its many members, all active in the same project. I saw Sal, Jocelyn, Blaise, and our other extraterrestrial colleagues from the five planets, similarly holding down their positions at key geomantic nodes. In fact, though I couldn't explain the mechanics of it, my attention or perhaps a copy of myself was also established at those eight other sites, holding down the "fort." Per my count, that made 11 copies of Fredrick, those eight plus me at Sun Valley, me at Tiwanaku as the usual-sized Frederick, and me here as the giant Higher Self size.

I laughed. At first I wasn't sure why. Then I caught up with my own thoughts which had been racing in many directions far ahead of me. I laughed because I realized I needed an executive secretary to keep track of all my appointments. I appeared to be in many places at the same time, lucidly aware of what I was doing, where, and with whom, and how things were progressing.

I still don't know how to account for these simultaneous Frederick presences, but they seemed to be necessary. Much was happening, and I needed to be there—at all the *theres* where these important events were unfolding. I was at Tiwanaku, Sun Valley, the realm of negative numbers, the Supreme Being's Throne, with the Solar Logos coating all the stars and planets with Christ Light, with my eight colleagues in their locales on this Earth and the other planets, and I was even keeping track of other Hierophancy members spread out across the galaxy and within the Ofanim's glittering diamond geode of angelic support. I laughed. That's a lot more than merely 11 Frederick copies. I filled a stadium.

If nothing else, we would keep those alien gods on their nonincarnated toes. I laughed again as I imagined I heard my executive secretary telling me, Mr. Frederick, sir, I must remind you of your two o'clock meeting with

Person X. And your two o'clock conference call with Professor Y, and your two o'clock....

Another change I noticed now that I was back at Tiwanaku was that the alien gods' Magic Square was vacuuming out all the numbers from Tiwanaku and elsewhere and then they were proceeding into that null realm of negative numbers. That seemed to be the ultimate destination of our algorithms; the Magic Square was a façade, a stopping point, maybe a train station, but the true goal was complete retraction from all manifest reality and a sequestering in the nonmanifested realm of negative numbers where they were removed from life.

All the while I was trying to persuade a conflicted, ambivalent Supreme Being to allow the huge realm of numbers to keep scripting incarnational reality. I was petitioning the Conflicted One on behalf of the stones of Tiwanaku, the Light temples of Earth, and the mathematics that scripted the geomantic reality. And I was petitioning Him on behalf of my having had afternoon high tea with Philomena, so I could still remember those fine times from decades ago, that they had happened because the arithmetical realm scripted the reality that served tea.

I got to work with the first thing that came into my mind. I made copies of the different Ofanim manifestations and projected them like movies onto the pale green half-sphere I had already projected from my green staff. As the human Blaise once told me, you can't go wrong if you do like the Ofanim do. We come in many forms, they always used to say to the human Blaise when he was young; so here are some of those grand manifestations, I said cockily to the alien gods.

Observe Hanuman the giant roaring-flying monkey, Airavata, the white elephant with six golden tusks. Take note of Uccaihsravas, the majestic winged white horse; Ganesh, the sitting-upright, rotund and jolly elephant god; Garuda, the ecstatic Christ Light bird; the Thunderbird, the fiercer, formidable bird form, standing as tall as the Sun. And I tossed in some Og-Min for the meditative temperament among the aliens, and a generous serving of standard issue silver-haired ten-foot tall Blaise angels with wrap-around sunglasses for those with traditional expectations. The Blaises once told our Blaise it's very bright where they are, hence the shades. These images danced and waved like banners in the rich ethers of the green dome. Probably the sunglassed Blaises winked at them.

I am sure I didn't do the next part but it happened anyway. The precise mathematical script that coded these image projections appeared on the backside of the horses, elephants, monkeys, birds, meditating monks, and clowning angels. This was the number coding for the images, not for the reality the images came from. It was like looking at the screen of a computer, enjoying the color image, then opening up the unit and seeing the "mother board" or central processing unit that ran all the image projections, the binary organization of pixels. Delightful image on the outside, arithmetic coding script on the inside.

At the same time, I felt I was part of a creative design team making a presentation for a proposed ad campaign, for print, television, the world computer net, and other media to an uncertain client who had to be convinced the idea of advertising itself was good before we stood any chance of selling him on our clever design proposals. Look guys, numbers and pretty images. We tried to draw the attention of the arithmetical gods to our presentation storyboards.

But while our presentation was attempting that, something else was happening. The metaphorical guises of the Ofanim I was seeing and projecting were only things I knew. I was seeing what I already knew but not seeing reality at all. I was settling for the established name and form mode of the Ofanim's reality. I was not truly seeing them, but only what I expected to see and thought I knew. They took that presumption away in a flash of brilliant Light.

Then that Light went away. No forms remained, no visible, describable presence, not even a thought. Yet the Ofanim were still out there as a nonformed and nonlocalized sharpness of attention. It was their *Dharmakaya* mode. You couldn't say anything about it. But it got the alien gods' attention. I saw them raise their eyebrows, even though they didn't have any or even have faces. But the Ofanim's empty, formless, crystalline presence secured their attention. It was as if the Blaises showed them a magic trick and the arithmetical gods nodded their approval. Nice trick, I could swear I heard the alien gods mutter.

It was as if the Blaises did a sleight-of-hand with a deck of playing cards then disappeared the cards and their own hands but let the visual impact of that trick remain. The cards, in the form of images and their mathematical coding, weren't there any longer, but the memory of them was. I couldn't see the Ofanim any more, and what they were doing seemed incomprehensible to me. Though formless, they radiated from within everything, the stones of Tiwanaku, the

platforms, the air around it, the green dome I had made and the star dome already there. The pictures of the Blaises in their clever guises and the numbers floriated all perceivable reality, like a full-on marketing campaign media blitz.

Instead of my seeing angelic forms or flying white horses or jolly elephants, I saw all the galaxies in the vastness of the universe through their formless attention. I could instantly focus on entire galaxies or individual stars, and each star in these galaxies was intensely bright, surrounded by an even brighter sphere of Light. As soon as I looked at one sphere, it immediately enlarged to a frightening size as if it somehow expanded to fill all available space, absorbing the individual star that it had been surrounding. This happened every time I focused on a single star, and it happened when I looked at galaxies. Each unit of organization was engulfed in this sphere of Light, and within this Light I glimpsed the Light grids and the arithmetical coding that produced them.

It was as if all the Light in Creation rushed to engulf the star I was looking at. This was taking place in the space occupied by a Blaise appearance only moments before. Then the sphere of white radiance flashed like a supernova and became a field of black; it might have been spherical but I couldn't tell because I was inside it. There was nothing to see, not even a field of radiant Light.

As for myself, I am misleading the reader when I use the self-referential term "I" to recount what was inside this new universe of black. It seemed empty yet at the same time it felt saturated, thoroughly filled, packed to the gills and stuffed to the teeth. Everything in the Creation had returned to this dark quiescent home. It was all in here but unexpressed, unmanifest, a potential only, I had awareness of this, but I had no sense of a separate self-identity any longer.

A curious quality of being here was that my mind was devoid of all questions. Not a single query arose, no desire to know anything or have something explained. I already knew everything possible and yet had moved beyond that, presumably forgetting it or discounting its importance or necessity. I had no questions whatsoever because I was implicitly part of everything. All the answers were preloaded into me and I was saturated in the field of answers.

Or maybe "I" had transcended the need to deliberately or actively remember anything I knew because "I" had become one with this knowledge and everything possible was implicit and nothing was outside me any longer. I was complete and I was beyond caring or noticing. It was both fullness and emptiness. Nothing was missing because the entire Creation was in here, fetal, quiescent, complete. It had not yet been rolled out and displayed gloriously for sentient creatures to behold. The Tree of Life and Arithmetic was in here in seed form—no, probably less incarnate than that: as an idea for a probable unfolding.

This was the Blaise's legendary Black Bowling Ball, as the Ofanim and the human Blaise jokingly agreed to call the triple *Ains* when Blaise first visited it. The Qabalists call this the Sphere of Negative Existence above the Tree of Life. In layman's terms, it is threefold: a realm of blackness, a realm of a single point of Light in a black sphere, and a realm full of Light. These are the three *Ains*. When we're in here with the Blaises, it's the black sphere *Ain* with one point of Light.

Then I bounced back to where I had been, sending out green sparks from my staff. I appreciated the conundrum this new development presented: How could I sell the Supreme Being on the merits of deploying the arithmetical realm when this ultimate display I had just witnessed was perpetrated by the Supreme Being? It was giddily tautological. The Old Boy is a tough customer, that's for sure. It occurred to me that perhaps I was the customer; well, not just me, the entire Hierophancy, that the intent here was to *show us*, persuade us maybe, the correct role and hierarchical placement of the arithmetical realm in Creation.

When I thought about it, it made no sense the Creator would second-guess Himself, have uncertainties and a wobbling of conviction and commitment to what He had done, launching the Creation, again in yet another episode of the Life of Brahma, the original Groundhog Day, the ever-popular situation comedy with all your favorite characters, renewed for another happy season, with universal syndication rights and streaming free into every home every day. The Old Boy never tires of the same program, reruns, the one He wrote, like a child saying to me, I never watch a movie I haven't already seen. The Old Boy, the original couch potato, can't get enough of his own Reality TV.

The arithmetical gods reacted queerly to this latest development. I sensed them around me in their forceful but formless manner trying to code me out of existence. Imagine a Qabalist using algorithms rather than spoken invocations in Hebrew to ritualistically exact a change in the order of reality, namely, me. They were trying to mathematically code me out of the picture. If it wasn't perilous to my continuity as Frederick, it would strike me as amusing.

Think of your genetic code as a mathematical script. Then code the opposite of this so that this contrary coding will erase your actual DNA and remove you from existence. It was like using arithmetical means to erase Light temples from a Light grid. Their coding numbers are rescinded. The alien gods, it seemed, figured if they took me out of the picture they'd be safe and their numbers inviolate and the Supreme Being would be convinced to stop and all this irritating fuss would be done and finished with and they could go back to their interrupted aesthetic appreciation of how amazing their numbers are.

I heard somebody laughing. I'm glad someone finds this funny. It was Blaise. Who else? But how could I hear him laughing if he was far away in Japan?

He was far away in Japan, and so was I. Somehow I had traveled there instantly, yet it seemed no further than if I had turned to the left and walked a few steps across a large room to stand next to him. I looked back and saw myself. The Frederick over there was wielding his green staff surrounded by the alien gods, again, not palpably present, only suggested, but strong enough so you could imagine what they would look like if they actually looked like anything.

I had barely understood what Blaise was doing when I read his letter. Now I was in the midst of this arcane mathematical Sumo wrestling match against an inserted arithmetical subscript with superscript to Earth's algorithm. It was running Earth reality much too fast, deeply unsettling all of the Earth's inhabitants. People were running their consciousness processes 11 steps faster than usual. Oh crap: that was still happening? I'd forgotten about that. It was worse than that. They were operating their consciousness on two versions of the planet, one the normal one, the other in hyperdrive eleventh power mode.

They were likely experiencing a split reality, experiencing life on two different tracks. That was the +2 subscript. The hyperdrive algorithm was designed to exhaust humanity so that they died, thereby releasing the managing equations to return to the waiting alien gods. That was the 11th power superscript. From his Pleiadian colleagues, Blaise had an anti-algorithm (the -2 subscript plus another) to stop this, and he had inserted a copy of himself into it and was now numbers-wrestling the gods. He was stripping off the expansion orders down from 11; he was making progress, but not enough to win the tournament.

I appreciate how bizarre this must sound to any sensible reader. I had to read Blaise's original letter many times before I could make sense of it. His words were clear and his sentences coherent; I refer to the concept of his actions. He was waging a battle within a mathematical construct, stripping a superscript of its domination over Earth reality, deploying an anti-algorithm for this struggle, and also trying to eliminate a superfluous artificially-generated fake Earth. This wasn't removing inimical spirits and energy configurations from Light temples, which was our normal activity; this was an arcane struggle pitched at the formative level where Light temples were coded by mathematics into existence.

As he wrote in the letter to me, the alien gods had added a "+2" subscript, and Blaise had countered with a "-2" subscript to take away the extra Earth copy. That removed any traction point for the alien gods' eleventh order superscript. So this was how things stood when I joined up with Blaise who was carrying on with the titanic corporeality of a Sumo wrestler about to pounce and crush. I guess everything we had just experienced took place outside of normal time. Now we were back in the thick of the time flow and the alien gods were kicking our asses something smart, winning the rope pull, arm wrestling, the works. If you recall, our four reports had each ended inconclusively, as if a final chapter had to be written. Now it would be written. Live action had resumed. It was bad.

Help of an unexpected nature arrived. It was my old mentor from the Baghdad House of Wisdom, Al-Khwārizmī, the inventor of algorithms. I said earlier he seemed to have algorithms streaming out of his fingertips. We could use some of that mathematical prolixity right now to tip the balance our way. He was like the proverbial itinerant Arab medicine man, his camel loaded with satchels containing medicines, ointments, salves, dried herbs, for all ailments. Except his satchels were brimming with items of mathematical cleverness. Here was our *hakim*, physician, sage, philosopher, metaphysician, hero-savior, or maybe better, our *khidr*, the wandering prophet and keeper of esoteric secrets, dispatched just in time from the *Bayt al-Hikma* with arithmetic to save our butts. His mere presence with us anchored me again in my own earlier Arabic form.

Al-Khwārizmī surveyed what Blaise had done so far and nodded. "Let us enrich the equation," he said quietly. Numbers streamed like filaments out of his fingers and seemed to inscribe themselves on the air itself which had become a writing tablet capable of registering the enriched equations he was generating.

It was an algorithm expressed in four dimensions, written all over a hypercube. It looked like a glittering number bauble to capture the alien gods' interest, but then I realized it was also a stealth agent designed to infiltrate their minds and start covertly rewriting certain calculations dominant in their current activities. It was like playing a game of chess in which while your opponent made his moves in present time, you made yours from the future back along the timeline towards the present, thereby staying many moves ahead of him, anticipating his gambits because you already saw them. It was a good advantage.

What was I doing in the midst of this arithmetical melee? I was applying the fresh equations streaming out of Al-Khwārizmī's nimble fingertips like paint on the teeming and nonbodily presence of the alien gods. They were present by inference, not manifest in any tangible sense, but I was laminating this ghost presence with the new equations coming out in 4D mode. More weirdness, I know, and this was a most arcane finger-wrestling match underway.

I sensed the alien gods were inspecting the new equations the way a feral dog might sniff offered food you hold in your palm, and at the same time they continued with their squirming and pulling as they attempted to regrow their diminishing superscript and reinstitute the alternative hyperdrive Earth.

My teacher had laid a clever trap inside his alluring new equations. It was an arithmetical version of the classic Chinese finger-trap where when you pull your fingers apart to release them the trap only grabs them tighter. The tactical equivalent here was that as soon as they started exploring the complexities of the new numbers display, it drew them into a concatenation of further calculations.

It was a type of arithmetical hypertexting. Key integers, once pursued, then immediately linked you to other related calculations. It was like a Qabalistic permutations table where you explored the meaning of individual letters, and then their constituents, until you found yourself in an unnavigable labyrinth. My teacher was counting on the irresistible fascination that new algorithms would hold for the acquisitive alien gods who would unravel them like a ball of yarn. That would draw them further into the distracting field of numbers and soon their attention would be captured and they'd be taken off their playing field.

I admired the daringness of Al-Khwārizmī. He was using mathematics to trick the inventors of all mathematics, or at least the holders of that arcane field. It was a slow-motion erasure he was executing, dangling intriguing number combinations in front of these endlessly acquisitive spirits, a tactical move that might be able to distract the alien gods long enough for Blaise to make significant inroads in undoing their work and gradually peel them off the Earth.

They would lose themselves in their adoration of mirror reflections of their own essence as numbers. A cunning trap, perfectly suited to their temperament. It was like trying to pry off ten fingers strongly gripping a surface, one finger at a time, coating each still gripping finger with a mathematical allurement, counting on the alien gods wanting to taste what you had painted on their finger. It was working. Their fingers were coming off the ledge; the alien gods were distracted. They were licking their fingers and tasting the numbers.

For myself, I noticed that now I seemed to be back in the study room at the House of Wisdom in Baghdad surrounded by my fellow apprentices as we listened to Al-Khwārizmī explain the theoretical basis of a capture algorithm. He had been mulling over the possibility of working out the arithmetical mechanics of such an equation and he jokingly said we might test it out on some local Djinn.

The principle of such an algorithm, he proposed, was that its special arithmetical processes would first grab the attention then the focused consciousness of the designated viewer. The number sequence would be designed in such a precisely specific manner as to be akin to what later scientists would call genetic targeting. You could tailor the activation and capture mechanisms of the algorithm to the mathematical peculiarities of your intended "target" recipient, somewhat like a fishing lure whose colors and patterns were appropriate to attracting certain fish and not others. You could design your capture algorithm to snag specific corresponding numbers by their coding.

The capture algorithm's focus lay somewhere between fishing lure and occult weapon with a little dose of hypnotism thrown in, so one must use such a device, cautioned Al-Khwārizmī, only with extreme circumspection. He may well have been saving this device for the future for a special circumstance. Well, our present situation certainly qualified as a special circumstance to use it. This would be wasted on the Djinn. We were up against arithmetical behemoths now.

Who would have thought the fate of the planet and even of many worlds beyond it would hinge on the deployment of a clever algorithm by dueling mathematicians? It was both awesome and ludicrous when I thought about it. Al-Khwārizmī grinned and extended his hand. A live algorithm squirmed in it. "Why don't you try it out, Frederick. I have been saving it for a special occasion."

The fact that he used my contemporary named suggested my encounter with Al-Khwārizmī was taking place in the present moment and was not a memory artifact. The algorithm throbbed with Light and intelligence; it resembled a coil of silken rope laying in loops and swirls, its fibers made of number sequences. Each strand of the ropelike algorithm had echoes of its shape, like etheric versions of the same pattern, or perhaps I was seeing the many dimensional aspects of the algorithm, indicating its ability to effectively unwind itself in a 4D spectrum.

The fact that this equation existed in dimensions beyond our familiar 3D meant that when it unwound, unfurled itself, spread out its long coils, it was far larger and more extensive than I could have imagined. It was like straightening out the fjords of Norway into a single long straight line: you'd be awed at how long that intricately folded, repetitive landscape actually was: 63,000 miles. It was the same with the capture algorithm: it must have been a hundred yards long when fully stretched out. That would do some fancy lasso work for us. I was confident it would properly confound our recalcitrant alien gods who would not be able to resist its fishing-bait allurements and grab onto its arithmetic coils as they deliriously hopscotched along that hundred yards of sticky mathematics.

I saw that my House of Wisdom colleagues were watching me carefully, like I was an athlete competing at the Olympics in a crucial elimination contest. I deployed the capture algorithm like a cowboy swirling the lasso onto a calf. Maybe a calf is too tame an image. How about Herakles going after Geryon's cattle? Their owner was a three-headed, three legged monster. The numbers glittered and sparkled; they called mentally to the alien gods like Sirens luring Odysseus and his easily tempted shipmates to give in and dive into the ocean.

I watched the alien gods examine the algorithm, looking at the curious sequencing of numbers. They studied it with the professional attention of collectors. They knew what to look for in advanced mathematical artifacts and they were sufficiently discerning as to not settle for cheap arithmetical simulations. They wanted to be surprised, taken by delight, see something new. They would never settle for imitation pearls no matter how good the paste work.

It looked like I had six arms and each was tossing out a lasso of numbers. The alien gods as a collective mental field were snapping at these like eager dogs being shown a delicious-looking treat just out of their jaw's reach. The capture algorithm's specifics hinted at arithmetical delights perfectly suited to the aesthetic tastes, and mental demands of these discriminating collectors.

The alien gods did not see that the numbers were sticky in an arithmetical sense. That when they put their focus on a particular sequence, it subtly grabbed their attention and followed it back to the mental core of their being. Once there, it clutched strongly and held it motionless. If the alien gods were deployed in one hundred points of attention on our capture algorithm, it would stick to them at these hundred nodes and hold them invincibly fast.

I had to remind myself that our goal was persuasion, not coercion. The alien gods had to be talked back into supporting the manifest world, allowing their numbers to be deployed in its service, accepting our assurance it would not irretrievably sully the admirable purity of all their precious corralled numbers. And through this we were supposed to assuage the Supreme Being's own vexed ambivalence about sending the numbers forth to incarnate the world.

If this were a diplomatic negotiation, you had to first get the other side to sit down at the table so we could persuade them. That first step might require strong-arming. But our strong-arm tactics had to be so subtle the alien gods didn't notice them. They would walk entranced right up to the conference table and sit down before they took stock of their actions. The capture algorithm would mesmerize them. They'd be halfway through the negotiations before they realized what they were doing. They'd already be holding the treaty-signing pen.

That was the theory, but it wasn't working out like that. A few of the alien gods were looking skeptical, surveying the algorithm with caution. I describe their collective attention this way though there were no individual alien gods as such; it was more a matter of diverting a portion of their collective attention to an alternative focus, namely, investigating whether this was a hoax. Most of them were going for the allurement of the capture algorithm, but these few beams of alien god skepticism were threatening to undo our capture work.

I saw that Al-Khwārizmī had hidden a fallback extra capture-stealth modality within the algorithm and was deploying it like reserve troops. This surprise portion of the number strands acted like an entrancing mirror: you look at yourself in it, and the reflection coming back is slightly altered but in such a way you don't notice it at first. This was how the reserve modality would seduce the alien gods' attention by exaggerating certain "facial" features.

The set-up reminded me of the wiles of Scheherazade, the clever courtesan who always had another story to beguile the king so he'd forget to execute her. Our capture algorithm was Al-Khwārizmī's version of Shahrazad, her Arabic name, and she had a thousand stories with which to distract and charm the king. Our mathematics "courtesan," Al-Khwārizmī, dangled before them an algorithm with a thousand additional capture nets and keen hooks.

We were like architects trying to convince a reluctant client to consider building a house, that is, commissioning us to design and construct one. This client had never had a house built for him, never even contemplated it. All that money and time and effort just for a place in which to live, he would say. I'm already living just fine here, and he would gesture to the wide-open ethers. We would display our scale models of proposed houses we could build for him, set them out on the conference table for his inspection. Some were quite elegant.

Our model houses are metaphors for the processes of consciousness, or the arithmetical gymnastics these algorithms could perform. We didn't have to sell the client on an appreciation of that: they were already raptly appreciative of this. We had to lure them into an interest in setting these algorithms into the manifest world where the adept processes could stage-manage actual life-forms. We had to cast a veil of enchantment over these conservative alien gods, show them a few intricate arithmetical processes, new combinations of their numbers and what they could do. Magic tricks, in a sense. Performance pieces.

Al-Khwārizmī had deftly embedded a shell game within this show. He set things up so the alien gods would think something clever was going on just behind the scenes, that these entertaining practice algorithms hid a complex layer of mathematical operations, one that kept disappearing around the corner. Hence the shell game aspect: Under which shell lies the pea? My teacher kept letting the alien gods have a peak at this elusive arithmetical pea but never a long gaze or detailed examination; only a hint, but sufficient to lure them in, to let their attention try to slip under the moving shells to grab it.

That pea was a mutating algorithm. Every time the alien gods put their attention on it, that triggered the algorithm to mutate into another form, to change its numbers and product, yet to retain just enough of its old form to seem like the same quarry. This constantly changing aspect would nail down their interest. Al-Khwārizmī must have read *The Odyssey*, the bit about Menelaus wrestling with Proteus, the Old Man of the Sea, an accomplished shapeshifter.

The Ever-Changing Watchman of Pharos and son of Poseidon, Lord of the Sea, kept changing his shape from bearded lion, a youth, a horned bull, snake, panther, boar, leafy tree, to running water, never settling into one fixed form. Such was the unfixed nature of our mutating algorithm, and it secured the alien gods' fascinated attention as they watched it make its next alteration in form.

That was not the full extent of Al-Khwārizmī's deviousness. The algorithm was not only mutating; it was self-propagating. The alien gods' attention triggered the original shapeshifting algorithm to generate more copies of itself, and these would run scurrying under the various shells on the table, changing into still new shapes and mathematical outcomes. I watched this spectacle in astonished admiration. I surely hope my mouth was not gaping. The algorithm kept spawning new variations, altering a few integers, just enough to keep the appearance and product different than any other copy of the equation.

This quality in turn got the alien gods to keep propagating more heads to follow the action. I'm speaking metaphorically. They didn't have heads of course, just attention, but every time their attention was freshly deployed in a new direction, to chase after a newly emerged algorithmic form, it was as if they sprouted another head to lean over the conference table to raptly follow the numbers. Dozens of alien heads peered over the table tracking the scurrying algorithms like a predatory bird keeping tabs on its lunch. My teacher was doing a good job keeping himself from grinning. He kept his face serious and concentrated, seeming to be worried about events, while inwardly he was filled with glee to see the alien gods falling for the trick.

This numbers circus was a long way from using arithmetic to generate complete Light grids for planets and phylogenies, but it was showing the alien gods what entertaining and ingenious constructions could be born from their precious, unsullied numbers if they let them out of the kennel for a good run. Al-Khwārizmī now generated an algorithm to create a simple Light grid. It would periodically spin out the image of a raised sword to indicate focused clarity, like a flash of incisive understanding or the ability to have that. This sharp-edged sword would flash regularly like a pulsar, indicating peaks of focus. I saw (or at least I felt without seeing it) the alien gods nodding in appreciation, as if murmuring among themselves, "Nice one. Crafty little sword flashing away."

Now Al-Khwārizmī raised the bets. He created simple Light grids, then a more complicated one that linked the smaller ones, then still bigger ones. In a few moments his algorithms had generated a sample generic planet born out of its own Light grid and pulsing various recognizable states of consciousness and cognitive thresholds. He led the alien gods carefully through this visual syllogism. If those guys had mouths they would have no doubt "Ahhed."

My mentor was a master salesman unpacking his caravan of trinkets and building appreciation on its way to astonishment. You see, my dear alien gods, his demonstration was implicitly saying, behold what your numbers can build. They studied this simulated generic planet running its consciousness processes. They examined it the way a skeptical investor would pore over the year-end balance sheet on a company to test it for likely profitability.

We were addressing the alien gods on two fronts. This one, dangling sample designed planets featuring their sacrosanct, hermitic numbers, and the other one, where Blaise was running capture and mutating algorithms to reduce the alien gods' hijacking of the Earth through the added algorithmic superscript.

We seemed to be making progress when I saw Jocelyn in this same room. It wasn't a room in any physically manifest sense; it just looked and worked like one. It was some kind of erasure of spatial distance zone in which no matter where our bodies physically were on the Earth, we were in close proximity in this room and as a result of the esoteric operation of this room. Can you follow?

You will recall I inexplicably found myself both at Tiwanaku and in this large room that contained Blaise and what he was up to. Now I saw Jocelyn in this "room." She had been working at Helgafell in western Iceland and now she was here. She had her own area in this space-erasing holographically-generated room, or perhaps it was her vertex of the rhombus. Jocelyn was accompanied by the Elohim and was embroiled in the dichotomy between trying to wrest the numbers away from the alien gods and identifying with them and understanding their passion for protecting the purity of the numbers realm. Like the rest of us, she was stuck, or at least poised, at the threshold of resolving the predicament she was in when her report concluded. Again, live action resumed.

She was halted between what she described as the pixellated universe, the one of images, forms, and manifestations, and the original quietude of the arithmetical realm where the numbers were pristine and entirely inviolate. She was wondering if the Hierophancy was a personification of the arithmetical realm, a way of representing their interests in the manifested world. She was occupying this uncertain landscape called the Planck boundary, though she kept fluctuating from alignment with the aliens to allegiance to the Hierophancy.

Jocelyn looked regal in her bright orange Ray robe with its gold flush. Her simulation of the Earth's Light grid with all its numbers streaming towards and around it was strong. Her simulation was extracting Earth's arithmetical "body" from the alien gods' Magic Square as if she were drawing bees from a hive. She had projected all these numbers and the grid patterns from out of herself, knowing a human carries a copy of the planetary imprint, and through this projection she was calling back Earth's legitimate numbers. The trouble is the numbers flowing back into her pattern were only ghost images of the real ones. The alien gods knew this and that was why they weren't responding to her grid.

Now I was standing behind Jocelyn, although bizarrely I was still with Blaise and occupying my own place at Tiwanaku at my rhombus node. How many different places was I standing in now? I lost track. The Elohim made a grand circle around her and their angelic forms held swords. These swords were upright and blazing, and in the center of this circle where Jocelyn stood there was another single Elohim sword, massive and adamant.

Nobody in particular held this sword, though it seemed the encircling Elohim and their swords provided support for this big sword which summarized theirs. Numbers comprising complex Light grid patterns streamed out of this sword. The numbers that made up the geometric shapes seemed to shout commands. They were like the old Norse berserkers running frenziedly into battle or like screaming Valkyries swooping down to collect the worthy dead.

As the Elohim issued their design commands, numbers flew out of the Planck boundary like a flock of startled birds rising all at once out of a tree. The Elohim's actions carried an implicit divine imprimatur, but then so did the reluctance of the alien gods to permitting the dispatch of their precious numbers. All I can say is it's God-awful when the Supreme Being Himself is ambivalent, occupying both sides of a polarity at the core of Creation or whether there even should be a Creation. The arithmetical realm holds its breath and all reality pauses, awaiting the resolution of this troubled moment.

Jocelyn was caught up in this polarity, or maybe she was playing out both sides willingly. She seemed to be standing on a carousel that kept turning in circles. On one arc of the rotation, she was calling all the numbers back to her Light grids, but on the other she was the arithmetical gods withholding the distribution of their numbers field, refusing their entry into any post-Planck- boundary realm. So what was crossing this boundary were only etheric shadows of the real numbers; the shadows lacked traction on scripting reality.

She came up with a clever tactic. Since she knew she was real and already created with all the numbers and grid patterns already implicit in her, a done deal the alien gods could not refute, she used her alignment with that unarguable reality as a way of intensifying her presence in this etheric ghost realm middle ground of the numbers and to make these numbers be real. She was transferring her personal ontological reality into this etheric realm like a blood transfusion for an anemic patient.

Since I am real and comprised of real numbers in algorithms scripting my Light grid reality as a human whose pattern mirrors the planet's, then I transfer this reality like an imprint or a hands-on blessing (though it's more of a mental one) to this weak stream of ghost numbers extracted from the resistant arithmetical realm and thereby endow them with vigorous, blood-enriched life. (This is my sense of how she was formulating her tactics to herself. I seemed to be standing directly behind her mental processes, monitoring their logic train.) Then she could draw upon the Elohim's sword-focused presence to strengthen her movements. Once she announced her spatial position, they could help her. That's the tricky imperative about the human design: we have to move first. Then the spiritual world can fall in behind us to give support and direction.

I think I started to understand the alien gods' mental state about this. The combined Elohim-Jocelyn demonstration was showing the alien gods that the deployment of their numbers into the scripting of Light grids and eventually planetary systems and phylogenies was merely an extension of the numbers. It was like stretching, but did not represent a fundamental change in their shape. They were starting to see the essential identity of the numbers did not change even when they were sent out past the Planck boundary to pixellate the world.

Prior to this they had interpreted the dispatch of the numbers as a grievous pollution of their essence, that manifestation and pixellation corrupted them and utterly changed their nature. Now they entertained the idea maybe it did not, that perhaps the rash deployment of the numbers realm beyond that perilous boundary was more like an imagination, a daydream, a bold but still playful experiment, a trifling mental peregrination in the realm of possibility. I didn't know how long they could beguile themselves with this alternate explanation of the worthiness of sending forth the numbers, but it was working.

The view had merit after all. From our point of view, the numbers were still pure. Jocelyn was like an orator swaying public opinion in an assembled crowd to her ideas. People were starting to flock towards her, agreeing with her position. She was drawing forth the real numbers to flesh out the etheric versions as they gravitated by resonance to her own completely real and empowered Light grid numbers. They called out to the sequestered numbers cowering behind the Planck boundary: Look, we are real, we survive, we flourish purely.

What a comedic dance this was. Jocelyn was luring the skittish numbers into incarnation, to step past the defensive boundary and take a risk. What clinched the deal was her unwavering conviction of the rightness of her invitation and the incarnation project; the alien gods responded to her surety.

Following her lead, the Elohim were in their world-generating mode, directing their sword to script Light grids out of the combinations of numbers. The alien gods, still jittery and restive, were, so far, going along with this work. I seemed to have wandered into Jocelyn's thinking process like it was a chamber. She started thinking of all the stars represented in the Earth's Light grid. She followed their holographic forms back to their galactic originals and into the arithmetic coding that generated and subsequently named each of them.

She quickened these numbers by inhabiting them, walking through them like landscapes, swelling them up with her extended human consciousness to conjoin with their stellar awareness. Her presence made them more animated, at least as far as the alien gods and their hold on the original deployment of the numbers. It made sense: since these particular stars were part of the Earth's Light grid and thereby implicit in its copy within Jocelyn's psychic constitution, the viability of their number constituents rightly came out of her consciousness. She made them stronger in her form, emphasized their reality and enhanced their number basis; this transferred to the galactic originals and did the same.

Everything looked bright, real, and unequivocally manifested. She realized she was seeing this from the pixellated side of the Planck boundary where it appeared reality had in fact already been manifested. But from the other side of that boundary, reality as we know it remained unmanifest, in quietude. The alien gods dwelled undisturbed in their arcane cave of all the numbers, and as far as they were concerned, nothing was in incarnation; it was just an idle notion of God's and not likely to amount to anything should He be rash enough to try it. So was reality *in fact* manifested outwardly, clearly in form, or not?

I realized it was the wrong question, or my query was put incorrectly. From the Supreme Being's point of view, reality would always be only a mental notion, an *eidolon*, a thought experiment, a clever little daydream He'd spun out. It was not manifested definitively; matter was not rock solid like we usually think such that we could tap on it with our knuckles and hear a sound. The arithmetical realm had been deployed outside the Planck boundary only by degree. It was not a sharply defined boundary; rather, it was porous, tentative. It was not a binary matter of reality being either on or off,

black or white; the Supreme Being was using a dimmer switch, manifesting it by degrees.

I wasn't happy to figure that out. How was I to tell if I was succeeding? Then a troubling thought arose, although, in retrospect, it was intriguing. Our Earth algorithm is heuristic, meaning it is self-learning and always adjusting its processes to accommodate the changing circumstances it encounters. What if this business about the theft from the Arithmetical Earth of its managing algorithm was to facilitate its self-awareness?

What if our self-learning algorithm sought to become a *self-aware* algorithm? To summon and burgeon self-awareness of its individuality and its sheer existence on behalf of a curious arithmetical realm that felt sufficiently daring to try this? Like monks wanting to try out the quotidian outside world, the alien gods were sneaking out into the manifest, incarnated, pixellated world to sample its blandishments and shortcomings through this self-aware algorithm.

What we have been casually referring to as the alien gods was our way of indicating the collective intelligence and awareness of the arithmetical realm. These "gods" are the presence and attentive state of the numbers realm. It is probably inappropriate to refer to them as gods. They are hardly Great White Brotherhood material; they never ascended because they never descended.

But now I was getting an impression of possibly their next step, at least regarding Earth. Up until the present it was as if the arithmetical gods had been dreaming they were running the Earth's Light grid processes through this special algorithm. That was on what we would call automatic pilot, like sleepwalking.

Now perhaps they were about to take the next step, to wake up from that dream, to look around and look at themselves looking around and experience a flush of self-discovery, like a dog looking in a mirror and recognizing himself. That would be the pivotal moment of the birth of self-awareness in the arithmetical domain, seeing themselves awake, alive, and active as this heuristic algorithm, as processing, calculating numbers alive in the world.

I laughed. A thought suddenly arose in me that seemed irresistibly funny. If the arithmetical gods become self-aware and all their number computations become aware of themselves as agents in reality, it means they will be in a form. It sounds obvious but maybe these guys don't get it. To be self aware, you need to be a self, which means a separate *incarnate* unit of aware consciousness. To get what they want, they will have to accept exactly what they stridently don't want.

They will have to step across that horrid Planck boundary that to them is anathema, the pit of contamination. They will now be incarnate intelligences, bearing incontestable *bodily* proof of the very thing they have been opposed to.

I didn't know if this was actually happening or was a simulation or a proposal or mock-up of a possible future event. I saw that it was an opening. I could use it to show the alien gods, if only in the merest introductory manner, that it might be desirable, possibly fun, and certainly educational, to sample the manifest world and see it and themselves through its pixellated context. It might start to disarm their militant resistance to entering the incarnated realm and sacrificing the purity of their numbers to service to the created world.

I was hoping they might see that the numbers would suffer no diminution of their purity from doing this, that it was only a kind of postulated hysteria on their part to assume the arithmetical realm would be corrupted permanently by this world. I was hoping they could see that their numbers could serve the world and remain uncontaminated at the same time, as if they were coated in an impenetrable wax. They couldn't just stand around bodily and do nothing with their numbers. Even if they lifted one finger that would be running an equation.

If the alien gods, acting as this particular algorithm, became self-aware while doing it, recursively attentive to their own existential condition as numbers, then they could participate wakefully in the consciousness processes their numbers were coding and then, and this is the exciting part, the part that might make all the difference in our retrieval of Earth's necessary algorithm, they would become susceptible to the Christ Light. Numbers would merge with awareness, then that would dissolve into the nondualistic bliss of the Christ Light. Oh boy: will that ever flummox these staunch resisters. Dissolved in bliss?

That requires self-awareness because, paradoxically, you have to willingly surrender this—dissolve yourself— to participate in the Christ Light condition, or what you might also call the primordial, original ground of Being. Should they make it to this stage, all doubts about preserving the purity of their numbers would be assuaged, as the Christ Light is the ultimate purity preserver. That's what we tried to do with the Solar Logos before; maybe this time it would work. This was two levels up the hierarchical ladder: from Solar Logos to *the*

Logos. The doubts won't be assuaged; they will be eliminated as if they never existed.

For the alien gods to become wakefully self-aware as the Earth's managing algorithm and with it, self-aware as the host of secondary algorithms, they would experience this sudden birth of self-awareness in the context of our planet's Albion, its composite goal and consummate expression. They would find themselves awake and alive and self-referentially aware as our Albion. They would appreciate how large a field of consciousness their numbers were serving. I should think that would be a salutary, even exciting, prospect for these stay-at-home curmudgeons. The scope of that awareness might open their eyes wide.

Still, maybe their resistance to deploying the numbers beyond the Planck boundary was a trepidation about this inevitable moment of self-awareness. Was it too challenging a prospect, overwhelming in its individuation implications? To stay asleep will probably always seem safer than the rude moment of waking up.

I hoped I wasn't spinning just a delightful fantasy with these speculations. You could never be sure about these arithmetical deities. I did have the impression, in this simulation at least, that there was no longer a discrete boundary between the numbers undeployed and pure in their own realm and the numbers organized to code and sustain a created world. They did not seem to have lost anything essential, nor did they seem tainted by the manifest world.

I couldn't help laughing again. It was a nervous laughter, almost giddy. Was this whole venue, the theft, our attempts to retrieve the algorithm for Earth, part of an educational opportunity for the alien gods to get them to

experience their implicit embeddedness in this original ground of Being, this primordial state of pure Light, as the Tibetan mystics say? Good God, were we pandering a "spiritual experience" for these guys, tempting them with Light?

To give them *Rigpa*, or knowledge of the primordial ground, a knowing of the original wakefulness, the spontaneous presence and primordial purity, the direct vision or self-existent reality, which is the Tibetans' abstruse way of indicating the Supreme Being without indulging in any personification? Was that what we were doing? That would make us not detectives chasing after number thieves, but tutors, or maybe just procurers. Had the Grand Master of the Universe set us up to be pedagogues to the alien gods, the Sirens of incarnation?

I heard somebody muttering further along in this room. It was Sal. "That bloody equation should have shaken loose their hold on the algorithmic set," he was saying to himself. He hated it when his mathematics failed to produce the results he forecast for them. It seemed a violation of a fundamental principle of good behavior on reality's part, that it would dance to the steps as dictated by his clever equations. Arithmetical specifications were supposed to be incontestable.

I saw the empty rolling plains of Alberta around him and the Omahk-Majorville Medicine Wheel and its piles of stones and swirls and circles in which he was standing. He was attired in his long yellow robe emblematic of that Ray and of his soul's ancient alignment with that quality and its Ray Master. He had positioned himself at a place in universal reality that came before the numbers. I understood his tactic, how he hoped that gave him an existential advantage.

He needed an advantage. His mathematical tactics had failed against these devious and devilishly clever number mavens. I found myself strolling into his mental atmosphere as I had with Jocelyn and Blaise. I hoped he didn't mind the intrusion. He had tried to con the alien gods with his 16th order magic tesseract packed with 218,750 numbered facets. It was just a flat tire now.

They were no more impressed with that or stymied by its sudden emergence than if they had indifferently bent over to pick up a few shiny pennies on the ground. His stealth reverse algorithm that he hoped would start retrieving all the numbers without the alien gods seeing it had dismally failed, and just as he was sneaking back through the arithmetical tunnel he had generated to penetrate their domain, he discovered he was caught in an illusion of mirrors, his hands empty. He had collected only leprechaun gold and the numbers were crumbling to dust. In sum, he had nothing to show for all his putative cleverness.

I saw the vexation on his face. A mathematics marvel, he was not used to procedural setbacks like this. He was up against mathematics itself with them. It was supposed to be the epitome of logic in fixed syllogistic equations, but it wasn't working that way. The arithmetical realm was unexpectedly obdurate, even creatively so, and the logical, procedural presumptions that seem to be inseparable with mathematics were rendered invalid in his exchanges with them.

Then he flashed into the yellow-robed figure with its spiritual regality, its antecedent position in the hierarchy of reality to the arithmetical realm and the confidence that positioning generated. There he was, sending out yellow sparks from his yellow staff at a place that preceded mathematics. But then he'd fall back into the realm where the arithmetical gods were getting the better of him and he was failing to retrieve the numbers we needed and set those alien gods on their backsides. Sal was locked into this dichotomy and flat on his backside.

It looked as if he was using the solidity of the Medicine Wheel and the Alberta landscape to push against with his feet as he tried to shift the arithmetical realm from its resistance to his intrusions into their numbered realm. He looked like he was straining, his legs pressing against the solid ground, to push over a vast wall made of numbers, the intransigent alien gods inside it. His dedication to the goal was admirable, but he was failing. He was holding the Medicine Wheel vertex position within that rhombus steady, but he was not gaining traction on the rest of the system, the reservoir of numbers beyond what Omahk-Majorville was able to hold steady.

I suggested to Sal, telepathically, that he take the opposite approach. Forget about trying to wrest the numbered realm back from them. Try to interest them in the prospects of an intelligent investment in Omahk-Majorville, show them how the numbers could create a delightful consciousness state through that designated geomantic node—in effect, show them that it wouldn't "hurt" to put their numbers into play at this site. As soon as Sal registered this proposal to shift directions, the Above People arrived.

All the Sky People appeared, the celestial and star-intelligences this site was aligned with and for which it acted as a seating chart and summoning center. As he had seen before, behind these many assembled Sky Beings were the algorithms running their realities and consciousness processes. They were continuously specifying the operational specificities of the Medicine Wheel. Their presence made the Medicine Wheel and its etheric counterpart feel cosmopolitan.

It testified to a richness of awareness, a diversity of perspectives and conclusions. It was like a festival as the Sky People brought holograms of their Light temples and the qualities of awareness these generated. It made the site a circular promenade of tents and bright pavilions offering treasures. The visitors brought their banners, decorated in arresting pictures of their life. This was the mythic layer, the psychic impression filter that the site created. This was the picture code that translated mathematics into sensible imagery, providing entry details for initiates meditating here.

Here is what this site produces in awareness, and here's how to enter the field, the mythic pictures were saying through their images. Even the bulls of Aldebaran were shuffling ponderously onto the site from all directions, as if they were walking out of the galaxy right into the grassy, stony field of the Wheel.

I waited to see what the alien gods would make of this merry spectacle. They were like astute investors who had parlayed some capital to fund a project. Here it was, completed and ready for presentation and in fact open for business. Would it prove that their "money" had been prudently invested? Filaments of Light started streaming out of the Medicine Wheel back to the arithmetical realm, to these invisible, formless watchers behind the algorithms.

What were these thin streams? Moments of insight, gestures of understanding, elevations of awareness, cosmic perception and participation from site users. People come to the Medicine Wheel, use its geomantic design correctly, and produce these filaments of Light as testimony to the enrichment of their souls. The site, saturated with this infusion, starts to emanate these qualities like flower scents. The celestial world draws near to enjoy the aromas, fluttering hungrily around the blossoms like feeding hummingbirds.

This, incidentally, demonstrates a prime development that happens when you use a site correctly and over a prolonged period. You generate this new quality of consciousness. You midwife the birth of a new feature out of the geomancy of the place and subsequent users of the site can immediately benefit from this lovely emission.

The alien gods were not usually interested in or impressed with anything pertaining to incarnation and its supposed blandishments, but I saw that this display was making a difference in their habitual resistance. They saw their numbers streaming back to them, untainted, and possibly—unbelievably, they thought—enhanced, as if, like tourists to Hawaii, they were returning home festooned with gorgeous *leias* and full of happy accounts of a wonderful time.

Sal was now acting like an attentive salesman in a showroom of alluring merchandise, furniture, kitchenware, clothing, cars, whatever. It was like a department store with everything displayed in the one room, in this case, the Medicine Wheel and what it was designed to produce, the world of material forms. See, this is what your numbers can make when intelligently deployed.

The alien gods were still skeptical, exceedingly conservative and reticent about this questionable use of their precious numbers realm, but they were *looking*, at least giving the display some consideration, even if it went against their judgement. I had to remind myself (this was more me, as Frederick, having this particular thought) that our ultimate customer, the One we really had to persuade, was the Supreme Being Who needed to be finally "cured" of His vacillating ambivalence. He was the Prime Customer with the fabulous bank account. One solid sale to Him and our fortunes would be made, reality saved.

Sal was shaking his head, rubbing his forehead as if to wipe perspiration. He wasn't sweating though. It was just a nervous gesture as he saw the enormity of the task. Convince the Supreme Being of the judicious wisdom of deploying the numbers? Few humans even think in terms of having an audience with the Big Guy, but we were tasked with trying to change His mind about something. The Olympians had failed impressively to budge Zeus off his iron decision to destroy Troy and terminate the Trojans, and they were gods with formidable powers of their own. What did we have to measure up against that?

It was worrisome, yet it was funny too, because it was He who employed us to convince Him to act other than His predilection about keeping the numbers at home. Our Supreme Being was proving to be supremely tautological. He was like a mistrusting father set on protecting the purity of his teenage daughter, not letting her go out on dates with boys or even to think about them. Very 1950s. And we were the boys trying to lure her out "to her destruction," he thought. Or he was a conflicted Zeus who invited us, mere mortals with a bit of cleverness at our disposal, to tell him why he should save Odysseus from ruin.

All the Above People were leaning in on the Medicine Wheel, pressing against its surface from the circumference. Each held a sheet of paper containing the equations coding their existence. They held them up forlornly. They looked dependent on Sal to achieve a resolution to this impasse. Deploy the numbers or end the world? Will we continue to exist or be sucked into the Nothing? As a mathematician, Sal was taking this dichotomy personally. Who wouldn't?

There He was, Mr. Supreme Being, infinitely creative and imaginatively fertile, spinning out an infinity of mathematical possibilities that generate realities, and there He was too, in a flush of extreme conservatism and hesitation, second-guessing Himself, retracting into a hermitic reluctance to commit anything to existence, and there Sal was, professional mathematician, trying to resolve this with brilliant equations, and they were all failing to work. The arithmetical gods, and even God Himself, seemed implacably set against letting the numbers into circulation, into that defiled world of incarnation and tarnished forms and lascivious teenage boys intent on deflowering all the innocent girls.

Sal fluctuated between trying to concoct super-adept, convincing, *salvific* algorithms to bring the Big Guy and the arithmetical gods around and reverting to his yellow-robed, yellow-staffed guise, sending yellow Ray sparks all over, occupying this primordially wise position in his own consciousness. In fact, all of us were doing that, alternating between trying to fix the problem and standing at a neutral reserve position transcendent to the vexed problem itself. Wasn't that just another way of saying we were stalled out?

Manifest the world or forget the whole idea? I felt this polarity swinging in me, the other three here, and the rest of the Hierophancy across the galaxy. I thought we had been chasing down a wily thief; this had dilated to the profound schism in the Mind of the Great Creator: Generate life or forget it? The Old Vacillator simply couldn't make up His mind, or maybe He didn't want to.

I shivered. Or maybe Sal shivered and I felt it. Jocelyn and Blaise looked worried. We were defendants in a court case charged with justifying our dubious existence before this Supreme Judge. He leaned across the high bench, like a skeptical Victorian British magistrate, the artificial curls in His hideously large white wig gleaming like worrisome ripples in a landscape, awaiting our defense. I felt like Rumpole, with nothing but his charm, Wordsworth quotes, and sharp wit up against the indomitably stubborn and not awfully bright Old Bailey Judge Bullingham. The schism we were charged with resolving came down to whether our existence would continue or if we'd be told to pack up things and leave.

Why should any numbers be allocated to maintaining the four of us? The air in the courtroom had grown suddenly chill. Dire implications now enveloped us. I was beginning to feel the existential worry members of the first-generation humanity, so accustomed to lives spent abusing the privilege of consciousness, must have felt when they first got wind of the possibility to the Supreme Being would drown their sorry asses in a world-engulfing flood to destroy their brood, that the network sponsoring their "show" had cancelled any more episodes.

Then this shifted to the opposite, a scene from an Elizabethan May Day frivolity, young men and women gaily dancing around a Maypole amidst a riot of early spring foliage, warm air, and lush prospects for enjoyable living. I heard the poetry of Robert Herrick recited jauntily in my mind. Light grids coding this physical reality and the consciousness processes the young humans were enjoying radiated Light and benevolence all about them. Other Light grids specifying important Light temples nearby similarly flashed brilliantly.

I saw the algorithms regulating their existence flaring confidently all around this, and I saw the collective "faces," the focused attention of the arithmetical gods behind that, like a group of old men peering curiously through cottage windows at this nonsense the young folks had gotten themselves up to. It was as if we held these alternate scenarios in an outstretched palm for the Supreme Being to examine. We were His art directors presenting our mockups, two different cover versions, for the client's approval, a difficult client frankly, but don't tell anyone. He thinks He's the only customer in town.

I wasn't sure if we were making any progress with the recalcitrant gods. Spontaneously, the four of us reverted to our robed and staffed presence and concentrated on emanating the Ray qualities these represented. When in doubt, bring in a consultant, and, amusingly, each of us in our higher wisdom body was our own consultant because where we stood in our individual Light temples of past-life accomplishments and the distillation of experience into wisdom was a place beyond or before the vexation and ambivalence of numbers. The colored sparks were flying, continuously launching flocks of brightly plumed birds. You could see the implicit rhombus our points created as we occupied our landscape sites around the planet as we also stood in this room.

I felt the strain of what we were doing. We were poised at our landscape sites and we were standing forthright emitting Ray sparks in this special room. We were straining at this, and I felt the stalemate. We were not prevailing. The alien gods, and I suppose the Supreme

Being since they are part of Him, were holding out, obdurate, unconvinced, possibly even disinterested in the idea. Deploy the numbers? Sorry, not interested. Can't see the point, really. Go away.

We did go away, suddenly, unexpectedly, like a stretched rubber band snapping back to a lax position. I was at my desk again at the Hierophancy offices where all this started. I appeared to be studying some papers; they looked like blueprints. Where did they come from? I couldn't remember. I felt a little anxious: wasn't I supposed to be worrying about something important? I couldn't remember at first. It felt like an ordinary day at the Hierophancy office.

14

Until it didn't. It seemed like that transition took about five minutes. I had forgotten we didn't have to solve this problem entirely on our own. We had colleagues. I saw L2, R1, the eight A representatives, Y1, Y2, and G1, and smiled. They were in this problem up to their necks just like we were. Their free-will planets were equally in jeopardy as the Earth. Maybe they had some new angles.

My attention was drawn to L2. He was the "guy" with the pulsing hypercube that he held in his hand combining fairy magic and calculator. He was the "guy" who tried to deceive the alien gods into thinking they had neatly acquired his planet's managing algorithm, meanwhile feeding them a false one. He was the alien colleague who had projected a house of Light from this handheld hypercube and invited us to enter it on the slopes of Bald Mountain.

As I noted at the time, it seemed to be a Light projection of his own mental space, and it was exquisitely and immediately interactive, like being inside his brain. It was an instantaneously responding holograph projector: whatever you wished to see, like geomantic outlines of the other free-will planets, it made this.

At the time when we first saw it, we had mistakenly thought the alien gods were trying to extract the mathematics of L2's planet to complete their Magic Square. Since then, their tactics have been better revealed to us. Finishing their vast Magic Square was only a step towards a larger goal. They didn't want to commit their arithmetical realm in support of the incarnated domain under any conditions, and in this resistance to number-coded manifestation they were representing the Supreme Being and His apparent diffidence.

In service of this absolutist goal, they were retracting all their numbers from reality. Against this one-way suction, L2's fascinating green ribbon, which I had likened to a tongue of numbers projected from his mind and by which he regulated geomantic affairs on his planet through adjusting their number coding, was proving ineffective and increasingly futile. That was where we stood now.

L2 was losing ground. It was like he was using a modest pump to keep the ocean water stopped at the beach so it wouldn't pull in his beachfront bungalow, and the alien gods were like the irresistible tidal pull, sucking in everything. They rolled the tide in, trying to swamp the bungalow, then suck it back with the outgoing pull of the tide. A mere pump could never prevail against such a force of Nature as that, high tide and low tide improbably hitting it at once. But that was only one way of looking at it, and maybe it was not even an accurate one.

I mentioned that L2 had projected his mind in front of him like a house of Light. In it he now displayed all the numbers involved in his planet's existence like a gallery hanging for a prominent artist just opening his new exhibit to the public. L2 gave these numbers that scripted his planet what is called "pride of place," but this display was not to exalt the wonders of his planet but its scripting numbers. He wanted the alien gods to experience that sudden intake of breath, the gasp, the sigh, the smile, the enthusiastic head nods, as they appreciated their own genius-level arithmetical glory revealed before them.

I saw the alien gods, even though they were only a collective mind, examining this display with interest. They saw the numbers, the equations that combined them in attractive clusters, the psychic pictures that they generated, and the actual living conditions on an alive planet that these two layers scripted. And they saw the resulting products of consciousness, the delicate exudates of awareness streaming out of the heads of the sentient life-forms as a validation.

They saw the spectrum from abstruse arithmetical design to consciousness states. At least they didn't automatically dismiss it after a few seconds' perusal. Maybe they hadn't ever seen the full syllogism of consciousness their numbers made possible, or they had never cared, until now. Yes, the numbers were forced into a "fallen" condition in support of incarnation, manifestation, and the dreaded pixellated universe, the aliens ruminated, but at least the numbers were foremost in this display. Everything was subsequent to their primacy of

display, like a thought inserted into the middle of a sentence by way of parentheses, meaning it was supplementary to the sentence's point and you could ignore it.

I had the impression the alien minds were strolling through this arithmetical art gallery, nodding their heads at times, their hands clasped behind their backs, entertaining the possibility, still vague and barely formed, that all this lavish investment in a questionable manifested world with their numbers might be acceptable. Any such scripted world would of course be of only finite duration; then the numbers would gallop back to their inviolate corral and it would be as if the unsavory experiment had never been undertaken.

They could look forward to that eventuality, the use of numbers like a short-term loan. I couldn't see them ever getting excited about how numbers could script realities; the best we might expect, it seemed, was a grudging tentative tolerance for this fueled by a narcissistic appreciation of their own mathematical magnificence. I didn't realize then how I was suffering from the anthropomorphic fallacy, attributing human-style emotions to the motives of these inscrutable mental gods. Narcissism would have no traction in their minds. I was suffering under a fallacy. You need an incarnated selfhood for narcissism. Can you imagine a computer strutting around in the aura of its amazingness? It simply runs the programs installed in it and which you order up by keystrokes.

Now L2 upped the ante in terms of the seductive appeal of the art display. He revealed his home planet as an exclusive manifestation of only numbers. It was an arithmetical planet, comprised of algorithms in dizzying complexity, a spherical terrain laminated in numbers and nothing else. There was no sign of a materially manifested world, of sentient, mobile life-forms, nothing to suggest the fallen state of the numbers in service of questionable incarnations. Only pure mathematics, a dancing pirouette of numbers alone.

The alien gods liked this display. They seemed to be nodding their heads, as if they had heads, I suppose, but I caught their essential gesture of tentative approval. Just numbers, thank you; none of that horrid incarnational riff-raff, you could hear them think. None of those vile bodies, they thought, as if bizarrely echoing Evelyn Waugh.

L2 winked at me. At least it looked like that, as much as a differently formed alien life-form could wink like a human person would. But I saw why. I saw why the alien gods were only seeing the numbered planet, nothing else. L2 had stealth-veiled the materialized planet, hidden it under a deflecting field. It was there, fully manifested, enjoying all the vile body corruptions of pixellation, but the alien gods could not see it or were sufficiently distracted to not try to penetrate this veil to see the awful truth, that their numbers had generated a world, and there it was complete, and, God forbid, *incarnate* under the numbers.

It was a droll trick, clever and, so far, successful. The alien gods thought it was just a world of numbers they were seeing, but for L2 it was that plus the world they generated. But was that the route to success and the continuation of the arithmetical world, this tactic of distracting the alien gods and thereby tricking God? Was God trickable in any sense? It seemed logically impossible.

L2's green tongue-ribbon was extruding numbers furiously like a brash launching of July 4 fireworks in any American community. He was prolific in numbers, like a Pentecostal surge of swirling equations to beguile the aliens. He was in a wroth of arithmetical glossolalia, channeling algorithms in all directions. Now it was my tongue that was hanging droopingly out of a wide-open mouth. Who could not be astonished at this spectacle of continuously emitted numbers?

Blaise, smirkingly put his hands together to make some mini-applause. Sal was frantically writing down as many of these novel equations as he could with the eagerness of somebody discovering another 20 mysteries by Agatha Christie, never seen before and only now emerging from some obscure Devon closet and promising to be spectacularly intriguing, her best ever. Jocelyn was making sketches of some of the psychic-mythic pictures being revealed.

"Just for good measure," L2 told me telepathically, "I changed many of the algorithms displayed in this arithmetical planet so our real planet would be undisturbed if the aliens decided to suck the numbers into their virginal realm. The numbers I displayed as this arithmetical planet were close enough to ours to fool somebody at first glance but would code a different planet or even a fake one. If they wanted to, they could play cat-and-mouse with this simulated, hypothetical planet, retracting the numbers then letting them snap back like a released elastic. But this 'cat' made of misleading numbers was an unreal cat.

"On our planet what you understand as individual consciousness is arrayed in a hexagonal pattern of six linked consciousness holders. This is the 'person' on our planet, an awareness comprised of six complementary parts. Our Light grid has features that reflect this sixfold quality, and the goal of spiritual development is to harmonize and unify the six aspects of this composite person.

"As the arithmetical gods started to remove the essential numbers from our system, these hexagonal units started to wobble and shred. The integrity of consciousness grew weakened and the bonds, even the filaments, linking the six unraveled. That means our algorithms have a special, sometimes only implicit, emphasis on six-functions, yielding products supportive of our sixfold structure of the psyche. I don't mean six as in the quantity of functions, but six as the dominant aspect. We are six. That is our basic unit definition, like your Blaises."

For a moment I saw L2 as sixfold, as if he had multiplied himself into five more identical copies, except that was likely his true appearance. I saw one L2 standing in the forefront as if he were their spokesman. I had the impression L2 smiled as I saw his true form, his sixness. His face didn't really support a smile as we would register this expression as humans. But I felt his mind brighten.

"We thought it would be easier for you if you only saw one of us, not the full six," he continued, his exotically couched thoughts streaming into my mind and then getting converted into English syntax that I could (probably) understand. "We can use this sixfold aspect to feed back into the alien gods' matrix and confound it. Congruent with this, we have six-based algorithms that have the peculiar property of grabbing hold of other mathematical constructs that try to acquire, extract, or delete them. In a functional sense and by analogy, they are like strong grasping claws that emerge

out of the mathematical construct to hold on tight to anything trying to unravel their system. We believe it will perturb the aliens, maybe stop them. They will try to grab our algorithms and the sixfold matrix will stop that, like laying down 12 hands with claws."

I don't know if L2's people laugh in any way like humans do, but I felt his mind grow mirthful. "It will be like trying to bite down on something and your teeth get no traction on a solid, intractable substance and it sticks in the mouth."

The sixfold matrix was acting like an impenetrable glass wall around L2's planet. I saw the alien gods leaning in from all directions, trying to extract the numbers, and failing. They seemed puzzled with this, but also intrigued. They were always alert to innovations and signs of high cleverness about numbers.

Their minds reminded me of cats trying to scratch and claw their way through a resistant barrier. You could almost hear the sound of long fingernails screeching against glass as the numbers remained alluringly inaccessible beyond them. The sixfold arithmetical finger-trap kept relaunching itself against the alien gods. It kept them out, and it was embroiling them in distracting calculations that sent their attention elsewhere or simply pulled it tighter into its nimble web.

On the other side of this glass wall of outward-projecting equations, the planet's essential algorithms appeared to run inviolate, unaffected by the aliens. But was this making any inroads in persuading the protectors of the arithmetical realm to allow their precious number "herds" to be deployed for the Creation?

I likened them to cats. Another feline nuance I observed was that they were toying with this reflective matrix the way a cat will push and pull a ball of yarn. They did this out of a relaxed, almost idle, amusement, as if they knew, whenever they were ready, they would take the complete number ball in a single swift grab. This likelihood argued against their progressing towards a convincing case that they should allow their numbers to go out into that horrid incarnational realm.

Then I saw that perhaps that was a premature conclusion. L2 had embedded another layer of persuasion within his sixfold reflective glass wall. As the matrix kept reformulating itself against each cat's-paw incursion, it spooled out a complex, multidimensional algorithm that looked like a 6D snowflake. It kept building, expanding in all directions, exponentially adding more numbers. I will tell you, it certainly grabbed my interest. It seemed to catch the aliens' too.

It was mesmerizing, like an exotic Hindu dancer flashing scarves and veils and making hand gestures and facial movements so you couldn't take your eyes off her. L2's special algorithm was generating an expanding mountain of numbers. The alien gods could see themselves reflected in its complex surfaces, and I think the mild narcissism this indulged, or perhaps proposed, captured their interest. They didn't look like anything and never would, being a collective awareness, but the beauty and majesty of the numbers in this hyperdimensional parade provoked a ripple of pride and satisfaction in their abstruse minds.

This extravagant acrobatic display of numbers didn't seem to commit them to any incarnational travesties while it made a nice exhibition of number prowess. It was as if, disdaining heartily to ever touch the ocean water, they had tentatively extended a foot and the tips of their toes were now enjoying the water sensation. So far they didn't feel irremediably tainted by the exposure.

I admired L2's tactical concept. On each side of the glass wall entirely different number activities were underway, planetary maintenance on one side, narcissistic indulging on the other. Different equations were deployed for both. The set-up had philosophical appeal. Don't mystics, especially Qabalists, suggest that the Supreme Being, ubiquitous and unique, wonders Who He is? That God created the universe, launched the Creation with its hierarchies of Light, to produce a mirror in which He could appreciate His Own ineffable essence? Because really the focus was the Supreme Being doing business as the numbers.

The arithmetical gods were the collective awareness of the numbers realm, so they must be searching for a reflection of their own identity too, to answer that same question, and L2 was providing them with such a reflection. This is who you are, see, watch the skillful, absurd dance of these frolicking numbers. L2's approach was a blend of sly trickery packaged in an alluring narcissism. Could he rope in the Supreme Being with this tactic and persuade Him to agree?

My attention was drawn away from this spectacle to something else. One thing you realize in dealing with agencies and problems at this level is that your "adversary" can attend to multiple tracks at the same time, as the alien gods were clearly doing. We were a team of salesmen making our own pitches to them at the same time, and the alien gods never seemed to be short of attentive heads.

R1 was next up, and he was making his pitch. He's the one with an index finger that was as long as a magic wand, and this wand projected a house-sized sphere with ruby-colored pillars around its equator, and these pillars were packed to the brim with numbers. These numbers effervesced with enthusiasm, smart, articulate algorithms petitioning to be released into the world to create wonderfully clever, long-lasting structures. Just give us a chance, you'll like it.

When we first saw this, R1 had released the numbers from the red pillars. They had started to write phylogenic scripts with equations, specifying the various life-forms of his planet, including his own. They were air paintings of the animals, plant life, and sentient, self-aware forms such as R1, as well as the Light temples necessary to support that consciousness life and to maintain his planet. They didn't look anything like what passes for life-forms and Light temples on the Earth, but I appreciated the essential similarity in terms of their function.

R1's master planetary algorithm enveloped these pillars like a head of Light. It managed all consciousness and life activities of his home world in a climate of free-will and self-determination. His was a burgeoning world, and I was alarmed to see the long fingers of the alien gods reaching for its numbers. Resistance algorithms streamed out of R1's pillars to halt the alien advance.

The last time I saw this R1 seemed nonplussed by this alternate coding. It seems since then he had devised a suitable response. It reminded me of juggling. He accepted the alien gods' algorithmic bid and juggled it on his own fingertips. The numbers bounced up and down on his fingers like delicate tennis balls. Every time they recontacted his fingertips he extruded another set of numbers into them, creatively contaminating them with different directions, making them run contrary to their original number coding, paralyzing contrary tendencies.

The alien gods' algorithms were now infected with puzzling antigenic equations, confounding their integrity, like an immune system seriously challenged by an exotic package of aggressive foreign cells. The alien gods studied these new number forms with curiosity; they did not notice, at least initially, that these strange formulations were commandeering their intended arithmetical functions and that this beguiling distraction was costly to them.

R1's tactic had layers to it. Outwardly, he was capturing the alien gods' attention and grabbing control of their algorithmic expansions into his planet. But that was only to get them to stop deploying numbers for a moment and to stop trying to remove all of R1's planetary equations. This gave R1 sufficient breathing space to insert sticky capture algorithms back into the alien gods' mental field and to launch other entertaining mutating algorithms as a sales pitch for the general utility and irresistible attraction of numbers cleverly deployed.

It evoked images of lively circus performances done in multiple rings. Each of R1's launched equations pirouetted into multiple forms and dimensions; it was like watching acrobats doing flying trapeze numbers inside a hypercube of numbers. While the alien gods reached for the new, attractively dancing numbers, R1 secured his planet's necessary algorithms, stuffing them covertly in his pockets.

Each new numbers foray R1 pushed towards the arithmetical gods soon captured another increment of their attention and gave him the necessary cover distraction to pocket more of his planet's required algorithms. It looked like the alien gods were slowly succumbing to the courtesan charms of R1's clever digits. The rest of us stood by, astonished and amused. We tried not to laugh noticeably in case it warned the arithmetical obsessives that something was underway.

R1's ruby pillars kept ejecting bubbles of numbers and equations like shaken bottles of bubbly, and the calculations kept getting more astute in their configurations and products, like he had a team of mathematicians making them. It was as if R1 were a master salesman in a department store, demonstrating each appliance, kitchen aid, vacuum cleaner, air conditioner, fan, everything, at once, for a customer who evidently had never ventured into such a magic tent.

His tactic was running on two levels. On one, R1 was entrancing the alien gods with an adroit display of what their own numbers could assemble. On the other, he was pocketing his own planet's essential algorithms without the alien gods noticing it, or maybe they did, but discounted its significance or assumed they could retrieve them later when they were done reveling in their opium haze of numbers distraction.

In the old American cliché, R1 was good cop *and* bad cop. The good cop was concatenating an elaborate arithmetical structure before the rapt alien gods; evidently, they had not imagined such creative uses of their numbers, and they seemed reassured the inviolate purity of the numbers was not in jeopardy. The bad cop was ruthlessly seizing all the equations his planet needed, like yanking apples forcefully from a tree reluctant to surrender them.

I turned my attention to the eight representatives from the "A" planet who were busy running their tactical approach. You may remember this comprised two groups called A1-4 and A5-8, which looked like two humanoid figures with four bobbling heads, each facing a cardinal direction. As I indicated when I first introduced these exotic extraplanetary colleagues, saying they had heads was an act of metaphorical exaggeration. Their attention was headlike.

Their "heads" were provisional personifications of their awake minds, of the air element, pure mentality marshalled into a coherent force and point of origin we might over-literally take for a head such as we know them. I'm sure their true reality was sublime in contrast. It was windy. I felt like I was standing in the midst of eight converging breezes, and in each of these zephyrs complex calculations were whizzing through their steps towards an inevitable conclusion, which was to retrieve their algorithms and confound the alien gods.

These eight heads looked like a single Cubist-style head arrayed in a circle around an implied single cranium. It was outgassing number formulations as effortlessly as breathing. These aliens were not mathematicians; their windy essence was numbers itself, though it was expressed on the other side of that perilous divide the alien gods were so staunchly and in such a fundamentalist manner hysterically defending. Their numbers streamed out of the incarnated realm.

For the eight A-aliens, the numbers already had been deployed. They were in a constant state of deployment. Every second of their attention exuded a riot of numbers. Their single cranium was like a circus tent that suddenly unloaded a thousand tumbling, jumping, somersaulting acrobats in gleeful whoops of calculation. I couldn't help becoming entranced. Sal and Jocelyn, and even Blaise to an extent, were similarly captivated by this wanton display of arithmetical creativity. Surely, the Big Guy Himself would be just a little spellbound by this testimony. Maybe the whoops were getting through to Him.

The A-representatives were mellifluous in numbers. Pentecostal even. They were eight magicians spawning universes of equations; their numbers went forth from their inventive minds like blaring trumpets, brazenly declaring the advent of a numbered universe, a world in which numbers ruled everything. I tried to imagine living on their planet, a zone where the mind was so quick it was surely a delight to be only mental, like the fastest game of table tennis and never a netball and each serve generated a new ball until there were hundreds batted back and forth, the balls always zooming, perfectly aimed.

The alien gods were intently following this accelerating demonstration. They were like conventioneers who strolling the booths had stopped at this one and were bedazzled. They were inspecting the merchandise with unalloyed interest, almost caressing the numbers, ultimately their property, it's true, and so ultimately it was themselves they were admiring with respect.

Behind the rapt alien gods was the God-in-Chief. We were like lawyers presenting our case before the Supreme Court, and He was all nine judges. He knew the law, He knew what lawyers could do and what they would try to get away with, and He was unwaveringly logical and judicial-minded. The Supreme Being sat on His high bench assessing whether we were making our case or not.

We might beguile the alien gods with our arithmetical tinsel and brassy trumpets, but not the Supreme Being. As the numbers realm this was the Supreme Being in His party face, sporting with algorithms. But in his deeper juridical mode, He was all seriousness. As Chief Justice, He was too sober to be easily swayed by merriment. I felt like we were a team of puppeteers running our Punch and Judy hand puppets through our antic routines fervidly trying to amuse a critical, grouchy audience. Our puppet *avatars* clanged each other on the head and shoulders, ducked and leaned, made angry faces, grimaced, teased, cried out, ridiculed, all of it a numbers dance desperate to beguile the audience.

I couldn't say the eight A-representatives were making any headway. I couldn't say they were losing ground either. I guess it was a draw so far, so I turned to see what Y1 and Y2 were doing. These were the "aliens" I called the Yellow Ones. Everything about their planet's Light grid, themselves, and the curious doors through which their algorithms ran was done in bright yellow. The yellow doors opened into geomantic provinces on their planets; I counted 36, and Y1 and Y2 somehow managed to stand like guardians before each of the 36.

When I say "stand" I don't mean to suggest they stood in a discrete bodily way. It was more a manner of a psychic countenance or an attentive diffuse presence. I can't say they had bodies, or anything upright and humanoid like we're used to. It was more a matter of the suggestion of a face and how that implies awareness, and the allusion to upright meaning their steady attention.

I found myself chuckling. It was about these 36 doors. It was like 36 wildly excited children all dashing out these doors at once, storming into a playing field. Imagine a house, better make it a circular one, with 36 equal-sized doors, evenly spaced. They are flung open at once with a loud bang and out dash the kids. It's the planet's ruling algorithms that are streaming out of these opened doors. You can't impute emotions to equations but these calculations seemed merry, eager to compute and code their planetary conditions, psychic pictures, Light temples, and the "physical" living conditions, with whatever quality those took. Y1 and Y2 stood proudly at these 36 doors, observing the cheerful deployment of their reality-scripting numbers as they ran out enthusiastically, like teachers watching children cavorting during recess.

Maybe I should liken the running forth of these algorithms to berserkers. They had that kind of crazed confidence, the kind that brooked no questioning. I think it was the yellow doors that gave them this brazen certainty. The doors looked unchallengeable, as rooted and immoveable as the monoliths of Stonehenge. They spoke of seniority, job security, tenure, a position that could not be dislodged. They were as solidly anchored as if they were sunk into the bedrock of reality itself, into the primordial foundations of the Creation.

That's the kind of imprimatur you have to bring to any contest with these gods. It was as if Y1 and Y2 were carrying around an assurance from the Creator, a certification of purpose that could not be revoked. Or could it? Would the Supreme Being go back on His Own Word and cancel this inviolate anchorage?

Y1 and Y2 were conducting planetary business as if this doubt never raised its head. They were acting like they were the first two cabinet ministers appointed. They had been with the Old Man since the beginning, and they and the Old Man were like this—you'll have to picture your middle finger wrapped over your index finger to suggest immoveable proximity. Surely that was a guarantee of constancy.

They were streaming numbers out the yellow doors like a home-run champion batting warm-up practice balls into the centerfield bleachers. Their unceasing, confident activity itself was the best argument for the Supreme Being Who was looking for reassurance that using numbers was a good idea. Proof by precedence: See, we've been doing this with such proficiency, that in itself is the best persuasion that the idea has merit and should be extended universally.

In terms of what we were doing, I was in a field of shifting metaphors. I was taken with the enthusiasm of Y1 and Y2. If they had ears, smoke would be steaming out of them. Now it seemed like we were figure skaters at a public competition and we had to execute flawless toe loops and triple axles to win high marks with the judges or else we'd be disqualified and have to leave the ice-skating rink. These alien gods and their sponsor, the Supreme Being, were tough judges; their reputation as hard-nosed critics impossible to please was justified. They were the kind of judges that would never put up the "10" card.

Skaters did not like coming up before their skeptical eyes, yet there were Y1 and Y2, spinning, jumping, extruding numbers prolifically out of their nimble minds, trying to win over the chilly judges. They were not even convinced there should be a skating competition at all. I hope you can keep up with my constantly shifting metaphors; they bewilder me at times too. These realities I have been encountering challenge the mind to come up with plausible ways to describe them, me pulling everything out of my metaphor bag to handle that.

Beneath their dazzle, Y1 and Y2 were recapturing the algorithms of the other five planets, including ours. It was like running a subset shadow algorithm that was quietly reacquiring all the essential number configurations for their collegial planets while outwardly they draped the attentive alien gods in glitter. At the same time they were deftly restealing the numbers, making a convincing sales pitch; I guess that means they were covering all the bases. Their fallback plan was that if the alien gods were not persuaded to "buy" their sales presentation, it wouldn't matter; they would have the algorithms back already.

They still had the obstacle of a certain immoveable brick wall, the God problem. They might be able to hoodwink the alien gods, for a time, at least, but the Supreme Being was an obdurate force Who owned the casino, the ice-skating rink, and the circus tent. They would still be up against that irrefutable fact at the end of their glittering show. It's the absurdity of a hand puppet rebelling against the hand wielding it. As a gesture, the defiance might be momentarily charming to watch, but it was still futile. It will fizzle out, leaving only wisps of smoke.

Meanwhile, as if deliberately discounting this fundamental fact, Y1 and Y2 were spinning out a proliferation of images, showing what their numbers could generate. They were like *piñatas* disgorging not toys and candy but a warehouse of psychic pictures, hands tossing piles of confetti with images on it into the air, letting the wind disperse the colored bits of paper, hopefully in the gods' faces.

Where did these guys get such confidence? I'll take a case of 12, thanks. Myself, I felt too beset with questions, doubts, queries, uncertainties. I wobbled. Blaise looked like he was pondering. Sal and Jocelyn seemed bewildered. The Hierophancy was up against the Ultimate here. I don't mean to sound histrionic.

But this problem, whether to commission the numbers realm to code reality and thereby Light grids and thereby the phylogenies these geometries supported, was the bedrock of what the Hierophancy deals with. Usually, we operated at the other end of this bedrock, adjusting the already existent Light grids when they got misaligned. Now we had to reconvince the Supreme Being these Light grids were warranted in the first place. If not, presumably He'd close up shop, turn off the lights, and start the next *Pralaya* early, right after lunch.

I turned my attention to our final colleague, G1, to see what he was doing. I had come up with this name as a compliment for his fabulous geometrical sense. G1 for first-rate geometer as he had crafted a planetary Light grid in hues of pale orange using one of the more complicated Archimedean Solids, one that almost defies seeing. By 3D humans, that is. His planet clearly was far more advanced than Earth and its humanity. It had received this geometrical upgrade in recognition of its achievements in consciousness evolution.

I said it almost defied seeing because its true form was in 4D, which requires nimbleness in perception and cognitive processing to see and understand or to walk around in. The many edges and vertices of this complex shape bore their arithmetical coding like watermarks on fine paper. It reminded me of a typical page in a book by C.G. Jung where often his footnotes took up as much space as the main text itself and often were even more interesting.

G1's planet kept asserting itself proudly against the alien gods' studied indifference. The alignment of its Light grid and physicality was seamless, and you could see much of the Light grid through the material mass of the globe. Its material aspect looked infiltrated with Light, as if its arterial network were transparent and you watched the blood flow through the see-through veins.

The planet, virtually in the faces of the alien gods, kept demonstrating the level of consciousness and cognitive processing the numbers realm made possible. It is what the business world calls proof of concept, the pilot project that shows the viability of the proposal, here, an advanced arithmetically-coded planet. See, skeptics, how smart this planet looks, how well the numbers work. How could you possibly say no to a project as bang-up masterly as this?

I tried to understand what was at play here. Say you're the Supreme Being, sublime generator of realities of all types, and You start second-guessing Yourself. Most of these realities consistently come up short. It's disappointing. You begin to wonder whether You should have

bothered. Is it worth mustering the required patience to sit around and play checkers against Yourself until the rest of the lot come up to speed and finally show signs of positive evolution?

Yes, G1's had merit. His was a good demonstration model in the new housing development of custom-built homes, but as for the rest, not so. They did not warrant the label "proof of concept;" rather, they refuted it neatly. If You needed a good reason to abandon the project, those other failures would do.

Would the Supreme Being second-guess Himself? Isn't that a human projection? You would think so except for the historical fact that The Boss did wipe out an entire generation of misbehaving humanity on the Earth, the brood of Lilith and Pandora and their Sumerian settlements like Sodom and Gomorrah. That was proof of wrath, a convincing display of Supreme God irritation. It shows He could, when sufficiently provoked, take steps, pull out all the plugs, drain the infernal human sink of all viability, life-force, and existential status. Were the rest of the Light-gridded planets for Him just more cities of the plain?

I couldn't answer that, so I stopped trying. It was time for the grand circus act for we six free-will trained planetary puppies to make our convincing display. We six, so we understood, came from planets that had higher than usual endowments of free will and Light grids of comparable sophistication. We'd have to serve as our own proof of concept. Had we been worth the investment?

What does it all come down to anyway, this gift of consciousness to us? Why bother? How is this better than the absolute non-consciousness "we" started with? You wouldn't know you had missed anything as you would not even exist. Work out that paradox if you can. Consciousness, then the history of its continuity and what principles you extract from it, then wisdom. Is that it? Again, is it worth it? Do it or not do it? The Supreme Being ponders the question. We would only know the outcome if He did do it, bestow consciousness on us.

The Light grid and its arithmetical basis follow from that decision. The Light grids of the many planets support the decision to bestow consciousness, to spread it around within phylogenies. The Hierophancy's job is to help maintain the viability of those Light grids to underwrite consciousness on the planets. But if we didn't exist, none of this would concern us. Should it concern us now? As to the possible desirability of non-existence, it's not the same thing as death. That is simply consciousness existing in a changed context, but it's still existent.

I shook my head. I know this is all sophomoric philosophical pondering. I'm not the first to come up against these paradoxes and throw platitudes at them. But the Supreme Being's apparent ambivalence has inspired these clichés. Is consciousness worth it? Why do people want to be conscious? To enjoy the 3D sensory world, most would say. But sensory blandishments are only a clever distraction, like the aromatic pollen and bright colors plants use to draw in birds.

Take the affective hormones out of the picture and it is all pretty flat and 2D. That's the disastrous moment when the dogs sprinting around the racetrack realize they're chasing an artificial lure. It won't taste like anything if they get it, and they begin to realize —*we* realize— that we've been perfectly duped by this. Screw

the dog race. I quit. I'll just lie down here in the sunlight and do nothing.

"Now you see why I spend all my free time in the Pleiades," said Blaise. "Less nonsense. You should lighten up, Frederick. You've become gloomy. You have to be careful with the Old Boy. Every time you think you've pinned Him down to occupying a describable, fixed position, He slips out of it like Proteus, and you're left with only the memory of shaped water in your hands: nothing. So you must be careful as to what conclusions you draw from the presumed data. The Old Boy is the perfect example of an antinomy, contradictory opposites existing, if paradoxically, in a reasonable, balanced relationship of Yes, No, *and* Maybe. He gives us all three with a smile and waits for us to come to terms."

I set out now to remember where I actually was, or at least seemed to be. I was in this room with Sal, Blaise, and Jocelyn, and each of us was occupying a vertex in that planetary rhombus of the four geomantic sites. Either my physical body or my Light body Double was out there in Tiwanaku and the other version of me was here. Either way, I had to re-anchor myself at both places.

Our respective sites and the arithmetical developments we had managed there were flashing in the room, a combination of strong-arm and dulcet sales pitch to these tough customers, the alien gods intent on retaining all their numbers. At the same time our 13 extraplanetary colleagues were doing the same with their planets, Light grids, and special "sales pitches" so that we comprised a team of 17 "salesmen" pressing our product upon an obstinate, irritating client.

I laughed again. The alien gods were nodding in satisfaction, seemingly flattered we had gone to such lengths to impress them with 17 delightful fronts. They had no problem attending to the 17 of us at once. I had the suspicion they regarded our presentations as nothing more than half-time entertainment, when the dancing troupe or acrobats flutter out onto the court and beguile us for 20 minutes, maybe accompanied by a smart band or singers until the game resumes.

Even though the four of us, ostensibly, were out at the four rhombus points, busy concentrating on our respective Light grid displays in this room, we were also huddled in a corner of this room discussing the latest developments, namely, the continued intransigence of the alien gods and the puzzling antinomy of the Big Chief for Whom we were applying all our talents.

My head was still reeling. It kept changing, what I thought we were trying to do. It had started with us trying to hunt down a thief, the one who had stolen our planet's arithmetical key. Now it seemed we were in an athletic performance demonstration, like figure skating, trying to garner the judge's high marks. It was surrealistic the way the playing field and rules of the game kept shape-shifting, and how the atmosphere kept modulating from Marx Brothers to Kafka to Glass Bead Game. We were antic, we were bewildered by unexplained demands, and we were possessed of a gravitas sufficient to playing a chess game for the world.

But who is the Magister Ludi here, the Master of the Game, or what is this trial about, or what will Harpo Marx next pull out of his voluminous clown's robe for us? God help me if numbers tumble out of his pockets. I shouldn't even use the word "or" because all three scenarios were equally relevant for us. It was a three-headed question with the faces of clown, judge, and philosopher.

"We should check in on the thousand participants Blaise rounded up for us," said the human Blaise. He was snickering when he said this. I could see the familiar outline of the amusement signature written on his face. He was referring to the project of rounding up a crowd of participating humans who would occupy key geomantic nodes and hold down the numbers there as a bulwark against further encroachment and removal from the Arithmetical Earth.

The angelic Blaises instantly transferred us to a small stadium, or maybe it was a large lecture hall at a university, big enough to seat a thousand people. Our adroit Blaises had rounded up those thousand and brought them in one of their bodies to this location. I guessed it was probably their astral Double. You will note my prevarication. Things had grown so fluid and instantaneous since we started out on this detective's troll for the thief of our planet's algorithm that I was reluctant now to make quick and sure interpretations of any phenomena. I was sure my score sheet would reveal me wrong far more often than I was right.

"These are unusual circumstances," said Blaise to the multitude of colleagues. "It is not that the Earth is under attack. It isn't in any normal sense. Rather, the Earth is being refuted, its managing arithmetical base called back to its source. All the numbers, equations, and algorithms that run the consciousness processes of our planet are being extracted by the mathematical gods who own them.

That is an odd way to put it, I know, but they own them because *they are* the collective consciousness that animates the entire realm of creative numbers.

"They in turn are the hand puppets of the Supreme Being Who is apparently now having a crisis of second-guessing and uncertainty, wondering whether the numbers should exist in the manifest world in service of the Creation or if He should call it a Day, or a *Life*, as in Life of Brahma, and go home to His *Pralaya* early and pack all the numbers in a box and slide it under His bed.

"We used to worry about the Nature Spirits revolting against humanity, throwing down their mandated responsibilities in protest against centuries of neglect and abuse by an uninformed or uncaring humanity. We got past that. This is worse. The elemental kingdoms superintend our physical form, emotions, and the organic containers for our awareness. The numbers realm runs our processes of consciousness; they manage the Light temples in us and their equivalents across the planet that support this conjoint Light grid operation of self-aware consciousness with which we and our Earth were originally endowed.

"That is now in jeopardy, or, as I suspect, it always has participated in this fundamental ambivalence, and it is only now, through the Hierophancy and our discovery of the master planetary algorithm, what I have called the Hierophancy heuristic algorithm, that we have perhaps penetrated to the core reality of the arithmetical realm. The Supreme Being has always been second-guessing Himself. As a one-man jury, He has never passed down a verdict. He's still deliberating and has been since the beginning. We're only now figuring that out.

We have to mount a convincing demonstration of the worthiness of the numbers and resolve that perpetual second-guessing and the threat of numbers removal. We have to persuade this jury to come in with a definitive 'Not Guilty' verdict."

Though there were more than one thousand of us in this large lecture hall, it seemed low-key, even intimate, like we were seated around a small oval conference table in a quiet room. The angelic Blaises had underlain our conference room with their Rotunda of Light and opened up its diamond geode to resemble a flowering diamond peony. The participants seemed only at arms-length from me and we were enveloped in the Ofanim's lovely diamond hexagons of Light. I only had to reach out to touch them. I saw innumerable images displayed around their heads and in their psychic fields, pictures and emblems of their many incarnations and what wisdom they had distilled.

I can't say I knew the names or particulars of all the participants, yet they seemed like friends, fellows of the Grail Quest and the Round Table, and certainly compatriots of the Hierophancy and our worldwide projects. Maybe over time, I had known them all, had experiences with each of them, worked important Hierophancy projects in various locales across the Earth.

One of them, a man about 50, started speaking. "I suppose we should see this situation as growth pains in the emergence of the new Golden Age. It started 45 years ago, but given its length of 1,728,000 years, it's still an infant. Right now it has colic or teething problems or some kind of complaint that you'd expect from a very young life-form.

"Our refashioned Light grid and the profound changes in psychic circumstances from the advent of the Golden Age in 2020—and let me not overlook the momentous unique incarnation of the Ofanim in believable human forms and I've been fooled many times by this—are still, like very young people, learning how to walk and make sounds and speak to us coherently. My point is we should have expected symptoms like these, because here they are and we as the 'parents' of this new offspring, our upgraded reality, have to find ways to cope with it."

"Yes, though the contrary interpretation seems just as valid," said a woman in her sixties. "As every parent knows, sometimes a fetus arrives still-born or if born successfully fails to prosper and suffers inexplicable crib death. Maybe that is what these perturbations by the arithmetical gods are about. A slow-motion crib death of the infant retooled Earth in the new Golden Age. A nice idea, good genetic stock, but somehow inherently flawed, and fatally so.

"The mythic records do record at least two failed attempts to create humans. These flawed phylogenies were quickly recalled, and even the third attempt, the brood of Lilith and Pandora, quickly enough proved defective too and was soon recalled. Maybe our new Golden Age is like that. Too many spiritual-genetic defects in the human psyche and the corresponding planetary Light grid argue for its removal. Maybe we, the fourth generation of humanity, are after all these centuries irremediably flawed and should be recalled too."

Another man spoke. "I used to lose patience with the bull-headed intransigence of humans and thought often of using that to justify packing it up, leaving the planet, and never looking back. Now it seems it's the arithmetical gods who are the masters of obdurate obstruction and I am losing my patience regarding their unyielding resistance. With all due respect, screw them and their stupid numbers. Let's all go home while the lights are still on. They could flip the switches any moment now leaving us utterly in the dark."

I grinned. I'm sure most of us had that thought tucked away somewhere inside and he had deftly, if crudely, voiced this suppressed frustration we all felt.

Another woman stood up to speak. "Yes, I'm sure we all share that sharp sentiment, yet we should not let it rule our actions. As members of the Hierophancy we made a commitment long ago to support incarnated existence. We agreed to maintain the interchange between the arithmetical realm and the world of Light grids, conscious life-forms, and dedicated planets requiring both. Dedicated as in appointed by the Designer-in-Chief to be places for incarnation.

"I submit it is our job, in this time of great indeterminacy and even wobbling at the highest levels, to hold fast to our mission to be the Revealers of the Holy Light, even if we have to reveal it once again to its own creator and the numbers gods. How do we know the Great Mystery is not running a Job-like loyalty test on us, pretending to doubt and waver and allowing His personifications as the numbers gods to appear to interfere with all Light grids and the planets they support? He is tricky, devious, multifarious, and, we must remember, He is an excellent card sharp. He empties the casinos every time. The winnings always pile up at His end of the table with Him sitting there grinning."

Sniggers and grins blossomed across the faces of our colleagues. She had nailed some key points with her pithy remarks. After all, He owns the game, the casino, and all of Las Vegas, the phantasmagoria of created existence. Mr. Antinomy, we should call Him: the intrepid poker player and sly game-rigger.

"We're in the position of pushing against an immoveable brick wall," said a man in the front. "We'll never push back this wall. We should walk through it."

His statement summoned images in my mind of the Hierophancy members confidently walking through this solid wall, the indomitable Berlin Wall at the far edge of existence, striding through its seeming impenetrability as if it were no more than a fog bank. It was possible, surely. Hadn't Blaise walked through a solid wall back in 2019 to escape that secure black-site prison in Utah?

A deep rumbling voice rose up amidst us as if from the floor. It was Blaise. The angelic ones, speaking from the millions of loudspeakers of their diamond geode which underlay our assembly. "Might we make a suggestion?"

Their many diamond facets gleamed with a brilliance like galactic suns. These guys know how to put on a grand show. The human Blaise was always telling me that. Though I suppose from their point of view it was simply their nature. Maybe it was God Who was showing off; He's the One Who made them. Their geode Light seared through my awareness turning clarity into a sword. I saw swords everywhere, so I assumed they did the same to all the Hierophancy. It felt good. The sword's edge of clarity came perfumed in the Ofanim's trademark Love from Above vibration, a delicious melting of consciousness into a state of bliss, focus, fondness, and the confidence you could understand it all.

That lush swell of confidence also brought a feeling of certainty, as if we were getting realigned with our mission and the mission with its purpose and its purpose with the original imprimatur from the Boss-in-Chief, free of wavering. As Hierophants, we were the Revealers of the Holy Light, and that Light was His. It was as much of His Mystery He was willing to divulge to the Creation, and we were charged, probably even created, to accomplish that disclosure. The Light grids and Light temples were the performance stages for that display. And the Blaises were here to sharpen the transmission of that grand divulgence to all sentient life-forms, even including ourselves when our comprehension faltered.

"We bring the Soma to create life-forms," said the Blaises. "Your job is to fit that Soma to the life-forms and where they live, which is their planets. Then to reveal that same Light in its original holiness to these conscious life-forms. And we help sharpen that revelation. You see, it all fits nicely together. We *like* that, not that we really have likes and dislikes, but if we did, we're sure we'd like it.

"The numbers are like the stitching that holds the fabric together, that keeps the Light grids fastened to the life-forms and their respective planets. It is easy to get entranced with the arithmetical realm. Qabalists have the same problem with their Tree of Life model. The mind can get entangled in its allurements, you can get lost in the endless permutations and the *Sefirot* thickets, and the numbers themselves can get a little self-absorbed with their importance.

"We offer these cautions often, and usually they are disregarded by most people. We say 'people,' but of course we refer to units of self-aware consciousness, like yourselves, like what you call the arithmetical gods, and like just about everything else in the Creation. They get tangled in the beard hairs. As you know, the Ancient of Days has such a long and, some say, scraggly beard."

I laughed. A lot of others laughed too. This was an obscure Qabalistic joke. It's the kind the human Blaise loves and was always coming up with. I saw an image of the Great Beard in which thousands of Qabalists and wanderers were struggling to machete their way out of the tangles. The *Zohar* makes great metaphorical usage out of describing the mystical significance of the Ancient of Day's Face, including His Beard upon whose hairs hang universes. The picture always reminded me of bearded college students with alfalfa sprouts bungee-jumping off their chins and getting stuck forever in the curling long whiskers.

But I think the meaning behind the joke is that the Supreme Being is complicated beyond any likelihood of us fully comprehending, probably the angels too. They probably stare at the Old Man and shake their heads. "His motives are beyond us," they might whisper to one another. And His Presence is ubiquitous, like a beard, His Beard, spreading out vastly and luxuriously across the chest of the universe. We'll get stuck somewhere in the vast unfolding syllogism, like trying to run fast enough to catch the end of *pi* and the last possible number *pi* could ever express. That's like mountain-climbing the Beard hairs in search of the Chin of the Great Smooth-Faced One. That is futile; there is always another digit in the infinite equation of *pi*, another tangled layer of hairs. I doubt the numbers gods will ever reach The Smooth Place either.

Blaise continued. "We awarded the Soma to innumerable forms of life capable of developing self-awareness and eventually achieving the nondual state of unitive consciousness. We are patient. The Life of Brahma is long; we can wait. Consciousness is the bedrock. It came first. Numbers tie it to worlds and grids. You interact with the numbers, grids, and consciousness, and we assist you.

"The numbers are implicit in consciousness like bones in a body, but awareness is senior. What enlivens the arithmetical realm is consciousness. What you call the alien gods of numbers is the collective awareness of that abstract numbers realm. We infuse that awareness, in fact, you could say we inspire it; we present it. We live within that awareness and see through the numbers, Light grids, and you. And, as you know, we have a lot of eyes to do that with."

By way of demonstration, the Ofanim increased the Light emitted from their diamond geodes. That Light seared through our awareness, turning it crystalline. I felt like I had many heads suddenly grown upon me like bulbs of Brussels sprouts on the stalk of my body. The same happened to everyone. Multiple heads, and each with a myriad of eyes. The Ofanim are famous for their eyes. They're called the Many-Eyed Ones, and many who have seen them agree.

They once told the human Blaise each of them has 8,466 eyes on their own manifestation form. I did the math on that ocular prolixity once: it comes to 341,271,097,344 eyes for the group. Can you imagine, one angel with that many eyes. There's more to their presence still: each Blaise angel, when they are dressed up for the angelic version of a gala occasion, such as now evidently, wears a robe with 3,456 sapphires and a crown with 14 emeralds. For a moment they flashed their full complement at us. The numbers are daunting but they paint the picture we had before us in the hall: 40,310,784 manifestations of the Blaise angels, 129,314,069,504 sapphires on the robes, 564,350,976 emeralds. You can potentially see this full spectrum in their Simorgh majestic divine bird form, the entire angelic family expressed as a single regal blazing Bird of Heaven. No wonder the "birds" went on pilgrimage to the Simorgh: God, what a bird it was.

Why so many eyes? So we can see things from all possible angles, they said modestly. They were seeing those angles. We were too. I thought it was a cognitive challenge to have a couple extra copies of myself running around in various places and dimensions. This was harder. I was seeing this spectacle of we 17 Hierophancy primary members, our 1,000 assembled helpers, the Blaise angels, the arithmetic gods, through 8,466 eyes. I needed a staff of a hundred to keep track of this dizzying proliferation of manifestation props and accessories. Each human eye has about 120 million rods; if I had as many eyes as a single Ofanim, that would be 1,015,920,000,000 rods I'd be deciphering the world from.

The spectacle of the Ofanim revealed in their full manifestation glory was arresting. I wanted to enter it and stay there forever. It was a vista of ultimate consciousness, the powers of awareness, bliss, focus, and Love from Above. It made the algorithmic thievery

we had been chasing seem moot, unimportant. It didn't affect the Blaises in the least, only professionally, in that that they had to help resolve the crisis, but otherwise they remained untouched by any of it.

It was a world in itself, this Planet Ofanim, this Blaise Reality, full of eyes, emeralds, wings, and sapphires, and always cheery. Let's not overlook the myriads of Light tendrils that stream out of their Simorgh form to connect with all manifest phenomena imparting consciousness to them. Lovely. Paradisal. Never a hermitic moment. There was no Supreme Being ambivalence in here, no arithmetical gods' duplicity. Screw both. I realized this fabulous zone was inside me, inside every human, just as I seemed to be inside it. I already had it. Really? I couldn't tell you what the difference was, maybe none, between inside it or out.

I was in a sphere of many hexagonal facets surrounding me. I must have been at the center with the closest ones pressing up against me like windows. I suppose this sphere was vast but I had no spatial frame of reference to estimate its size. It could just as well have spanned the universe as be the size of an atom. The main characteristic of it was I felt fabulous inside it. I could stay here always. It had a lovely stasis, a permanency, a complete wakefulness and assurance to it.

I felt like already I had been in here forever, and I wanted that forever to go on. I felt like I was wearing these many crowns, emeralds, and sapphires, and I was looking out through all those eyes. A Blaise angel with these attributes stood inside each crystalline hexagon. I was at the center of this spherical concatenation of angelic attributes and a consciousness with 40 million forms beholding existence through them. Strangely, it felt like I was in meditation too.

"You are in the *Ains*, the still, unmoving serene center of the Creation." It was a voice, oddly familiar, speaking as if all around me, though a bit muffled. Gradually, I realized it was the human Blaise speaking like a commentator for a travel documentary. He continued: "That center exists before the Creation, in the sense of being located in time before the emergence of the Tree of Life and Cube of Space. It lies outside this. Before this and senior or antecedent to this. Of course you love it. I do as well. It's what we still call the Black Bowling Ball.

"Note that it is surrounded by a collar of the angelic Blaises with all their finery. Robes, sapphires, crowns, emeralds, and all those eyes. That is the Blaises in their *Hokmah* guise, within the Tree and inside the Cube, though it lies still two chakras above your crown chakra. So there you are, in the full rich dark of the *Ains*, and surrounded by the fully illuminated glory of *Hokmah*. Here is a secret about this place: it is the womb of the numbers. The arithmetical realm is not born yet, reality is not deployed; both exist only as a potential inside the *Ains*. Nothing else has been manifested yet. The *Ains* is the great fetal sac of reality. It contains everything that will be; it is the home to which everything when created eventually returns. It is wonderfully implicit in this great black ball of nothing."

The human Blaise was laughing. All of his eyes looked merry. His laugh must have pulled me out of the trance I was saturated in while in the sphere.

"This is how you beat the antinomy. Do you see? You do it by seeing it from all possible angles. It's a field application of Zeno's Paradox. You cross the uncrossable distance by taking tiny steps. In this case, you bridge the seemingly intractable dichotomy in minute degrees, one eye at a time, until your 8,466 eyes encompass the polarities and thereby erase the distinction between both. The antinomy is thus overcome. No standing room remains for it to occupy. The eyes own the field. They eyeball every single degree lying between Yes and No."

I don't know how they did it, because the Ofanim looked like hexagonal diamond facets each studded with 8,466 eyes, and multiply that by 40 million, but they seemed to be applauding, or at least wiggling, squirming perhaps like puppies in a basket to whom the chance of a surprise treat was announced. What I'm trying to say is they were pleased the human Blaise got the connection. They started parading out of their facets with placards and bright banners that proclaimed "We Beat the Antinomy!" The words were wreathed with stars. Was I really hearing the triumphant blare of trumpets and toboggan-slide trombones?

The Ofanim are always entertaining, but they had made a vital point. This was the demonstration, the pilot project, for defeating the recalcitrant alien gods. And it wasn't even a defeat we were contemplating; we didn't need a defeat. The Ofanim showed us how to stitch the apparent discord and disparity between the arithmetical and manifested realms with multiple, minute angles of attention. In an outer world sense, it was laying innumerable pebbles to create a crossing over a stream. Patiently put down enough pebbles and you have a usable footbridge.

This way the two opposites would seamlessly blend or at least operate as an integrated whole. The Blaises would roll through our assembly of one thousand Hierophants like a field commander walking among the troops massed in the field, although as far as metaphors go, I would prefer we be a huge *commedia dell'arte* troupe and the Blaises our director, acting coach, prompter, and even the lighting technicians (and why not the audience too: they'd like us).

I say "roll" deliberately for the Ofanim are the Wheels of the *Merkabah*. That is the distinguished name for the Supreme Being's mobile Throne, the Chariot, and as the human Blaise once told me, the angelic Blaises as rolling wheels move the Ancient of Day's energy and attention throughout the universe. That means when they convey the characteristic *Sat Cit Ananda*, or what we simplify as focus, fondness, and amusement, they are "channeling" their Boss, rolling His ineffable vibration throughout the created worlds they roll through. It's as if the Blaises say, "We come as Love from Above, and so does our Boss."

It's genuinely mysterious, to me at least, but though the Ofanim of course were created by the Ancient of Days they still add their own inimitable touch to the rolling, a certain unmistakable quality of levity, focus, and fondness to the proceedings, revealing a key nuanced expression of the Boss-in-Chief. Or, to use a different metaphor, as Ganesh, they remove all the obstacles to consciousness, namely to us, our 13 extraplanetary colleagues, we mortals, apprehending the set-up, the plan, what's going on, what's expected to happen, and then staying awake and focused while it unfolds, maybe making jokes too.

Speaking of our 13 colleagues, they seemed acquainted with the Blaises. Even though, compared to us, they were only abstractly or cerebrally present with us, they acted like they knew the Ofanim well and liked them fine. Blaise had told me the Ofanim work with "people" on many planets, so here were some of them. I was curious what kind of jokes the Blaises offered them for merriment. The frame of reference for "alien" humor would likely exceed my grasp, but I suppose mirth and gaiety are emotional states deeper than language or culture.

I can't say I saw our buddies smiling, but I felt however subtle their cheerfulness. The Blaises have that effect on people; it's like a friendly effervescent infection. They look at you and suddenly you're full of bubbles, each a sun of amusement. I have learned you have to be lighthearted to prevail in this work; you don't want to get captured and sink disconsolately into one of those serious gravity wells. The Blaises say amusement is a pre-condition to reaching them. That is the baseline vibrational platform of where they stand in the world.

Chariot mysticism insights were not forthcoming from this outing, but the Blaises did seem to give all of us a quick ride to our respective geomantic tune-in locations. I enjoyed the roll; it loosened up my mind from its dire fixations. Sal, Blaise, Jocelyn and myself were back where we probably never left from, while the Blaises dropped off the one thousand Hierophants across the Earth. They knew the seating chart; they had probably drawn it up in the first place.

They also had a surprise for us. More Blaises showed up to accompany us, but these were the human-embodied Blaises, the ones who had incarnated starting in 2020. Each of us would have the company of a human-embodied

Blaise angel to hold down the respective digit in the Earth's algorithm at our local site. I imagined the jokes would work just as well on the embodied ones.

"This should kick some antinomy butt," said the human Blaise, grinning.

These extra thousand helpers suddenly appeared among us. They looked like people, men and women, but you could see the extra bits, the angelic parts. Inside each human form stood a translucent angel with flaring wings, eyes like stars, and lots of eyes, by the way, and a toroidal cycling of lilac Light in them. Their vibration was unmistakable, and it was delicious. I'll take a lifetime supply. I was a presold customer. I think everybody else was too. How do these guys do it? They feel so deliciously blissful, focused, serene, yet as smart as 40 million Ph.Ds. who could recite to you the full history of the world and universal reality over lunch and then finish with a toast to the Old Man and a few good jokes.

15

I found myself lying on the ground on my back when I woke up. How had I gotten into this position? Did I fall over or did somebody knock me down?

I didn't know. My head was a blur, spinning a bit. The one thing I was sure of was that we had failed. Despite our utterly impressive turn-out, the massing of 1,017 Hierophants, we had lost our supposedly winning hand and the arithmetical gods had grabbed Earth's algorithm again and taken all the numbers away with them. The Earth was bereft of its infrastructure, like its bones had been removed. I didn't see any of my colleagues, though they were never at Tiwanaku anyway. I looked around the site. At least they left us the stones of Tiwanaku. I should count them to make sure they're all still here. It felt bleak.

How could we have failed? We had everything going for us, hadn't we? Everything looked downcast, though I was probably viewing the situation through my own glum mood. Let me try to reconstruct what happened.

We deployed to our sites. The Ofanim provided transportation for the 1,017 of us, seemingly at the same time. I suppose they produced duplicates of their Rotunda of Light for this, whisking us off to our destinations like a fleet of taxis going in all directions, and while it was a kind of Chariot mysticism for us, an authentic ride in the Big Chair on Wheels, since their Rotunda, their Wheels, were a key component of the Old Man's *Merkabah*, I can't say I remember having any grand insights. The view was nice. I just remember arriving here quickly.

Somehow I was able to see everyone else arriving at their locales around the planet, settling in, preparing to fine-tune their awareness to the site's number. I saw my colleagues at their sites, the algorithm's number displayed behind them like a banner shimmering in the ethers, the number etched in neon, or maybe it was more like a wrap-around cylinder encasing the entire site so that the number was broadcast to the site and its features from all directions at once.

I may not have made this detail clear, but our 13 extraplanetary colleagues were deployed on their own planets, though in some strange but delightful way, those five planets seemed to be co-present with us wherever we looked on the Earth. It was as if the physical distance between them and Earth had been erased and the six planets enjoyed a shared space, the five being like guest sacred sites on Earth, and the reverse too, the Earth being present in their respective worlds.

I don't know how this was possible, but I found myself walking among these thousand sites like a field commander inspecting the troops. No, there was nothing military about our deployment, and maybe a better metaphor would be an athletic one, that I was the coach for a soccer team doing their practice drills, a very large team which was spread across a playing field the size of the planet. At every site the angelic Blaises had installed a copy of their diamond geode under the physical features and the Light temples so that every participant could draw upon the Light and sharpness of awareness the Ofanim's geode emitted. They were like a sponsor providing free brand new shiny sneakers to all the players.

Seen collectively and from a distance above, as if I were hovering in the atmosphere, these diamond geodes sparkled around the globe like a thousand large diamond rings. That deployment alone would have tremendously sharpened the feeling of consciousness on the Earth and would surely be registered by many people so they would feel suddenly, inexplicably, and delightfully, bright, lucid, and confident. That would be a subliminal effect pleasantly welling up into daytime consciousness that now felt wonderful.

I am thinking of those times when you feel unaccountably edgy, as if either the planets are mal-aligned or the Earth had borborygmy. There was none of that edginess now. Reality felt silken and happy. The people meditating at these sites expanded their consciousness field to encompass the site's assigned number so that I saw an ethereal outline of their incarnational form co-present with the official integer. Each site had a Hierophant, one digit from the master

algorithm, and many Blaises. It seemed like a strong alignment, even invincible.

Both digit and person seemed to occupy the same space and you could see one through the other, and both occupied the physical site like a beacon of Light, and this Light in turn illuminated the Light temple or complex of such features, turning them into brilliant sources of illumination. A number of Blaise angels (it looked like six) stood with each site meditator, and they didn't mind showing off a bit as their wings were flared out majestically like yachts in full wind, and the lilac toroidal cycling of Light through them was like a celestial fountain releasing gold and silver sparkles which dazzlingly gave their presence a dynamic aspect. Let me remind you that our 13 extraplanetary colleagues were co-present with us, as well as their planets' Light grids, and we were present on their planets.

I never thought the Ofanim were much given to singing, so it must have been the movement of the lilac Light in this forceful manner that sounded like an oratorio. Music emanated from them, somehow, delightful, merry sounds that cheered the participants; you could see the joy flushing their faces. Even Bach would grin to hear this. I saw Nature Spirits, elementals, and landscape *devas* watching from the edges. Were they tapping their toes in rhythm with the music? Maybe humming along? I probably imagined that. The results of this collective tune-in would surely affect the quality of their lives in a good way.

The Ofanim must have helped me with this because I was seeing the 1,017 of us as deployed across the planet at our sites. As I mentioned, around each person and site was a translucent cylinder comprising the integer from the algorithm. This cylinder was larger than the physical site which, for many locations, meant it was very big such as at Tiwanaku which spanned many acres. The designated number comprised the cylinder itself so that at whatever angle you observed this cylinder, all you saw was the wrap-around digit. Mine was 33. I felt this "33" encapsulated the full essence of the geomantic node I occupied.

The geomancer holding space there seemed to wear the numbered cylinder like an auric sheath, and you looked through his translucent body and saw the Light temples of the place and through them the physical features. The cylinder gave the impression of securing the site, person, and number to the Earth, like a deeply set bolt anchoring the location; it was as if the Earth's master algorithm was now fastened tightly to the Earth through these thousand bolts, and each was like a watermark uniquely identifying the site and its function. As instructed, each participant had also visualized the rhombus inside the hexagon, and these mind-projections surrounded each person like another temple of Light.

Encircling this planet-wide placement of the geomantic bolts were the alien gods. They were peering intently, curiously, at the display from the outside, and it was as if they had manifested a thousand faces with which to look in on it. Their faces spoke of interest, dismay, intrigue, fascination, puzzlement, and disdain—an unsettled mixture of reactions. They seemed slightly under duress, as if our competent, even forceful, display had a slightly coercive effect on them. I suppose they didn't like being forced to do anything against their own interests, and here we were, drawing their attention to a display they probably disfavored,

all of it designed to get them to seemingly act against their interests.

Each of the thousand geomantic sites was like a magnifying glass focused on one number in the complex algorithm. Collectively, this algorithm flashed around the Earth like a living arithmetical banner, plugged into a thousand electric sockets. Its illumination, its electrical charge, supported myriads of life activities around it. Each of our thousand colleagues was truly acting as a Hierophant. Their strong alignment with the site, its number, and cylinder was revealing the Holy (Numbered) Light, broadcasting it in concentric circles of illumination.

The design and intent of each site was thereby revealed to the landscape and all the life-forms and intelligences in the area. The display was like a grand parade, as floats rolled past proudly displaying the activities of the many civic organizations, its members dressed in their finest, flags rippling, banners announcing their names, bands playing marching tunes, sightseers waving. Here like bright ornaments were Earth's prime Light temples and Landscapes of Light.

Then the power went out and the Earth grew dark. The sites went black. I saw what had happened but I didn't believe it. It looked like the alien gods had as a group and all together at once grabbed the cylinder numbers, turned briskly around, and walked away from the Earth and the other five free-will planets. I am tempted to use the word "flounced" to describe their attitude in retreat as they stomped off clutching the digit cylinders like long uprooted tent posts.

A thousand alien god faces (I never saw any bodies, just the faces) were moving petulantly away in all directions from the Earth, each clutching a number from the composite algorithm, leaving the planet endarkened, its grid turned off. It was as if a thousand hands imperiously had reached out simultaneously and grabbed the numbers; then the alien gods turned as a group and stormed off. I had to give it to them: it was wonderfully choreographed, nice dramatic flourish, even though it spelled the doom of the Earth and the other planetary Light grids.

Yes, "doom" is a ponderous word, but the peremptory removal of the algorithm's numbers seemed to guarantee planetary disaster and dissolution. The Norse seers would say here comes the doom of the Light grid upon us. The Sun appeared to be still shining on the planet, but it felt dark; its psychic field was dimming. A kind of fearful, perhaps unprecedented, psychic anemia was setting in. The Light temples started to look thin and flaccid, becoming unstable and unmoored. A few seemed to be floating or bobbing like boats on a rough sea. The inherent chaos of pre-Creation was reasserting itself. I appreciated the degree to which the Light grids had established and preserved necessary order. As the Egyptians might say, horrible Isfet had returned to claim our Earth life.

I held something in my hand. It felt like a coin I must have picked up here. It looked like a gold medallion. It was quivering, even humming, possibly singing. It wasn't a coin or medallion, but only vaguely resembled those forms. It was a sphere made of Light that winked in and out of a vague materiality. I suppose it was somewhere between Light and matter, what physicists call plasma. At first I didn't remember where I got it from, then it came back to me.

I had been hanging in a large tree like an apple ripening in the delightful sunlight. I was in proximity to other apples also maturing on the boughs. They felt familiar, friendly, even collegial, in an odd way. My friends are all apples. What on Earth did this mean, hanging applelike on a tree? For some reason, the sheer strangeness of this impression didn't concern me, only that I didn't get the apple symbolism. Then another odd thought intruded itself into my mind.

Myself, as this singing apple, I was like a single richly intoned note from a fabulous aria, something musically delicious, from Puccini perhaps? It was just that one note but all the beauty it encapsulated and ravishingly alluded to was just beyond itself, as if on the next bough. I was holding this apple in my palm, and it only remotely looked like a found object An apple? In fact, it was much larger than an apple; it was an immense sphere, one whose size kept burgeoning further outward as I relaxed into its mystery. It was more like a singing soap bubble, a sphere of Light and sound the size of a house, maybe a planet. I expected numbers to be associated with it, to script its shape and function, but I didn't see any yet; it had the level of design and complexity that suggested them.

Let me explain what I think this singing Light bubble was. Imagine a sphere of Light that somehow summarized your entire existence, all your lives in whatever life-form you tried out and on whatever planet those forms lived. Not only did it contain the future and eventual complete historical record of all those incarnations, your own personal *Akashic* Records library, but it presented their overriding theme and all the secondary themes too, the complete inventory of purpose motivating your serial incarnation odyssey through universal time. It was the germplasm for a soul's incarnational odyssey, its unique perspective.

Distill the actions, thoughts, emotions, traumas, and extracted wisdom from those eventual lives into a single focus, a particular, perhaps unique, angle of attention and pure feeling quality, an original nuance, not an emotion but a sensibility of consciousness, a scent, the way flower blossoms have their own distinctive aroma. Think of roses, how one aromatic whiff summons to mind all roses, the essence of rose, Roseness, you might say. That's what this sphere did.

This scent, sound, note, feeling quality, however you evoke it, was deeper than any sense of yourself you might have concocted in a phenomenological sense, in the context of being a selfhood collecting experiences or pursuing specific goals. It was deeper than that, antecedent, primordial; it was your foundation. It was how the Supreme Being sees you, how He first created you, when this "you" was a perfectly crafted bubble of eventual pure consciousness, and the "you" you would gradually become and knew yourself to be now, was merely a sketch in the mind of your Higher Self in consultation with your spirit. It was God's Idea of you, of your soul's unique formulation, different than all the others, even if by just one gene or spiritual angle of sight, but necessary to the complete pattern of Creation He had in mind when He got up this morning.

I settled into this mystery of original Being as if it were a relaxing bath. It was a complete environment of sound, scent, awareness, and assurance. How often we look for that quality, the complete assurance of the worthiness of what we are doing, of what we are, that reality itself is justified and not inimical to us. An end to doubt and second-guessing, to feeling incomplete, missing something.

This was a moment before the travails of incarnation, before the alien gods who were the recalcitrant faces of the arithmetical realm, before they became a problem. This was a purity of consciousness as if you had just emerged, still dripping wet, taking the cure, from the hot tub of the primordial *Ains*, that most exquisite spa, and you were flush with certainty, conviction, and imprimatur.

The incarnated worlds had not yet begun. Everything was still deliciously fetal. An idea perhaps, something to look forward to, to step into and sample, but not yet. Still, I knew somehow that the particular organization of this bubble of sound, scent, music, and pure feeling that "I" was, even before I had generated a self, was special. I don't mean that in any elitist sense, as better or more chosen than others, but simply in a functional sense, like one tool in a large toolbox that when the moment arose would be just the tool the carpenter next reached for or like I played the humble triangle in a symphony orchestra and a moment would come in the concert when that simple bright tingling was perfectly called for and I had to stand ready to gently clang this triangle of metal at that precise moment. A moment will arise some day when precisely what I am is just what is needed.

Let's say the Supreme Being has an infinity of angles of attention. One of them is you, or in this case, me. At some point in the vast unfolding saga of the Creation, your angle of attention will be called for, will be acutely relevant. Your name will be sounded.

This sphere is like a name, but not in words or numbers.

An essential vibrational signature, a unique watermark, not unique in general terms but definitely unique at the minutest level of particularity, with perhaps just one slight difference from all the other names, that one angle of attention. When that moment arrives, perhaps billions of years in the future from your starting point, *you* will step forward, without even thinking about it, and take *your* place, adding yourself to the unfolding syllogism of universal Creation.

Raised arms with clenched fists surrounded me as I sat in my bubble. I heard a roar, many roars, the vibration of mighty wings, a rich flush of heat. Innumerable diamond wings fluttered underneath me and it seemed my bubble bounced gently on a rising platform of identical diamond facets like hexagons. That was the Ofanim of course, and the fists, roars, and heat flush belonged to Hanuman, their guise of a mighty flying monkey and ardent devotee of Rama.

He has a monkey's head set on an upright human torso. His strength is fantastic; he can shapeshift, fly, move entire mountains; he's ugly on the outside, divinely radiant and beautiful inside; and his *bhakti* towards Lord Rama is unwavering. Hanuman was not so much aggressive or defensive in posture, just fierce, and his passionate avowal of the primacy of consciousness aligned with Christ-Rama was unsurpassed in the pantheon of Hindu gods. The Ofanim, as the Blazing Star, are the way for humans to reach the Christ. In their Hanuman guise, they amped up that fact and highlighted the ardency and devotion it had.

It's as if Hanuman was declaring without even speaking, These bubbles exist, and are supposed to exist, and they are gloriously existing, and we shall uphold this. Under their aegis I flushed forward into the present moment of Frederick existence at Tiwanaku and the whole Light grid and arithmetical fiasco, then I retracted into the inviolate cosmically fetal primacy of the bubble.

I noticed the bubble was slightly different now, as if it had been deformed in a subtle way, and now that deformation was corrected and perfectly spherical. It was like tuning a piano where one or two keys are slightly off perfect tone, and now they are adjusted to their intended vibration. My bubble felt fixed like that. In retrospect, I think I was viewing the bubble's history along its own timeline, from creation to deformation to restitution of its original perfection of form.

I popped from fetal quietude into ferocious incarnation again, seemingly spanning billions of years of unfolding cosmic life and my own incarnation saga. Only a millisecond transpired. I fluctuated from being immersed in the awful dilemma of the arithmetical gods extracting all the numbers from the incarnated world and existing before that was even a flickering thoughtform in the postulating mind of the Planner of cosmic reality. I felt like a yo-yo spun out then retracted or like a Jack-in-the Box snapping out brusquely into the manifest world —Hi! I'm Frederick. I'm incarnated.— then yanked back into the box.

The arithmetical world was a problem and it wasn't a problem, but in both the extrapolation into the incarnated world and its retraction back into the serene nonmanifested domain Hanuman accompanied me, fists raised, roars sounding. He is the remover of all obstacles to consciousness and its destiny to participate in the nondualistic blissful singularity of Christ Consciousness, the Rama Reality. I had a tremendous problem and I had no worries in the world. I was becoming antinomial myself, in emulation of the Great Antinomy Himself.

The arithmetical gods were draining reality of all its numbers, but Hanuman, the Ofanim dressed up as the fearsome monkey-god, didn't need numbers to exist. Hanuman existed, as did copies of Hanuman surrounding innumerable Light bubbles. Numbers could come along later. All these individual names, the notes, frequency signatures that hung like vibrant apples alongside me on this vast tree of the cosmos, the Tree of Souls most likely, were flanked by roaring Hanumans who held them like beach balls of great value.

Inside each of these beach balls was a spirit like myself, in the sense of existing in a pure form before taking on a recognizable life-form, such as human, and each was holding its little coin-like sphere comprising its name. It's as if the Supreme Being invited all of us to a grand birthday party and gave each a name badge to wear prominently on our chest so everyone knew one's name. Then He assigned Hanuman to be the party's security chief and general host, smiling or scowling as appropriate, and maybe roaring occasionally for effect. I looked at my sphere again. It did not contain any numbers, yet I suspected in some manner when it was "plugged" into the proper receptor, it would generate a series of numbers, perhaps even an equation that contributed to the algorithm.

I felt sad about this. It seemed like a lost opportunity. It had looked great, and now it had fallen flat. We were staring at a disaster. I wouldn't get to do it. I didn't see my immediate Hierophancy colleagues either. I suppose Sal, Blaise, and Jocelyn were at their respective geomantic nodes within the rhombus similarly surveying the wreckage of our plans and the imminent demise of the planet as its Light grid had all its numbers sucked out through this alien straw. Our immediate prospect seemed to be watching the Earth grow anemic, then faint, then eventually start to collapse, its consciousness project defeated. The bright promise of Hanuman and his beach balls was dissolving around me.

Earth would not be alone in this dismal outcome. All the planets supporting consciousness were in the same predicament as their life-force got drained out. Prior to 2020, people used to come up with all sorts of grim futures for the planet, darkly envision the ways in which planetary life would collapse and get miserable. It had always seemed to be a strikingly clichéd failure of the human imagination to conceive of a brighter future. The darkened negative Apocalypse everyone imagined was distressingly widespread in those years. People seemed to expect, to *want*, complete disaster and civilization collapse.

Now it looked, impossibly, implausibly, to me, like they were right. I doubt anyone thought it would play out like this, this global exsanguination of the Light from the planet's etheric body and organizing grid: their numbers gone, the Light grids stop working, and gradually planetary life, consciousness, and viability drain out of the Earth's geomantic and ecosphere systems as we go the slow-motion blighted way of Maldek. Anyone want the movie rights?

The outline of our geomantic rhombus was growing faint. The Light temples at the respective locations the four of us occupied were unmoored. They seemed to float above the sites and looked tilted, crooked, out of alignment, as if somebody kicked them or the gravity field securing them to the ground was off. All across the planet it looked as if the bones were coming out of Albion's body and were massing in a confused jumble of shanks above the planetary form. You'd need a forensic anthropologist to reconstruct his original form from this.

I saw the same thing happening on the other planets. There were too many to see. It was a general impression I had that these many planets were losing their Light grids. I had the impression the geomancers for these planets looked dismayed as they witnessed their planets being disassembled before their impotent eyes. They understood the mechanism of this dismantling, but couldn't do anything to stop it. They watched as the operational numbers got vacuumed out of their Light grids. Reality was being sucked down the cosmic drain.

I tried to figure out where this left me and the Hierophancy members. Out of a job, it looked like. Out of a life mission. Short one viable planet. I was close to 90 and Blaise was 115, so maybe it was time to call it a day. Leave the Earth. Take care of the *Bardo* paperwork and see what comes next. Maybe nothing. Maybe our hierophantic work was done. If there were no Light grids in operation because their managing numbers had been recalled, probably there were no viable incarnational venues and maybe even the higher subtle worlds were now in jeopardy. No Light to reveal. The Supreme Being had retreated invisibly behind

His *Pargod*. Pack things up and trudge back to the Throne and go home.

What is the ultimate fallback position? Inside the Throne. Pack things up and return to the Supreme Being. We'll have to do it one day. The only thing of interest against that ultimate return is my sphere of Light with my name. I was still holding it in my outstretched palms as if it were an offering in search of a temple. It looked slightly deformed again or dented perhaps, and it was not fully illuminated. I didn't understand what it was any longer or what I was supposed to do with it. All I was sure about was that it felt incomplete, yet it was mine.

Why did I mention the Throne? Because that's where these bubbles came from. The Throne is a metaphorical way of representing the Supreme Being. The Old Boy is formless after all; you'll never see Him, only what C.G. Jung called God-images. Anyway, He's inside the Throne, and when you return to God, that's where you go. Into the Throne and its primordial unitive consciousness.

It's funny, in a sense, because our fate now seemed to be worse than what happened to the generation of Lilith and Pandora. They got removed from the physical world and refused any further incarnation in the human phylogeny on the Earth. They remained exiled on some astral islands, according to the myths. But they could still look through the "windows" into our world, see what was going on. The world kept going; the Earth still had its numbers and Light grids. They just couldn't be part of that anymore. But our exile will be more profound than that. There will be no outside world any longer, no windows to look through. We didn't misbehave and trash the place; God just lost interest in us.

My sphere didn't roll properly and when it glided through the air it seemed lopsided, like a poorly packed moving truck. A few areas were opaque, like windows somebody had sprayed white paint over to insure interior privacy. I felt the vibration of my name (be sure to know I don't mean "Frederick" here) was off, missing a syllable, being repetitively mispronounced, wrongly accented.

Everything about the bubble and its contents was slightly subluxated from its original alignment, its starting "factory" condition. I felt a little brown in tone. Brown as in heavy, gravity-dominated, somber, and trudging. Brown is a slow vibration and people who are in a brown study are gloomy, deeply absorbed in a melancholic reverie, in common usage, spectacularly down. I used to come across this phrase in Agatha Christie stories from the 1940s, and I even had to look it up. People didn't say that anymore. Except I was in one now.

What had happened to my Light bubble? Somewhere along the line it had degenerated, suffered knocks and bruises, pushing it out of alignment. Even though I wasn't in a body while my attention lay inside the bubble, I felt I was standing crooked, as if leaning to one side or one shoulder was slightly lower. I felt brown smudges on my mood, as if I'd been besplattered by a spew of mud.

Certainly I had grounds for despondency given the recall of all the numbers, but my brown study did not originate from that. It pre-existed that development. I shivered. Had this brown study predisposed me in some subtle, unsuspected way to fail in my role at convincing

the Supreme Being to keep the numbers in play and order the arithmetical deities to get their heads back in the game of life?

Then my thoughts plunged into an even darker place. The others in this hierophantic field project must have had their own brown smudges, surely. It couldn't all have been due to my grim contamination. Or could it? Could one person's brown study distort an entire hierophantic field of input?

I was feeling mortified. Shit. That's the last thing I'd ever want to do, screw up the whole project and wreck the prospects for my colleagues and their home planets. It was at this point I began moving towards the Throne, wherever it was. I called out for it. Okay. It's my fault. Take me back for purification, realign my wheels, change the oil, put in new sparkplugs, or bench me for the remainder of the game. I willingly accede to my own disqualification. I'm guilty.

The last thing I remember was a flash of Light, first golden, then silver, then white. I was blinded. I felt my bubble getting washed clean absolutely. It was like a baptism that restarts the world. Then just before I winked out, I knew that everything was reversing itself, that I had perceived the pattern completely backward. I had misread everything. It was like the surprise resolution of the inexplicable case in Agatha Christie's *Murder on the Orient Express*. Seriously?

Surely one or at most two passengers in the Calais coach had committed the stabbing, yet Hercule Poirot could not convincingly prove that, or anything. Everyone could have done it but nobody seemed definitively to have. Then the true pattern emerged, and it was the opposite of what the cleverly designed crime had suggested. It wasn't one person. He had misread the crime scene. Poirot sat back in his chair and appreciated the clever picture puzzle, its true outline and the correct placement of all the pieces as now revealed to him. He could now announce the culprit and explain the intricacies of the baffling case.

16

Blaise was looking at me with a half-concealed smirk. He seemed pleased with himself. "It was you, Frederick, all along. You. You stole the algorithm. It is you we have been following, detecting. You have been at the core of this case."

What? You will not be surprised, I trust, when I tell you I had nothing to say in return. I heard his words but my mind hadn't processed their meaning. Eventually, it did. Blaise was saying I was the guilty party, the key suspect at the core of it all. But how could that have been? I was chasing after the alien gods along with the rest of the Hierophancy. I wasn't one of the arithmetical deities. I was a principal detective on the case of first-degree thievery. What had I done?

Blaise allowed me a few more moments for my flummoxing to wane.

"You will excuse my little pique of drama, dear Frederick," said Blaise in a conciliatory tone. "I couldn't resist the opportunity to play it out. Here is why it has all lain at your feet. It's that Light bubble you were holding in your hands. You saw that it was slightly out of alignment. Its vibrational signature was crucial to completing the Light grid pattern and securing all its arithmetic to it.

"That's because when it was first extrapolated *your* specific contribution was a final step in the activation of the system. We had to take *you* through all the steps by which the Earth's Light grid and ruling algorithm were devised to retrieve this and purify it. You were unlikely to actively remember it all, so we helped. We simulated a convincing scenario in which you would have to retrace your steps through the long process by which the arithmetical realm coded the Earth's Light grid and put it in working relationship with the five other worlds.

"We took you through the steps, here on the Earth and elsewhere, by which we devised the Hierophancy heuristic algorithm, with the full support of the Supreme Being and the vexatious alien arithmetical gods, as we have enjoyed calling them. In truth, they have been most cooperative in our retrieval project. For a time, though, we let you form a notion of them as Arithmetical Angels, the alien oppositional gods, possibly even once mortals who got upgraded, who acquired knowledge of mathematics and then used it to undermine humanity. This often happens in investigative work anyway: the detective entertains then eventually discards notions of the perpetrators, assigns tentative identities to the presumed bad guys, then later discards all of this when they clue in on the truth.

"We introduced a small amount of deviation and disruption to the arithmetical matrix to make a convincing demonstration of the supposed problem. You had to buy the problem for this retrieval process to work. You had to believe it. We made sure this structured deviation was easily, quickly reversible. We have already corrected for this controlled burn on the algorithm's systematic integrity. The Earth is not in peril; all its Light grids and temples are working perfectly.

"Similarly, regarding some planets you saw divested of their arithmetical infrastructure by the numbers recall and their physical aspects left withered and their dominant species disappeared and without biological forms, that was an inverted perception too. Rather, you were seeing the steps originally taken to code those worlds to support life-forms; you saw the arithmetical 'blood' being *infused* into their Light grids and reality structure to enliven the biological forms.

"A few planets, though, failed on their own account, but not from alien god sabotage. You saw them in their devastated condition. Their consciousness phylogenies failed, like progeny of Nature, offspring that was too weak or poorly constituted genetically to survive their incarnation. When the species failed, the numbers failed because they were no longer in the vitalizing reciprocal loop of consciousness and numbers that keeps both healthy. That's why they failed.

"These last three months you were reviewing all the steps you as a soul and acting through a succession of lives as a Hierophant and geomancer took to help us devise this final master algorithm. We helped you where we could. You thought you were moving forward in time, towards the future on your timeline over these last three months. Certainly the calendar moved forward a hundred days, but in your experience you were moving the opposite direction on your timeline, into the far past, going in reverse against the current of the syllogism that led you to this moment, passing through all the layers and connections of your participation in the creation of the Arithmetical Earth and its Light grid.

"Your Light bubble was a key component, one added towards the end of the complex mathematical syllogism that yields the heuristic algorithm. It took a lot of digging through your time records to unearth it. It needed cleansing. But you had to unwrap many layers in your past life experiences to get to it. Think of it in terms of stratigraphy. It lay close to the bedrock layer of yourself. Your experience was like walking a labyrinth. There is a point when it seems you are the furthest you could be from reaching the center; you have just nudged it in a walk-by and now you're out on the periphery again. Then in one loop you're in the center, finished. That's when you found the bubble. It looked the darkest then, that you and the rest of us had failed; in truth, you were only steps away from the labyrinth center and completing the mission, and now here you are."

Then Blaise grinned. "The only confusing bit was you saw this in reverse. I suppose there was no way around that distortion. You reversed the causal sequence and saw all the components that had necessarily and in perfect accordance with divine rationality contributed to the syllogism of generating the algorithm as if every component was taken away from you, leaving nothing. You saw it as a disassembling process, but in truth it was a coherent assembling. You examined all the parts that comprise our wonderful, really masterful, algorithm. You saw the awesome extent to which the arithmetical realm infiltrates all reality, though, seeing it in reverse, it seemed like it was opposed to the Creation and sought through a myriad of clever tactics to remove reality from arithmetic.

"You saw you could never beat the alien gods. That was frustrating. They always undid or countermanded whatever clever tactic we came up with. We almost wanted to kick their butts too. That's because you were up against the invincible, inextricable, and completely necessary binding of numbers and reality. They cannot be separated ever, except at the conclusion of this round of the Life of Brahma. They are *meant* to be intermeshed like this. You were seeing all the nuances of this required, inseverable connection, but because you saw everything in reverse, it seemed a conspiracy against you, all cards opposing you.

"You spent a fair amount of mental time trying to construe the agency involved in this theft, trying to fit some personification on the invisible intruders. Ultimately, you were entirely wrong in all your attributions, although it provided a focus to sharpen your investigation. Somebody has to be at fault. The arithmetical gods were the prime miscreants and cosmic reality lay in ruins. You saw them acting like a metastatic cancer infiltrating the body mass of the planet's arithmetical system. You saw them rewriting the Light grid coding, taking over everything mathematical in Earth reality. You saw it all backwards, in a mirror.

"The frightening prospect of their corralling all the planets, their Light grids, and arithmetical codes in a universal Magic Square was a misperception. Read it in reverse. You were actually seeing the innate embeddedness, the perfect congruity, of all arithmetically scripted planets in this universal matrix. Think of it as the master Light grid that houses and organizes the arithmetical realm. This Square is a library of the possible mathematical models for patterning the Light, the complete permutation table. You saw it as a totalitarian-style prison for planets, but in fact it is the natural, God-mandated anchorage point for all created worlds. It has a necessary, benevolent role in the Creation, a matrix for mathematics, but in your quest as arithmetical detective, you saw it in reverse.

"You further thought the aliens were out to steal God, capture Him and lock Him up in this cage. To inexorably advance on His infinity of numbers and claim as much of this ever-expanding domain as possible. A truly fascinating idea, Frederick, but see it again in reverse: this was the innate original context, entirely mandated, for all these mathematical permutations. They were in God's Big Hands. Who else but the Master Magic Square Master, the famous Chief Permutationist, could hold them? They didn't have to run after God's infinity.

"They already had it. They were the arithmetical domain, infinite and self-aware. They *already are* the intelligence of that infinite realm of numbers in all their possible combinations. You saw them trying to acquire this. The truth is they have been this from the beginning, but either way, you now appreciate their infinite extent.

"It was the same with your Maldek memories. You thought they intruded a corruptive geomantic gene or formula into the arithmetical matrix to eventually ruin the Earth by stealing its heuristic algorithm. Again, the truth is the reverse. We incorporated the *best* of the Maldek mathematics into our new Earth formula. Why not? It was viable; it worked, produced good results; it was achieved wisdom of continuing practical value in this new geomancy. In truth, you were retracing your original steps by which we generated the master algorithm that runs the Earth's Light grid. You reviewed all the steps involved except in your understanding you reversed the causal sequence. There was no way around it.

"It was particularly necessary to introduce you again to the nexus of six planets and the implicit seventh their relationship generates. These were our 13 alien colleagues from the other high free-will-endowed worlds. You thought the arithmetical deities were ruining this beautiful cosmic snowflake of six planets and their implicit mother-seventh and that if they took the meta-algorithm or one from any of the six planets, including the Earth, it would compromise the unit. You will see more of this seventh planet shortly; you'll see it plays a crucial role.

"The truth was you had to retrace your steps through this starting point of the sevenfold nexus, the sphere-packing business, the equation and what it meant. It was important that you realize the connection between Earth's scripted algorithm and the system that links these five and the seventh they all generate because our algorithm derives from that higher assemblage of algorithms and it has special trap-doors opening into that of the other five and the seventh planet.

"This was part of the arithmetical background, the originating context, in which our Hierophancy heuristic algorithm was born. So you had to review this again. Even that seeming three-week fugue where we went about in a daze and lost track of ourselves and the algorithm problem was part of this; we had to go along with your distraction because it was part of your mental retrieval process.

"The arithmetical realm, though possessed of a collective consciousness, is constrained like the angelic orders to complete obedience to the divine dictates. It cannot rebel and act against the prescribed interests of the Creation and Creator. This realm is a numbers extension of the Supreme Being's Mind. They are the Supreme Being expressing Himself mathematically, perfectly executing His intentions in the enumerated realm. But we subtly encouraged you to personify their seeming actions a little more than was accurate to provide suitable motivation for your quest. Every mystery needs both a good detective and a convincing villain. So you helped create the bad guys, that of the disobedient, rebellious numbers, while you fulfilled the role of the able detective.

"Then you moved on to considering the theft an act of cool, neat revenge by the outraged gods, nonplussed something shocking by the Supreme Being's gift of Soma to the upstart, undeserving, ignorant brats of the cosmos known as human beings. The alien gods stole the algorithm to ruin human chances on this new planet, and they took it at just the right moment to exert maximum damage. That was wrong, too. Do you see now? Many of those gods helped, even voluntarily, in fact, the Earth and humanity, and worked to sustain the operational integrity of the Arithmetical Earth and its Light grid deployments.

"You may have wondered why we had such minimal input from Ray Master Hermes, the Pleiadians, and Elohim. Under other circumstances they would have done much more but because this was your quest for memory retrieval, we had to leave the bulk of the onus and pressure upon you, Frederick. That's why it often seemed these able masters were simply standing around, whistling and shuffling their feet when they could have been helping you.

"Sorry about that. Certainly, the Pleiadians could have told us who took the algorithm. Can you appreciate the irony? Nobody took it. But they were in on our little deception; that's why they refrained from telling you what the game was. The Pleiadian expertise in mathematics was another grid component you had to touch on in your retracing of the steps that led to our Light pattern. It wasn't necessary for them to tell you anything, only for you to review this, to appreciate the important role they played in the creation of Earth's Light grid.

"We also had to nudge you up against that fundamental paradox of the Supreme Being. Is He for or against the numeration of an outer reality? Is the Old Man gripped by an unresolved dichotomy, a basic antinomy between pixellation and dissolution, and were the arithmetical gods in fact His agents, and in fact was the Hierophancy too, and we had it all embarrassingly backwards and now finally got it right that we were allied with the arithmetical gods and charged with safeguarding their forays or refusals to be active in the outer world?

"But here it was important for you to remember how the arithmetical realm came out of the Supreme Being, how it is a mental personification, His Mind in action enumerating the cosmos. Of course the numbers do His bidding, but that bidding, as you saw, is complex, convoluted, even seemingly altogether contradictory. Antinomy is a constant of the Supreme Godhead; we can't fix it or change it. To see it then accept it as an unalterable fact of reality is crucial.

"A being who is infinite in extent and duration will manifest every possible trait, so from this viewpoint, He will be rife with contradictions, big, glaring turn-abouts and inconsistencies where it appears He's walking North and heading South and saying Yes, No, and Maybe to all questions which logically would seem to stalemate all forward progression, yet you look at your feet: they are moving. Our job in the Hierophancy is to work within this basic antinomy, to keep both ends of it as balanced and reciprocal as possible. But we let you explore the full nuanced expression of this contradiction, all the way to the point where you just about concluded the Supreme Being was our enemy.

"It seemed to me at the end that everything I tried had failed," I said.

"Yes, that would have been dispiriting," Blaise replied. "That was the way it seemed because you were still locked into the misperception of the problem. The opposite was true. Every step you took succeeded brilliantly; you just didn't understand the intended outcome. You were looking in the wrong direction. You saw all the steps in the great arithmetical syllogism, but you saw them inverted."

I suddenly took stock of where I was. I was back in our Sun Valley offices. So were

Sal, Jocelyn, and Ray Master Hermes. They looked like they had just heard a fine joke and were still marveling at the unexpected, adroit punch line. I wondered if I had ever physically left this office or had all this been in my mind? I took stock of myself. How did I feel hearing this disclosure? It feels quite odd, unsettling, really, to be fooled to this shocking degree when you're 90 years old. You don't expect that. I never guessed, never suspected, that I had everything backwards, and that Blaise, the Ofanim, and presumably the Big Guy Himself, were running a misdirection program on me. Still, I appreciated the tactics now.

"You had much to do with creating the algorithm in the first place," Blaise continued. "You were not a mathematician in this life, but in certain earlier incarnations you were and quite a capable one. The Arabic life was one of those. We followed you through your recollection process, walking with you through your mental processes and data storage retrieval like we were all in a hologram.

"We had Sal, Jocelyn, and myself deploy to three key geomantic nodes and reveal the workings of the numbers and the Light grid scripting. You went to the fourth. This was to give you a fourfold illumination of more key processes. That rhombus is a valid geomantic fact of the Earth's energy design. That was genuine, but we had to reacquaint you with its four locational aspects. Still, it was inefficient to send you alone to the four so we divided it up and our reports gave you a live holographic window into the arithmetical realities of these nodes.

"You explored three more nuances of the structure of mathematics and the derivation chain of our master algorithm by seeing through

their eyes. We contrived our experiences to seem fraught with jeopardy. You saw them in the context of the fourth, you at Tiwanaku. Nice, don't you think, in terms of special effects, heightened drama, and misdirection? All four of us encountered some high drama and seeming failure despite our awesome cleverness. That was hard for Sal. He is truly a mathematics wizard so being stymied like that was a stretch. These four sites to which we dispersed are crucial to the Light grid upgrade. The geomantic rhombus was not just a flimsy stage prop set up for this performance.

"The Blaises told me at the onset we had to gently but steadily induce you to remember the starting point, that key ancient moment when your Light bubble extruded from the Supreme Being's Throne and manifested itself, bearing that key vibrational component. Try to conceive of that as a vital component; it's like we divided up the opening code for a lock into four parts, and the lock will only open when all four parts are inputted. You had one of the four and had to remember it so we could reconstitute the complete opening code. Follow?

"Think of this experience as a long, careful recommencing of the planetary system, one whose first step was to purify one vibrational field and restore it to perfect alignment. We knew that somewhere along the line of your involvement in the algorithm something had gotten out of whack. We had to isolate it then correct it. We did. You did, and here we are, merrily delighting in the return of reality as we have grown accustomed to the Old Dear, all numbers in their place. Crucial to that restarting was your retrieval of *your* Light bubble from the Tree.

"Everything you saw, all the evidences of opposition, betrayal, subterfuge, and theft you mistakenly saw as reversed in a mirror. The truth is they are all stages in a long cooperative syllogism that yields something wonderful. Your guided misperception goes all the way back to Valles Caldera and then the Maldek intruders into the Earth Light grid. You were construing everything you saw within the initial framing parameters of a grievous theft, an action inimical to the planet; thus the thieves were evil, their acts contemptible, the results disastrous. Your compounding perceptions were built on this original mistake.

"It's quite interesting actually, because that's what happens to myths. They start out going left to right in the spiritual world, then when we get them down here, they seem to go right to left. All backwards. The causal sequence seems reversed. You see it all the time in the Greek myths: somebody is said to be somebody's father, but it turns out they are the brother or son; or the story says they killed someone, but in fact it means they achieved new seniority over a fixed position in consciousness, completed the next stage in their initiation. They 'killed' their identification with that now outmoded, worn-out stage of identity.

"It looked, at first, that these were steps in a long-term swindle, one set of grasping hands after another reaching into Earth's pockets and taking out all the numbers. This plausible misperception of the actual situation led you all the way through to the ever increasingly subtle machinations of the alien math gods and even the suspected indifference bordering on ambivalence of the Supreme Being to the use of the arithmetical realm to create and sustain reality or anything.

"Yet that was valuable, to appreciate how intimate and intricately involved the Supreme Being is in the arithmetical realm, that numbers are His Mind at work. The presumed indecision and second-guessing of the Old Man, His flawed antinomy, are actually unavoidably necessary attributes of an Infinite Being. Our job as Hierophants is to reconcile reality and ourselves to this fact. It is a finer aspect of the disclosure of the Holy Light, to see it is antinomial."

I felt the need to interrupt Blaise at this point with a question. "But the Valles Caldera episode—that seemed so clearly to have been a violation of Light grid protocols and a danger to the planet. Are you saying it wasn't?"

Blaise grinned, then nodded. "Got it in one, mate. Initially, long ago it was, as you understood. But we took the fangs out of the corrupting algorithms it ran. We made a copy and tried it out in a safe place, off-planet, in fact, quite a distance. We ran it in a safe room, the mathematical equivalent of what scientists and manufacturers of sensitive equipment use to exclude all air-borne particulates. We ran this program in an environment in which it would be utterly unplugged from actual reality; all it could produce was a holographic simulation, the mathematical equivalent of a hypothesis, as if the program said, 'Consider if this....' Well, out of curiosity, I suppose, we wanted to see what it generated.

"Our numbers experts (which included Sal, in an earlier guise) isolated the dangerous bits, the arithmetical hooks that could have undesirable traction on Earth's actual, real-time algorithms, and removed them or rewrote them so they would be ineffectual. It was fascinating to watch this corrupt mathematical program generate a simulated but alternate-looking planet and its Light grid. At first glance, it looked like the Earth, the way we designed it, but when we studied it more carefully, we were astonished, then shocked, then *appalled*, by the ways it *wasn't* like our familiar planet. Dangerous stuff, I'm telling you.

"So when you and I revisited the Valles Caldera vault, it was mainly to be sure nobody had tampered with our reformatted, defanged version of this program. But for the purposes of keeping you on track, I let you believe it was still a threat, though, I assure you, we'll never let it out of its protective cage."

"But it seemed as if the alien gods, as we construed them at the time, had in fact released this capture algorithm," I said. "It seemed like we were dealing with a disaster already unfolding, trying to stop it from getting worse."

"Yes, that is how it seemed. We allowed you to form a wrongly weighted interpretation of the situation. We thought it would provoke old memories of the arithmetical system you had helped create millions of years ago. Mostly, what you were seeing was the hypothetical extrapolation of this capture algorithm, and the parts that were real took place off-planet at our safe room, as I said. In fact, you were studying its mathematical architecture, but what it seemed to you that you were doing was registering shock at its contamination protocols. Do you see? Your memory distorted what actually happened, and we helped that along.

"To return to my point about the Supreme Being: Yes, it was a bit grim, wasn't it, when it seemed the Supreme Being Himself was behind the whole problem, having grown disenchanted with His arithmetical realm and seemingly ordering the complete recall of the enumeration infrastructure that organized reality and held it in place and ran its consciousness operations and that the true task of the Hierophancy was to chaperone the arithmetical realm back home.

"Your shock at this prospect and its implications was genuine which, since in fact it's not happening, served to clarify and refresh your appreciation of the structure of reality and the absolutely crucial role of the Supreme Being in continuously validating and maintaining His own good idea to use numbers. It was like you got your head in there, inside the machinery of reality, and had a good look around at the mechanism, evaluating it as a good geomantic engineer.

"Now we turn the mirror inside out and you see you were retracing all the steps in the order we originally followed, you as a key component, to create the Light grid, and then over time leading up to that pivotal moment in 2050 when we completed the Hierophancy heuristic algorithm and set it running the grid. I admit I am still a bit astonished to be reminded of how many factors went into generating this managing algorithm, how many alien intelligences and planets. You gave us all a nice refresher tour of the steps we took to get this algorithm."

My mind was still sluggish, slow to catch on to the implications of all this. "Are you saying that the Earth's algorithm was never in jeopardy or stolen?"

Blaise nodded. "Correct. Never stolen or in peril. But there was still a key reason you had to retrieve the exact memory and restore the pure status to your bubble. We are about to institute an upgrade to the heuristic algorithm and we had to clear the system of all defects and misalignments before we launch it. That is the actual reason behind the three-month detective hunt we set you on."

"What about all those people, the thousand Hierophants we had deployed across the planet? Was that all an artifact of my imagination in my retrieval?"

"No, as a matter of fact. Those people are out in the field, waiting for us. They will tie down the respective digits of the algorithm at the geomantic nodes, but it will be the upgraded algorithm. But we had to get through all this first. We had to take you through the entire history of setting up the algorithm in the first place, to meet all the players, visit the key sites, remember the logical process that yielded this high-order managing algorithm and its extraplanetary links. They are all waiting in place for the next phase of our master plan: the upgrade.

"Yes, I know: the unasked question. Why didn't we tell you we were doing this? We thought if you knew you would unwittingly obstruct it or try to direct it and thereby get in your own way. So we let you believe it was a real-time problem. You were indispensable and irreplaceable in this retrieval project because you were the one who made the key input to the heuristic algorithm long ago. In many respects your role was the central, geomantically instrumental one of all. One link was out of phase, but we didn't know which one at first so we had to walk you through the complete sequence back to the beginning of the Creation to find it. Then we could correct it. You see, only you could find it because it was you, albeit an earlier version of yourself, who first inputted it."

Again, I couldn't say anything. I was processing this news. Astonished, relieved, and, gradually, excited. So, the world was not finished after all. Good. I had grown despondent after seeing every feint we made against the arithmetical gods fail, including the last one which seemed so certain of eventual success. Now none of that represented failure, but stages in a long retrieval process. Well, double shit. On one side, I was relieved it wasn't a giant failure; on the other, I was peeved at being misled for three months. On still another, it was rather fun.

Those had been the steps in the lengthy syllogism by which the algorithm was attained in the first place. We had to review the steps, apparently in reverse order, back to the beginning to find the precise place where things deviated. It was, I suppose, like taking a complicated engine apart to examine all the parts, inspect for faults, clean and oil them, then reassemble the whole machine.

"There is one other aspect to this little program of ours, Frederick. Again, it directly concerns you. Think of it as job training. As another initiation. The time is coming when I will be leaving the Earth end of the Hierophancy. I will still be part of the larger project, but not working out of this planet. I have been grooming you to take over my position when I leave. In addition to the other prime reason for this three months of concentrated detective work, this was to solidify your confidence and resolve to work Hierophancy problems, to take a major share of the responsibility to complete them, come up with tactics, assign duties, and work towards a conclusion, as you did nicely in the present outing."

So there we were again, back in our familiar offices. The angelic Blaises were here too, and I felt the arithmetical gods lean in towards us from the circumference. It was their own circle, and they stood on its margins. I wouldn't say they were discretely personified, that I could see any detail of their presence specifically, but I had the strong impression they were focusing their attention on our group and, most importantly, their entire attitude towards the numbering project had changed. So those fuckers are actually our allies and always have been. That will take some getting used to on my part. I had them figured for the arch-enemies of all the Hierophancy stands for and now we're best buddies again? Had been from the beginning? They willingly deployed their numbers?

You will appreciate the irony of those statements. Their attitude had not changed because it had never been aberrant from our intentions or needs at all. It had been an illusion of mine, due to the veiled procedure I was taking part in. I felt their vibration now to be helpful, cooperative, even, if remotely, friendly. I had to keep shaking my head to dispel my now quite clearly demonstrated wrong impression of them. They are our colleagues, our arithmetical associates. I may have fantasized this next part, but I thought for a moment a few of them were offering me the square root of *pi* served up on a silver platter as a peace offering. That got my attention: the solution was worked out to 2,200 decimals.

Our extraplanetary colleagues were here with us too though I suspect it was by long-distance holographic projection because I could see their planets' Light grids through their ethereal forms and maybe ethereally was how they had always been with us. It didn't seem to effect their ability to work with us. I blushed as I realized those 13 extra-planetary friends probably were in on the secret all along and were too polite to even pass me a hint that I was being had. Blaise started talking so I turned my attention to him, as did everyone else.

"Now that we have isolated the flaw in the algorithm and fixed it, and let Frederick in on our little caper, we can move on to the main event. Yes, all that which we have done was not yet the main event, but preparation. Funny, isn't it. It seemed so dramatic and fraught with peril and dire implication. Anyway, the first part of the main event is the upgrading of Earth's heuristic algorithm and the corresponding and simultaneous upgrading effect that will have on the algorithms of the other five free-will planets and more subtly on all the Light grids of the galaxy. That's why our 13 extraplanetary colleagues worked with us.

"The improvements to our algorithm will effect the other five planets by means of the Light grid that joins the six planets. Changes in that master Light grid will then reciprocally feed down into the individual Light grids, make changes, and these will feed back up into the master Light grid. Things will bounce around like that for a while as the systems adjust to the upgrade. That's the reciprocal nature of its design. Our job is to supervise and modulate those reciprocal bounce-backs and make sure all the reciprocal systems stay balanced.

"We had to clean out the existing algorithm before we could introduce the upgrade. Otherwise it wouldn't hold and there would be friction between the two or some kind of mathematical incompatibility. The new system will work faster, smoother, be more fluidic sideways across space and time, and facilitate a greater scope of awareness, penetration, discernment, and mental equanimity. It in turn will make possible an even bigger development scheduled to start soon. This is the second part of the main event. You could call it the *main* main event.

"Sometime in the next 10-20 years, possibly sooner. It's the return of the domes. That requires a commensurately sophisticated Light grid managed by a super-efficient algorithm because when those domes come back 'in the flesh' reality will change. Or I should say reality will finally start to come back into its true planetary state. More of how the Earth was originally designed will be revealed to Earth people. Our planet will finally start to awaken from its long trance state, like a coma patient regaining daytime sunlit world awareness. The return of the domes will remind people of how the Earth was meant to feel: full of Light, understanding, all the finer qualities of the Creation intended for us.

"I emphasize that the timing of this is approximate and subject to change. Whether it's in 20 years, or sooner or later, depends on a myriad of factors. The entire planetary system, its Light grid, all the arithmetical structuring, the collective state of humanity, have to be in perfect condition and complete receptivity and occupying just the right vibratory niche for the return of the domes. Yes, the system is exceedingly fine-tuned, even twitchy, you might say. But as the effect of the return of the domes is so momentous energetically, everything must be in a state of perfect preparation to accommodate them. The goal is for the Earth to safely integrate their strong energy, not reel into chaos."

Blaise was pointing to aspects of a complex projected hologram in the center of the room. A sphere about 20 feet in diameter, it was big enough to comfortably walk around and observe from all sides which is what I was doing. It showed the Earth with its basic geographical features and the Light grid superimposed over it, emphasizing our rhombus of four geomantic sites. It displayed the key arithmetical components, and if you pressed on the right point in the hologram it would display the subset of support equations and go into as much mathematical detail as you wished.

You could, if you wanted, see all of it, the complete arithmetical scheme of the planet, the numbers that scripted the Light grid that supported the biosphere and human and all life consciousness. I pressed on that right point and walked around the hologram of our Arithmetical Earth, a planet comprised of numbers and equations ever birthing consciousness.

That wasn't even the extent of this hologram. It displayed the other five free-will planets and their Light grids and arithmetical aspects, and it showed the hexagon Light grid that linked the six planets (that included our Earth) into this special pattern. Further, it showed that special seventh planet born out of this web but also its mother, perpetually birthing its sixfold structure of heightened free will and comprising the fulfillment of the six linked worlds it had birthed.

This hexagonal grid was different from the individual planetary grids, yet it superintended them, looked after their collective relations, their reciprocal exchanges, and constant interactions. This grid featured its own set of equations and algorithms, and if you pressed the right node on the display they would be instantly presented in their complexity. This grid alluded to the seventh planet.

The alien gods, I knew, were leaning in attentively from the room's circumference to study this display. They were no longer our enemies, our problem, or our focus. They were as they should be, our designated non-corporeal colleagues in this project. They were like investors who had already agreed to put their money into our project and were appreciatively reviewing our forecasts and expected results. Or they were the engineering firm that had agreed to provide the necessary expert workforce to build the Light patterns, and these workers were now deployed into the field to begin the construction work.

"Now watch what happens when we upgrade the Earth's algorithm," said Blaise. He was standing inside the hologram as if inside the planet itself. Knowing him, I wouldn't be surprised if he momentarily fancied himself as Antaeus, the prototypical man, giant, or god of the Earth itself, his feet rooted in the planet, his invincible power steadfast as long as he remained anchored in the ground of his mother, the Earth; or maybe he pictured himself as the arisen starry Albion, admiring his planetary estate richly endowed with Light temples.

Blaise always liked to explore the implicit mythopoeic aspect of any situation. He had begun his geomantic training undertaking what he called "myth-living" the Arthurian mythos, living into and experiencing firsthand the initiatory realities that the outer myth veiled yet alluded to, all couched in the geomantic landscape. The myths and their mythic heroes revealed this terrain.

All the displayed equations and sub-algorithms started to change. The numbers changed like a new readout on the stock market when all the share prices had risen dramatically. The master algorithm changed too, growing in complexity and length, many of its key components altered and more complex. This had two effects proceeding in opposite directions.

The first effect concerned the Earth. The Light grid, its temples, Light lines, zodiacal star patterns, and other geomantic features brightened, sharpened, and clarified. They seemed to snap into a stronger focus, grow more streamlined, somehow take a few steps closer to palpable daytime seeable outer world reality, as if they were landscape *devas* nudging up closer to human perception to say a cheery *Hello!* to us. It was like watching a teenager of perhaps 16 suddenly grow into a 36-year old adult, maturity flushing across his face, his posture confident, his emotions pacified, his life path and purpose well established and on track.

The other effect was outward and concerned the composite Light grid linking the six planets. That grid expanded, added complexity, more numbers; it was flushed through with more Light now and what it most suggested, though the comparison might seem odd at first, was the Earth was gaining land mass.

As mentioned earlier, Persian, Hindu, and Aztec lore speak of extra veiled continents that accompany our planet and which lie at a right angle to the Earth's axis of spin. These continents, known as *dvipas* or islands, are legitimate parts of the planet, of what you might call the Higher Earth, populated with humans in more subtle forms, celestial mountains of Light, enclaves of enlightened deities. When the composite Light grid of the six planets took up the reformulated algorithm, it was as if these hidden lands were suddenly majestically revealed. Reality grew wider, bigger, richer, and in basic terms, there was now *more* of it.

Not only were the *dvipas* now more potentially seeable by incarnate humans, but the implicit enlarged extraplanetary landscape of the six linked planets was too. The planetary bodies and the Light grids of our five linked planets now seemed to be added to the visible "mass" of our Earth. It had grown in size at least ten times. It was now embedded in this secure nest of six planets.

The Earth would never again seem like a solitary planet fending for itself in a hostile or indifferent universe. It would never again be the "silent planet" that nobody in the solar system ever heard from, as C. S. Lewis saw it in the late 1930s in his famous science fiction novel. It never had been solitary, though many people had felt this, falling for the lie put forth by dark agencies. But now we had five hardy, dependable co-travelers in our galactic odyssey, watching our back, as the expression goes, and we had full visitable access to their psychic and geomantic landscapes and possibly one day to their physical landscape as well.

The effects of the Earth's algorithmic upgrade on the six-planet Light grid then fed into each of the other five planets and began a cycle of reciprocity. It was like both systems were sending a stream of messages and updates to each other, new numbers, conditions, parameters, frequency settings, possibilities. It was a multi-global event, each planet teeming with new information and discussion, and the Light web linking it with the other five also participating in this geomantic colloquy of new conditions, that, it seemed, everyone was liking. I had the impression they had been patiently awaiting this upgrade, like one might have, as when I was young, and my computer was running far too slowly and I had been promised a newer, faster one with lots more memory, and got it.

This was all simulated, I had to remind myself. It hasn't happened yet. But the results looked excellent and seemed likely to be taken up without resistance.

Blaise ran through a few alterations in the upgrade algorithm, and we observed their effects. There were six proposed algorithmic upgrades for the Earth and we were tasked with evaluating them and deciding which one would work the best. They were not terribly different, one from another; it was like listening to six superb pianists each performing their rendition of a Chopin polonaise. You admired the nuances of style, speed, technique, and musical brightness in each pianist, but it was still Chopin's genius underneath their fingers' dexterity, and we had to judge which pianist most perfectly captured all of Chopin's nuances.

The simulated upgrades to Earth's master algorithm not only affected the Light grid linking the six planets but the neighboring stars around this grid too. Our changed numbers delivered a specified reality, a new feel to consciousness, and this sent ripples out beyond the confines of our single planet and even of the six. The galaxy itself felt the change, and it shivered in a frisson of delight.

Yes, I exaggerate a little, I'm sure, but it is still a fact that the stars near to this grid and even far away registered the upgrade, noted how it changed local conditions for them. It was like how your neighbors would register your changed social status if you had just come home after graduating college or finishing your M.D.'s internship. They looked at you differently. They awarded you a higher degree of respect. I chuckled. They might ask about office hours.

The upgrade to Earth's algorithm would similarly affect the relations and consciousness potentials of all the stars, not just the ones in immediate proximity. As Ezra Pound said of literature, it should be news that stays news. Our Light grid upgrade would be news that stayed news for some time. I saw the ensouling intelligences of the many stars, what myths would call their star gods, leaning forward to observe these developments, many of them nodding their approval. The changes to our six-planet Light grid and its operating algorithm would have reciprocating effects on the quality of their galactic conditions.

The galaxy has a Light grid that connects all its stars in a complex web too, and this galactic web was receiving modulations in response to the changes we made. Numbers were being adjusted everywhere; the arithmetical deities were busy, like waiters bustling through a popular restaurant at its frantic rush-hour.

It was such a reversal to see what we had somewhat derisively called the "alien gods" now cooperating fully, even lavishly, with our commission. I was struck too with the irony of this because they did not have a big mind change; they had never been in opposition to the Hierophancy in the first place. I had just removed the filter through which I wrongly perceived their actions and plans. They were not our enemies; they were our confederates in the Hierophancy.

I saw their numbers everywhere, like decorations and tinsel draped on the Christmas trees of the myriads of stars in the galaxy, and these stars were paying attention to what we were doing, even at this simulation stage. The galaxy is alive, and I felt that aliveness as a steady attention, like spotlights trained on us. I likened this sensation of presence to we in the Hierophancy being a sports team and the star gods and their retinue the rapt assembly of fans seated in the stands.

We selected the algorithm we would use. It was the one that produced the most balanced results while at the same time catalyzing advances in awareness. My mind was gaining traction on where we stood with the project, but I was still fuzzy as to the definitive location of my body. Was I at Sun Valley or Tiwanaku? And those thousand colleagues I saw deployed around the planet at the algorithm integer-geomantic nodes—were they in fact there, or had that been only an artifact of the complex memory retrieval experience I had gone through?

Blaise had anticipated my confusion. "Yes, Frederick, they are out there. Bodily, just as you saw. I sent them in advance of you completing your memory retrieval because I knew you'd get through it and I wanted us to be ready to take the next steps. Which is what we are about to do. You saw them in the context of your imagined scenario of the hostile arithmetical gods; now you can see them in their correct context, as willing allies of our friends, the mathematical deities. In many ways you were seeing twofold the whole time, as through a double layer.

"One layer was the film of your recollection process. The other was reality as it actually is.

The face-slap version of reality. As you now see, some of your interpretations were correct for the perceived context, but wrong as far as actual definitive reality and context were concerned. The Hanuman touch was nice. You can always count on our pals, the Blaises, to provide just the right garnish and emphasis and a little jollity for our work. We enjoyed hearing their roars."

I hadn't thought of Hanuman as a figure of jollity, but with the Ofanim they could shift valence in an instant and turn Hanuman into the happy Ganesh. I was always grateful for their strong presence and enjoyed their participation, though I doubted I would ever understand them the way the human Blaise did. We trooped out of our Sun Valley offices and got ready to input the algorithm. Don't ask me how, but I was immediately back at Tiwanaku as if I had never left.

I was at Tiwanaku, among the big stones and the high altitude and the stillness, but I was also out in the galaxy. I don't think I ever before realized how implicit the rest of the galaxy is in anything that happens on our Earth or other planets. Our activities are not exempt from exerting an influence on the whole system. To make a change as big as upgrading the planet's master algorithm would ramify across the star fields, ripple the webs connecting all the stars and their life-forms and consciousness states. Everything is entangled, implicitly connected, as physicists would say, always touching, always still in touch, because that's how everything began, everything in touch with everything.

The upgrade to our algorithm and the corresponding changes that exerted on the six-planet Light grid would send cascades of influence across the galaxy. It reminded me of the Three Stooges who had to sleep three to a bed and that bed was big enough for only one and every time one of them turned the others did. They had to shift to accommodate the change in bodily position in the tiny bed.

So the many stars were expecting to shift their positions in consciousness slightly as we entered the upgrades to the Earth's algorithm. If you were sufficiently sensitive, you'd know the entire galaxy would feel a little different after this. I felt a lot of eyes on us. What an understatement. The galaxy was watching. I felt we were a soccer team girding ourselves for the other team's penalty kick, our bodies poised, our concentration locked, awaiting the destiny of that ball, the eyes of 50,000 fans in the bleachers intensely locked on to us.

I relished the fact, the changed condition as far as my perception was concerned, that the arithmetical gods were now on our side, working with us. In fact, we were all on the same side; there was no opposition to our project. The Supreme Being had authorized the upgrade and He was with us, sleeves rolled up. I didn't know what to expect, what the change would look like as it happened. I imagined it might be like watching numbers change on a digital clock. One minute it flashes 2:46 and the next it blinks 4:47, or maybe the upgrade would show up as a tiered set of numbers like a 4D mathematical axis.

Actually, as I was pondering this, the upgrade had already happened. Imagine you're in that sports stadium I have evoked a number of times. All the fans stand up to better see an exciting play on the field or to applaud a player. They notice the stadium is girt round with neon numbers as tall as buildings. It's as if a crowd of arithmetical spirits form a circumference around the stadium, and these numbers are alive, running equations that script the processes of reality, and the fans are part of that reality and they feel the inputted changes.

They were numbers certainly, digits, integers, arrayed in complex formulas, but I sensed the intelligence and attention behind them, the intangible faces of the arithmetical deities, how they were concentrating on instituting these updates, the planned deliberateness and assiduous care they demonstrated in this inputting. You felt like you were participating in the living core of reality, that nothing was being served up to you as a *fait accompli* but you were working the dials, moving the levers, entering new scripts for perceived reality.

I felt I was becoming accurately entrenched in the true conditions of reality, that I was more richly embedded in the processes all the Light temples created, and that my consciousness was profoundly focused on the truth of existence and the actual conditions of incarnation from bodies to stars. A layer of indefiniteness, of vagueness and uncertainty, was being peeled off from me, like a fusty film of obscuration and complaint that was now gone.

The Light temples were brighter, more sharply defined. They even looked bigger. I appreciated them as like at a car wash: you drive your car onto the automated track and it moves through a strong jet of cleansing water and soap then buffers. Similarly, the Light temples cleansed then amplified our consciousness states. Our car, our incarnational "vehicle," gets scrubbed clean, freshened up by the processes of consciousness the Light temples convey to us.

Somehow I was aware of my colleagues across the planet. I saw them all, and I could look at individual colleagues too, but what I noticed about them, and I presume this was true of myself as well, was that inside their Light forms, which were growing brighter and more pronouncedly alive, I saw the particulars of the geomantic node they occupied and the corresponding numbers that ran that site and that they were being upgraded.

Inside their human forms were the same outer conditions, the stones, sky, numbers gods, the digits, the expanding equations, and inside this outside I saw my colleagues. I hope I am not confusing you with my way of saying this, but I am trying to evoke the sense of simultaneity of inside and outside, of their co-participation in the same burgeoning, upgraded reality. You could see one through the other. It was a perfect demonstration of the Hermetic Axiom (as amended years ago by Blaise) that says, "As above, so below, and in the middle too." Here I was seeing the equivalence of mesocosm (outer world) and microcosm (our inner world and constitution) as both received the upgrade better aligning us with current conditions in the macrocosm (the Above world).

I heard talking, a lot of it. It was like crowds of people all talking at once. Some of them surrounded me, and others stood in circles around the colleagues I was viewing. It took me a while to realize what I was seeing. The upgrade had rendered the shadow reality of all the past lives myself and the others have had into a seemingly living reality, a friendly crowd of our predecessors standing around us, commenting, instructing. All our past-life selves had come to join us.

The force of the enhanced consciousness precipitated by the algorithmic upgrade had brought this latent content to the surface and all our selves were talking to us. Each of us was like a Greek drama in which we had our own instructing chorus, the embodiment of the public offering comment and criticism of our hero actions. Except now it was useful information, tips, reminders, historical anecdotes that would help us understand current conditions. For each of us, our selfhood had radically dilated. We felt broad, wide, completely open.

I now saw revealed further constituents of our incarnational self. The Higher Self appeared, standing regally and paternally about each person, and with this august angelic figure a council of advanced spirits presided, like a ministry of advisers who accompany the soul through its incarnations. I saw angels of various orders around each person, a few Ofanim, a couple Serafim, and other spirits, depending on the person's and their alignments and contracts.

I saw them surrounded by the local *devas* and Nature Spirits they worked with and who depended on their human-flavored interaction for guidance. It was a vista of our actual entourage as humans, or at least as Hierophants, now lushly revealed to us in these vivid group portraits for each of my colleagues. No, not just them. I now saw this disclosure was presented for all humanity; people had different degrees of entourage, but the generic fact of this held true. The upgraded Earth Light grid was now acting as a Hierophant, revealing the Holy Light in each person and the full spectrum of their incarnation.

As people became aware of the details of this disclosure, it strengthened their consciousness,

sense of self, manifested presence, and overall awareness level, and this fed back into the galaxy and started to affect the stars. The stars were able to manifest a stronger presence within human consciousness, and people started to become aware of the pre-existent habitation of these star energies, these star intelligences within them, what they stood for, what they meant, and what actions they took that affected or benefitted them.

That broadened the human's self-definition and embedded them further in actual reality, divesting them of the cobwebs of illusion and partial perception that had characterized their notion of the world for so long. They were waking up to the structures of consciousness, which included their own psyches, the Light temples, the Light grids that supported these temples, the arithmetical realm that ran the processes of these Light temples, and the heavenly-cosmic originals. Even more acutely, it showed people how exquisitely reciprocal are the relations among the holders of consciousness, namely, people, *devas*, and stars. Changes in state in any of these groups will tremble the intricate connecting web.

Quite a dilation of awareness was underway, and I saw that for some their attention was already expanding, growing like trees into the *Akashic* Records which enveloped them like a sky touching ground level. It was as if their heads had just spontaneously popped into this vast cosmic library and they were starting to read the cosmic histories. Isn't that one of the biggest failures of human education, how little we know of anything beyond the planet, what life has been like on the myriad other sentiently occupied planets? Even the history of the Earth has been vastly abridged, edited, deleted, and rewritten with a fake storyline to keep us in the infernal dark, childlike and utterly uninformed. That would start to change now as more people bravely foraged in this truth library.

I felt the Earth tremble and even shudder. What was this about? I heard the angelic Blaises speaking in my mind: "The Earth is starting to correct its wrong tilt. It has been tilted off its true axis for a long time, as you know. Its original design did not call for a 23.5-degree tilt off its true axis. That was an imbalance produced by the force of aberrated consciousness put forth by first-generation humanity compounded by their removal from physical reality.

"Their abuses of psychic power and their subsequent destruction tilted the axis. The force of that generation's misalignment with the planet's Light grid, its misuse of psychic powers, shifted the planet into that disastrous tilt, throwing off all the geomantic numbers which had been keyed to the umbilicus of 360 days in an Earth year. The Light grid is based on nines, on 360, not the unnatural 365.25."

For a moment I felt what that had been like. Maybe I was remembering. It was like reality had just been ripped open, torn, slit with a knife, rendered with the kind of noise you hear when you wrench nails out of an old two-by-four. I felt ripped inside, like I was a piece of paper deftly torn down the center. I felt I wasn't standing up straight any more, that I was listing to one side. I felt dizzy.

I felt like I was in a building made of steel girders and someone had just shoved it to one side, like a giant leaning rudely into it, twisting and bending the whole thing, and the sound of all that wrenching metal was horrific, unhuman. You felt the structures of life and reality were being attacked, taken apart, demolished. It seemed I was seeing double in everything my eyes took in. I couldn't focus them. I felt sad, enormously grieved, as I knew my familiar reality was now dissipated. And I felt the displeasure of the Supreme Being, the ire focused on all humanity, the resolution to remove us from the Earth plane and put us in permanent exile.

"The planet has lived under this deviation too long," the angelic Blaises continued. "It has suffered with this. You have taken it for granted, no longer notice its baleful effects on you. Humanity has endured it like a crooked house, tilted by an earthquake and never righted. It's still standing, but it's slanted, not straight. Now you feel the planet starting to finally correct that ancient disturbance. The planetary house will no longer stand crooked. The force of corrected human consciousness, the fresh algorithmic upgrade, the work of the Hierophancy, the many other factors you are aware of now, are producing this. Say goodbye to the awful Precession of the Equinoxes. That farrago has presented its last parade. People will now, finally, walk straight up again."

The human Blaise used to talk about this a lot. The planet's tilt, the Precession, the four seasons, are not normal conditions of the planet. The Earth's Light grid was designed with 360 being the ruling number. Then the planet tilted off its axis and all the numbers were skewed from Earth reality. The tilt averages between 22.1 and 24.5 degrees over a 41,000-year cycle, and currently measures out at 23.5 degrees of obliquity, as the scientists call the tilt. People have gotten so used to this aberration they think it's the normal state of the planet.

Blaise would show the kind of irritation over this an architect might display if you kicked over his scale model rendering of a proposed complex of buildings. This tilt is the physical evidence, the truth, of what theologians call Original Sin, the abuses of psychic power effected by our ancient ancestors taken out on the Earth. He took this injury to the Light grid design personally, like somebody had trashed his house or broken his porch beams and written graffiti on the walls. As one of the planet designers, this axis aberration disturbed him.

It might sound odd at first, but most of the Hierophants would have some degree of personal memory of their primordial involvement in the design and construction of the planet's Light grid and would similarly feel incensed about this damage and be cheered that at last this deviation from its design was fixed. Then Blaise laughed. "I wonder if we'll get the part where the mountains melt down into molten metals and Earth is rendered flat again, like the Persians said."

He was referring to a Persian prophecy that one day the killed Gayōmart, the Cosmic Man and container of Light, and his celestial bull, Gavaevodatta, the two original inhabitants of the Earth (archetypes of humanity and the entire animal kingdom, the bull signifying the forceful vitality of life), would be resurrected and their arch-enemy and killer, Ahriman, definitively repulsed.

The planetary aberrations that resulted from that original double homicide, which included the rising up of the mountains and the start of the seasons and the end of the permanent springtime of the planet and the onset of the vagaries of daily weather and probably the disastrous planetary tilt as well, would be undone, and perfection restored. Because it was perfection, the original perfect design for Earth-Human reality, the one that had been exquisitely well thought out by the creative geniuses of the universe and implemented here with divine approval. Gayō Maretan, the original Avestan name for this cosmogonic figure, was the first human, the first *shah*, and the ideal form of all humanity. He was Keyumars to the later Persians, and Gayōmart to the Zoroastrians, and we will recognize him in the possibly more familiar guise as our Earth's Albion.

Technically, we've been living on an aberrated planet for many millennia, languishing in the distorted psychic atmosphere consequent to this primordial homicide. The Greeks remembered that paradisal original time when Man and Bull were alive as Hyperborea. That was the Land Beyond the North Wind to which their bright god Apollo travelled every year. On a physical level, that landscape was the British Isles, parts of Western Europe, and Scandinavia, Greenland and Iceland; but it was more basically a planetary condition of Light.

The Greek historians record that the Hyperboreans were always happy, spent their time gamboling and playing music in the lovely permanent springtime of the world and enjoying the regular six-month visits of Apollo who had a special affection for them. He is the Ray Master of the Pale Blue Ray, and his association with Hyperborea suggests he might have been a primary superintendent of this early Earth condition. He is the leader of the Nine Muses, the creative *divas* of the classical arts, so we may assume Apollo brought that lively artistic impulse with him to Hyperborea.

The Persian seers said the unnatural mountains would melt their seven constituent metals (which represented the chakras, associated with the planets and metals, signifying states of fallen, fragmented cognition), the landscape would be rendered flat again, as it was at the beginning of the planet, and instead of peaks it would be covered with a milk-like sea that only the "righteous" could survive when attempting to cross or wade. By righteous, they did not mean anything morally priggish and elitist as Judeo-Christianity construes it, but people aligned with the truth of the Light grid and its primordially pure structures of consciousness, outside on the Earth and inside as the human, the complete Holy Light that the Hierophants seek to reveal.

Remember what I said earlier about Ma'at and her original conditions of *ma'at*? Alignment with Ma'at's correctness of design and intention is "righteous," and anyway, that is likely a translator's ineptly chosen word for a Persian concept. The Persians had their own term for *ma'at*: they called it *asha*. It means truth, properly joined, right working, a true statement, and it has a deity personification known as Asha Vahishta, one of the *Amesha Spenta*, a high-ranking category of celestial spirits, whose name means "Best Truth." Their bad guy equivalent to the Egyptian Isfet was known as *Druj*, the "liar and deceiver."

The "righteous" would survive because they could match the new cyclopean condition of consciousness in which all the metals, the chakras, were melted back into one chakra. In this view, the seven chakras, the seven metals, and all the planet's mountains were aberrations, proofs of the grievous fallen and fragmented condition of humans and planet, the mechanism of our split vision. The renovation of the world would undo these unnatural conditions. The Earth would be flat and smooth again and

humans would be cyclopean, and Albion and the animal kingdom (as Gavaevodatta) would be restored to primal health. When Gayōmart was killed by Ahriman, the seven chakras came out of the one; the unified state of consciousness was sundered and fragmented vision resulted.

With the renovation of the world, all this would be corrected. The Earth would be inundated with that milk-like singular sea of molten metals no longer differentiated as seven which meant the planet would be suffused with unitive consciousness, cyclopean perception, single-eyed comprehension of the universe. The seven differentiated metals, namely, gold, silver, copper, mercury, tin, iron, and lead, would be melted down into a single condition of molten fluidity, a film of higher, lucid consciousness and sharp perception laying upon the surface of the Earth like a dispensation from the heavenly realms to encourage humans to live wakefully. That was the meaning of "milk-like sea," nutriment and Light.

It was the goal of the Light grid, why it was installed, its design outcome. It's what the Persian mystics called *Xvarnah*, the glorial Light infusing the world. Originally, the Persian seers tell us, that was the quality of Light across the planet. With the foretold renovation, the Earth would spontaneously fulfill the seven stages of alchemy's Great Work. The planet's landscape, geomantically templated, would be hierophantic again, on fire with the purest celestial Light. The Earth would once again be celestial, the embodiment of an Angel, its soul.

Could the Persian seers have seen true this far into the planet's future? It did seem likely that with the correction of the Earth's tilt this sea of unitive consciousness would, at least experientially, gradually become the norm again.

I felt the planet wrenching incrementally back into its intended alignment, slowly chipping away at those unwanted, perturbing extra 5.25 days that acted like an authorized signature on the tilt that first-generation humanity's abuse made. Cyclopean consciousness wouldn't happen overnight so we must be patient. The *Satya Yuga*, which we entered 45 years ago, lasts 1,728,000 years, so we had time.

It was as if a giant plumber (Gayōmart's older, tougher brother perhaps?) was applying force to a wrench the size of the planet as if it were a twisted pipe, and he was gradually pulling the axis back into its true alignment, straight up, facing North. I mean Cosmic North, the Orient, the true orientation with the Holy Light. The planet itself would once again become hierophantic. It would take some time, years, maybe decades or more, to finish this. You have to approach all geomantic matters organically and think like plants. A little at a time, assimilate, adjust, then another increment, growth and emergence in gentle steady stages like a dimmer switch turned gradually to illuminate a room.

Say you had a stroke at an early age, much younger than most people are when this heart attack in the brain happens. One side of your face is pulled up slightly, your speech is slurred at times or thick and slow and stumbling, and perhaps your shoulder and one arm are tilted, twisted, or slanted downwards. You still function well, live your life, are productive, reasonably resemble a human being. Then comes a healer who miraculously undoes this deviation. Your body resumes a fully upright posture, your face relaxes and regains its symmetry, your speech is mellifluous, even honeyed, and has no bumps in it.

You had lived for so long with the stroke-delivered aberration you forgot it was not your original condition. You had resigned yourself to it as a body permanency. Now that is all gone. I picture the correction of the Earth's tilt as being like this. Humans have been living under post-stroke conditions. Now our planetary stroke is undone, its facial conditions normalized, the brain fixed.

Miraculous is not a word I use often. It reeks of hyperbole, yet to a degree we were witnessing the arithmetical realm rewriting the physical reality of our planet, and it argued for the privileged use of the term miraculous. The installation of the new algorithm, the upgrade, was precipitating a cascade of effects (impressively foreseen millennia ago by the Persian seers) that would transform, by way of purifying and awakening, human consciousness. You could feel the renovation of the Earth underway, like carpenters repairing your house. The restoration of the planet into a hierophantic world will seem miraculous.

The planet will be healed of a physical deformity it has endured for millions of years, having accepted it reluctantly as the new normality, however unbalanced it was. Human consciousness as a generic planetary condition would gradually dilate into cyclopean perception, as our fallen, fragmented condition of the "seven metals" was healed. We would see with one round eye again, like our godparents, the Elohim, the original Cyclopes, our cyclopean mentors and geomantic tutors. Gayōmart in effect would be resurrected, our planet's Albion would grow in wakefulness, and, gradually, increasing numbers of humans would realize this and regard the improved conditions, only then appreciated, as being for the best. People would start to sample unitive consciousness, seeing as the Elohim see, appreciating themselves and the world as a single awake reality.

"They're complexifying the Light temples, said Blaise, with a studious look. "They are adding dimensionality to the features, like new rooms to visit."

I saw that the Light temples (and I'm not even sure which ones I was looking at, it was more of a general impression) were growing, like a plant putting out new branches and leaves in a springtime spurt of growth. In geometric terms, it was probably a dimensional expansion from 4D, their norm, into 5D and 6D which were far more complicated but intriguing shapes, both in terms of their mathematical scripting and, experientially, in terms of their use.

The algorithmic upgrade was affording a commensurate deepening of the revelatory nature of the planet's Light grid. That is one of its main purposes after all: to reveal in progressive, initiatory degrees the cosmic architecture and processes to illuminate human consciousness which bears the mostly dormant microcosmic equivalent. The Light grid has always been intended for us as an interactive mirror. More of reality can now be disclosed, more veils dropped, and more existential nakedness tolerated by a strengthening human psyche.

Light temples burgeoning into complex dimensions means our awareness can similarly gain adroitness and cognitive flexibility, take in more of the truth of higher reality, the celestial realms and our Sponsor. Human consciousness has been awarded a promotion; in the old language of governments and their secret agencies, we've been "read into" more

covert programs now, covert only because to understand them and navigate through their complexities, our consciousness has to be more athletically nimble, our paradigm for reality greatly widened. So through the algorithmic upgrade we've been read into a lot more programs.

"These changes are making the Light temples look more like the hostels and *sidhe* of Ireland's Tuatha de Danann," said Jocelyn. "Especially in terms of how you described them to me, Blaise, after your first trip to Ireland." He had told me too. He had never seen Light temples like those. They were like 5D Escher drawings which usually only hint at a 4D-level geometric bewilderment. The temples seemed to grow like hair out of the Tuatha deities themselves, and it was hard telling where the "god" ended and the temple configurations began.

The Tuatha were the first godly inhabitants of Ireland and for a time lived on the surface of the island and interacted in a friendly, helpful manner with humans. Then they went underground, back into their *sidhe*, which meant they stepped back from being perceivable in the physical to dwell in the etheric background. But their Light temples remained inside the Hollow Hills of Ireland, and you could still visit them by psychically entering the numinous portals of their *sidhe*. Their level of disclosure, based on their Light temple design, Blaise had conjectured, lay beyond the cognitive ability of most humans for a long time. Now that revelatory threshold just might be assimilable for a number of people.

"This new algorithm has equations in it I've never seen before," said Sal. "Somebody is pretty bright on the Old Man's mathematical staff. There's more. It's like a checkerboard pattern has been laid over planetary reality. One color is regular reality, your normal sense of yourself and the regularity of spacetime. The other color is a door out of spacetime and that kind of familiar continuity. It is like a gap. These gaps occur regularly; that's the smooth orderliness of the checkerboard pattern, but inside one of these gaps everything is wildly different.

"It's like you've burst into the undifferentiated realm of unitive consciousness. You stay there for a while, though it could be an eternity as it is timeless; then you bounce back into the other colored square, the one of individuative consciousness, your self as you normally construe it, a separate 3D time-awareness unit. I think it's a way of getting us acculturated to this fluctuation of consciousness states, like bouncing back and forth from chakras to cyclopean-style perception with the long-term goal of converting Earth reality to this one. Maybe that's the meaning of the molten metal lake inundating the Earth. These gaps are regularly spaced, which means they are predictable. The key number here is 23. That's the number that cracks open this new pattern.

"Blaise, remember—you told me this from what the angel Blaises told you in the early 1980s. 'Magic exists in each gap of your time. In each moment there are 23 gaps. Magic is imperative.' Those gaps are this checkerboard pattern. The gaps are like grace notes, priest's bolt-holes, secret chambers behind bookshelves. You could step into one of those gaps and be gone for millennia and only a fraction of a second would have passed back in normal 3D spacetime reality. But in one of those gaps

you could access, I should think, the *Akashic* Records, the full library and all its holdings, the histories and explanations of goddam *everything.*

"You could visit ontologically evanescent 'aliens' in all manner of dimensions. Investigate zany Light grid designs, exotic life-form phylogenies, hopscotch your way along the timeline of reality backward into the past or into the future. You could reanimate past lives as if they were *avatars* of your current self, stand among them as with a dependable fellowship of alumni from some prestigious college you graduated from. You could study the probable timelines from unfolding reality, see which one best suits the design intentions of Earth.

"Or, and this one especially appeals to me, you could visit the library of all mathematical possibilities, a kind of arithmetical warehouse where all conceivable algorithms, equations, and number combinations are displayed for the inquiring numbers-obsessed mind, like me. You could see the Elohim, those consummate reality creators and merchants, proudly display their new designs for consciousness structures, phylogenies, planets, and Light grids, their templates and the epiphanies of understanding these bring.

"The more I studied this pattern, the more I realized each square in the checkerboard pattern has another square inside it, and that one has 23 squares. It is a hidden grid of 23 squares. It's like the Blaises said, inside each moment, the checkerboard pattern, is another checkerboard with 23 gaps, 23 timeouts from ordinary reality and its obligatory style and rules of perception. The algorithmic upgrade is making this implicit pattern visible now, bringing it to the surface of Earth reality. I doubt anyone suspected its existence before. I certainly didn't.

"Somewhere in this new algorithm there is a sub-routine that scripts this presentation, brings it into the foreground. It also intrigues me that 23 is a prime number. So few of these occur as Light grid numbers. This is like discovering a secret extra floor upstairs in a building you thought you knew well. It suggests all sorts of possibilities for exploration and reality excursions."

The situation I was observing suggested being inside a computer, not the physical aspect of it but among the bytes and binary processes that run its intelligence, and watching the escalating ramifications of a systems-wide update. You saw every aspect of its function being affected, improved, streamlined; all the numbers changed, and their outputs and linkages with other parts changed. It was a living process; you were upgrading an alive system as it remained alive.

The alive system in this analogy is human consciousness as supported by the Earth and its Light grid, all the mechanisms of awareness by which we take in the world, and now we'd be able to take in a much expanded world, even many worlds. If we were among those ancient Toltec seers of Mexico Carlos Castaneda used to write about almost a hundred years ago, we'd be delighted; they existed, he wrote, to constantly gain more awareness, to be aware of more things, to have greater scope, to enlarge their awareness because it was why humans existed. As far as they were concerned, it was the only worthwhile pursuit. These bold changes to the Light grid would facilitate that desirable expansion of awareness.

"You know what this upgrade is doing?" said Blaise. "It's making the entire planet a platform for gaining more awareness. Our Light grid is the mechanism of that enhanced awareness. The planet itself is a cognitive organ. It's like an eye that can see in all directions and into many dimensions at will. We operate that composite eye, turning our attention to whatever topic we choose. This was always the implicit intent of the Light grid, but only now, with this upgrade, can it move into the foreground and assume its rightful prominence.

"The whole Earth now can act like a Toltec seer intent on deploying its awareness. More awareness means we can enhance what we know; we can know much more, and knowing more means we get more traction on our life purpose, why we are here, what we're expected to do, and better, what we *want* to do, why we incarnated, this time, and all times, why we wanted to leave the Supreme Being to explore the myriad created worlds as individualized units. Don't you see? That's what has always hindered us, held back all humans, not knowing enough of their true context, and that was from insufficient awareness.

"This algorithmic upgrade to the Light grid changes all that. Now we can know. And with that knowing comes power, a co-creative power, true hierophantic power to participate in the maintenance of planetary, cosmic, and higher reality. You cannot deploy power intelligently and constructively until you understand your context, the mechanism you're trying to adjust, the goals you want to achieve. Otherwise, you're casting spells in the dark like an idiot, or worse, like a sorcerer's apprentice, a magician-manqué, making things worse.

"As Hierophants, we not only reveal the Holy Light. We fine-tune it so it delivers the optimal benefits to embodied consciousness. But to do that effectively, we need to be maximally well-informed, briefed on as many topics and nuances of those topics as possible. Now the Earth itself will handle those briefings for its ascent into illumination."

I saw a Hierophant standing on the Earth. He had a white staff with a white crown on its top. The crown had upright petals or crown points but they were on fire with a white flame. He wore a robe of brilliant gold suffused with orange like a blushing undercoat. This was the Ray color of the Ray of the Hierophant, the Grail Knight, and the geomancer, superintended by the Ray Master known as Kuthumi, Elijah, and Levi. The diamond-white crown atop his white staff suggested heavenly mansions and sublime vistas. It was a landscape in itself and the ability to perceive and participate in it.

He stood on the Earth, as a person ordinarily would, yet I saw the complete physical Earth and its subtle Light grid inside him, as coterminous with his form, comprising his insides. It was a living revelation of the Holy Light and its structures for consciousness. Then for a moment it looked like his head, greatly enlarged, was the Earth itself, and his arms were made of algorithms, with constantly changing numbers flowing like blood, as if his arms were sending and receiving arithmetical information, dispensing numbers as energy.

His body was made of all the Light temples on the Earth, and his awareness was the enlivening presence inside these many temples, and, more so, the composite radiating attention of the full array of temples. Behind that like a skeletal system of radiance was the arithmetical coding of those processes. How reassuring to see the numbers gods working cooperatively with the Hierophants.

It was like a spotlight bright and expansive enough enough to illuminate the Earth, and the Light temples were like brain cells that ran his awareness. This Body of Light was vivifying the planet as the Earth continuously received this energized presence like drip irrigation or an IV-feed or maybe it was more like a flood that was enlivening the galaxy, washing Light through it. Behind it you saw the numbers ticking like a stock market tape. It was an elegant picture of geomantic symmetry and the reciprocal maintenance of interdependent realms, an image of the designed Light system working properly.

I realized that Jocelyn had been studying me with extra attention. Then she smiled. "That image you were seeing, Frederick, is an example of the new psychic pictures and geomantic icons that will emerge from this numbers upgrade. Human consciousness will be exposed to a new set of pictures, like a Tarot deck freshly reconceived with new images to quicken human attention.

"It will be a new assortment of Major Arcana images that evoke our updated reality. It will be interesting to watch how this image you're seeing gets insinuated into human culture, how it starts to appear in mass consciousness like a watermark on fine stationery, like a new product logo that pops up everywhere, mysteriously or perhaps miraculously etched on consciousness during sleep or perhaps in daydreams or for some sensitive people as waking-time lucid visions arising in the sunlit daytime hours.

"We could be seeing crop circle images directly imprinted into the mind. The neurons will be the waving grain the images are stamped on. It could even become as popular and revered as the Virgin Mary apparitions once were in the previous century. I foresee apparitions of the white-staffed Hierophant will be popping up all over the place, imparting mystery and inspiration to its viewers."

I held out my arms. I saw the equations streaming out of my fingertips like electrons. They immediately started scripting Light temples and their circuitries of consciousness. My head felt as large as the Earth, and all the planet's Light temples, which number in the millions, filled my head like excited neurons. It was a dizzying image and rather funny too because I knew I was seeing this new psychic picture superimposed over my Frederick form, trying it on like a new suit. This image of mathematical arms and planet-sized head was an *avatar*.

I saw the long-reach of these arithmetical arms of mine extended to the other five planets in our six-planet Light grid across the galaxy. These numbers were streaming into the Light grids of those planets, adjusting their scripting codes. I tried not to be facile in my thoughts, but I couldn't help wondering how my arms had gotten so long as to reach across such a vast distance of galactic space to touch the managing grid patterns of these worlds. The new equations streaming out of my arms were adjusting the existing algorithms in place. We knew the upgrade to Earth's ruling algorithm would have a reciprocal effect on the other five planets in this system, and I was now seeing how that played out.

I saw how it was affecting R1's planet. This alien colleague had been co-present with Jocelyn at Helgafell in Iceland and I now saw her

co-present with "him" within his home planet's Light grid and focused through a specific node. The two sites seemed superimposed upon each other, linking the two planets. The upgraded Earth algorithm was having a secondary affect on the Helgafell coding and new equations were circulating through that site, and now they were streaming around and through the many red pillars that characterized R1's grid.

The last time I saw R1 on his planet he had been distracting the alien gods with alluring false equations to keep them from pulling out all the numbers. He didn't have to fake them out this time; they were willingly supplying all the numbers. So instead he was taking Earth's changed algorithm and his own planet's existing arithmetical matrix and choreographing them into a dazzling balletic movement. Imagine the changing sequences and products of a long equation as akin to a troupe of leaping, pirouetting dancers, and as the numbers changed and the equation outcomes modulated, so did the identities of the dancers. They were shapeshifting prolifically with the numbers, which meant the consciousness conditions on his planet must be protean and malleable now.

R1's "people" kept changing their appearance as the numbers computed through the red pillars. Nobody seemed to mind; they looked invigorated by this dazzling inconstancy of form, their changing bodies like a series of verbally prolix metaphors spun out by a hyper-articulate word master. The Light temples also kept adjusting their shape, size, and dimensionality. My impression was that R1's people were accustomed to an unfixed reality, one subject to constant fluctuations in form, and that they enjoyed this shapeshifting.

It was wonderful and unsettling to look at these people and watch them change shapes almost with each passing moment, as if they were running through a lexicon of possible shapes, trying on all the costumes in a catalog. Their Light temples modulated their shapes to match these form changes, altering their architectural details to reflect modulating consciousness conditions. It was unsettling because we Earth humans like our fixed bodily forms; maybe we'll tolerate or even indulge small cosmetic changes, not wholesale alterations of our entire appearance. That's why it was wonderful to see because as it was so contrary to our fixity; it was liberating to watch this, though from a safe distance.

I laughed. I was looking at my arms and hands and the streaming integers. The arithmetical gods were riding the numbers like they were stallions; these gods wore wild, almost crazed, gleams on their faces. I suppose that was the image of their enthusiasm, and of course, they were not riding the number horses but were identical with them, so I should say I saw their faces grinning from within the numbers or as equivalent with those faces. It was a cheering prospect, though, to see them finally working with us, on our side. Or maybe it was the glee of the supremely creative mathematical genius, the Supreme Being, delighting in the amazing, exciting things He could do with all these numbers.

They were committing themselves, the vital, sentient numbers of reality, their own "flesh" as much as that was possible as they had no forms, to the creation of higher states of consciousness and richer forms of manifestation as Light temples, and they were performing this benefic deed with no reservations.

The Supreme Being seemed pleased with Himself. I knew I was imputing a truckload of anthropomorphic projection onto the Ancient of Days, and I remembered my perspective during this detective hunt for the algorithmic thief had been skewed and these alien gods had never opposed us nor had The Chief and they were now, as He was, as they had always been, performing their duties.

The fluidity of form and identity on R1's planet made me dizzy. The "people" kept morphing from one form to another, none of them resembling the familiar human appearance, not that they should, and their Light temples also kept transfiguring themselves into a wild assortment of architectural shapes, many of them physically impossible on our 3D-biased Earth. Even stranger or entertainingly, some of R1's "people" assumed Light temple shape.

They expanded their own manifestation shape into a visitable Light building, and I saw other still morphing "people" enter these unstable, protean shapes. I presume they went inside these buildings to be exposed to the quality and process of consciousness that Light temple conveyed, to meditatively immerse themselves in the uplifting vibration, or maybe it was like shopping and the Light temples in their fluctuating forms were boutiques inside a posh mall.

I realized I was struggling to apply analogies to the strangeness of what I was seeing. It did not operate on human presumptions or Earth habits, so it was difficult to make any definitive sense of what I was only sketchily seeing. R1 seemed confident in what he was doing, streaming numbers out of himself into the red pillars to feed his planet; anyway, I knew his effervescent vibration suggested he was smiling on whatever kind of face he had.

I saw the mechanism that led to these upgrades on R1's planet. The upgrading of Earth's algorithm fed into the Light grid connecting these six planets, and it changed its geometry. It did not alter the fundamental shape but added secondary tiers and extensions and strengthened the form. This improvement then fed down into R1's planet and precipitated the changes I've described. Then those changes reciprocally fed back into the Light grid of the six planets and got distributed to the other five planets. Everyone benefitted from it.

It was a living system, constantly keeping track of even the most minute alterations and entering them into the inventory of the linkage's current status. It noticed everything; it accommodated all nuances. I bet even my attention to this feedback loop, the fact that I was observing it, was noticed and entered into the balance sheet as an input capable of altering it, however slightly. The system was exquisitely sensitive to nuances, even minute rises in participant awareness.

Jocelyn would have liked what I saw next. I hoped she was seeing it. The red pillars on R1's planet were emanating psychic pictures, mythic icons, into the subtle atmosphere, pictures that described, even extolled, the new reality creation underway. They not only reflected what was happening, they seemed to feed it as well. The occupants of the planet were prolifically morphing across a repertory of shapes, including those of the Light temples, but they were also moving in and out of identifying with the physical mass and subtle bodies of their planet. I saw their "heads," though it was more of a mental space they intensely occupied,

as co-present with the visible sphere of their planet. The images flashing out of the pillars showed this complex consciousness form.

Then I saw the same thing happen with perhaps 100 stars. The "people" flashed into the stars, one at a time, stars that formed a functional constellation of influence for their planet and its prospects for consciousness, and as they became each star, they shared the mental space with the ensouling intelligence of that star and beamed down upon the planet the particular vibration of that heavenly body. Viewing this spectacle I realized this planet's primary life-forms did not have a fixed shape or identity in any normal Earth-human sense of that. They were moving adroitly through a repertoire of forms and identities but settling on none of them in any permanent sense. They were emulating the Ofanim, metaphor masters, continuously running through a retinue of different forms to model consciousness and its powers. We are *like this*, they're saying.

That meant their fixed identity was consciousness itself, taking on all these masks. It was consciousness, unmoored to an unvarying body, playing 100 roles in a planetary drama, moving nimbly from one guise to the next, always being the actor though never identifying with the temporary new part. It meant to appreciate the fullness of their character acting you had to see this in 4D, as a multiplex across time and space, seeing the 100 forms happening at once.

Who they are is the complex of 100 faces seen simultaneously in one space, though that singular space straddled a large planet and 100 related stars. The upgrade to Earth's Light grid apparently freed up more of this delightful morphogenetic fluidity on R1's planet, allowing the changes to happen faster and perhaps to encompass a larger region of space and involve more stars. R1's people could expand their consciousness field to take on more guises at once. I still hadn't comprehended the fullness of this upgraded disclosure.

This array of R1's planetary consciousness zipping among all the guises, the 100 stars, the different Light temples, and the varying incarnational guises, had as a goal the generation of a new constellation, but along fresh, unique lines. It was not a deliberate pattern of stars only, but of consciousness-bearing forms, even if they were vexingly protean, and the planet's many Light temples.

It was a constellation comprised of an awakened, shapeshifting planetary consciousness, and it would shine in galactic space suggestive of a face, a focused awareness surely, and this is the most sublimely exciting aspect, it would be a Light temple accessible to people on the Earth through our planet's Light grid, possibly by way of one of those 23 gaps or checkerboard squares between moments of life. Earth humans would be able to visit this exotic Light temple.

They've made a Light temple out of their phylogeny. This is the R1 planetary Light temple, we might call it, and this composite Light temple of the entire planet was now open for business and accessible from Earth. Humans would be able to walk through this structured space and experience the spectrum of fluctuating forms amidst a constancy of consciousness presence.

I could see that such an experience would, for example, instill a sense of fluidity of identity that might make it easier for people to remember and integrate details of

pertinent past lives and construe an identity that straddled their own timeline. It would be like an interactive "museum" of the life and consciousness of R1's people. Not stultifying like most museums, preserving artifacts of the past, but a Light temple capable of imprinting its consciousness signature on human visitors so we would emerge from this initiation center feeling we'd seen more of the Holy Light and its innate patterns. Our human presence, any insights we had, consciousness surges, would be registered in the system and incorporated, R1's phylogenic Light temple adjusting to our input.

It would start to free humans from a fixed affiliation with only their current form and personality characteristics and help them see themselves instead as multifaceted embodiments over time. I saw that a few selected geomantic nodes on the Earth would have a secondary trigger aspect that once you had penetrated their primary Light temple you then could access this secondary one in a gesture of geomantic hypertexting. Access to R1's new planetary Light temple would be on offer to people using this primary temple. It would be like referencing a book in a footnote for further study on a given topic, then offering the reader instant access to it.

My attention shifted to L2 and what he was doing on his home planet. He had been co-present with Sal in Alberta at the Medicine Wheel and on his planet. He had expanded his handheld hypercube to the size of a large building of Light, and his green ribbon of number extruders was floriating the space with complex equations and doing this as prolifically as a tree releasing springtime pollen. I have mentioned that on his planet the consciousness-bearing forms appear as hexagons of six linked units of awareness; that is what constitutes a person there. The goal of "spiritual" development is to awaken and unify the expression of these six. L2's House of Light was now prolix with thousands of these hexagons.

Now that the arithmetical gods were cooperating and not hindering his planet's life, L2 was going all out to extrapolate the potentials for his phylogeny. His green ribbon was extruding numbers at a furious rate, like he was seeding an entire world in a single morning. The hexagons were building larger structures; they looked at first like greater linkages of hexagons, like upward-building fractals, but then they shifted into higher dimensions, 5D and 6D hexagonal composites. They were becoming difficult to see; they were in constant motion.

In an odd way, for me it was like standing in a burgeoning crowd. The crowd was intensely populous with units of awareness, "people," I was tempted to call them, but the keynote was this crowd was exceedingly orderly and well-behaved. That was an artifact of the geometry that ordered its construction. Its precision in shape and perfect measurements was the product of the green-ribbon numbers.

L2 was building something with this continuously expanding hexagonal web. It was as if each basic hexagonal frame of genuine consciousness units was putting out octaves of echoes, harmonic extensions of itself like subtle bodies. These were rapidly burgeoning ever outward to fill the planetary space and beyond that, into the gravity well of its system's principal star. The hexagonal web was starting to extend all the way out to the parental star which meant, if I understood this correctly, the consciousness field of the inhabitants of L2's planet was infiltrating the complete gravity well of its own solar system.

In human equivalent terms, this would be like human awareness investigating and then occupying every square inch of planetary and solar space, filling it with our human-flavored awareness and enabling us to be hyper-aware of this great life. It would be the inverse of astrological modeling, or perhaps our conquest of what the Gnostics once termed the baleful influence of the dark, inimical Archons of the planets, an influence they sought to overcome. How novel, or was this the evolutionary end-goal of the system, that consciousness-bearers become a viable astrological force in themselves, modulating the planets? There are hints of this in the esoteric lore of Magic Squares, that mastery of these invocatory and mathematical matrices enables one to influence the planets, even to direct their emanations to benefit oneself or larger collectives of awareness.

Our consciousness would spread out to fill the gravity well of our Sun, incorporating into our burgeoning awareness body all the planets (the solar system correlates of the seven metals of the Persians) lying troublingly in their niches in the prescribed tiers of the great solar system well. My point is the planets would now be subject to our fluctuating influences. If we did this, we could proclaim, perhaps cockily, I am hereby conjuncting Mercury, and loving it. Hey, smart guy, watch me while I walk backwards for three weeks—like it? The solar system, under new management, would no longer tolerate retrogrades, and no planets would be allowed to walk backwards skewing Earth sensibilities.

Soon this vast web of hexagons filled the solar system's space. It was like a honeycomb that had rapidly grown out to fill the gravity well's space, but instead of honey or bees you had the focused awareness of the planet's residents. This awareness oversaw every aspect, every square inch of that interior space. It filled this space as the unified, attentive presence of sentient life in that system. The upgrade to Earth's algorithm had enabled the algorithm of L2's planet to finish extrapolating this intended result; it had been planned since the inception of this planet but now conditions were suitable for this expansion of awareness.

It was as if the fans at a completely filled baseball stadium were now standing in all available spaces inside the sun's gravity well, like the seats had been transferred to this new location and the size of the stadium radically enlarged to fill the Sun's gravity well, and the sixfold units of consciousness were all on their feet, the way fans at a baseball game might stand if somebody whacked a grand slam. Out on the playing field were the planets of the system, neatly identified with number and team emblem and color, batting and chasing.

The fact that the hexagonal fractals had expanded to fill the gravity well's space also meant they lushly surrounded their home planet. They fully attended it. Appreciate the significance of this gesture, if you would: their home planet was fully looked after by its dominant phylogeny; it was geomancy the way it was supposed to be administered, consciousness taking responsibility for its physical home, maintaining the viability of its Light grid and Light temples.

The next thing I saw startled me at first. This vast crowd of inhabitants was singing.

They were singing to their own solar system and planet, offering a grand chorale to their incarnational context. Maybe I attribute too much purposefulness to this. Maybe they were not so much singing as expressing their innate vibrational quality because they were in perfect alignment with the truth of their existence. Those congruent, harmonious choralic sounds couldn't help but be expressed. Whatever the motivation, this music was fortifying the matrix. It was the Grand Ma'at Oratorio, as precise and mathematical as the best of Bach. The Persian seers would have loved this spectacle: these guys were righteous.

It was a sonic nutrient that was strengthening and thickening the hexagonal web. The linkage of hexagons in turn was feeding back into the assembled singers, infiltrating them with more of the structures of consciousness the grid supported. It was an elegant picture of geomantic reciprocal maintenance, with both components, the consciousness-bearing life-form and the Light grid mirroring that achieved form, fortifying each other in a continuous loop between the conjoined pair. The effect was to generate a third living form.

This was the awakened, well-maintained solar system itself, comprising the planet's self-aware inhabitants and the planet's illuminated Light grid, the awareness of both expanded to fill the solar system interior with this delightful quality of singing. This too, like I saw with R1's planet, now became a Light temple in itself, and one accessible to Earth humans who felt daring enough to explore one this big. It was like a Light temple comprising astrological, singing sheet music. The Earth and its humans had access to this exciting Light temple.

This would have the effect of broadening the scope of geomantically grounded human awareness with our attention now deployed on other planets as well. It would be like teaching consciousness new tricks, innovative martial arts moves or yoga postures in a fabulous calisthenics regimen to expand us. Our geomantic self-definition, how we construed ourselves based on our interaction with our indigenous Light temples (meaning the projected structures of consciousness), would now include input from these affiliated planets. Do you see what I am excited about? What it means to be a human would expand.

The singing, I gradually realized, comprised the sounds of the hexagon units. Here is what I mean: take this vast matrix of linked hexagons as a permutation table of all the possible soul vibrations that can exist on this planet. It is their planet's version of the Tree of Souls. Each hexagon unit of six linked awareness facets expresses a specific vibration, one that can be mathematically scripted. All the permutations of this vibration are worked out, as are all for the other hexagon units; you end up constructing this concatenating hexagonal web, and it was this that was offering the grand chorale to its own solar system.

Remember the Light bubble I retrieved at the end of my odyssey through the seeming disaster? That was "my" vibration plucked from the Tree of Souls. This array of soul vibrations on L2's planet was their world's basket of Light bubbles.

All the possible differences in expression of the planet's dominant phylogeny were singing to their host context, the gravity well of their sun. They lined the streets, packed the stadium, took up all the standing room. It was a terrific turnout, everybody agreed afterwards. It was a gesture of gratitude and validation, like a college graduate walking around her hometown proudly displaying her graduation certificate to those who had watched her grow up.

It was a marvelous sight, the way this planet's dominant life-form filled its solar system with its awakened presence. It transformed the solar system, or perhaps it gave mature expression to what was always latent within it, a seed. The solar system became a delivery vehicle for the expression of this soul group.

I am being overly literal now, but it was as if a single awakened, singing face now filled the interior of this solar system. It was the face of L2's planet's people. I tried to imagine what an entire galaxy of solar system "faces" would be like. Maybe that was the goal of these phylogenies, to have each solar system awake with the singing of its major life-form; if so, the Creator was very patient. It would take some time to get these choruses organized and properly trained so they could give the Old Man, generous sponsor that He was, a proper concert.

Behind this fullness of hexagons was a field of arithmetical codings. If the array of hexagons was singing, the arithmetical backdrop was the music scoring for their chorale. That probably meant the arithmetical scoring lay just outside their solar system, wrapped around it like an etheric numbers net. I saw in this net a myriad of equations running their numbers in a live process, and I saw how these alive equations and algorithms fed into the singing hexagons, and how their singing in turn fed back into the arithmetical net and changed it, causing some of the flashing numbers to alter and the algorithms rewritten to match.

This happened continuously. It was a pattern of reciprocal interaction and constant exchange. My impression was that this was what an achieved Light pattern was supposed to look like, when the consciousness forms, Light grid patterns, and managing numbers were in synchrony, flourishing in this living pattern of constant flow, reciprocally adjusting to the minutiae of changes.

My attention was now drawn to a strong flash of yellow. That was all I could see at first. The yellow hue was pervasive. Then I saw the Yellow Ones, Y1 and Y2, standing at their doors. You may recall those doors numbered 36 the last time I saw these colleagues who had appeared like guardians at these portals. You may also remember I said they did not precisely have visible bodies, certainly nothing like a human form, but a strong nonspecific sense of presence.

The algorithms that run their planet appeared to be streaming out these doors. These 36 doors seemed as anchored and permanently fixed into the planet's manifest reality, as unchallengeable a continuing presence as Judaism's 36 Hidden Righteous Men. This holds that at all times humanity maintains a secret cabal of 36 *Tzaddikim*, or Righteous Men, to testify to the worthiness of humanity to a Supreme Being Who might be having second thoughts about keeping us around. The public never knows who these *Lamed Vavniks* are, but they are always present, substitutions made when the old ones die off, but always petitioning the Supreme Being, making our case, standing up for us. I presume the *Tzaddikim*'s parameters for "righteous" would be congruent with what the earlier Persian seers had in mind, those aligned with the Ma'at-Truth.

The 36 yellow doors were performing a similar function for the Yellow Ones' planet. Except now, with the effects of Earth's algorithmic upgrade entering into this planetary Light grid and its geomantic system, that number of doors had multiplied. Their number now was dizzying to contemplate and hard to count. I didn't have to count them. I'd still be at it if I had to. The doors numbered 36^6, which comes to 1,679,616, the angelic Blaises courteously told me.

People used to speak disparagingly of micromanagement. I remember some of my Dartmouth colleagues leveling those criticisms at our department head, that she put too much attention on picayune details of department procedures or spent too much time monitoring exactly how we delivered our lectures. The expansion of the number of doors on the Yellow Ones' planet gave the term a new meaning, freed it of criticism. This was the kind of micromanagement that I could respect. I saw the need for it, the smart thinking behind its deployment, and if I lived there, you wouldn't find me complaining.

The planet's primary algorithm was now fractally deployed through these many new doors. Instead of having a sales force of only 36 to cover a vast territory, this "company" now had a prolific sales force of 1,679,616 salesmen out in the field, going door to door. That meant the algorithm could be focused on nearly every important detail of planetary life and Light grid input, and it could be slightly modified for local applications just by varying a few key digits.

That struck me as like translating difficult Greek phrases into English for a seminar. Why put the class members at a disadvantage trying to fathom the meaning of obscure classical phrases? Effectively, there were now 1,679,616 versions of the one algorithm; it was creatively adapting itself to the needs of local conditions. Y1 and Y2, though they didn't have heads or bodies, stood at these many doors (they had copied themselves as well) and nodded gratefully as they worked. Things were going well on their planet.

The micromanagement that led to having this many versions of the master algorithm deployed at such minutely localized receptor points also guaranteed that these nodes would each have a holographic copy of the engineering map for the planet. They would get a model download of the planet's Light grid. That way the sites and their sentient attendants, what we would call landscape *devas*, were well-briefed on the local and global energy patterns. They would undertake their localized work with knowledge of the planetary context. Or, to give this more of a personified quality, it would be like each geomantic node had its own docent on hand to answer operational questions. You would always have a thoroughly informed expert present to handle your queries, so ask anything.

The many copies of the algorithm were affecting more than just space. They were affecting the time aspect of reality as well, opening doors into all sorts of nuances of the timeline of "people" and the planet itself. The algorithmic variations were scripting access points into the past and future conditions, and they were coding for future or hypothetical conditions as well. That meant possible or probable outcomes but ones that had not happened yet.

It did the same for the present moment, writing arithmetical specifications for parallel realities for the present, what people used to call alternate universes where possible alternative outcomes, other than the ones that "officially" happened in their local reality, were played out. All the branching variations from any action were demonstrated. The algorithm for the Yellow Ones' planet was providing these specialized nuances.

I kept in mind the fact that this expanded Light grid would be available to daring Earth-human adventurers like an advanced metaphysical theme park. It would surely keep human visitors on their cognitive toes to keep track of all these variations in space and time. I easily imagined myself getting hopelessly lost in its myriad of nuances and alternate outcomes; on the other hand, I marveled at what a fabulous laboratory (or theater) for the exploration of reality permutations this expansion of the Yellow Ones' grid pattern now represented.

The arithmetical realm was making this radical dilation of consciousness possible. I saw many of the "consciousness units" on this planet entering these pathways. How refreshing to observe a planet on which the pursuit of greater awareness was a national pastime, even, perhaps, a recreational option for the wide-awake. I was tempted to dispatch a "Thank-You" card to the arithmetical gods for making this possible, but I held back. I was still recovering from coping with their (as I now know, misperceived on my part) odious culpability in the removal of Earth's managing algorithm and the stress retrieving it had cost me.

These avenues for multiple forays into the vagaries of time and space made something else possible. I saw this complex array of pathways turn inside out. The timeline of this planet was now revealed as a single landscape. It was a landscape of consciousness, but all the details and potentials of the past, present, and future were arrayed upon it like trees, hills, mountains, and lakes. The "people" on this planet could now live within this spacetime-liberated land.

I tried to imagine that possibility on our own Earth, with all the truths and possibilities across the time spectrum displayed as living forms amidst ourselves. What a difference this would be to what is usually the norm, that the past and future are at best rumors or speculations, but mostly we live oblivious to them. When we do turn our attention to them, they appear fixed and inaccessible. We may summon their details to mind, but we cannot actually go forward or backward in any experiential sense. There's a Berlin Wall type of barrier blocking us in both directions. You had none of that on the Yellow Ones' planet. Here among the Yellow Ones all that was open and was shared common knowledge.

At least one human was already taking advantage of this dispensation. I saw Blaise at the Hokkaido site among the Ainu grinning as he explored these avenues. He checked out many of these pathways like an avid collector at a book sale. He examined dozens of volumes, putting many in his bag for checkout. Then I saw myself at Tiwanaku—it's more accurate to say I remembered I was there—and I was observing the effects of Earth's upgrade on G1's home planet.

G1 was the "alien" colleague who was an expert in geometric design, whose planet was flushed with an orange hue, and whose Light grid was one of the complicated Archimedean Solids whose minimum expression started in 4D. The characteristic of his planet was the interpenetration of Light grid and material reality such that you did not have to be clairvoyant to see the subtle landscape. It was much more easily perceived by ordinary daytime awareness than anything we could conceive of yet on the Earth. It was at your fingertips.

Numbers in algorithmic format streamed out of the vertices of this figure. They were the coding of the Archimedean Solid and its intimate relationship with the material world on that planet, and it was doing something else. It was coding for additional geometric shapes to appear. These were as complicated as the first one, and after a while I realized these were the other 12 Archimedean Solids. G1's planet was getting encased in the spectrum of these higher Solids.

Just as Earth's classical Light grid comprised a nesting of the five Platonic Solids, G1's planet was growing a nest of the 13 Archimedean Solids, a higher octave version of a complex Light grid pattern expressing itself principally through geometry. It would be too overwhelming if all 13 of these forms were simultaneously and equally available to embodied consciousness; access to them was staggered. They appeared arrayed in vibrational tiers, escalating octaves of expression. Or, seen from the other end, from the top down, it was a cascade of geometric forms, each imparting its specific condition of consciousness.

You could climb this stepped pyramid of octaves or descend it. In either direction you would be passing through a stepped series of vibrational changes, like plateaus each with its own quality of consciousness. I marveled at the calisthenics opportunity presented to consciousness by this form of structuring.

I tried raising my awareness of these Solids up one layer at a time. The distinguishing characteristic of an Archimedean Solid is identical vertices, but these convex polyhedrals displayed differing numbers of components. The one nearest to me had four triangles and four hexagons and 18 edges bounding them. A few levels further up I saw a figure made of 12 squares, eight hexagons, six octagons, and 72 edges describing their overall shape. Further up was a figure with 20 triangles and 12 pentagons and 60 edges; a few more layers up one figure had 20 triangles, 30 squares, and 12 decagons framed by 180 edges, and the one at the top of this nest consisted of 80 triangles and 12 pentagons with 150 edges.

Try to keep in mind this is not just a high-level version of a jungle gym. These geometrical forms are primary modeling agencies for consciousness at that level. They structure how consciousness feels and what it can do at each level. We have always lived under the influence of the nest of the five Platonic Solids on Earth, but this fact has never been part of public knowledge, though it is now. On a geometric level, the Archimedean Solids are clearly more complicated than the Platonic Solids which means their shaping effects on awareness will be stronger, and the product of that shaping, how you perceive reality, will deepen.

Each geometric form created a different quality of awareness within its confines. Each form defined reality differently, presented different existential conditions. It's hard to describe the impact on consciousness of these changing geometric forms. Maybe I could compare it to *mudras* and hatha yoga postures.

Mudras are hand gestures that accompany body postures to convey certain spiritual principles. The yoga positions or *asanas* affect the whole body. Each bodily gesture along these lines expresses a condition of awareness and in fact evokes it. The nest of 13 Solids was like a choreography of body postures that generated specific but differing effects on how you felt, how reality seemed.

One after another, this is how reality is, this is its feeling quality, each Solid instructs its planetary recipients, then the next, through the 13. Or maybe I should liken it to changing sets on a stage for a theater production: first it's a Victorian drawing room, then a 1950's American ranch-style house, then a Southwest pueblo-style beige-hued flat-roofed house with curving edges. The nest of Solids was the integration of these 13 different reality set changes.

To put this in perspective, the Light grid upgrade to the Earth that began in 1986 consisted of installing only one of the Archimedean Solids. G1's planet had all 13. That says something about the carrying capacity of the consciousness of that planet's residents, that they could handle a fixed cascade of all 13 Solids. Fixed as in it would be there all the time, as a planetary and awareness reality.

Adventurous people on our Earth could visit this array and climb the tiers like kids in a playground exploring the slides and jungle gyms. It's one thing to intellectually know about these Solids; but it's another to experience them as direct realities you find your consciousness embedded in and affected by. I tried to imagine what it would be like wielding free-will on a planet like this, to have that many geometric facets bearing down on your sense of free-willing self.

It would be like, I imagined, living on a planet with a 13-tiered reality structure. On each tier your perceptions and experience of existential conditions would be different, but then think of how flexible that would make your consciousness. It would be like an actor so skilled she could switch fluidly among 13 characters, playing each one convincingly, with changed body, postures, and personalities, transforming herself into one and then the next.

Behind each layer of Solids was the mathematical script, like a backlight. I won't dwell on the specific details because I cannot claim to understand much of it, but for example the equation for one of the Solids involves the square roots of two, five, 10, and 37, and another the square roots of five and 58, another of 22. This is what I saw displayed as if in neon behind each layer of Solids, complex equations in parentheses, brackets, and square root indicators, the scripts of consciousness as expressed through geometric forms, all of which, at this point, were squeezing my head, like I was wearing 13 tight-fitting caps.

I said I wouldn't dwell on the details, but I will provide these to give you a sense of this bizarrely stimulating geometric environment. My head, my awareness, was now capped by (neatly encased in) 792 edges, 452 faces, and 558 vertices. That's the sum of the facets the 13 Solids encase you in on this planet.

I felt like a child exploring a house with that many walls, rooms, and corners, and I knew that it would take me a long time to tour the entire house, to touch it all, but I also knew, or at least suspected, that it would be great fun. With a Light grid as complicated as this, I was no longer surprised that the "people" of G1's world seemed to have no discrete living forms, "bodies" as we knew them. With this many edges, faces, and vertices bearing down upon you, I doubt their consciousness would be able to sustain a single fixed form, but would be subject to wild, protean fluctuations among a repertory of diverse forms, none lasting.

This nesting of the 13 Archimedean Solids had the geomantic effect of creating a planetary skin of 13 layers, which is to say a planet of 13 variations. In practical, experiential terms, this meant 13 different planets laid as a palimpsest. It was also a consciousness and initiation gradient or the equivalent of a stepped pyramid with each layer of planetary reality coded by one of the Solids and exhibiting specific aspects for awareness to master. You climbed this tier of layers as you mastered each preceding layer, and gradually mastered the complete nest. You explored 13 related planets without ever having to leave your home planet.

There was still more to this design. Each of the Solids in the planetary nest circumscribed a specific set of constellations, many dozen star patterns for each. These were not the constellations we are familiar with; their layouts were novel. The layouts were not even the point of this. It was the star gods that were the point. The ensouling intelligences and celestial spirits arrayed in affinity groups were the point, and each Solid and planetary layer afforded access to this group.

Several dozen constellations were in each Solid layer with hundreds of stars in them and 13 layers with variations on this pattern. That's a lot of stars leaning down. It was like having an appreciative, encouraging audience for all your acts of consciousness as you dwelled in one of the 13 planetary layers on this world. It was having access to the consciousness states and initiation wisdom of hundreds of star gods, their knowledge and celestial expertise at your beck and call. It would replicate what I always thought was a delightful cosmic picture from the *Mahabharata* where the gods looked down on human events and applauded the ones they approved of with flower blossoms and ringing bells. It was the closeness of the observing gods, their abiding presence, I liked the best.

It's only an estimate but with an average of 36 constellations per layer and 20 stars in each (720) times 13 layers, you get 9,360 star gods to consult. The count could easily be much higher. Whatever the amount, I admired the rich potential for thorough cosmic knowledge among G1's people. Each planetary layer afforded access to up to 720 star intelligences, which suggests the geomantic map of the planetary landscape would have that many tune-in points or what we call geomantic nodes, providing people access to these star gods. It would be like going to a specialized college and having access to 9,360 tutors.

Each of the 13 layers was also a complete and different planet. In each you would feel you were exploring an entirely different, freshly formulated world. Not only would the conditions of consciousness be varied, but the nature of the material world itself, the elemental aspects of reality, the feel of the wind, the density of stones, the brightness of sunlight, would be different in each Solid tier.

With each level you climb the visible world will appear and feel radically different, as determined by the geometrical necessities of the ruling Archimedean Solid. Before you could with justification say you knew your home planet, had visited all of it, you would have to navigate these 13 adjacent but wildly varying worlds and comprehend their distinctions and match their consciousness. Just to live on G1's planet with its 13 tiered realities would be an initiation experience. The goal, I imagine, proof of planetary mastery, would be to live simultaneously on all 13 layers in the sense of maintaining a detailed holographic record in your consciousness of having mastered each level and being able to call upon it at will.

Since the "people" on this planet don't seem to have material bodies, why would they need a material world to surround them? For one thing, it's not that material; it is quite ethereal and suggests a Pure Land or Buddha Field as you encounter in Buddhist geomantic descriptions of worlds permeated with Light. But these spirits still needed an environment to contain them, to provide them boundaries for their consciousness to push against, however subtle these were.

In a sense, each of the 13 tiered worlds on G1's planet were etheric versions of a material world, bearing the subtle scripts for the elemental conditions, but keeping them at the non-physically manifest level as thoughtform suggestions. This subtlety factor will add extra "spice" to any human explorers venturing into these stacked worlds; humans would have to master 13 levels of etheric reality. I could imagine prolonged package tours by humans, people spending months, years, exploring these 13 congruent worlds, undergoing the transformations in consciousness and identity exposure to this tiered world would induce in them, returning home to tell their friends about it. This would give new impetus to adventure tourism as an initiation expedition.

I saw spirits from G1's realm already exploring these many new levels to their planetary reality. As if they had bodies, they moved their awareness across landscapes in which stars scintillated like mountains of Light in every direction. Each star contained a Light temple, and in that province stood a star intelligence awaiting any visitors who might stop by and inquire about cosmic Mysteries.

I know, it sounds a bit odd, even cavalier, putting it that way, but it seemed clear that these ensouling star *devas* were genuinely committed to enlightening the residents of G1's planet regarding any questions they might pose about existence. Each layer of this 13-tiered planet had its own distribution of stars, temples, star-god docents, and the types of information and Mysteries that might be revealed. It was refreshing, bordering on astonishment, to see a planet in which the pursuit of this type of information was the paramount activity of the people living there. Why am I here, and what is this *here* anyway? The planet with its 13 reality tiers of Solids is your do-it-yourself answer.

People are starting to pose these basic questions on the Earth in greater numbers but the level of inquiry is nothing like what I was seeing on G1's planet. Here it was the consensus reality that posing questions was the purpose of being alive, and they now had a planet properly prepared to enter into that dialogue. Can you picture it, inquiring of your home planet the reasons for your existence and getting practical answers such as recommendations of Light temples to visit? Technically, our Earth was designed precisely to facilitate that through its geomantic terrain and its correspondence with the human structures of consciousness, but up until now few people knew this and took advantage of it, or considered the questions worth asking or even likely to get useful answers.

Their equivalent of an Albion, their world's personification of the collective consciousness of the phylogeny set in the cosmic design container of a Body of Light, comprised the contents and experiences of the 13 layers of their planet. For a "person" on G1's planet to get a comprehensive picture of "his" own identity, "he" would have to traverse these 13 tiers and experience then assimilate it all. Their Albion was a 13-layered collective, with all those stars and their *devas* and the revelations those thousands of awakened spirits had to offer.

Each spirit had to build this planetary Albion on their own, yet their individual construction of that body of Mystery and disclosure contributed to the definitive fleshing out of this collective Person for the entire world of the 13 parts. One individual's Mystery initiation contributed to the initiation of the collective, making it easier for the next person who tries it. On Earth people used to call this additive impact the "hundredth monkey effect," that the achievement of a few spreads rapidly through a population like a positive infection, reaches a critical threshold, and suddenly everybody can do it easily, whatever it was. I saw that the life of the "people" on this planet was now devoted to this pursuit.

Every Archimedean Solid not only affected the tier of planetary reality it structured, but it was coincident with that layer, part of the surface landscape. You could not accurately say the Solid existed above you, as it were, in or part of the atmosphere; instead it was in the same place as the traversable landscape, and the squares, triangles, pentagons, and hexagons of the various figures defined the geomantic provinces and architecturally acted like Light temples. Each Solid was the energetic framework for the planetary reality of its tier. Add to this picture the consciousness impact of all the stars in each tier, more than 720 on average, and their star gods, and you have a richly hierophantic landscape. Can you image living on a planet that offers 13 sequential layers of revelation?

Around this entire 13-tiered planet, like a series of lotus blossoms encompassing the planet's achieved Albion, were the thousands of Ofanim diamond hexagon facets rising up around the world like hands gently cupping the figure in Light that the planet had now birthed. These Ofanim diamond hands cupped the individual geomantic provinces, the components of the Solids, and the planetary array. That was only the beginning of what they were doing.

Picture this scene turned around so that the diamond facets each bore a copy of the complete planet and its 13 tiers, the Solids, their facets, and the 9,360 stars in those facets. These Blaise facets are offering this dazzling array of consciousness states to the cosmos like pollen on a ripened flower blossom. They hold the completed 13-tiered display like seeds ready to be launched into cosmic space, not to seed other worlds to copy this one, but as inspiration, examples to show them what could be achieved: Look at this marvel of Light. You can do it.

I tried to picture seeing such a seed approaching the Earth. I saw the 13 Archimedean Solids wrapped around a material globe and rolling through space. Each layer bearing its load of secondary geometric figures and the 720 stars and the star gods in their

Light temples, and don't forget to be almost overwhelmed by the myriad of outstretched diamond-angelic hands cupping this spectacle, imparting great Light to it. It would be a fantastic apparition in our sky, and I wouldn't be surprised if people took it to be a monstrous spaceship. It would certainly evoke that interpretation, this rolling colossus of Light and form, or perhaps people would see it as the final, prophecied approach of all the gods.

How could anyone come to the correct conclusion that it was a copy of a planet? That its purpose in arriving in the cognitive proximity of our planet was to inspire us to copy its level of achievement in mastering the rungs of awareness implicit in the geomantic design of the planet itself? Then I thought, perhaps the heightened cognitive conditions the Earth's algorithmic upgrade will deliver to Earth people will make us more able to comprehend this unusual appearance and appreciate it as a benign planetary visitation, a *Hello!* from an old colleague.

We will be able to see things, marvelous, extraordinary things we never could before as this big change to the operating conditions of our geomantic Earth continues to expand. I wrote myself a mental note to keep my eyes focused on the sky around Earth for the arrival of G1's planetary entourage. It would be something to see it while (presumably) still occupying my physical body. I was looking forward to resuming cognitive business in a fully embodied state.

Then I reminded myself that this planetary epiphany G1's entourage was sending us was in fact already present across the Earth. About one-third of the 48 dome caps per dome present the holographic reality of the Light body of a planet; there likely already were other planetary apparitions as complex and marvelous as G1's blazing their presence across the subtle Earth, but we just hadn't seen them yet. Possibly the sight of G1's outlandish planetary arrival in Earth's psychic atmosphere might train people in seeing the Light bodies of planets and make it easier, even, eventually, more routine to see them under the dome caps they've been living under for untold generations but not seeing them. Every planet's Light body will be a challenge to human-style cognition but a mind-expander and keen source of illumination once you do see them clearly.

There's more to this than merely seeing an extraplanetary Light body as if it is only a curiosity in a museum. The Light bodies of these planets are each a visitable Light temple laid out for us upon the Earth's geomantic landscape. We could enter and tour the facility of each, and, better, take in its special experience. Each Light temple is designed to deliver an experience in consciousness, to saturate us in the particular process of awareness that Light temple performs.

Each immersion like this deepens our understanding of reality and activates yet another "codon" within our innate geomantic template. Every planet is relevant to us, and the experience of their Light body progressively wakes us up further. I envisioned people devoting their time to this new style of geomantic tourism; you no longer need to travel to remote and exotic places on the Earth. Just find the nearest dome and you could spend the rest of your life exploring its "caps." You could visit strange and exotic planets in their Light body manifestations just by walking around within a 33-mile area of landscape.

It was time to see what the last of our extraplanetary colleagues, A1-4 and A5-8, were up to. These "guys" actually resembled a humanoid appearance, with large heads that seemed to bobble and turn fluidly in all directions, though I figured out the first time I saw them that this head quality was meant to evoke the reality of their mostly mental state of existence, that their manifestation was primarily wide-awake, focused mind, and the semblance of linked heads was probably mostly metaphorical. This was the Air planet, as I mentioned before, and its life was all of the mind, as swift and clear as the flowing wind.

When you looked at them as a group, it was like a Cubist painting of eight heads showing up as different angles on a single large cranium looking in eight directions. At the same time, two heads accompanied each of the four of us at our rhombus sites around the planet, which meant I enjoyed the company of two A-heads at Tiwanaku, although for the most part I was seeing them at their home planet where they were industriously extruding numbers with a dizzyingly prolific enthusiasm. You'd feel you were playing tennis against 100 champions, and they were backhanding so many balls just over the net you couldn't keep up.

The sword is the elemental talisman for air, and I was seeing lots of them. Thousands of sharp bright swords rose up out of the planet like porcupine quills. Soon the planet was surrounded by upraised swords of Light, and the planet itself now looked like an adamant sword that seemed to face out in all directions ready to cut through ignorance, confusion, illusion, glamour, and misperception.

The planet was a sword of Light searing through the galaxy, dispelling darkness. It represented the power of mind to cut through all obfuscation and confusion. It did *not* represent an aggressive, hostile, challenging stance. If that were a spaceship approaching Earth I would expect to see people running. To get away from it, that is: this degree of cognitive clarity could be intimidating. Here comes a planet of swords that will slice through all our illusions about reality. On the other hand, if you're weary of reality being so confoundingly comprised of bullshit and lies, this sword-planet's arrival would feel liberating and welcome.

How did things look in the other direction, in the interior of the A's planet? I saw a multitude of minds at work. They were focusing on a library of schematics. It was as if the Supreme Being let them pore through the archives of cosmic design and intention, His personal files, and study the blueprints for realities, including those proposed, underway, or achieved. Their nimble minds were digesting this wealth of design, this creative proliferation of reality plans. I saw they had a sponsor or perhaps a reference librarian. It was our own mentor, Ray Master Hermes, Lord of the Emerald-Green Robe and the Emerald Tablets.

He walked among the researchers in this cosmic architecture library, answering questions, indicating correlated plans the researchers might like to consider. These minds gave the impression that they wanted to know everything, read every report, study every blueprint, and that they had endless mental digestive abilities, that they could assimilate even the Mind of God, if given enough time. The infinity of that Mind and its contents did not daunt them. They would start today, this minute, and keep working every day until they had thoroughly plumbed the riches of knowledge and fact in that Mind.

They were spreading this spirit of mental acuity and acquisitiveness as the planet of swords rolled through the galaxy. To be precise, it was multiple copies of this that were now touring the galaxy imparting this clarifying quality. That probably understates its impact. Imagine a planet of swords, sharp, bright, adamant, appearing suddenly in your world's atmosphere, its very existence clearing the air, sharpening minds, slicing through misunderstanding, the razor-sharp mental edge of its presence cutting you clear down to the bone of truth, that inviolate part of you put there by the Supreme Being to be the touchstone for reality no matter what the external conditions of world and psyche might be.

The swords of this planet did not, technically, move any closer to any planet they visited, including Earth, as I pictured myself standing on the Earth as it approached, but it was as if somehow the swords' potential effects were extended outwards so that the etheric edges of the swords were cutting through planetary confusion. I saw a multitude of copies of this sword's-edge planet traversing our galaxy, like an entire sales team dispatched from headquarters to offer clarity to all the worlds it encountered, each carrying his own sample case.

All of this was made possible, and instantaneously so, it seemed, through this marvelous web of relations among the six free-will planets that began when Earth got the upgrade to its algorithm. One planet's progress makes possible major improvements and the achievement of evolutionary thresholds on another. The A's planet was waiting for us, for

Earth, to upgrade; then we could enjoy the benefits of this improvement in our cognitive abilities and get the mind-clearing (and searing) impact of their sword-saturated world coming to visit us soon.

Speaking of our home planet, I saw big changes happening on the Earth. The main thrust of the algorithmic upgrade was to prepare the planet for the return of the domes in the immediate future. This had been long foreseen; it was part of the long-term plan for the planet, and the angelic Blaises had alluded to it in their early briefings with the human Blaise back in 1984. They said the domes had been here three times already in the long history of the Earth, and would return for a fourth visit not too far in the future. That was 81 years ago. Then it was a fascinating rumor about our planet's future, a tomorrow too far ahead on the timeline to feel real at the time; that tomorrow was now. We were nearly there.

I could understand why they had to make provisions for the Earth to receive the domes again. It would be a major energetic input to the planet. It would rock the grid and perturb human consciousness, not from any ill intent but from the sheer force and magnitude of 1,746 actual domes of Light arriving. They were not spaceships or only etheric canopies of Light, though they did resemble both; in construction, they were something in between matter and Light, perhaps like how we conceive of plasma, and each was 33 miles wide.

You would be able to see them though I don't think you could tap your fingernails on their surface and expect the kind of sound you'd get if you did that to your car. Probably you would be able to walk through them yet they would provide a "palpable" membrane,

some kind of noticeable consciousness gradient. Blaise said in his training he had often been inside domes, except he had been in his visionary body (possibly astral) and the membranes were porous.

Each dome would convey the real-time holographic presence of a star and its ensouling intelligence, and we're talking about the major players of the galaxy. The big shots of the galactic body, the high-magnitude boys, gigantic galactic presences like the star Arcturus whose diameter is 21.9 million miles or Canopus at 61 million miles, or Rigel at 67 million miles across. One of the returning domes will convey each of those. Try to conceive of compressing that actual star presence into a Light canopy no more than 33 miles wide, how intense that concentrated holographic presence would be on the Earth and for people. You have to appreciate the likely impact of that real-time presence times 1,746.

It's one thing to see the stars in the night sky or to interact with their holograms in a landscape zodiac. But with the domes here again, those star presences will be intensified by many orders and that will impinge mightily on consciousness. Aspects within us that have been long dormant will suddenly spring to life. It would be like, I imagine, immediately becoming aware of the throbbing, pulsating presence of 1,746 wide-awake energized and illuminated cells in your body, each of them bearing the face of a star god and its Light.

Each of these domes would be 33 miles across, 16.5 miles high. That was their original size here, though their residual imprints have mostly shrunk over the years since their last arrival to about half that size. Many, returning to their pre-arranged, original locations, would overlap settled areas, cities, highways, even individual homes. The human-settled Earth's surface over the many millennia since they were last here (which was many millions of years ago) had grown up and out, though mostly oblivious to these indigenous energy emplacements, except for when the domes were co-present with mountains, which, in fact, they caused to rise up from out of the Earth in the first place.

I suppose it is the 83,808 secondary dome caps that would principally "land" over the Earth's settled surface areas. The entropic subluxation of Light grid with physical topography might pose some problems because for the most part human settlement has proceeded oblivious to this distribution pattern and only the Earth remembers where the domes and dome caps originally set down. The domes and dome caps had to return to their original places because the whole pattern was scripted before the domes ever came even the first time. The Light grid of the dome imprint was a fixed-form meta-grid of consciousness designed to envelop the planet like an intricate lace doily of stars and Light lines.

None of this would physically obstruct human life and its logistical mechanisms, but it would have an immediate impact on consciousness, Nature, and biosphere. The upgraded algorithm would accommodate the introduction of this radical and tremendous Light source on all aspects of planetary life and its Light grid, and it was already starting to make those accommodations years in advance. Not too many years, but not literally tomorrow either for the return. The upgraded algorithm was coding flexibility and expansion potential for the Light grid; far more factors and a higher consciousness gradient would have to be taken into consideration when the domes arrived like a fleet of cosmic trucks.

I saw our thousand Hierophancy colleagues at their geomantic nodes. It was a general impression, a group photograph that spanned the planet, and I could focus on any individual I wished to see how they were getting on. I tuned into a man meditating at a wooded mountain site near Lake Tahoe in California.

It was an odd sight to see a geomancer defending a single digit. It wasn't that this number within the upgraded algorithm was in jeopardy, but it did seem like the man's meditative attention had the effect of constant attention on this figure. The single digit encompassed the Light temple at this site as if strongly backlit. Inside the Light temple (it was a copy of the Celestial City of the Sun and thus a geomantic feature of considerable size and importance), everywhere you looked you saw the translucent digit, upright like a skyscraper made of glass.

You have to remember that geomantic work of this type is very subtle. There is no heavy lifting, no straining or effort, no heroic meditative exertions. You just have to keep your awareness focused on an intended topic and outcome, in this case, the presence of this single digit and its anchorage in the Light temple at this site, all of this framed by the rhombus and larger hexagon.

I saw what the man was doing. He had entered the Light temple, anchored his awareness in it, added certain geomantic features such as a large blue dish underneath it (spanning a mile in diameter, made of combined human and Ofanim consciousness), and a copy of the Ofanim's Rotunda of Light on it which provides a dependable interaction mode for people working with this site.

Then he toured the Celestial City and further anchored his presence within this large golden citadel, close to the "solar furnace" aspect of this facility. Next he expanded his awareness outward in all directions to move into the skyscraper-like presence of the single digit (a "9") that was coordinated with this geomantic node and was thereby his responsibility to maintain. His "9" looked formidable, a towering digit in Light surrounded by his focused attention.

It looked like he entered this digit from a hundred different points and stood there. Once you make all your alignments, what remains is to hold your attention there steady. It was as simple as paying attention to your breathing in yoga or conventional meditation; here, instead, you keep your awareness on the presence, the duration, the existence, of this translucent digit, appreciating the fact that it is one number among at least a thousand in a live running equation.

I had the odd impression (it bordered on the whimsical, you will likely think) that the purpose of this Tahoe site was to be squeezed with focused consciousness until it extruded this one digit, like popping a pea out of its pod, a number necessary to the continuance of the world and reality even though it was but one number in a global equation of a thousand digits.

All the other geomancers were making the same meditative gesture. It had the effect of linking them up in the flow of this algorithm, like in a grand parade. This image might have been subject to my whimsy, but it looked like these people were marching along merrily holding up their digits like bright banners.

They paraded across the Earth's surface proudly bearing their standards. Maybe if you were in psychic space above the Earth you could read the full algorithm.

Then it seemed they walked inside the translucent column made by the digit, and these digits weaved in and out of one another in formations that resembled constellation patterns or perhaps the way you could look down on a swimming pool and see trained swimmers make an elaborate, beautiful, kaleidoscopic pattern in the water based on the collective positions of their bodies. Synchronized group swimming, they used to call this. The new algorithm was manifesting an elegant symmetrical digital pattern like that on the Earth, and the planet's surface was a parchment upon which the numbers were coded.

The man I was observing looked exceptionally healthy. His body exuded Light and vitality, like he had a miniature sun inside him. I wasn't sure what his age was, fifties, perhaps, but he looked like he would enjoy a rich longevity. I had the same impression from others I looked at. A combination of factors, the Golden Age advent in 2020, the various Light grid upgrades since then, and now the upgrade to the planet's algorithm, was playing out in human physiology.

People were looking healthier now, more vibrant, more wide-awake. Myths tell us that during previous Golden Ages humans lived to extreme old age, into the hundreds of years, even, though it's hard to believe, into the thousands of years. The Hindu time model of the *Yugas* or Ages says humans lived 100,000 years in the *Satya Yuga* or Golden Age; for 10,000 years in the *Treta Yuga* or Silver Age; 1,000 years in the Bronze or *Dwapar*; but only 100 in the recently ended *Kali Yuga* or Black Age. Maybe they lived 100 years, but that would be early *Kali Yuga* because it hasn't been our longevity norm, but they weren't years of delight and enlightenment, generally speaking. Troubled, vexed, disturbed were more typical qualities, complemented with lots of pathologies.

Without trying to prove the validity of any of these numbers, it seems reasonable that a Golden Age plus the additional correctives we have seen (and helped) in the last 45 years will have a positive effect on human health and life viability. People will remain healthier, live longer, have less disease, probably require less sleep, and then sleep less troubled than in previous generations, and during waking hours exhibit more sharpness and clarity of attention, and have probably a marked improvement in cognition and intelligence. The status of a planet's Light grid and how fast it runs will usefully modulate all these factors.

The speed of the Earth's Light grid will push through the unprocessed karma from people's bodies and enable them to clear out old business faster. At a deep level the stuckness of this old material is what causes illness and disease and clogged, stagnant, and rebarbative states of mind in people keep them glued to old ways, conservative notions, fixed, even archaic, beliefs and rituals.

The Light grid upgrade is like a powerful fire hose pummeling water through the caked mud and detritus blocking the drainage channels in the roads. Or it is like a controlled burn smartly excising dead, dry brush that cluttered up forests. I felt this in myself, whatever analogy I used to describe it: I felt a lightening of spirit, a brightening of awareness, a sharpening of intelligence, a lovely ripening, a deep and thorough karmic housecleaning of my burdened psyche and body as it gladly yielded up intransigent stodgy old karmic content.

I was observing the immediate effects of the Light grid upgrade on the members of the Hierophancy out in the "field" affecting the anchoring of this change. Soon these benefits would start spreading out, foliating into the general population, and the Earth would feel unarguably different, better, richer, uplifted. That in turn would make any subsequent modulations easier to implement and faster to assimilate by the population. Earth would have a flow, once again participate in the refreshing reciprocal cascade of effects from multiple levels and linkages (higher Light grids) the Earth was now set into.

The Hierophancy members were demonstrating this dexterity in consciousness, the fluidic ability to move into and through the conjoined layers of Earth reality and the six-planet free-will Light grid, and to hold these layers together. As an example of this growing geomantic proficiency I saw the man I already had been watching shift into the digit his geomantic node anchored, then into its Light grid specifics, the temples and processes of awareness the structures ran, then the psychic images that emanated from this complex to illustrate the site's identity, function, and its role in cosmic life.

More of the life of the cosmos, its true reality, and the human role in it, will start dawning in people, and it will be a marvelous, refreshing revelation as people start to get an accurate orientation to reality, the planet, and higher intentions. This will be the true end of the Dark Ages, those millennia of Kali's blackness. People will be living happily in the

Apocalypse, enjoying their incarnation in a thoroughly self-revealing landscape of Light and consciousness.

Reality will be finally revealed in its true details, the original design disclosed, and people will start to find that salutary, a source of orientation, and a pleasure. The Apocalypse was never a destructive event, certainly not on the physical level. It was to be a revelatory moment, definitively displaying the true structures of reality. The *Kali Yuga* inspired a darkened interpretation and expectation of this; the truth was the Apocalypse was always intended to be a hierophantic event. All I can say is, thank God reality is now apocalyptic and the Earth hierophantic every day. It makes all the difference in my quality of life, my daily routine, how well I can execute the responsibilities of my job, and the longevity and success of our Sun Valley project, and, I wager, in yours too. Can you see my eyes twinkling? Look in the mirror. Are yours twinkling now?

Meanwhile, I was stepping into a new Light temple, a grid pattern that straddled the six free-will planets that had been crucial to our algorithm upgrade. The design of the six-planet Light grid challenges the mind to describe it properly. It is an architectural space, an implicit hexagon encompassing a great deal of galactic space, comprising six key features, and, as far as I can tell, existing or conducting business mostly in 5D. That means as a time landscape, you can enter this at any desired node, in the past, present, or future, as simply as choosing a marked door and entering through it, what the Ofanim call a "now-ledge," a portal into the time landscape from outside it in 5D reality.

I was now surrounded by the complexities and beauties of the Light grid improvements to the other five planets. It was like you're in a pentagonal building and at each of its five corners it opens into another building, five more in total, though that's too literal a 3D analogy. It's more like you can see these five adjacent Light grid buildings as if transparently overlaid at the five corners; the moment you focus on one of them, you are already inside it, walking around.

Then I realized I had the count wrong. It's a building with six corners. I was no longer implicitly centered in the Earth Light grid building. I was instead in the center of this composite architectural space made by the six linked planets. Correctly put, we now had a *seven*-aspected Light grid spanning the six planets.

See if you can picture this. The six planets and their upgraded Light grids were no longer only in the corners, transparently overlaid; now they filled the interior. I was in a consciousness field described by the interpenetration of these six grids. They were each running their complex consciousness processes, scripting their planetary realities, and they were doing this in an integrated collective manner. This harmonious collective manner in turn generated the seventh, a summation of the life and processes of the six.

I had the singing hexagons, the shapeshifting spirits and Light grids, the 279,936 doors, the sphere of swords, the 13 layers of Archimedean Solids, the Earth's own upgrading Light grid, the nest of five Platonic Solids morphing into one of the Archimedean Solids, the planetary tilt correcting itself, and the planet preparing for the return of the domes. I had all of that. I was immersed in that. It was as if I was now on a planet in a Light grid comprising these six Light grids.

The realities of the six collegial planets were now integrated into one big reality. It shared—it *integrated*—all the consciousness processes of the six linked worlds. In this composite "building" the contents of the six corners now filled the inside. It was as if the corners and contents had been pulled to the space's center.

Each of the six planets had their own Albion, a personification of their collective consciousness, expressed essentially as a face or focus of attention. These Albions filled the composite Light temple, making a six-headed form. I saw the Light temple from the outside; a spirit with six heads looked out of it. Each head occupied a 60-degree section of the interior space. The heads were different, in accordance with their host planets, yet collectively they were the same, a focus of planetary attention, seeing reality in an integrated sixfold way but through a cranium of Light comprising a cosmos of pertinent stars and *devas*.

Like another layer within each head I saw the dominant sentient life-form of the planet. For Earth I saw a generic human filled with stars and chakras, and for the other planets, I saw forms that were too cosmically feral to decode into images I could even attempt to describe. But they all had wide-awake self-awareness distributed throughout individual units (bodies) that carried this.

Inside the composite Light temple, I experienced "myself" to have these six heads and to be seeing out across the galaxy from these six linked cranial perspectives, each covering a 60-degree swath of galactic space. These six heads comprised the composite temple, and if I could experience the six all at once, it would yield a seventh "head." No, it already did yield a seventh; I meant I could potentially expand my awareness to see through these interlinked six eyes.

Yes, this was the seventh head, the implicit seventh planet we had met earlier in the sphere-packing perception of our six planets and how they yielded a seventh. It was the same expansion logic as Qabala's 50 Gates of *Binah*. You had seven *Sefirot* or chakras each expressed through seven nuances; there's 49, then your entire system of the 49 makes the 50th. That's how we got the seventh here.

This was the seventh sentient spirit, or perhaps the first, the conjoint culmination of the integration of the six free-will planets and their Light grids to create a seventh, and all of that comprising a larger Light grid. This was a new body of consciousness, a new fusion of elements, a new Head. It was like being one of six children, compatible, psychologically consanguineous, and you could move your awareness among any of the six, and, the key part, you could also be the summation of these six, the seventh composite integrated child, the six children together, fused into one, by parthenogenesis birthing a seventh child.

I want to be sure you can follow this, the architecture of "where" I was. I was on the Earth, at Tiwanaku or Sun Valley, I don't know for sure, maybe both. Our planet occupied a corner in the hexagon that though it spanned a vast extra-galactic space, gave the impression that the other five corners and their planets were right here, as if leaning over my shoulder in support and cordial interest. In functional and energetic terms, the planets of our five colleagues were with us on the Earth; the hexagon had drawn their remotely spaced planets to the Earth.

Then I moved over to the next vertex. This was Rl's planet. The other five planets, including the Earth, were leaning over his shoulder, and the hexagon of six planets loomed over him like a shield of Light. The situation was the same for the other four planets; on each, you had the impression the other five were there. That meant, experientially, I found myself on six planets simultaneously and I experienced my position in this hexagon as having six points of focus or view.

Then came the marvel of it all. The hexagon was framed spherically by the seventh head. The six planets were six heads comprising its larger seventh head, and I experienced myself as occupying this head too, along with our 13 friends. I was in six places at once (as were my colleagues, and that includes Blaise, Sal and Jocelyn, so I should say I was with my 16 friends), and overviewing this multi-spatial reality from a seventh vantage point. This head was the place you occupied to experience the other six simultaneously, not linearly, as I have related it here, but all of them at once as you see through six linked planet heads.

This seventh head was self-aware, aware it was looking through six heads as a seventh, and it gave the spectacle the sensation of stillness, even stasis. It was just the one seven-headed presence touring the galaxies while being anchored at six widely separated planets with a high free-will quotient. Shining through this seventh head were the six "heads" of the six planets, but more precisely, it was the phylogenic face of the collective consciousness of each planet, their equivalent of our Albion, the summation of their Light grid.

I was glad Albion had some company, the fellowship of his peers, but I also marveled at how my awareness was simultaneously occupying the summation of six planetary consciousness forms, and, for as long as I could hold my attention, the seventh which was the experience of the six all at once, knitting these distant galaxies together into this unified seven-planet presence, a snowflake of planets.

This seventh Head, this consciousness, was the fusion of six nuances of free will. These six planets were not the only planets among the untold number that had free will in significant amounts awarded to its dominant life-form, but there was something special about the nuances represented by these six. You could read the anatomy in the reverse direction: our seventh was the mother planet that birthed the six progeny, each carrying a 60 percent part of it.

Either way, here it was, alive, awake, and broadcasting. It was speaking to the galaxies. I wasn't the only person inside this Head observing events. All our thousand Hierophancy colleagues, Blaise, Sal, and Jocelyn, were in here watching. The Blaise angels were watching this with some glee too. Watching what? The act of conscious co-creation exercised under conditions of free will.

Free will means you can act unencumbered by necessity, karma, or compulsion. Your actions are not blindly driven by Shadow considerations. This Head compounded of six free-will planets was now acting that way, freely. For one, it was generating copies of itself, images in Light of its sixfold composition. A newborn consciousness-bearing form, something brand new to the cosmos, it was speaking to the galaxy in a kind of glossolalia about the joys of freedom. It dispatched pictures on its words, and I'm not sure it was even words it "spoke."

The pictures showed "people" of the six worlds that comprised this Head moving about in their Light temples, interacting with the facilities, seeing deities. Their heads enlarged as they filled with Light and their body forms grew more ethereal, and you could see the Light temples they visited as if now inside them. They created new Light temples as if they were master architects working in Light, and they empowered these new forms to run processes of awareness. They did this as easily as a master chef trying out new sauces in the kitchen.

This co-creative space was like an imagination matrix, a holographic generator of desired realities, proposed realities, conjectural, experimental ones—anything. We could create situations anywhere along the timeline, as if using the *Akashic* Records as raw material and story seeds for our "film" scripts and creating life "movies" out of them.

We could create situations that were personally desirable, such as, for me, a lovely day at the beach, perhaps a quiet *motu* in the Tahitian island cluster, or scenarios that were of initiation significance or revelatory impact for students. Let's say somebody was trying to decide on a course of action, follow course *a* or *b*, and she could not make up his mind. We could simulate the outcomes for both choices and let her experience the ramifications along their respective timelines.

None of it would count in terms of a permanent entry in the *Akashic* Records of actual reality, but this sampling of outcomes would be instructive. It would be a live-action version of how architects used to create 3D interactive computer models of proposed homes in which the prospective buyer could "walk" through the house. We could generate images of Grail Knights experiencing the Holy Grail, healing the Wounded Fisher King, leaving these images in place to inspire others later. We could fashion simulations of successful interactions with any of the Light temples, their distribution grids, and linkages among them, all of which built finer, more sophisticated awareness platforms.

Our minds now possessed the requisite mathematical dexterity to create these situations. Once we would have to depend on computers to generate these holographic realities. Now we could do it ourselves. We had use of the numbers. The arithmetical gods were on our side; they willingly cooperated with our plans. Science fiction writers once used terms like "holodeck" and "holosuite" to denote designated creative playgrounds for reality simulations based on computer code and holographically projected light. You could take the storyline of books, such as detective stories or adventure tales, and project them this way, then interact as characters within this defined matrix. But it required complex technology and energy inputs to pull it off. Now we could do it with our mind.

Thought and energy were now arithmetically coded into simulated realities, and, when appropriate, into actual realities, ones that would last and be recorded. But maybe the simulated realities were entered into the *Akashic* Records as well, as just another branch, perhaps under experimental simulations, the way scientists would record all their experiments and hypotheses, regardless of outcomes. You could check the *Akashic* files under Simulations and Conjectural Realities.

God is a meticulous diarist, writing down every last event, however minute. Samuel Pepys, Virginia Woolf, André Gide, all the mellifluous and prolix diarists over time, would be outdone in an instant by His punctilious scribblings. After all, per the model of quantum physics that every possible alternate action in a scenario requiring a crucial choice branches off to form its own universe to play out that alternate outcome, surely the Chief Diarist records these multiplying alternative worlds, maybe adding an annotation, "Interesting. Clever. I might try that sometime."

If so, then what we spawned from our experimental mental holographic projections would be worthy of entering the public record and would have a palpable effect on overall reality, and He'd have twice as much recording to complete for each day. He'd have to hire some executive helpers. Maybe we could get writing credits or even author's royalties for the ideas.

We created many pictures, complete scenarios with action and drama, and left them in a freeze-frame format hanging like bright banners in the ethers. You put your attention on one banner and it would activate the reality-movie to start running. That was the mission of mythic images left to us from our ancestors and the *Rishis*, to serve as initiation portals for our understanding to move into and realize the pictures depicted live realities, still crucially pertinent to Earth.

Now the message of these mythic images, these freeze-framed psychic dramas, was more than that. They had a meta-message. That was to suggest human consciousness has the power to create these scenarios and more, per our imagination, desire, and purpose, and along lines that would benefit the planet and humanity and not harm either. Even better, they would be fun to experience. When was the last time we thought reality was fun? Not recently. Drudgery until yesterday, I should think. No doubt the prolific array of Ofanim images and metaphors the angelic mentors presented the human Blaise over the years of his training were created like this in a spirit of creative fun and great enjoyment.

We were travelling—the sevenfold Head, that is—to many planets in the Milky Way Galaxy and apparently in other galaxies as well simulating realities. We were a theater troupe touring the provinces, staging our exciting production in a bracing round of summer stock theater. It was a good play, this one. Our performances were custom-matched to the particulars of each planet, to its style and structures of consciousness, its level of picture understanding, and its Light grid. Somehow, without any noticeable effort, we got into alignment with those particulars and generated our mythic images and holographic simulations to match their consciousness style. The numbers we needed were always at hand.

The arithmetical gods were astonishingly cooperative, compared to their earlier attitude, and the suitable myth pictures and psychic initiation maps came easily. Could this be the same guys, once recalcitrant, now our best friends? Say a choice needed to be made. Before it was, we simulated images extrapolated into the future showing the ramifying consequences of either decision; the "client" could watch how each decision played out then decide his course on that basis.

I chuckled. What we were doing was still hierophantic. It was high level, certainly, compared to what we used to take for hierophantic work on the Earth, but it was still revealing the Holy Light only with a changing repertoire of mythic images and metaphors. The Holy Light, I now understood, is a generic condition of consciousness, its powers to be self-aware, to create, to comprehend. It's like adjusting product advertisements to correlate with local demographics.

Ultimately, it seems the focus of this Holy Light is itself, to facilitate embodied consciousness to gain lucid awareness of its own ability to gain this awareness. Yes, it is circular, and that can seem dizzying at first, but this Holy Light inevitably leads you back into a paradoxical singular space, a nondualistic realm. There you find yourself not contemplating the august presence of the Supreme Being, but better: you're one with the Ineffable Creator as the Holy Light. You don't witness the Holy Light's disclosure: you *are* that disclosure.

You participate in the Supreme Being's ecstatic hierophantic act, Here I am, like this. You reveal the Holy Light, you are embedded in it, you are this Holy Light, and you realize, with a shock perhaps, that reality itself is hierophantic, and all the Light grids and Light temples across the worlds are the mechanism of that disclosure and your work as a Hierophant is to make sure they keep disclosing that Holy Light and illuminate and fully wake up everyone.

Eventually, disclosure leads to identity, and you and the world, you and the Creator, you and the particulars of the geomantic template, are identical. It makes sense: the whole point of the hierophantic landscape is to present a mirror image of yourself as a cosmic intelligence. Behold, pal, this is you as we see you.

I hope you can follow this but it now seemed to me that this ability to generate simulated realities and alternative outcome projections was itself a type of Light temple. After all, a Light temple is a structure in Light that conducts you through a specific process of consciousness with the intent of making you fully cognizant of all its aspects and allowing its transformative effect to work on you.

Each Light temple and its process reveals a component of the Cosmic Human as expressed in the microcosmic you. It is a continual revelation process. The Light temple is only a delivery vehicle for this revelation; after you get it, enter the process it displays before you, the Light temple is irrelevant, like an envelope a letter came in. Your assimilation of the process is paramount. Our work of releasing suitable mythic pictures, accessible reality simulations, and psychic signposts is one of populating a given world with more Light temples. A mythic image is a Light temple; its components, its implicit drama, can enlighten.

A mythic tableau—a hero slaying a dragon—can strongly reveal the Holy Light. When you *get* what that picture means, it can feel wonderfully illuminating. Your mind widens as the Holy Light fills it to saturation with a bright understanding. The Qabalists tell us that the Ancient of Days is always looking for new ways to reveal Himself to mortal consciousness: Here I am! The Hierophant's job is to help that along, nudging, clarifying, pulling back curtains, so the Supreme Metaphoricist can spread out His billion card images of Himself.

The Hierophant is always hosting a new Light temple for visitors. He is docent, mentor, instructor, even mechanic, assuring it delivers the Holy Light. These images we were generating and proliferating across the galaxies were Light temples. Consciousness could enter each, rendering it instantly alive and interactive and capable of providing the illumination of mind it was designed to.

The galactic sky was copious with revelation points like lightning bugs on a summer's night. The ethers were bursting with star points of disclosure. The Supreme Being was speaking in a billion voices, hinting, explaining everything. Just listen; enter the nearest Light temple; put your attention on its processes.

As a former professor of comparative mythology, even though it was decades ago when I last faced a seminar room full of mostly eager students, I found it fascinating to realize that mythic images themselves are Light temples. Usually, I thought of a Light temple as an architectural space done in Light; it delivered a process of consciousness, held up a mirror to the corresponding version of that in a person, and invited a person's awareness into its field for a creative, hopefully edifying, encounter. A mythic image is like a psychic snapshot taken by an initiate at the peak of the interactive cycle of consciousness with the features of a given Light temple and its residents or superintendents.

Often a psychic picture hinted at the kind of experiences it offered. Think of the Greek picture of Hephaistos at his solar forge accompanied by three Cyclopes inside the terrible volcano, Mount Etna. There he toiled at making all sorts of objects for the gods, shields to thrones. That mythic picture, that residue preserved in Greek myth, is a clue to this site's use. You go into the subtle aspect of Mount Etna, into the forge of Hephaistos, to have that celestial fire put in you.

It was the Greeks' way of representing *Swarga*, the Hindu name for a high realm of solar effulgence, a domain of spiritual riches, opulence, and pure golden Light. It is Indra's paradisal realm, a high Heaven, one of the eight exalted god-planes whose entrance is guarded by Airavata, the golden-tusked white elephant, who is Indra's mount and our pals, the angelic Blaises. The Cyclopes (Elohim) stand by as design consultants. This powerful *Swarga* Light is available to anyone prepared to use it: start your apprenticeship as a smith of the forge.

The point that was exercising my admiration at the moment was that a mythic image like this itself is a Light temple. Enter the picture, live its myth: that experience is the Light temple and you can then dispense with the contrived architectural space. The point is to derive the experience in consciousness; the Light temple is the delivery vehicle for that, but if you get it without the temple and using the initiation picture instead, that is fine. You still get the exposure.

Again, the usual custom is you enter a Light temple as a defined and shaped interactive space, have an experience, then summarize and memorialize its quality and details with a psychic picture. That's what the Vedic *Rishis* did: they deliberately created pictures that would resonate a long time in human culture and intrigue consciousness, such as the golden Cattle of the Sun. I'm saying this works in both directions: temple to picture and picture as temple, and the fun part, the grown-up satisfactory aspect of it, was we were doing that.

For the particularly adept among the Light temple visitors, we copied the 13-tiered Archimedean Solids and its 9,360 stars of G1's planet. We replicated that then strolled through its many halls and layers putting up psychic pictures like we were hanging paintings for a retrospective opening of a famous painter.

We ambled through the higher, complex dimensions and geometries of these Solids and hung our images, knowing that some "souls" would make it up here. I hope this isn't confusing, but the Solids have their own higher geometries, what we might call their own etheric bodies, something like how a 4D cube looks different, definitely more complicated, than the familiar 3D cube version of this. These higher levels of geometry were like hypotheses posed to consciousness, proposals for alternate branching realities, as if saying, consider this possibility.

Thoughts are realities, and these are Light temples for experiences. Our hierophantic work was spawning then revealing these realities, opening up more possibilities for embodied consciousness to revel in the Holy Light, for all of reality to be a continuous bright disclosure of the Higher Mysteries and Presence. We generated psychic pictures as hints for how to use the Light temples, as sketches of the mechanisms in consciousness and the likely outcomes of this use. In a sense, they were advertisements for the psychic products of the Light temples, the way a restaurant will publish alluring photographs of its food fare.

After a while, though, you realize that however gripping, the psychic images and Light temples are dispensable or can be left behind in the wake of your actual experiences. They are the packaging, the means of delivery, for these higher experiences, and once you have these, you don't need their carriers any longer. They are TV programming of the sixth chakra. You move up to the crown chakra where you don't need images but have direct knowing and certainty.

The fresh experience becomes part of you and you realize it has always been a constituent of your true manifestation, but you needed this temple mirror first to reveal it to you. You have just awakened an indigenous but dormant part of yourself. You walk about the galaxy digesting temples and mythic images, consuming these packages of Holy Light disclosure like canapés at a party.

I heard a clunking sound. Then something pulling on my shoulder or perhaps it was only a tap. It made me remember I wasn't particularly in my body, and that made me wonder where I left the old form anyway. I seemed to have lost track of my physical nexus point in the midst of these vivid disclosures. Then I came into focus and found myself standing in the Hierophancy's office in Sun Valley, my hand raised, finger extended, to make a point or highlight a line I'd written on a blackboard, with Sal, Joceyln, and Blaise standing there, smiling.

17

At first I thought they were smiling at me for the charming way I had lost track of my body. Then I realized it wasn't that but a recognition they had done the same. We had all been transiting the higher realms of design and Light. I was just the last of the four to return to my physical anchor point, known as my body. Ray Master Hermes had returned with us too, though he didn't have these odd quandaries of bodily location and physical anchoring as his body was of Light and he could be anywhere at any time and in any form he desired.

That thought triggered a memory of something I had been only recently watching. Minutes ago, I suppose, though my time sense was vague and skewed. But I was sure it was part of this most recent episode within the sevenfold Head. It had to do with time layers, being able to experience different time frames in a simultaneous manner, like thin slices of reality sandwiched together.

Here's what I mean. Say you were doing something pleasant, like reveling at the oceanside, enjoying the waves, sand, and sunlight. Then you are back at home, remembering how you had been at the beach only a few hours ago. You imagine yourself back in the salty, swelling water, baking under the hot sun, lying on the malleable sand, nudging your back, shoulders, and elbows against it to shape a comfortable position. Still, you know your body is now at your home, not at the beach. Your sense of time continuity is firm, your imagination supple.

Under this new fluidity provided by the sevenfold Head of planets, these separate time nodes can now be in the same place, like stacked layers. You are at the beach, you are at home recalling being at the beach, you are making your next trip back to the beach in what you used to think was the future. They are not memories, richly recalled. They are all present realities, as vivid and palpable as experiences happening to us right now usually feel. Usually, we only have one at a time; now we could have multiple simultaneous experiences. This is a modest example. Expand it to include the history of a geomantic node, a narrow-band focus of the *Akashic* Records for a single location, its complete time dossier, all the layers of its palimpsest of use and interaction immediately present to experience.

It's not just a matter of seeing these layered time frames, say, a thousand-year stretch of events here, but it's being in all of them, and here's the key part: you experience them not successively but all at once. Every single time layer is right now. You are in all of them equally and at the same moment. It's being a book and you look out through any or all of the pages that comprise your form.

You can look through, *be*, all the pages at once, if you wish. You can occupy a great number of different time nodes (think of the divisions of a ruler) on the timeline of that site simultaneously. They are not memories vividly recalled; they are present-moment realities. You have dissolved the time boundaries you used to believe were fully fixed to the point of intransigence. All moments are here now. You are a timeshifter; it's like a shapeshifter who can change his shape and appearance at will, but this change is across the timeline. You can shift your manifestation to chosen points on the timeline, stack them up like juggled balls, keeping them all up in the air as you co-occupy many points.

Then it got even more interesting. This was still a mostly linear layering. There was flexibility in the time spectrum, but the presentation was still in 3D. Now it shifted up to 4D and took on a geometrical form, maybe a hypercube. I could transition into any time node regardless of linear proximity. Now it was more like a picture gallery in a 4D cubic art gallery. I could see effects before causes; I could see events 5,000 years in the future, then 5,000 years ago, just by shifting which facet of this constantly shifting hypercube I put my attention on.

The complete saga of a geomantic node was accessible to me, even, from my 3D viewpoint, of time periods that had not happened yet in actual 3D clocktime. This also included the alternate moments in branching timelines, in what we sometimes call parallel universes, that quantum field where all the possible alternate outcomes for given events are played out. You could walk into these as you wished, as your curiosity drove you. It was like standing in a building of complex geometry, maybe more than 4D, possibly 5D, with all the time nodes for this geomantic site displayed, and you could instantly move your awareness to focus in detail on one facet, then move to another, while at the same time experiencing all of them at once, being the awareness of the building itself.

"...of a picture that was psychically generating a new reality." Somebody was speaking. I wrenched my focus away from the complexities of this time building and realized Jocelyn was talking and probably had been for a while. She smiled at me when she saw I had caught up with the fact she was speaking. I gathered she was giving us a report on her impressions of what we'd just done.

"The pictures we were generating to hint of or depict the psychic processes underway at given nodes could hypertext your attention to related images. It was like a live illustrated textbook of the riches of comparative mythology. Any images from the many cultures of the Earth that were germane to the new ones were immediately linked, and you could explore, for example, all the different ways of representing a Grail Castle found in myths and its process of deep soul memory recall that it facilitates when you use it. I was sure you would like that feature, Frederick, with your fine Dartmouth résumé."

She looked at me with that look of slight irritation flushed with amusement that I remember I used to get from schoolteachers when I zoned out and completely missed hearing anything she was saying while I tried some swift new moves with my yo-yo or perhaps daydreamed I was on a celestial chariot.

"It was like a visual lexicon of synonyms for the given mythic picture, all these alternate ways of 'saying' the process and the experience it offered people there. This would make a fabulous printed book, but I think you could not create a comparable interactive format as this live version I witnessed in the ethers. You could move into any of the synonym versions of a given myth image, enter it like a room or a landscape, really explore it with the sense of your truly being there.

"You move into the experience coded in the pictures and dispense with all the images. They were designed to get you *here*, to point the way to the living experience. They are like signs, billboards posted along the road to the luxury hotel you're heading for; once you reach the hotel, you forget about the alluring signposts. You experience the 'hotel,' the Light temple and what it offers you.

"But now the experience, fully realized, awake in you, feeds back into the lexicon of visual synonyms and illuminates them. Each refers more mightily to the truth. This is another nuance to our hierophantic work, revealing the Holy Light in the mythic pictures. They are meant to shed Light into consciousness. Some of the new images we generated through this unique sevenfold Head had no correspondences to Earth psychic pictures, as far as I could tell. They referred to formulations of 'alien' experiences and how they fit into existing structures of consciousness not found on the Earth, so there were no synonym link-ups here.

"I sampled some of these, trying to figure out what the objects and gestures meant. They were exotic, metaphysically feral, exciting in an inarticulate, dumb manner. Dumb in the sense that I was 'dumb' or inert to their reality significations. It was like visiting an 'alien' world and walking around but without an explainer. Everything caught my eye, but I didn't understand it.

"But others did, the ones from the host planets. I saw them—they had some kind of vaguely discernible form to hold their consciousness, that is, as far as I could see—standing in these pictures, immersed, like you would in a swimming pool. The picture, or water, had special effects on them, as if it were full of minerals. They seemed to remain in one picture for a set time then move to another. They appeared to be going the rounds of consciousness exposures, like nutrient baths. I knew they were strolling through pictures illustrating the structures of their consciousness, the mechanics of their own psyche displayed outside them for the purposes of illustration, instruction, and direct experience.

"Oddly, I found in some manner I could psychically digest these images. It was as if I possessed some dormant genes in my make-up that now came on line to help me comprehend these unusual images and foreign formulations of awareness. It was like having computer software you never knew you had. For all I know, 'I' in some manner and time had a life among these different species.

"Like the immune system when it is exposed to a novel antigen, it learns defense, creates proper antibodies to neutralize the pathogen the next time it's encountered, so maybe I subconsciously could call on these dormant antibodies to help me comprehend what I was now exposed to. They were psychic antigens. They certainly challenged my cognitive framework of how I pictured reality.

"I suspect for some people, though maybe it's a small number, these exotic Light images might prove comprehensible and people will activate dormant cognitive genes to help them navigate the unusual configurations.

"For such people, exploring these extra-planetary mythic images would be beneficial. For others, though, they will seem like a brick wall of incomprehensibility, like an unfathomable mystery involving different laws of space, time, and awareness. Still, the mysterious *numen* of their unfathomed presence will act slowly like a sliver in their consciousness, wedging itself gradually deeper until one day they are inexplicably ready and a person feels ready and they enter a picture and it starts to make sense and they get the Light. You realize the universe has a prolixity of hierophantic exposures awaiting us, as if it is dying to show us this awesome diversity of metaphors for consciousness.

"I saw pictures begin to link up and form successive image narratives. They seemed to be describing a syllogism of initiation and consciousness, as if laying out the steps in a long process of how you wake up to reality on this planet and under these conditions. The pictures mapped out the progression. You could sample it by stepping into each, though because these pictures were real, carried a jolt of actuality in them, you might find that a bit formidable.

"It reminded me of the Masons' metaphysical cue cards, a variation on the Tarot. It was encouraging, I thought, and should be for the residents of the given planet. The steps to higher consciousness and illumination are known and mapped out. Here is what they look like; sample them in advance, affirm your progress later by stepping into them and seeing you can comfortably remain in their field. It is a picture-card primer on the basics of higher consciousness. It reminded me of how in the late 19th century, before seamless moving pictures were perfected, you could watch a series of quickly flipped sequential images to create the illusion of a continuous image flow. Here is the initiation movie.

"These were scripts for retooling a planet. Cultures can get tired, worn out, in the doldrums with lifeless clichés of description, reference, and experience. We saw this on Earth up to 2020. Everything was exhausted, empty of meaning. People kept repeating the same dire images, the same projections of disaster, the same notions of what people used to call universal heat death, the falling-apart end of things. A large portion of the Hollywood movies were just reruns of earlier ones. People copied the old patterns, afraid of anything new. Language, body gestures, social roles, styles of communication, all were clichéd.

"I felt the tiredness in the psychic atmosphere of the country every day. Everything was repetition; people were lost in the same vitiated preoccupations and distractions, celebrity status, rampant narcissism, self-promotion, power and control struggles, and the acquisition of wealth and material possessions. Everything was clogged; the culture was stagnant. That happens to all these planets eventually; the remedy for it is already in hand. In other words, I was seeing a familiar pattern, repeated often across these worlds.

"Then at last came renewal with the change that began in 2020. The Golden Age began; the Ofanim incarnated. These new images will serve the same renewal purpose. They will invest the tired planetary cultures with new life, fresh impetus. A vibrant, original set of metaphors will spring up to enliven the mind, reinvigorate life, move the planets forward in their social evolution.

"I was participating in making mythic pictures for six planets. I began to feel that I was a legitimate resident on these different worlds, like a press agent. Each was a client and my job was to represent it in public, among the customers. Forgive me my lame analogy. By customers I mean the inhabitants of that world. Perhaps it would be more accurate to say I found myself suddenly articulate in six different languages and I understood each world's style of metaphors.

"The pictures we created for each of these six worlds were capable of linkage. You could follow the thematic development on one world into the next as a daisy chain. There were consistencies among the six worlds, certain generic patterns were repeated, but there were unique image blossoms on each that were not repeated. Just when you thought the pattern was predictable, along came a big surprise.

"Overall, you could see the outlines of a complex, higher stage of consciousness development as expressed in these six linked mythic systems. Here is what six congruent nuances of free will in embodied form can yield, they said. The images from these worlds broadcasted that display across the galaxy. You can follow the developmental sequence for the human on Earth, go into stages we haven't reached yet and may find hard to imagine. That is only one.

"Then you repeat the process for the other five, look back and appreciate you have been constructing an awesome figure in Light and of awareness here, one that has abilities and a range of awareness and cognitive processing fluidity that you wouldn't have thought possible if you had only the Earth for reference. You realize others across the galaxy, or perhaps from many galaxies, are studying this. You are an artist who has just put into a gallery display an arresting piece of work and the connoisseurs are flocking to look at it.

"The experience was exhilarating. It was like being a writer, maybe a poet, and suddenly you find your vocabulary has been radically expanded and all sorts of new words with evocative meanings leap forward and you realize you have all sorts of new things to say now that you have these new words. You feel like you can describe anything, evoke everything in the world with these words.

"In the same way, this new pictorial lexicon of initiation possibilities stretched my conception of what a conscious being could be, how one could feel. I generally resist hyperbole, but I have to say, it was like being reborn in Eden as a fresh human being, newly conceived, invented, you might say, by the Creator. You take stock of yourself, your mind, your range of perception, your body, and you feel your eyes widen in amazement and maybe your cheeks even blush. You have just received a generous, unexpected inheritance; you are flush in funds.

"The array we were generating was a gestural alphabet, like a picture book of yoga postures, but here the postures were for consciousness to occupy. Here is a repertoire of movements and consciousness attitudes to take on, each one embodying a different nuance of awareness. Our job is to shine Light in this new gestural space. Think of it like this: take the image of Hanuman, the mighty flying monkey-god from *The Ramayana*. He's strong enough to move entire mountains; people hear his roar across the worlds; he is fierce, strong, and loyal.

"Hindu myth left us vivid pictures of Hanuman and his deeds, but they are like 2D images, flat, lifeless, a celebrity report on somebody else, not ourselves. Except it is ourselves. The point of this picture is for us to *become* Hanuman. Not just to step into the Light temple of his mythic image, but to become him fully. Hanuman is a metaphor for a power of consciousness. We can have that power; Hanuman is the role model. We enter his mythic image and become one with it and now we are Hanuman. We no longer need the image.

"Our job as Hierophants is to sufficiently illuminate that mythic picture so people can realize it has 3D and even 4D expressive possibilities, not to stay at only 2D. So it was with the new psychic pictures and myth images we were generating. They have to be fleshed out, inflated into a 3D and 4D format for their recipients. Then the designated 'users' enter the images, expand their awareness to fill the space, and become the image or gesture or process or power the images portray. This way they digest the picture, make it part of themselves. The pictures, the processes they evoke, are only intermediaries between their consciousness as it is and what it can become, as our hierophantic work shows."

Sal was nodding enthusiastically. He seemed like he had a lot to say. "That is so right. But for me I was like a technician working the stage lights for your performance of the Mystery rites of the mythic pictures, Jocelyn. I was working the arithmetic behind the scenes of the initiation drama. I loved it. All those numbers in new combinations, quite unexpected, original ones at that.

"I felt like I was at a conference table with a dozen 'guys' from the cabal of what we've been calling the arithmetical gods and we were heatedly working out equations. I mean it in the sense of with great enthusiasm, concentration, and dedication. We were a think tank commissioned to execute a great public work, a new reality. We were spinning our algorithms to accommodate the ramifications of this blazing sevenfold Head comprised of the six free-will planets.

"Our new number formulas encompassed consciousness and matter. As the Earth started to correct its axis and gradually erase that perturbance of 23.5 degrees off alignment, this affected the other five planets. They made slight adjustments in their tilt and orbital patterns. They had not been as misaligned as the Earth, but they had been subject to some entropic drift, like slack on the line. Earth's prolonged misalignment had imparted a chronic destabilizing effect on them and now that could be corrected. It was like, I should think, having to stand in a crowded bus with your shoulders hunched in one direction for the duration of the bus ride. You get off the bus, or everybody else does, and your body has the room to stretch and correct its posture. Your body comes into balance again.

"We wrote code for the 'people' on the five planets to appropriate the complex stacking of reality layers on G1's planet with the 13 Archimedean Solids. That is not only complex to see but intricate to experience. We wrote code like laying in staircases, signs, guideposts, and information stations, kiosks for consciousness to find its way as it climbed this elaborate Light grid edifice. It is an initiation challenge on each level, thresholds that must be mastered before you can cross them, but it would do nobody any service if people lost their way.

"Our code had to allow both for initiation challenges and sufficient guidance, and it had to be interactive, even heuristic, adapting to the changing needs of users. We devised mutable codes for each of the six planets, adapting it to the framework of seeing the other five planets in a reciprocal relationship with the sixth one. On each planet you feel you're at the center of the universe, or at least the web; so you construct your mathematics from that centrist perspective.

"Except there were six centers of this planetary web, so the holographic center shifted according to where you stood in the hologram. You could easily get disoriented trying to figure out where you were in this complicated shape. We created six sets of self-adapting maintenance algorithms for this web. They were constantly in reciprocating proximity with one another, always adjusting.

"Then we moved on to something more ambitious. Stacked algorithms. In many respects similar to the stacking of the Archimedean Solids on G1's planet. We created interlocking tiers of equations. Each one in itself was complex, but it had an interactive connection with the tier above it, and when certain criteria were achieved in the first layer, it unlocked access to the next one in the stack.

"These openings to the next tier were keyed to achieving evolutionary thresholds. When certain vital markers were surpassed in the expansion of consciousness in that planetary system, the next layer of algorithms was initiated and started to code planetary reality. The first remained operative; it was a 13-story building. We had just moved up a floor. You don't discard the first floor just because you build the second, third, and on. They all became dovetailed.

"We had such a wealth of number combinations to draw upon. The mental sphere we worked in was like a fully-stocked warehouse. It was packed to the ceiling with algorithms and equations we could pull down for formulas. Everything was at our fingertips. I'd never felt such facility with mathematics.

"That's funny, I suppose, as I've spent my life to date working with numbers. But this was crazy-rich with numbers; they were streaming out of my ears and fingers. I was creating formulas of such complexity I had never seen in books. I was mellifluous in numbers. I couldn't stop their outpouring. I was in the realm where these arithmetical deities live all the time. Get me a room there; I'm moving in now. I'll commute back to Sun Valley on weekends, maybe.

"The arithmetical deities might have been showing off a little. They knew I was enthusiastic about this work. They created a 10D algorithm. Imagine that. An algorithm that required a 10D-cube space to be written in. It's a dekeract or 10-dimensional hypercube. It has 1,024 vertices; 5,120 edges; 11,520 square faces; 15,360 cubic cells; 13,440 tesseract 4-faces; 8,064 5-cube 5-faces; 3,360 6-cube 6-faces; 960 7-cube 7-faces; 180 8-cube 8-faces; and 20 9-cube 9 faces. *And* there were numbers coded all across this almost unfathomable spherical space. I *loved* this: it was like a 10-dimensional jungle gym combined with a magical funhouse.

"To follow the complete algorithm you had to traverse all the parts I just listed. Yes, it is a sphere; at a certain point, at about the 6D level, the expanding square and cube become a sphere. Another mystery solved: squaring the circle. What was this beautiful monstrosity coding? I don't know yet. Jacob's Ladder maybe. The complete five Trees of Life. Every Qabalist would be in awe of this.

"They weren't really showing off. That's my projection. This form was commissioned. God's Own idea of a Rubik's Cube. They generated this as a Mystery sigil to float around in the universe like a Jack-in-the-Box. Figure it out and you get a surprise. They probably know what the product is, though I don't. The idea was to leave this 10-cube algorithm as a puzzle for mathematically clever minds from any phylogeny to figure out. The cube could replicate itself too. People could take home a copy, palm-size or as big as your own planet. They can work it out in their leisure, solve the mathematical puzzle the gods left them.

"*And*," Sal said this standing, holding something glittering in his hand, "*look*: they gave me a holographic copy of that astonishing cube to work out here in my Hierophancy office. It's almost too complex even to look at. The eyes struggle. But speaking of eyes, do you see how it looks like a vast Eye of God filled with numbers, thickest at the center, which draws your attention into it like a vortex.

"The coolest part is I can expand it to any desired size, as big as a house if needed. Then you guys can walk around in it, inspect some of the 13,440 tesseract 4-faces. I can invite all sorts of clever people to our offices and give them a tour of the cube. I can expand it to barn-size and people can really lose themselves in its

bewilderment of numbers and equations. It's a Light temple made of an arithmetical puzzle of staggering complexity. Initiate that! Maybe somebody will work it out and Sun Valley will see an anomalous explosion of Light and a streaming of digits as this vast arithmetical house slowly explodes.

"Then we had to work out algorithmic extensions to put adjacent planets and other galaxies in congruence with the upgrades to the sevenfold Head. Its presence immediately had a cascading effect throughout all the planetary systems since everything is connected to everything else in this vast energy web. We made these extension algorithms heuristic so they could constantly adapt to changing circumstances and even creatively modulate them while adjusting to their requirements. Better, they could do this without our monitoring them.

"In fact, the algorithms could rewrite themselves to an extent (within parameters we installed in the equations) to stay in tune with feedback coming from the multiplicity of planets as the consciousness-bearing forms on those planets made progress in extrapolating the possibilities of their designed consciousness structures. It sounds formal, putting it that way, but it was great fun, and the system was made wildly creative. The algorithm became a sub-creator in the system, and as it unfolded, it added to the complexity of the whole.

"We could lean back and watch this riot of creative self-adjustment going on everywhere we looked. We set it in motion, then let it run on its own learning. It was like being a teacher in a school for the exceptionally gifted. Every planetary Light grid and its mathematics was an exceptional student. A teacher's dream, no doubt. One major upgrade, the sevenfold free-will planetary web, moved ahead in its processing ability and began to ramify throughout space.

"Each planet posted its developments, its need for Light grid settings that allowed for more Light and consciousness, and the attentive algorithmic system immediately responded, dispatching the heightened frequencies. It was organic, natural, like your body telling you to drink more water and take in more calories when you exercise vigorously, perspiring, burning up calories, and you comply. It was hard keeping all this in my head. So many Light grids were involved.

"I was lucky to even keep track of the total count of maintenance systems. The details of this proliferation of algorithmic Light grid maintenance systems seemed beyond my ability, though, I was confident, not for the arithmetical gods. For them it seemed no more a logistical demand than juggling three balls; they kept those three balls in constant motion with the minimum use of attention.

"For the Earth we prepared a number of contingency Light grids. It is hard to tell precisely which direction conscious evolution will take; you can estimate probabilities, but it is difficult to guarantee them. We extrapolated probable alternative outcomes and generated Light grids to accommodate them. We left them in place, rather like how you put something in a footnote or maybe a parenthesis; it is available but not necessarily for immediate or urgent use. These contingency Light grids hovered in place like understudies in a drama, ready to step in if the principal actor, the Light grid, wants to make a change.

"The probability Light grids lined the path of the parade like supporters. I am likening the development of consciousness on the Earth and the other planets to a parade. It is certainly a pageant, a delightful spectacle most of the time, and the designers of the parade floats, which is to say, the particular structures of consciousness as determined by the Light grids, understandably wanted to watch their creations roll by, displaying their attainments. Maybe I'm taking this analogy too far, but this display was akin to cheerleaders twirling batons. Their dexterity at keeping the batons in motion was an index of consciousness mastering its Light grid and making optimal use of its awareness endowment.

"You appreciate the necessity of design when you're talking about form. It is ineluctable, no way around it. Forms must be generated by designs, and those designs are executed by numbers. Algorithms, equations, all making Light grids. Maybe this is already obvious to you, but watching this parade, this deft twirling of the batons of the Light grids, I was struck by this sheer fact. What fact is that?

"That everything, even my reflective thoughts on the primacy of mathematics, is dependent on Light grid designs based on equations. I mean, the human form itself, *humans*, all the structures of human-style consciousness, are themselves a Light grid, and that Light grid was coded by mathematics to deliver an experience in consciousness to the users of this temple. *Us.* The human form is hierophantic. Numbers did it. This doesn't mean we, as humans, are no more than automatons produced by clever coding; that is only the infrastructure for the freedom of consciousness meant to operate within these structures. So we master these structures and learn to use them as creative tools, and some day we will join the ranks of the arithmetical gods and set out designing new Light grids.

"At first I was concerned about how intricately structured all these realities were. It didn't seem to leave much room to move. Then I realized the free element, the part that could will itself anywhere in the system, was awareness. It is unbounded, as broad and eternal as the Supreme Being's because it is a copy of it, a little drop of infinity put into mortal form. Awareness can scramble over, up, through, and down all the playground swings, climbs, jungle gyms, rope ladders, with the nimbleness of a squirrel.

"It was a case of being both immanent and transcendent, just like the Supreme Being, to use the words of the theologians who have fretted over this dichotomy forever. It's not a dichotomy: both are true. Our awareness is immanent, embedded in all the systems coded for it, functionally identical with all the infrastructure, the Light grids and form designs; and it is transcendent, more than all these scripted forms, utterly unbounded, unfixed, filled with freedom. It moves about this minutely coded landscape in unrestricted liberty. It enters a Light temple freely, whether it's a body, a palace of the gods, or a planet, receives its designed experience that enriches awareness, then leaves for another.

"It's like saying we're in the system and outside it, moving in and out as we choose. That is the Supreme Being's little secret with His created forms: Look, you may have it *both* ways, like Me. I'm in. I'm out. I'm a Buddhist. Form is emptiness, and emptiness is form. *Bodhi svaha*! Gone beyond, baby. And isn't that

just amazing. I felt I was experiencing the Old Boy's delight as I realized this.

"That changed my perspective on this intricate, almost absolutist, coding I was participating in with the arithmetical gods. It was not restriction by numbers. Consciousness in all its forms was unbounded by these algorithmic fences. It could stay within those confines and go through and beyond them, as if they did not exist, and do both or all the variations simultaneously. *That* was the set-up. You didn't have to color within the lines set out in the coloring book. They were only suggestions, general indications, merely hints at possible parameters, but the Management was perfectly okay with people ignoring or exceeding them. You could use the coloring book or dispense with it altogether.

"Consciousness was like this hugely bright spotlight moving through the intricacies of our mathematical design, lumbering, it usually looked like, though sometimes it leaped nimbly like a ballet dancer with a perfectly trained body. As it progressed through our jungle gym infrastructure, its spotlight highlighted nearby regions like mini-sunrises illuminating the first edges of a big landscape.

"New aspects of the algorithms were constantly being revealed, and eventually this burgeoning, highlighting consciousness would reveal the entire landscape. In this manner, the immanent, constantly expanding outward, became the transcendent, exceeding the framework established by the number matrices. I hope this analogy is not too droll, but consciousness is like a dog sniffing a bone. It will insist on finding it, stuffed in the master's pocket perhaps or in his hand. The bone of course is the Creator of all this, the

Great Arithmetician of Infinity. Consciousness will inevitably reach Him with its beam, claim the bone, and gnaw on it contentedly back in its rightful original home."

I spoke next but since I have already reported my impressions in the preceding pages—all that business about the peripatetic sevenfold planetary Head like a snowflake—there is no need to repeat that. Blaise reported next.

"I went off with the Blaises who had me participating in some seeding. They wanted to install copies of their diamond geode at the six vertices of the hexagon that linked our six free-will planets. This emplacement would be different from the *Nimitta* or diamond installed within the planet's Light grid. Off the surface, in etheric or higher space but in proximity to each planet. It would be a key component in the hexagonal Light grid linking these six planets. I'm tempted to compare them with space stations in low orbit around a planet.

"They allowed me to make copies of myself. I counted six to start with, with me as the seventh acting as a field monitor for what I was elsewhere up to. As for them, the Blaises were lavish in their replications. I saw thousands of Blaises. They were standing in the diamond hexagons clustered at the center of each vertex where they would install the diamond geode. They were supervising its landing, like it was a massive but elegant spaceship slowly descending.

"The Blaises stood within the hexagons serenely observing their own descent, though I'm sure about half of them winked at me. A few may have fluttered their wings. They can't help themselves. They can't keep a straight face. I had the impression they were preparing themselves and me for something higher. Higher in the sense of at the next level in the hierarchical tier of reality.

"Soon I found out what that was. They were opening a door for these six planets to the Great White Lodge. This is, to us, an exceedingly arcane group of evolved celestial spirits involved in recondite levels of cosmic life supervision. We know of the Great White Brotherhood. This is based in the Great Bear with principal 'offices' at the star Megrez, King Arthur's home base. This Brotherhood is the huge assembly of Ascended Masters superintended by the 14 Ray Masters. The Norse seers called it Asgard, the Enclosure of the *As*, gods, or *Aesir*. The 'white' of course refers to the ascended pure form of their Light bodies. Their manifestation forms possessed the pure white of the highest realm, *Kether*.

"They came out of the Lodge to form this larger conclave of cosmic directors. My assumption is that the Lodge consists of perhaps ten percent of the membership of the larger Brotherhood. Apparently, it is a more arcane, exclusive collegium. Norse myth says there were 614,400 warriors of Asgard, based on how many valiant residents of Valhalla could rush out its many doors at once when Ragnarok starts. The *Prose Edda* says that for the 640 doors of Valhalla 960 warriors will rush through each, "champions advancing on the monster." I think we can safely interpret that monster to be *Isfet*, the agent of chaos and entropy.

"As I understand it, the Brotherhood is an expansion of the Lodge, which began first but with fewer members. The Great White Lodge had to do with special projects pertaining to the Light when it started and its members, again it's my assumption, were even more developed than those in the later Brotherhood, though, believe me, from our point of view, they are all hyper-developed, even the secretaries and go-fors, compared to humans as we now perceive ourselves.

"The Blaises tell me the Lodge began in Ursa Major but was first focused through the star Sirius in Canis Major, the Greater Dog, and our galaxy's brightest star. I guess that was its first area of application, a recipient of its consciousness beam. Later, it created the larger conclave of the Brotherhood.

"The Blaises wanted to take advantage of this great opening in consciousness that the unification of this new Light grid of the six free-will planets represented and use it as the occasion to open the six up to the Lodge. They wanted to unveil the Lodge or open the door to their arcane chambers. I shouldn't say 'wanted' because the Ofanim were merely executing the Supreme Being's orders. The time was now ripe, the Ancient of Days believed, to do this.

"The Blaises let me have a glimpse of a meeting of the Great White Lodge. I suppose they are always meeting since they communicate by telepathic sharing of pictures in Light, what the Blaises call the Language of Light. The information packets are even more subtle than pictures made in Light; they are the ideas behind the pictures, the facts of higher reality before images are even conceived.

"Thoughts and images seemed to roll through this assembly of cosmic adepts like ocean swells. It was silent but vigorous. It had a suggestion of music, something evocative of a blend of Debussy and Wagner. The Lodge members were clearly in a state of bliss, the way Buddhist cultures depict their high deities, but they also seemed sharply focused, fully concentrated on their task. They weren't talking or sharing notes. They weren't putting up images. It was more like they were co-participating in the generation of new reality scenarios. They were already in such a scene, observing, strengthening, and validating it.

"This was different from what Jocelyn reported about generating new mythic pictures. This was reality-steering at the level of huge wedges of the cosmos, like they were piloting a massive ocean liner, one that takes a long time to turn itself. The ocean liner analogy is apt. Such a ship carries thousands of passengers; such a ship is massive and ponderous to maneuver. Our seven-headed planetary colossus, impressive to us, was but one of its passengers.

"Similarly, this wedge of the cosmos contained thousands of planets with their own phylogenies on board and the Lodge members were 'steering' their evolution and thus that of the cosmos as a whole now in a changed direction. Changed in the sense of refined, upgraded, with added momentum deriving from the success of aligning our sevenfold Head and the fluidity of the mathematical constructs that go along with everything we have finished doing. I appreciated once more how entangled everything is in the universe, how one change ripples throughout the web of consciousness, enabling it to advance.

"The Lodge members were not only navigating this cosmic wedge. They were infiltrated throughout its slow-moving mass. It was as if I saw their heads of Light peering out from all the portholes on the ocean liner, a whimsical though, oddly, an accurate image. They had permeated the system entirely, like water saturating a sponge. They flashed images like neon billboards of possible or desirable evolutionary states through this cosmic sponge to its passengers. It gave the consciousness units, the myriad life-forms, ideas on how to develop.

"I could swear it sounded like they were singing, almost like beer-hall songs coming out the portholes, but I know it must have been my imagination glossing things. More soberly put, I hope, is the likelihood I was hearing the vibrational framework around the images the Lodge members were releasing.

"Back at the Lodge, the members were strengthening the alignment of planets with the Sirius system. Sirius is a kind of umbilicus in the galaxy. Not only is it the brightest star, but as the Dog-Star it is the guardian of the cauldron of stars, as most myths about this star attest. It is the site of Hinduism's Shiva who does his legendary four-armed dance inside the flaming hoop of the galaxy which it turns out corresponds to our crown chakra. Look up: you have a dog dancing on your golden crowned head in a circle of fire at the core of the galaxy.

"What does it mean at the galactic level? The crown chakra is the front door, the primary place of entry, and Sirius is the doorkeeper and guardian for all entries. Inquiries from outside the galaxy apply at the front door of Sirius; there the Lodge members assess the suitability of all claimants to entry into our system. I know: that's a bit overly formal. Let's say the Dog checks out visitors.

"Domestic dogs usually know if somebody is friendly or not, should be welcomed or not. Similarly, Sirius, through the Great White Lodge, studies external forces. Will they benefit the galaxy, find its energy settings congruent and compatible? In a large sense, external energies must pass through the Lodge members who act as a sieve, filtering out the inimical qualities or redirecting wayward ones. Well, of course extraplanetary travellers can physically enter our galaxy as they wish. The Lodge at Sirius monitors their access to its Light system.

"Let's say you can enter a great Gothic cathedral and walk around the corridor on its periphery, but if you propose to go down to the Holy of Holies at the High Altar you need a pass from the Lodge monitors. I'm only speculating here, though. On the other hand, probably the dangerous intelligences seeking to enter our galaxy won't be coming in material forms anyway but as energy waves or massive bodies of consciousness or hyper-dimensional manifestations, and these guys definitely will have their IDs checked carefully at the Sirius front door.

"Two dozen Lodge members now surrounded our great white hexagon. Even though, in strictly spatial terms, they stood very far apart from one another, they appeared to be close enough to knock elbows should they wish to be that familiar. They were infusing our hexagon of relations with Light from the Lodge. You could feel the edges of the hexagon brighten, as they engorged with Light.

"I felt it as a thickening of awareness, as if I could perceive and understand more, as if the range of my attention, the degree of sharpness with which I could focus my awareness and the general sense of self-presence, were intensified. I couldn't say I had any particular notion of the mathematics of this presence. Their attention seemed beyond the arithmetical realm and the algorithms we've been concerned with, though I suspect equations were implicit in their focus.

"These 24 Lodge members surrounded our sevenfold Head of the six planets, but the

Ofanim surrounded the Lodge members like hovering white birds. They were in their angelic guises and they hovered in space around the Lodge members, a sphere of white birds with their wings swept back in the motion of flight but as if the flight were freeze-framed, so that when the wings swept forward they would deliver a breezy burst of encouragement. You would feel fanned, everything in the hexagon would feel fanned, by their Light, like a great tailwind on your sails as your yacht glided swiftly across the water.

"It was an unforgettable sight, the Blaise angels seen through the Lodge members. Their upright presence began to look like pillars of Light, then these pillars enlarged and grew closer to one another, creating an almost wall-like effect, like they had fused into a cylinder of Light, with the Ofanim pressing upon it from all sides with the eager insistence of hummingbirds fluttering before a source of sugar water hung from a tree in somebody's lovely garden.

"I had the impression the Blaises' job was to taste the consciousness coming out of our hexagon, to see if it had attained the desired sweetness of focus and force. I reminded myself they are the Soma masters, its original dispensers. They were not there to consume this sweetness, only to measure its attainment. That sweetness would be produced through the cognitive force of our collective awareness, the combined focus of the six free-will planets. The Ofanim's task was to help that, facilitate its achievement, removing obstacles to our success as they shifted into their friendly Ganesh mode as humanity's helper.

"I could see their angelic bird guises looming strongly through the Lodge pillars, as if they were peering right through it, moving their attention straight against us, the hummingbirds hovering against the windowpane as we watched them. It was like observing ourselves in a state of hyper-attention, of achieved focus and concentration, seeing what we will look like—what we do look like—emulating them. But that isn't it. We emulate them only to realize our own true nature. They hold up a clear mirror for us to see our true form. We emulate that. Any form the Ofanim take is purely metaphorical for a power of consciousness. For each of the life-forms on these linked planets, that form would look different in accordance with what their 'bodies' look like, but in essence it's the same form.

"Much of what the Lodge members were doing was beyond my ken. It was high-level, arcane, and no doubt encompassed many adjacent dimensions. But they did leave us with an imprint of their presence, something we could call on in the future. You know how we each found ourselves wearing a robe of a particular Ray color. I saw that on mine two strips of white had appeared running right up the front in two parallel lines, one on either side of the clasps.

"It was a vertical strip of white on each side of where the two robe halves joined. You should be able to notice the same on your robes. Have a look. These two white strips have the ability, when I concentrate on them with the earnest focus of the Ofanim, to enlarge into two pillars of Light that seem to stand both in front and behind me, as if they had multiplied themselves into a dozen pillars, and I am able to transmit their powerful Light onto whatever I concentrate on.

"It's a way of introducing the Lodge presence as a factor in our geomantic work. Sites, and even people, for that matter, will be exposed to a quality of Light they would be otherwise very unlikely to ever encounter. It is entirely new for us. When we activate those two white strips on our Ray robes and they enlarge into Light pillars, we make it possible for people and sites to experience this Light. Merely to touch this Light, even to register its tingling aura at your fingertips, will start to change your sense of reality, identity, and your prospects. It illuminates a stratum of your mind you probably never suspected was there.

"That was my experience. It seemed foreign at first; then the Blaises helped me get anchored in this new expanded reality and I began to take delight in this. The Lodge is making its presence known, and we're part of that new hierophantic episode in the continuing disclosure of the spiritual worlds. These pillars have an unshakeable strength and enduring presence as if they were the columns within the Supreme Being's own Temple of Light. I shouldn't say 'as if,' for I think now my first perception was correct: they are those Temple pillars.

"My correlation of these pillars with the Supreme Being is not only an analogy. It points to the Light that the white pillars contain. It is *Kether* Light, the unsullied White Light from the top of the Tree of Life. This is the Holy Light. It is what our hierophantic work is all about, what the Hierophancy strives to show. It is as adamant and simplistic as a strong upright pillar, and it is universal in meaning and implication, a source of infinite, unending revelation. The white pillar is similar to our white staff with the White Crown on the top, but while the white staff is mobile and we can plant it wherever we need to, the white pillar when installed at a site remains there as a new permanent addition to that node.

"You feel such a stability of consciousness in this dual alignment of the Ofanim and the Lodge members expressed as Light pillars. Reality feels solid. You feel like you're on an expedition, one that is challenging, somewhat fraught with jeopardy, and with an uncertain though desired outcome, and you have these two guys along who have done it, done all conceivable expeditions, and that fact alone is marvelously reassuring, filling you with confidence. I guess you can put this on the 'emptiness is form' side of the registry. As far as consciousness taking any form goes, this form imparts a feeling of conviction. It erases all quivers of doubt, uncertainty, worry, anxiety, and faltering of purpose.

"On an immediately practical layer, we can install these Lodge pillars around our Hierophancy offices in Sun Valley as a permanent support feature. I suspect their presence will help us align deeper with our purpose and possibly be able to receive fuller, more thorough, and even different types of instructions for our next phase of work, like being able to tune into altogether new channels.

"These pillars will enter a reciprocal relationship with the dome over our local Boyle Mountain. It will strengthen the dome's beneficial spiritual emanations, and the dome, by virtue of its radius of influence, will impart a quality of boundary and definition to the pillars. It will do this through its spirallic network of 48 dome caps and their planetary Light bodies and stars. Both of those factors will enhance the concentration we'll experience here.

"It also makes the Hierophancy headquarters a newly commissioned geomantic node with special conductance of the Great White Lodge, the star Sirius by extension, and of course as another focal point for the seemingly omnipresent Ofanim, all of which are complemented by the dome overhead. That should equip us for the imminent return of the domes to our Earth.

"We will already have a geomantically secure location for the receipt of Boyle's dome when it 'materially" arrives. When the domes come back, it will tremble the Earth to receive so much Light in one gesture after millennia of virtually existing in the galactic dark as a planet. The Boyle geomantic terrain, with these Lodge pillars, will be a stabilizing factor for this strong upgrade."

"It is not only here at Boyle Mountain and its dome," said Ray Master Hermes. "Nor is it only your small group here in Sun Valley that gets the two Lodge stripes on your robes. All the Hierophancy cooperators who just worked with you on this project with the cosmic hexagon of planets also get the stripes. In the next few years we will gather more participants so that by the time the domes arrive there will be at least one Hierophancy member at each dome.

"Each person will be able to extend their white robe stripes into the Lodge pillars and thereby welcome and anchor the incoming dome to its intended node. That geomantic welcome will greatly reduce the otherwise unavoidable trembling the Earth would experience when the 1,746 domes return after millions of years of absence. It will also pacify turbulence roused up in humans from this event. That much Light suddenly introduced into the collective and individual psyches of humans will trigger a considerable purging of accrued darkness, negativity, stuck karma, and recidivistic habits of being. It's unavoidable and ultimately healthy, but we have to make provisions for this inevitable sudden release of the content from millions of humans under domes.

"If you look out upon the Earth's surface now you will likely see the arithmetical pattern that prescribed the location of all the domes the last time. It was a distribution pattern worked out long before the domes arrived the first time. As you know, they have come and left three times in the planet's history to date, and their arrival and settlement locations were organized in advance by this pattern. The pattern was a mathematical coding, an arithmetical grid, a seating plan, if you wish, for 1,746 stars. Over the millennia since the domes 'left,' this grid diminished, shrunk, as you like to call it, Blaise, and compacted, pulled in on itself, and some domes went dormant, got damaged, or built over.

"The dome imprints, their residual presence in Light, are generally now only half their original size. They still carry a strong charge after all this time. That placement grid is now being rescripted with fresh algorithms to identify where all the incoming domes will go. It will be to the same places as before, but the planetary pattern has to be refreshed, the numbering codes reactivated.

"When Hierophancy members reiterate this pattern of the White Lodge pillars and the encircling Ofanim presences, it will greatly help this rescripting. It imparts a solidity, a certainty, and a quality of steadfast anchoring to the pattern. In a sense, it reassures the arithmetical realm of the correctness of their work. You already noticed that the White Lodge members exercised a quiet seniority over the numbers realm, and this authoritative assurance enabled the spirits of the numbers to deploy their formulas with ease, confidence, and no resistance."

I looked out upon the Earth's surface and saw the arithmetical grid. It was a grid in the sense it had a properly and intricately designed geometry, and it was an Arithmetical Earth I was seeing because this geometrical grid was comprised of innumerable equations and master algorithms running them. It was a living system of Light, consciousness, and mathematics I was seeing, a skin of numbers and processes in Light laid over the physical planet's landscape.

The equations were preparing the contact points and anchorages for the domes which would then fit snugly ("land" without untoward consequence) into them. The contact points were coded with equations as well, and they seemed to be slowly expanding, enlarging in all directions to the optimal doubling in size. The domes when they arrived would each require a 33-mile wide anchor-down node, and many dome anchor points were at present barely half that in diameter. I saw the designated spots where the Hierophancy members would stand when they were ready; some were already there, in their places, at least in spirit form.

Provisions had been made in this Arithmetical Earth for the members and the White Lodge pillars and encircling Ofanim angelic presence that each site needed. I chuckled. I guess there were equations specifying that special activity as well. I saw that should they wish to the Hierophancy members at their nodes could evoke the larger alignment of the Earth Light grid with the hexagon linking it with the other five free-will planets and impart the energetic qualities that august array embodied. Our 13 extra-planetary colleagues and their worlds could be present with us, like witnesses and supporters, when the domes came.

Gradually, people would discover that already existing higher Light grid like a backdrop to the more "outer" geomantic aspects of these sites. They might regard it with great interest and wish to explore it in detail. Everything would already be on hand to accomplish that, and every exploration like this would benefit the anchor site and deepen its connection to this hexagon. That would give site users access to a two-tiered hierophantic experience, the "traditional" geomantic template and the newer Lodge-enhanced one lying behind it—well, three, actually, because the freshly arrived dome was another Light temple.

Lodge members for the first time in many millennia of Earth history would be available for consultation by inquiring humans. I don't mean they would be just standing around like docents in an art museum and you could walk up to them and have a chat. But they would be accessible to meditative concentration; if you met them perhaps half-way, you'd have a reasonable chance of contact and guidance.

Even if you couldn't reach them in a wakeful condition, their presence would impart a standing emanation, like a wave of spiritual influence, and this would flavor your experience of a geomantic site and you would gain assurance of the rightness of things, that reality had a plan and a destination, and it wasn't half bad, well thought out even, when you got down to it and studied the details.

And there's always the Blaises. I shouldn't say "always." I should say, thank God for the Blaises. Or maybe I should say always. The Blaises are always here when we need them. The Light touch, the shiver of amusement and profundity they bring to any activity. I saw them now in their diamond geode manifestation. They were going for broke in the number of hexagon facets they were showing. They had their duplication machine running on overdrive.

Millions, easily, with a Blaise angel inside each one and the whole array surrounding each geomantic node was staffed by a Hierophancy member. Yes, they were cheating again in their number of permitted copies, and it seemed okay. I didn't see the Old Man stepping up to bust them for their happy excess.

Each node with its Light temples was enveloped by this marvelous diamond lotus with upraised petals gently surrounding and holding the site in the Ofanim's trademark blend of focus, fondness, and amusement. This is the vernacular for the august *Sat Cit Ananda*, or Being, Consciousness, and Bliss, in short, what God feels like, the basic vibrational signature of the Creation. I was glad we could count on this fortifying presence in our Hierophancy work, but then, how could it be otherwise. The Blaises have been here from the beginning.

About the Author

Richard Leviton is the author of 29 books on myth, consciousness, and the global geomantic landscape, notably *The White Staff Nudge* (2017), *The Green Knight Expedition* (2016), *Theosophon 2033* (2015), *The Mertowney Mountain Interviews* (2014), *The Blaise Conjunction* (2013), *My Pal, Blaise* (2012), *Hierophantic Landscapes* (2011), *Walking in Albion* (2010), *Santa Fe Light* (2009), *Welcome to Your Designer Planet!* (2007), *The Galaxy on Earth, Looking for Arthur, The Emerald Modem, Signs on the Earth, Encyclopedia of Earth Myths,* and others.

He is the director/founder of the Blue Room Consortium, a cosmic mysteries think-tank based in Santa Fe, New Mexico. A trained and certified clairvoyant, Leviton teaches clairvoyant tools and development as well as their applications with geomantic protocols to engage responsibly and effectively with the planet's energy body—to "plug in" and make a difference. Since 1984, he has been interacting with and describing the Earth's Light body, its energetic anatomy, and through workshops, trainings, and geomantic field trips, facilitating people to have directed visionary encounters with the planet.

He may be contacted at: blaise@cybermesa.com or blaise@blueroomconsortium.com or the website: www.blueroomconsortium.com

The Blue Room Consortium

The Blue Room Consortium, based in Santa Fe, New Mexico, and founded/directed by Richard Leviton, is a cosmic mysteries think-tank for Earth energies, mapping, and interaction. It's the authoritative information source for the Earth's visionary geography, providing an experiential guide to interacting with sacred sites and their Light temples and for understanding the Earth's geomantic plan and function. It teaches effective methods to beneficially interact with the planet. The Blue Room offers research, workshops, classes, field trips, tours, designer pilgrimages, geomantic maps, trainings, consultations, initiations, publications, and articles.

Clairvoyant Readings-Healings: Professional-quality clairvoyant readings (in 120-minute sessions conducted by telephone) that look at psychic conditions and the roots of problems or difficulties in making positive energy changes, then correct, adjust, or eliminate these factors so a person can take their next step.

Clairvoyant Tools and Development: Foundational acquisition of psychic tools and introduction to energies, psychic pictures, maintaining one's energy space, and more, in a structured one-on-one program of 12 two-hour classes (over the telephone).

Geomantic Immersions: Six-day field programs of active engagement, experience, and interpretation of geomantic features throughout the greater Santa Fe landscape through four different week-long formats, focusing on intensive introductory immersion and landscape zodiac work (an interactive terrestrial star pattern), given in a one-on-one format, meaning, one instructor to one participant.

Annual Geomantic Initiation Immersion Weeks: One week of intensive teaching, training, and field experience at each site for small group "boutique" workshops, given during the summer months, from April-September, to: Glastonbury, England; Avebury, England; Oaxaca, Mexico City, and Teotihuacan, Mexico; the Rondanes, Norway; and Chaco Canyon, New Mexico. These weeklong immersion intensives provide you with a comprehensive experience in the protocols of the Christed Initiation in the Buddha Body and field application of geomancy practices. One 7-day program is given per month, although the two England programs may be given together.

Christed Initiation in the Buddha Body (CIBB): A unique (i.e., nobody else teaches it) three-part training intensive in a one-to-one format featuring direct acquisition of the living Christ Light and presence within you. The program is free of all dogmatic or religious content and is correlated with the Santa Fe geomantic landscape which also benefits from your initiation. The Christ Light is the preeminent tool for working with the Earth and its energies.

CIBB-1: A 6-day program in which you "access" the Christ Light.

CIBB-2: A 10-day program in which you "embody" the Christ Light.

CIBB-3: A 7-day program in which you "wield" the Christ Light.

CIBB-4: A 7-day program in which you "create" with the Christ Light.

The four components of the complete CIBB training can be done all at once or with gaps (of any length) between each segment.

Email: **blaise@blueroomconsortium. com; blaise@cybermesa.com**